INDIA'S WARS II

'*India's Wars II* manages to deliver an almost action-movie kind rush for its readers in what is essentially an academic enterprise and manages to cover the entire sequence in a fast-paced summary of Indian military history. Overall, it is a fascinating read, a deeply researched book that sets a solid foundation for more body of work to come from Indian scholars in this area.'

– *The Hindu*

'*India's Wars II* is not only about stories of courage and valour. It is also a serious examination of senior military leadership and how they orchestrated battles and campaigns under trying circumstances. Arjun Subramaniam does not eulogize or indiscriminately criticize in his book because he understands what it means to have served in the Indian military.'

– *Economic Times*

'Arjun Subramaniam's viewpoint is especially interesting because he is an airman. He has, therefore, a deeper understanding of the use of air power and of combined ops, or jointmanship as it is called in the defence services. In this respect, he's outstanding.'

– *Business Standard*

'It is a one-stop read for those seeking a professional perspective on contemporary Indian military history sans the usual verbosity. It is a must-read for all officers of the armed forces, for citizens who aspire to know more about India's armed forces, and the strategic community of policy-makers in the realm of national security.'

– *Swarajya Magazine*

'*India's Wars II* mirrors the myriad reflections of India's military leaders who have witnessed momentous events in diverse battle spaces over the last five decades. Covering a vast landscape that ranges from India's strategic compulsions to joint operations and intense personal experiences of combat, the book offers policy and operational planners a detailed lens into the past as they chart the future of India as a leading power.'

– **General Bipin Rawat**, former Chief of Defence Staff

'Arjun Subramaniam has done it again. Through meticulous research he has uncovered telling details that vivify the familiar story of India's post-1971 conflicts in a new history that does justice – and honour – to all of India's armed forces. Both scholars and policymakers will benefit greatly from this intimate window on modern India's military operations.'

– **Ashley J. Tellis**, Tata Chair, Carnegie Endowment for International Peace

'After his maiden "opus", *India's Wars I*, Arjun Subramaniam picks up the thread to take the reader on a fascinating journey of our post-1972 conflicts. In battle zones ranging from tropical jungles of the north-east to dizzying heights of Himalayan outposts and from neighbouring Sri Lanka to worldwide UN missions, Indian servicemen have served silently and often unsung by their countrymen. Recorded for posterity here, we have, in meticulous detail, first-hand accounts of military operations calling for courage, fortitude and uncommon leadership.'

– **Admiral Arun Prakash** (retired), former Chief of Naval Staff

'Air Vice Marshal Arjun Subramaniam in his meticulously researched book highlights the many complexities, innovations, challenges and eventual outcomes of the several wars and conflicts that India has experienced since 1972. Enriching the institutional memories of military/strategic thinkers and enthusiasts, Arjun brings out the leadership traits of many charismatic military leaders, captures memorable battles/skirmishes, and busts many myths in his own inimitable style. This book is a treasure trove of military history.'

– **Air Chief Marshal Fali H. Major** (retired), former Chief of Air Staff

'A fascinating analysis by a former military officer of the internal and external wars India has faced since the early 1970s. This is essential reading for those wishing to understand India's security challenges, which have accentuated over the years in large part because of the country's failure to learn from its past experiences. The book offers insights on how India could draw the right lessons from its handling of both internal conflicts and the silent wars its regional adversaries have waged against it.'

– **Brahma Chellaney,** author and geostrategist

'Arjun Subramaniam has come up with another riveting account of India's military operations over the years. While his first book covered the major wars, the new one gives an unparalleled insight into many unknown aspects of India's numerous military campaigns in scenarios other than war. A must-read for those interested in strategic decision-making, military leadership and India's recent history.'

– **Nitin A. Gokhale**, author and strategic affairs analyst

'Arjun Subramaniam deserves kudos for writing back-to-back volumes on contemporary Indian military history. He has done yeoman service in recounting the contributions of the Indian armed forces in service of the nation. *India's Wars II* is an honest appraisal and analysis of events with no attempts either to glorify or unfairly criticize any individual or action. Painstakingly researched to bring forth individual and collective efforts which charted India's recent conflict landscape, *India's Wars I* and *India's Wars II* are perhaps among the best chronicles of modern Indian military history in recent times.'

– **Air Chief Marshal B.S. Dhanoa** (retired), former Chief of Air Staff

'*India's Wars II* is Arjun Subramaniam's "second pass", which means he still had ammunition left after his first. His soldier-scholar insights richly contribute to the burgeoning genre of contemporary Indian military history. Writing this must not have been easy because military operations of India's recent past are still shrouded in secrecy. Arjun uses a mix of regimental archives, official documents, personal diaries, books and personal interviews with over 100 serving and retired soldiers to uncover operations from the Naga and Mizo insurgency, to Op Blue Star, Op Meghdoot, Sri Lanka, Maldives, Kashmir, Kargil and the Doklam standoff. The book underscores how India kept missing the opportunity to leverage its tactical and operational successes into long-term strategic gains, and shows the way to the future.'

– **Shekhar Gupta,** Editor-in-Chief, The Print

'Indian history is written almost exclusively as political history. Therefore, it is refreshing to read Arjun Subramaniam's new book on the military history of India. His writings combine a lucid understanding of the wider geopolitical context with the practical knowledge of a man who has spent decades in uniform. It is a must-read for policymakers, military history enthusiasts, journalists, academia and, most importantly, the next generation that they may know the origins of the challenges that they will face.'

– **Sanjeev Sanyal**, economist and bestselling author

'*India's Wars II is* an eminently readable book that does full justice to the outstanding service that India's armed forces have rendered in the rise of the Indian nation-state. The joint narrative is unique and devoid of unnecessary military jargon that would distract a lay reader. Fair in his assessments and measured in his criticism, the strength of the book lies in Arjun Subramaniam's ability to convert his exhaustive interviews into chronologically arranged, factually correct and gripping personal stories and accounts of operations and combat.'

– **Lieutenant General D.S. Hooda** (retired), former General Officer Commanding-in-Chief of the army's Northern Command

1972–2020

ARJUN SUBRAMANIAM

First published in hardback in India as *Full Spectrum* by
HarperCollins *Publishers* 2020

Published in paperback in India as *Full Spectrum* by HarperCollins *Publishers* 2022
4th Floor, Tower A, Building No. 10, DLF Cyber City,
DLF Phase II, Gurugram, Haryana – 122002
www.harpercollins.co.in

This edition published 2025

2 4 6 8 10 9 7 5 3

P-ISBN: 978-93-6569-632-5
E-ISBN: 978-93-5357-806-0

The views and opinions expressed in this book are the author's own
and the facts are as reported by him, and the publishers
are not in any way liable for the same.

Other than the official Indian boundaries depicted on the maps,
few boundaries are as per the author's own findings and study. The author and
the publisher do not claim them to be official/legal boundaries of India.
The maps are neither accurate nor drawn to exact scale and the international
boundaries as shown neither purport to be correct nor authentic
as per the directives of the Survey of India.

Typeset in 10.5/13.5 Adobe Caslon Pro at
Manipal Technologies Limited, Manipal

Printed and bound at
Replika Press Pvt. Ltd.

This book is produced from independently certified FSC® paper to ensure
responsible forest management.

For my father,
who helped me realize the power of the written word

CONTENTS

LIST OF MAPS AND SKETCHES

PREFACE TO THE PAPERBACK EDITION

Recent conflicts in Iraq, Syria, Afghanistan and Ukraine have clearly underscored the proposition that the utility of force and its widespread use as an instrument of statecraft remains an enduring paradigm in inter- and intra-state relations. With terms such as 'all measures short of war', or 'no war and no peace' largely reflecting the existing geopolitical rivalries, the title of this book stands vindicated as a contemporary reflection on the character of war. The sheer elasticity of this character has created a diffused and often confusing understanding of war in all its hues. After almost seven years of attempting to undermine the sovereignty of Ukraine through low-grade and hybrid warfare, President Vladimir Putin of Russia declared war against Ukraine in the conventional sense in early February 2022 with a calibrated show of force. Frustrated with the resolve of the Ukrainians, he intensified his military campaign with widespread and a reportedly indiscriminate application of firepower against urban targets. When the US and Europe imposed widespread economic sanctions, and accelerated the supply of defensive weaponry to Ukraine, Putin called it a 'declaration of war' and put his nuclear forces on full alert. The outcomes and pain that the West sought to impose on Russia without physically entering the conflict is a typical example of full spectrum conflict that encompasses the military, diplomatic, economic, technological and cognitive domains.

In that sense, *India's Wars II* is a forward-looking narrative that seeks to proliferate a broader understanding of war and conflict as multi-dimensional, multi-spectral and complicated activity that merits repeated examination. The application of widespread firepower in Syria and Afghanistan; deployment and use of air power, armour and conventional artillery in Ukraine; massing of troops, armour and artillery along the Line of Actual Control; and the sudden proliferation of drones and space-based targeting methodologies indicate that after a hiatus of a few decades, conventional conflict is back in focus. As a rising power with serious security challenges along two continental fronts, with a rapidly emerging maritime front along the Indo-Pacific, India's basket of security conundrums is overflowing and cause for serious concern. It is in the above context that security practitioners and policy makers would do well to revisit India's battlegrounds of the recent past and derive lessons for the future.

Despite a release during the pandemic, the hardback edition of this book seems to have struck a chord among several groups of readers, including practitioners who have fought in and lived through the conflicts I have written about, common citizens who have wondered whether India has fought a 'real war' after 1971, or millennials with an inherent curiosity to learn more about India's armed forces. The response has been heartwarming, and I am humbled by the acceptance of my narrative. With the release of the paperback edition against the backdrop of an increasingly conflict-prone global and regional security landscape, it is hoped that a wider readership gets a sense of war and conflict as an inescapable instrument of statecraft, albeit still being the last resort to resolve disputes in an increasingly intolerant world.

Arjun Subramaniam

New Delhi
March 2022

1

INTRODUCTION

'Our own generation is unique, but sadly so, in producing a school of thinkers who are allegedly experts in military strategy and who are certainly specialists in military studies (also called Strategic Studies by some) but who know virtually nothing of military history, and who do not seem to care about their ignorance.'[1]

– Bernard Brodie

India's Wars II: A Military History, 1972-2020 is the second part of what is envisaged to be a holistic attempt at understanding war and conflict in contemporary India. *India's Wars I: A Military History, 1947-1971*[2] was the first, and it struck the right note by setting the stage for a sequel, one not unlike a 'second pass' over a target area by fighter aircraft.

A second pass is carried out when there is ammunition left, to ensure that the target is destroyed. However, if the first pass is not good enough, this move is fraught with danger because the element of surprise is lost. Unless a new attack pattern or an unpredictable flight profile is adopted before a second attack, the enemy could be lying in wait with interceptor aircraft and ack-ack (military slang for anti-aircraft guns) or surface-to-air missiles (SAMs). The first kills achieved by the Indian Air Force (IAF) in the 1971 war with Pakistan were the result of a four-aircraft Pakistani Sabre aircraft formation carrying out repeated passes in a predictable pattern over an Indian Army brigade in the Boyra Sector of the erstwhile East Pakistan. It was this careless bit of tactical flying that allowed the Indian Gnat aircraft (affectionately called 'the last real fighter' by the fighter pilots who flew them) to pounce on them from above. The Sabres paid a heavy price for their complacency.[3]

As fighter pilots pull out of an attack and reposition for a second pass, most do a quick recap of the previous attack. They first try to assess the damage they have caused while simultaneously checking their Radar Warning Receiver (RWR) for any lock-on from an airborne fire-control radar or the tracking radar of a SAM. A deep breath and check of engine and weapon parameters follows. In the meantime, if the attack has been controlled by a ground-based Forward Air Controller (FAC), pilots wait for feedback on the previous attack. All this would typically take about 30 to 45 seconds before the next attack commences. Everything happens in a blur at speeds of 700-850 kmph.

The second pass is done rapidly and all ammunition expended, following which they duck down to tree-top level and head home after regrouping with other formation members. There is no relaxing till they cross the border and hear the calming voice of a friendly radar controller, who guides the formation back to base. After landing, the adrenalin is still pumping, knees are generally wobbly, and overalls invariably drenched with sweat. One of the most important factors for an effective second pass is the speed at which the pilots assess any changes in the environment, the impact of their first attack and the configuration of the next one – whether they should stick to the same pattern, or do something different. *India's Wars II: A Military History, 1972-2020* is much like a consistent second pass. It adheres to an applied military history narrative that weaves the strategic and operational dimensions of war and conflict in contemporary India with tactical vignettes and credible personal perspectives to create what is hopefully a coherent mosaic of contemporary Indian military history.

All conflicts that India fought before 1971 were mostly conventional wars that could be sequenced chronologically. The only departures from this were the two insurgencies in the north-eastern states of Nagaland and Mizoram, and the India-China skirmishes at Nathu La and Cho La in 1967, which I could not cover in my first book. I have respected reader feedback and covered them in this volume along with a few United Nations (UN) peacekeeping operations in the 1950s and 1960s as part of a larger examination of India's combat experiences in pursuit of global peace in troubled lands.

As was the case with *India's Wars I*, this volume retains a practitioner's flavour and is reinforced with scholarly rigour. The credibility of the narrative rests on three pillars – triangulation of facts and authenticity derived from the available primary sources (mainly regimental archives, official doctrines, personal papers and interviews); deep mining of secondary sources and existing literature; and a practitioner-scholar's unique perspectives on war and conflict. This is so because much of the actual fine print of how the Indian state has conducted military operations is still shrouded in secrecy and has not been regularly declassified. Unrestricted access to Lieutenant General Rostum Nanavatty's meticulously preserved diaries and recollections gave me the much-needed primary sources to dissect operations in those sectors and construct my narrative. Interviews and conversations with almost a hundred serving and retired officers and men (some of whom wished to remain anonymous), including former chiefs from all the three armed forces, served as highly credible primary sources for land, air and naval operations.

The Indian Army has over 1.2 million personnel, the Indian Navy has about 100 frontline combat ships while the IAF has over fifty squadrons and 800 aircraft. These are large forces that have been in a near constant state of readiness and seen much action. I have tried my best to write a representative and running history that does justice to all the three services without fear or favour. I reiterate my deepest respect for all the regiments, fleets and squadrons of India's armed forces, and any omissions are only because there was just no space to fit in all that I wanted to write about. Some warriors emerge as larger-than-life characters in my book, but that does not in any way suggest that others stood on the sidelines and watched. This is essentially a book about India's contemporary soldiers, sailors and airmen, and I have tried to ensure that they occupy pole position in the book. Writing about war and conflict, especially when one has witnessed success and failure from the inside, has been perilous. Many of the protagonists I have written about are battle-hardened professionals and practitioners, and my contextual and measured criticism in hindsight may appear harsh at times. All I can do is seek their indulgence and magnanimity.

This book is also about how the Indian nation-state and its armed forces have coped with the changing contours of modern conflict in the decades since 1972. During this period, India's democracy has flourished, surmounting many challenges even as multiple geopolitical fractures have plagued the world. One needs to look no further than the Soviet Union, the Balkans, West Asia and the Caucasus to situate India's predicament and progress in the right strategic context. This book asks the same questions, but from an Indian perspective, that Sir Lawrence Freedman asked in the introductory chapter of *War*, a 1994 compilation of essays: 'What are the causes of War? How have they been fought and what are the prospects for the future? Are there basic principles which should shape the conduct of war if it is to be successfully prosecuted?'[4]

The narrative also offers a changing perspective of how India has approached the conduct of war and conflict in contemporary times. This includes the 2016 'surgical' or cross-border strikes across the Line of Control (LoC) with

Pakistan by the Indian Army's Special Forces, the face-off with the Chinese at Doklam in 2017, the pre-emptive punitive strikes by the IAF against terrorist camps in Pakistan in 2019, and the large-scale aerial engagement between the IAF and the Pakistan Air Force (PAF) the following day. The structure of the book offers readers a choice of either embarking on a comprehensive and chronological examination of war and conflict in contemporary India, or doing a selective reading based on specific timelines or campaigns. Considering the rather secretive role of India's armed forces in the development of India's nuclear capabilities, these have not been discussed in the book. Space and cyber capabilities are still fledgling areas and remain predominantly in the highly classified domain. They do not find mention in what is primarily a historical narrative. India's Central Armed Police Forces (CAPF) and paramilitary forces (PMF), particularly the Assam Rifles, Border Security Force (BSF), the Central Reserve Police Force (CRPF) and the Indo-Tibetan Border Police (ITBP), have done a sterling job along with some state police forces in complementing India's armed forces in a wide range of operations. I could not possibly have done justice to their exploits in this volume.

This book is a tribute to the soldiers standing vigil through the night at lonely outposts, not knowing when an enemy sniper could bring one of them down, while the rest of the country celebrates Diwali, Gurpurab, Eid or Christmas (festivals celebrated in a secular India). It is an ode to the unsung helicopter and transport pilots who snake through narrow valleys in poor weather to drop sacks of flour and potatoes or a bagful of letters, which are then read by the soldiers within the confines of a thermal tent at 19,000 feet. Finally, it is a salute to the sailors helping their captain on the bridge, navigating their frigate through a stomach-churning storm on the high seas whilst on an anti-piracy mission. It is hoped that the book will fulfil its primary objective of serving as a historical narrative of war and conflict in contemporary India; one that appeals to a wide spectrum of readership in India and elsewhere.

2

CHAMELEON WARS

'She (Indira Gandhi) defended Indian interests and security when threatened. For that the nation must be grateful to her. In her ability to anticipate security problems … and the need to build up Indian power she truly reflected the Indian intelligentsia.'[1]

– K. Subrahmanyam

Indian Perspectives on Contemporary Conflict

It is now widely accepted that thinking about large-scale conventional wars is back in fashion in the backdrop of the emerging military rivalry between the US and China and a resurgence in Russian military posturing. Equally clear is that limited wars and sub-conventional conflicts in varied terrain, including the vast maritime spaces, will constitute the main template for conflict in the twenty-first century. This will all take place under the nuclear shadow looming large over the India-Pakistan security relationship.[2] These scenarios remain a distinct possibility given India's adversarial relationship with its two powerful neighbours, a rising China and a revisionist failing Pakistan. Making it even more important to understand the complexities of contemporary conflict is the likely impact that the Covid-19 pandemic is going to have on warfare in general.

Sub-conventional conflict, irregular warfare (IW), fourth generation warfare (4GW) and even fifth generation warfare (5GW) are merely generic terms encompassing armed conflict and non-contact warfare. These are above the level of peaceful coexistence and below the threshold of conventional or structured war between nation-states.[3] Hybrid war, cyber war, proxy war, border skirmishes, armed militancy, insurgency and terrorism are contemporary manifestations of such conflict. These wars are characterized by asymmetric force levels between the regular state forces and the irregulars, wherein the force applied and the violence generated depends on the motivation, intent and capabilities of the combatants. The modus operandi of non-state actors is often marked by irrationality, indiscrimination, unpredictability and ruthlessly destructive behaviour, while states respond with restraint or ruthless force, depending on the state architecture (democracy, dictatorship, majoritarian or communist) and the laws that govern the actions of their armed forces.

I support the 'realist' argument that India's emergence as a potential global power would be dictated not only by its economic rise and the exercise of 'soft power' but also by its calibrated exploitation of force as a visible and potent tool of statecraft. India's conventional warfighting strategy in the post-1971 era has revolved around deterrence by limited coercive and punitive action, primarily to protect its geographical boundaries and sovereignty. An example of this was the limited high-altitude campaign during the Pakistan-initiated Kargil conflict in 1999. The large-scale deployment of conventional forces along India's northern and western frontiers against powerful, unfriendly neighbours is an inescapable imperative. Force employment and application strategies against insurgencies and secessionist movements have been markedly restrained and calibrated, even when there has been clear evidence of external abetment. The performance and conduct of the Indian Army in the troubled areas of the north-east and Jammu and Kashmir (J&K) reflect this strategic maturity and restraint.[4]

What this means in very simple terms is that India's armed forces must be constantly prepared for what is commonly termed as 'Full Spectrum Operations'. It is important to understand the basic characteristics of some of these genres of conflict if one genuinely wants to comprehend the complexities and ambiguities of modern warfare. None of these forms are new – they have been practised for millennia in some form or the other. For example, the Oxford historian Sir Hew Strachan argues that 'all war is potentially asymmetric, in that an intelligent opponent should try to maximize the enemy's vulnerability rather than play to their strength'.[5] He goes on to speculate whether 'hybrid wars are those which occupy some middle point in the spectrum between regular and irregular, or whether they are characterized by simultaneous activity on both ends of that spectrum'.[6]

Conventional Conflict in Contemporary India

Conventional conflict generally denotes a conflict between the standing armed forces of two nation-states. It is invariably a classic fallout of the failure of political negotiations and diplomacy.

India's experience with conventional conflict since Independence has been varied. It has a large standing army, navy and air force, which were initially trained to fight conventional wars across varied terrain. It has two acknowledged adversaries, Pakistan and China; it has fought four wars since 1947 with the former, while the 1962 war remains the only conflict with the latter. These wars have been fought over territorial and sovereignty issues that are deep-rooted and highly emotive, making a negotiated resolution highly difficult over the years.

Three of India's major wars with Pakistan have been fought on multiple fronts (1947-48, 1965 and 1971). It has also fought a limited but high-intensity conflict in Kargil (1999). Kargil was interwoven with the ongoing Siachen high-altitude slug fest, continued infiltration along the LoC, and the covert war that Pakistan has been waging against India in J&K since 1947. With China, the conventional war across two fronts in 1962 has not been repeated. It has, however, resulted in a protracted cat-and-mouse game of deterrence that has effectively prevented conflict between the two nations. Embedded in this tension have been interludes of posturing in the form of numerous skirmishes, face-offs and encounters. Confounding many security analysts is the astounding fact that not a single shot has been fired across the Line of Actual Control (LAC) with China since the last firefight at Nathu La in 1967,[7] although pushing and shoving is commonplace at numerous border posts. Whether that signifies the success of deterrence or whether it is just another move on a complex strategic chessboard, it is another example of the ambiguities of the India-China conundrum.

What are the significant takeaways from India's experience in conventional conflict? Despite being dragged into war barely months after Independence, the Indian Army and the IAF leveraged their experience gained from WWII and thwarted the larger Pakistani objective of wresting the entire state of Kashmir from India. Large tracts of territory though remained under Pakistan's control as Pakistan-occupied Kashmir (PoK).[8] The performance of conventional forces in battle depends largely on the synergy between the political leadership and the armed forces as instruments of statecraft. When there is abject neglect of this tool, defeat is almost always inevitable, as was the case in the 1962 war with

China.[9] The build-up of conventional forces is a long-drawn process that takes decades to translate into effectiveness on the battlefield. The 1965 war was an example of such a process wherein a strategically nimble Pakistan sought to leverage its conventional superiority on the ground and in the air to achieve a stated political objective of redrawing boundaries. It is a testimony to India's resilience that it turned an operational stalemate into a strategic advantage by successfully focusing on intangibles like leadership, morale and political will. Despite Pakistan having reached the limits of its warfighting potential, the Indian military was reluctant to go for the jugular.[10] Political diffidence during crunch-time negotiations too failed to convert operational gains into decisive strategic outcomes.

The deft synergizing of all instruments of statecraft – and a final blow delivered by conventional military forces across multiple fronts – saw the dismemberment of Pakistan and the creation of Bangladesh in December 1971.[11] However, the Simla talks in 1972 saw India's prime minister, Indira Gandhi, being outmanoeuvred by her wily Pakistani counterpart, Zulfiqar Ali Bhutto. Convinced by Bhutto's assurances that he would soon come up with a mutually acceptable plan for the resolution of the Kashmir problem, she failed to convert India's decisive military victory and the 93,000 POWs into tangible geopolitical gains. India would pay a heavy price over the years for this – a fact that has for long, and quite deliberately, been underplayed in contemporary Indian strategic discourse. Realizing its inability to achieve any strategic objectives through conventional warfighting across wide fronts, Pakistan came up with limited war options by initiating the Kargil conflict in 1999 by forcing its more powerful adversary to limit the application of combat capability to a small area. When that too failed to deliver the desirable strategic outcomes, Pakistan realized that a limited war with conventional forces against an exponentially more powerful adversary like India was a non-starter. It would have to deploy other means to wage war against a nation that it perceived to be an existential threat to its survival.

Orchestrating the Big Battle

Operational plans for conventional conflict are generally made well in advance and disseminated to field formations, which then go on to evolve tactics and drills that are assiduously practised in exercises and sand-model discussions.[12] When hostilities are imminent, defences are strengthened and offensive formations are moved closer to the border. When diplomatic parleys fail, the nimbler and more aggressive protagonist invariably makes the first move by launching a pre-emptive strike that signals commencement of hostilities. These strikes could be land-based, aerial or maritime, depending on which offers the greatest element of surprise, shock and destruction of enemy combat potential. Air strikes have often been the first choice for pre-emption, as seen in the 1967 Arab-Israeli war or the India-Pakistan wars of 1965 and 1971. The land option has also been exercised, by the Egyptians in 1973 when they crossed the Bar-Lev Line on Yom Kippur. Conventional conflict generally involves set-piece moves, where speed, surprise, firepower, manoeuvre and the destruction of the adversary's combat potential hold the key to conflict termination.

Three concepts in modern conventional warfare have interested the Indian military in recent decades. These are the air-land concept of joint operations propagated by the US in the late 1970s and early 1980s,[13] sequential military operations[14] and parallel operations.[15] The Air-Land Battle concept or doctrine was first articulated in the US in the late 1970s as *Field Manual 100.* Its stated objectives were to meet the challenges of a possible conflict on the plains of Europe between the North Atlantic Treaty Organization (NATO) and the Warsaw Pact countries. It also sought to address two weaknesses that plagued the US armed forces, which had by then emerged as the predominant bulwark against the mighty Soviet war machine that constantly threatened to steamroll across the plains of Europe. Next was to rethink its existing warfighting strategies in the aftermath of the Vietnam debacle. This it did by advocating manoeuvre, leveraging the emerging technology revolution to drive tactics and creating synergies between the army and the air force to maximize their fighting potential.

Finally, it needed a strategy to combat the overwhelming might of the Soviet army and its amassed armour and artillery in the Tactical Battle Area (TBA). By advocating the concept of 'Deep Battle', it sought to use air power to punch holes in enemy defences, interdict 'follow on' forces and create space for manoeuvre, which would then be exploited by a combined arms assault. The doctrine was an effective deterrent against conventional Soviet military strategy as it opened offensive windows for NATO.

Both India and Pakistan were quick to draw lessons from *Field Manual 100-5*. While the Indians acted first under General K. Sundarji, their talismanic army chief in the mid-1980s, Pakistan would soon evolve its own version based on its traditional pre-emptive philosophy. Sundarji, who was attending a course at the US Army War College in the 1970s at the time when the Air-Land Battle concept was being debated, saw it as an opportunity to change the stagnant mindset that had taken deep root in the Indian military. He knew that on India's western front its military top brass was more comfortable with attrition warfare and fighting the 'holding battle', while waiting for suitable opportunities to launch limited offensives. During his tenure as chief, he sought to drive home the importance of manoeuvre, offensive action and the need for the IAF to commit more resources to winning the land battle.[16]

Complementing Sundarji's views on offensive action was another brilliant military mind from the IAF, Air Commodore Jasjit Singh. Though Jasjit preferred to view air power through the lens of the 'big battle' – with deep strategic strikes and air dominance being the key determinants of the employment of air power – he was also among the first to acknowledge the necessity of supporting the army in the TBA directly, or by interdicting reinforcements before they joined the battle.[17]

A follow-up of the Air-Land Battle was what militaries across the world termed as 'sequential operations', which sought to systematically degrade and destroy the enemy's combat potential. Sequential warfighting relied heavily on what came to be known as Effects-Based Operations (EBO).[18] EBO used military power to systematically and speedily destroy target systems with a debilitating impact on an adversary's capacity to sustain military operations. Air power emerged as a key element of this style of warfighting and was used to good effect during Operation Desert Storm in 1991. The IAF embraced this concept in the 1990s and tried unsuccessfully to convince the Indian Army that ground forces could be effective only if they first allowed the air force to win the air battle before launching an offensive with its strike elements.

Experiences during the early decades of the twenty-first century do suggest that long conventional wars are a phenomenon of the past. Militaries now must plan and execute military campaigns that offer speedy conflict termination to political leaders. Parallel operations offered such an option wherein land, sea and air power would no longer be sequenced, but applied simultaneously to create overwhelming pressure on adversaries and force them to capitulate under shock without necessarily suffering heavy casualties. US military operations in Iraq in 2003 delivered one such template by mounting combined land and air assaults during Operation Iraqi Freedom, which led to the collapse of Saddam Hussein's forces.[19] Following the inability of the Indian Army to mobilize rapidly after the suicide attack on India's parliament by Pakistan-sponsored terrorists of the Lashkar-e-Taiba (LeT) and Jaish-e-Mohammad (JeM) in December 2001, there was a need for a recalibration of its strategy based on mobility and logistics on the Western Front. The Indian Army now seeks to embrace some elements of an orchestrated and synergized application of combat power, bolstered by the significant power of the Indian Navy and IAF.[20] More about this strategy will emerge in Chapter 19.

Understanding the Strategic Milieu

The end of the Cold War saw the emergence of a fragmented world dotted with numerous localized, but seemingly intractable, conflicts arising from the fundamental differences of religion and ethnicity.[21] Terrorists, insurgents and freedom fighters found remarkably new ways of combating the coercive capabilities of established states and coalitions. While powerful nations such as the US, Russia, India and Israel have been building full-spectrum military capability to calibrate escalation and prevent extended conventional wars, their opponents have been employing sophisticated tools and techniques of limited hybrid war that gradually nibble away at the fabric of the state. Such forms of warfare, while existing in some form or the other across millennia, have now emerged as effective asymmetric counters to coercion, and the tools used are unlike those of conventional coercion, be it diplomatic or military. Mao's peasants and Tito's guerrillas have all waged limited wars against stronger adversaries and achieved asymmetric outcomes.

In recent times, such limited wars have become the focus of attention in the study of war and conflict. By the end of the twentieth century, several military historians in the West declared the death of large-scale conventional conflict and questioned the need for big-ticket military acquisitions, particularly in the air and maritime domains. India though has never had the space to reflect on and debate the need for limiting the development of 'full-spectrum' capability. Until there is clear political and strategic guidance to India's armed forces in a post-Covid-19 world that it should discount the possibility of waging conventional conflict on multiple fronts, India can ill afford to go easy on developing robust conventional capabilities to deter its neighbours' aggressive strategic designs. Concurrently, it has developed capabilities to tackle the entire range of conventional and sub-conventional threats to national security.

The Paradox of Sub-Conventional Conflict

It is easy to be confused by the plethora of definitions of the various genres of conflict below the level of conventional conflict. Some academics – such as Professor Dan Stoker, a former professor of strategy at the US Naval Post-Graduate School at Monterrey – like to club everything that is not 'Total War' under the heading of 'Limited War'. Others in the US like to use terms like 'small wars', 'irregular wars', 'operations other than war' and 'fourth generation warfare'. India prefers terms like 'sub-conventional conflict', 'low-intensity conflict' and 'proxy war'. 'Hybrid war' has also gained some traction in recent doctrinal pronouncements. A scan of these definitions offers an insight into the ambiguity and uncertainty that dogs contemporary conflict and the challenges that countries like India face.

The Indian Army doctrine defines sub-conventional operations as:

> Armed conflicts that are above the level of peaceful coexistence amongst states and below the threshold of war. These include militancy, insurgency, proxy war and terrorism either employed as part of an insurrectionist movement or independently.[22]

The Indian Ministry of Defence (MoD) expands the definition used by the US and NATO and defines insurgency as:

> Armed rebellion by a section of the population against the legally constituted Government, with the support or sympathy of the local population, obtained voluntarily or by coercion. It covers the full spectrum of conflict from subversion to full-scale guerrilla war, including the emergence of guerrilla bands into regular units.[23]

Taking the debate further, the Indian MoD defines low-intensity conflict as:

> Low-intensity conflict encompasses a variety of violent and low-level conflict situations. In most cases, such conflicts fall under the category of 'politico-military confrontation' between contending states or groups. Such conflicts are at a much lower scale than conventional war but are above the routine and peaceful competitions among states. One of the parties to the conflict may not be a state, as in an insurgency situation. It frequently involves protracted struggle of competing principles and ideologies. Low-intensity conflict ranges from high-grade internal-struggle situations to

> extensive employment of the armed forces in counterinsurgency operations. It is waged by a combination of means, employing political, economic, informational and military instruments. It includes terrorism but excludes purely criminal acts.[24]

Finally, terrorism is distinct from insurgency and relies on coercion rather than popular support. It shares similarities with violent and organized crime, and is defined in a variety of ways, depending on interpretation, focus and perspective. For the Indian MoD, terrorism is defined as:

> The wanton killing of persons or involvement in violence or in the disruption of services or means of communications essential to the community or in damaging property with a view to putting the public or any section of the public in fear; or affecting adversely the harmony between different religious, racial and language groups or overawing the sovereignty and integrity of a nation.[25]

A more nuanced explanation is offered in the Indian Army's sub-conventional doctrine, which is similar to the one offered by the US Department of Defense:

> Terrorism is the unlawful use or the threatened use of force or violence against people or property to terrorize, coerce or intimidate governments or societies; this is most often resorted to with the aim of achieving political, religious, or ideological objectives.[26]

Praveen Swami, one of India's most accomplished journalist-scholars, has been studying and writing about the ongoing proxy war and terrorism in J&K for almost three decades. His interpretation of the terms 'terrorist', 'insurgent' and 'militant' is relevant as they are used indiscriminately and interchangeably in South Asia.[27] He writes:

> I define terrorism to mean a political strategy that involves the use of violence to coerce civil society into submission to the ideological agenda of its adherents. Armed groups in J&K and Punjab have principally directed their violence at civilians, hence the term 'terrorists'.

By such a definition, LeT, JeM and Hizbul-Mujahideen (HM) are all terrorist groups irrespective of whether they fight the Indian Army or kill innocent civilians because their aim is to wage jihad on the Indian state and force the secession of J&K. The bottom line is that India is familiar with terror. In the north-eastern states of Assam, Manipur and Nagaland insurgencies have demonstrated chameleon-like characteristics and left a window open for terrorism to take root. Terrorism has occasionally reared its ugly head and demonstrated subnational, communal and ethnic overtones. The Indian state, however, has managed to control it. In central India, left-wing extremism is an example of terrorism as an instrument to bring about social and economic reform. Punjab in the 1980s and J&K after the 1990s remain the most emphatic examples of terrorism faced by the Indian state. J&K will remain a covert war for the foreseeable future with tools changing from insurgency to terrorism. Finally, it is assessed that Pakistan will continue to employ terrorism as an instrument of state policy to destabilize India until a black swan event forces it to abandon the strategy.

Covert, Proxy and Hybrid Wars

Complicating conflict genres further for countries like India are two other derivatives of limited conflict – proxy war and hybrid war. It is important to understand the finer nuances of the two as it is the proxy element that usually facilitates the hybrid means. Very rarely are low-intensity conflicts decided in a few months. Most often these conflicts last for years, or even decades, as we have seen in Malaysia, Vietnam, Northern Ireland, Sri Lanka, J&K, Nagaland, Iraq, Afghanistan, Syria and so on. Involvement of proxies can have a significant impact on the outcome of such conflicts, as they provide additional resources, military heft, international recognition as well as more ways to put opponents under pressure and reduce their effectiveness. These proxies could be governments, non-government organizations or individuals with resources and personal influence. They have varying motives but they can prolong the conflict, change the outcome or even become contestants themselves.

Independent India's tryst with covert war began in 1947 when Pakistan hatched its plan to sever Kashmir from the Indian Union by aiding and supporting raiders backed by armed militia. This was repeated in 1965, shelved for a while, and then revived in the early 1990s as a strategy for a protracted armed struggle in J&K. Pakistan's proxy war in Kashmir is merely a sophisticated derivative of covert war that uses the instrument of terrorism to sap India's growing power by 'bleeding it with a thousand cuts'.[28] When a large power like China joined the fray as part of Pakistan's security strategy,

India had no choice but to be alarmed. It therefore does not have the luxury of letting up on building military capability.

The word 'hybrid' is derived from the Latin root *hibrida*, meaning the offspring 'of a mixed union'. Hybrid warfare is a combination of two or more 'dissimilar' elements from those of conventional, asymmetric, irregular, information, non-linear and 4GW.[29] The first step in the transition to a hybrid conflict is escalating an insurgency or a covert war with external ideological support, supply of sophisticated weaponry and finances, and training. It gives the non-state actor the wherewithal to scale the conflict up to levels that resemble conventional conflict in many ways and yet retain the flexibility and ambiguity not available to regular state forces. Frank Hoffman explains the finer nuances of hybrid warfare and argues:

> A distinctive feature of hybrid warfare is that it blends the lethal nature of conventional force employed by the state with the fanatical and protracted fervour of irregular warfare.[30]

The most recent examples of hybrid wars have been the conflicts in Lebanon, Georgia, Crimea and Syria. Offering a practitioner's perspective of hybrid war, David Kilcullen in his seminal work *The Accidental Guerrilla* suggests that:

> ...the tendency towards hybrid forms of warfare combining terrorism, insurgency, propaganda and economic warfare to sidestep Western conventional capability is not only an Arab or Muslim phenomenon.[31]

In 1999, two colonels from the People's Liberation Army (PLA) wrote a book entitled *Chao Xian Zhan* (Unrestricted Warfare)[32] that directly countered the dominant Western way of warfighting by introducing the disruptive maxim of 'no rules and nothing is forbidden'.[33] These diffused forms of warfare bring to the fore the cognitive dissonance and non-traditional means like information warfare and even biological warfare. When embedded in conventional strategic thinking it drives military leaders into 'fighting the war they wanted to be fighting, rather than the war they actually were fighting'.[34]

Constitutional Mandates and Code of Conduct

The Indian Constitution has clear provisions for the deployment of the armed forces in various contingencies and eventualities. However, its founding fathers had little inkling of the ways in which the nature of both internal and external conflicts would evolve. While there have been periodic amendments and modifications, there is a disturbing disconnect between the judiciary, the executive, the legislature, the military, the media and civil society regarding the various aspects of the application of force as an instrument of statecraft. There is also a widespread lack of understanding of the difference between deploying the armed forces for maintaining law and order during civil disturbances, and deploying them to combat internal armed conflict. While the former is mandated under a strangely worded Criminal Procedure Code of 1973, the latter is governed by the Armed Forces Special Powers Act (AFSPA).

The AFSPA was first passed in 1958 to declare the Naga Hills District of Assam as a 'disturbed area', and was later imposed in several other areas.[35] Despite the attempts by Pakistan to wrest Kashmir from India in 1947 and 1965, the AFSPA with respect to J&K was only promulgated in 1990, when levels of violence necessitated large-scale deployment of the Indian Army to counter the externally abetted armed rebellion in J&K.[36] The debate on whether to declare an insurgency-ridden area as a 'disturbed area' to empower security forces is often shrill, uninformed and adversely impacts national security.

A perusal of the AF(J&K)SPA is instructive when it comes to categorizing 'disturbed areas'. Para 3 clearly enunciates, 'If, in relation to the State of Jammu and Kashmir, the Governor of that State or the Central Government, is of opinion that the whole or any part of the State is in such a disturbed and dangerous condition that the use of armed forces in aid of the civil power is necessary to prevent activities involving terrorist acts directed towards overawing the Government, or striking terror in the people or any section of the people, or alienating any section of the people or adversely affecting the harmony amongst different sections of the people... It also includes activities directed towards disclaiming, questioning or disrupting the sovereignty and territorial integrity of India or bringing about cession of a part of the territory of India or secession of a part of the territory of India from the Union or causing insult to the Indian National Flag, the Indian National Anthem and the Constitution of India.'[37]

Activists like Sanjoy Hazarika have been highly critical of the insistence of the Indian state to continue with AFSPA and argue that it is time to take a relook at its relevance in the north-eastern parts of India, where peace and normalcy are fast returning.[38] However, in J&K, even a cursory glance at the conditions that have forced the Government of India to promulgate the

AF(J&K)SPA in 12 of the 22 districts, and the existing patterns of violence, will indicate how difficult it is to review its notification district-wise.[39]

Lieutenant General Rostum Nanavatty urges caution while labelling genres of contemporary conflict. Writing in his academically robust book titled *Internal Armed Conflict in India,* he argues that 'indiscriminate use of terminologies does little to foster comprehension of the new forms of conflict'.[40] Finally, Clausewitz too recognized that war and conflict would be governed by both continuity and change.[41] This reflects India's struggle to define for itself the limits of war and conflict as an instrument of statecraft in contemporary times.

3

INDIA'S MILITARY RENAISSANCE

'We have become a very soft people and we must realize that nations are not built through soft options, nor are the country's frontiers secured by a soft line.'[1]

– George Fernandes, Defence Minister of India

The Initial Bear Hug

The Indo-Soviet Treaty of Friendship and Cooperation of August 1971 formalized almost a decade of close defence cooperation between India and the Soviet Union, even though the former steadfastly refused to align itself politically with Soviet Russia. It also opened the floodgates for licensed production of Soviet military equipment (not to be confused with technology transfer), which was supposedly designed to boost the indigenization of India's military-industrial complex and industrial infrastructure. The first Indo-Soviet military deal was based on a $140 million loan from Russia to be repaid over ten years, at a measly interest rate of 2 per cent per annum. After the US refused to supply C-130 Hercules transport aircraft and additional Bell helicopters in the late 1950s, the IAF became the initial beneficiary of the India–Soviet military cooperation.

It was the Russian IL-14 and An-12 transport aircraft and Mi-4 helicopters that sustained the Indian Army during the 1962 war, along with American C-119 Packets and the few Bell helicopters that were acquired in the 1950s. After the initial lot of MiG-21s were inducted in 1963 and used very sporadically in the 1965 war with Pakistan, additional MiG-21 squadrons were quickly raised along with a few squadrons of Sukhoi-7 fighter ground-attack squadrons. Finally, one of the most impactful acquisitions from the Russians in the early 1970s was a hardy helicopter, the Mi-8, which would continue in service for over four decades and serve as forerunner to the Mi-17/25/35 class of helicopters. The Indian Navy soon got its share of the pie too, with the induction of the Foxtrot-class diesel submarines in 1967 and the OSA-class missile boats in 1970.[2]

Though the Indian Army received large numbers of Soviet T-54 and T-55 tanks, India's armoured divisions preferred the more reliable Centurion tank and the newly inducted indigenous Vijayanta tank. The only Russian tank that made a difference in the eastern sector during the 1971 India-Pakistan war was the PT-76, which was a lighter and smaller tank with significant amphibious capability.[3] One of the biggest impediments to effective manoeuvring on the ground for the Indian Army, as experienced in the 1971 war, was the lack of Infantry Combat Vehicles (ICVs). Though the Indian Army had a few Czech Topaz ICVs in 1971, it was only in the mid-1970s that the highly effective Soviet BMP-1, with a lethal 57mm gun and anti-tank missiles, was inducted. These were followed in the early 1980s by the potent T-72 tank and the BMP-II ICVs, which would form the mainstay of the Indian Army's mechanized punch and mobility for almost three decades, till the former was replaced by the T-90 Main Battle Tank (MBT). The foundations of India's ground-based air defence systems were laid by the induction through the 1970s of the medium-range (15-40 km) SAM-2 and the short-range (2-15 km) SAM-3 missiles, the ZSU-23 self-propelled ack-ack guns, and a mobile SAM-6 variant with its launchers mounted on a BMP-1 called Kvadrat.

The Stagnant 1970s

In 1973, India's armed forces were just under a million strong with the national population being approximately 600 million. The Indian defence budget of $2.4 billion was approximately 3.75 per cent of GDP, rising over 50 per cent by the end of the decade in real terms but marginally declining as a percentage of GDP to $3.72 billion (3.5 per cent of GDP). The Indian Army's offensive punch comprised one armoured division, with a second one being raised a few years later, while five independent armoured brigades were largely assigned to standard infantry divisions as their manoeuvre arm in the plains. Near-obsolete Soviet T-54s and T-55s made up over 50 per cent of the inventory, while the equally aged British Centurion and French AMX-13 constituted almost 30 per cent of the force. This meant that the 500 indigenous Vijayanta medium tanks were the spearhead of India's armoured corps.[4] Though the tank was much appreciated by India's tankmen and almost 900 were built by the end of the 1970s – mainly to replace the Centurion and T-54s – it had too many flaws, such as a light armour and a suspect engine, to be developed into a futuristic tank.[5]

The Indian Army's artillery arm mostly had thousands of obsolete towed and self-propelled 25 Pounders and Abbot 105mm guns of British origin. Along with several hundred Russian 100mm and 130mm guns[6] they constituted the main fire-support element for both attacking and defensive formations. Complementing these guns were Russian recoilless anti-tank weapons and obsolete air-defence artillery guns, which were complemented by the end of the decade with the highly effective Russian radar-controlled ZSU-23 air defence guns.[7]

The vanguard of the Indian Army had also only marginally increased from fourteen to sixteen infantry divisions along with the eleven mountain divisions[8] that made up an eight/nine-corps-sized force, with two corps deployed in the Eastern Theatre and the rest arrayed against Pakistan along the disturbed western and northern frontiers. Interestingly, though several divisions manned the contested frontier with China on the eastern front, only one division defended the entire LAC with China in eastern Ladakh. The primary infantry weapons were the 7.62mm self-loading rifles and a variety of near-obsolete light and medium machine guns.

The successes notched up by the Indian Navy in the 1971 war acted as a catalyst for the expansion of the Indian Navy. In the early 1970s, the aircraft carrier INS *Vikrant*, a few near-obsolete British destroyers and frigates, two modern Indian-designed Nilgiri-class frigates, efficient but ageing Soviet Petya-class light destroyer escorts, the Osa-class missile boats with Styx missiles and four Foxtrot-class submarines comprised the primary combatant fleet. These were complemented by patrol boats, minesweepers and landing craft of WWII and 1950s' vintage. By the end of the 1970s, the transformation of the Indian Navy was well under way with two additional modern Nilgiri-class frigates and four Foxtrot-class submarines joining the fleet along with several smaller ships (Soviet minesweepers, missile boats and corvettes) boosting the strength of the western and eastern fleets. The Soviet influence on naval aviation had not yet crept in, with British Seahawks and French Alizes continuing to be the main carrier-based fighters, and the ageing American Lockheed Super Constellation constituting the fixed component of maritime reconnaissance. Modern British Sea King anti-submarine warfare helicopters and French-design Chetak helicopters (Indian derivative of the Alouette-III) formed the rotary-wing component.[9]

The IAF fleet of the 1970s comprised mainly Soviet and British aircraft. The indigenous element petered out by the end of the 1970s because Hindustan Aeronautics Limited (HAL) could not address the deficiencies in the indigenously designed and manufactured HF-24 (Marut), which had performed creditably in the desert sector during the 1971 India-Pakistan conflict.[10] Though HAL was able to scale up production beyond the initial figure of seventy and manufactured over a hundred aircraft, it was unable to support the IAF beyond equipping three squadrons and delivered the last aircraft to the IAF in the mid-1970s. Though the Marut remained operational into the early 1980s, it remained an aircraft that promised much but failed to deliver. This was primarily due to HAL's inability to develop or reverse-engineer a suitable engine to replace the underperforming Orpheus engine.[11]

Driven by necessity and ageing platforms, the IAF looked to exploit many of its fighter and bomber platforms in multiple roles. The obsolescent but reliable and battle-proven Canberra bomber continued to be the only offensive-cum-recce platform that could fly reasonably deep (over 400 km) into enemy territory, while the Hunter MK 56A and MiG-21 FL emerged as multi-role platforms. The Sukhoi-7 and HF-24 remained tactical ground-attack aircraft, with the Gnat Mk 1 and the MiG-21 FL assigned to point air-defence roles. However, by the end of the 1970s, the ground-attack variant of the MiG-21, called the MiG-21 M or T-96, had also been inducted. Acquisition of the multi-role MiG-21 Bis, the MiG-23 BN strike aircraft, MiG-23 MF interceptor and the MiG-25 strategic recce aircraft meant that Soviet fighter aircraft formed the mainstay of the IAF combat fleet (around thirty-six squadrons). The IAF's airlift capability was in serious trouble in the 1970s with obsolete and ageing American C-119 Packets and Dakotas, British Avros and Soviet An-12s making up the twelve squadrons that struggled to cope with multiple requirements. Soviet Mi-4 and Mi-8 helicopters, complemented by the Chetak light communication helicopters, were the mainstay of the IAF's twelve helicopter units.[12] An overall assessment of the time reveals that the IAF had a hybrid mix of Western and Soviet platforms, flown by operationally proficient pilots, with a penchant for adapting Western aerial tactics on Soviet platforms.[13]

Though the 1970s were marked by economic stagnation, the security landscape in the subcontinent and South Asia evolved quite rapidly after the Soviet invasion of Afghanistan in 1979. The arming of Pakistan as a frontline and proxy state by the US was a Cold War strategy that resulted in much of that capability being leveraged by its military dictator, President Zia-ul-Haq, against India. Consequently, India was forced to embark on a rapid military capability build-up. Across the Himalayas, there was also a realization within a resurgent Deng-led China and the PLA that it ran the risk of being left behind in its quest to emerge as a global power by the end of the twentieth century unless it built credible military capability.

Muscular 1980s

India faced its most diverse security challenges between 1984 and 1990, and it can be argued that there was little scope for cutting defence spending. Strangely, that is exactly what happened as the defence budget declined from 3.79 per cent of GDP in 1980 to 3.28 per cent in 1989[14] even as the GDP grew almost threefold – from $100 billion in 1980 to almost $280 billion in 1989.[15] Despite serious structural problems that necessitated defence budget cuts in the closing years of the decade, speedy and pragmatic acquisitions were made between 1980 and 1987. Driven by rising forex holdings and the political backing of the military as a critical instrument of statecraft under Prime Minister Indira Gandhi and her son and successor Rajiv Gandhi, the Indian armed forces acquired the necessary muscle before the slump of the 1990s.[16]

Under Deng Xiaoping, China embarked on a reform process in the PLA in the 1980s, with defence budgets varying from a low of $12 billion to a high of $20 billion, or between 3 and 5.25 per cent of GDP.[17] Revisiting this comparison in 2000, 2010 and 2016 would reveal the emerging non-linear asymmetry in military modernization between India and its principal adversary. For the first time, India's armed forces crossed the million mark, with the Indian Army accounting for over 80 per cent of this strength. There was some force restructuring because of the counterinsurgency and counterterrorist operations in Punjab, Sri Lanka and Nagaland, and the creation of larger manoeuvre forces in the form of mechanized infantry regiments and the Reorganized Army Plains Infantry Divisions (RAPIDS). The latter was the brainchild of the farsighted General Sundarji, the army chief from 1985 to 1987. They were raised to support offensive operations in the plains against a rapidly modernizing Pakistan Army. Older infantry battalions from all major regiments were converted into mechanized units, a move that caused some heartburn within the traditional infantry constituency.[18]

Sundarji also expanded the army's integral air arm and formed the Army Aviation Corps by convincing the IAF to part with its attack helicopter fleet of Mi-25s and giving the Indian Army's strike corps (1 and 2 Corps) operational control over them. The major acquisition for the Indian Army in the 1980s was the Russian T-72 tank which replaced the obsolete T-55s and the Vijayanta as its MBT. By the end of the decade the Indian Army had 700 of these tanks as its main offensive force. The acquisition of the BMP-II ICVs in large numbers and the addition of the versatile 155mm FH-77B Bofors artillery gun added significant punch to India's strike corps for offensive operations in conventional conflict scenarios.

The 1980s also saw the emergence of a robust maritime discourse within India's strategic establishment, as scholars like K. Subrahmanyam and Raja Menon emphasized the need to focus on the Indian Ocean as a maritime space of great relevance if India wanted to emerge as a power of consequence in the years ahead.[19] The Indian Navy rapidly expanded in both the surface and sub-surface domains. With the induction of the refurbished INS *Viraat* (formerly HMS *Hermes)* of Falklands vintage, the Indian Navy could deploy an aircraft carrier-based fleet on both its eastern and western seaboards. Replacing the Seahawks and Alizes with the battle-proven British-made Sea Harrier jump jets was a major step towards the expansion of naval aviation.

With eight indigenously designed Nilgiri-class frigates, three Godavari-class frigates and five new Kashin-class destroyers, the Indian Navy's surface fleet was in fine fettle. Its capabilities now more than outmatched those of both the Pakistan Navy and the PLA Navy. Realizing that the Indian Navy's submarine fleet was in danger of being outclassed by both Pakistani and Chinese submarines, the old Foxtrots were replaced by eight Kilo-class and four silent German HDW type-1500 submarines, not forgetting the leased nuclear-powered Charlie-class Soviet submarine, INS *Chakra*. Maritime reconnaissance got a fillip with the induction of the huge four-engine Tu-142 and the reliable Il-38 aircraft in addition to the expansion of the Sea King fleet for tactical reconnaissance and anti-submarine warfare.[20]

Building on the impetus given to air power by Air Chief Marshal P.C. Lal during the 1971 war, the IAF emerged as an independent arm of warfighting, and a critical enabler in joint operations. This was forcefully argued by Air Commodore Jasjit Singh, a self-taught practitioner-scholar and protégé of K. Subrahmanyam, who was arguably the pre-eminent security strategist of independent India.[21] The acquisition of the British Jaguar deep-penetration strike aircraft in large numbers from the late 1970s through the 1980s, along with variants of the MiG-23 and MiG-27 aircraft, strengthened the IAF's offensive punch. Procurement of MiG-25s for strategic reconnaissance, MiG-29s for air superiority and Mirage-2000s as fourth-generation multi-role combat aircraft transformed the IAF into the most advanced third-world air force.

Induction of the heavy-lift Il-76 aircraft and the medium-lift An-32 aircraft gave the air mobility fleet inter- and intra-theatre capability, while the introduction of medium-lift Mi-17 and Mi-25 attack helicopters provided significant rotary wing flexibility and enhanced air maintenance support to the Indian Army in remote deployments along the LoC and LAC. The IAF's tactics and combat development establishment – which was formed before the 1971 war and developed some innovative tactics during that conflict[22] – expanded its repertoire significantly.

More impactful in the 1980s though was the attempt by Indira Gandhi and Rajiv Gandhi to proactively leverage this transformed military capability to support an aggressive foreign policy, albeit with mixed results. However, the sudden flurry of military actions from 1984 onwards shook the Indian military out of its post-1971 slumber. A mix of successes and failures prompted the drive for a recalibration of both equipment profiles and operational strategies. The successes included the occupation of the Siachen Glacier in 1984 (Operation Meghdoot*)*, Exercise Brasstacks, a massive air-land exercise, the thwarting of an impending Chinese move in Arunachal Pradesh in 1986-87 (Exercise Falcon) and the air-land operation in the Maldives in 1988 (Operation Cactus). But the disastrous storming of the Golden Temple in 1984 (Operation Blue Star) and the failure of the extended military intervention in Sri Lanka from 1987 to 1990 (Operation Pawan) had a greater strategic and national fallout.

The 1990s and Beyond

Plagued by an economic crisis and a lethargic national security apparatus, the 1990s were marked by a negative non-linear growth in defence expenditure, which reflected an apathy towards building hard power as an element of Indian statecraft. From 1990 to 1998, while India's GDP increased from just under $300 billion to around $420 billion (an increase of over 40 per cent in real terms), the defence budget rose from $9.25 billion to just $10 billion, a measly increase of around 7.5 per cent. It needed the Kargil crisis to precipitate a much needed 20 per cent boost in the defence budget in 1999. Yet the defence spending as a percentage of GDP hovered between 2.5 and 2.8 per cent, as compared to the almost 3.7-4 per cent that was maintained in the previous decade. Even Japan spent more on defence in the 1990s. For the first time, the official Chinese defence budget surpassed that of India, even though it was widely known that PLA spending was completely opaque till the first decade of the twenty-first century.[23]

Following the break-up of the Soviet Union, replacing and even maintaining the Soviet inventory became problematic, as India went shopping for spares of MiG and An-32 aircraft and T-72 tanks to Russia, Ukraine and Romania, among other countries.[24] India's inability to reverse-engineer systems and components, and the slow progress in India's indigenous fighter aircraft and tank programmes, meant that it would have to rely on its Soviet inventory for longer than could be logistically supported. Faced with a covert proxy war of terrorism in Kashmir since the early 1990s, the Indian Army raised a counterinsurgency force in 1990 called the Rashtriya Rifles, which was initially deployed in Punjab.

General B.C. Joshi, the army chief in 1993-94, played an important role in initially expanding the Rashtriya Rifles to thirty-six battalions and assigning it specific areas in both South and North Kashmir.[25] Its role gradually expanded to counterterrorist operations in J&K. General Joshi's son, Akshay Joshi – a former lieutenant commander in the Indian Navy and now a joint secretary in the National Security Council Secretariat – recollects that his father was among the first few military leaders who likened Pakistan's support for the violent secessionist movement in J&K to a proxy war. As the name suggests, proxy war is a form of war; therefore, he argued, the army was the right instrument of the state to combat it.[26] He believed that combating terrorism in J&K differed from terrorism as experienced elsewhere in the world. Arguing forcefully that this was a 'legitimate task' for the army, he suggested the restructuring of the force to fight this menace more effectively.[27] It is for this reason that General Joshi spent much time and effort in creating the Rashtriya Rifles and nurturing it initially as an effective counterinsurgency and counterterrorism force in the Kashmir Valley.

The force was designed to ensure constant and uninterrupted flow of intelligence and use of superior knowledge of terrain and capabilities of all arms and services of the Indian Army to fight insurgency, instead of using only the infantry for this purpose. According to a former defence minister, 'The Rashtriya Rifles has provided the requisite continuity in the low-intensity conflict/internal security grid and allowed the army to retain a strategic reserve for other border [conflict] variants.'[28] By the end of the 1990s, Rashtriya Rifles had grown to over fifty battalions divided across four counterinsurgency forces identified as Victor, Kilo, Delta and Romeo. While the Victor and Kilo Forces operated in the Kashmir Valley north of the Pir Panjal range, the Delta and Romeo forces were responsible for the areas south of the range, comprising the regions of Doda, Rajouri and Poonch. The army would add on one more division-sized force called Uniform Force in the 2000s for Udhampur. The army also raised an additional strike corps HQ and a corps HQ in the north-east during the 1990s.

The main equipment acquisitions by the Indian Army during the 1990s were the Pinaka multi-barrel rocket launchers, an entire range of surface-to-air missile systems for air defence of the tactical battle area (SAM-6, SAM-8 and SAM-13) and battlefield surveillance radars for monitoring the extremely active and volatile LoC in Kashmir. After much inter-services recrimination following the Kargil conflict, the Indian Army would also get its own Searcher unmanned aerial vehicles from Israel.

The Indian Navy continued its dual acquisition spree as it modernized its surface fleet with indigenous and Russian-built frigates and destroyers, and added two additional Kilo-class submarines to its sub-surface fleet. The navy fleet comprised twenty-six principal surface combatants (aircraft carrier, destroyers, frigates and large corvettes), fifteen submarines of three classes and thirty-eight patrol and coastal combatants (small corvettes, mine-warfare ships, coastal patrol boats and amphibious support ships).

The IAF made few major purchases in the 1990s apart from the first Su-30 squadron equipped with the Russian Su-30K, which was inducted in 1999. Other minor acquisitions included a few VIP and electronic warfare Boeing aircraft, Mi-35s as replacements for the Mi-25 attack helicopters, the upgrading of the Jaguar fleet and completion of deliveries in all other fleets. Its combat fleet increased to forty squadrons, almost at the authorized limit of forty-two. The acquisition of six Il-78 aerial tankers was a milestone for enhancing the combat reach of the IAF's fighter fleet. It addressed its major operational weakness – the lack of a robust ground-based air defence network that could be comparable with the PAF's well-networked system, which had multiple tiers of radars all linked to provide a composite picture. Air Marshal Patney reflects that if there was one thing he was immensely satisfied with in the 1990s it was the improvement of the IAF's air defence network.[29] The integration of multiple radar pictures by using high-frequency radio on to one screen, known as TADIDS (Tactical Air Defence Integrated Display System), helped operationalize the control and reporting centre concept. This allowed multiple radars to be networked with adequate redundancy (satellite, radio and visual reporting). This ensured that the IAF slowly embraced networks involving fusion of data and caught up with the PAF in the realm of air defence. Fusing these networks with fourth-generation aircraft like the

Mirage-2000, MiG-29 and SU-30 gave a significant fillip to India's lagging capabilities in air defence.

Entering the New Millennium: China Looms Large

By the beginning of the 2000s, India's strategic establishment had got over its Pakistan obsession and realized that India's major strategic and security challenge would emerge from a resurgent China. Voicing his concern openly for the first time in 1998, India's combative defence minister George Fernandes declared that 'China and not Pakistan was India's principal adversary'.[30] Highlighting one of India's major concerns about the collusive threat that could emerge in the decades ahead, he added, 'China has provided Pakistan with both missile as well as nuclear know-how. We have become a very soft people and we must realize that nations are not built through soft options, nor are the country's frontiers secured by a soft line.'[31]

When Deng handed over complete power to his successor Jiang Zemin in the early 1990s, the modernization of the Chinese military was on an upward trajectory. In 1990, China had a reported defence budget of $6.13 billion – which could well have been twice that amount – as against India's reported defence budget of about $9 billion. Relying heavily on its nuclear arsenal, mass and a manpower-intensive army for deterrence, the only area where it was both qualitatively and quantitatively better placed than India was in the realm of rocket units and submarines. Supported by a galloping economy that had grown to three times the Indian economy by 2000, China's defence budget, according to the respected *Military Balance*, had increased from $12.6 billion in 1999 to $14-15 billion in 2000. Chinese defence spending remained non-transparent, and official accounts substantially understated real military expenditure, which was estimated at more than $40 billion in 1999 – three times the official figure. As against this, India's defence budget remained relatively stagnant, at around $12 billion.

By 2010 China's armed forces had showcased the progress of their accelerating military modernization drive and caught the world's attention. The comprehensive set of military capabilities that were demonstrated at the sixtieth anniversary celebrations of the founding of the People's Republic of China put the world on notice that China was ready for power projection on the global stage. China's defence budget had skyrocketed to what most defence analysts agree was at least twice the officially stated figure of $70 billion – i.e., almost four times that of India's officially stated figure of around $35 billion.

The PLA, PLA Air Force and PLA Navy had modernized at a startling pace with an eye on closing the gap with the US even as China jostled for clear leadership in Asia.

India, on the other hand, appeared content to continue to build military capability primarily for deterrence and protection of its interests rather than any kind of power projection. By 2016, China's official defence budget had more than doubled over the preceding six years to $145 billion, keeping pace with the growth in GDP, as against India's budget of $51 billion, which had increased only by 37 per cent despite a GDP growth rate that almost matched China's.[32] Even if one considers the actual Chinese defence budget to be 1.5 times the official figure, it is still four times the Indian defence budget.

The modernization of the Chinese military has resulted in sweeping top-down organizational changes that have ensured that the PLA is now part of integrated theatre commands and shares leadership space with the much smaller PLA Air Force, PLA Navy and the PLA Rocket Force. However, in India, integration is still a work in progress, hampered as it is by turf battles between the three armed forces and other stakeholders in national security. Some movement towards better synergy is visible on the horizon with a slew of reforms announced by the Modi government and the appointment of a Chief of Defence Staff. However, it is too early to assess its impact on operational capability. Much of the asymmetry that has emerged between India and China in land-warfare capability can be attributed to the rapid expansion of the conventional element of the PLA Rocket Force – earlier known as the Second Artillery – which forms part of China's first-strike capability. India has no force to match this capability other than its meagre inventory of Prithvi and BrahMos cruise missiles. The Indian Army's artillery has been another area of stark asymmetry that India has finally addressed by inducting two highly mobile guns, the US-built M777 Howitzer – a 155mm 39-calibre towed gun – and the heavier K-9 Vajra 155mm 52-calibre towed gun. While the former is being assembled in India by Mahindra Defence Systems, the latter was developed by Samsung Techwin of South Korea and is being manufactured by the Indian engineering giant Larsen & Toubro.[33] With 245 of these guns scheduled to be produced within the next three years, the Indian Army can be more confident of being able to respond with adequate firepower to a rocket/artillery assault – the preferred option of the PLA.

The PLA Navy has undergone the most aggressive expansion among all arms of the PLA, reflecting China's resuscitated thrust towards expanding its maritime influence.[34] Protection of its sea lines of communication and ensuring the safety of its expanding infrastructure interests in the form of the Belt and

Road Initiative seem to be the overriding focus of this expansion. It has grown into a modern navy with one operational aircraft carrier, around sixty-five submarines of different classes and capabilities, eighty principal combatants and 450-500 support vessels comprising coastal defence, amphibious craft and logistics support ships. Apart from its traditional watch areas in the East and South China Seas, a confident and resurgent PLA Navy now makes regular forays and deploys in areas that converge with the Indian Navy's areas of interest, influence and deployment – the entire Indian Ocean Region (IOR). In contrast, force levels in the Indian Navy have remained relatively static over the past decade with one aircraft carrier, fourteen to sixteen submarines, forty-five to fifty combatants and around ninety to hundred support vessels for a protect-and-influence role. Despite having the most vibrant indigenous manufacturing programme, which has resulted in the induction of the Delhi-class destroyers, Brahmaputra- and Shivalik-class frigates and the Arihant-class nuclear sumbarines, the budget share of the Indian Navy has remained within the narrow range of 14-17 per cent over the past decade. This does not support the conversion of doctrine into capability. If there is an area of strength that India can build on, it is in the realm of maritime surveillance and anti-submarine warfare. With eight aircraft, the Indian Navy operates the world's second largest fleet of Boeing P-8 Orion maritime reconnaissance aircraft.

For long the IAF was sanguine in its conviction that it was a superior fighting force as compared to the PLA Air Force on every parameter except numbers. The last two decades, however, have seen the PLA Air Force acquire indigenously manufactured (mostly reverse-engineered) fourth- and fifth-generation fighters, Airborne Warning and Control System (AWACS) platforms, aerial refuellers, highly sophisticated and reverse-engineered missile systems, long-range air-launched weapons, significant airlift capability, high-altitude long-endurance and medium-altitude long-endurance UAVs. When compared with the significant decrease in the number of fighter squadrons in the IAF during the same period – without any replacements – and the sluggish indigenization of aircraft, weapons and sensors,[35] the IAF's competitive advantage is seen to be fast eroding.

The impending induction of two state-of-the-art squadrons of the French-built Rafale multi-role fighters and the ongoing induction of the indigenously designed and built Tejas light combat aircraft are likely to stem the slide. Where the IAF is in good shape for some decades to come is in the air mobility domain with the induction of the C-17 and C-130J aircraft, and the Mi-17 V5 and Chinook helicopters. Along with the most recent induction of the Apache attack helicopters, the air mobility component of joint operations is more than comparable to what the PLA Air Force has. However, more needs to be done if the IAF is to match up overall to the PLA Air Force in the years ahead.

One area in which all three arms of the Indian military are significantly better placed than the PLA is in terms of actual battle experience across the spectrum of conflict. Their learnings from friends and strategic partners during the extensive joint exercises held since the early 1990s have added significant value to their fighting potential. The purpose of President Xi Jinping committing Chinese troops to UN operations over the past decade has been to enable the PLA to gain vital overseas operational experience.

Iconic Platforms

Soldiers, sailors and airmen across the world have stories to narrate about their favourite military platforms, and there are three stories about platforms that need to be told. The first two are pre-1980 stories, while the third is the story of an imported artillery gun that has performed brilliantly in the most inhospitable terrain. The first story relates to the Nilgiri-class frigate programme – which stimulated indigenous design and production in the Indian Navy. The second tells the tale of the MiG-21, which has demonstrated the IAF's ability to do 'more with less' as it operationally exploited the MiG-21 well beyond what the Russians did. The final tale is of the controversial Swedish gun, the Bofors 155mm FH-77B medium-range howitzer.

The Nilgiri Tale

The development of the Indian Navy's Nilgiri-class of frigates was a defining moment in indigenous warship design. Modelled on the British Leander-class frigate – which was among the most widely operated frigates across navies in the 1960s – it displaced around 2,500-2,700 tons in its original version. They proved to be versatile ships in their various roles that included anti-submarine warfare, air defence and fleet picquet. What the Indian Navy did right was to lead the design process by sending several talented officers to study warship design in the UK and US and thereafter it orchestrated their entire careers either in naval design or in leadership roles at various dockyards. This move not only ensured the success of the Nilgiri class of frigates but also paved the way for the entire design, development, production and maintenance processes to be user-driven – a method that was to elude both the Indian Army and the IAF.

The first ship in this series, INS *Nilgiri*, was designed, developed and built as a collaborative effort between the Indian Naval Design Bureau (NDB), Mazagaon Docks and a British consortium of Vickers and Yarrow (lead shipyard). It was launched in 1968 by Prime Minister Indira Gandhi, and commissioned four years later in 1972. The *Nilgiri* was followed in 1974, 1976, 1977, 1980 and 1981 by the *Himgiri, Udaygiri, Dunagiri, Taragiri* and *Vindhyagiri.*[36] All six ships were equipped with the full range of basic shipborne weapons and an electronic suite comprising guns with different ranges, torpedoes, sonar, surface-to-surface radars, electronic support measures and basic electronic countermeasures.

Admiral Arun Prakash, a former chief of naval staff who commanded the last of these ships, the *Vindhyagiri,* in the late 1980s, has fond recollections of his time in command and recounts the two biggest enhancements on the *Taragiri* and *Vindhyagiri.* The first was the widening of the helicopter landing and storage areas to accommodate the larger Sea King ASW helicopter; the other was the integration of Indian electronic and weapon systems within the inherently British electronic architecture.[37] All six ships served the Indian Navy with distinction for over three decades – except for the *Nilgiri,* which was decommissioned after twenty-four years of exemplary service.

The Nilgiri class was followed by what were initially known as Project 16 frigates, which later came to be classified as the Godavari class. The hull design was essentially the same, but at a maximum displacement of 3,800 tons, it was heavier than the Nilgiri class by over 1,000 tons. This permitted the widening of the rear deck to accommodate two Sea King helicopters, surface-to-surface missiles (SSMs) of Russian origin (it could accommodate four Styx P-15 missiles), SAMs and other advanced electronic architecture designed by Bharat Electronics. The *Godavari, Ganga* and *Gomti* were further modernized, modified, adapted, strengthened and weaponized into the Brahmaputra class of frigates, which were similar in looks and mode of propulsion (steam turbines).

These were followed by the Shivalik class of frigates with stealth design features. Not satisfied with designing 4,000-tonne warships, the NDB decided to amalgamate the best features of the Godavari-class frigates and the Russian Kashin-class destroyers. This, in the 1990s, led to Project 15 – the Delhi-class destroyers that were the first gas turbine-propelled large combatant ships in the Indian Navy, displaced 6,500 tons and could carry sixteen Uran missiles. Almost concurrently, it built the Brahmaputra-class frigates, followed by the Kolkata-class destroyers – all of which were built at the Garden Reach Shipbuilders in Kolkata. India is justifiably proud of its frigate and destroyer development capability, which has allowed it to project maritime power and diplomacy to great effect over the years. These ships have done India proud and symbolize India's indigenous naval capability, particularly when they call on foreign ports as the vanguard of India's military diplomacy.[38]

A Bird for All Seasons: The MiG-21

The second story narrates how the IAF took a simple aircraft like the MiG-21 and made it do things that its original designers could never have imagined. Fighter pilots have a respect for the MiG-21 aircraft that is enduring and always evokes nostalgia. Many pilots moved on to later-generation aircraft like Jaguars, Mirage-200s, MiG-29s and Su-30s but many would come back to MiG-21s at various stages as flight commanders and commanding officers and renew their love affair with the most widely produced and operated fighter aircraft in the post-WWII era. Air Chief Marshal Tipnis, a former air chief, called the MiG-21 'My Fair Lady'. He was known to jump into one and fly solo when he visited a base.

Unlike the smooth evolution of the Nilgiri-class frigates into a design-and-development project, the MiG-21 acquisition and licensed production followed a different trajectory, driven as it was by strong political considerations. IAF historians like Pushpindar Singh have chronicled the note of diffidence[39] from the IAF leadership when V.K. Krishna Menon, the acerbic defence minister, first suggested the MiG-21 in August 1962 as a counter to the Western aircraft (F-104 and F-86) that Pakistan had procured. Correctly analysing the geopolitical situation, the Soviets made a mouth-watering offer to help set up massive plants in India to manufacture the MiG-21 under licence, but without any assurance of technology transfer. This clinched the deal and the first six MiG-21s, also known as Type-74s, arrived in India in 1963.

After an initial sojourn in Chandigarh, the first squadron – 28 Squadron, commanded by Wing Commander Dilbagh Singh (a subsequent air chief) – consolidated operations at Adampur. The initial induction was accompanied with ambitious plans to set up manufacturing plants for various parts and components of the aircraft at Nasik, Koraput and Hyderabad. This initial aircraft was a very basic design; it had limited fuel capacity (1,800 litres) and endurance, was equipped only with two primitive heat-seeking missiles without any radar guidance and – as one early pilot put it – handled 'like a sports car'. Noting Indian concerns, these were soon followed by the MiG-21 FL, or T-77, which had a basic airborne fire-control radar and an underslung gun-pack that housed a lethal 23mm twin-barrelled cannon that could fire at the rate of 3,600 rounds per minute. Air Marshal Patney and the late Air

Marshal Rathore, both Vir Chakra gallantry award winners from the 1965 war with Pakistan, were among the second lot of pilots who went to Russia to train on this variant. Speaking about the aircraft, Patney said, 'It was a fun aircraft to fly! Get the air speed indicator down to zero and carry out a slow speed loop at 2,000 feet. We did a lot of insensible things on the bird that surprised even the Russians.'[40]

Over fifteen years later, I would go up as a rookie fighter pilot in my first fighter squadron in a MiG-21 twin-seater trainer variant with Rathore, then a group captain, and see for myself what it could do in terms of pure manoeuvring. On an overcast day with the cloud base at just over 500 metres, Rathore asked me to level off below clouds at a speed of 700 kmph and transfer my attention to the instruments. He then proceeded to talk me through a loop relying only on my instruments – the artificial horizon and angle of attack indicator. As we turned into the top of the loop, his voice was calm as he said, 'Easy, boy, don't pull back, look at your angle of attack, keep it within the range I told you,' and before I knew it I had levelled off below clouds at the same height as where I had commenced the loop. I was sweating like hell and it had started raining. From the rear cockpit, RatC – as Rathore was popularly known – calm and collected as ever, talked me through executing my first landing in a MiG-21 in pouring rain!

After assembling over thirty of these variants, the IAF would go on to manufacture under licence 197 T-77s between 1966 and 1974. The love affair of the IAF with the MiG-21would continue with the induction of a dedicated ground-attack version – the MiG-21 M, or T-96. It had four underwing hard points and one underbelly station to carry a variety of bombs, rockets and even electronic warfare pods. The MiG-21 Bison followed with a more powerful engine (R-25) and air-to-air missiles like the R-60 and R-23 that matched some Western missiles in performance. Fifty-seven years after the first MiG-21 was inducted, the IAF still flies the last variant, the MiG-21 Bison, which operates alongside fourth-generation aircraft such as the Mirage-2000 and the SU-30 MKI. Interestingly, US Air Force pilots who flew mock air-combat drills in 2008 against the MiG-21 Bison marvelled at its adaptive capability despite its vintage and, more importantly, the ability of IAF pilots to keep the MiG-21 relevant. A US Air Force colonel described it as 'pretty neat… very manoeuvrable aeroplane'.[41] The MiG-21 saga in the IAF could not have asked for a more befitting finale than when credible IAF evidence showed that one of its MiG-21 Bisons downed a Pakistani F-16 during an aerial engagement on 27 February 2019.

The Controversial Gun

Seeking to add firepower to the Indian Army's growing offensive capability in the 1980s, the quest commenced for an artillery gun that combined mobility, improved rate of fire and enhanced ranges. This led to a fiercely contested international tussle between France, Sweden, Austria and the UK for the large contract of almost 400 guns. After an exhaustive evaluation and price negotiation, the Swedish Bofors 155mm gun was chosen over the French model.[42] This deal has not been without controversy, with the scandal that broke out following allegations that a commission of Rs 64 crore was paid to undisclosed entities in the Congress party, and that Prime Minister Rajiv Gandhi and his family were involved.[43] Controversies aside, the gun has performed brilliantly under varied conditions.

Till the mid-1980s, Soviet-origin guns and multi-barrel rocket launchers – such as the 100mm, 122mm, 130mm and GRAD – were the mainstay of the Indian Army's 'fire arm', the Corps of Artillery. The conversion of field and mountain guns to 105mm calibre was the next step, keeping with prevailing global trends of developing guns that would be effective against armour and fortified defences. Armed forces across the Western world gravitated towards the production of 155mm guns. Consequently, the FH-77B 155mm field howitzer – as the Bofors gun is technically called – was inducted into the Indian Army between 1986 and 1989 to complement the Soviet 130mm guns.

In a bold and unprecedented decision, the Indian Army chose the path of acquiring a complete 'gun system' from AB Bofors (today BAE Systems Bofors). It acted not only as manufacturer of the guns (410 were purchased by India in total), but also as the major single-point supply contractor for globally sourced items. These comprised equipment such as the Saab-Scania gun-towing and ammunition-hauling trucks (approximately 600 trucks in different variants), Barracuda camouflage nets, Marconi command-and-control systems, Quickfire fire-control systems, Fairey Australia muzzle-velocity radars, BEAB sighting equipment, surveying equipment from Wild of Switzerland and navigation equipment from Ferranti UK.[44]

A highly mobile platform despite its weight of 12 tons, the Bofors gun can be driven at speeds of up to 70 kmph on paved roads – with excellent off-road mobility too. The gun's USP is its high rate of sustained fire of six rounds per minute – it is said to have sustained a short rapid rate of fire of fifteen rounds per minute during the Kargil conflict.[45] Capable of achieving ranges of slightly over 30 km, it has been known to hit targets at 35 km in the rarefied atmosphere of Siachen and Kargil.

The first consignment of the guns and ammunition was dispatched by the manufacturer in August 1986 and landed at Bombay in September and October 1986. The 285 Medium Regiment was the first regiment to receive these guns at Deolali, Maharashtra – where the School of Artillery is located. Officer-instructors trained in Sweden drove this equipment from the railway sidings to the unit location, then trained the soldiers on this totally new and what was then considered a highly complex system. The initial priority of acquiring these guns was for deployment along the western borders in support of conventional operations in the plains and the Desert Sector.

However, in June 1986, the Sumdorong Chu (Wangdung) incident[46] in the Tawang Sector of Arunachal Pradesh along the Sino-Indian border (covered in detail in Chapter 9) and the intensified pace of operations in Siachen changed the deployment priorities. After a quick orientation training and test firing in Deolali field-firing ranges, a battery of 285 Medium Regiment was inducted into the Tawang sector of the Tezpur-based 4 Corps in the winter of 1986-87 as part of the proactive Indian response to Chinese incursions into the Wangdung area of the Sumdorong Chu Valley. After the crisis ended, it handed over its guns to 218 Medium Regiment in the same area, which was officially declared as the first Bofors unit.

Next, 79 Medium Regiment became the first regiment to be equipped with the complete 'weapon system'. The regiment inducted these guns in Sikkim as part of 33 Corps in the Nathu La Sector. The deployment in this sector was led by Captain (later Lieutenant General) Anil Ahuja, who took these over rickety wooden bridges of unknown classification and along landslide-prone narrow roads, with many a night spent on the bed of the Teesta River during the movement. Three more regiments (285, 230 and 36 Medium Regiments) would soon follow as the Indian Army equipped more than twenty regiments over the years with these superb guns.

The procurement and induction of the FH-77B Bofors guns by the Indian Army is an example of a well-planned and meticulously executed acquisition, only disrupted subsequently due to the political controversy generated around it. Ahuja, an accomplished artillery officer who provided first-hand information and analysis of the induction of the gun as one of its pioneer operators, is emphatic about the professionalism with which the system was inducted and operationalized. He stated: 'The most important takeaways from the Bofors acquisition are meticulous perspective planning and continuity of commitment, identification of operational needs, diligent contract planning, detailed training curriculum and lastly, incorporation of transfer of technology and indigenization. We had plans for additional manufacturing of 1,500-2,000 guns, which did not get executed because of the political fallout. However, the "ghost" of the Bofors deal has finally been exorcized with the successful induction of the indigenous Dhanush 155mm gun – which owes much to the original Bofors gun.'[47] The guns have since performed brilliantly in the Siachen and Kargil conflicts and in punitive responses during the artillery duels that rage frequently across the LoC.

Having sampled an overview of how the Indian military coped with the rapidly transforming global and regional landscape of war and conflict and equipped itself to fight these wars, it is time to dive headlong into the heart of the book – the various conflicts beginning with the Naga insurgency in the steamy jungles of north-east India.

4

THE NAGA REBELLION

'India's stand on the Naga question is based on the honest conviction that the Nagas are as much part of the Indian nation as the Assamese or the Manipuris.'[1]

– *D.R. Mankekar*

Author's Note

The north-eastern region of India comprises the seven distinct states of Assam, Meghalaya, Arunachal Pradesh, Nagaland, Tripura, Mizoram and Manipur, also colloquially known as the 'Seven Sisters'. Sikkim became part of the group after it joined the Indian Union in 1975. Except for Meghalaya and Sikkim, which have been relatively peaceful, all other states have witnessed strife of varying intensity and duration. While the common thread across the region is one of a governance deficit and neglect by successive governments in New Delhi, it is the secessionist, cultural, religious, ethnic, foreign illegal migration and demographic fault lines that have given rise to internal armed conflict of various kinds.

The Naga insurgency continues to be the wellspring of much of the unrest along India's north-east frontiers, all of which warranted the use of force by the state. In all subsequent insurgencies in the region – such as the Mizo uprising, the rebellion in Tripura, tribal strife in Manipur and the ethnic strife in Assam – the state governments have sought the help of the Indian Army and the IAF to counter the protracted violence. Due to space constraints, I will focus in detail only on the joint operations in Nagaland and Mizoram.

I have served in and visited the north-east frequently – as a fighter pilot posted to Tezpur on two occasions, as a student officer and faculty member at war colleges and on numerous trips to Arunachal Pradesh, Nagaland, Meghalaya, Tripura and to the extremities of our frontiers at the trijunction of India, China and Myanmar at Kibithoo. I have trekked in the Dirang valley and spent time with army course mates and air force comrades from the helicopter stream at Imphal, Zunheboto, Mukokchong and Chakabama. My experiences there are nothing compared to the hardships faced by uniformed personnel who are posted there for years and civilian folk who invariably get caught in the crossfire of an internal conflict. What they have given me, however, are perspective, empathy and an understanding that goes beyond mere historical analysis. I have extensively referred to Indian forces as 'security forces' as operations in the north-east over the last six decades have involved troops from the Indian Army, Assam Rifles and state police forces.

Rumblings of Dissent in NEFA (1950s)

Operation Mop was conceived in the early 1950s and executed by Major Bob Khathing, the administrator of the erstwhile North Eastern Frontier Agency (NEFA). The operation aimed at amalgamating the tribal areas of the region into the Indian Union in the 1950s before China could execute its creeping strategy of co-opting Tawang and large parts of NEFA as 'Southern Tibet'.[2] Khathing was a Manipuri Naga who had assisted Field Marshal Slim's XIV Army during the Burma Campaign of WWII as part of Victor Force, a small covert unit that provided information and intelligence on the Japanese advance. He was subsequently commissioned as an officer in the Kumaon and Assam Regiments of the Indian Army. Khathing retired from the army after Independence to steer the integration of NEFA into the Indian Union as a bureaucrat and administrator. He was later appointed India's high commissioner to Burma (renamed as Myanmar in 1989) and is one of independent India's lesser-known nationalists.[3]

Before the Chinese, however, the Indian state had to contend with the Thagins, a fierce tribe in the Siang Frontier Division that lay south of the McMahon Line astride one of the Brahmaputra's major tributaries, the Subansiri. In the years following Independence, the Thagins had fiercely resisted any attempts by the Assam Rifles – India's first paramilitary force – to bring them under control, and even inflicted some casualties on the force. The tipping point, however, was the massacre of a large column of Assam Rifles – including an officer and some local government officials – by a raiding party of Thagins, who ransacked the Aching Mori outpost on 22 October 1953 and took a few hostages. Alarmed at the turn of events, the NEFA administration swung into action and ordered the Assam Rifles to raise a strong force and send it into the affected area to free the hostages and maintain the peace.[4]

A battalion of the Assam Rifles – with troops on attachment from the Indian Army and officials of the political department – advanced on Aching Mori, with direct offensive air support provided by the Spitfires and Harvards of 14 and 17 Squadrons respectively. Five Dakotas from 11 Squadron based at Jorhat, an IAF airfield in Assam, dropped paratroopers near the troubled area, where they helped construct an advance landing ground (ALG) by 14 November. Additional troops were then flown in from army formations around Jorhat and other areas in the north-east. Clearly, much joint planning had been done to ensure the success of this operation.[5] The mandate of the force as it converged on Aching Mori was not to kill or lay waste to the land, but to threaten, deter and finally coerce the more belligerent among the tribals into submission. Before and during the approach march, troops demonstrated their firepower to tribal audiences so that the more recalcitrant among them would be duly cautioned, while the friendlies would be reassured. Air power demonstrations were also staged at selected spots. The targets chosen were unpopulated areas like hilltops and other prominent natural features. Spitfire Mk XVIIIs from 14 Squadron, which were deployed at Jorhat airfield in Assam, attacked these 'targets' with rockets, bombs and 20mm cannon in a show of force.[6]

But these measures did not always have the desired effect. Interestingly, local witch doctors cashed in on these 'near misses' of the IAF, saying that it was their charms that kept the rain of bombs away from the villages. The slow-moving Harvards dropped leaflets over both hostile and friendly villages, highlighting government initiatives and proposed welfare schemes. There was some exchange of fire as the hostiles ambushed patrols and made one determined bid using rifles and Sten guns to dislodge troops from their positions on the night of 15 December. The column returned the fire with mortars and light machine guns, followed by low early-morning passes and strafing by the Spitfires and Harvards. This blunted the attack and soon the security forces had the tribals on the run. By the end of December 1953, they had ceased to offer any resistance. This was the last 'operational' task of the Spitfire in the IAF before it flew into the sunset of its glorious existence.[7] In January 1972, NEFA became the union territory of Arunachal Pradesh, and was declared a federated state of India in 1987. Barring a few stray instances of Naga violence, that spilt over into the state, it has remained peaceful and stood steadfast as a north-eastern bastion, defying the territorial aspirations of a revisionist China.

The Longest Insurgency

It was over six decades ago that two companies of 17th Battalion of the Rajput Regiment (17 RAJPUT) marched through nearly 250 km of unfamiliar jungle and mountain terrain in Nagaland, marking the beginning of independent India's first prolonged counterinsurgency operation. In April 1955, the small force set out from Amguri – a sleepy town on the border between Assam and what is now the state of Nagaland – and headed east. Marching to Mokokchung and Aghunato through Naga territory – inhabited mostly by the Ao and Sema tribes – it swung north and headed into Tuensang province, the wild and uncharted area bordering Myanmar and home to the fierce Konyak tribe.[8]

Tucked away in the extreme north-eastern part of the Indian subcontinent, where the sun rises before the rest of India wakes, lies a pristine and beautiful land. The rolling hills rise to a maximum of 10,000 feet, while verdant and lush subtropical forests offer a breathtaking variety of flora and fauna. The terrain is dotted with evergreen forests that are denser in the northern part all along the India–Myanmar border. The young hills pose a military challenge in terms of their broken contours, frequent crests and densely forested slopes. The defining feature of this land are its people, the Nagas. Their tribal diversity is astounding as no less than seventeen tribes make up the demography of Nagaland, with six of them – Konyaks, Aos, Semas, Angamis, Chakesangs and Lothas – constituting almost 70 per cent of the total population of Nagaland.[9] Tribal loyalties, distinct customs and fierce territorial possessiveness were the prime reasons for the lack of cohesion among the Nagas, during the nineteenth and twentieth centuries. Their relative isolation from development and modernity resulted in a feudal and violent system of decision-making and conflict resolution. Headhunting was prevalent till the early part of the previous century, particularly among the Konyaks, who inhabited the area of North Tsuensang in the north-eastern corner of the state.

It was in this rather inaccessible and remote part of north-east India that the first organized and sustained rebellion against the Indian government gained momentum. Organized loosely under the leadership of a slippery and ambitious Naga separatist leader from the Angami tribe, A.Z. Phizo,[10] it was supported over the years by both Pakistan and China and would tie up tens of thousands of Indian Army troops for years. *Time* magazine described the rebellion as follows:

> ...a Mau Mau-like war of terrorism against villages and Indian government posts, wielding their razor-sharp daos (axe-like knives) or shooting off Japanese and British arms pilfered from World War II caches. They were led by one A.Z. Phizo (who, lacking a Christian name, took the first and last letters of the alphabet). Phizo, 56, a mission-educated Naga, guided his warriors on ruthless raids in which they slaughtered hundreds of villagers and Indians, then retreated into the jungles and pathless mountain terrain. Afraid that the Naga revolt may spread to other tribes and give Red China an opening to step in on the disputed Indo-Tibet border, Prime Minister Nehru last week called on the Indian army to join Assam's armed police in an offensive operation against the rebels. Next day Naga terrorists kidnapped seven pro-government villagers in broad daylight, and beheaded four of them.[11]

The robust response of the Indian state during the early years of this rebellion must be judged through this lens, and not solely through the lens of regional media that selectively reported the heavy-handedness of the Indian Army while ignoring the violence perpetrated by Phizo's band of secessionist insurgents.

Colonial Rule

The late-medieval history of the Naga people is closely linked with the rise and fall of the great Ahom dynasty, which ruled over Assam and most parts of north-east India for almost six centuries till its collapse in the early nineteenth century.[12] For much of this period, the Nagas were remotely subjugated by the Ahoms and paid tribute in return for non-interference in their animistic and tribal way of life. The collapse of the Ahom dynasty around 1830 – and the subsequent conquest of Assam by the British – marked the eastward expansion of the British Empire. The British made their first military foray into the region around 1840, establishing a few strong outposts across the Naga Hills as they attempted to subjugate the tribes as a precursor to establishing political dominance.[13] By the turn of the century, much of the southern and central Naga Hills regions were under British control. Only a few tribes – such as the Konyaks and the Changs – remained in the northern regions that bordered Myanmar and extended northwards towards the trijunction of India, China and Myanmar.

The advent of Christianity around 1850 led to the Naga society slowly opening up to education and the Western way of life. Dedicated Christian missionaries combined their religious zeal with a genuine attempt to usher in some form of development in the region. It gained further traction with the arrival of American Baptist missionaries in the 1870s. Although the number of Christian converts was a mere 579 in 1901,[14] the spectacular march of Christianity in the region was revealed by the 1961 population census, which revealed that over 2,00,000 Nagas – or nearly 50 per cent of the total population – had converted to Christianity.[15] Interestingly, these missionaries were encouraged by the British to go into tribal areas to protect the tea business. It proved to be a cheaper method of preventing attacks on the tea plantations as compared to deploying the police or Assam Rifles.

By the Indian yardstick, Nagaland is a small state – occupying an area of no more than 17,000 sq km and extending about 450 km from the trijunction in the north to the border with Manipur in the south. It is approximately 325 km from the border with Assam in the west to the international boundary with Myanmar in the east. Though the tribal solidarity movement in the north-eastern region started as early as 1900 in what is now Meghalaya, the first armed uprising took place in the Naga Hills. Till the outbreak of WWII, the areas east of Assam were viewed by the British as merely a frontier that must be monitored. The relentless advance of Japanese divisions through Burma had them knocking on the Crown's frontiers by early 1944, and forced the British to reinforce the garrisons of Imphal and Kohima. This brought the Nagas into contact with other Indians for the first time, as tens of thousands of Indian troops streamed into the region as part of Field Marshal Slim's XIV Army.

However, a select group of Nagas had already been recruited by Subhas Chandra Bose, a breakaway Indian nationalist freedom fighter, for his Indian National Army (INA), which had allied itself with the Japanese. Among them were the young Phizo and his brother who had escaped to Rangoon after committing a few transgressions in Kohima,[16] and had started providing intelligence to the INA about British troop deployments in Nagaland. April 1944 saw some of the bloodiest battles being fought around Kohima as the Second Indian Division of Slim's mighty XIV Army pushed the Japanese and the INA out of India in one of the greatest battles of WWII. At the other end of the spectrum were the exploits of Naga soldiers and officers like Major Bob Khathing who were part of Slim's 'Victor Force' that conducted covert operations behind Japanese lines.[17] Phizo was imprisoned after the war for collaborating with the Japanese. He was released soon after and remained in Burma for a few months. In deciding whether to lead the Naga freedom struggle on a communist platform or retain the tribal, ethnic and Christian flavour of the movement, he chose the latter. Returning to Nagaland, he led a secessionist movement that would trouble the Indian state for over six decades.

Beginnings of Insurgency

The winds of freedom that swept across the Indian subcontinent in 1947 blew across Nagaland too. An opportunistic Phizo – with very little sense of history, geography or nationhood – sought independence from colonial rule for his motley bunch of tribes by professing that 'historically Nagaland has no connection with India'.[18] He was emboldened by a meeting with Mahatma Gandhi – who empathized with the Nagas and promised to help them achieve their aspirations without endorsing their cry for freedom – and issued a slew of petitions to the British. He went on to form the Naga National Council (NNC) in early 1947 and declared an independent Nagaland on 14 August 1947.

The declaration of independence was a non-starter, given that the British had amalgamated large parts of Nagaland into the administered state of Assam. The new Indian government too deemed Naga territory as part of the state of Assam, and not as an area that had the option to exercise self-determination outside the Constitution of India. Mainstream India's political dispensation was too preoccupied with the horrors of Partition and the ongoing conflict with Pakistan over Kashmir, and there were a host of other problems in the princely states of Hyderabad, Travancore and Junagadh, to have the Nagas anywhere on their minds. Sir Akbar Hydari, the suave governor of Assam, did offer an olive branch to Phizo in the form of a nine-point agreement[19] that offered to review the status of the Naga problem ten years after the NNC had agreed to amalgamate with the Indian Union.

However, Sir Hydari passed away in 1948, and Phizo used this opportunity to interpret the agreement on his own terms and convert his struggle into a popular movement. He had the active help of the Church in the complete absence of any government machinery or capability in the region. Phizo and his charismatic deputy, Sakhrie, sensed that the collective mood of the Naga tribes favoured self-determination and they sought a referendum. This rattled New Delhi, and in a contentious meeting with Phizo in 1951, a brusque Nehru clearly stated that he was not prepared to accept any referendum that endorsed a breakaway from the Indian Union. Phizo nonetheless went ahead and held a dubious referendum in 1952, in which 99 per cent of the Nagas voted for independence. Phizo then appealed to the international community to intervene. When that move did not yield any result, Phizo decided that an armed struggle was the next logical step. It was a move that would bring untold misery to the people of Nagaland for over six decades.

The various tribes of Nagaland have always been valiant fighters, skilled in archery and spear-throwing. It was customary for warring headhunting tribes and factions to settle disputes through violence. So, all that was needed to set this tinderbox aflame was a spark. This was provided by a charged Phizo and his initial band of insurgents, who were committed to the idea of an independent Nagaland. Among these were an erudite and articulate Sakhrie, who wrote an impassioned letter to Gandhi; a young Kaito Sema, who would go on to become one of the most feared and wanted guerrilla leaders in the Naga Hills; and Scato Swu, who was the moderate voice of the Naga struggle from the 1960s onwards. Waiting in the wings were young student leaders like Muivah and Mowu Angami, who would give up promising student lives to join the secessionist guerrilla movement. Alarmed by Phizo's rise, the Indian intelligence agencies tracked him closely as he repeatedly crossed over into Burma in the 1950s to organize the armed struggle and garner help from Naga outfits there that had rallied together under the Eastern Naga Revolutionary Council (ENRC). Tipped off by intelligence from Burma, Phizo was arrested by the Indian government in late 1952 for a second time.[20] However, he was fortuitously released the following year on compassionate grounds when his wife met with a terrible accident.

Nehru's conciliatory visit to Kohima in 1953, where he was accompanied by Burmese prime minister U Nu, went awry after he was booed by thousands of bottom-smacking Nagas for turning up late at a public meeting where he was to explain the Government of India's stand on the Naga issue. Humiliated, Nehru would not forget this slight.[21] Following Nehru's visit, Phizo melted away into the jungles of northern Nagaland and Myanmar to build the most formidable insurgent outfit that the Indian Army would face for decades. The legend of Phizo unfolded over the next few years, as the newly formed Naga National Army (NNA) and its invisible headquarters (or 'Oking') caused immeasurable attrition in the Assam Rifles, which was tasked with border security and management.

The years 1953 to 1956 would see escalated violence all over Nagaland as Phizo's NNA held sway even in the capital, Kohima. Scholars within the movement – such as Sakhrie – were among the first to realize the futility of waging an armed struggle against the might of the Indian state, and raised their voices for reason and peace. Crying treason, Phizo had Sakhrie assassinated in early 1956, sparking off the first of many internecine killings among competing Naga groups. Tensions began to simmer between Angamis, Semas and Tangkhuls – Naga fighters on the Indian side – and the Konyaks and Aos, who were Nagas from Myanmar. In 1955, sensing an opportunity to exploit the intra-Naga strife, the Indian Army moved into the region in large numbers.

The Indian Army Moves In

What about the military dimension of the Naga insurgency? A review of the forces ranged against each other would reveal a typical counterinsurgency profile that is now easy to analyse. A few thousand well-armed and well-trained insurgents who knew the terrain intimately and used the land and its people as both a logistics chain and a shield were ranged against a 'perceived occupier' with nascent counterinsurgency capabilities. The Indian Army in the 1950s had a peacetime cantonment culture and severe budgetary constraints that seriously impacted its operational capabilities. It was an army trained to fight on the borders and not against militias and insurgents embedded in the civilian population. To move into such a situation at short notice without any specialized training and indoctrination was a momentous decision taken by the Indian government, one which the Indian Army obeyed without fully realizing the magnitude of the task.

During the initial years of the insurgency, the insurgents possessed a huge stockpile of WWII vintage rifles, light machine guns and mortars. These had been recovered from abandoned and dispersed caches of Allied and Japanese weapons in the jungles of Burma and Nagaland. Although devoid of any formal military training or inclination, Phizo had nevertheless studied the mechanics of revolutionary warfare as conducted by Mao, and had also closely observed the Japanese jungle-warfare tactics. Deeply impressed by Phizo's revolutionary zeal, hundreds of Naga youth joined the movement across the state. Led by young commanders like Zuheto Sema (Phizo's intelligence chief), Thungti Chang (head of the military wing), Kaito Sema (a ruthless frontline commander) and Mowu Angami, the force expanded into an imposing cadre of fighters,[22] intelligence operatives, guides and trackers numbering over 15,000 in total. By July 1955, the Naga insurgency had reached a point of no return. The modus operandi for violence followed a predictable pattern – Naga villagers in remote areas would refuse to pay taxes; the local administration would then send police or paramilitary forces to investigate the issue, and these forces would then be waylaid by insurgents and brutally killed. Despite the beefing up of the paramilitary forces in the Naga Hills,[23] the raids and ambushes continued unabated.

The governor of Assam, Jairamdas Daulatram, had to finally call on the army in its constitutional role of aid to civil authorities. The easternmost bastion of the Indian Army in the early 1950s was the 181 Independent Infantry Brigade at Shillong. It was this formation that shed one of its battalions in the middle of the monsoon of 1955 and rushed it to the Naga Hills to douse the fire of rebellion. Marching through the Naga Hills via Mokokchung to the troubled district of Tsuensang and the Central Naga Hills, 17 RAJPUT attempted to restore some normalcy with the help of the already deployed Assam Rifles battalions.

The mandate for the battalion was outlined by Chief of Army Staff General Shrinagesh: 'You must remember that all the people in the area where you are operating are fellow Indians. They have a different religion and may pursue a different way of life, but they are Indians. The very fact that they are different and yet part of India reflects India's greatness. Some of these people are misguided and have taken to arms against their own people and are disrupting the peace of the area. You are to protect the mass of the people from these disruptive elements. You are not there to fight the people in the area but to protect them. You are fighting only those who threaten the people and those who are a danger to the lives and properties of the people. You must, therefore, do everything possible to win their confidence and respect to help them feel that they belong to India.'[24] This is one of the earliest official pronouncements by the Indian Army on what would emerge as an enduring principle of counterinsurgency operations across the post-WWII world. This later came to be known as the 'winning the hearts and minds' strategy (WHAM).

Realizing that a single battalion was woefully inadequate for tackling determined Naga resistance, three more battalions were sent into Nagaland by mid-1956 from forces under the command of the general officer commanding the Assam Area. These were the 2nd Battalion of the Sikh Regiment (2 SIKH), 1st Battalion of the Third Gorkha Rifles (1/3 GORKHA RIFLES) and 3rd Battalion of the Bihar Regiment (3 BIHAR). By early 1957 there were two undermanned brigades in the region based at Kohima and Mokokchung respectively.[25] Skirmishes continued, with the Indian Army taking heavy casualties despite destroying several camps. The violence was escalated by the brutal execution of Sakhrie under the nose of the Indian Army, and the situation further exacerbated by the unfortunate killing of a respected citizen, Dr Haralu, by the Indian Army during a curfew.[26] Encounters became fiercer and rules of engagement were cast aside.

Despite claims by the Naga insurgents that they had killed numerous Indian Army personnel by early 1956, Indian Army records indicate that it was only in February 1956 that the Indian Army lost its first soldier when a young lieutenant from 3 BIHAR was killed in action in an ambush near Kohima. Soon after, in June 1956, Kaito's fighters ambushed a unit payroll convoy and fatally injured Lieutenant Colonel Chitnis, the commanding officer of 1/3 GORKHA RIFLES, during a prolonged engagement. Chitnis had led a Gorkha counterattack and successfully stormed one of Kaito's hideouts, killing numerous insurgents before succumbing to his injuries. Chitnis was awarded the Ashok Chakra – India's highest peacetime gallantry award – for leading the operation against the much-feared Kaito.[27] The gloves were now off and Kohima was virtually under siege by night. The Indian Army found it difficult to differentiate between a common citizen and an insurgent as Phizo and his cadres roamed around the streets wrapped in colourful red-and-black shawls in the winter, spreading the stern message that whoever supported the Indian security forces would meet Sakhrie's fate.

Sensing that it was only a matter of time before the Indian Army tightened its noose around him, Phizo decided that it was time for him to leave the area to scout for international assistance from India's adversaries and those sympathetic to the Naga cause. Despite the dragnet that the Indian Army had laid out for him around Kohima, Phizo made a remarkable escape. He headed south-east towards the Cachar hills of Assam via Dimapur, ending up finally in the extreme north-eastern parts of East Pakistan's Sylhet district. He was a prize catch for the Pakistan government and was welcomed with glee as it had secured a proxy to wage war against India. Phizo was followed into East Pakistan by a few NNA leaders such as Mowu Angami, who were then armed, trained and routed back into Naga territory to escalate the conflict against the Indian Army. After two agonizing years of indecision and strategizing in East Pakistan, Phizo chose to flee westwards in early 1960. He first went to Zurich and then onwards to London, where he set up the Naga Revolutionary Council (NRC) in exile. He was assisted in this westward transition by a Christian missionary, Reverend Michael Scott – who was so taken in by the movement that he saw himself as the conscience of the Naga people – till he was deported for anti-India activities in the late 1960s.[28]

In a setback to Phizo, Mowu Angami was captured in 1957 by Indian security forces as a parallel movement for a peaceful reconciliation with the Indian government gathered momentum. A general amnesty was announced for all insurgents, including Mowu Angami. There was a misplaced confidence in New Delhi that a political resolution was around the corner. Delhi's assessment was off target as the Indian government had not reckoned with the military capability of Phizo's other commanders – led by the enigmatic Kaito and the elusive Zuheto Sema – who remained at large and continued to inflict heavy casualties on the Indian Army. The heaviest of these were taken by the 9th Battalion of the Punjab Regiment (9 PUNJAB), one of the battalions of the two additional brigades that had been inducted into the area. It lost one junior commissioned officer (JCO) and thirty-two men in April 1957 when an entire road protection party was brought down by well-directed fire from one of Kaito's ambush groups.

The hard truth was that in almost eighteen months of counterinsurgency operations, the situation had not stabilized. The Indian Army was beginning to realize that it was up against a bold and innovative adversary who had the support of the local populace. The absence of any government machinery to support military operations made matters worse. This hampered the achievement of the overarching political objective of integrating the Nagas into the Indian Union.

Joint Operations

Guerrillas and insurgents across the world are largely prepared to live and die by the sword. When the battleground and sanctuaries span international borders, the risks are even greater, and this was understood by Phizo's commanders. They constantly flirted with danger as they shuttled between the Naga Hills and sanctuaries in East Pakistan and Burma. It was during one such crossing in August 1958 that Zuheto Sema and Thungti Chang were killed in an encounter with the Assam Police following a tip-off. It was a body blow to the insurgents and infuriated Kaito. He immediately stepped up operations against the army and suspected informers were dealt with brutally whenever caught.

In 1959, the Indian Army responded to the growing ferocity of combat by increasing its troop density to over three brigades. It also revived the famous 23 Indian Division from WWII, appointing Major General D.C. Mishra as its first commander post-Independence.[29] At that point, the Naga insurgents had never attacked the strongholds of either the Indian Army or the Assam Rifles. Instead, they resorted to ambushes and classic hit-and-run guerrilla tactics, inflicting asymmetric casualties and significantly eroding the morale of army troops. The siege of Purr (now traceable as Phor on Google Maps) signalled a change in strategy. Purr is located on high ground in the northern part of a mountain range east of Kohima, very close to the existing India–Myanmar border. The post was occupied by two platoons of Assam Rifles and supported by two other posts in the vicinity. In late August 1960, in a well-executed pincer-and-isolating operation, a large force of almost 500 Naga insurgents comprising Semas, Angamis and Tangkhuls first cut off the post by destroying a linking bridge, and then laid siege to it for over four days till the post ran out of ammunition and supplies.[30]

The IAF – which had not joined the fight till then beyond routine air maintenance – responded to an SOS from divisional HQ by sending two DC-3 Dakotas of WWII vintage from 43 Squadron to drop essential supplies at Purr on 28 August 1960. Flying extremely low, the Dakotas tried to drop supplies and ammo with mixed success, and then had to take evasive action as over a hundred insurgents opened fire with their rifles and light machine guns. One of the Dakotas was badly hit, while the other miraculously managed to get back to base. The damaged Dakota lost both its engines and crash-landed a few miles south of Purr in hostile territory. Captained by Flight Lieutenant Singha, with Flying Officer Raphael as his co-pilot and Flight Lieutenant Chandrasekhar Misra as navigator, the aircraft had six others on board – including an under-training navigator, a flight signaller and a dropping crew of four Indian Army men. The entire crew survived the crash. They were taken prisoner by a large group of hostiles under an emerging commander, Zuheto Sema, and held captive for 617 days deep in the Myanmar jungles before being released sometime in mid-1962.[31]

Numerous search-and-rescue sorties were undertaken over several months by all kinds of aircraft to locate Singha – a high-profile captive, as he was the brother-in-law of Dev Anand, a Bollywood superstar. It is alleged that he was released after the superstar paid ransom money to Phizo in London.[32] Though the experience was harrowing and took a psychological toll on the crew, Misra acknowledged that they were treated well and suffered more from boredom and the weather. More than anything, the episode boosted the war-waging reputation of the Nagas, as numerous attempts to rescue the hostages had failed.

Following these events, there was a hardening of resolve in New Delhi. Offensive air power began to be used against Naga insurgents in areas where there was sparse habitation. Though there is very little information in the open domain, many IAF fighter pilots who served in the region – at bases like Tezpur, Kumbhigram and Jorhat – have confirmed that they were often flown by helicopter to the brigade HQ located at Mukokchong and briefed by the army on possible hideouts and rebel locations.[33] Two fighter squadrons based at Tezpur began operations in late 1960, with a third joining the fray in 1961. Toofanis (the Indian name for the French Ouragan fighter) and Vampire trainer-jets were the main aircraft deployed, while a slow-moving Harvard trainer was used for visual reconnaissance.[34] Major General D.K. Palit, a soldier-scholar of accomplishment, writes: 'The IAF was brought into action in a tactical role, bombing and strafing rebel oppositions.'[35] Highlighting the close cooperation between 23 Infantry Division of the Indian Army and Eastern Air Command, the operational record book of 29 Squadron for the quarters ending December 1961 and March 1962 records numerous air strikes on rebel locations. Indian troops reported extensive explosions and damage to rebel positions with several casualties being evacuated in an easterly direction, possibly into the thick jungles of Burma.[36] Innovative tactics were employed, such as using the Harvard propeller aircraft as target locaters and pathfinders with additional assistance from ground troops via VHF radio links. Locations of these targets were ascertained based on Indian Army grid references of 1961 converted into coordinates. When now extrapolated on Google Maps, they are seen to be accurate.[37]

29 Squadron had moved from Kumbhigram in southern Assam to Tezpur in northern Assam for two reasons. Firstly, Tezpur was the airbase closest to the Tawang area – where the India-China crisis was brewing; secondly, it was also close to central and northern Nagaland, where most of the fighting between the Indian Army and the Naga insurgents took place. Some key observations from the operational record book make interesting reading. On the night of 12 December 1961 the air force approved 23 Infantry Division's demand for an air strike on a hostile camp consisting of one large basha (tent) and five small ones.[38] The strike was carried out the next morning by seven Toofanis along with five Vampires of 101 Squadron. A total of 1,500 rounds and nineteen T/10 rockets were expended, the target was seen to be on fire and hostile casualties were estimated at sixty killed.[39] Follow-up attacks with greater coordination with ground troops were carried out six days later against larger camps that were closer to the India–Myanmar border.

Jottings in the operational record book reveal that attacks were carried out on Target Alpha, which had eight bashas, and the second target, or Bravo, which had seven bashas. On this strike, a Harvard also acted as director and proved very useful. Target Alpha was reported to have been destroyed completely with sixty to eighty hostile casualties. An interesting feature of the strike was the good air-to-ground communication that helped pinpoint and strike the targets.[40] Slow-moving Otters of 41 Squadron were modified and converted into mini gunships for carrying rocket pods and cabin-mounted machine guns. These gunships escorted Mi-4 helicopters and Dakotas that dropped supplies to garrisons under siege in the Naga Hills.[41]

Several Indian Army units performed exceedingly well during 1961-62. These included units like 8 ASSAM RIFLES, 2 GRENADIERS and other units in 11 Mountain Brigade commanded by Brigadier N.C. Rawlley. He would go on to lead the brigade in a splendid rearguard action at Walong during the 1962 war with China. As war clouds loomed large on India's northern borders with China, the 23rd Mountain Division left Nagaland and headed for NEFA. Phizo cleverly used this time to recoup and reorganize his forces to politically orchestrate events from London.

Searching for a Solution

Though the first group of Naga insurgents entered East Pakistan in 1958 and were trained in a camp in the Sylhet region,[42] the post-1962 period saw a hardening of militant Naga nationalism and increased training support from East Pakistan. Formal military training in these camps empowered the Naga insurgents to go beyond ambushes and frontal engagement with the Indian Army – they moved on to tactics like bombing trains and planting explosive devices to create panic in the civilian populace. Alarmed by the formation of a Naga Federal Government (NFG), the Indian Army wasted no time in sending its battle-weary units back into action in the hills of Nagaland despite the bruising it had received at the hands of the PLA in 1962.

Rostum Nanavatty, a former commander of the Army's Northern Command, retired as a lieutenant general in 2002. He is unarguably among the most operationally accomplished, articulate and scholarly Indian generals of recent times. My engagement with him over six years took me from his flat in Pune to the sylvan surroundings of his home in Dehradun, aptly named 'Saltoro' after the daunting Saltoro Range that flanks the Siachen Glacier where he commanded a brigade from late 1988 to 1990. Nanavatty was commissioned into the 2nd Battalion of 8 Gorkha Rifles (2/8 GORKHA RIFLES) as it retreated on orders from Menchuka during the 1962 war with China.[43] He was thrust into leadership roles in the Naga hills that he never imagined he would have to assume so early on in his career. His battalion, along with 2 MADRAS and 1 JAKRIF, was among the first battalions to return to Nagaland between December 1962 and January 1963.

He reminisces: 'We trucked from Dinjan (the army cantonment near the town of Dibrugarh on the eastern tip of Assam) to Dimapur, where we received our new commanding officer – the previous one had been killed in action during the Battle of Walong. We then distributed web equipment, boots, raincapes and mackintoshes to our stoic Gorkhas and set out on foot to Tamenglang along the Kohima–Imphal highway. Having established a grid to intercept Naga gangs which had slipped into East Pakistan for training and recuperation, a ten-man section from the unit had its first scrap with an approximately thirty-strong gang in Tamenglang. Outnumbered, we pulled back and ran into another gang. This time around, the Nagas melted away into the jungles, avoiding a firefight. We were then ordered to march to Zunheboto in the Sema heartland, where I was put in charge of a double company post. We experienced constant skirmishes, which included the stealing of weapons from under our noses. The Nagas were constantly needling us, and we had to ensure that every man remained on duty or patrol all the time. After a year in the Satakha-Zunheboto area, the battalion relocated closer to the Myanmar border, to the town of Mukokchong.'[44]

Forever in Operations

In 1963, the Army HQ swung into action under General J.N. Chaudhuri and took steps to consolidate state presence and improve the command-and-control structure of the forces in the north-east. It deployed the newly raised 8 Mountain Division with three brigades in Nagaland under Major General K.P. Candeth. Candeth had seen success as a commander during Operation Vijay, which had been undertaken for the liberation of Goa in December 1961.[45] One of the best narratives of the operations of an Indian Army division after Independence has been penned by Colonel R.D. Palsokar, an infantryman who won a Military Cross in WWII as a young lieutenant in the Myanmar theatre. Titled *Forever in Operations*,[46] the book tracks the sterling exploits of 8 Mountain Division during its early years in Nagaland and during the 1971 war in the Eastern Theatre. The division went back into counterinsurgency operations in Nagaland, Manipur and Tripura after the 1971 war to stem insurgencies that showed signs of resurgence, abetted in no small measure by an interfering China. Redeployed into the Kashmir Valley in early 1990, where the insurgency had intensified with active Pakistani support, the elite division also featured in the Kargil conflict of 1999.

The period between 1965 and 1970 saw pitched battles being fought between units of 8 Mountain Division and Naga gangs, who liked to describe themselves as battalions of the Naga Army. After its initial formation, the division settled down at its HQ at Zakhama, with three brigades at Zunheboto, Dimapur and Ukhrul. There were also several battalions of Assam Rifles, the CRPF, the Railway Protection Force (RPF) and even a Kerala Police battalion that had been moved there during the 1962 conflict. Their principal adversaries were Naga gangs with regional commanders under the unified political leadership of Phizo. These gangs had a clear division of political and military responsibilities, attributed by Indian intelligence to the training received in East Pakistan and China.[47]

Between 1963 and 1968, the central government made several attempts to hold elections. Ceasefires and interlocutors attempted to broker peace, but all these efforts failed in the face of increased insurgent activity. Making matters worse was the breakdown in Naga unity, which led to the creation of splinter groups of Angamis – who were pro-Phizo and NFG – and Semas – the anti-Phizo breakaway faction led by Kaito Sema. The latter called themselves the Revolutionary Government of Nagaland (RGN), and they vied for the support of the Naga people and external entities like Pakistan and China. By 1969 the journey across north Burma to China was becoming extremely hazardous for Naga insurgents. When the self-styled NFG commander-in-chief Mowu Angami attempted to return to Nagaland through Burma with a 600-strong gang, he was met with determined opposition from the locals. He reportedly lost about half his gang in a series of battles. Tia Ao, the son of the NFG 'elder statesman' Imkongmeren Ao, was killed in this encounter. At the same time NFG cadres looted Rs 1,00,000, from the two towns of Tiddim and Falam.

When the insurgents reached the border of Nagaland, they found their access routes effectively blocked by the Indian Army. The RGN scouts then apparently contacted General Mowu and his band and persuaded them to take 'sanctuary' in the RGN camp, which was protected by a ceasefire agreement. While the full story has not been told, it appears that the Indian authorities learned of the arrival of General Mowu and his 162 NFG men and orchestrated their capture with minimum resistance, aided in no small measure by the 'treachery' of the RGN. Shortly afterwards, eighty-three insurgents of a second contingent of China-trained Naga cadres were captured, but their leader, Isak Swu, eluded security forces and managed to slip into the Naga areas of Manipur with about a hundred of his men. The capture of large contingents of NFG insurgents substantially altered the political balance in Naga politics. Morale in the NFG dipped to a new low, enabling the RGN to recruit NFG defectors.

The RGN leaders – who desperately wanted to get the peace talks started again – soon discovered that the Indian government under Indira Gandhi saw no reason to resume the talks. Even as storm clouds gathered in East Pakistan, a hopelessly fragmented Naga secessionist movement resulted in an improved security situation in Nagaland. Instead of exploiting the situation, Indira Gandhi procrastinated. The Indian prime minister may well have lost a golden opportunity to transform the concerted military action into a lasting political solution.

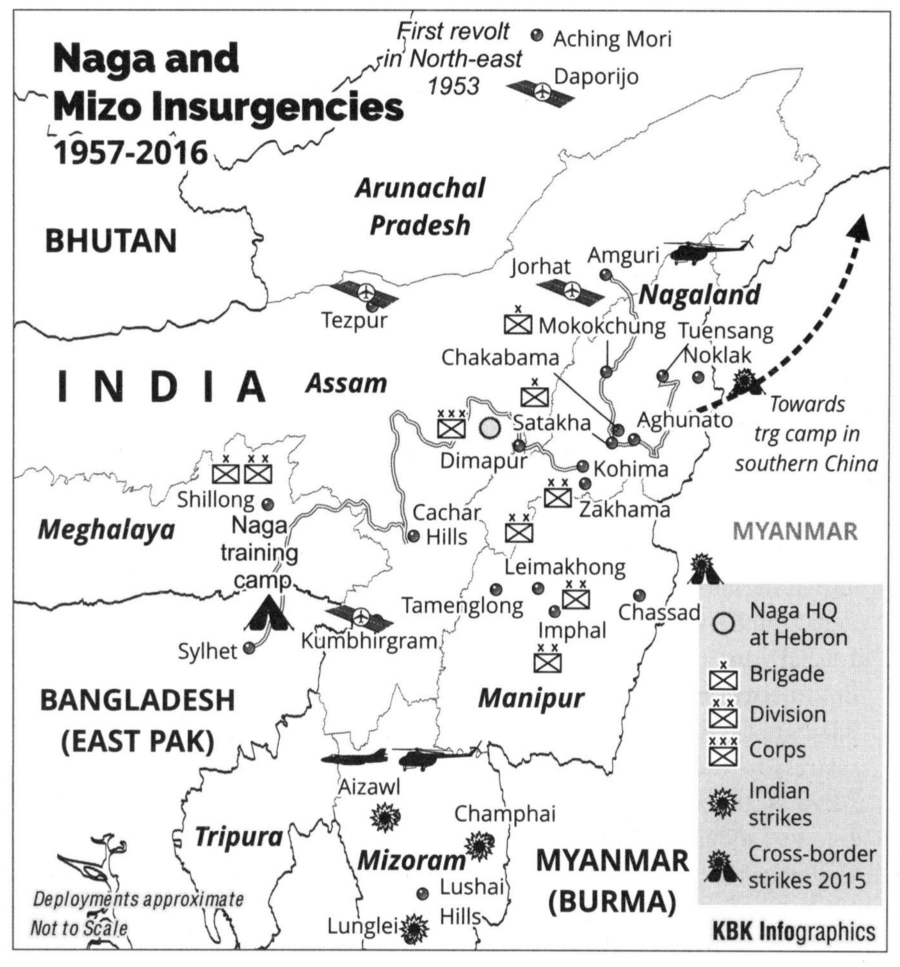

This map is for representational purposes only and does not purport to depict political boundaries

5

MIZO ANGST, NAGALAND FESTERS

'The Mizo Accord so far remains the only successful peace accord of its kind in Independent India's history.'[1]

Insurgency in Mizoram

Mizoram is a hilly state flanked by Manipur and Assam to the north, Tripura and Bangladesh to the west, Myanmar to the east and Bangladesh again to the south. Unlike Nagaland, Mizoram was demographically stable during the early years after Independence. The Lushai tribe constituted over 60 per cent of the total population, while no other tribe formed more than 8 per cent of the residents.[2] When the Mautam famine swept through the Mizo Hills in 1959, it caused great distress to the people. Government apathy led to the emergence of the Mizo National Front (MNF) as the militant voice of the Mizo people.[3] Led by Laldenga, a former havildar of the Indian Army, the MNF would challenge the might of the Indian Army after the 1965 war with Pakistan.

Indira Gandhi had taken over as prime minister of India following the death of Lal Bahadur Shastri during the Tashkent peace talks. Seeking to seize the initiative in the wake of political uncertainty in New Delhi and riding on the wave of Naga turbulence, the MNF sounded the bugle for an armed revolt on the night of 28 February 1966. It declared independence, seized the treasury in Aizawl and laid siege to the Assam Rifles garrison that was located next to it. Armed cadres simultaneously moved into the other important towns like Lunglei and Champhai in what the rebels called Operation Jericho, overwhelming the Assam Rifles companies that were located there. BSF posts in other towns were also overrun as the MNF saw the rebellion as the first step towards the formation of the state of Greater Mizoram, which sought to include parts of the neighbouring states of Assam, Tripura and Manipur.[4] Prime Minister Indira Gandhi reacted promptly and flew into the area with her defence minister, the experienced Y.B. Chavan. Accompanying them were the home secretary and the chiefs of the army and air force. Lieutenant General S.H.F.J. (Sam) Manekshaw, the head of Eastern Army Command, advocated a swift and hard response during discussions with the prime minister and her team. New Delhi was rattled by the MNF operation, which had taken Indian intelligence agencies by surprise. To the prime minister's credit, she did not hesitate in employing force to quell the rebellion. She is reported to have struck an immediate rapport with the no-nonsense Manekshaw, a relationship that would yield rich dividends during the 1971 war with Pakistan.

Manekshaw entrusted the operation to 101 Communication Zone, a division-sized force that oversaw operations in the region. 61 Mountain Brigade was promptly ordered to undertake a heli-landed operation to relieve the siege and retake the treasury. 105 and 110 Helicopter Units – equipped with Mi-4 helicopters – were tasked to fly in two companies each of 8 SIKH and 5 PARA in several waves to relieve and reinforce the Aizawl garrison. The initial waves of helicopters flew in on 5 March 1966, but had to return to base as they were fired upon by more than a hundred Pakistan-trained Mizo insurgents and Indian Army deserters from the MNF. They had surrounded the treasury and five other posts nearby, even firing at and damaging a Caribou transport aircraft of the IAF carrying senior army and IAF officers for a recce mission over Aizwal.

Lieutenant General Mathew Thomas, who would go on to command the Indian Army's only parachute brigade in the 1971 war, was a lieutenant colonel in 1966 and in command of 5 PARA. Disappointed at not being able to participate in the 1965 war, this was his opportunity to give his troops a battle inoculation. He was surprised by the response from the MNF cadres, who, he recollects, had 'planned well, executed the plans swiftly and fought cleverly'.[5] Given that the IAF had conducted extensive offensive operations against Naga camps in the early 1960s, it did not take long for Manekshaw to reach out to his counterpart in Eastern Air Command, who readily agreed to provide offensive air cover for another attempt at heli-landing 5 PARA and paradropping of ammunition and supplies at Aizawl.

Air Commodore D.J. Sarma, who commanded the IAF's 33 Squadron and Air Force Station Guwahati in later years, was flying Dakotas with the

49 Squadron at the time. He joined the six-aircraft detachment at Kumbhigram soon after the first abortive heli-landing attempt. He recollects that they had 'predawn Met briefing by hurricane lamps in the bamboo gazebo with glasses of tea' before being 'airborne by dawn to drop ammo and provisions on to the drop zone at the camp under siege. On the final run-in, two Toofanis flew abreast of the Dakotas and slightly ahead, firing their guns as protective fire.'[6]

While Toofani fighters from Kumbhigram escorted the heliborne force and Dakotas, Hunters from 17 Squadron based at Jorhat carried out their first strikes on Aizawl on 6 March 1966. Air Marshal Teshter Master, who retired as the IAF's director-general of inspection and flight safety, was a flight lieutenant at the time. He recounts, 'We were briefed that air support/supply by helicopter and Dakota aircraft had been met by small-arms fire from the rebels. The Assam Rifles unit was in danger of suffering casualties and needed close air support. The unit was in barracks with a clear area around them the size of a few football fields. It was decided to use rockets and guns to attack the rebels and provide relief to the surrounded troops. The army unit would put markings on the ground to indicate the target. The markings comprised an arrow to show the direction of the target and strips laid diagonally below the arrow to indicate distance. If I remember right the baseline was 1,000 yards and each strip was plus-100 or 200 yards. So, if there were two strips below the arrow, the target was 1,200 or 1,400 yards in that direction.'[7]

Master's logbook confirms that he flew two strikes on 6 March and used rockets and guns for strafing the designated area that was identified as a rebel camp. 17 Squadron also carried out armed reconnaissance runs along the main highway leading to Aizawl to interdict vehicular movement, but found no targets. The squadron received messages that its missions had been successful and that the besieged army unit had been relieved. These operations successfully intercepted MNF cadres on the move and introduced an element of speed and urgency into the operations.[8] Air Marshal Bharat Kumar, an accomplished air-power historian and fighter pilot who was part of a squadron based in the eastern sector, recollects, 'The situation at that time was really grim. Not only did the Mizos want to announce their "own government", there was real danger to the local army and police as well as some civil servants who were surrounded – it was feared they would be massacred. It was a difficult decision, but the Mizo struggle frittered away immediately after the air attacks and the talks started soon after.'[9] There is no official record of any civilian or rebel casualties during the air attacks, although locals vaguely insist that there were several without being able to provide any kind of evidence of numbers.[10]

Colonel Vivek Chadha interviewed several locals during the research for his book *Low Intensity Conflicts in India: An Analysis*, including Brigadier Sailo, the son of Laldenga and a future chief minister.[11] Apart from a feeling of hurt and indignation, there is little to suggest that there was much collateral damage. In the final analysis, the gravity of the situation forced Manekshaw to use all means available with the necessary restraint to ensure that troops under his command were not massacred by the Mizo rebels, who were disorganized, angry and liable to engage in indiscriminate killing.

By 7 March, additional troops had linked up with the heli-landed troops and relieved the siege at Aizawl. Troops from Gorkha Rifles and Bihar Regiment then moved towards the towns of Champhai and Lunglei, while paratroopers secured the areas around the border with East Pakistan the following day.[12] By 17 March, intense military operations in Mizoram had ended, though limited operations would continue till military resistance from the MNF ended almost a decade later. It would, however, take years for peace to be restored in Mizoram as Laldenga escaped first to East Pakistan, and then westwards to London, where he remained in exile for almost two decades. After the low-grade insurgency petered out in the face of a resolute Indian Army, a proactive Church convinced the MNF to lay down arms and join the mainstream political process. Laldenga became the first chief minister of Mizoram after signing a historic accord with the Rajiv Gandhi government on 30 June 1986.[13] Mizoram has been largely peaceful since then, barring stray occurrences of infiltration, drug-running and arms-smuggling.[14]

China Factor in Nagaland

Emboldened by their military victory over India in 1962 and seeing the ease with which Naga insurgents slipped into East Pakistan and returned to Nagaland after military training, the Chinese saw an opportunity to deliver a double whammy on India. They offered to train the Nagas in camps in the Southern Yunan province. Along with the military training, serious attempts were made by the PLA to indoctrinate the senior Naga leadership in Maoist ideology. Leaders like Kaito Sema, Mowu Angami and Thuingaleng Muivah were taken to Beijing and exposed to interaction with Chinese government officials and leaders of the Vietcong in North Vietnam. For over two decades, this policy of aiding the Naga insurgency waxed and waned, as China attempted to make inroads into the various secessionist movements that were springing up along India's north-eastern periphery. Following the crushing of the armed rebellion in Mizoram and the eventful birth of Bangladesh, training grounds in erstwhile East Pakistan dried up. The Naga movement looked to China for sustaining the armed struggle.

Based at Chabua airfield, the 105 Helicopter Unit was given the twin tasks of maintaining army units on the frontier with China and supporting counterinsurgency operations in Nagaland. Equipped with Mi-4s, the unit maintained a large detachment alongside 81 Mountain Brigade at Chakabama, which was located on the northern fringes of the operational area of 8 Mountain Division. A senior IAF group captain was co-located at the 8 Mountain Division HQs in Zakhama as the air force liaison officer and coordinated the complex daily tasking. Pilots like Flight Lieutenants Harry Ahluwalia and Anil Bendre spent weeks at Chakabama undertaking several risky missions over insurgent-infested areas. On 20 May 1974, the new divisional commander, Major General Girish Narain Sinha, was severely injured when rebels shot at a Mi-4 helicopter piloted by Bendre as they were flying low in the Zunheboto Valley. A bullet brushed Bendre's helmet, while another pierced Sinha's arm and exited through his back. More bullets damaged the communication box but luckily none hit the engine and Bendre could bank sharply and get out of the valley. Sinha was rushed to the divisional HQ, where he was operated on immediately by a surgeon. As a result, he had to hand over command to Major General G.S. Rawat. Later it was discovered that they had flown right through the area of a well-trained unit of Sema fighters who had just returned from China.

'Ganjoo' Rawat – as he was known because of his bald pate – was a proactive commander who liked to take the battle to the enemy. During his tenure (1974-76), several rebel gangs attempted to sneak through a well-established counterinsurgency grid as they returned after training in Yunan. He aggressively employed the IAF's Mi-4 helicopters for aerial reconnaissance and for positioning his troops to cut off routes to and from Myanmar.[15] The IAF got further involved in operations in the Naga Hills after the Mi-8 helicopters were inducted in the mid-1970s. The 118 Helicopter Unit operating out of Guwahati was employed in the reconnaissance and troop-insertion roles, and it played an important role in blocking egress routes and logistically sustaining small teams that were engaged in missions behind rebel lines. As hectic operations continued through the late 1970s, Bollywood made another appearance in Nagaland with Major General Ashoke Dutt – the younger brother of the renowned character actor Utpal Dutt – assuming command of 8 Mountain Division.

Reconciliation, Factionalism and Revival

On 11 November 1975, moderate elements from within the NNC – who were tired of the two-decade-long insurgency and the relentless Indian Army action besides being disillusioned with Phizo's remote leadership – signed the Shillong Accord with the Indian government. Led by leaders like Zashei Huire and driven by a dominant Indira Gandhi, the accord offered much promise – but it did not translate into peace and stability for two principal reasons. The first was the inability of the Indian government to rapidly usher in good governance and spur development in the region; the second was the inability of the Naga people to rise above tribal and ethnic loyalties. The promulgation of the Emergency in 1975 by Indira Gandhi and the political chaos that followed led to her ouster in 1977 and stalled the peace process. Widespread violence returned to Nagaland as a series of weak coalition governments in New Delhi neglected to convert the Shillong Accord into something permanent.

Prior to signing of the Shillong Accord of 1975, the Indian government announced that 800 guerrillas had surrendered between October 1968 and March 1969 and that another 2,316 guerrillas had surrendered over the two-year period ending 16 December 1969.[16] Almost 2,000 of the surrendered rebels were inducted into three battalions of the BSF between 1969 and 1973. It was a move that promised much but failed to make a dent in the combat potential of the various Naga groups. 111 Battalion of the BSF located near Zunheboto has over eighty former insurgents who are still serving at past seventy years of age.[17] A major split took place within the Naga movement in 1980, when dissatisfied militants of the NNC broke away to form the National Socialist Council of Nagaland (NSCN) with the blessings of Phizo. Led by Thuingaleng Muivah, Isak Swu and S.S. Khaplang, the NSCN was emboldened by the limited support from China. This marked the next phase of the armed struggle between the Nagas and the Indian Army. All factions of the NSCN gave the Indian Army a hard time with their sophisticated guerrilla tactics and significant firepower. The violence would last for almost two decades until the next comprehensive ceasefire of 1997.

Lieutenant General Narasimhan, a hardy infantryman from the Madras Regiment – who retired in 2016 as the director-general of military intelligence and is now the director-general of a government-sponsored China think tank – admires the fighting capabilities of Naga insurgents. Among the few officers in the Indian Army to have served ten years at a stretch in his first battalion, the 25th Battalion of the Madras Regiment (25 MADRAS), Narasimhan served as company commander, 2 I/C and commanding officer as the unit moved between various insurgency-prone areas.[18] He has also served in the Counter Insurgency and Jungle Warfare School (CIJWS) and has a deep insight into the minds and operational philosophy of the numerous militant groups in Nagaland and Manipur. Narasimhan clearly recollects that, after the death of Phizo in 1991, the NNC – which represented the political face of the secessionist movement – no longer enjoyed the confidence of the Naga people and the original cause of an independent Nagaland faded away. Reminiscing about his early tenures in Nagaland, particularly in the Chakabama and Tsuensang areas, Narasimhan recollects that Naga insurgents – unlike the local and foreign terrorists in J&K – adhered to a battle code of conduct. They would issue warnings before attacking and respect fallen soldiers.[19]

Lieutenant General Prakash Katoch, who was commissioned in December 1969 into the 1st Battalion (Special Forces) of the Parachute Regiment or 1 PARA (SF), first experienced counterinsurgency operations in 1983, in Nagaland. He was part of a team which was tasked with undertaking reconnaissance patrols along the Nagaland–Manipur border with Burma from Mon province in northern Nagaland to the southern limits of the Manipur hills. Operating out of Chakabama in Nagaland and then moving to Leimakhong in Manipur, Katoch recollects that his team had a few skirmishes with both Naga and Manipuri insurgents. His understanding of the situation on the ground corroborated the assessment that New Delhi had lost a major opportunity in the 1970s to leverage the capabilities of surrendered Naga insurgents to resolve the Naga problem.[20] He reckoned that after that lost opportunity, the NSCN increased attacks on the Indian Army during the final period of full-fledged support from the Chinese.

Factional rivalries, tribal loyalties and reduction in support from China started to cause rifts in the NSCN. After a series of deadly strikes by the Khaplang-led group comprising Konyaks, Aos and Burmese Nagas on the Tangkhul and Sema factions led by Muivah and Isak Swu, the NSCN splintered into the Khaplang (K) and Isak and Muivah (I&M) groups in April 1988. India's intelligence agencies too played their part by undertaking a disinformation campaign that sowed the seeds of doubt in the minds of competing groups. The main operational areas of the NSCN(K) were restricted to the northern parts of Nagaland (Tsuensang and Mon) and the overlapping Naga-inhabited areas of Myanmar and Arunachal Pradesh. The NSCN(I&M) group dominated the larger swathe of territory in the Sema and Tangkhul Naga areas spanning the hill districts of the adjoining state of Manipur. More than anything else, this split precipitated a violent reaction from indigenous Manipuris (Meiteis), making Manipur another hotspot in the north-east.[21]

The splintering of the NSCN into multiple factions based on tribal loyalties was accompanied by an ideological vacuum even as the Chinese – who had invested heavily in the insurgency as a means of maintaining pressure on India's eastern frontiers – stopped their large-scale assistance. This was more out of a desire to cut their losses rather than any altruistic design to appease India. Running camps for Naga rebels in Yunan was proving to be an expensive proposition without any tangible payoffs. With external funding drying up, the Naga factions turned to extortion, illegal taxation and drug trafficking to generate finances. This gradually eroded their credibility. Feeling the heat from sustained Indian Army pressure in the early 1990s, Khaplang fled to Myanmar, while Isak and Muivah escaped to Thailand.

In 1989, the Congress party made inroads into Nagaland by convincing local parties like the Progressive United Democratic Front (PUDF) to merge with it. Politicians like S.C. Jamir and Hokishe Sema were at the forefront of the political process. They dominated the political stage as chief ministers of Congress-led coalition governments till Hokishe Sema joined the Bharatiya Janata Party in 1999 following differences with Jamir. While Jamir aligned himself with the NSCN(K), Hokishe Sema had no choice but to support the NSCN(I&M). It was clear by now that local politicians and political parties had little interest in fulfilling the aspirations of the Naga people. They were more open to consorting with insurgent groups for personal gains, while national parties invested little in the political process. Consequently, the security situation remained stressed, and the army continued to be involved in stability operations in the absence of robust policing and internal security structures.

3 Corps and the Long Road to Peace

When 8 Mountain Division celebrated its twenty-fifth anniversary in 1988, it was the Indian Army division most experienced in counterinsurgency operations. Its services were soon requisitioned in another hotspot – J&K. Consequently, even as the Army HQ decided to move the division to J&K in late 1989, it assigned 3 Corps with its HQ at Dimapur on the border between Nagaland and Manipur with the task of fighting of insurgencies in the north-east. This formation would emerge as the largest corps in the Indian Army with the dual responsibility of countering insurgency and defending large portions of the LAC in Arunachal Pradesh.

3 Corps was initially formed with two divisions at Dinjan and Zakhama – 2 Mountain Division and 57 Mountain Division – to manage insurgencies

in Nagaland, Manipur and parts of Assam. Its first corps commander was Lieutenant General B. Joginder Singh. The corps soon expanded to include one additional division – 56 Mountain Division – to oversee operations in eastern Arunachal Pradesh, and a division-sized complement of Assam Rifles to defend the border with Myanmar and conduct counterinsurgency operations in Nagaland and Manipur. It has a huge area extending from the central parts of Arunachal Pradesh to the Lohit division in the east at the trijunction of India, China and Myanmar, covering the states of Nagaland, Manipur, Tripura, Meghalaya and areas of Assam south of the Brahmaputra.

Operations across the Naga Hills and into the Kohima plains are now run by Inspector General Assam Rifles (IGAR) (North), who commands a large division-sized force of Assam Rifles. Similarly, IGAR (South) is located close to Imphal to combat the ongoing insurgency in Manipur along with IGAR (East), another recently formed division-strength force. Sitting in New Delhi, it is easy for armchair critics to question the need for such large forces in this region. Considering the several security fault lines in the region, such elements of state power are essential not only for conducting counterinsurgency operations but also to assist in maintaining law and order, and in preventing the outbreak of violence in the absence of effective policing and governance.

In 1995 when the Indian Army came under flak from citizen groups in Nagaland over some excesses against civilians, General Shankar Roychowdhury urged New Delhi to extend an olive branch to the Naga insurgents. Facing immense pressure from a well-established counterinsurgency grid – much like during the period preceding the 1975 Shillong Accord and the time of the split in the NSCN – the NSCN(I&M) entered into a ceasefire agreement with Prime Minister Atal Bihari Vajpayee's government in 1997 and claimed leadership of the Naga movement. 3 Corps, however, continued its operations against the NSCN(K), much to the ire of the Nagaland chief minister, S.C. Jamir, who was an Ao himself and had failed to rise above sectarian loyalties. Commanding 3 Corps from September 1997 to June 2000 as a lieutenant general, Nanavatty recalls that Jamir put much pressure on him to 'go easy' on the Khaplang group. He also remembers meeting Hokishe Sema, who represented the political aspirations of the NSCN(I&M), and found him to be more balanced than Jamir.

While there have been numerous reports on the heavy-handedness of Assam Rifles and the Indian Army during the initial years of operations against the Nagas, including the use of offensive air power by the IAF, these must be seen in the light of the heavy casualties that Naga groups inflicted on the security forces. Instead of pushing under the carpet this transition period of the

1950s and 1960s – when under grave provocation the security forces followed a scorched-earth strategy in retaliation – it is also critical to acknowledge the remarkable restraint shown since by the security forces in operations.

Characterizing instances of human rights violation by the Indian Army while dealing with civilians in the north-east as 'unfortunate and unacceptable collateral', Nanavatty is emphatic about the broader restraint shown by the Indian Army. He says, 'Our record is nothing to be ashamed of. We do not now use offensive air power, tanks or heavy weapons in our operations any more and are paying one hell of a price for this restraint. The Indian Army does its best to punish human rights violations and I personally recollect numerous instances where I had to severely punish officers because of a variety of transgressions. I recognized that large organizations, including armies, do tend to "cover up" and have a "hota hai" [it happens] attitude, and came down quite heavily whenever aberrations came to my notice.'[22] He went on to recall an incident: 'A classic example of "regular force retaliation" after suffering significant casualties was when, on 27 December 1997, a unit under my command lost their commanding officer in an ambush and firefight with insurgents of the Naga army and the attackers then slipped away into the villages around. A disproportionate response from the unit followed, which caused several civilian casualties. This is the ambiguity and the fog of war in counterinsurgency operations that every professional army in the world has had problems dealing with. The Indian Army has been no different.'[23]

Acknowledging that he faced much trouble while dealing with transgressions in the north-east because of societal differences, he emphasized that it was essential for any commander in such circumstances to display fairness and firmness as part of an overall strategy, even if it involved sacking officers with outstanding operational records. He remembers that on one occasion village elders asked the commanding officer of a battalion in his corps to reduce the punishment meted out to a soldier who was accused of groping a woman at a road-opening point.[24]

Almost the End

5 June 2015: As a convoy of the Indian Army's Dogra Regiment wound its way through a densely forested road at Chandel – close to the border between the north-eastern Indian states of Manipur and Nagaland – it was ambushed by insurgents from three diverse rebel groups: the NSCN(K), the Manipur-based Kangleipak Communist Party and the Kanglei Yawol Kanna Lup, also Manipur-based. Eighteen Dogra soldiers lost their lives in the murderous

ambush. Little did anyone then realize that they would indirectly become the catalysts for the possible termination and resolution of what has been the longest insurgency in the post-WWII era. The incident unleashed a chain of events that would lead to a swift retaliation and a recalibration of the way the Indian state would consider punitive action in sub-conventional warfare.

While the NSCN(K) and NSCN(I&M) represented the Naga secessionist movement, the other two groups involved in the attack represented the Manipuri Meitei elements of a defensive movement that sought to protect themselves from Naga and Kuki insurgents. The political dynamics of these groupings indicated their desperation to remain relevant in an increasingly fractured Naga polity that had emerged after the signing of the Naga Framework Agreement between the Government of India and the dominant Naga group, NSCN(I&M), in August 2015.[25] The NSCN(I&M) has progressively diluted its secessionist stand over the years and replaced it with the demand to integrate all the Naga-dominated areas of north-east India – including parts of Manipur, Assam and Arunachal Pradesh – into a Greater Nagalim. Marginalized in this discourse, the NSCN(K) – comprising primarily Nagas from northern Nagaland and the adjoining areas of Myanmar – refused to endorse the agreement and joined hands with Manipuri and Assamese insurgent groups to disrupt the fragile peace in the region.

General Bipin Rawat – India's current Chief of Defence Staff, and commander of the Dimapur-based 3 Corps at the time – had his reservations about the robustness of the loosely worded ceasefire and recollects having discussed the same with the central government interlocutor.[26] His worry was that no clear red lines had been laid down for the rebels, who flaunted their weapons with impunity and imposed ridiculous restrictions like declaring a 'no-fly zone' over their HQ at Hebron, barely 20 km from Rawat's HQ. Deciding to ignore this restriction, Rawat made it a point to fly over Hebron every time he visited one of his formations. When the rebels complained that he was flouting the ceasefire agreement and ran the risk of drawing fire, Rawat dared them to try and fire at him.

In a wide-ranging interview with the author, Rawat recollects that he had been uneasy about the regrouping of various Naga rebel factions months before the 2015 attack. Adding to the rising tension was the continued extortion by the groups within their respective areas of influence. The tipping point came when the NSCN(K) attacked a Corps of Signals convoy of the Indian Army and a post of Assam Rifles in the heart of Kohima in May 2015, killing several soldiers. Realizing that many units in his formation had been lulled into a false sense of complacency, Rawat directed IGAR-North in Kohima to launch an informer-guided and intelligence-driven operation against an NSCN(K) camp in a nearby forest. The operation had to be aborted as the informer chickened out barely 500 metres from the camp and fled, indicating that it was highly likely that an ambush was in place. Concurrently, Rawat commenced planning for a punitive operation and identified six or seven rebel camps along the border with Myanmar as likely targets. He reckons that he would have launched a punitive operation even if the Chandel incident had not taken place.

Determined not to fritter away the advantage gained from the various peace initiatives after the Chandel strike,[27] the Indian Army planned a swift operation to hunt down the perpetrators of the ambush. Several options were considered. These included hitting selected NSCN(K) camps with attack helicopters and then following up with special heliborne operations. Rawat was given a free hand by the army chief and the eastern army commander. He worked closely with Air Marshal Kler, the Senior Air Staff Officer at HQ Eastern Air Command in Shillong, who ensured that Mi-35 attack helicopters were speedily inducted into the 3 Corps Zone from their home base at Pathankot. Operating from Imphal, Kohima, Leimakhong and other helipads built for supporting such operations, they carried out reconnaissance missions and live firing practice.

However, the two days spent in mulling over the various options at a time when the government was looking to smoke the peace pipe were enough for the rebel groups to disperse and melt away across the border. Drawing on extensive human intelligence and other reliable aerial and space-based recce assets, it was not long before two major camps were pinpointed for targeting. Situated less than 10 km across the Myanmar border with Manipur and Nagaland, the camps were said to be buzzing with insurgent activity. While the northern camp lay opposite the town of Noklak in the district of Tsuensang, the southern camp had sprung across the town of Chassad in Manipur. Once the targeting was complete, the attack helicopters continued to operate normally to instil a sense of status quo. The rebels assumed that the search missions would continue without crossing the border as had been the norm in the preceding decades, even when the provocation had been as grave.

Rawat chose the night of 6 June to attack the camps after receiving the requisite clearance from all levels including the national security advisor (NSA) and the prime minister. However, he had to postpone the attack by a day due to operational reasons. Luckily for him, he was able to alert his teams to delay the operation by twenty-four hours. At the tactical level, there was never any doubt that the operation would be entrusted to teams from the two Special Forces units under Rawat's command. While one of the units had honed its fighting skills over decades in the north-east, the other had only recently taken on the role and was hungry for action.[28]

Two teams of around sixty men each from both units were selected for the mission. The main aim of each team was to carry out fire assaults on the camps from a stand-off distance with mortars and rocket launchers, while performing various supporting roles such as setting up blocks, ambushes and supporting exfiltration. The idea of a fire assault did not appeal to Lieutenant Colonel N*, the tough second-in-command of one of the units that was leading the southern prong of the mission. The target was a large camp with large numbers of insurgents from the Manipur-based groups that had combined with the NSCN(K) for the Chandel ambush. Rawat recalls that when he briefed N, the latter said, 'Sir, what is the point of Special Forces doing a fire assault from a stand-off distance, you may as well use mortars or artillery from here. I will go in close and hit them with surprise and stealth.' Though Rawat had orders from the chief that it had to be a fire assault as otherwise the risks of taking casualties from close combat were too high, he respected N's proposition as a soldier and told him, 'Go ahead, but ensure no casualties are left behind in the adversary's territory.' The soldiers' arrangement was that N would overlook orders and Rawat would back him if something went wrong.

After the go-ahead from the prime minister on the evening of 7 June and a call from the NSA to confirm the green signal, the mission was launched with complete radio silence. All contingencies were in place, including helicopter support for casualty evacuation and extrication. Though the southern camp was barely 4 km from the India-Myanmar border, N and his team chose to detour via some high ground that would allow them good visibility of the camp and retain the element of stealth and surprise. Setting out at 7 p.m. on 7 June, the group encountered two local hunters and their dogs. They tied and muzzled them up and left four men to guard them. Once in visual contact with the camp, the group settled down for the night in the dense foliage, covering themselves with repellent as they had snakes, leeches and insects for company. Rawat recollects that despite the repellent all of them were covered with boils and insect bites when they returned. The lead recce party found the forward sentry huts empty, but detected two sentries on trees. They were promptly taken down with silenced Israeli sniper rifles.

It was 6 a.m. on 8 June by the time the assault group entered the camp and it still appeared deserted. This prompted N to alert Rawat that things may not be going their way: 'The camp is empty, sir. I am going in deeper.' Rawat

* A person has been referred to only by an initial wherever he has requested anonymity

replied, 'You guys will get us into trouble.' N replied before signing off: 'Don't worry, sir – no casualty will be left behind.' A trifle apprehensive about the turn of events, Rawat alerted the IAF attack helicopters, the Army Aviation's Advance Light Helicopters (ALH) and the extrication team to be ready for a contingency. As the commandos crept in closer, they heard the clatter of utensils and saw a single guard outside what seemed to be a large dining hall. N assessed that about thirty or forty insurgents had gathered for their morning meal. Silencing the guard with a knife, the assault group surprised the insurgents by firing their weapons, and then picked out the insurgents as they fled. Rawat reckons that the firefight was over in minutes. Still, instead of heading straight back, N perceptively chose to exfiltrate through the longer route to avoid running into villagers or other insurgents. The return journey was uneventful, with the more fatigued among the force being extricated by the army's ALH while others just trekked back. N's force suffered no casualties and – after a Bara Khana (a traditional Indian Army celebratory meal) with some very welcome rum and whiskey thrown in – it was business as usual the following day.

The northern group had a longer but uneventful walk to the high ground from where the target area was to be engaged in a fire assault. However, when the lead assault group carried out a reconnaissance, they only encountered two guards – who were neutralized. They only saw a few women at the camp, and concluded that either the insurgents had left the camp after a tip-off or they had trooped out for their daily firewood collection chore. After a brief wait, realizing that discretion was the need of the hour, the team leader decided to call off the mission. The group headed back to base with no casualties. When asked how he felt about the lack of success on the northern prong, Rawat was fully supportive of the decision to abort made by the man on the spot. As far as he was concerned, the operation was more about demonstrating intent and serious political signalling. Lieutenant Colonel N was awarded the Kirti Chakra (second highest gallantry award during peacetime operations) while six others received gallantry awards for their exploits during the operation.[29]

Following the success of the cross-border strikes of 2015, there was no let-up in the pursuit of rebel groups that threatened the fragile peace in the region. Adding heft to this was the ability of the Indian government to take on board the Myanmar Army and assist it in a series of joint operations that destroyed camps belonging to the Kachin Army, a rebel group that has been a thorn in the flesh of the Myanmar Army for decades. Acting on credible intelligence tip-offs that the Kachin Army was looking to link-up with anti-India insurgent and terrorist groups such as the NSCN(K) and attack infrastructure projects along the Kaladan Multi-Modal Transit Transport Project, the Indian Army launched Operation Sunrise in early March 2019.[30] Involving units of India's Special Forces, the Ghatak (specialized commando) Platoons from units in 3 Corps and ALHs from the Army Aviation Corps, the operation demonstrated the commitment of the Indian Army to be the sword-arm of diplomacy in an environment that had great economic and geopolitical promise.

Furthering India's ambitious Act East policy – and executed jointly with the Myanmar Army – it pre-empted attacks by rebels along the corridor connecting the Indian port of Kolkata with Sittwe, a port in eastern Myanmar.[31] When queried as to how this operation differed from the 2015 operation, General Rawat said: 'This time around, the Myanmar Army was fully on board as we too supported operations against insurgents who were suspected of attacking the Myanmar Army. We also supplied and sustained many units of the Myanmar Army through the winter rains as they combed the jungles for insurgent camps.'[32]

Peace and Lessons

At the politico-strategic level, it is ironic that in the past the reason for the Naga tragedy was the inability of Nehru and Phizo to understand each other. Both were men on a mission. While Nehru had the power of the state, Phizo had a myopic and messianic view of Naga sovereignty. Though many believe that the Naga struggle may have taken a different course had Phizo not left his homeland, others argue that it would have only been a matter of time before he would have either been incarcerated by the Indian government or come around to realize the futility of waging an armed struggle.

The Naga insurgency lost its separatist sting in the late 1990s following the split in the NSCN and the marginalization of the NNC after the death of Phizo in the UK on 30 April 1990.[33] The idea of 'Nagalim' resurfaced after the break-up of the NSCN in 1988 along with the emergence of the NSCN(I&M) as the pre-eminent group. Isak and Muivah channelled the aspirations of Naga communities across north-east India and Myanmar to push for a 'Greater Nagalim' comprising 'all contiguous Naga-inhabited areas'. In addition to Nagaland, this includes several districts in Assam, Arunachal Pradesh and Manipur, as also a large tract of Myanmar. The unrealistic aspiration – periodically endorsed by the Nagaland assembly – looks at expanding the footprint of Nagaland from the current 16,527 sq km to about 1,20,000 sq km.[34]

As the movement degenerated into a criminal and terrorist movement, New Delhi failed to seize the initiative and let it drift aimlessly for almost two decades, despite some good work during the tenures of Prime Ministers Narasimha Rao and Atal Bihari Vajpayee. Vajpayee would provide the much-needed balm in 2003 when he became the first prime minister to visit Nagaland since Nehru was booed away in 1960. Speaking at a public reception in Kohima, Vajpayee warmed the hearts of the Nagas by speaking in the local language when addressing them: '*Ami laga bhai aru boyni-khan, aami Nagaland-te matiye karone besi khusi paise dei* (My dear brothers and sisters, I am very happy to be amid you on the soil of Nagaland).'[35] Unfortunately, the lack of follow-up by subsequent governments in the next decade and the extension of the 1997 ceasefire into Manipur allowed the insurgencies in Nagaland, Manipur and Assam to combine.

Lieutenant General D.S. Hooda, who retired in 2016 as the Northern Army Commander, was the Divisional Commander of 57 Mountain Division under 3 Corps in 2009-10. Operating out of the town of Leimakhong in Manipur, he was witness to the exacerbation of the existing fault lines in that state. The NSCN(I&M) joined hands with the pro-Naga groups in Manipur – who dominated the hilly areas around the plains of Imphal – to exert pressure on the Meiteis, who held political power and claimed to be the rightful and original inhabitants of Manipur. Meitei groups in turn aligned themselves with the NSCN(K) and insurgent groups from Assam – such as the United Liberation Front of Assam (ULFA) – to fight the Indian security forces and counter the expansionist concept of Nagalim.[36] Years of extortion and terror continued as pro-Nagalim and Meitei groups clashed with one another as well as with the Indian security forces.

When speaking of the fractured polity in Nagaland during his tenure as the commander of 3 Corps in 2015-16, General Rawat highlighted the near-absence of the rule of law and structured governance. He was shocked to find that even government servants and men serving with the National Cadet Corps (NCC) were paying 10 per cent tax to whichever NSCN faction dominated an area. The division of these spoils was based on tribal domination. Extortion from transport contractors and trucks plying on the lucrative Myanmar–Kohima route was rampant. The NSCN(K) set up an operations base in Ukhrul, Manipur, to intercept these convoys by exploiting the ambiguities in the peace accord. The Semas of the NSCN(I&M) controlled Dimapur and the outskirts of Kohima, the Aos of the NSCN(K) dominated Kohima town while the areas from Peren to Mon were under a conglomerate of tribes that went by the name of Eastern Peoples Naga (EPN).

Prime Minister Narendra Modi's government made some bold moves in 2015 by initiating a settlement that promises to bring peace into the region – despite some stonewalling by the disgruntled Naga and Manipuri rebel groups.[37] Extinguishing the last embers of rebellion in the region is imperative for the success of India's Act East Policy. The last-mile challenge for the Modi government will be to dismantle the proposition of Greater Nagalim, rein in the NSCN(K), and usher lasting peace and prosperity into the region.

India's counterinsurgency strategy in Nagaland has evolved gradually and in several phases. The Indian Army – which in the initial phases had little to no intelligence on the area or the people – was shocked by the initial attrition at the hands of surprisingly skilful Naga insurgents. The few initial units retaliated by pursuing a scorched-earth policy wherein entire villages were burnt down and reprisals were ruthless.[38] Indian troops and convoys were frequently ambushed and never saw their attackers. This led to the establishment of road-opening parties that were tasked to sanitize stretches of road and protect the convoys that traversed them. A structured counterinsurgency grid was established following the formation of 8 Mountain Division in the early 1960s and 3 Corps in the late 1980s. This allowed the Indian Army to put in place a dual strategy that sought to weaken the military component of the insurgency and win the hearts and minds of the local people.

Tactically the Naga fighters excelled in marksmanship and setting ambushes, and often disengaged to fight another day during the initial decades of the insurgency. However, their fighting skills declined as the insurgency became criminalized. Gradually, the Indian state has worn down the Naga insurgency with a calibrated mix of what Shekhar Gupta calls 'the force, persuasion and concession strategy'[39] that seems to be working. Finally, the Nagas themselves seem to have realized that they were missing out on much of India's spectacular growth and development and that they needed to seek a resolution that met the requirements of all stakeholders. Namrata Goswami argues that 'a counterinsurgency strategy of trust and nurture based on democratic political culture, measured military methods, special counterinsurgency forces, local social and cultural awareness and an integrative nation-building approach will result in positive handling of India's various internal security problems'.[40]

It would be reasonable to assess and hope that with the death of Isak Swu in 2016, and the squeezing of the NSCN(K) by security forces from both India and Myanmar, the insurgency is in its final phase. However, tribal and ethnic loyalties are still deeply rooted and will be the biggest stumbling blocks in developing a cohesive Naga identity and reaping the benefits of economic prosperity. Contrary to public perception that China no longer looms large on the north-east horizon with its support for the Naga secessionist movement, there is still a free flow of arms from southern China into Nagaland and Manipur. Bibhu Prasad Routray, a security analyst with a focus on tracking terror and insurgent networks, argues in a recent piece that Beijing could well be 'gradually unveiling a grand design to revive the battered (north-east) insurgencies'. Going on to highlight rather alarmingly, he cautions, 'Provision of safe houses, supply of weapons and even playing a more prominent role in directing attacks on security forces could be emerging as Beijing's instrumentalities to disturb peace in the fragile north-east.' Clearly, there is little room for the security forces to let their guard down.

On a more positive note and reflecting the mood of the populace in the region, Colonel Sanjeev Hazarika argues in the *Infantry Journal* why this is as opportune a moment as any to take the peace process forward:

> After having faced the brunt of insurgency for seventy years, the public is yearning for peace. Incidents of public outrage against militants are on the rise and offer opportunity for mobilizing them against militants by effective psychological operations and deft handling. The dynamics of ceasefire with the militant groups and the political process that is in progress cannot be underrated. However, at the tactical level, security forces must cater for contingencies, build up intelligence and ensure a high state of operational preparedness at all times.[41]

6

OPERATION BLUE STAR: OURS IS NOT TO QUESTION WHY

'Operation Blue Star can perhaps be classified as one of the most traumatic, sensitive and thankless missions ever undertaken by any army in the world.'[1]

– *Lieutenant General K.S. Brar*

Brewing Crisis

It was the autumn of 1981 and Lieutenant General S.K. Sinha had come a long way from his time as a major, when he had coordinated the aerial move of the 1st Battalion of the Sikh Regiment (1 SIKH) from Palam airfield to Srinagar in the early days of the first India–Pakistan war of 1947-48. Sinha was now commander of Western Army Command,[2] the Indian Army's largest command. He was facing a crisis of sorts as Darbara Singh, the chief minister of Punjab, wanted him to dispatch troops to arrest a violent and troublesome Sikh preacher named Jarnail Singh Bhindranwale. Bhindranwale – the head of the Damdami Taksal,[3] a fundamentalist Sikh religious organization[4] – was holed up in a gurdwara at Mehta Chowk, some 50 km from Amritsar, Punjab. He was accused of allegedly masterminding the killing of Lala Jagat Narain, a Hindu newspaper editor in Jalandhar who had been exposing his divisive and sectarian politics.

Not only was Bhindranwale targeting Hindus, he was also alleged to have killed a rival Sikh preacher of the Nirankari sect – who were considered non-conformists and heretics.[5] Bhindranwale and his ragtag bunch of armed followers had escaped from a guest house in the neighbouring state of Haryana minutes before a posse of the Punjab Police arrived on the scene to arrest him. Frustrated by the inability of the police to execute the task and control the hostile crowd of Bhindranwale's supporters who had gathered at Mehta Chowk, Darbara Singh was forced to turn to Sinha to assist his police force with armoured escort vehicles from the Indian Army. Rightly deeming this to be highly inappropriate, Sinha politely refused, arguing that the military must intervene in internal security operations only if the primary instrument of law and order in states – the police – failed to execute their mandate.

Darbara Singh appealed to Delhi, and a day later Sinha received a directive from the vice chief of the army to plan a military operation to arrest Bhindranwale. Sinha stuck to his guns. He impressed upon his chief, General Krishna Rao, that such action would be detrimental to the image of the Indian Army and must be carefully thought through. To his credit, Krishna Rao conveyed the same to Prime Minister Indira Gandhi, who abandoned the plan.[6] Bereft of any operational plan, the Punjab Police force sent to arrest Bhindranwale had to wait for forty-eight hours as the cult gathered over 30,000 followers outside the gurdwara. The cult leader then triumphantly surrendered to the police in full view of the restive crowd. This was to be a defining moment as Bhindranwale was released within a couple of days – allegedly under instructions from Delhi – much to the chagrin of Darbara Singh. Darbara Singh was the first Congress politician to recognize the ominous threat that Bhindranwale posed to the security landscape in Punjab. Sadly, his warnings went unheeded by Delhi and one can only wonder whether events would have panned out differently had Indira Gandhi realized the danger sooner. Sinha, though, some years later rightly assessed that even had the army arrested him in 1981, Bhindranwale would nonetheless have been released given the vitiated and fractured political environment.

Indira Gandhi was shaken and rattled by her political decline and crushing electoral loss following the infamous Emergency of 1975. But she stormed back to power in 1980 after five years of misrule by a series of coalition governments. Among the early political challenges in her second tenure was to ensure the primacy of the Congress over the Akali Dal, a regional party that was rallying the Sikhs of Punjab around a largely sectarian narrative that sought a separate state for them. After the passing away of Akali leaders such as Master Tara Singh and Sant Fateh Singh, the Akalis were afraid of the marginalization of the Sikh ethos in Punjab. This feeling was strengthened after the state of Haryana was carved out of the post-Partition state of Punjab in

1966. Responding to the changing political and demographic dynamics, they passed the Anandpur Sahib Resolution in 1973. This resolution marked a shift in Akali strategy – whereby fundamentalism began to erode the traditional values of harmony and tolerance – and set in motion a polarization process to wean the Sikhs away from Congress influence.[7]

Wary and fearful of growing Sikh militant behaviour was the Jan Sangh – a predominantly Hindu party – which also began mobilizing cadres in Punjab. Adding to the prime minister's woes were two rival heavyweight Sikh leaders within the Punjab Congress, Darbara Singh and Zail Singh. While the former was chief minister of Punjab, the latter was the home minister in the central government and a close confidant of the prime minister and her powerful son – Youth Congress leader Sanjay Gandhi. Zail Singh would soon become the President of India, and it was this combination of Zail Singh and Sanjay Gandhi which emboldened Bhindranwale to counter both the Akalis and Darbara Singh. They encouraged Bhindranwale to peddle his inflammatory and muscularly separatist narrative as an alternative to the emerging Akali narrative, which was a trifle restrained and based on the Anandpur Sahib Resolution.[8] The resolution in its original form was no more than an expression of Sikh angst and identity politics to overcome other constituencies in the region comprising Hindus, lower castes and the migrant population. The Akalis and the Congress had sowed the seeds of separatism and terrorism and were soon to reap a whirlwind.

Defiling the Sanctum

Emboldened by his release, Bhindranwale realized that he had a window of opportunity to seize the leadership in the fragmented political space. Consequently, as debate and discussion exited the scene, rhetoric, coercion, violence and religion became the framework of a new discourse that Brigadier R.K. Chopra termed as a 'plain vanilla secessionist movement'. In his National Defence College course thesis, Brigadier Chopra writes, 'The terrorist movement in Punjab led by Sant Jarnail Singh Bhindranwale was not linked to any redressal of grievances or attainment of additional civil liberties. It was a plain vanilla secessionist movement demanding a separate state for the Sikhs from the Union of India.'[9]

Unleashing a reign of terror from within the confines of the Guru Nanak Niwas – a rest house on the periphery of the Golden Temple in Amritsar – Bhindranwale assassinated several prominent Sikh and Hindu activists who spoke or wrote against him. Among over 192 civilians killed were H.S. Manchanda, a Sikh leader of the Congress party in Delhi, Ramesh Chander, the fearless editor of *Hind Samachar*, and Summan Singh, the editor of another Punjabi magazine.[10] The hijacking of an Indian Airlines plane to Lahore in September 1981 by Sikh separatists owing allegiance to the Dal Khalsa,[11] Bhindranwale's primary terrorist outfit, allowed Pakistan to make an entry into the terrorist movement even as it slapped life imprisonment on the hijackers.

The growing movement for an independent Sikh state of Khalistan started to gather a lot of overseas support, particularly from UK-based separatists such as Jagjit Singh Chauhan, who established strong links with Pakistan's Inter-Services Intelligence (ISI).[12] The hijackers, Tajinder Pal Singh and Satnam Singh, were released from prison in 2000 and deported to India, where they continue to face trial for a variety of offences. As the violence spread in Punjab in the wake of Bhindranwale's incendiary speeches and the abysmal lack of counter-narratives from either the Punjab government or the central government, the secessionist flavour began to permeate government organizations. The Punjab Police was eventually proved complicit in the lack of intelligence about the terrorist-military build-up within the Golden Temple complex that Bhindranwale had commenced in mid-1983.

According to Praveen Swami, much of the pre-1984 help provided by Pakistan was in the form of low-grade weapons,[13] with heavy weapons reinforcing the arsenal only when an illustrious but disillusioned war veteran, Major General Shabeg Singh, joined Bhindranwale. The South Asia terrorism portal assesses that the number of fatalities between 1981 and 1984 – the period of the first round of the 'Khalistan war' – was around 650, which includes a conservative estimate of the deaths following the operations in the Golden Temple in June 1984.[14] This figure would be contested by the media and the Sikh community, although the numbers closely match those provided by the Indian Army.

Blowout

Indira Gandhi realized that she was staring at rebellion by the end of May 1984. Following the spate of killings and a complete breakdown of law and order in Punjab, the shaken prime minister directed her army chief, General Arun Vaidya, to flush Bhindranwale out of the Golden Temple. She had little choice but to assign the task to the Indian Army as India did not at the time have a dedicated counterterrorism force like its current National Security Guard (NSG) that could have undertaken the very complex mission.

Deferring to the prime minister's orders without first discussing the issue with his principal staff officers at Army HQ or mulling over the consequences, Vaidya immediately assigned the task to Western Army Command under Lieutenant General Krishnaswamy Sundarji. That Sundarji wanted to micromanage the operation was reflected in his choice of commanders and formations for the operation. Instead of tasking the corps commander of Jalandhar-based 11 Corps to oversee the operation, he chose his chief of staff, Lieutenant General Ranjit Singh Dayal. Inexplicable was also the decision to assign Meerut-based 9 Infantry Division with the task of storming the Golden Temple – instead of the Amritsar-based 15 Infantry Division – and recalling from leave Major General K.S. Brar, the divisional commander of 9 Infantry Division, to execute the mission. 15 Infantry Division was instead tasked with sealing Amritsar off from the rest of Punjab and plugging any infiltrations from across the international border. As both his trusted lieutenants and planners were Sikhs, Sundarji was confident that the plan they would come up with would be viable.[15]

Recollecting events on the day prior to the storming of the Golden Temple in an article in the *Telegraph*, Mark Tully wrote:

> The next morning, I found the Golden Temple complex surrounded by the Bihar Regiment. Bhindranwale held a defiant press conference in the Akal Takht at which he promised to give the army a fitting reply. I could see how heavily fortified it was, and thought that there was bound to be a bloody battle unless Bhindranwale cracked. The army was in too much of a hurry to bother about public relations, so all the journalists were then bundled out of Punjab. As we drove through Amritsar, we heard intermittent small-arms fire and the occasional whoof of a mortar. The government had clamped a strict curfew on the whole state. Frequent army checkposts ensured that there was no traffic on Kipling's Grand Trunk Road.[16]

Brar had roughly two brigades for the operations and he assigned the task of storming the temple to four infantry battalions (9th and 15th Battalions of the Kumaon Regiment (9 KUMAON and 15 KUMAON), 26th Battalion of the Madras Regiment (26 MADRAS) and 10th Battalion of the Regiment of the Guards (10 GUARDS), a para-commando battalion (1 PARA) and the Special Group (SG) from the Special Frontier Force (SFF).[17] Reinforcing this assault force was an infantry battalion of the Bihar Regiment that threw an outer cordon around the temple, a battalion from the Garhwal Rifles and select CRPF and BSF companies to assist in storming selected locations on the perimeter.[18] The para-commandos and SG were to breach the Akal Takht (seat of power) where Bhindranwale and his core group were manning defences and to ensure the safety of two senior Akali leaders, Harcharan Singh Longowal and Gurcharan Singh Tohra, who were holed up in a wing adjoining the Akal Takht. Keeping these leaders alive was considered essential for post-conflict negotiations as they represented the moderate face of emerging Sikh separatism.

Led by 10 GUARDS, 1 PARA and the SG were to follow closely behind during the first attack, assaulting the main temple complex from the northern entrance with multiple objectives. Among these were clearing the Parikrama (walkway around the Harmandir Sahib, the sanctum sanctorum in the centre of the temple complex), capturing the Darshini Deori (entrance to the sanctum), securing Harmandir Sahib and clearing the Akal Takht of all terrorists. That last objective would prove to be the most difficult to achieve, as it was the main centre of gravity of the defenders and the command-and-control centre. It was where Bhindranwale and his military commander, Shabeg Singh, were controlling the battle from, along with a large force of over a hundred heavily armed fighters.

The southern and eastern assault force comprised 26 MADRAS and 9 KUMAON, which were later reinforced by 15 KUMAON, armoured personnel carriers and Vijayanta tanks when the assault floundered. Their objectives were to clear the hostel complex and capture the Akali leadership, enter the Parikrama, secure the eastern and southern flanks without damaging the library located on the southern flank of the Parikrama and provide support to the force assaulting the Akal Takht. The main operation was to commence around 10 p.m. on 5 June and end by daybreak on 6 June, a period of six to eight hours.

Formidable Enemy

After his deployment in Nagaland, Major Katoch was back with his battalion, 1 PARA, in Nahan, a cantonment town in the picturesque state of Himachal Pradesh. But it was not long before he was in action again, as 1 PARA was asked to move to Amritsar without any preliminary briefing[19] on the night of 2 June – forty-eight hours after the decision was taken to storm the temple. Heading to Amritsar in their convoy with three tons of explosives, the commandos were prepared to blast their way into the target area rather than engage the enemy in a frontal assault. Over a quarter of 1 Para's troops were Sikhs, and the unit moved with its granthi (priest) to Amritsar. Along the way, the officers of the unit took great pains to sensitize their Sikh troops on what was happening and what they could expect in the days ahead.

On arrival in Amritsar the next day (3 June), the commanding officer and Katoch, who was second-in-command, were shown a hazy photograph of the Golden Temple complex that was marked 'Secret' – but, as Katoch recalls, there was nothing secret about it. It was only after walking around the periphery of the complex that the para-commandos realized that they were faced with a well-prepared and tactically proficient enemy, who had dug in with sandbags and fortified the watchtowers around the complex with light machine guns and other weaponry. It was only later that Katoch understood how lucky they were not to get shot during their walk – no one had briefed them about the seven CRPF soldiers who had been shot at a couple of days earlier during a recce of the periphery. The terrorists had perhaps been instructed not to target the Indian Army until it initiated combat operations.

Given the heavy fortifications, it was clear to the para-commandos that the only way to get Bhindranwale was to blast their way into the Akal Takht from the rear. This, they reckoned, would surprise the defenders and help them seize the initiative after having eliminated the leadership and left the defenders rudderless. Katoch was surprised when their plan was rejected by Brar on the evening of 3 June. Instead, they were asked to be part of a frontal assault on the Akal Takht via the main north entrance along with 10 GUARDS and the SG commandos. The SG had surprised Brar by declaring that they had briefed the prime minister about a plan to storm the Akal Takht by using gas canisters that would immobilize the defenders. What they had not factored in was the wind direction and limited availability of gas masks, which could make the accompanying assault troops vulnerable to gas ingestion. Most importantly, the SFF had not realized that the Akal Takht would be sealed. Luckily for the para-commandos, a consignment of masks arrived on 5 June and was distributed among the para-commandos and 10 GUARDS who were expected to be in the vicinity during the gas attack.

What of the military pedigree of the defenders? Some angst within the Sikh community emerged after the 1982 Asian Games in Delhi, when several decorated war veterans and accomplished senior officers were randomly stopped and frisked. Much displeasure was expressed during a meeting of Sikh ex-servicemen at the Golden Temple in October 1982 in the presence of Bhindranwale. While there was general disagreement when Bhindranwale proposed direct armed confrontation, his belligerent posturing attracted two senior retired paratroopers, Major Generals Jaswant Singh Bhullar and Shabeg Singh. While Bhullar left Bhindranwale's flock before the final showdown, Shabeg stayed on. An ex-paratrooper from 1 PARA, Shabeg had an excellent reputation as a combat soldier and tactician. He had also trained and commanded the Mukti Bahini forces in Bangladesh.[20] Angry and bitter at being sacked from the military for petty misappropriation of funds, he was drawn to the secessionist movement led by Bhindranwale and emerged as among his most radicalized lieutenants. Bhindranwale had found his military strategist, one who would prepare him to challenge the might of the Indian Army.[21]

A hot and cloudless day on 5 June saw the Indian Army closing in on the target area much like a conventional operation in a built-up area. There was absolutely no surprise element, with loudspeakers warning civilians to exit the temple while they had time and outer-ring targets being engaged by the paramilitary forces. By the evening, Shabeg's reinforced and well-armed watchtowers – on top of two minarets and a water tank that offered excellent views of the temple complex and surrounding areas – had been reduced to rubble by 106mm recoilless launchers and howitzers. By all parameters Brar thought he had the operation under control.

The final assault commenced at 10.30 p.m. with 10 GUARDS attempting to breach the Parikrama and having to withdraw when faced with well-directed fire from multiple directions and levels as they climbed the stairs of the main entrance. Captain Jasbir Raina – a young Sikh officer who led the assault and had only the previous morning carried out a daring reconnaissance of the defences inside the temple – was the first officer casualty. He was followed by many others. They were evacuated by a team of 1 PARA that followed on to the Parikrama. The para-commandos and the SG met with a similar fate as casualties mounted, but the gritty Guardsmen, SG and para-commandos made their way to the Akal Takht and Darshini Deori along a closed veranda and the riskier open Parikrama. Here, well-placed snipers from the Harmandir Sahib and Akal Takht picked out troops in the moonlight. Katoch also recollects that some of his divers had been alerted that they would have to swim across the Sarovar (tank) and secure the Harmandir Sahib, a proposition that seemed preposterous as the battle unfolded. Staying alive was now the prime task for Katoch's men as they absorbed the initial blast of Shabeg's defensive plan. As the battle progressed and the troops advanced with their cumbersome 7.62mm self-loading rifles, they were met with fire from light and medium machine guns and AK-47s. Katoch was the next to fall in the early hours of 6 June as he approached the Darshini Deori, a vantage position from where both the Akal Takht and Harmandir Sahib could be engaged. Taking two bullets in his right shoulder, he was quickly evacuated by his troops out of the temple complex and thereon to the Amritsar General Hospital. He lay there bandaged for the next thirty-six hours before being taken to the Jalandhar Military Hospital, where he underwent surgery. There was no medical evacuation plan and he recollects that as the battle progressed, there was chaos in the hospitals and clinics in Amritsar, which had not been warned either by the army or the local administration. Katoch wryly remarked that he had to salute Indira Gandhi with his left hand when she visited the unit after the operation.[22]

The paratroopers had taken thirteen casualties in the initial assault, with 10 GUARDS bearing the brunt. The SFF would take heavy casualties too as they attempted to assault the Akal Takht soon after. Several troops were cut down by the firing at knee level from holes cut in the marble as they ran up the stairs. A conventional assault was being torn to shreds by a clever and tactically proficient enemy who had been grossly underestimated by the Indian Army's leadership. The other frontal assaults from the southern and eastern wings by troops from the Kumaon and Madras Regiments faced similar fire from concealed positions. There were strict initial orders that no rocket launchers – such as the highly effective Carl Gustaf – would be used, and that armoured personnel carriers would not be permitted to provide covering fire, as they would damage the marble stairs and walkway. Sundarji had assumed that the early capture of Harmandir Sahib would be a symbolic victory that would hasten the capitulation of Bhindranwale and his terrorist fighters. The plan to capture the Harmandir Sahib using para-commandos – who were expected to swim across the tank with flippers and light weapons and take the defenders by surprise – was shelved as the early battle went awry.

Dawn Breaks

As Brar's plan of clearing the temple by daybreak faltered in the face of a determined enemy, he was faced with a dilemma. His troops were scattered around the Parikrama – some in the covered veranda and others caught in the open – and they would be easy pickings for Shabeg's well-concealed fighters. Withdrawal was one option, but that would have meant a humiliating defeat for the mighty Indian Army. He was determined to accomplish his mission even if it meant a fight to the finish. Taking clearance from Sundarji, Brar deployed a few ICVs and Vijayanta tanks to provide covering fire to troops as

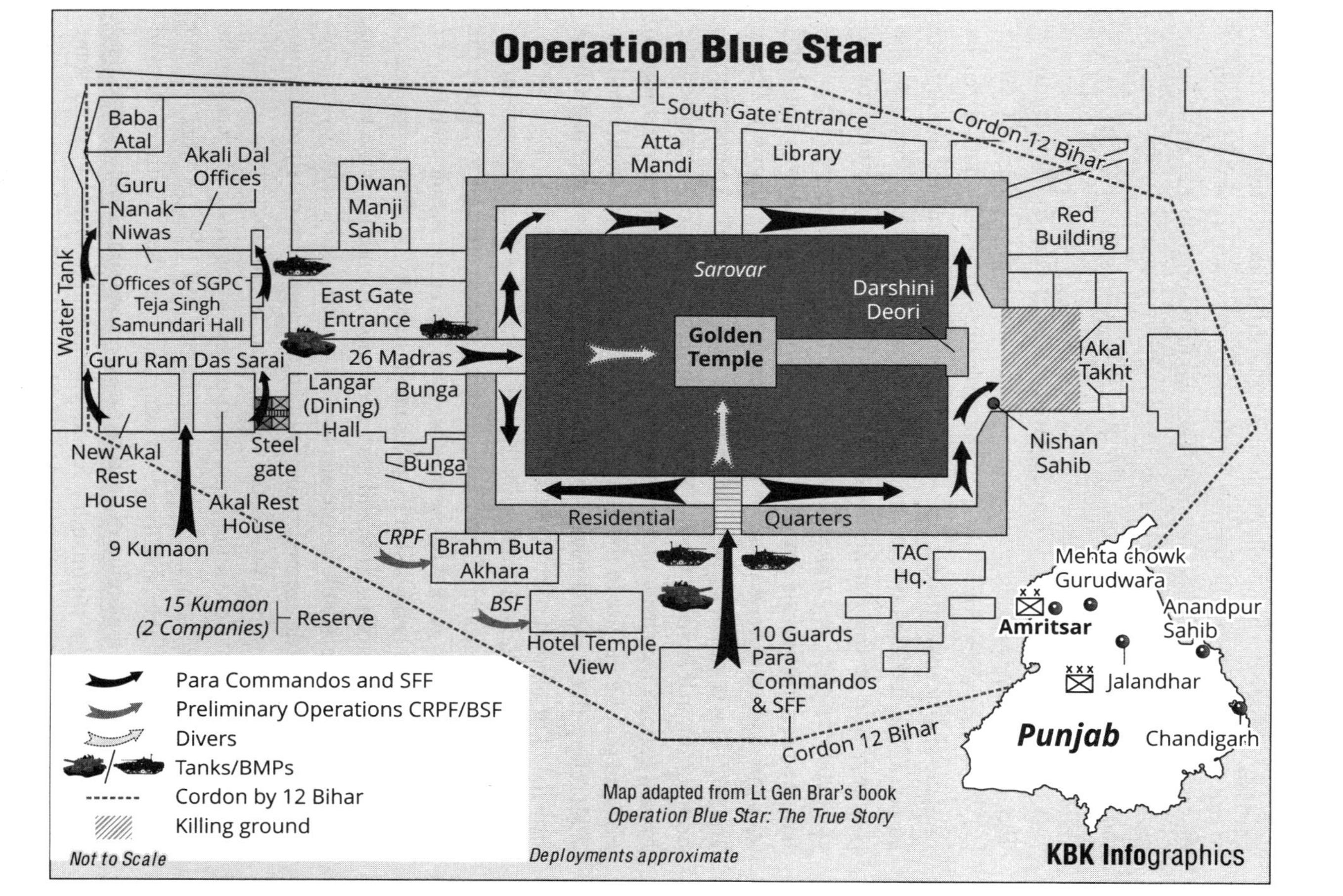
Operation Blue Star
South Gate Entrance
Cordon-12 Bihar
Baba Atal
Akali Dal Offices
Guru Nanak Niwas
Atta Mandi
Library
Diwan Manji Sahib
Red Building
Water Tank
Offices of SGPC Teja Singh Samundari Hall
East Gate Entrance
Sarovar
Darshini Deori
Golden Temple
Akal Takht
Guru Ram Das Sarai
26 Madras
Langar (Dining) Hall
Bunga
Bunga
New Akal Rest House
Steel gate
Akal Rest House
Nishan Sahib
Residential
Quarters
9 Kumaon
CRPF
Brahm Buta Akhara
TAC Hq.
15 Kumaon (2 Companies)
Reserve
BSF
Hotel Temple View
10 Guards Para Commandos & SFF
Cordon 12 Bihar
Mehta chowk Gurudwara
Amritsar
Anandpur Sahib
Jalandhar
Punjab
Chandigarh
Para Commandos and SFF
Preliminary Operations CRPF/BSF
Divers
Tanks/BMPs
Cordon by 12 Bihar
Killing ground
Not to Scale
Map adapted from Lt Gen Brar's book Operation Blue Star: The True Story
Deployments approximate
KBK Infographics

they advanced towards the Akal Takht. Prior to the deployment of tanks and the limited use of heavy weapons, Brar had announced a temporary cessation of firing to allow the hundreds of devotees trapped inside the temple complex to exit the area. Seeing the writing on the wall, many terrorists slipped out of the complex along with the devotees. They would go on to form part of future resistance to the Indian state as they joined various terrorist outfits – such as the Khalistan Commando Force (KCF) – and continued their secessionist struggle for another few years.[23]

Once the heavy weapons were deployed, it was curtains for Bhindranwale. Though Sundarji would later tell course participants at the College of Combat in Mhow that every round fired by the tanks was personally authorized by him, the reality was different as the tanks and ICVs had provided fire support based on the situation on the ground. The destruction of the library on the southern side of the Parikrama could have been one of the unfortunate collateral effects of this move. While several Sikh chroniclers and historians have accused the Indian Army of intentionally burning it down, first-hand accounts and interviews point at several snipers operating from the library and targeting troops of 26 MADRAS and even their brigade commander. The prolonged battle is likely to have started a fire that eventually destroyed the library. Katoch recollects that an injured Sikh tank commander told him in hospital that he did fire in the direction of the library. Katoch said, 'I told the Sikh officer that I would have done the same in a Hindu temple had I been ordered to in support of comrades who were being cut down.'

Troops from 26 MADRAS finally approached the Akal Takht from the southern wing at around 7 a.m. and were the first to attempt to silence the machine-gun posts located below the staircases. The entire assault team was cut down, with a JCO being killed in gruesome fashion by dynamite strapped to his body by the terrorists. It would take a few more rounds from the Vijayanta tanks and another assault before silence fell on the Akal Takht. By 11 a.m. on 6 June, the battle seemed to be finished as many terrorists jumped into the Sarovar and swam towards the Harmandir Sahib. They were promptly cut down by fire. At the same time, good progress was made in clearing the eastern wings of militants.[24] Troops from the SG and 1 PARA were the first to enter the Akal Takht shortly after noon, and what they saw there shocked them. Apart from the bodies of dead terrorists – including Bhindranwale and Shabeg Singh – the commandos found several bodies of women and some skeletons in the rubble within the Akal Takht. Clearly, Bhindranwale and his men had also converted the sacred temple into a den of iniquity and vice.[25]

Katoch laments the fact that media access to the operation was denied, as there was no one to provide a real-time narrative. Instead, a few reporters who managed to remain within the Golden Temple complex fell for the information provided by the extremists that focused on alleged atrocities committed by the security forces. Killing of cornered terrorists or those attempting to escape in such a situation cannot be discounted, nor can the death of civilians in the crossfire or in debris caused by tank shells. However, most officers – both Sikh and non-Sikh – are quite emphatic that there was no spontaneous execution of civilians after the Indian Army took over the temple, as suggested by some.[26] Sporadic fighting continued through the day at locations like the langar (dining area) till it dawned on the terrorists that their leaders were dead. Many terrorists slipped out through tunnels, while others surrendered. Mopping-up operations continued through till 9 June.

The visit of the President of India to the Golden Temple on 8 June was a solemn moment that signalled the end of the battle. However, the President, Giani Zail Singh – a Sikh himself and the commander-in-chief of India's armed forces – may well have been among the chief architects of the disaster that was Operation Blue Star. According to the Indian government's white paper on the Punjab agitation, the Indian security forces suffered significant casualties, losing eighty-three personnel with 248 suffering injuries. However, with 493 terrorists killed and another 592 apprehended, the terrorist movement experienced a significant setback. Others – such as Harminder Kaur, a journalist – insist that the casualties on both sides were much higher.[27]

Operational Postscript

This was the most difficult chapter to write as I was posted at the Adampur airbase outside Jalandhar for much of the time when Punjab was in flames. Most of us at the airbase were relatively insulated from the simmering discontent and violence. A few of us who had a latent curiosity about the happenings around us would pick up stray comments that reflected angst and fear among the civilian orderlies, waiters and casual workers, most of whom belonged either to minority communities or were migrants from other states. The more affluent Sikhs were perplexed and alarmed at the turn of events, particularly at the unchecked rise of Bhindranwale and his brand of bigoted, inflammatory and sectarian discourse. They seemed confident, however, that the crisis would soon blow over, given the sacrifices and contributions made by the small Sikh community to India's military and economy. They could not have been further from the ground reality.

At the military level, my first opportunity to explore the dark corridors of Operation Blue Star was in the most unlikely of places – the Defence Services Staff College at Wellington, in the salubrious Nilgiri hills. It was the summer of 1993 and I was doing the 49th staff college course, a mid-career professional military education course for officers of the rank of major (army), squadron leader (air force) and lieutenant commander (navy). General Krishnaswamy Sundarji, the former army chief, had settled there after retirement in a bungalow that had been dubbed Alcatraz by members of the course. Eloquent as always, Sundarji had just released his book *Blind Men of Hindoostan,* but rarely entertained visitors except for groups of student officers who wished to intellectually engage with him. Most comfortable when asked to expound on manoeuvre warfare, nuclear strategy and the integrated application of firepower, he would turn reflective when asked about Operation Blue Star and Operation Pawan, the Indian peacekeeping-turned-military intervention in Sri Lanka.

Looking around his large walled compound with dense concertina barbwire and security towers, he said to us one morning, 'The government says that I need all this to insulate me from the Khalistanis and the LTTE (the Liberation Tigers of Tamil Eelam). Unfortunately, after what happened to Indira Gandhi, Arun (General Arun Vaidya) and Rajiv Gandhi, I have no choice in the matter.' While the first two were assassinated by Sikhs in 1984 and 1986 respectively, Rajiv Gandhi was blown up by an LTTE suicide bomber in 1991. I was part of a study group on insurgencies and terrorism in South Asia and wanted to hear Sundarji's views on the storming of the Golden Temple as the head of Western Army Command at the time. To Sundarji's credit, he stuck to his guns and said that as an operational field commander it was his mandate to execute a difficult task that had been assigned to him.

When asked whether he had doubts about succeeding in what was the Indian Army's first real experience of dense urban warfare, he replied in the affirmative but said that the conservative soldier in him forced him to push away those doubts. He emphasized that those were troubled times, the kind that the Indian state had never experienced before, and that even though numerous moral and ethical dilemmas did cross his mind as operations were being planned, the sheer brutality of Bhindranwale's cadres and the impunity with which they had started challenging the writ of the state pushed those dilemmas away. What remained with me, though, were his parting words when he said, 'I hope no Indian field commander is ever asked to execute such an operation again.' Little did Sundarji anticipate that much of the warfare that India's armed forces would wage in the decades ahead would involve several decisions and ethical dilemmas like those faced at the gates of the Golden Temple – albeit with varying intensity.

Several officers who were thrust into action on those fateful days in June 1984 are critical of General Vaidya's acquiescence to what was a panicky decision by Indira Gandhi to storm the Golden Temple without adequate planning and preparation. They argued, 'General Vaidya had three choices when ordered to flush Bhindranwale out – say yes, say no, or ask for more time to shape the environment in a manner of his choosing.' In hindsight – and these officers acknowledged that reflecting on military actions in hindsight was much easier – the last option would have been the most suitable, given that the Indian Army had never been involved in such a major operation in urban terrain and that too in a less-than-war situation, where there would be no clear rules of engagement.

Many suggest that a few weeks – or even a few months – of concentrated military strategizing on how to defang Bhindranwale would have had greater chances of success than a force-on-force engagement that ran the risk of alienating the Sikhs. Moving beyond the strategy of laying a long siege to the Golden Temple, they argue that embedding Sikh volunteers into Bhindranwale's force to assess the impact of Shabeg's shrewd military mind, or even planning a covert operation to eliminate the leadership may have yielded better outcomes. Dwelling on command-and-control issues, Vaidya may have erred in delegating the operation completely to Sundarji, who had assured him that the operation would be over in hours. Both were the operational products of the 'big battle' and, however competent they may have been, this was uncharted territory for the entire Indian Army leadership.[28]

According to Katoch, the only man who could have infused some caution into the plan was the chief of staff, Lieutenant General Ranjit Singh Dayal, a hero of the 1965 war. That he did not do so even after all the ominous bits of intelligence trickled in between 3 and 5 June reflected the operational hubris that existed within the Indian Army of the time. Brar too had built up a reputation as a 'cool and competent' commander; one wonders whether he ever contemplated going back to Sundarji, either after the initial recce reports indicated well-concealed fortifications, or when the initial assault met with unexpectedly heavy fire. Having studied the Indian military leadership closely, one aspect that merits attention is the fear and stigma of command failure that prompts leaders to persist with suboptimal operational plans. Had Brar gone back to Sundarji and asked for time, most reckon that Sundarji would have sacked him and brought in another divisional commander to continue with the operation. For Sundarji, at that time, there was no going back.

Retired Lieutenant General Ghei, a Sikh and a paratrooper of some accomplishment, is scathing in his indictment of Operation Blue Star thirty-five years after the operation. He says, 'It was a political blunder but was possibly a hasty reaction from the government after the intelligence agencies had lost a senior officer (Deputy Inspector General Atwal) at the gates of the temple. The timing was totally wrong – the day was the celebration of the birth (Gurpurab) of the fifth Sikh guru, because of which there were many peasant devotees inside the temple when the assault was launched. One cannot understand the urgency. There was no justification for that, nor for the use of artillery and tank main guns. They (meaning the army chief) should have told the prime minister to wait till they had a correct assessment and a better plan to execute the mission. The military hierarchy from the chief downwards did not display professional prudence.'[29]

General Brar has been more than honest in his analysis of the operational lessons from Operation Blue Star and this section will cover only some of the important ones. Of the three army divisions in the area, 15 Infantry Division was located at Amritsar, 9 Infantry Division was at Meerut and 7 Infantry Division at Ferozepur. Why 9 Division was chosen to execute a task that could have been assigned to a division that knew the area better (15 Division) has baffled many. It may have been a result of General Sundarji's personal preference for Major General Brar to lead the operation. As the planning process morphed into an operational plan, it barely conformed to the principles of the existing army general staff manual on fighting in built-up areas. There was no study either of earlier operations conducted in 1973 by the Indian Army to put down the Provincial Armed Constabulary revolts in the Uttar Pradesh towns of Bareilly, Meerut and Agra.[30] Comfortable with classic semi-urban cordon-and-search operations, the trio of Sundarji, Dayal and Brar seem to have ignored all available intelligence that pointed at heavily fortified defences and trained and radicalized terrorists who were prepared to fight to the last man.

Hoping to clear the temple in six to eight hours as envisaged by Sundarji was certainly going to be a bridge too far. Thirty-five years later, Katoch is emphatic that the best strategy would have been to cut off the water and electricity supply for a few days, given that it was peak summer. Having sapped the will of the fighters, the commandos could have blasted their way into the Akal Takht from the rear, while 10 GUARDS could have created killing grounds along the Parikrama and the corridors should the terrorists have attempted to flee. Instead of concurrently entering from multiple directions, the operation could have been commenced with the sole objective of eliminating the adversary's principal centre of gravity – its core leadership led by Bhindranwale. Once that had been achieved, a combination of psychological warfare through loudspeaker announcements and selective assaults would have resulted in the speedy capitulation of the remaining terrorists.

Over the years there has been speculation in the media that Indira Gandhi sought British Prime Minister Margaret Thatcher's assistance in planning the operation. British Special Air Service (SAS) experts are said to have assisted in planning the operation.[31] Responding to these claims, Katoch said, 'I was in the thick of planning in Amritsar from 3 June and did not see any British operatives. If at all they were around, it could only have been to advise the SG at their home base before the balloon went up.'[32] In any case this is more of a political issue in Britain, where the Sikhs are one of the largest immigrant groups. They form a significant vote bank and include a small group of seditious elements that sparked the Khalistan movement after Operation Blue Star.[33]

Mutiny

The Sikhs are courageous fighters, emotional and easily provoked. As news of the storming of the Golden Temple filtered out of Amritsar, there were ripples of dissent among the large complement of Sikh troops in the Indian Army. Mostly distributed among two exclusive regiments – the Sikh Regiment and the Sikh Light Infantry Regiment – there were Sikhs in many other regiments, but it was mainly in the Sikh Regiment that trouble brewed. Ganganagar in Rajasthan was home to the 9th Battalion of the Sikh Regiment (9 SIKH), and it was here that the first major mutiny broke out in the absence of effective officer leadership. Troops ransacked the armoury on 7 June and set out in large numbers towards Delhi in convoys, with Mark Tully even suggesting that some may have found their way into Pakistan.[34]

In the absence of any official communication on what had happened at Amritsar from the officers to the troops, it is highly possible that the unit granthi (ceremonial reader of the Sikh holy book) was transmitting rumours about atrocities being committed by the security forces in the villages, which infuriated the soldiers. It was not too long before they were disarmed and rounded up by other regiments of the Indian Army without much shooting or loss of life. In the absence of social media, news of the mutiny travelled rather slowly and it was only on 9 June that the second major mutiny broke out in Ramgarh, Bihar, where the regimental centre of the Sikh Regiment was located. It was here that the Indian Army faced its sternest internal threat since Independence, as almost a thousand young recruits led by a radicalized young soldier looted the armoury, killed the commandant of the regimental centre and injured a few others in a shootout.

Setting out in a large convoy towards Amritsar, they were engaged along the way by artillery and effectively stopped by several roadblocks set up along the way. According to official figures, over thirty-five mutineers were killed. The official court of inquiry attributed the mutiny to poor officer leadership and inadequate sensitization rather than any seditious or externally abetted rebellion. A few other combat regiments of the Indian Army – particularly the Punjab Regiment – also saw sporadic uprisings that were speedily put down. With no availability of official records on the operation at either the defence ministry or the home ministry – other than a hastily stitched up white paper that was released in July 1984 – narratives of the operation have been varied.

While General Brar's book *Operation Blue Star: The True Story* remains the only credible narrative to emerge from the Indian Army, Mark Tully and Satish Jacob provide an honest and objective blow-by-blow account of what happened during those tragic hours and their aftermath in *Amritsar: Mrs Gandhi's Last Battle*. The Sikh narratives by journalists such as Harminder Kaur and Kunwar Sandhu, whether written or in the form of YouTube videos, are instructive but clouded by emotion and make vastly exaggerated claims of the number of deaths resulting from the alleged indiscriminate firing by the Indian Army and other security forces within the Golden Temple.

Arguably one of the most objective academic pieces on the causes and consequences of the operations is 'The Indian Armed Forces' Sikh and Non-Sikh Officers' Opinions on Operation Blue Star' by Professor Apurba Kundu, currently acting dean at East Anglia University, Cambridge.[35] The three fundamental questions Kundu asked his sample group of ninety-six officers – comprising non-Sikhs and Sikhs in a ratio of 5:1 – were: was the military action justified; were the means employed the most optimal ones; and why did the post-operation mutiny by Sikh troops take place and whether it damaged the ethos of the Indian Army? To the first question, all non-Sikh respondents and one Sikh respondent answered in the affirmative. The second question was more contentious – only a few non-Sikh officers approved of the direct military action while most others were unanimous in their criticism of the means employed and the haste with which the operation unfolded.

The third question elicited the most interesting response. Most respondents concurred that the mutiny was the result of poor leadership and did not have any long-term adverse impact on the ethos of the Indian Army. One Sikh respondent very emphatically stated, 'The role of the Sikhs in the military is not compromised.'[36] The declining Sikh enrolment in the Indian Army since is a result of societal and economic factors such as the rule assigning vacancies to each state as per its recruitable male population, and not any disillusionment with the institution.

Colonel Gurnam Singh, an ex-paratrooper, motivational coach, active blogger and a Sikh himself writes very emotionally about the solidarity that was seen among all religions and communities within the Indian Army in the aftermath of Operation Blue Star. He remembers the occasion of the first Sikh festival to be celebrated after the operation, and writes in a blog on 'Secularism in the Indian Army', 'The number of army personnel of every religion that thronged the regimental gurdwara of the nearest Sikh battalion was the largest I had seen. I distinctly remember each officer and soldier who put his forehead to the ground to pay obeisance appeared to linger a wee bit longer than usual. There was that empathy... that appeared to say, "You are hurt and we all understand."'[37]

Aftermath

Though Operation Blue Star had left Bhindranwale's secessionist movement in disarray, the army action left a deep psychological impact on the masses. The assassination of Indira Gandhi by her Sikh bodyguards on 31 October 1984 galvanized the extremist struggle into a global movement that would trouble the Indian state for a few more years. The resurgence of extremism in Punjab took a while to manifest itself and peaked around mid-1986, almost a year after an Akali government supported by the Congress came to power and the Rajiv Gandhi–Longowal Accord failed to strike a chord with either the people or the secessionists.[38] The accord had sought to address most of the long-standing demands of the Akalis but was sabotaged by hardliners within the Akali Dal and the extremists, leading to the assassination of Longowal in August 1985 by Sikh terrorists. The Sikh extremists – who were initially led by the All India Sikh Students Federation (AISSF) – had regrouped with Pakistani help. The other groups that later emerged or rejuvenated themselves were the KCF, Khalistan Liberation Force, Dashmesh Regiment, Babbar Khalsa and the United Sikh Army. Wasan Singh Zafarwal and Labh Singh emerged as dreaded terrorists from among the 350-400 hardcore terrorists identified by the Punjab government in1985-86.

The main weapons used by the groups were semi-automatic rifles, Sten guns, pistols and country-made weapons. These were mostly carried under chadars or shawls and used in daring motorcycle- and scooter-borne attacks in broad daylight. There were enough sympathizers and sanctuaries in both rural and urban areas for the attackers to escape and hide. A five-member Panthic Committee was formed to coordinate the move towards the declaration of Khalistan, which reflected firm intent on the part of the secessionists. They banned any dialogue with a government that did not have Khalistan on its agenda, and gradually made the Akali government irrelevant. The rise of Hindu groups such as the Rashtriya Swayamsevak Sangh (RSS) and Shiv Sena across Punjab, particularly in the urban areas of Amritsar, Jalandhar, Hoshiarpur, Batala and Gurdaspur, worsened matters.[39]

Pakistan's military dictator General Zia-ul-Haq was pleased to have a readymade hunting ground for his policy of 'bleeding India with a thousand cuts'. He adopted a four-pronged strategy to wage a covert war against India in Punjab that was followed till his death in 1988. The first was to provide safe havens to hundreds of disgruntled Sikh youth and Bhindranwale's remaining terrorists and set up training camps to provide basic training for handling small arms, explosives and other subversion techniques. The second was to create and spread a narrative in rural Punjab that revolved around Bhindranwale's legacy and the atrocities committed by Indian security forces inside the Golden Temple. The third prong was to support infiltration by trained Sikh terrorists along the porous international border, particularly in Rajasthan. The terrorists would then carry out bombings and other terrorist acts, targeting the Hindu community in Punjab to exacerbate the communal divide. The last prong was to support the Khalistan movement globally by providing financial and propaganda support to Sikh secessionists in Europe, Canada and the US.

External support was given by wealthy and influential Sikhs like Jagjit Singh Chauhan in the UK and Ganga Singh Dhillon, an influential US-based Khalistan ideologue. The ubiquitous ISI was the conduit through which this strategy of creating a mass movement was to be executed.[40] Consequently, it helped sponsor the Lahore-based Akal Federation and facilitated the Babbar Khalsa and Damdami Taksal (Bhindranwale's original outfit) to set up training camps in Sialkot and Narowal in Pakistan with about 700 Sikh youth and the few disgruntled armymen who had crossed over after Operation Blue Star. Matters finally came to a head in March 1986 when fierce clashes erupted between Sikh terrorists and Hindu social groups across the state of Punjab, with the latter bearing the brunt of organized killings by AISSF-led mobs.

According to *India Today*, fifty-three civilians lost their lives that month. Thousands of Sikh farmers laid siege to the industrial town of Batala for over a week till security forces dispersed them, but not before eleven Hindus were killed on the outskirts. The Akali government was a mute spectator to this violence. This emboldened the Panthic Committee to raise their war cry of secession by formally declaring Khalistan on 29 April 1986. They increased attacks on civilians (mainly Hindus and dissenting Sikhs) despite the presence of a weakened and dysfunctional Punjab Police. In a clear case of revenge killing, two motorcycle-borne terrorists of the KCF shot the retired army chief General Arun Vaidya as he was driving home in Pune on 10 August 1986. After it was assessed that over 800 civilians had lost their lives in Punjab from January to May 1987, Prime Minister Rajiv Gandhi declared President's rule in the state in May 1987. Brigadier Chopra is scathing in his assessment of why Punjab continued to simmer:

> The Government and its policies towards solving the Punjab problem are, so far, like rowing a rudderless boat. It has failed to provide protection, neutralize terror networks and create public awareness.[41]

Punjab limped back to normalcy in the late 1980s and early 1990s and did not go the Kashmir way, and here the role of two outstanding police officers, Julio Ribeiro and K.P.S. Gill, cannot be overlooked. While the former was brought in by the central government in 1986 as the Director General of Police (DGP) in Punjab, he was elevated to the post of advisor to the governor in 1987 after surviving an assassination attempt. Gill then took on the operational role of DGP, transforming the Punjab police from a demoralized force to an effective semi-urban counterterrorist and counterinsurgency force. Countering terror with terror and using hard-line methods to persuade the civilian populace to desist from aiding Sikh terrorists, by the end of 1988 Gill had either eliminated hundreds of cadres, or driven a large chunk of them into Pakistan.[42] A significant number, however, decided to make a last stand at the Golden Temple in Amritsar, which was off the government radar after the 1984 debacle. As a result, 1986 and 1987 saw the extremist and AISSF leaders use the Golden Temple as a hideout under the very noses of the Akali government and the Punjab Police.[43]

May 1988 saw the government swing into action as the Golden Temple once again was turned into a fortress. This time around it was the recently formed NSG and elite commandos of the Punjab Police who were entrusted with the task of clearing the temple complex in Operation Black Thunder.[44] Within the NSG, it was mainly 51 Special Action Group (SAG) – comprising army commandos led by Major General Naresh Kumar – that executed the operation over ten days. It was an intelligence-driven operation, with the SAG planting an operative inside the temple for two days and gathering vital information on the defensive dispositions and approximate terrorist strength in the temple. Intelligence was complemented by political patience, a whole-of-government approach, snipers and psychological warfare. Adequate windows were periodically offered either for the terrorists to surrender, or for trapped devotees to leave the temple safely. Restraint was the hallmark of the operation, with the prime minister, Rajiv Gandhi, and the director-general of the NSG, Ved Marwah, monitoring the operation.

In his book *Uncivil Wars,* Marwah puts the operation in the right perspective:

> The most important difference between the two operations (Blue Star and Black Thunder) was that the former was conceived in haste, underestimating the militants' determination and capacity to fight, and the latter was meticulously planned with inputs from all concerned (including the IAF, which sent in clear recce photographs).[45]

Despite the extremely effective strong-arm tactics of K.P.S. Gill and the Punjab Police during the post-Operation Black Thunder phase, the terrorist movement did not lose steam as the offensive action by the security forces was not complemented by good governance and political stability on the ground. Making matters worse was the complete absence of effective communication directed at weaning away the mostly patriotic and nationalistic non-urban Sikhs from the secessionist narrative. With Rajiv Gandhi preoccupied with Sri Lanka, it would take a few years for the Khalistan movement to peter out.

Pakistan reignited the covert war in J&K after realizing that it would not be able to sustain the Khalistan struggle. Quitting while the going was good was an excellent move by the ISI. The Sikh religious elders also gradually came to shun the Panthic Committee. The sealing and patrolling by the BSF of over 600 km of the border from Hussainiwala to Chhamb Jaurian, and the gradual success of the campaign to win hearts and minds, led to peace in Punjab. It was to the credit of Prime Minister Narasimha Rao's government[46] in the early 1990s that Delhi empowered and supported a strong Punjab state government led by Beant Singh. They implemented a two-pronged strategy to bring peace to Punjab: cracking down on terrorism and simultaneously impressing on the people of Punjab that they ran the risk of being left behind in the ongoing economic liberalization programme that Delhi had embarked on. It proved to be a winning strategy. By the mid-1990s, Punjab was back on track.

7

SIACHEN: AN ICY BATTLEGROUND

'Fighting and dying at breathtaking altitudes, Indians and Pakistanis are locked in an icy stalemate over a disputed Himalayan boundary. Who will compromise?'[1]

– EDWARD DESMOND IN *TIME*

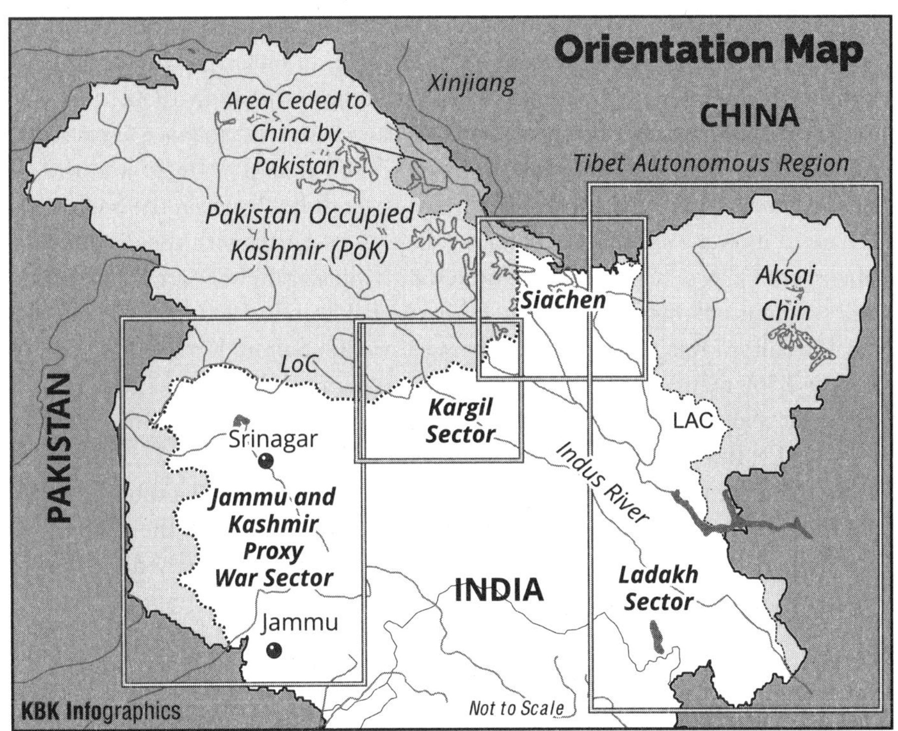

This map is for representational purposes only and does not purport to depict political boundaries

Cartographic Dispute

The Russian tundra is a most unforgiving battleground for armies. Hitler's defeat at Stalingrad in the bleak winter of 1942 – his Panzer divisions destroyed by the hardy and acclimatized Russian forces – proved to be among the critical turning points of WWII. The battles fought by Major General Thimayya's Sri Division (later 19 Infantry Division) against invaders from Skardu and Gilgit across the snowbound passes of J&K and Ladakh in the early summer of 1948 are standout examples of endurance and courage. So are the battles fought by the Indian Army in 1965 and 1999 in the Kargil sector at altitudes of 13,000 to 15,000 feet – where every breath is an effort. These examples, however, pale into insignificance in comparison with the India–Pakistan face-off on the Siachen Glacier, where even the soaring Himalayan Eagle does not dare to venture.

Running at an average altitude of 15,000 to 17,000 feet above mean sea level, the Siachen Glacier was discovered in 1821 by the British explorer William Moorcraft. The parts from the snout northwards were first surveyed by another Englishman, Dr Tom Longstaff, in 1909, when he climbed to the Bilafond La, a pass on the Saltoro Range that would see much action in the years ahead.[2] And it was Professor Giotto Dainelli, an Italian geographer and naturalist, who mapped the glacier to its northernmost point in 1930.[3]

In the local language, 'Siachen' means 'the land with an abundance of roses'. The Siachen Glacier drains into the Nubra River that goes on to join the Shyok River, a major tributary of the Indus River. It lies between the Saltoro Range to its west and the Karakoram Range to its north, with the disputed Shaksgam Valley to its northwest. Interestingly, Shaksgam was part of Jammu and Kashmir before being ceded to China by Pakistan in 1963.

The Saltoro Range is dominated by the towering Saltoro Kangri that rises to over 7,500 metres (25,000 feet) and includes many peaks above 23,000 feet, the most relevant ones being the Sia Kangri and Sherpi Kangri. The Indra Col, Sia La, Bilafond La and Gyong La – at heights of 18,000 to 22,000 feet – are the most prominent passes on the range. The range flanks the glacier, shielding it from Pakistan-occupied J&K to the west, and joins the Eastern Karakoram Range at Indra Col. It then runs in a south-easterly direction till the Karakoram Pass. The southern tip of this range is a geographical grid square designated NJ 9842, the last point up to which the LoC was delineated.

In the ceasefire agreement signed on 27 July 1949 after the first India–Pakistan war, the Ceasefire Line (CFL) was demarcated on maps up to Grid NJ 9842.[4] Thereafter, the agreement went on to state, rather ambiguously, that the CFL would continue 'thence north to the glaciers'. In 1972, prior to the signing of the Simla Agreement between India and Pakistan, the CFL was redrawn – with both sides retaining the areas they had captured on either side of the line – and designated as the LoC. The vague description beyond NJ 9842 remained unchanged and lent itself to differing interpretations by either side, causing problems several years later. Had some care been taken to extend this line northwards along the Saltoro Ridge, the Siachen conflict could well have been avoided.[5]

The Indian claim line is based on the universally accepted watershed principle of demarcation that runs northwards from NJ 9842 for almost 110 km along the Saltoro Ridge. It was India's view that from NJ 9842, the LoC (now known as the Actual Ground Position Line or AGPL) ought to follow the Saltoro Range ridgeline, i.e., the watershed of the Dansam and Nubra Rivers. Pakistan, however, asserted that the LoC should continue in a north-easterly direction as the crow flies till the Karakoram Pass. As a result, the Pakistanis claimed the Saltoro Ridge and the Siachen Glacier that constitutes the Nubra River Basin and the magnificent climbing areas that surround it. Thus, Pakistan began allowing foreign expeditions to trek in the area from the late-1970s onwards. These expeditions would climb the Saltoro Kangri and Teram Kangri and then go on to explore the glacier by descending through the various passes.[6] In an article in *Pakistan Horizon* – a journal brought out by the Pakistan Institute for International Affairs[7] – Dr Omer Farooq Zain further reinforced the glacier's Islamic connection. He claimed that a Muslim saint, Syed Ali Hamadani, had travelled along the glacier from Kashmir to Kashgar, while spreading the message of Islam and constructing mosques.[8]

Operation Meghdoot Unfolds

Lieutenant General M.L. Chibber, the Northern Army Commander in 1983-84, is considered by many to be the brain behind Operation Meghdoot (Cloud Messenger),[9] the Indian Army's stunning high-altitude pre-emptive operation to occupy the Saltoro Ridge and the Siachen Glacier. In one of his very few personal reflections on the operation in Siachen, Chibber wrote in the *Indian Defence Review* of January 1990 that he became interested in the area as early as 1978, when he was the director of military operations.[10] In September 1978, the mountaineer Colonel 'Bull' Narinder Kumar provided Chibber with a bird's-eye view of the area after leading an expedition to Teram Kangri, a 24,000-foot-high peak located on the north-eastern flank of the Siachen Glacier. Chibber then set in motion a chain of events that would alter the way the world looked at high-altitude combat.

Flying Officer Manmohan Bahadur (later Air Vice Marshal) was at that time posted to 114 Helicopter Unit. Called 'Siachen Pioneers' after it moved to Leh, it is the most decorated Helicopter Unit (HU) of the IAF and has been equipped over the years with a fleet of Chetaks, Cheetahs and Cheetals.[11] Little did Bahadur imagine that on 26 September 1978 he would be part of the first IAF crew to land on the glacier as Bull Kumar's expedition traversed across it.[12] For the next few weeks Bahadur would be co-pilot to three experienced squadron leaders of the unit, carrying supplies and mail for the expedition as the team made its way past Camp 1, Camp 2 and Camp 3. Since the Chetaks did not have skis, they would fly low and hover over the glacier and roll out the stores. In response to an SOS for a casualty evacuation mission on 6 October 1978, the Chetak picked up two casualties from the northern tip of the glacier after a long sortie (two hours and fifty minutes as per Bahadur's logbook) and evacuated them to the Thoise airfield. There, they were admitted to a forward base hospital. Bahadur went on to become an accomplished test pilot and commanded 114 HU from 1994 to 1997.

Following the expedition, Bull recommended that India occupy some of the heights immediately to pre-empt any Pakistani move to do the same. The plan was considered but shelved – as it was rightly assessed that the posts would be unsupportable in winter – though regular summer patrols were authorized. Bull Kumar was revered by the Indian mountaineering community, particularly in the Indian Army. The mere mention of his name raised the temperatures of Pakistani military officers involved during the early years of the operation. Speaking to Kevin Fedaranko, an American photographer and high-altitude trekker-cum-journalist, at a Pakistani post on the western slopes of the Saltoro Ridge in 2002, an officer fumed, 'Colonel Kumar is the man who started all this, I have no wish to meet him – that bastard.'[13]

Things remained quiet till Chibber returned to the region five years later as the Northern Army Commander. He had hardly settled in when he was alerted to a protest from Pakistan regarding Indian patrols in the Siachen area. This was followed by another one in August 1983 that was a trifle alarming: 'Request instruct your troops to withdraw beyond Line of Control south of line joining NJ 9842 and Karakoram Pass. Any delay in vacating our territory will create a serious situation.'[14] A few days later, in came another protest note clearly laying claim to the entire Siachen Glacier and reiterating that the line joining NJ 9842 and Karakoram Pass be treated as the de facto LoC. When this was followed a few months later by intelligence reports that the Pakistan Army was seriously scouting around for high-altitude equipment from European manufacturers, Chibber realized that something was cooking.

India's military attaché in Bonn was alerted about this development by German intelligence, which corroborated that a large Indian advance order for mountaineering equipment was being hijacked by the Pakistanis at exorbitant rates. Given a free hand by India's army chief, General Arun Vaidya, Chibber – along with Lieutenant General P.N. Hoon, the corps commander of 15 Corps in Srinagar – brainstormed a pre-emptive plan to occupy the 100-km-long Saltoro Ridge overlooking the Siachen Glacier.

Pakistan displayed tactical nimbleness and dispatched a small force with machine guns and mortars in the winter of 1983 to occupy Bilafond La or Sia La, two of the highest passes in the Northern Sector of the glacier. It is believed that the force had to turn back due to inclement weather and the logistical inability to support the force.[15] Had this force succeeded, Pakistan may well have gone on to occupy the entire Saltoro Ridge, as access to it from the west was more comfortable than from the east. India's attempt from the east was to come a few months later.

Making Military Sense of the Siachen Glacier

Many believe that the Siachen Glacier is one long and menacing stretch of snow that is separated from Pakistan by the Saltoro Range and that both armies assault the ridge from their own sides. However, mountain ranges do not spring up – they gradually unfold. A few kilometres north of the snout of the glacier, the glacier floor keeps rising from around 11,000 feet to 15,000 feet until it abruptly ends at a point where it branches out as a fork-like glacial feature. One prong leads to Sia La, while the other heads towards Indra Col, where the Saltoro Range blends with the Eastern Karakoram Range. Along the way, it is joined by subsidiary glaciers emanating from the Saltoro Range. All Indian posts are approached via these subsidiary glaciers – known as G-1, G-2, Lolofond and G-3 – from north to the central glacier and further south via the Gyong Glacier. Of greater relevance from a military perspective are the glaciers to the west of the AGPL in Pakistani territory, i.e., the Kondus Glacier, the Dong Dong Glacier, the Bilafond La Glacier and the Chumik Glacier. It was from these glaciers that the Pakistan Army launched attacks from 1984 to 2003 to displace Indian troops from heights along the Saltoro Ridge. A peak on the Saltoro Ridge appears close as you walk along the main glacier, but reaching it on foot is only possible via a subsidiary glacier.

The winter of 1983 saw hectic parleys between Chibber and New Delhi on how to prevent Pakistan from physically occupying the Siachen Glacier and the major passes around it without escalating the situation beyond a localized conflict. After wargaming the situation extensively, it was decided that the only way of ensuring control over the region was by occupying the two pivotal passes of Sia La and Bilafond La in the northern section of the Saltoro Ridge. A decisive Indira Gandhi gave the go-ahead sometime in early 1984, and thus began Operation Meghdoot.

Assault and Whiteout

The essence of a sound military plan lies in its simplicity, surprise, sustainability and clarity of purpose in terms of likely strategic and operational outcomes. From these emerge other operational imperatives like force levels, contingency plans and costs – both human and material. Chibber reckoned that the surprise element was essential for capturing Bilafond La and Sia La as it would give India a lead time of about two weeks to beat back any Pakistani attack, however strong it was. This would allow Indian troops to dig in, stock themselves and create a logistics base for resupply. Induction by helicopter right to the pass was the only way to make this plan work. There were many who felt that the operation was doomed as such an audacious attempt to combat the natural elements of weather and terrain was too risky. Chibber thought otherwise and believed that these challenges could be overcome with adequate preparation and training, especially when there was no enemy firing. He drew on history to validate his proposition – arguing about the accomplishments of mountaineers and Arctic explorers – and reinforced the idea that this move would spook the Pakistanis, who were not used to such aggression from the Indians.

Brigadier Vijay Channa, the commander of 26 Sector with its HQ at Turtok, also had the Siachen Glacier under his command. The two units under him – 4 KUMAON and the Karakoram Wing of Ladakh Scouts – were well-acclimatized and familiar with the region, having regularly patrolled the area up to Sia La and Bilafond La in the summer of 1983. Many of the officers and men in the two units were accomplished mountaineers – among them Major A.N. Bahuguna and Captain Sanjay Kulkarni, who had just climbed Stok Kangri, a 7,000-metre-high peak on the Saltoro Ridge. Channa did not know about the plan till March 1984, when he was summoned to the Corps HQ in Srinagar and briefed by Lieutenant General Hoon, the corps commander. It was left to Channa to choose his teams and the date of the assault in a window between 1 and 30 April. Channa chose 13 April as it was Baisakhi – a holiday to mark the harvest in Punjab that was celebrated in Pakistan too – which he reckoned would provide the surprise element. Captain Kulkarni led the first wave on to Bilafond La with his company from 4 KUMAON.[16]

It was also decided that there was no possibility of undertaking a helicopter recce of the likely landing spots close to the passes, as that would take away the element of surprise. Channa reckoned that landing spots could be found on firm snow during March and April. He agreed to the plan of landing almost sixty troops of 4 KUMAON and Ladakh Scouts on Bilafond La and Sia La respectively. Squadron Leader Rohit Rai was among the handful of pilots chosen for the Helicopter Task Force that was put together from four units of the Indian Air Force – 114 HU, 131 FAC Flight, and 662 and 663 AOP Flights. The Helicopter Task Force at Thoise was led by Wing Commander C.S. Sandhu with Colonel G.S. Ghuman, the seniormost army pilot on the task force, acting as the force commander. Comprising six to eight Cheetah helicopters and about thirteen to fifteen pilots, only Ghuman and Sandhu may have known of the detailed plan in the first week of April. The day of 10 April saw all the helicopters moving to Thoise from their respective locations in Jammu, Udhampur and Srinagar. Though several of the captains and co-pilots had earlier flown in the Nubra and Shyok Valleys and in Subsector North of Eastern Ladakh, the Siachen Glacier and the Saltoro Ridge was virgin airspace for all of them. It was only on 12 April that Rai had a glimpse of the possible landing areas around Bilafond La and Sia La along with officers from 4 KUMAON and Ladakh Scouts during a recce sortie.[17]

In an interview with Nitin Gokhale, Kulkarni highlighted the importance of being well-kitted and equipped for such an operation. He said, 'I remember they (the kits) arrived on 12 April evening, barely hours before we were being launched into Operation Meghdoot. Thermal coats, thermal pants, very nice balaclavas, excellent tents, ice axes, goggles, the works were bought from Europe. The weapons, however, remained the basic Indian Army 7.62mm SLR. Of course, we had mortars, MMGs, missiles, Grad P rockets. Some of the weapons came by air, some came through porters.'[18] Soon after being heli-landed at Bilafond La, Kulkarni and his team were cut off from the rest of the world by a blizzard and experienced whiteout conditions for four days. They almost immediately lost a soldier to frostbite and had to have their radio operator evacuated on the first day, losing radio contact with the rest of the force. Had they not been so well-equipped and familiar with the terrain, it is unlikely that many from the team would have survived. By the time the weather cleared on 16 April and reinforcements and medical help arrived, twenty-one of the remaining twenty-eight men had suffered some degree of frostbite. It was only when Kulkarni radioed for the evacuation of a fallen comrade did the Pakistanis discover that the heights they coveted had already been occupied.

Rai's logbook entries from 10 to 30 April reveal a stupendous fifty sorties flown in support of the initial induction during Operation Meghdoot in what he recollects were 'incredibly challenging operational and weather conditions'. After inserting the Kumaonis on Bilafond La on 13 April, the weather clamped down. It was a frustrating wait before the task force could fly in the Ladakh Scouts on to Sia La on 16 April after evacuating the first casualties from Bilafond La. Once the heights were occupied, the Cheetahs settled into a routine of taking off in the early morning from Thoise, refuelling at Base Camp, and getting their tasking for the day depending on the requirements at Bilafond La and Sia La.[19]

Exploiting the window of good weather on the same day, Bahuguna and his company from Ladakh Scouts were heli-landed on to Sia La and a lower camp. Joining the effort that day were two Mi-8 helicopters that carried supplies and ammunition from Thoise. A total of forty sorties were flown in two days to insert the two forces around Bilafond La and Sia La. After occupying Sia La, the rest of the force linked up at the Forward Logistics Base (FLB) on the glacier and set up two more camps that would support both the Bilafond La and Sia La locations. The Kumar FLB – as it came to be known – also emerged as the battalion HQ for the Northern Glacier Battalion. It remained so until relocated along with the logistics base a few kilometres east, away from the glacier floor and out of range of Pakistani artillery. In view of the increasing PAF air activity, Kumar FLB was reinforced with towed ack-ack guns (ZU-23) – the first induction of such guns on the main glacier. Some posts higher up were given SAM-7 shoulder-fired missiles too. The years ahead would see a variety of guns in action from both sides.

As units of the Indian Army settled to a routine, the climatic conditions, life-threatening physiological effects, terrain and enemy action all began taking their toll. The lack of oxygen degrades psychomotor performance and induces altitude sickness – also called high-altitude pulmonary oedema – while frostbite and gangrene set in rapidly following exposure to temperatures in the range of minus 15 to minus 40 degrees Celsius. Blizzards, fog and whiteouts disorient both the soldiers on the ground and aviators, while terrain hazards include avalanches, rockfalls, crevasses, ice falls and ice walls. The typical operational routine at such posts would involve patrols, the manning of observation posts, sentry duties and casualty evacuation. The regular camp routine comprised activities such as personal health and hygiene, water heating and periodic maintenance of weapons and critical equipment. The relief and rotation of manpower at high posts was carried out every fifteen days. Casualty evacuation was a challenging task during the early days, sapping energy and morale as it involved carrying a casualty to a lower post or a helipad in inclement weather conditions.

Taking risks, flying without oxygen at times and suffering losses along the way, the Helicopter Task Force, which included Mi-8s from 128 HU, performed magnificently during the initial months. Wanting to see for himself the action on the glacier, Air Chief Marshal Katre, the Chief of Air Staff, flew in to the Base Camp in late September/early October and experienced first-hand what it meant to face enemy fire on the Saltoro Ridge. Flying with Rai to Sia La, his helicopter had to return from 200 metres short of the post as it was being targeted by enemy mortar fire.[20] This would be the normal till the ceasefire of 2003. The exploits of this task force have been among the most underrated operations during the several decades of Operation Meghdoot.

Narratives and Counterattack

In his book *Fangs of Ice*, Lieutenant Colonel Syed Ishfaq Ali gives a Pakistani perspective that is typically jingoistic and Kashmir-centric:

> The Siachen dispute is basically a manifestation of Hindu hegemonistic design and has now become a complicated affair and a sedimentation of various unsettled issues like the Kashmir problem.[21]

He then goes on to deftly add a 'China and Soviet perspective' to India's pre-emptive move by arguing rather fancifully:

> It is commonly believed that one reason of Indian presence in Siachen is to ultimately pose a threat to the Karakoram Highway. Taken at its face value it appears rather preposterous because there are over 155 miles over inaccessible glaciated mountain ranges that no army can cover in any manner. Thus, the Indian move on Siachen was a flanking manoeuvre meant to pave the way towards a future cutting off of Pakistan's strategic lifeline to China. Moscow, motivated by much the same concerns as its military ally, is obviously well placed in the Wakhan Corridor to facilitate Indian designs.[22]

Adding Soviet designs to India's occupation of Siachen at a time when they were entrenched in Afghanistan was a masterstroke that drew US scholars into the Siachen debate.

Has Pakistan been nimbler than India in generating military narratives for most of its bilateral disputes with India? After reading *Fangs of Ice,* I immediately checked on the first authentic Indian account of operations in Siachen – Lieutenant General V.R. Raghavan's book, *Siachen: A War without End.* Though the book is an academically robust and a measured appreciation of the Siachen conflict, it was written in 2002 – almost eleven years after Ishfaq Ali's book. It is quite evident that Ishfaq Ali had state assistance to churn out the book, so it is perplexing why the Indian Army or the Indian government did not create its own Siachen narrative in the 1980s despite having several fine soldier-scholars. Militarily, India surprised Pakistan, but Pakistan supplemented its military counterattacks with a diplomatic and military narrative that proved effective.

Even as Chibber was planning his operation, President Zia-ul-Haq, Pakistan's military dictator, had assembled a battalion-sized force at Skardu. Called the Burzil Force, it was named after the Burzil mountains that separate the Gilgit and Baltistan provinces of PoK from the Kashmir Valley. Comprising SSG commandos and a sprinkling of soldiers from the Northern Light Infantry (NLI) who had specialized knowledge of the region, the force commenced training for high-altitude and glacier operations in early 1984. The final assault was planned for April or May that year. Frustratingly for Zia, the Indians beat him to the Saltoro Ridge.The first probing counterattack from the Burzil Force came at Bilafond La on 24 April, which was beaten back easily. Realizing that a frontal assault was next to impossible, the force was expanded over the next few days and split into company-sized groupings with names such as Asghar Force, Hafeez Force and Shahbaz Force. Despite extremely spirited attempts, these were repulsed by the entrenched Indians.

By the end of August 1984, the Burzil Force realized that they would be better off occupying the lower ridge lines of the Saltoro Range and a few higher posts. Located at some distance from the glacier, these posts would enable partial observation of Indian activity in the region and support periodic attacks whenever the opportunity presented itself. With Dansam as the brigade HQ, the force had to first establish routes of ingress and set up suitable logistics hubs and camps along the Chumik and Bilafond Glaciers. In 1984, it was the Bilafond Glacier that became the centre of action. Consequently, Gayari – at the snout of the two glaciers – was chosen as the FLB to support ingress on both routes, while Naram was an intermediate camp en route to Ali Bragansa at approximately 16,000 feet. From here the final assaults were to be launched to occupy the posts on the Saltoro Ridge that were either not occupied by the Indians or to capture some vital Indian posts. Following the failure of multiple attacks to dislodge the Indians from the heights, a Pakistani general reflected, 'When we saw the Indians at those heights, we knew they came to stay.'[23]

Much of 1984 and 1985 was spent by both sides in consolidating their positions, enhancing force levels to that of a large mountain brigade, getting artillery guns into position and engaging in localized firefights. On the Indian side, 26 Sector was converted into 102 Infantry Brigade and Brigadier Jal Master took over command in May 1985. Pakistan formed the 323 Infantry Brigade to look after the Siachen operations along with the SSG, complementing the infantry battalions in all the assault operations. The first pilot casualty in Operation Meghdoot was Major S.K. Gadhiok, who died on 30 August 1985. Gadhiok was shot by a Pakistani sniper through the head as he was directing artillery fire on Pakistani posts from his Cheetah helicopter in the Central Glacier. The co-pilot, Captain Guleria, flew back to the Base Camp with Gadhiok slumped forward in the captain's seat.

The glacier was divided by the Indian Army into the Northern, Central and Southern Sectors. The Northern Sector – which saw most of the action during the initial years of the conflict – comprised the Sia La complex, the Bilafond La complex and the G1 complex, all named after subsidiary glaciers. A complex in the Indian military lexicon signifies a cluster of posts. Subsidiary posts are located to protect the approaches to the main posts, while observation posts (OPs) may be located at vantage points that can accommodate only a few people and are difficult to access. A large post can typically accommodate a maximum of twelve men and have a helipad that can receive a light helicopter, while a subsidiary post is large enough to house six to ten men. OPs would generally have dug-in shelters to accommodate four to six men and are occupied during fair weather, when the visibility is good and it is possible to observe enemy movements or direct artillery fire.

Prominent posts in this area are Sia La, Bilafond La, Kumar, Sonam, Bhim and Bana, along with a few other subsidiary OPs on the northern shoulder of Bilafond La. Cheekily, the last Indian drop zone on the glacier floor was for long called Benazir. This was probably because Benazir Bhutto came to power on the back of a political campaign that castigated President Zia-ul-Haq for losing Siachen to India. It serviced the Sia La complex – including Tiger Saddle, the northernmost Indian post in the complex – and was later renamed Rani after Benazir was voted out of office in 1997. The battalion headquarters of the Northern Sector battalion along with its complement of artillery support was located at Kumar for almost two decades before it moved eastwards in 2001. While the Indian brigade had infantry battalions that cut across regions – the Sikh, Dogra, Garhwal, Gorkha and Madras Regiments, to name but a few – the Pakistani brigade drew most of its personnel from the NLI, which comprised various sects of the Gilgit and Baltistan region. While there has been an attempt to widen this base over the years and ensure that all units of the Pakistan Army serve on the glacier and in the Kargil sector, the

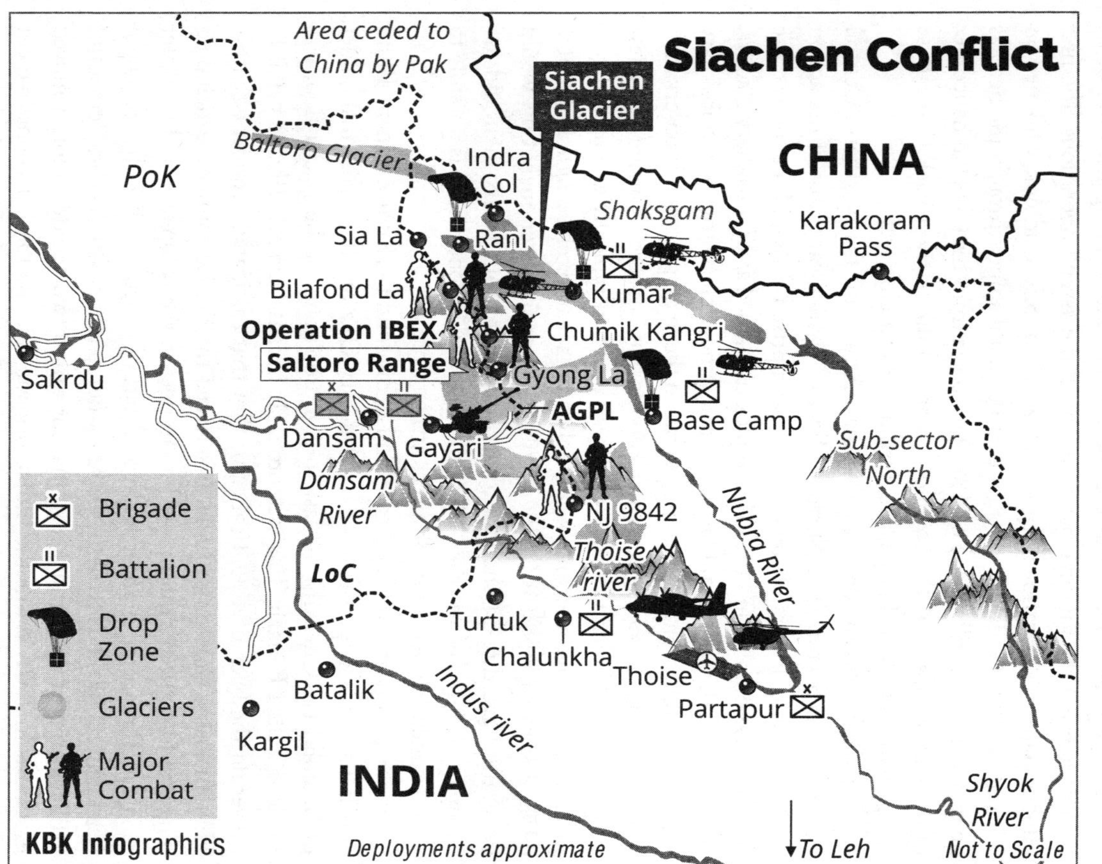

This map is for representational purposes only and does not purport to depict political boundaries

Punjabi-dominated military establishment of Pakistan has often been accused of putting the NLI in the line of fire.

Among the most significant achievements of the Pakistan Army during the initial years of the conflict was the occupation of the Quaid Post (at approximately 22,000 feet) in April 1986. Measuring no more than sixteen feet in radius and towering over the Indian posts in the Bilafond La complex, it served as an observation point from where it was possible to observe parts of Kumar FLB and the surface routes to the forward posts of Bilafond La over the Lolofond Glacier. Based on observation from Quaid Post, the Pakistan Army could direct effective artillery fire – till then most of the Pakistani artillery fire was speculative. Quaid Post emerged as an irritant for the Indians and its capture was high on the list of objectives for Brigadier Chandan Singh Nugyal, the brigade commander of 102 Infantry Brigade.

Courage on Uncharted Heights

It was early 1986, almost two years after the likes of Kulkarni and Channa had established Indian dominance over the Saltoro Range. In a daring but completely unsustainable operation, Ladakh Scouts attempted to establish posts at over 20,000 feet on the lower slopes of the Saltoro Kangri massif that formed part of the Northern Sector. Navkiran Singh Ghei was a young captain and paratrooper posted to Ladakh Scouts after finishing his tenure as an instructor at the National Defence Academy. Ghei went on to command a para battalion and the Indian Army's only parachute brigade, a division in the north-east in counterinsurgency operations and a corps in Punjab before signing off his illustrious career after a three-year stint as the commandant of the National Defence College.

Ghei spoke about his experience of opening and maintaining a small post at 20,000 feet for over six months with hardly any backup or logistics support along with five 'Nunnus' (as Ladakh Scouts soldiers are affectionately called).[24] By then, operational ideas about how to dominate the entire glacier were flowing thick and fast from both the Northern Command and the Army HQ. It was considered important to establish more posts in the Northern Sector as that would enhance visibility of the communication lines that extended towards the Pakistani posts on the Central Sector, and on Saltoro and Baltoro Ridges and improve the direction of artillery fire. The height chosen overlooked Indian posts on the northern shoulder of Bilafond La and offered visibility over the Pakistani logistics line that ran up the Bilafond Glacier on the western slopes of the Saltoro Range towards the Quaid Post.

At the time, Ladakh Scouts had its headquarters in Leh and was divided into two forces of eight to ten companies each. These were known as Karakoram Force and Indus Force, after the areas they patrolled and defended. After a period of acclimatization at the Base Camp and Kumar FLB,[25] Ghei and his platoon – with Subedar Sonam as platoon commander and four Ladakhi troops – set out on an arduous climb from 15,000 feet to 20,000 feet. At around 8 p.m. on 26 February 1986, they reached their intended summit of Point 6135 (20,245 feet). Having pitched their three-man arctic tents, they burrowed in for the night little realizing that they would endure whiteout conditions in appalling weather for the next three days. Ghei recalls that they could not see beyond a couple of feet and had to make do 'without a pee or a crap for days'. It was a surreal experience for the six men as they huddled in their small tents wondering how they were going to survive a week, leave alone a couple of months. Realizing that they had bitten off more than they could chew, Ghei radioed for assistance and asked for a larger tent, some supplies and reinforcements.

As the weather cleared, they established camp for the long haul and hoped that the team would be rotated every few weeks. Unfortunately, Ghei's replacement was struck down by acute mountain sickness and had to be evacuated to the Base Camp and onwards to the military hospital at Thoise. This meant that Ghei remained on station for much longer. On a clear day, the team had a good view of Pakistani supply lines along the Bilafond Glacier, and directed artillery shoots on these lines. The rarefied atmosphere posed significant challenges for Indian gunners as the lower density meant that the shells encountered lower drag. They often overshot the target by miles as there were no calibration charts for those altitudes. 'Drop 300 metres, drop 500 metres' were common radio calls that Ghei made to the artillery gun posts to aim much shorter. The gunners invariably transmitted back to him that the firing picture they were getting had an impact point that was in friendly territory, sometimes even coinciding with his own location. It was a period of uncertainty and virgin territory for India's gunners and it was only gradually that ballistics were worked out to ensure acceptable levels of accuracy.

One month turned into two and then almost six, as Ghei and his team continued to man the post like zombies. When asked how they managed to keep on, he said that the Ladakhis were amazing survivors and seeing them gave him the courage to lead from the front. Deprived of sleep, suffering from periodic hallucinations and surviving on milk powder and the odd paratha that the Nunnus made for him, Ghei lost 10 kg and suffered partial memory loss at the end of his extended six-month vigil on Point 6135. After they returned and reported the conditions, the post was abandoned and never manned again.

Vertical Assault and Courageous Defence

Major General Chandan Singh Nugyal of the Sikh Regiment is a Pahadi (a person from the hills in colloquial Hindi) and one of the most decorated major generals in the Indian Army. A fine mountaineer and an outstanding commander, he was the brigade commander of the Siachen Brigade during the years of fiercest fighting in the Northern Sector (1986-87). While the most talked about operation during his tenure was the capture of Bana Post, the fierceness of the other battles across the Bilafond La complex in the summer and autumn of 1987 tested Nugyal's leadership skills to the maximum. The access to the complex from the Bilafond Glacier was easier from the Pakistani side when compared to the tough climb from Kumar FLB via the Lolofond Glacier.

The capture of the Quaid Post by a five-member team of the 8th Battalion of the Jammu and Kashmir Light Infantry (8 JAKLI) under Naib Subedar Bana Singh and its defence by an equally worthy opponent is a well-chronicled saga of sheer bravery and close combat in icy conditions. Bana Singh's exploits during the operation – which lasted three days, from 23 to 26 June 1987 – have made him a legend. Now almost seventy years old and leading a happy retired life, he still patiently recounts the operation in detail to anyone who comes to him. Of all the narratives of his exploits, the most riveting one is by Major General Raj Mehta, written in 2013 for the Centre for Land Warfare Studies, Delhi.[26] Equally interesting is probably the first full-fledged interview given by Bana, published in the *Illustrated Weekly of India*.[27] The narrative that follows draws heavily from both these pieces as well as from the unit diaries.

After a month of preparation and preliminary probing attacks, Lieutenant Colonel A.K. Rai – the commanding officer of 8 JAKLI – chose three teams of thirty men for the assault. Major Varinder Singh was the leader of the mission and Bana was one of the section commanders. Armed with only light machine guns, 9mm SAF carbines and grenades, the teams commenced attack on 23 June 1987. After a couple of failed night assaults that involved climbing near-vertical ice walls and losing a few men to enemy fire, the force had already spent over thirty-six hours in assault mode. Desperate times call for desperate measures, so in a decision that could have well led to the decimation of Bana and his team, Rai ordered an assault in broad daylight.

Still recovering from two successive night assaults, the eight defenders on Quaid Top – which was 300 metres above a post they called the Quaid Base – were not expecting a day assault. Naib Subedar Atta Mohammad of the SSG commanding the Quaid Post and its subsidiary OP was supremely confident of beating back any attack as he had reinforced the post with four SSG commandos a week before the assault. The Quaid OP – where all eight SSG commandos had dug in – was accessible from only one direction. Mohammad knew that an attack was imminent because there had been continuous artillery bombardment of his post over days, albeit with limited accuracy. His commander, Major Irshad, had alerted him on 20 June to prepare for a final battle.[28]

Biting cold and a raging blizzard sapped their energy as the SSG commandos took turns to shovel snow and keep the areas around their igloo navigable and combat-ready once the weather improved. Making matters worse were the Indian howitzers and guns as they attempted to soften the Quaid OP and block any reinforcements that Irshad wanted to send up. The Indian firing took its first casualty even before the assault, and Mohammad was left with only six men to ward off the repeated attacks. By the time the second attack took place, Atta had lost one more commando to Indian artillery fire. Despite their own artillery succeeding in pinning down the Indian attack, the relentless Indian fire made it appear that a much larger force was assaulting the top.

When Bana led his section for the final assault on 23 June 1987 in what was expected to be broad daylight, the weather turned murky and the operation commenced in darkness at noon. Bana recalls the appalling and wet weather conditions and a lack of clarity whether to follow SOPs for day or night operations, given the ambient light conditions. Also, from the sustained artillery shelling, he realized that the Pakistanis knew something was going on. Bana led his men through an extremely difficult and hazardous route, climbing in near darkness in a snowstorm. Reaching the single deep bunker on the top after a two-hour firefight, Bana recalls that the defenders were quiet until he and his five-man team assaulted the bunker with grenades and single-shot light machine guns. They overcame some spirited resistance from Mohammad and his remaining commandos in an intense close-quarter battle. It lasted only a few minutes but seemed like an eternity to Mohammad and his doomed comrades.[29]

The Pakistani narrative alludes to the possibility of Mohammad having been the lone survivor battling Bana and his men when they stormed the bunker, with the rest having been killed before the assault either by artillery fire or during the prolonged exchange of fire. It also claims that the assaulting troops numbered in the hundreds and suffered well over thirty casualties.[30] However, the Indian narrative says it was a firefight with several defenders and resulted in a dozen Indian casualties. Numbers really lose their significance in such battles, and even seasoned soldiers marvel at the sheer guts required for attacking and defending at such altitudes. The satisfaction of victory did not dent the battle ethics of fair play and chivalry, and 8 JAKLI 'handed over the body of each *shaheed* (martyr) after giving it a military salute'.[31]

If there was one difference between the Pakistani defenders and the Indian attackers, it was the officer leadership. Why there was no officer at this toughest and highest post baffles many even today, particularly when the Pakistanis knew that an attack was imminent. While Bana led the final assault, the presence of two officers in the assault teams was a significant force multiplier. Bana recollects that it was the 'roaring voice of Major Varinder Singh and Captain Anil Sharma encouraging us along which gave us strength and hope'.[32] The capture of the Quaid Post came at a heavy price as 8 JAKLI lost a young second lieutenant, a JCO and eight other men in the various assaults. It is even today the most highly decorated unit that has seen action on the glacier. Bana Singh was awarded the Param Vir Chakra (India's highest gallantry award in war), while Major Varinder Singh and eight others were decorated with Vir Chakras (the third highest gallantry award in war) for that one operation. Naib Subedar Atta Mohammad was awarded Pakistan's highest peacetime gallantry award, the Sitara-i-Jurrat. Quaid OP was renamed Bana Top and Quaid Post became Bana Base.

The Pakistan Army's riposte for the loss of Quaid Post came fast and strong. In September 1987, it attacked two Indian posts on the northern shoulder of Bilafond La while an overstretched and battle-weary 8 JAKLI, long overdue for relief, was handing over to the Third Battalion of the Fourth Gorkha Rifles (3/4 GORKHA RIFLES). One of the attacks was beaten back after fierce hand-to-hand fighting at one of the posts. Major Krishna Gopal Chatterjee – the company commander of 3/4 GORKHA RIFLES who was awarded a Maha Vir Chakra (India's second highest gallantry award in war) after the attack – recalled the action in a conversation with Nanavatty when the two met in Delhi prior to the latter assuming command of 102 Infantry Brigade. When Chatterjee saw the unmistakable signs of an attack developing, he spoke to his lads and said that if anyone of them was not up for the fight, this was their chance to leave quietly. Not a man flinched. During the fighting, a Pakistani soldier managed to clamber on to the post. He felled Chatterjee with a blow to his body but was cut down by one of Chatterjee's fellow Gorkhas with his khukri. Despite taking heavy casualties, the Pakistanis continued to engage the Indians in the area with sporadic attacks and artillery fire. Interestingly, the Pakistani brigade commander at the time was Brigadier Pervez Musharraf, the future Pakistani army chief and president. On that day, Musharraf came out second best in his duel with Chandan Singh Nugyal.

Holding Firm

Brigadier Rostum Nanavatty assumed command of the Siachen Brigade from Nugyal in late 1987. He recollects that while the Sia La complex in the Northern Sector remained quiet, fighting on the northern shoulders of Bilafond La continued unabated. He remembers flying to all the posts in the area – which were now manned by a battalion of the Garhwal Rifles – and seeing for himself how difficult it was to survive on those icy heights, leave alone fighting to defend them. It was during an intrusive aerial recce of Conway Saddle – a Pakistani post opposite Tiger Saddle (Indian Army's northernmost post in the Sia La complex) – that Nanavatty witnessed aerial activity on the Pakistani side that remains etched in his memory. He says, 'We had a Pakistan Army medium-lift chopper hovering directly below us over the Conway Saddle helipad just as two PAF fighters streaked westwards over their high-altitude training camp in the Baltoro Glacier area – a magnificent sight.'[33]

Nanavatty adopted an aggressive approach right from the start. He wanted to test the effectiveness of the SAM-7 shoulder-fired missile at extremely high altitudes and told a post equipped with the missile to engage an enemy helicopter should it come too close. Though the missile missed, it did send a message to the enemy. However, Major General V.R. Raghavan, Nanavatty's divisional commander, was not amused. Nanavatty recalls, 'General Raghavan admonished me because he thought my action ill-considered. He believed it could escalate matters and adversely impact our air logistics support. Considering our greater dependence on air support, this would be to our disadvantage.'[34]

Nanavatty communicated simple tactical objectives for his battalions as his key result areas. 'By occupying the extreme high ground on the Saltoro Ridge, we were paying a high price in terms of casualties from terrain and weather as well as air logistics support,' he says. He adds, 'It was imperative therefore that we exploit our tactical advantage to completely dominate the enemy by fire and observation. The rules of engagement were simple – interdict all observed enemy activity within range by direct and indirect fires. The authority to open fire was suitably delegated.'[35] He recollects being at a forward OP for the first successful Bofors firing by the 36 Maratha Medium Regiment, which had a battery at the Base Camp.

Brigadier Devender Kumar, an officer from the Brigade of the Guards, was a captain posted to the 7th Battalion of the Brigade of the Guards (7 GUARDS) in mid-1988 after completing his young officers' course. The battalion was entrusted with watching over the Northern Sector. After a customary period of acclimatization, Devender found himself as the post commander at Sonam, at almost 20,000 feet the highest Indian post that had a helipad. He recalls that the Sia La complex was relatively quiet and mainly saw long-range artillery duels as the access from the Pakistani side was difficult.[36] Much of the damage on either side was caused by mortar fire from distances of 3 to 5 km. Devender remembers that some of his men even ventured out on moonlit nights and targeted Pakistani posts on the lower slopes of the ridge lines with the Russian Grad P rocket launchers.

Typical tenures on these posts varied from forty-five to sixty days, followed by a period of rest, recuperation and continued training at the Base Camp. 7 GUARDS caused significant attrition to the enemy, though Devender admits that they also lost twenty men during their six months on the glacier. Some perished during enemy firing, but most were lost to the weather, altitude and terrain. The one incident that remains with him is a casualty evacuation in bad weather. Devender and a few others navigated down the Lolofond Glacier on a snow scooter. As soon as the weather improved, a Cheetah helicopter from 666 AOP Squadron appeared and the casualty was evacuated within minutes to the base hospital at Thoise. Over the years such exploits became the norm as the IAF and Air OP squadrons mastered the art of casualty evacuation in extremely difficult conditions.

The Central Sector assumed great operational importance in 1988 following the failed attempts by Pakistan to dislodge the Indian Army from any posts in the Northern Sector. Desperate for an effective strategy of interdiction, the Pakistan Army established two posts to the south of the Bilafond La Ridge on the higher slopes of the Chumik Glacier. These were designated North OP and South OP by the Indian Army. These posts allowed the Pakistanis to contest the domination of the Indian Army and direct effective harassing fire at them. This area emerged as the next hotspot on the glacier and saw maximum fighting from 1988 to 1995.

The major posts in the Central Sector were K, D, J, G3 and C.[37] The battalion headquarters was located at the Base Camp (11,600 feet) along with the HQ of an artillery regiment. Most of these posts had small helipads that could only accommodate the smaller Cheetah helicopters, but did have the space to receive drops from Mi-17 helicopters. The force multiplier in this sector was a troop of Bofors guns located at the Base Camp that had the range to engage targets well across the Saltoro Range and along the length of the glacier. Supplementing the Bofors were other medium artillery guns. The maximum loss of life on both sides during operational engagements was caused by artillery fire and not close-combat engagements. Broadly speaking, normal posts in the Northern and Central Sectors were at heights between 16,000 and 18,000 feet while a few higher posts were located above 20,000 feet.

The Southern Sector to the west of the Nubra Valley included NJ 9842 and had a set of heights that could enable vigil over the LoC in the Turtok Sector. R, B and G are the prominent posts in this sector with large helipads that can accommodate the larger Mi-17 helicopters, while Chalunkha serves as the base camp, logistics hub and battalion HQ for this sector. Chulung La is the southernmost pass held by India along the AGPL and the western approaches to the glacier are along the Shyok River. Chorbat La (16,700 feet) is not part of the Southern Sector but has seen much action over the years, as both India and Pakistan have repeatedly made attempts to alter the LoC in this area.

On the Indian side, road connectivity to the glacier is provided by one major road that runs eastwards from Turtok and Chalunkha, connecting the brigade HQ of Partapur to the base camp. The road network on the Pakistani side is far more elaborate because of the lower heights, and extends to a town called Gayari at the base of the Bilafond and Chumik Glaciers. This means that Indian posts had to be maintained by the medium-lift Mi-17 helicopters, which carried loads from the base camp or Thoise to the FLBs. Some FLBs such as Kumar, Sonam and B still have loads taken up by foot, snow scooters or by smaller Cheetah helicopters. 129 and 130 HUs were the two Mi-17 units supporting Siachen operations from a detachment at Thoise. Generous in his praise for these units, Nanavatty recalled some daring Mi-17 helicopter drops to the Southern Sector that were made to reduce the load on the Cheetahs. He recalled a valley-hugging sortie to the B helipad and drop zone. Staying low in the valleys was the only way to avoid detection by the enemy, who held the western slopes.

Operation Ibex (April-May 1989)

The highlights of Nugyal's tenure as brigade commander were the capture of the Quaid complex and the complete domination of the Indian Army over the Northern Sector with aggressive action. However, during Nanavatty's tenure, Operation Ibex in the Central Sector was triggered because of a misunderstanding. The catalyst for the operation was an uncorroborated intelligence assessment of an impending Pakistani operation by the Indians and a desperate attempt by Pakistan to secure a foothold on the Saltoro Range prior to the impending talks at the political level.[38] The central section of the Saltoro Ridge has two prominent glaciers that dominate access to the various heights occupied by the two sides. The Gyong Glacier leads to the Gyong La Pass occupied by the Indians, from where they can thwart any northwards move. The Chumik Glacier allowed the Pakistanis to set up camps that could serve as springboards for taking control of the few unoccupied heights. This posed a threat to the Indian Army's logistics line from the Base Camp to both the Northern and Central Sectors.

In early 1989, the Pakistan Army took over two unoccupied OPs – Victor and Sher, called South and North OP by the Indians – on a ridgeline overlooking Indian posts. Colonel J.K. Sharma, the officiating brigade commander in Nanavatty's absence, reckoned that their next move would be to seize a prominent unoccupied height known as Point 6400 (21,000 feet)[39] and consolidate their position in the area. He assessed that this position could dominate the lower Indian posts of D and K and disrupt support to the Gyong La Subsector.[40] As a morale-boosting ploy, these posts were called Baniya and Sadhu (trader and mendicant) by the Pakistan Army to highlight the non-martial profile of the Indian Army. Major General Jamshed Ayaz Khan, the commander of Force Command Northern Areas in the Pakistan Army, also called FCNA, had directed his forces to dig in at these posts. This hinted at a prolonged occupation, which did not augur well for the Indians and alarmed them.[41]

In the absence of Nanavatty, his divisional commander, Major General Raghavan, and the corps commander of 15 Corps, approved an operation proposed by Colonel Sharma to try and disrupt the Pakistani camp with occasional artillery bombardment. These attempts, however, failed to prevent the build-up. By mid-March, there were reports that the SSG was being inducted into the region. On Sharma's advice, Raghavan took the call to pre-empt the likely Pakistani move to capture Point 6400. Leading this assault was the freshly inducted 2 DOGRA, which had recently replaced 3 MADRAS and had been in the region for barely a few weeks. Complementing the fresh but inexperienced Dogras were about twenty-five seasoned mountain warriors from Ladakh Scouts and a few instructors from the Siachen Battle School. In support were two 81mm mortar platoons, a battery with 105mm and 130mm medium guns and a few Bofors guns. Assisting the force were

Cheetah helicopters of the Army Air OP Squadron and Mi-17s of 129 and 130 Helicopter Units.[42]

The month-long operation had three objectives. First, to occupy the highest point on the same ridge (Point 6400) to negate the advantage the Pakistan Army had gained by setting up Victor and Sher. Located as it was on a difficult ridgeline, capturing Point 6400 would demand the highest possible mountaineering and survival skills. The second objective was to protect the two main Indian posts of K and D, which could become easy targets should Pakistan get to Point 6400. The last objective was to evict the Pakistanis from South and North OP and destroy the Chumik Camp with sustained artillery bombardment that could be directed from Point 6400. When Nanavatty returned from leave, he was presented with a fait accompli.

What this operation demanded of officers and men is reflected in the citation that Nanavatty wrote for a tough young Dogra officer, Second Lieutenant Deepak Thapa, who for almost a week attempted to keep the supply lines to Point 6400 open:

> For his inexhaustible strength, stamina and endurance; his outstanding military mountaineering skills; his professionalism and organizational ability and leadership in the task of organizing the defence of Point 6400; in opening the hazardous route from Kaman to Support Base; and in establishing line communications and ferrying vital stores to Point 6400 under the harshest imaginable conditions of combat, I recommend Second Lieutenant Deepak Thapa for the award of Yudh Seva Medal (YSM).[43]

The motley group of Dogras, Sikhs and Ladakhis led by Captain Vijayant Singh first made their way to the Kaman Post, climbing and clawing their way over sheer ice walls and crevices. They braved avalanches that buried seven of their comrades, whose bodies were never recovered. They then traversed a hitherto uncharted southern approach to the ridgeline to establish a support point at Thapa Base (named after Deepak Thapa), from where they could assault Point 6400 unobserved by the two posts that Pakistan's 323 Infantry Brigade had set up. By mid-April, following a series of risky heli-insertions and a treacherous eight-hour climb from Thapa Base, they had succeeded in ensuring a section strength of six to fifteen personnel, which included three officers.

Mainly sustained from Thapa Base via Cheetah landings at a lower helipad in good weather, the post managed to beat back repeated attacks by the Pakistanis from the north and the west while continuing to direct intense artillery fire on all Pakistani posts through the last week of April and early May. This forced both brigade commanders to call for a local ceasefire. This was followed by three meetings at Kargil between Nanavatty and his Pakistani counterpart from 323 Infantry Brigade.[44] Apart from several citations for 2 Dogra, including a Vir Chakra for Captain Vijayant Singh, Nanavatty put up eight citations for gallantry for the Karakoram Wing of Ladakh Scouts. Captain Vijayant Singh vividly recollects the recovery of an Army Aviation Cheetah helicopter from Point 6400 after it developed engine problems.[45] Nanavatty reckons that it was a stupendous task and matched the recovery of an IAF Cheetah from Amar helipad in the Northern Sector.

The Pakistani narrative is expectedly different. In an account of Operation Chumik, as it was called in Pakistan, Lieutenant Colonel Syed Ashfaq Ali narrates a tale of equal courage and daring in three chapters: 'The Razor's Edge', 'The Overreachers' and 'Crowning Triumph'. This includes the setting up of the posts of Victor and Sher, the helicopter assaults on Naveed Top (a post slightly below Point 6400) and uncorroborated firefights that forced the Indians down from Point 6400.[46] According to Kevin Fedaranko – the first Westerner to be given access to both Pakistani and Indian posts – three teams of Pakistani soldiers attempted to reach the summit to thwart the Indian operation but failed: one team was wiped out by an avalanche; the others halted by cornices (overhanging ridges of ice). A last-ditch decision was made to airlift troops to a point just below the top of the mountain (22,185 feet) by French Lama helicopters that were modified to fly no higher than 21,000 feet, like the Indian Cheetah helicopters. The air was so thin that the pilots feared they would crash if they attempted to hover.

Nanavatty contests the Pakistani claims with great clarity. He says, 'The truth is that our patrol held Point 6400 from the time we occupied it until the time it was decided at the third flag meeting to disengage and revert to the status quo, i.e., the previously held positions in the subsector. Apart from the continuous pounding by enemy artillery, the only direct attempt made by the enemy to occupy the position was after the brave and innovative heli-insertion of the Pakistani patrol on a feature to the west of Point 6400 (presumably Naveed Top). This attempt was thwarted by Captain Vijayant Singh and a small team using the 84mm Carl Gustav at close ranges. There was no other close-quarter battle. The earlier attempt made by the enemy to approach Point 6400 along the ridgeline from the direction of their South OP had stalled because of terrain difficulties at least 1,500 metres away from the objective. On my first recce the morning after my return, I flew over this enemy column and drew small-arms fire. I realized that they posed no threat – they were going nowhere but down where they came from.' Continuing to explain the rationale for speedy de-escalation, he adds, 'Multiple avalanches caused by the heavy artillery exchanges had by this time obliterated Thapa Base, causing casualties and completely disrupting the tenuous surface routes of communication. Even resupply using helicopters was proving very difficult. One helicopter had malfunctioned and had to be recovered after repairs in situ. A question mark hung over our ability to sustain the patrol logistically. In my mind was just one thought – it simply was not worth sacrificing the lives of our men for an overreach on our part. This is what I conveyed to the army commander on his first visit after my return.'[47]

Weapons and Gunners

Most early commanders on the glacier bet on the Carl Gustav rocket launchers as the most effective close-range weapons at those altitudes and temperatures. They hardly malfunctioned, and caused significant damage during assaults and close-range fighting. The Grad B rocket launchers were also particularly effective at medium range, and caused great damage from ranges of 500 to 1,000 metres. The main personal weapons used were the 9mm SAF Sten carbines and 7.62 SLRs. While the former came in handy only at close ranges, the latter jammed frequently and had to be kept warm by placing them either next to a stove or inside a sleeping bag. After repeated complaints against the 7.62 SLRs, they were replaced by a limited number of AK-47s. LMGs and MMGs functioned well, and 81mm mortars were frequently used for harassment fire, causing significant damage to igloos and personnel.

Artillery has been the prime means of destruction and dislocation for both sides on the glacier, but the role of gunners has often been underplayed when compared to the raw and primordial nature of close-quarter combat at the various posts. Nothing can be more demoralizing for a post at 20,000 feet than to see an igloo or a bunker shattered by a single shell or to see a comrade suddenly lose a limb to a sudden burst of artillery fire from across the crest line. Much like the impact of air power, it is the physical and psychological shock of artillery fire that proved to be a decisive force multiplier for the Indian Army in Operation Meghdoot.

The 155mm Bofors gun has been the most effective and reliable gun on the glacier. The maximum range of these guns at those altitudes varies between 30 km and 35 km and can effectively clear all the crest tops. In mid-1988, one battery (six guns) was airlifted to Thoise for deployment in support of operations on the Siachen Glacier.[48] The 130mm medium guns are normally deployed at Chalunkha to support operations in the Southern Sector, and at the base camp to supplement the Bofors. The field guns that proved the most mobile of the lot were the 75/24 Howitzers, which were used initially along with the 120mm and 105mm Indian Field Gun (IFG). The 105mm gun has good loft characteristics to negotiate the heights. It has a range of 10-12 km and can be dismantled into three or four modules for transportation. Artillery support has always posed a challenge as the guns were flown and dropped in dismantled condition at the gun positions and then assembled.

Brigadier V.K. Sharma was a captain in 1988 when six 105mm IFGs were flown in by Mi-17 helicopters of 129 Helicopter Unit and dropped at a partially prepared post later named Sehjra (17,000 feet). He recollects that the guns were carried dismantled and as the ground was ascertained unfit for landing by the large Mi-17 helicopters, were dropped from a low altitude. Of the six, only three guns could be assembled as the others were lost in crevasses or damaged by impact. The firing and maintenance of these guns was a tremendous challenge. The moment things quietened down in the area, the guns were withdrawn to Kumar FLB, which also served as the battalion and battery HQs.[49] In 1989, the entire gun position along with its complement of personnel was submerged under an avalanche following a shoot. There were no survivors and the Sehjra Gun Position was abandoned. However, the guns were recovered later. Located even higher were the ZSU-23 ack-ack guns and SAM-7 shoulder-fired missiles that Nanavatty had positioned after noticing increased enemy air activity in the area. Adapting to the situation, the ZSU-23 guns would also be used against surface targets.

Artillery engagements on the glacier are either punitive, deterrent, counter-bombardment or speculative. Punitive engagements cause maximum destruction to the enemy's combat potential, while counter-bombardment targets the enemy's gun positions. Speculative engagements are undertaken when target observation is absent and targets are picked based on OP reports. Deterrent engagements precede an ongoing ground operation or large-scale aerial resupply operation. A typical shoot would involve an OP report of troop or logistics load movement along with the calculated coordinates. During the initial months of the conflict, there was an attempt to place an artillery officer in most OPs, but later most young infantry officers and even JCOs were trained to direct artillery shoots. On clear days, Air OP Cheetah helicopters would direct shoots too. Through a continuous method of trial and error, enemy posts would be registered and then engaged, often with deadly effect. Edward Desmond reports a conversation he had with an Indian officer: 'The rules of engagement are clear-cut on both sides: if there is a target, fire. Artillery observers posted on peaks and ridgelines keep watch day and night with night-vision equipment after dark for the other side's patrols and supply columns. We wait for them to be well out in the open where they cannot run for cover.'[50]

The fiercest artillery battles on the glacier – particularly in the Bilafond La complex (Northern Sector), K and D Posts (Central) and R (Southern) Post – took place in 1989 and 1990. For a rough idea, 1990 saw approximately 190 incidents of small-arms exchange of fire as against over 400 exchanges of artillery fire in the Bilafond La complex. The Indians fired over 5,000 rounds and the Pakistanis retaliated fiercely with over 6,000 rounds. The Pakistanis expended larger rounds not because they were more aggressive but because they had a larger number of Indian posts to engage.[51]

Lifeline Providers

Engineers are always a critical combat support arm, particularly in hostile terrain such as deserts or mountains. Never had engineers from the Indian Army cut their way through glaciers, ice and crevasses to facilitate mobility as they did in Operation Meghdoot. They had no doubt opened the Baltal-Zoji La axis in 1948 and facilitated the defence of Leh, but this was a different ballgame. Brigadier A.K. Ramesh, a former chief engineer at 14 Corps in Leh, is a soft-spoken and articulate sapper who highlighted some of the major engineering tasks that can make or break operations on the icy heights.[52] The toughest tasks were what he described as 'lifeline and survival tasks' for facilitating mobility, connectivity and living. These included providing crossings over crevices larger than 80 feet at places, constructing helipads at altitudes never attempted before and fabricating living and observation shelters with the ingenuity and intelligence that India's sappers have displayed since WWII. In the initial years, the engineers used extendable aluminium ladders with fabricated sockets, perforated steel plate sheets, empty jerrycans as well as natural shelters, fibreglass sheets and drop parachutes to supplement the fabricated and insulated arctic tents as they built living areas that were to be 'home' for the boys in olive green. Apart from the many other routine tasks, the engineers also maintained the snow scooters that are indispensable on the glaciers.

Supporting the Indian Army's resolve and dogged determination are the air warriors of the IAF and the Indian Army's Aviation Corps. Flying in and out of Siachen is hazardous in the extreme. Appreciating the challenges faced by aviators on the Glacier, Nanavatty is effusive in his praise for them: 'Air operations call for nerve, courage and exceptional flying skill. There is no margin for error and even less hope of recovery. Routinely pushing man and machine beyond all known limits they really are "our magnificent men in their flying machines".'[53]

8

FLYBOYS OVER THE GLACIER

'For the men confined to the white wilderness, the characteristic shrill whine of the single-engine Cheetah and the flutter of its rotors as it comes in to land is as soothing as a mother's heartbeat is to her infant child. The Base Camp helipad notches up as many as seventy landings and take-offs, making it the busiest helipad in the country, if not in the world.'[1]

– W.P.S. SIDHU IN *INDIA TODAY*

ANGELS FROM THE SKIES

There was much action in the early 1990s in the areas around the Central and Southern Sectors of the Siachen Glacier.[2] The Indian Army had established several helipads across the entire glacier and there was hectic flying by Cheetah helicopters of 114 HU, several Mi-17 helicopter units of the IAF and 666 Air OP Squadron from the army's aviation arm. It is a matter of great pride for any helicopter pilot from the IAF or the army aviation corps to be posted to these units as the assignment is one of the most challenging assignments in the world. By 1984, 114 HU had been re-equipped with the Cheetah light utility helicopter, a variant of the Chetak with skis. It could land on tiny makeshift helipads at dizzying heights of over 21,000 feet, which even the manufacturers considered to be well beyond the capabilities of the helicopter.

Air Commodore Shashank Mishra was posted as a young flying officer with the Siachen Pioneers (114 HU) between 1990 and 1992. He recollects that new pilots were whisked straight to the station sick quarters, where a mandatory inspection by the friendly doctor was followed by three days of restful acclimatization.[3] Mild diarrhoea and a headache were common because of hypoxic (lack of oxygen) conditions. Food comprised regular but small portions of packaged food that included powdered eggs and pre-cooked chapattis, with regular treats awaiting the pilots at the army helipads they landed at. Usually most of the unit would fly off early in the morning, leaving behind three or four pilots who were either recuperating from illness or had flown the maximum permissible of sixty hours a month. Very rarely did anyone who was fit and available find himself on the 'not-on-programme' list.

Flying on the Glacier

There were three approaches to the Siachen Glacier for the flyboys. The Nubra Valley ended at the Base Camp and enabled access to the Northern Sector. The highest posts in the glacier at heights of between 18,000 and 21,000 feet lay here – Amar, Sonam, Gyong La, Bilafond La, Sehjra, Sia La, Camp V, among many others. Immediately west of the Base Camp was access to the valleys leading to the Central Sector. Major helipads here are at J, C and G III posts. Then there was a narrow valley leading steeply to Z helipad, the highest in the sector at 18,000 feet. There was also a southern approach to the glacier through the Shyok Valley from Thoise which is a critical airbase near Partapur, at the head of the Shyok River and headquarters of the Siachen Brigade. Halts were made en route at Chalunkha, which served as the logistics base for this sector for support through the valleys that led to the important posts of G, B and R, all of which are at heights of between 14,000 and 15,000 feet.

The first sortie to the glacier had to be earned, but kitting was the first part. The NATO suit – so called because it was procured from Europe – was the standard cold-weather kit for NATO air forces. However, these were in short supply with the IAF, so pilots usually inherited a used jacket along with the trousers and the inner layer. These had to be altered and repaired for use. Buying shoes for cold-weather operations from Chandigarh was the next step. The acceptance check by the squadron commander was followed by general handling to get used to aerodynamic and engine characteristics at those altitudes and low temperatures. That done, pilots began their journey to bag the coveted title of 'glacier captain'. It started with 100 hours of flying over the glacier as a co-pilot, assisting the captain with safety procedures, power management, monitoring load cards for various helipads and closing doors. If the youngsters got lucky, a magnanimous captain would hand them the controls for a while, which did wonders for their confidence. It was tough going, and co-pilots had to earn the confidence of their captains before they were certified as being fit to fly the machine in tough weather and terrain conditions. The glacier overawes most pilots with its unforgiving, dangerous and gaping blue ice crevasses. The feeling of whiteout is common, and it must be recognized.

In the early days, the army helipads at the posts were made of flattened cardboard cartons and marked with embedded coffee powder, which would stand out in the snow. They could barely accommodate the skids of a Cheetah helicopter. Helipads were often elevated with 'gullies' on the sides, where the waiting troops could protect themselves from the icy downwash of the rotors during landing and take-off. The approaches and take-offs were tricky and any unplanned variation could have catastrophic consequences. These were discussed at length during pre-flight emergency sessions. Young pilots dreaded these sessions, because one wrong simulated action incurred the wrath of the flight commander.

In winter, pilots were woken at around 4.30 a.m. by the orderly with a steaming cup of solja (a local tea) and an effervescent greeting of 'Jullay saab le' ('Good morning, sir'). While the 'saab' tried to muster up the courage to emerge from under a 5 kg quilt and into the freezing environs of the room, orderlies would light up the bukhari (traditional Kashmiri wood heater). Soon the room would be warm enough for pilots to crawl out of bed and finish their morning chores. Mishra could hardly think of a bath in such conditions, but recalls braver souls who would pour the leftover hot water over their bodies and consider themselves bathed. Local orderlies would then give the first weather brief, which was generally as accurate as the official briefing that followed. While walking to the briefing hall pilots would try and guess the prevailing temperature by the degree of pains in their limbs. Anything lower than minus 15 degrees Celsius would mean more pain. Pre-flight briefings at 5.30 a.m. were followed by a quick bite, a hot cup of tea and a concurrent sortie briefing before heading out for the day's task. The unit engineering officer (EO), warrant officer and the gang of early-morning ground crew would reach the unit an hour before the pilots in numbing cold and be ready to see off the helicopters after completing the pre-flight servicing and checks.

Usually a four-ship formation would be readied for departure, with Nos. 1 and 3 being the commanding officer and flight commander. Younger captains would be wingmen (Nos. 2 and 4) while rookies would generally be co-pilots. The first challenge was negotiating the steep ascent over Khardung La, which lay 16 km east of Leh and had to be crossed at 18,500 feet. This was followed by a descent and a relatively comfortable ride down to the Nubra Valley. Along the way, an air traffic controller in a mobile station at Thoise would exchange a few pleasantries and some banter before his voice faded away as the helicopters entered the Nubra Valley.

An hour later, the helicopters would land at the Base Camp at an elevation of 11,500 feet. Since 114 HU also kept two to three helicopters at Thoise, they would have a lead time of about an hour over the Leh formation. As the Leh formation approached the Base Camp, they would often see their comrades disappearing into the mouth of the glacier for their first mission to Amar and Sonam. These two highest helipads could not be negotiated easily after 11 a.m., and the small window from dawn had to be exploited. The helicopters from Leh would follow with a mission comprising four to five approaches to Amar and Sonam.[4] The late breakfast at the Base Camp between missions was unique. An igloo served as the crew room-cum-cafeteria, and the troops on duty would make them a scrumptious 'Maggi omelette' – which, as the name suggests, was Maggi noodles stuffed into a fluffy omelette.

Pushing the Envelope

Each battalion on the glacier had a loadmaster, usually a JCO who was an expert in prioritizing loads and weighing each bag with his eyes. He had an eye for detail, and could easily juggle between loads and even ensure that an odd soldier was accommodated on board. These little things made him everyone's best friend. Mishra recalls, 'One morning, while landing in whiteout conditions, an army captain who was the post commander had tears rolling down his cheeks and insisted that I accept a bag of cashews as a gift. This was a helipad where perhaps a sortie landed a few times a week. Troops would look forward to mail from home and it was heart-rending looking at bleeding lips and faces covered in black polish to ward off UV rays while we were clad in NATO suits and shaven fresh as daisies. We were grateful that we served those who defended the borders in such difficult conditions, and they for the little conveniences we offered in terms of an occasional pick-up to the Base Camp – saving days of treacherous treks – or simply a letter or a cake delivered just in time.'[5]

Maintaining radio silence while flying led to the development of a unique system that warned of enemy shelling at an intended destination. Helicopters approached for landing from below the helipad, gradually climbing till they could barely discern the top surface of the helipad. Then they would fly in for a hover and landing. One of the co-pilot's secondary tasks was to count the black marks left by artillery shells on the white snow around the helipads on the AGPL. If there were several, it would indicate that the area was unsafe and the approach would be terminated. The army troops at the post would place a red flag in the centre of the helipad as a warning to the helicopters should they miss the black marks. They would then radio the Base Camp for artillery support from the Bofors or 130mm guns to silence the enemy guns and ensure that the helicopters were able to land. Most of the enemy gun positions were registered and the enemy also knew what was about to happen. In a way, it was like a black comedy.

The capacity of the Cheetah squadron to carry loads was rather limited and could be compared to small ants going about their business with grit and determination. The Cheetahs would deliver about 40 tons of supplies a month to posts that could not have been sustained by the heavier Mi-17 helicopter drops. They were truly a lifeline for the higher posts. Mishra relived some dangerous moments faced by 114 HU. On 3 June 1990, an IAF Cheetah was hit by a burst of enemy groundfire while coming in to land at the Amar helipad (19,500 feet), experienced engine failure and had to force-land at the helipad. Troops of 11th Battalion of the Sikh Light Infantry (11 SIKH LI) and an IAF maintenance crew carried out an engine change at those hostile altitudes and made the aircraft airworthy within days.[6] It was flown out just as 666 Air OP had done from Point 6400 the previous year, during the final phase of Operation Ibex.

A couple of years later, in early August 1992, Indian fire brought down a Pakistan Army Lama light-utility helicopter with Brigadier Masood Anwari, the 323 Infantry Brigade commander, on board. Expecting an escalation after the incident, flying was stopped for a while over the glacier by both sides. This caused great hardship and forced the director generals of military operations of each country to speak to one another about possible de-escalation. Flying was resumed on 14 August 1992, after both sides realized that it would be prudent to de-escalate or lose men at air-maintained posts. The Southern Sector too witnessed intense action from 1996 over unoccupied heights and ridgelines that dominated the approaches to the Indian posts of B, G and R. On 26 August 1996, the occupation of one of these ridgelines by Pakistani troops resulted in the shooting down of an IAF Mi-17 that was on a supply mission to one of the posts.[7] Another Indian Cheetah helicopter was suspected to have crashed in the same sector on 2 July 1997 due to enemy fire.[8]

The Workhorses of Siachen

The versatile Russian Mi-17 helicopters proved to be an excellent replacement for the Mi-8 helicopters in 1987. The latter variant had done a wonderful job till then, but had started to develop serious engine and other problems because of their age. Three Mi-17 units initially took on air maintenance duties on the glacier from the late 1980s onwards. These were 127 HU commanded by Wing Commander Fali Major, who later became the first helicopter pilot to become chief of air staff; 128 HU commanded by Wing Commander Mike Dutt; and 129 HU with Group Captain Harpal 'Harry' Ahluwalia at the helm. The initial units maintained detachments at Thoise in rotation that comprised a bunch of very senior pilots who had combat experience on Mi-4 and Mi-8 helicopters. Ahluwalia and Major recollect that they were almost permanent members of the Thoise detachment, preferring the adrenalin rush of flying on the glacier to the urban environment of the air force station at Hindon near Delhi, where the units were based. Operating a detachment from Thoise gave the Mi-17s access to all parts of the glacier. Ahluwalia was surprised to be ordered by Air Vice Marshal Dushyant Singh, the seniormost air force officer in J&K, to prepare to move further north from Thoise to the Base Camp and set up a detachment there. Ahluwalia was convinced that this was operationally unsound, but moved anyway. He flew a few missions to all parts of the glacier from the Base Camp before preparing a decision matrix that clearly indicated that it was not feasible to operate a permanent detachment from there. His stand was vindicated when the Western Air Command concurred, after the chief of staff of Western Air Command flew a mission with Ahluwalia on one of his visits to Leh.[9]

In addition to the operational constraints, an early-morning inspection at 5 a.m. to facilitate a 6 a.m. take-off was almost impossible at the Base Camp. The wind chill factor prevented technicians from climbing up to inspect the rotor blades, an exercise which was possible on the smaller Cheetahs from 114 HU. This defeated the very purpose of moving forward to the Base Camp – which was to exploit the early-morning window. Dushyant Singh was furious, because he had requested Nanavatty to build a hangar at the Base Camp at considerable cost and engineer effort, which would now go to waste.

The typical load profile for Mi-17 parachute or free drops was 1.8 tons of ammunition boxes, dismantled artillery pieces and dry rations. All dropping zones were on the glacier floor except at J and G-3, which were on subsidiary glaciers that were part of the Central Sector. All the valleys were narrow and loads had to be taken up to higher posts like Amar and Sonam on snow scooters as they did not have helipads or drop zones for Mi-17s. This exercise demanded exceptional skills, and it never ceased to fascinate the Mi-17 crews seeing the scooters reduced to specks across a white landscape as they disappeared up the subsidiary glaciers. Ahluwalia recollects that 1988 and 1989 were particularly tough years at the Base Camp as Pakistani artillery periodically targeted it from gun positions on the Chumik Glacier. In response, he remembers that Colonel K.S. Jamwal, the commander of 36 Maratha Medium Regiment – the Bofors unit at the Base Camp – let loose six rounds of rationed ammunition across the AGPL to welcome Ahluwalia when he landed there. He particularly recollects that enemy mortar firing would commence the moment they heard the helicopters heading towards the valleys close to Amar and Sonam, which were key posts in the Bilafond La complex. This forced the helicopters to take a different route every day. When I asked him about Brigadiers Nugyal and Nanavatty, Ahluwalia replied, 'They were tough guys, great soldiers.'

The winter of 1988 brought terrible flying weather and the backlog built up tremendously. As soon as the weather improved, there was a frenzy to catch up. To support Operation Ibex in the Central Sector, the posts at Kaman and Thapa Base had to be reinforced. These were lifelines to the isolated section on Point 6400. On 22 April 1989, Ahluwalia flew thirteen sorties. He remarked, 'We loved it – flying, switching off, refuelling, loading, dropping and back again. We made up for the winter shortfall that month. Along the way, we were once buzzed by fighter aircraft, albeit accidentally, when an IAF MiG-23 from Air Force Station Adampur, piloted by one of the commanding officers on a routine reconnaissance, decided to descend and see what it meant to streak across the glacier floor at 800 kmph as we were on a dropping mission. It was a narrow shave but all's well that ends well. At the end of Operation Ibex, Air Marshal M.M. Singh, the Air Officer Commanding-in Chief (AOC-in-C) of Western Air Command and Lieutenant General B.C. Nanda, the Northern Army Commander, flew in to Thoise to congratulate the unit on some stupendous flying. The AOC-in-C even wrote me a nice letter.'[10]

The Fixed-Wing Heroes

The IAF's heavy-lift transport aircraft, the IL-76, was the mainstay of the Indian Army's continuous troop induction on to the glacier, while the versatile An-32s complemented the Mi-17 helicopters in air maintenance operations. They dropped varied loads at the drop zones at the Base Camp, Kumar FLB (supporting the Bilafond La complex) and the northernmost Rani (supporting the Sia La complex). Group Captain K.S. Lamba recently commanded 48 Squadron (the Camels), which is equipped with An-32 aircraft. An old glacier hand, waking up bleary-eyed at 4 a.m. on cold winter mornings to make a 5 a.m. briefing and a 6 a.m. take-off for a drop sortie over the glacier was routine for Lamba.[11] Waking up two hours before their commanding officer, the technical crew would prepare the aircraft for flight even as the loadmaster and the logistics team from the army loaded up the aircraft. From a fixed-wing aviator's perspective, the Siachen Glacier was not as difficult to negotiate as the narrow and misty valleys in the north-east. However, the loss of power or an emergency were great everyday risks. As one squadron pilot put it, 'Every risk we faced in our pressurized cockpit paled in front of the existential threat to life that officers and men of the Indian Army face on the glacier.'[12]

While the main logistics lifeline for the Leh-based 14 Corps is the Srinagar–Leh National Highway 1A, it is complemented extensively by air maintenance from Chandigarh, where a major chunk of the IAF's air transport assets are located. This base is home to one of the heavy-lift IL-76 aircraft squadrons, the only heavy-lift Mi-26 helicopter unit, and the ever reliable and recently upgraded An-32 medium-lift transport aircraft. Loads are prepared here for sustaining life and operations in Siachen and the desolate areas of Eastern Ladakh even as troops assemble there and embark for the move to Thoise. A regular day for the Camels begins as early as 3 a.m. as the aircraft are prepared for the forward-area drop missions. The operational room is active by 4 a.m. with a never-ending flow of coffee, tea and sandwiches. As the crew prepare and brief for the mission, dozens of army trucks position their loads on the huge tarmac. The loading process is both manual and mechanical, demanding good teamwork from the flight engineer-cum-loadmaster and their army counterparts. By 5 a.m. all the briefings and weather reports have been assessed, and the aircrew are all set for take-off as the first rays of sunlight filter through the grey sky.

A normal flying day involves two waves of four to five aircraft each as the squadron attempts to beat the weather, which normally starts deteriorating by noon. Climbing to almost 30,000 feet, the An-32s cross the breathtaking Zanskar and Ladakh Ranges in a north-easterly direction, turning north at Leh and crossing the Khardung La Pass. Then they descend to fly over Partapur, Thoise and the Base Camp at speeds of approximately 550 kmph at around 1,000 feet above the glacier floor. Along the way, they cross the mountain passes of Rohtang La, Kunzum La, Chang La and Khardung La, the winding Sutlej and Chandra Rivers and the scenic valleys of Spiti, Indus and Nubra.

The lakes of Kartso and Tso Morari en route are an equally enchanting sight. The crew, however, seldom have time to take in these views. Instead, they compete with one another to assign peculiar names for easy identification of landmarks while flying. These would come in handy during emergencies. So, it is common for IAF crews to identify landmark peaks and mountains as an ice cream cone, a temple, a tiger or an elephant.

The activity level picks up as the aircraft approaches the drop zone. The captain initiates a quick revision of the escape routes in case of engine failure or emergency decompression. When confronted with such contingencies, the aircraft will have to descend below the hill crests to make a crash-landing. Sighting ground features beyond a certain distance is therefore mandatory for the crew, since this visual acquisition also determines the feasibility of the drop. Weather, winds and air traffic determine the drop plan. There is another quick brief in the air by the captain while the loadmaster gets busy preparing the load. Troops at the posts and the drop zone keep their ears open for the sound of the engine of an An-32 aircraft. The drop zones are marked with an orange 'T', and smoke is blown to help the aircrew assess wind speed. Strong winds at such altitudes are the norm, and even a small difference in wind speed can drastically affect the precision of the supply drop. This activity requires a lot of skill, coordination and composure.

When the cargo ramp door is open, the entire crew must use oxygen. Severe turbulence close to the terrain and deteriorating weather in the afternoon present significant challenges as the captain makes the final alignment along the line of run. The countdown to the drop zone is called out aloud in the cockpit as the aircraft is held steady in a gradual descent with the cargo ramp fully open and the load skids raring to go. As the load exits the aircraft, the orange-and-white parachutes deploy – there is no better sight for the waiting troops below than to see them land in sequence in the designated drop zone. The route back is equally tricky and the crew cannot afford to let their guard down till they clear the Zoji La Pass. By 9 a.m. the steel birds touch down at their home base. The machines are prepared for the next mission while the crew use this time for a quick bite before their second sortie of the day. An-32 operations on the glacier epitomize the spirit of jointmanship that is so strong at the tactical and operational levels. The author describes jointmanship in his earlier book as:

> ...a term exclusively used within the Indian armed forces to highlight synergy and interoperability between the three services.[13]

Rare Atmosphere – IAF Fighters Pitch In

There is a misconception that it is only the helicopter and transport fleets of the IAF and the helicopters of the army's aviation corps that have participated in the Siachen conflict and the continuous tension that prevailed along the LoC in the area. During my tenure in 108 Squadron, a MiG-21 squadron in Adampur (an airbase near the town of Jalandhar in Punjab) from 1983 to 1985, we shared the base with 223 and 224 Squadrons, the two MiG-23 MF squadrons. They were at the time the main air defence fighters of the IAF, as both the MiG-29 and the Mirage-2000 had not yet been inducted. They used to call themselves the first 'air superiority fighters' in the IAF – a term that evoked much mirth when the Mirage-2000s and MiG-29s came in.

The MiG-23 MF was a brute of a machine, weighing a monstrous 15 tons with an engine that generated a thrust of almost 13 tons. It was quite a formidable platform at high altitudes since it had a powerful engine and the flexibility of varying the lift. It had a variable geometry wing – the wing could be swept to 14, 45 or 72 degrees depending on the manoeuvrability requirements. For example, the aircraft could achieve top speeds only when the wings were swept back to 72 degrees. It was, however, most manoeuvrable when the wings were swept forward to 14 degrees and cruised best at 45 degrees sweep angle. During the mid-1980s, it was the only IAF fighter which could have fought the significantly more advanced F-16 that had recently been inducted into the PAF.

Several contemporaries of the author spent their formative years flying the MiG-23 MF at Adampur and flew missions about which they had very little prior knowledge. The evening before, all they would be told was that they were to escort a Canberra bomber-turned-reconnaissance platform on a mission 'up north'. It was on one such morning in April 1988 that Wing Commander 'Cheech' Brar and his No. 2, who is still serving in the IAF, took off from Adampur. They carried out an aerial rendezvous with a single Canberra well before crossing the LoC. Climbing to 26,000 feet, they headed north over the Burzil Range that separates the Kashmir Valley from the Gilgit-Baltistan areas of PoK. Using the Nun Kun peak as a navigational aid, they ducked down to 500 feet above the ground as soon as they crossed the range to avoid radar detection. Skardu is less than 150 km away from the closest point on the LoC, and takes barely ten minutes at 850 kmph an hour – the optimal speed for fighter jets at low level. This time, however, the MiG-23s had to cater for the slower speeds of the Canberra; as a result, the formation had to intrude into hostile airspace at speeds of around 700 kmph.

The plan was for the Canberra to carry out a high-speed run over Skardu, photograph some infrastructure that was supposed to have been newly added and head back southwards at top speed. The MiG-23s would form a defensive shield against the possibility of being intercepted by PAF F-16s – which, according to intelligence reports, were occasionally deployed in Skardu. Unknown to Brar's formation, there was another formation airborne on a similar mission from the other squadron on base. They were streaking towards Skardu along with another Canberra from the same squadron, but along a different run-in direction. After flying along the Nubra Valley into the Siachen Glacier area, they crossed Kumar FLB and turned on to a westerly direction, crossed the Bilafond La complex and ducked down as low as possible to head for Skardu airfield. Brar's No. 2 was the first to spot a glint in the east and was instinctively tempted to tell his leader over radio that there was a likely threat emanating from the right. He decided to wait a couple of seconds and soon recognized the MiG-23s. However, to be safe, Brar asked the Canberra to turn back. The PAF was not amused, but they rarely interfered with these missions because they did not have enough radar cover to prevent such intrusions.[14]

On another occasion, one MiG-23 pilot recalls seeing two F-16s parked on the tarmac at the Skardu airfield – they were part of a small detachment that the PAF would maintain at Skardu during the good weather months. During the 1980s, the strike version of the MiG-23 – called the MiG-23 BN – would buzz Skardu occasionally. MiG-23 MFs would also escort the MiG-25 high-speed and high-altitude reconnaissance aircraft during photo runs over the glacier and during intrusive missions towards Skardu and Gilgit. In later years, MiG-21 and MiG-29 squadrons regularly entered the Siachen Glacier area and flew along the Nubra Valley. They did so to familiarize themselves with the terrain in what were known as 'milk runs' because of the absence of any action in the air. The IAF fighter fleet thus acquired some high-altitude operational experience during Operation Meghdoot, albeit without engaging in combat or carrying out attacks on ground targets. This would come of some use when the IAF was called on over a decade later to assist the Indian Army in evicting Pakistani troops from the Kargil heights not far away from Siachen.

Forward Air Controller at Kumar FLB

In October 1988, Flying Officer Tejinder 'Tango' Singh, a rookie fighter pilot with No. 5 Squadron, was eagerly looking forward to finishing his air-to-ground firing sorties on the Jaguar aircraft. However, he was instead sent to Siachen as a Forward Air Controller (FAC).[15] After the standard acclimatization at Thoise, it was time to head to the Base Camp at the snout of the Siachen Glacier. He was kitted with the standard Koflach snowshoes, a thick down jacket that was stiflingly hot in October, and Kortina goggles. Tango would soon realize that these were essential for survival in the weeks ahead. His role at Kumar FLB was to be the FAC-cum-weatherman who would not only control IAF fighter aircraft whenever they chose to do their runs till the northern tip of the glacier but also provide accurate weather reports to the Base Camp to facilitate helicopter and transport operations.

Tango's last day at the Base Camp was Diwali. It was celebrated with ATC flare pistols and tracers from an air defence gun being fired in lieu of firecrackers. A helicopter sortie with 114 HU to the Northern Sector from the Base Camp was the last bit of familiarization for the young Jaguar pilot, as he was flown over the most treacherous terrain he had ever seen. He recollects, 'As the helicopter headed north on to the vast white sea of snow, there was not a speck of land. It was all white from horizon to horizon with small black dots – possible camps for those trekking up – as we reached close to what was and still is the highest battalion HQ of the world's highest battlefield, also referred to as Kumar FLB.'

Dropped at Kumar FLB, Tango was in the care of 7 GUARDS. Tango felt a bond as the seasoned Guardsmen got him accustomed to life there – wearing two layers of socks, how to avoid frostbite, how not to walk, what to eat and drink, and identifying symptoms of things going wrong. The reality of the glacier hit Tango early into his tenure. A JCO of 7 GUARDS had ventured out to a post barely 200 metres away to hand in a situation report and was on his way back when a blizzard hit the area. As per drill, he was to stay put till the weather cleared. However, being an expert mountaineer, he decided to continue heading back in whiteout conditions... and lost his way and his life in the battle against the elements of nature.

Tango recollects that despite the availability of snow scooters, the Northern Sector was mostly maintained by airdrops from fixed-wing aircraft and low-hover drops by Mi-8, Mi-17 and Cheetah helicopters. Clear skies after a spell of bad weather spelt excitement for Tango as he controlled airdrops by An-32s over 'Benazir' and sorties by MiG-21s and MiG-23s, which came and disappeared in a flash. There was a general cheer when many consignments were successfully dropped, but also occasional tragedy when retrieving parties reported a missing man – who often would be found frozen to death in a crevice days later by search parties. Violating the maxim of not trying to retrieve a package from outside the earmarked drop zone could mean death.

The troops from the 13th Battalion of the Grenadiers Regiment (13 GRENADIERS), which replaced 7 GUARDS as sentinels of the Northern Sector, were mostly from Rajasthan. Shaving was not permitted and everyone sported a beard. Baths were a luxury – Tango had only one bath during his stay at Kumar FLB. Troops were advised to drink adequate fluids and take regular doses of multivitamins. The morale among officers and troops was always high and Tango does not remember a sombre moment, except of course when tragedy struck and buddies were lost to combat and nature. While letters normally brought cheer and hope, they were also bearers of sad news. Letters were routinely censored, not only to ensure that no classified information was shared but also to manage the impact of bad news. Tango clearly remembers even today how the unit tried its best to soften the blow suffered by one of the men when news about his daughter's death following a prolonged illness came in through a letter.

The day at Kumar FLB started with a hot cup of tea and a weather check from the window. Then there was a weather report from each post and a clearance for flying. Breakfast was typically paranthas, puris, vegetables and pickles, after which Tango would make the 200-metre trek to the control cabin next to the helipads. The cabin was called Diwan-e-Khas – a 20 sq ft platform that provided a clear view of the glacier and all the passes and valleys. The IAF detachment ensured that fully charged batteries were fitted in the radio set, and would also guide the army unit in preparing the helipads – which were elevated cuboids made with jerrycans full of snow that froze into ice. They were held together by layers of parachutes lashed securely and stuck together with an adhesive. Radio conversation was easy-going, with mandatory greetings and an accurate indication of the wind velocity. The helicopters never switched off at Kumar FLB, and after offloading their consignment, they took supplies that had been airdropped by An-32s to individual posts. After about three shuttles on a good weather day, they would return to the Base Camp with a load of mail – and invariably a casualty or someone who was sick.

Chilblains and frostbite requiring the amputation of a toe, finger or even a limb were frequent medical occurrences, while high-altitude pulmonary oedema and high-altitude cerebral oedema were the most common killers. Tango clearly remembers being briefed repeatedly about watching out for signs, like accumulation of fluid in the lungs, frothy coughing, leaks from blood vessels, severe headaches and hallucinations. The day generally ended with a halt at the officers' mess, which also served as the commander's living quarters. The afternoons and evenings were spent playing bridge, watching movies and taking regular stock of situational reports from the posts. Tango's experience on the glacier is what inter-service camaraderie is all about in the Indian Armed Forces.

The Storm Subsides: Point 5770 Falls

Thirteen years after Operation Blue Star, Lieutenant General Prakash Katoch found himself commanding the Siachen Brigade at a time when the Northern and Central Sectors were relatively stable. The action had shifted to the Southern and the Chorbat La Sectors.[16] Katoch's tenure from late 1997 to November 1999 also coincided with General Musharraf's attempts to create an arc of instability from the Mushkoh Valley in the west to the Southern Sector of the Siachen Glacier. This would cost the Indians dearly and culminate in the Kargil conflict of 1999. Katoch got his first glimpse of the glacier in 1990. Interacting with Nanavatty – who was the Siachen brigade commander – was inspiration enough for the combat-proven paratrooper to set his sights on the command of this elite formation. Seven years later, in July 1997, Katoch volunteered to command the brigade. After a turn of events, he found himself at the helm of affairs, replacing Brigadier Randhir Singh.

Assessing that the Southern Sector merited attention, he foresaw that it would emerge as an extended battlefront if the Indian Army neglected it. In his initial operational assessment, he identified two areas as particularly vulnerable. The first was Point 5770 and the ridgelines that ran west, south and north. The second was the under-patrolled gap of over 40 km at Chorbat La, between the western limits of 102 Infantry Brigade's area of responsibility and the eastern limits of the Kargil Brigade. Making matters difficult for him was the temporary cessation of operations in the sector by the IAF in 1997. They had been forced to do so after Pakistan shot down an Indian Mi-17 helicopter during a supply drop sortie to B and G posts in retaliation for the loss of their brigade commander. This meant that for months the Southern Sector had to be maintained on foot and by the occasional Cheetah sortie.

Soon it became clear to Katoch that Point 5770 stood like a sentinel in the area and should the Pakistanis creep up to the top, they would be able to dominate several Indian posts and logistics routes by directing effective fire on to the area. Anticipating this, he assembled an assault task force comprising the 27th Battalion of the Rajput Regiment (27 RAJPUT), Ladakh Scouts, a team of high-altitude warfare school instructors and 5 PARA. This taskforce advanced on Point 5770 via its southern and northern shoulders. Throughout 1998 the Indians made concerted attempts to reach Point 5770, but failed because of the physical challenges posed by the terrain and the weather. Instead, the teams managed to set up small posts along the route as launch pads for further assaults. Katoch though was not done with Point 5770, particularly when the Pakistanis set up a post 600 metres to the west of Point 5770 in mid-1999 as the Kargil conflict raged.

Colonel K.H. Singh, the commanding officer of 27 RAJPUT, reported to Katoch a few weeks after the commencement of the Kargil conflict that the Pakistanis had indeed reached Point 5770. This galvanized Katoch into action. He decided that the only option to surprise the enemy was a vertical assault during the summer from the east with a small team. After a speedy approval for an assault from the divisional headquarters, Katoch and K.H. Singh put together a crack assault team comprising Major Navdeep Singh Cheema (27 RAJPUT), Captain Shyamal Sinha (Kumaon Regiment), Havildar Dola Ram (1 PARA) and a small group of six or seven additional men. Their instructions were clear – launch a vertical assault in broad daylight from the east, where the enemy would least expect it from.

The assault team climbed for seven hours in full combat gear carrying AK-47s and carbines. They reached the post at 2 p.m. and took the defenders by surprise. Eleven defenders were killed in close combat. The attackers found communication lines and sangars (rock shelters) a short distance away from the summit. Among those killed was Captain Taimur Malik, the grandson of a Pakistani politician and the brother of Pakistan's defence attaché in Washington. Three letters were found on his person. One was from his father, who had fought the Indians in Bangladesh and then had taken up arms again as a jihadi after his retirement from the Pakistan Army. In that letter, the father exhorted his son to continue fighting the Indians. The second was a letter from Malik's mother, enquiring about his health and well-being. The third was a note from Taimur himself that said, 'We have reached the top and are going to give them hell.' Responding to a request from the Pakistanis for a return of the bodies, Katoch transported the bodies to Kargil, where they were handed over during a flag meeting. Katoch sadly had to fight hard to get the necessary recognition for the assault team in the din of Kargil: Cheema and Sinha were awarded Vir Chakras, while other members of the team were given Sena Medals. Colonel K.H. Singh was awarded a Yudh Seva Medal for his inspiring leadership of 27 RAJPUT.

The discussions on joint operations and synergy with the IAF evoked a mixed response from Katoch. From his perspective and experience, it was clear that the trajectory of jointmanship, whether in peace or conflict, was determined by individuals and not by inbuilt mechanisms. On the other hand, Air Chief Marshal Fali Major has fond recollections of his time spent with the army as the base commander at Leh. He reflects, 'With regard to inter-services relations, I had an excellent tie-up with 14 Corps, 3 Mountain Division and the Batalik and Siachen Brigades. With army stalwarts like Rostum Nanavatty, Katoch, Panag and Arjun Ray, it was great going and I really enjoyed my association with them. My previous experience of commanding two MI-17 units and operating in the same area of my responsibility now was an added benefit and no one could poodle-fake me! I spent three winters there!'[17]

Colonel A. Jayaram is a seasoned army aviator and a rotary wing test pilot. He was the commander of 666 Air OP Squadron at Partapur and saw much action during Katoch's tenure as brigade commander. He took over his unit from Lieutenant Colonel Sharma, who was relieved of his command for pushing the envelope during a casualty evacuation sortie that the latter undertook at great personal risk. Even though Katoch backed Sharma and fought to retain him, Army HQ did not relent. Though the area of responsibility of the unit extended from the Batalik Sector eastwards across the Siachen Glacier into Subsector North in Eastern Ladakh, almost 70 per cent of his flying was in support of the Siachen Brigade. When asked about Katoch, Jayaram said, 'He was always on the move and wanted to be where the troops were. He visited almost all posts and would fly out to an accessible helipad. Then he'd walk up to inaccessible posts to see for himself how his men were doing. I recollect that he even spent a few days at Sonam, one of the highest posts in the Northern Sector.'[18]

Jayaram recollected that the most challenging missions were casualty evacuations in inclement weather and during twilight hours. He explained, 'The stakes were high – those were course mates with whom we have broken bread, stayed on our haunches and rolled together at the NDA and IMA; regimental colleagues, bodies lying in the same bunker and much more.' Highlighting some of the risky missions undertaken by his unit during Katoch's tenure, Jayaram reflected, 'We continued to selectively break existing peacetime rules and launched missions even late in the afternoon. We would then come in to land at Partapur in the dark with an improvised electrical flare-path and not kerosene lamp goosenecks, as the wind speed was too high and we ran the risk of starting a fire. It was action all the way and immensely satisfying.'

Training

Commanded over the years by some of India's most hardy and courageous commanders from all parts of the country, the 102 Infantry Brigade remains a prestigious and coveted command even today. A survey of the units deployed on the glacier between December 1989 and February 1993 reveals a mix of ten different regiments.[19] Brigadier V.M.B. Krishnan, a recent commander of the brigade, spoke to the author on life, training and the travails of commanding troops on the icy heights of the Saltoro Ridge and the Siachen Glacier. He emphasized, 'The key to survival and efficiency on the glacier were fitness, mental agility and situational awareness.' He continued, 'Upper-body strength and oxygen retention capability were more important than classical endurance. Coping with contingencies brought about by the weather and medical emergencies were the ultimate tests of mental agility, even more than facing fire. On the glacier, every man had to extract that extra bit all the time, to survive the three to six months that constitutes a normal tenure.'

Thoise remains the gateway to the glacier as the aerial maintenance hub. A steady stream of IL-76, An-32, and in more recent times the heavy-lift C-17 aircraft, come in loaded with troops, guns, rations and letters from Chandigarh to sustain life and operations on the glacier. Partapur today is a bustling military camp at the confluence of the Nubra and Shyok Rivers and remains the HQ of India's Siachen Brigade. There is a hustle and bustle at Partapur as long convoys line the road from there to the Base Camp. A similar scenario unfolds at Dansam across the LoC, where Pakistan's 323 Brigade is located. Convoys keep plying to Gayari, a battalion HQ and the major logistics hub on their side of the warzone. On the Indian side, new units of soldiers and officers eagerly make their way to the Siachen Battle School a short distance away on the upper reaches of the Base Camp for a three-week high-altitude inoculation module. Every soldier is very serious about the programme because he knows his life depends on it. Failure to complete the module is a stigma that is hard to shake off.

The school was set up initially by Brigadier Nugyal and expanded by Brigadier Nanavatty with Major Basil Hobkirk from the Regiment of Guards as its first commanding officer. The scope of its training programme is wide and all-encompassing. The initial focus is on mountain awareness, ice craft and rock climbing. Next are survival training, weapons and equipment training and high-altitude leadership and administrative training for officers and JCOs. Once that is done, it is time for tactical training on reading the battle, situational awareness, setting up of posts, night operations and directing of artillery fire. The pre-induction training process for an infantry battalion commences with a three-week training programme for instructors, including the firing of all specialized infantry weapons like MMGs, HMGs, 81mm mortars, Carl Gustaf 84mm rocket launchers and sniper rifles. This group then takes on the responsibility of training the rest of the battalion in the second phase of the pre-induction training. Artillery units have their own training programme that incorporates specialized modules after completion of the two weeks of standard training. These are for firing and manning gun positions, snowmobile operations and managing helicopter operations. The whole process of inducting a battalion or artillery regiment takes about two months from the time the instructors start their acclimatization till the battalion disperses to various posts.[20]

Over the years, the Indian special forces have gained much low-temperature, high-altitude fighting experience on the glacier. Nanavatty played his part here too, by translating into SOPs some of the experience he gathered in the UK after observing the Special Boat Service (SBS) train in Arctic conditions in Norway. Posted to the UK in 1985 as Indian Army liaison officer but with no clear charter, Nanavatty concentrated on understanding how the Royal Marine commandos and the elite SBS trained and fought, particularly in the mountains and the Arctic. Spending two weeks in Norway in the middle of winter was nowhere close to the conditions in Siachen, but was an eye-opener nevertheless. Impressed with their training regimen, situational awareness and fighting skills, Nanavatty was struck by the easy understanding and familiarity within units and the outstanding leadership skills displayed by non-commissioned officers, who shouldered great responsibility. Developing junior leader skills has been among the most challenging tasks for every Siachen brigade commander.

Leadership and Motivation

The main leadership challenge on the glacier was to keep the troops motivated to fight fear, isolation, monotony, superstition, passivity and foolhardiness. Subedar Major Satheesan from the Madras Regiment is a winner of the Shaurya Chakra, for the gallantry he displayed in the Kashmir Valley during counterterrorism operations in 1996. Enrolled initially into the Assam Regiment in 1988, he served on the glacier in 1992. He boarded an aircraft for the first time in his life at Chandigarh as his battalion was inducted into Thoise and then sent to the Base Camp for the customary acclimatization. He recollects having spent a month at Hathi Post (19,588 feet) along with eight other soldiers, and a further two months at a post that was only air-maintained and where firing was random and sudden.

Being better educated than the others, Satheesan was assigned the task of ensuring daily letter writing and reading sessions to maintain morale by sharing family and village happenings. Another havildar was responsible for ensuring that no one went on an empty stomach despite the frequent loss of appetite. Dried fruits were a vital source of energy. Satheesan remembers that there was a superstition that the spirits on the glacier shaved off two years from the lives of those who dared to live on the heights. Whenever morale slipped, men drew strength from the various exploits of the soldiers who, with nothing but grit and determination, had secured the heights they now occupied. Evacuation by foot or ropeways was dreaded, particularly in adverse weather conditions. Whenever sections were relieved at their posts for rest and recovery, the first stop after the descent to a base camp was the unit's place of worship.[21]

After basic survival training and the maintaining of morale, the next set of challenges was building professional pride by instilling alertness, self-discipline and display of controlled aggression with the courage and will to win. Junior and senior leaders have no option on the glacier but to set a personal example in terms of physical fitness, mental agility and robustness to plan, organize and execute in a manner that 'your men will follow you to hell and back'.[22] Also required was the ability to empathize and show genuine concern through sound administration and welfare activities. Echoing the words of Napoleon, Nanavatty said, 'On the glacier, there are no good or bad battalions, only good or bad officers.'[23]

A Price to Pay

The Indian Army – and the IAF to a lesser extent – have had to pay a heavy price for their domination of the Siachen Glacier. The Indian Army has lost over 850 officers and men, with several still suffering from the ill-effects of their tenures on the glacier. Most lives have been lost not to enemy fire but to the unforgiving elements of nature. Avalanches, crevasses, blizzards and whiteouts have been the main killers. The medical conditions that most affect soldiers are high-altitude pulmonary oedema, hypoxia, frostbite, hypothermia, altitude sickness and deep vein thrombosis. Between 1984 and 1990, the Indian Army lost 433 personnel, with another 1787 injured by a combination of enemy action, terrain accidents and climatic conditions. Of these, only 102 personnel fell to enemy action, with 195 wounded. Reflecting the ethos of the Indian Army, officers led from the front and put themselves in the line of fire. Eleven officers lost their lives with another 100 injured. Latest figures compiled by the *Times of India* by extrapolating various sources – including figures placed before the Indian Parliament and reliable Pakistani sources – puts the total number of Indian soldiers killed till 2016 at 869, including 33 officers and 55 JCOs. Pakistan lost an average of three to four personnel more per year.[24]

Though there was a sharp decline in the number of deaths between 2014 and 2015 (with only one loss of life in 2015), an avalanche in 2016 left a battalion of the Madras Regiment mourning the loss of over ten soldiers. The avalanche also saw the miraculous rescue of Lance Naik Hanumanthappa after he had been buried in the snow for over six days. However, Hanumanthappa succumbed to multiple organ failure a few days later. His death sensitized the nation to the perils of serving on the glacier and revived the debate on the futility of holding on. In addition, the numerous amputations caused by frostbite, gangrene and associated effects have left hundreds of soldiers maimed for life. There are also the unrecorded psychological disorders that are inevitable in such unforgiving conditions.

Much of the modern survival equipment to ensure soldier comfort and efficiency was bought during the tenure of George Fernandes as defence minister from 1998 to 2004. He stated in Parliament that the daily cost of sustaining operations in Siachen was Rs 3 crore. Various reports have pegged the cost of three decades of conflict on the glacier at over Rs 15,000 crore. While the current costs of maintaining existing force levels are an estimated Rs 700 crore to Rs 800 crore per year,[25] other estimates pegged the costs at around Rs 2,000 crore annually during the peak years of conflict. The environmental degradation caused by the occupation of the glacier has been precipitous, despite laudable attempts by the army to minimize it. However, anyone who flies over the glacier during the summer can clearly see the extent of the destruction of a pristine area. It would be safe to assume that Pakistan faces similar challenges and tribulations to those faced by India.

Resolving the Siachen Imbroglio

Following the loss of around 150 Pakistani soldiers and civilians in an avalanche in the Gayari Glacier area in 2012, the Pakistani military establishment led by General Kayani put forward a proposal to demilitarize the glacier. But the proposal was without any promise of taking India's views on the position of the LoC into account.[26] Before this massive hit in terms of the number of casualties, Pakistan always postured that it would be doing India a favour by agreeing to talk for resolving the Siachen imbroglio. It invariably linked this to the larger issue of Kashmir, a proposition that is still unacceptable to India.

Interestingly, Kayani was the director general of military operations when the historic ceasefire along the international boundary, LoC and AGPL between India and Pakistan was declared in November 2003, but never formalized in writing. Kayani's proposal was no different from what had already transpired in the eight rounds of talks held between 1989 and 1998. The deadlock was strikingly similar every time – before delimiting the LoC beyond NJ 9842, Pakistan wanted India to vacate the heights first, refused to share maps and wanted to go back to the 1971 deployment. Pakistan's view of de-escalation solely rested on an Indian pull-out, which was a preposterous proposition to the Indian side.[27]

Katoch has some very interesting vignettes to narrate on the time when India and Pakistan were exploring ways to defuse tensions on the glacier. One such narrative revolved around a visit to the area in 1998 by the defence secretary, Ajit Kumar, and a team comprising officers from the Ministry of External Affairs and Army HQ. This was also the time when the Americans were trying to get involved as interlocutors and the visit, though unrelated, coincided with the visit of the US chairman of the joint chiefs of staff to Leh. During the briefing, when the defence secretary asked whether the Indian Army could vacate the Saltoro Ridge, he got diverse opinions. While the HQ representative immediately replied, 'Yes sir, we can and will occupy the hillocks around,' Katoch was asked to give his views. He offered a scathing rebuttal and explained why it was a losing proposition because of the possibility of the entire sector being enveloped from the west and south by Pakistan and by China from the east, putting Leh within artillery range.

He declared rather alarmingly, 'Withdraw this brigade and you will barely have one battalion from Chorbat La to Khardung La against two Chinese divisions in Eastern Ladakh.'[28] Katoch is also quite dismissive of the 'Mountain of Peace' initiative as part of the Track II dialogue floated when Manmohan Singh was prime minister. He describes it as a meaningless initiative involving people who have never served or been to the glacier. He represents a hard-line view that has largely dominated the discourse through the years following the 2003 ceasefire. Former Indian foreign secretary Shyam Saran made a rather startling disclosure in his book *How India Sees the World.* He revealed that during the brief India-Pakistan entente that lasted from 2003 to 2008, the Manmohan Singh-led Congress government had almost succeeded in sealing a deal with Pakistan to vacate the Siachen Glacier as part of a larger 'peace process'.[29] The deal was scuttled following 'realistic' inputs based on the reports of field commanders and objections from the Indian NSA M.K. Narayanan.[30] The glacier, barring a few incidents, has been quiet since 2003. However, a permanent solution is still nowhere in sight.

China is accelerating its 'dream project' of the Belt and Road Initiative that seeks to connect Tibet and Xinjiang province with the Arabian Sea at Gwadar port. This road will run through the Baltistan region of PoK as part of the China-Pakistan Economic Corridor (CPEC). The current operational position is that Pakistan holds a few posts on the western slopes of the Saltoro

Range ridgeline that are extremely vulnerable to both fire and avalanches. India's position is almost impregnable, as it holds the four highest passes along the entire Saltoro Ridge, apart from numerous other positions along the eastern ridges.

Glacial modelling has revealed the formation and deepening of glacial lakes in the region. One such lake on the Rimo Glacier – which feeds the Shyok River – merits close monitoring. With both the Nubra and Shyok Rivers being prone to flash flooding, much of the Indian Army's infrastructure in areas like Partapur and the Base Camp is vulnerable to being washed away. Twenty-three soldiers of a Bihar regiment were washed away during the Leh floods of 2010. Though these floods were not linked directly in any way with the melting of the Siachen or other glaciers, it indicated the vulnerability of the region to climatic change and global warming. The lake on the Rimo Glacier could be a disaster waiting to happen, because a minor earthquake or heavy rainfall could lead to a flash flood.[31] Will the gods finally intervene?

Is there a solution to the problem? In a hard-hitting article written for the *Indian Defence Review* in May 2014, Brigadier Kharb reckons that the presence of Indian posts in the vicinity will be a deterrent for China's ambitions to connect Aksai Chin to Baltistan through the Karakoram Pass and Shaksgam Valley.[32] Nanavatty argues that real distances debunk the theory that the heights of the Saltoro Ridge offer great tactical advantage in terms of visibility into the Shaksgam Valley. While questioning the ability to watch over the Karakoram highway, he maintains that any settlement on Siachen cannot be reached in isolation nor can it be based on altruistic aspirations. General Hooda highlights that negotiations on de-escalation between the Indian and Pakistani armies continued till 2007, but stopped when the Indians realized that no headway was being made on mutually marking existing posts on the map and agreeing to them as the AGPL. This, he argues, is the first step, which could then be followed by an LoC extension and demarcation process. Only then could any kind of troop withdrawals be discussed, considering that access to the Saltoro Ridge is much easier from the Pakistan-controlled western slopes.[33]

Brigadier Javed Hassan, a commando from the Pakistan Army's SSG, argues that 'the only way out of this morass is to demilitarize this area with the UN acting as the guarantor'.[34] This proposition irks the Indian side, as they deem it a bilateral dispute with no scope whatsoever for any kind of international mediation. The broad consensus in India is that unless there are dramatic concessions from Pakistan and reasonable guarantees from China, it is unlikely that the current Indian government led by Narendra Modi will yield any space on the desolate battleground. Giving teeth to India's insistence on holding on to the Saltoro Ridge is the hectic PLA construction activity in the Shaksgam Valley that abuts the glacier. The area was ceded to China by Pakistan in 1963.[35] Though the proposed road does not lead towards the Saltoro Ridge or the Siachen Glacier, it is provocative action as it would run through disputed territory. However, the sheer absurdity of the conflict demands a resolution and a closing argument.

Nanavatty writes in his notes that 'the conflict is essentially over preserving territorial integrity and upholding national military pride. It is an irrational conflict in subhuman conditions with significant costs and little prospect of military solution. Its perpetuation does no credit to political and military leadership at the highest levels in both countries.' He goes on to suggest that 'India's approach to a final settlement should be based on demilitarization of a limited, well-defined and mutually agreed area following a political agreement. There should be a lasting ceasefire, delimiting, demarcation, disengagement, redeployment, verification and joint monitoring and administration. The bottom line is that peaceful resolution of India–Pakistan disputes is only possible when the two countries cease to view each other as military adversaries.'[36]

In contrast, an intransigent and jingoistic Pakistani perspective is offered by Omer Farook Zain: 'Particularly, Indians are paying a heavy price for enjoying the beautiful landscape of Siachen. For Pakistan, Siachen glacier is worth the blood spilled over it, and to give it up would be nothing short of giving up its coat of arms.'[37] The deterioration in India–Pakistan relations in recent years – and the enhanced proxy support from Pakistan to the secessionist movement in J&K – has ensured that Siachen remains unresolved despite the ceasefire. Indian and Pakistani soldiers will continue to patrol the glacier, and the best the two countries can do at this juncture is to minimize the human price they pay by ensuring that living on the glacier is made easier. This is a proposition that many who have served on the icy heights laugh at and say, 'You have to live there to realize that for those few weeks and months you have no choice but to draw on all your reserves with a constant prayer on your lips.'

9

STANDING UP TO THE DRAGON

'Operation Falcon was to occupy a forward position in the Tawang Sector to prevent intrusion, improve defensive positions and assert our claim on the McMahon Line. It increased the risk of a war with China.'[1]

– Lieutenant General J.M. Singh

Rising Tension

Lieutenant General S.H.F.J. Manekshaw moved to the Western Army Command in November 1963 as its commander-in-chief. The defence minister, Y.B. Chavan, was impressed with Manekshaw's understanding of the continued Chinese threat, and asked him to move to the eastern theatre in late 1964. Manekshaw was entrusted with the task of deterring China from opening a second front, should India and Pakistan head for another conflict. Some civilian narratives suggest that Manekshaw was moved out after troops from Western Command were deployed in Delhi to control crowds following Nehru's death, alarming some within the security establishment.[2] Had there been any truth in that theory, Indira Gandhi would surely not have chosen Manekshaw to lead the Indian Army a few years later. Manekshaw had two corps and two divisions under his command. While 4 Corps in Tezpur was entrusted with the defence of NEFA (present-day Arunachal Pradesh) and parts of Assam, 8 Mountain Division and 101 Communication Zone controlled counterinsurgency operations in Nagaland and Mizoram, and maintained vigil along the international border with East Pakistan. 33 Corps had the 17 and 27 Mountain Divisions under it to control operations in the Sikkim Sector, which included the vulnerable Chumbi Valley.

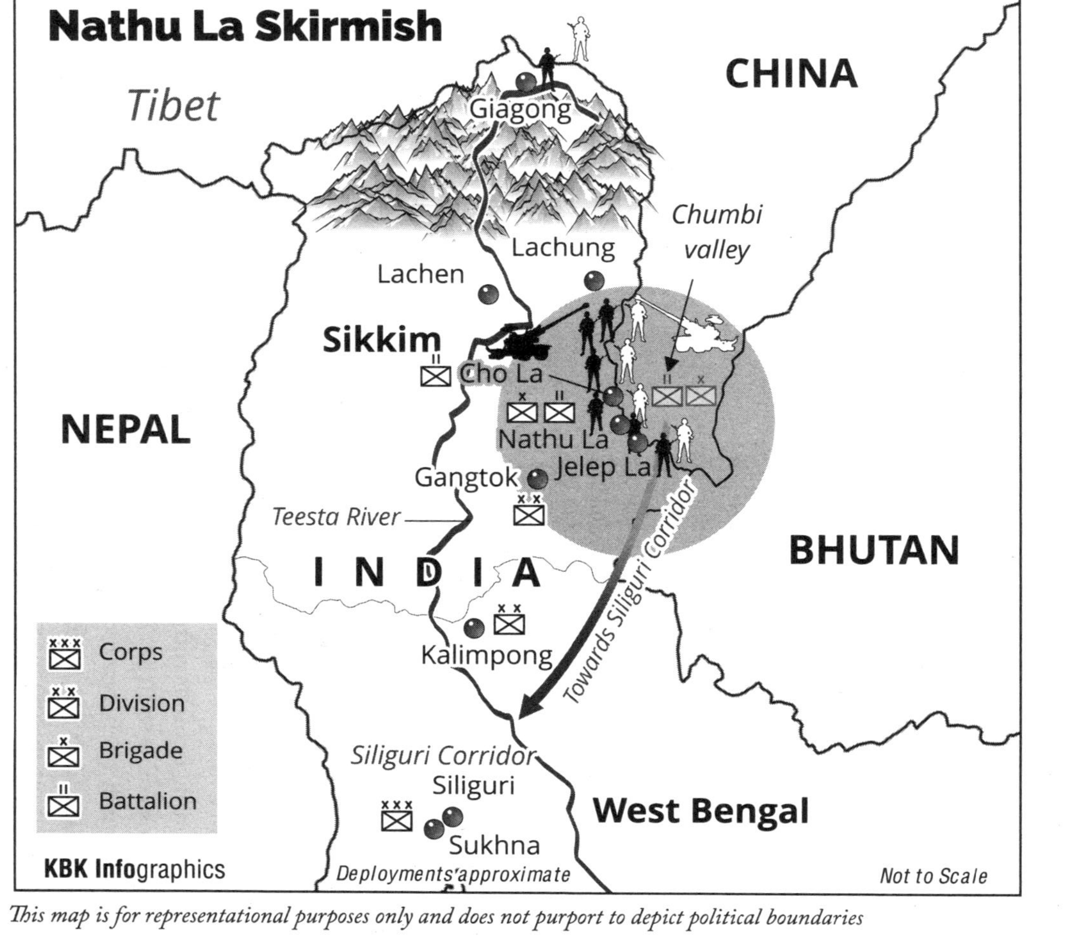

This map is for representational purposes only and does not purport to depict political boundaries

Prior to the outbreak of the India-Pakistan conflict of 1965, Lieutenant General Bewoor was in command of the corps, while Major Generals Sagat Singh and Harcharan Singh were in command of the 17 and 27 Mountain Divisions respectively. It was Manekshaw who assessed that a swift Chinese operation through the Chumbi Valley had the potential to sever communications between eastern India and the rest of the country. Following demands by the Chinese in 1965 that India vacate Nathu La and Jelep La and other passes on the Sikkim–Tibet border, the Indian Army increased vigil along the LAC. Largely unknown and unchronicled, and subsumed by the unfolding crisis on the western front that led to the India-Pakistan war of 1965, sustained pressure on the Indian defences forced 27 Mountain Division to vacate Jelep La and withdraw some distance south of the watershed.

Sagat, however, refused to vacate Nathu La and comply with his corps commander's operational strategy of fighting a defensive battle along a line south of the watershed. This surprised the PLA, which had by then amassed forces along the LAC in Sikkim, and forced it to desist from attempting a crack at the Indian defences along the LAC. A few skirmishes and firefights did take place between September and December 1965, but Sagat had planted a seed of doubt in the PLA's mind about the firmness of India's defensive resolve.[3]

Nathu La Skirmish

In September 1967, clashes between the PLA and the Indian Army across two high-altitude passes in Sikkim – Nathu La and Cho La (15,000 feet) – left hundreds of dead on both sides. It was the first time since the 1962 war that the two nations had exchanged artillery fire. It remains the most recent exchange of fire in what has turned out to be an intriguing military stand-off between the two large neighbours. There has been continued hostility and recurring face-offs without bloodshed across what is probably among the most inhospitable stretches of frontiers on this planet. It was a peculiar calibration of conflict between two rising powers.

The likely trigger for the Nathu La and Cho La clashes was the political situation in Sikkim at the time. The state visit of the Chogyal and his American wife to India in September 1967 led the Chinese to believe that the unpopular monarch had decided to cosy up to the Indians in an effort to consolidate his position in return for abdicating more powers to the Indian state.[4] Due to Chinese ambiguity and the lack of any official accounts, it is still difficult to ascertain if the skirmishes took place because two aggressive local commanders were responding to an evolving tactical situation on ground. Or

Prime Minister Indira Gandhi with troops in Jammu and Kashmir close to the Line of Control in the 1970s

Admiral Sergey Gorshkov with Air Chief Marshal P.C. Lal, Defence Minister Jagjivan Ram and naval chief Admiral S.M. Nanda

Wing Commander Dilbagh Singh, commanding officer, 28 Squadron, explaining the cockpit layout of the initial lot of MiG-21s, called the Type-74, to Defence Minister Y.B. Chavan at air force station Adampur in January 1964

Chavan being introduced to the initial lot of pilots kitted in their pressure suits

PM Indira Gandhi at the commissioning ceremony of INS *Nilgiri* in June 1972

A broadside view of the *Nilgiri* on her first sailing

Five of the seven variants of the MiG-21 flown by the Indian Air Force over the years in formation

The Bofors Gun: 155mm Field Howitzer (FH) 77B during induction training at field firing ranges

Indian troops in Nagaland cleaning their weapons in the 1960s

Lieutenant M.A. Zaki after a twenty-one-day pursuit of Naga rebels in 1957

Naga insurgents undergoing training in southern China, led by Thuingaleng Muivah (bottom left)

Publicity and propaganda photograph of Chairman Mao recovered from captured Naga rebels

Flying out captured Mizo insurgents for interrogation in 1967

Joint operations in Mizoram: Flight Lieutenant M.D. Aiyanna and P/O D.P. Gadkari of 110 Helicopter Unit (Mi-4) with army colleagues

IAF Hunter Squadron (17 Squadron) that took part in operations against the Mizo National Front. Flight Lieutenant (later Air Marshal) Teshter Master is seated second from left

Indian Army helping Mizo villagers relocate during Operation Security in 1967

A cheerful group of Mizo children on their way to school in 1967

OPERATION BLUE STAR

Jarnail Singh Bhindranwale's fighters monitoring the Indian Army build-up from the towers on the periphery of the Golden Temple complex

Major General K.S. Brar (right) briefing army chief General Arun Vaidya (centre) and Lieutenant General K. Sundarji (left) inside the temple complex after the operation

Captain Devender Kumar of 7 GUARDS at his post on the Northern Glacier in 1988

A breathtaking view from Captain Devender Kumar's post

Enjoying a photo moment during a card session at 19,000 feet

Squadron Leader Rohit Rai of 114 Helicopter Unit seeing off Air Chief Marshal L.M. Katre at Thoise airfield after the latter's visit to Siachen in September 1984

Wing Commander Manmohan Bahadur, commanding officer of 114 Helicopter Unit, preparing to carry an underslung snow scooter from the lower heights to the higher posts of Amar and Sonam

The IAF's Cheetah helicopter on a supply mission at a Schilka air defence gun position on the glacier

Training at the Siachen Battle School at Base Camp

Brigadier Rostum Nanavatty (centre) briefing Lieutenant General M.A. Zaki, the corps commander of 15 Corps, at Bilafond La

Nanavatty with his divisional commander, Major General V.K. Raghavan, at Base Camp. The wild rose bushes are what give the glacier its name

Nanavatty with his troops at Gyong La

Troops at the Siachen Battle School at Bara Khana (a community meal) on the completion of their training

MiG-29s on a routine Combat Air Patrol mission over Siachen

Light-weight bridges for crevasse crossings of snow scooters

A page from Group Captain Harpal 'Harry' Ahluwalia's (commanding officer, 129 Helicopter Unit of Mi-17s) logbook of 21-23 April 1988. Notice that he flew thirteen sorties on 22 April

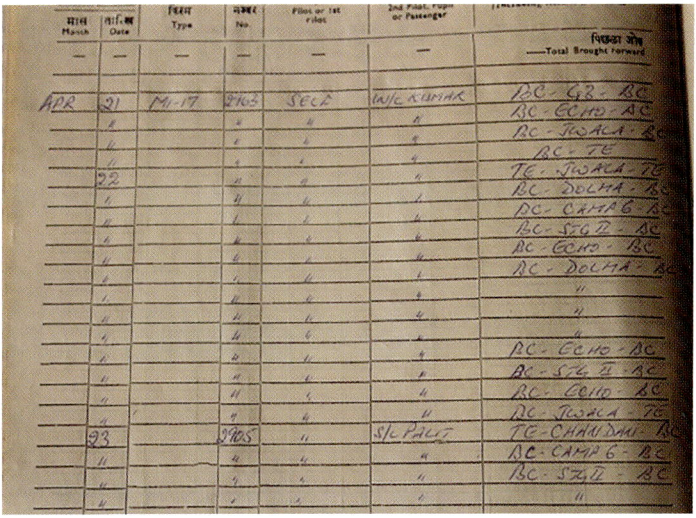

माह Month	तारीख Date	किस्म Type	नम्बर No.	Pilot or 1st Pilot	2nd Pilot, Pupil or Passenger	पिछला जोड़ —Total Brought forward
—	—	—	—	—	—	
APR	21	Mi-17	2963	SELF	W/C KUMAR	BC - G3 - BC
	"		"	"	"	BC - ECHO - AC
	"		"	"	"	BC - JWALA - BC
	"		"	"	"	BC - TE
	22		"	"	"	TE - JWALA - TE
	"		"	"	"	BC - DOLMA - BC
	"		"	"	"	BC - CAMP 6 - BC
	"		"	"	"	BC - STG II - BC
	"		"	"	"	BC - ECHO - BC
	"		"	"	"	BC - DOLMA - BC
	"		"	"	"	"
	"		"	"	"	"
	"		"	"	"	"
	"		"	"	"	BC - ECHO - BC
	"		"	"	"	BC - STG II - BC
	"		"	"	"	BC - ECHO - BC
	"		"	"	"	BC - JWALA - TE
	23		2905	"	S/L PALIT	TE - CHANDAN - BC
	"		"	"	"	BC - CAMP 6 - BC
	"		"	"	"	BC - STG II - BC
	"		"	"	"	"

Hazardous crevice crossings using collapsible ladders

Always on time and over target: An-32s from 48 Squadron on a dropping mission over the glacier

Indian and Chinese troops at Nathu La. Note the threatening Chinese posture

The final warning from the Chinese to stop laying the fence at Nathu La in September 1967

Major General J.M. Singh (left) with his corps commander, Lieutenant General N.S. Narahari (centre), and other officers from 5 Division at a forward post in the Tawang Sector in September 1986

J.M. Singh with Gorkha troops during one of his visits to a forward location in the Zimithang Sector

J.M. Singh flanked by Mi-8 crew from 118 Helicopter Unit

Officers and men of China's People's Liberation Army (PLA) on the lower slopes of Lungro La that was occupied speedily by the Indian Army in August 1986

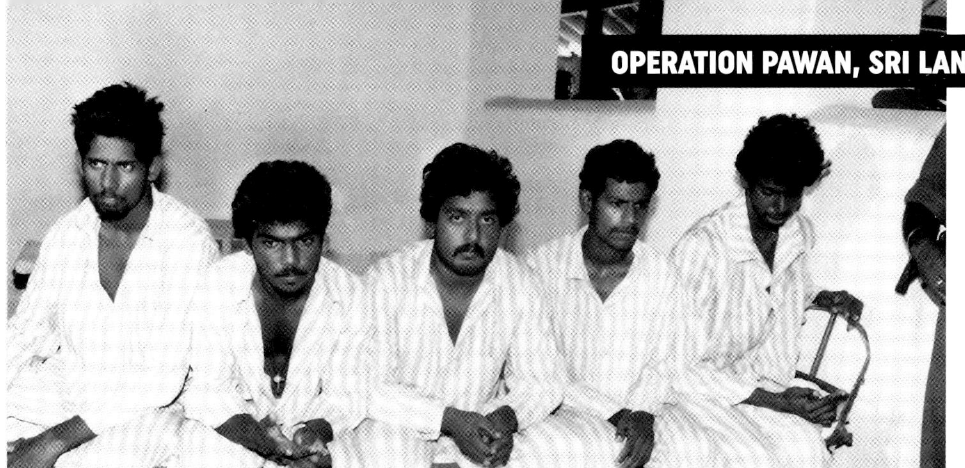

Cadres of the Liberation Tigers of Tamil Eelam (LTTE) captured by the Sri Lanka Navy and handed over to the Indian Peace Keeping Force (IPKF). They would swallow cyanide pills later when they came to know that the IPKF would hand them back to the Sri Lankan security forces

A lethal cache of weapons recovered from the LTTE

A captured LTTE flag with an intimidating caption

A routine vehicle search operation in Jaffna by an Indian Army patrol

High Commissioner J.N. Dixit with Lieutenant General A.S. Kalkat and troops in Jaffna

Chief of Army Staff General K. Sundarji with officers of the IPKF in Jaffna

An IAF Mi-17 offloading supplies at a divisional helipad

Flight Lieutenant A. Samtani (right) of 125 Helicopter Unit with a captured AK-47 and squadron mates at Trincomalee

Indian Marine Special Forces in their Gemini rafts on a mission off the Jaffna coast

Jointmanship around an Mi-25: Naval Lieutenants Prakash Chandavarkar and Anup Verma (in blue overalls) with IAF Flight Lieutenants A. Samtani and K.N. Rao (with belts) at Palaly

was the Chinese aggression a part of Mao's coercive signalling strategy? Inder Malhotra, one of India's most respected political commentators, thought that the Chinese might have intended to use the incident to warn Sikkim.[5]

Lieutenant General Jagjit Singh Aurora, a calm and phlegmatic soldier, had by then taken over command of 33 Corps from Bewoor, while the aggressive Sagat Singh had continued as the divisional commander of 17 Mountain Division and knew his area of operation like the back of his hand. The latter was entrusted with the defence of the Nathu La complex comprising Nathu La, Cho La and Sabu La. The entire complex was under 112 Mountain Brigade, which was commanded by an armoured corps officer, Brigadier M.M.S. Bakshi, a Maha Vir Chakra awardee from the 1965 war. Nathu La was defended by the 2nd Battalion of the Grenadiers Regiment (2 GRENADIERS) under the command of Lieutenant Colonel Rai Singh, while Cho La was held by the 7th Battalion of the 11 Gorkha Rifles (7/11 GORKHA RIFLES) and commanded by Lieutenant Colonel K.B. Joshi.[6] Across the border, opposite 17 Division, was the PLA's 11 Division. PLA intrusions increased in late July 1967, prompting the move of an additional battalion, 18th Battalion of the Rajput Regiment (18 RAJPUT), to Nathu La in August.

In an article in *Indian Defence Review*, Major General Sheru Thapliyal – then a second lieutenant – wrote that as things began to heat up around early September 1967, Bakshi decided to fence the area south from Nathu La towards Sabu La along the LAC.[7] This decision was precipitated by a series of heated exchanges between the English-speaking political commissar of the PLA and Rai. The tipping point for the crisis came on 11 September in a round of pushing and shoving in which the commissar was allegedly roughed up by Indian soldiers. The PLA quietly withdrew after the scuffle and the Indian fence-laying party of 70 Engineer Regiment continued their fencing operation along with 18 RAJPUT. Soon after, the PLA opened fire with MMGs accompanied by mortar and artillery fire, inflicting about forty casualties on the Indians. Rai was injured and two young officers were killed in action while rallying the troops. It took a while for the Indians to calibrate a suitable response. In the ensuing riposte, scores of PLA soldiers are said to have been killed by well-directed Indian artillery fire,[8] which blasted Chinese bunkers and silenced MMGs in a display of outstanding gunnery. Clearly, the PLA – which had stunned and shocked the Indian forward defensive line in all the sectors in 1962 with a professional display of gunnery – had received a taste of its own medicine.

P.K. Roy, an Indian reporter for the *Baltimore Sun*, wrote quite disparagingly about the fitness and preparedness of the PLA soldiers as compared to their

Indian adversaries. He observed that the Chinese 11 Division was stationed near Nathu La, but most of the Chinese soldiers seemed to be less acclimatized in the high altitude than the Indians. Chinese soldiers had been seen gasping while climbing.[9] The impact of good leadership, fitness and morale of the Indian troops at Nathu La was telling, as was the decision to surprise the Chinese with artillery fire.

On 12 September, an Indian overture for a ceasefire was rejected by the PLA and fierce artillery duels raged for the next two days. When the Indian Army did not back off or blink, the PLA stopped firing on 14 September and sought a flag meeting to defuse tensions. Two weeks later, in a concerted attempt to hit back after the reverse at Nathu La, the PLA attempted to overrun another Indian position at Cho La – which was the highest pass on the Sikkim-Tibet border, located at a height of over 15,000 feet. By then, the Indian Army had reinforced their defensive positions with crack paratroopers who along with the determined Gorkhas pushed the PLA 3 km back. Brigadier Vivek Sapatnekar, who commanded India's Parachute Brigade in the mid-1980s, was at Cho La as a young officer during the skirmish. He recalled that the Indian Army used its positional advantage to blunt the Chinese attack and once again effectively used mortars and field artillery.[10]

In a telling assessment of the larger strategic picture, Joseph Lelyveld – better known for his controversial biography of Mahatma Gandhi, *Great Soul* – praised India for its firm stand at Nathu La in what he described as a Himalayan street fight. He wrote in the *New York Times* that in their military and diplomatic posture, the Indians sought to reflect firmness and restraint. Emphasizing this, he wrote, 'This was not just posturing. In 1962, when they were woefully underprepared to meet the Chinese, they engaged in a good deal of braggadocio; the Chinese ruthlessly made them eat their words. This time, after five years of building up their Himalayan defences, the Indians felt no need for brave words.'[11]

India's politico-military leadership of the time demonstrated great self-assurance during the skirmishes. As the firing peaked on 14 September, Manekshaw, Aurora and Sagat Singh visited the scene of battle. This gave much cheer and confidence to the Indian troops, whose morale had remained high through the skirmish despite the loss of two officers and the wounding of a battalion commander. Prime Minister Indira Gandhi made her first major public statement about the skirmish only after the Cho La incident on October 1. In Bombay, she said that she 'hoped that it would only prove to be a local affair like the previous exchange at Nathu La'.[12] She also went ahead with her plans to visit Ceylon (now Sri Lanka) even as Defence Minister Swaran Singh, and the Chief of Army Staff, General P.P. Kumaramangalam, continued their official visits to Moscow and France respectively. Clearly, all of them had immense confidence in Manekshaw.

The Chinese threat to bring the PLA Air Force into the fray was completely discounted by India's operational planners. This was because the military airfields in Tibet could hardly support the launch and recovery of fighters and bombers that could effectively interdict Indian positions. However, Indian fighters (MiG-21s and Gnats) and fighter-bombers (Hunters) could easily operate from the Bagdogra airfield in West Bengal. They could reach their target areas around Nathu La within thirteen to fifteen minutes to provide air defence or attack PLA positions. An IAF Canberra photo reconnaissance aircraft from 106 Squadron in Agra did carry out a few missions over the area to ascertain the Chinese build-up. Though there is no archival record either in the PLA Air Force or the IAF to suggest that any kind of aerial flare-up was expected, IAF fighter squadrons were ready to intervene in case the need arose.

Notwithstanding the robust response, an all-round analysis of India's defence preparedness was undertaken within its military and strategic establishment. There was a realization that India would never be able to confront the Chinese on equal terms if it had to defend a border with too many forward positions. From the divisional headquarters at Gangtok (6,000 feet), it is an arduous drive of several hours followed by a climb of 8,000 feet to reach Nathu La. The PLA faced no such challenges, as its divisional HQ opposite Nathu La was located on a plateau and connected to forward locations by a network of steel-top roads. However, the Indian positions in the Nathu La Sector were well fortified and had adequate fire support; they were also logistically well stocked, and proved to be more than just a numerical match for the PLA forces. Indian commanders realized that the PLA did not have the requisite force ratio of 5:1 required to overrun the strong Indian positions. Leadership at all levels was resolute and officers at the battalion level led from the front. A less explored consequence of the showdown is the analysis from Washington, DC, that China's belligerence may have prompted a cornered India to accelerate its attempts to acquire nuclear weapons capability.[13]

Joint Response at Sumdorong Chu

Almost two decades after the Nathu La incident, China was irked by the certainty that the Union Territory of Arunachal Pradesh – which they claimed large portions of – would become the twenty-fourth state of the Indian Union. Chinese troops encroached into Indian territory in Arunachal Pradesh in late

June 1986 and set up a camp.[14] The area of dispute was a grazing ground north of Tawang at Wangdung on the Sumdorong Chu rivulet. It was a remote and inaccessible valley not far from the infamous Namka Chu of 1962.[15] Wangdung was literally a 'no-go' area till then for the Indian Army, as patrolling the area[16] constituted a provocation.

Angered that Wangdung was being used by Indians during the summer, the Chinese rapidly built a post in the area and, in a first, used helicopters to stock the post. India's response was swift and deliberate under the leadership of its army chief, General Sundarji, and two exceptional field commanders – Lieutenant General N.S. Narahari, the corps commander of 4 Corps, and Major General J.M. 'Jimmy' Singh, the divisional commander of 5 Mountain Division at Tenga. Jimmy Singh's recollections of the face-off are remarkable.[17] He clearly remembers that the Limits of Patrolling (LOP) laid down for the Indian Army in the early 1980s stopped short of all disputed areas. He also recollects the winds of change that had started blowing in 1982, when Indira Gandhi gave the go-ahead for Operation Faulad in the Tawang Sector. The operation was a modestly calibrated move to build adequate infrastructure to support a limited forward posture by the Indian Army against Chinese attempts to make inroads into disputed areas along the LAC.

5 Mountain Division was still defending the main ingress route that the PLA had employed in 1962 – from Bum La to Tawang. It also held the Tawang Garrison with one mountain brigade. Construction of permanent defences for the deployment of the remaining division at Tenga began in 1983. Work had continued during 1984 and 1985 and was ongoing when Jimmy Singh took over command of the division. He recalls that the Sumdorong Chu Valley, which lay forward of the LOP, was 'disputed' at the time and was uninhabited. However, Chinese patrols had been visiting Wangdung every year since 1980, as yak grazers from both sides used several grazing grounds in the valley. In 1982, after a Survey of India team confirmed that Wangdung was on the Indian side of the LAC, a seasonal Subsidiary Intelligence Bureau (SIB) was set up there in the summer of 1984 to watch, inform and run a covert trans-border network of sources. In the summer of 1986, the SIB's role in alerting the Indian Army to increased Chinese presence would prove timely and critical.

Proactive Defence of Tawang

Jimmy Singh spent the first two months of his command walking the entire divisional sector, as there were no roads beyond Tawang except for an operational track to Bum La. He immediately realized that his defences were weak, and vulnerable to being overcome by Chinese forces. Jimmy's first presentation to General Narahari after the latter took over 4 Corps focused on the need to adopt a genuine divisional forward position in the Tawang Sector. It was critical to moving one of the brigades that was then occupying defences on the western flank of Tawang northwards to the Hathung La–Kyhpo Ridge astride the Zimthang Valley. He reckoned the move would give depth to the Tawang Garrison. Such a move was possible only with secure logistics lines, artillery support, adequate air mobility and assurance of close air support. While Narahari agreed to the proposal, the Eastern Army Command and Army HQ were tentative about this forward posture.

Irritated by the earlier presence of the SIB, the Chinese increased their patrols in May-June 1986. They commenced some track-building activity in the Sumdorong Chu Valley before the seasonal SIB post was set up. Not wanting to unnecessarily provoke the Chinese, the SIB – who were not under Jimmy's command – did not revive their Wangdung Post in 1986. Alerted by some local grazers and the SIB, the Indian Army also discovered tell-tale signs of Chinese patrolling around Lungro La, a pass which offered access into the Sumdorong Chu Valley from the Indian side. This was alarming as Lungro La offered ingress routes that could threaten Tawang's defences from the north-west, an area that was not defended as it was beyond the LOP. The saving grace was that Khypo – a high feature which overlooked Lungro La – was defended by the Assam Rifles. Wangdung lay right at the bottom of a steep approach to the Sumdorong Chu Valley and would be tactically indefensible if the surrounding slopes were held by the Chinese.

On 23 June, when the Indian Army had still not moved forward, the SIB reported that the Chinese were in the process of establishing a large camp at Wangdung. Though the information was unverified, Jimmy immediately ordered the occupation of Lungro La by a protective patrol. He gave the patrol commander discretion to open fire with small arms if the Chinese approached the pass. He also ordered the deployment of 81mm infantry mortars to provide fire support. Though he readied one infantry battalion to move to Lungro La – which was 15 km from the nearest roadhead – a track to facilitate the deployment of field artillery guns still needed to be laid. Work commenced in early July without the approval of the command headquarters in Kolkata (then Calcutta). Infantrymen doubled up as porters and mule convoys were used for ferrying building materials. An army officer was embedded with the Assam Rifles at Khypo to act as the division's forward intelligence input.

As anticipated, a Chinese patrol soon came up to Lungro La. They retreated when challenged by the Indian troops deployed there.

In August 1986, the surveillance officer at Khypo reported a stream of Chinese helicopters flying into Wangdung despite inclement weather. Jimmy was not aware of the existence of a helipad at Wangdung, and after grilling the officer and other witnesses on the phone, he accepted the information as verified. As his corps commander, General Narahari, was on leave and everyone up the chain of command was dithering on the immediate action to be taken, Jimmy ordered an acclimatized infantry company to reinforce Lungro La supported by fighting porters and mules. They were deployed within twelve hours.

Jimmy assumed responsibility for deploying troops across the LOP (called 'Laxman Rekha' by the troops) because his operational orders directed that he defend Indian territory and Tawang. He says that he was convinced that he would be failing in his task if he did not take timely action to prevent the Chinese from occupying the tactical ground that extended from Lungro La to Khypo – even if it meant marginally transgressing the LOP. 'History was staring me in the face,' he says, 'and I had to cater for a worst-case scenario that could lead again to the capture of Tawang.'[18] Narahari's operational orientation had the hallmark of his engineering expertise, and this was leveraged fully by Jimmy. This ensured that within three months a 13-km-long class 9 operational track[19] to the base of Lungro La was complete. Available engineering expertise and explosives were used to construct tracks, with the manual work being done by the infantry. A battery of 105mm IFGs was also deployed.

Instead of commending the initiative shown by their field commanders, the reaction from higher authorities was not encouraging. Narahari and Jimmy were advised not to provoke the Chinese, cross the LAC or open fire. The existing orders authorized the divisional commander only the use of small arms, machine guns and infantry mortars, while the corps commander had the authority to use artillery. This mandate remained unchanged despite the gravity of the situation. In spite of the operational diffidence displayed by higher formations, Jimmy wanted to firm up his operational strategy before the winter set in and visited the entire deployment along with Narahari before the snow came in. Narahari then sent a personal message to Sundarji, who visited Tawang in the first week of October for a briefing and operational discussion.

Jimmy commenced the most important briefing of his career by emphasizing that despite Operation Faulad, only one of his three mountain brigades was garrisoned at Tawang and another battalion covered the Bum

La Axis. The battalion was modestly supported by short-range artillery guns, a company of engineers and signal and logistics components. With forward divisional defences coming up at a very slow pace, the rest of the division was at Tenga. The existing operational philosophy was to have a first line of robust defence along the Sela Ridge, well to the south of Tawang. He then argued that he may not be able to defend Tawang with the existing positions.

Sundarji responded by declaring, 'Then I will sack you.' Narahari requested Sundarji to hear Jimmy out, who then outlined the aims of the division: to prevent intrusion, improve defences in case of a full-scale war and assert India's claim along the McMahon Line. Sundarji said, 'You are the divisional commander. Who is stopping you? Why don't you go forward?' Jimmy replied, 'I do not have any roads. I would require more than 1,200 mules just to maintain the force level, as also longer-range artillery to support the Zimithang Sector. I will not deploy troops in a forward position unless I can provide them with artillery support.' Narahari added that it would also take a long time to build up, to which Sundarji responded, 'Why are we talking about mules in this era? Let's talk about helicopters.'[20]

They discussed heli-lifting guns, ammunition, supplies and water, and Sundarji reassured Jimmy that the newly inducted Mi-17s had just arrived in India and would be made available. All issues raised and resources sought by Narahari and Jimmy were approved by the chief, including a fourth mountain brigade, additional artillery guns, close air support, air defence guns and additional signal resources for command and control. Also approved was the quick conversion of the first 155mm Bofors medium regiment, which was then allotted to 5 Division.

Soon after, Air Chief Marshal Denis La Fontaine, the Chief of Air Staff, visited Tawang. La Fontaine was pleased to see that Jimmy had initiated work to build an aviation fuel supply chain and the requisite infrastructure for helicopter operations. Ordering the immediate deployment of forward air controllers (FACs),[21] La Fontaine assured Narahari and Jimmy of logistics and close air support. Jimmy was told that six Mi-8s and Mi-17s would be arriving the following day; he had to request the IAF to delay this by a week as he had to build up refuelling stocks and get the forward maintenance base (FMB) organized.

General V.N. Sharma, who took over as the army chief from Sundarji, was at that time the commandant of the College of Combat in Mhow. He recollects flying down to the area and reconnoitring it as a precursor to an exercise that he was planning at Mhow. Clearly supportive of the initiative taken by Jimmy and Narahari, he advised them to hold firm. Little did he know that he would soon come in as the army commander of Eastern Command and oversee the final phase of the crisis.[22]

The Falcon Takes Off

A tough but doable strategy of proactive deterrence was behind Operation Falcon. This strategy essentially involved the adequate deployment of infantry and firepower based on a minimum force level. Infantry deployment had to be accompanied by a rapid logistics build-up of artillery, ammunition, mines, supplies, water and stores to build defences. The construction of helipads, and mule and foot tracks along with extensive landline communications were important to ensure that forces did not get cut off and isolated. The robust and responsive organization headed by Jimmy's deputy had representatives from all services – the air maintenance cell, artillery, engineers, signals, and transport companies. Operation Falcon commenced on 8 October 1986 with the occupation of Lungro La by an infantry battalion. This was followed by the integration of the Khypo defences with the Lungro La defences and their extension down the slopes and spurs leading to Wangdung. On 31 October, the Chinese reacted by attempting to establish posts on the lower slopes overlooking their camp at Wangdung, moving up the slopes towards Lungro La. On 8 November, the Indians opened a burst of dissuasive fire with small arms on Chinese troops creeping up the slopes. This compelled the Chinese to remain on the lower slopes.

Jimmy then ordered the brigade commander to aggressively patrol and establish defended localities leaning on the Chinese posts. Despite a tentative clearance from Sundarji, there still was scepticism in the army and command headquarters about this aggressive posturing. Added to that was immense pressure from the China Study Group – supported by the Ministry of External Affairs – that was attempting to push détente with the Chinese. The Chinese made a final attempt in November to occupy an unnamed rocky feature that dominated Lungro La. A young Indian officer with a platoon pre-empted the Chinese with a daring display of rock climbing and occupied this feature. Thereafter the Chinese remained pinned to the bottom of the Sumdorong Chu Valley.

Not satisfied with occupying the Lungro La–Khypo Ridge, Jimmy shifted his attention to the Zimithang Sector. He had another battalion occupy the Hathung La Ridge that overlooks the Namka Chu Valley, where Indian posts had been destroyed by the Chinese in 1962. This was followed by aggressive patrolling of the Namka Chu Valley and the blocking of the southern

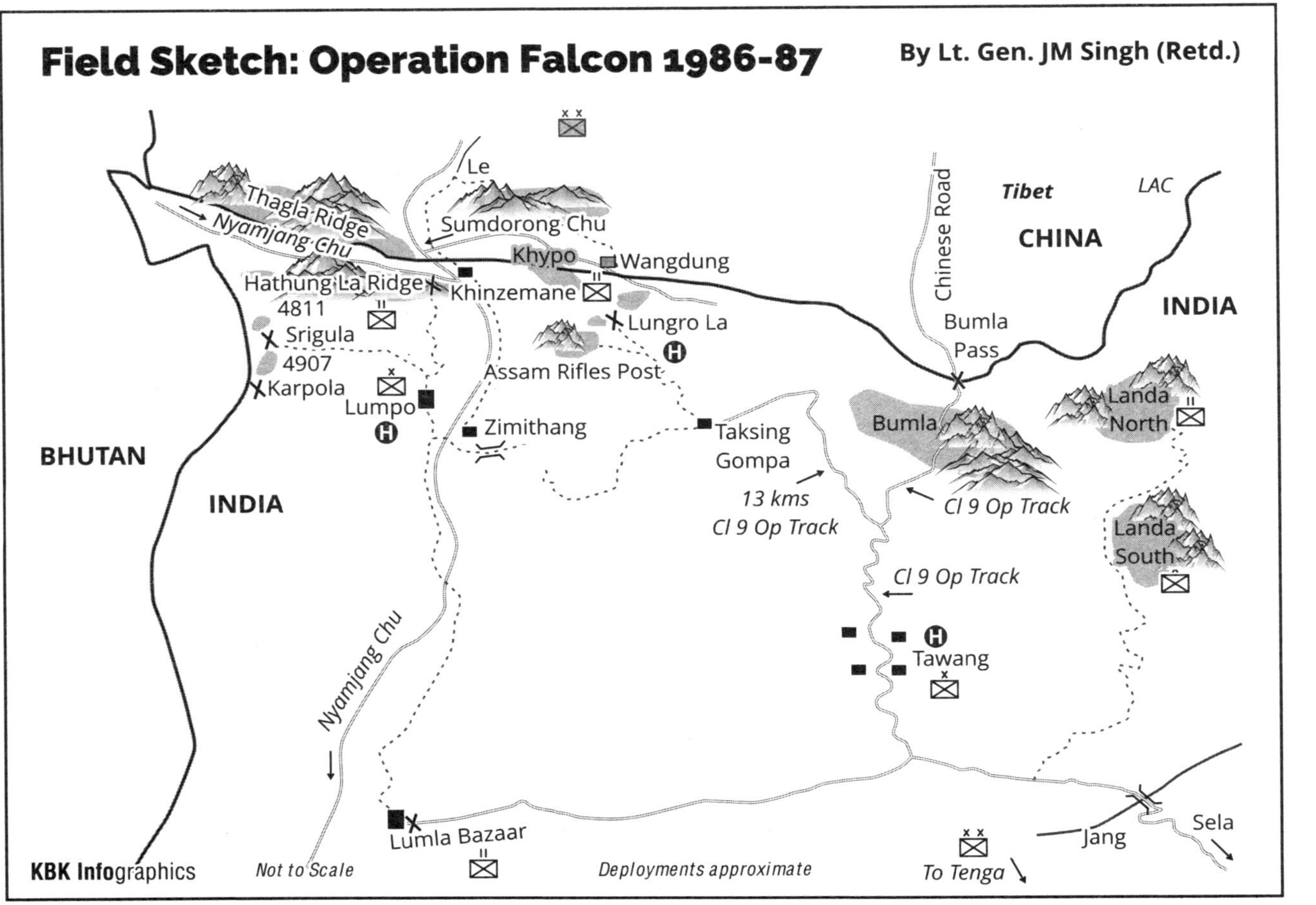

This map is for representational purposes only and does not purport to depict political boundaries

approaches by another infantry battalion. All forward deployments in the area were carried out on foot on a man-pack basis, with Mi-17 helipads constructed within twenty-four hours to enable air-landed build-up. Maintenance by paradrops and free-drops from helicopters was kept as a standby option. The Mi-8s and Mi-17s landed on the quickly built helipads made of corrugated galvanized iron sheets. Mule tracks were then developed to ensure routine maintenance and water supply, which freed up the helicopters for more important tasks such as the moving of dismantled artillery guns, mortars and ammunition stocks.

Lumpo was developed as an aerial hub with a main helipad that could take the giant Mi-26 helicopter and a large drop zone for An-32 drops. Later, another battalion was tasked to cover the western approaches to Tawang. This was a most difficult and daring operation carried out in November to occupy features Point 4811 and Point 4907 (about 16,000 feet). It was to block approaches from the west through Sirgu La, Gorgyi La and Karpo La, which were high passes used by yak graziers. This high ridge provided direct observation over the Lumpo helipad, the drop zone, gun areas, brigade HQ and the Indian Army's maintenance area. It could enable the Chinese to outflank the Hathung La defences and disrupt the rear areas. The infantry battalion that had been deployed to protect Lumpo cut its way through snow and ice to occupy Point 4907 and Point 4811, and even built small helipads close to the heights.

On Jimmy's request, the Rimpoche (chief priest) of the Tawang Monastery directed every family in the Tawang area to send three members to build the maintenance lifeline. The sturdy Monpas (local inhabitants) ferried loads for more than a month to Point 4907, surviving the prolonged exposure to harsh snow and ice conditions by spending the long evening hours praying in the local gompa. They lived and worked on faith, refusing Jimmy's offer of high-altitude clothing and snow boots as they felt it would deprive fighting troops of their protective gear. They were the unsung heroes of Operation Falcon and had to be persuaded by Jimmy to accept payments for their services once the crisis blew over.

By the onset of winter, 77 Mountain Brigade was entrenched in the Zimithang Sector. They were on the heights, the slopes and in some valleys, ready to take on whatever the Chinese could throw at them. Jimmy usually spent half the day visiting forward formations down to company localities. These visits provided vital inputs for decision-making, which enabled him to fine-tune the orchestration of logistics. Daily induction tables were reviewed and cross-checked with receiving formations after the last air maintenance sortie. The next day's induction table would invariably be finalized around midnight after approval from Jimmy. Last-minute changes were accommodated after speaking to the formation commanders and catering to their priorities.

Jimmy's overall assessment of the first phase of Operation Falcon is measured, and reflects a quiet sense of pride at what was accomplished. The swift induction of troops on foot followed by a rapid build-up took the Chinese by surprise and there was no reaction from them except for 'a feeble attempt at probing gaps in our defences'.[23]

Realising the IAF's Potential

The IAF's support for the operation was measured and swift. 5 Mountain Division was allotted tonnage for An-32s based at the Jorhat airbase by the HQ 4 Corps at Tezpur. All the demands for the division were met by the air maintenance unit at Jorhat – the IAF's largest transport base in the east. The An-32 was the latest medium-lift transport aircraft, designed by the Russians to cater to the IAF's requirements for air maintenance in the mountains. Mi-8 helicopters were initially rushed into the sector from three units in Assam, with some even being co-opted from the VIP squadron at Delhi to bolster the numbers.

Raju Srinivasan was a flight lieutenant posted to the 110 HU at Kumbhigram. He was among the first lot of pilots to be briefed on the ongoing operation by Narahari at the corps HQ in Tezpur. Srinivasan offers a glimpse into his experience of flying in support of Operation Falcon. 'We were tasked to carry ammunitions to the forward helipads at Hathung La, Lungro La and in the depth of the Bum La and Landa sectors,' he recalls. He adds, 'It was a melee in the valleys as helicopters from 118, 105 and 110 Helicopter Units criss-crossed in the sky. I recollect around ten Mi-8s during the peak build-up period apart from the giant Mi-26 that came in for a trial landing but was not used subsequently. We flew in field artillery to the Zimithang and Landa sectors. I was there for three weeks and it was a wonder that there were no accidents, because every Mi-8 exceeded their flying limits in some respects.'[24] While the Mi-8s operated from Tezpur and Guwahati, it was not long before the newly inducted Mi-17s joined the party as promised by Sundarji and La Fontaine. With its more powerful engine and better high-altitude capability, it was the perfect machine to operate from Tawang – where 127 Helicopter Unit maintained a regular detachment for almost a year.

Air Chief Marshal Fali Major fondly remembers those hectic times when he commanded and operationalized the first Mi-17 unit of the IAF. 'While our main task was in support of Operation Meghdoot in the Siachen Glacier, the unit was also inducted into the Tawang sector in support of Operation Falcon,' he recollects. He adds, 'This dual tasking to the unit was because of the envisaged high-altitude operations in Tawang and the Mi-8's payload restrictions at these altitudes.' They had ten brand-new Mi-17s, but only a few qualified pilots, and it was an onerous task to maintain two continuous detachments of three Mi-17s each at Thoise and Tawang. Each pilot in the unit used to average almost 100 hours a month during the initial days, switching detachments between Thoise and Tawang with a couple of days of rest and recuperation at Hindon. Fali adds, 'The good part of this deployment was that my pilots were battle-inoculated in almost warlike operations of a new type almost immediately after the induction. I was indeed very fortunate to have a fine team.'[25] Jimmy is highly appreciative of the IAF's contribution, and he says the system worked so smoothly that he never bothered to find out who controlled the air effort. As he had meticulously recorded events and stored data, he was able to provide load statistics and flow patterns of the air maintenance activity during the various phases of the operation.

During the initial induction and build-up in the 77 Mountain Brigade sector, 605 tons were lifted by mules, 1,838 tons by helicopters and 1,027 tons were dropped by An-32. In the Zimithang Sector, Lumpo was developed as the brigade maintenance area. All stores dispatched by An-32s from Jorhat and by Mi-8 and Mi-17s from Tawang were received at the drop zone or the helipad at Lumpo. Thereafter, they were sent by mules to the forward infantry battalions. Buffer stocks at both Tawang and Lumpo were maintained to cater for irregular aerial delivery and initial losses due to inaccurate drops. The losses became fewer as the crews gained experience, and the fast-track construction of storage sheds ensured logistics redundancy to cope with bad weather and the onset of winter.

Jimmy recollects that helicopter operations would start at dawn, with Mi-8s delivering both landing and drop loads of 600 kg. The Mi-17s would take on commitments at altitudes above 3.7 km, landing 200 kg and dropping 1,600 kg. Load tables for each sortie had to be carefully adjusted to create the desired mix of dropping and landing loads in keeping with priorities. Cheetahs, Mi-8s, Mi-17s and An-32s were all flying and dropping in the Zimithang Valley in the morning hours. However, the Tawang air traffic control centre managed well and there were no accidents. Jimmy recalls, 'Jointmanship was evident at each level. No mission was ever refused and risks were taken during the induction and build-up phases to land with priority loads at forward helipads hastily hewn out of the mountains. I always felt that the air force crew were a part of my division.'[26]

Contours of a Neo-Forward Posture

As Operation Falcon stabilized, 5 Mountain Division's forward position improved significantly compared to the haphazard deployment in 1962. 5 Mountain Division had three brigades deployed in 'hot war' locations ahead of Tawang by the beginning of 1987. The earlier focus of the Tawang Brigade in the Central Sector was to defend the Bum La Axis and Tawang. However, it now moved an infantry battalion forward to occupy defences at Lungro La and Khypo – overlooking Wangdung and Sumdorong Chu – to block any Chinese attempts to climb up. It had an operational class 9 track with ready defences and artillery support.

One infantry battalion held the Bum La Axis with a well-established logistics set-up that relied on a combination of vehicles and mules. Another one was deployed on the same axis to offer a layered defence. The main challenges in this sector were to cover Bum La and the new deployments overlooking Wangdung by improving the operational track and building additional feeder tracks to the Lungro La maintenance base and the main gun areas. With 120 guns with 300 rounds per gun deployed in this sector, it was an enormous task as the guns had to be stripped and loaded in vehicles. Two tractors were then employed in tandem and the guns were winched up slopes. Finally, they were put into emplacements by the soldiers.

In the flanking western sector, 77 Mountain Brigade was initially moved forward to the Hathung La Ridge and then to the critical Zimithang Valley to cover the western approaches to Tawang. It merged its defences with an Assam Rifles battalion located at Khinzemane, the last border post in the Zimithang Valley. Though the Zimithang Sector was accessible by mule track, the turnaround time was six days, making it unviable and operationally the most vulnerable to a possible Chinese incursion. The IAF together with Narahari and Jimmy put in place a template for a brigade maintained and supported by air. They built a large helipad and a drop zone at Lumpo along with additional Mi-8 and Mi-17 helipads constructed at forward locations.

The Eastern Sector under 11 Mountain Brigade still had no roads. It was served by a supply chain that relied on mule transport and good mule tracks. It was further constrained by partially ready defences constructed during Operation Faulad. The concept of logistics in this sector was to pre-dump ammunition and supplies, create buffer stocks and storage and build helipads prior to induction of troops, who walked up to the posts. Finally, the artillery guns and ammunition were partly heli-landed and partly moved on mountain artillery mules. A total of seventy-two artillery guns were deployed in this tough sector, with 300 rounds per gun.

Later, during the consolidation stage, command and control was adjusted to bring the Khypo–Lungro La area under 77 Mountain Brigade to ensure a single command over the Zimithang and Sumdorong Chu Valleys. The relieved infantry battalion was reverted to the Tawang Brigade, its parent formation.[27] When Jimmy handed over command in early 1987, the division had adequate artillery – including the newly inducted Bofors 155mm guns – to support both offensive and defensive operations. Major V.K. Ahluwalia led a battery of Bofors guns to Tawang through Misamari, Tezpur, Bomdilla and Se La to support operations that were planned in the sector. It was the first time that these heavy guns (the gun-train weighs approximately 31 tons) were moved in such a difficult mountainous terrain.[28]

The guns were installed at a place called PTSO, midway between Tawang and Bum La along the Central Axis of the sector. The excellent ranges of the gun meant it could support operations along the Western and Eastern Axes too. Considering the altitude of 11,000 feet, the rarefied atmosphere resulted in extended firing ranges of up to 35 km. The command and control of the guns necessitated a good second tier of command, with additional fire direction centres. An additional 697 km of communication cables were laid during the induction phase for this purpose. Radio communications had to be boosted for defensive fire tasks, and infantry officers were trained to fill in as additional observers to direct artillery fire from their locations at remote localities. Two Engineer regiments with machinery, infantry troops and some civilian labour worked tirelessly during the ninety-day period of induction and consolidation (September-November 1986). They constructed bunkers, gun pits, mule tracks, class 9 tracks and helipads for Mi-8, Mi-17 and Cheetah helicopters. Linking helipads with regimental aid posts enabled the speedy evacuation of critical casualties to the military hospital at Tezpur and onwards to the command hospital at Kolkata. There were only a few cold-related or altitude-related injuries per month – remarkable statistics considering there were nearly 16,000 personnel in the division.[29]

Leaders and Possibilities

After the flawed operation that was Operation Blue Star, General Sundarji seized the opportunity to support empowered subordinate commanders. Jimmy shared some of his recollections of Sundarji and Narahari. 'In many ways both the generals were alike – professional, upright, well read, knowledgeable, open to new ideas, clear thinkers with courage of conviction and great team makers,' he says. He adds, 'I first met General Sundarji when he was commanding 33 Corps and I was posted under him to command 164 Mountain Brigade in 27 Mountain Division on the Sikkim border. Always willing to question established norms, he expected a high standard of professional conduct and serious application of mind, and backed ideas and subordinates to the hilt. Witty and a good conversationalist, he loved to socialize, and was a friend when off-duty.'[30]

Though Narahari and Jimmy were contemporaries, the latter had immense respect for his corps commander. He recalls, 'Narahari and I were both commanding officers in the same division. I found him to be an unassuming and highly capable soldier who was well informed and had enquiring mind. His clear thinking, determination and courage of conviction were behind the success of Operation Falcon. He supported me throughout the operation, but never intruded into my command.'

Building on the success of the proactive defensive positions, Narahari and Jimmy also thought of a limited offensive action to evict the Chinese from Wangdung and secure the Thag La Ridge. Sundarji agreed with this plan and moved one brigade from Shillong, placing it under Jimmy's command for counterattack tasks. Jimmy recollects that he had 100 guns ready to boom in support of his initial offensive, with a total of thirty-seven fire units (222 guns) and 1,200 tons of ammunition available to him for a sustained operation. However, as the Chinese did not persist with their provocative moves, the operation was shelved. Sundarji firmly stood by Narhari and Jimmy as they promoted the concept of sustained helicopter-based maintenance in the mountains and provided enough resources for making it a success. While much was validated in defensive operations, the duo was unable to test this concept in a limited offensive as New Delhi was tentative about needlessly provoking Deng Xiaoping, who by now had emerged clearly as Mao's successor and was someone the Indian government felt they could negotiate with.

In the summer of 1987, Lieutenant General V.N. Sharma, the new Eastern Army Commander, hosted the prime minister, Rajiv Gandhi, at Tawang. The prime minister had flown in to see the situation for himself and interact with the troops. De-escalation took place a few months later after flag meetings where India demonstrated a firmness not seen earlier. Local Indian commanders laughed off threats by the Chinese that they would consider using tactical nuclear weapons if the Indians failed to pull back, telling their

Chinese counterparts that the prevailing wind pattern would take the radiation into Chinese-held areas.

The Big Picture

While it has never been confirmed whether the initial intrusions into Wangdung were with Beijing's concurrence or whether they were the handiwork of an aggressive local commander, the Chinese did not expect the resultant escalation by the Indian side. It triggered a disproportionate mobilizing response by the PLA as it rapidly moved two underprepared divisions into eastern Tibet. However, Deng Xiaoping, Mao's successor as China's paramount leader from 1978, had just started his strategy of modernizing China and did not want a flare-up with India. This was even more so as India's armed forces were bold, motivated and better trained. Deng rightly realized that the Indians would be no pushovers in a limited high-altitude engagement. He took the first opportunity to de-escalate once India demonstrated a willingness to negotiate a mutual pullback. The meeting between Deng and Rajiv Gandhi during the latter's visit to Beijing in 1988 was positive, and there appeared to be a willingness on both sides to move forward on the border issue.[31] There was clearly a newfound respect for Indian resolve and capability, and better border management followed Operation Falcon.

India seized the initiative and deployed in strength around Wangdung after correctly assessing that the PLA was not about to launch any major attack and was merely testing Indian resolve while showing solidarity with its strategic ally, Pakistan. Building on the success of Operation Falcon, Sundarji expanded the debate on how to militarily counter China by conducting Exercise Chequerboard in the Eastern Army Command with the assistance of Lieutenant General V.N. Sharma, who was now the army commander. It was essentially an operational and tactical brainstorming exercise based on an earlier exercise conducted by Sharma at the Army War College. Jimmy Singh – who had relinquished command of his division – was posted as the Chief of Staff at Eastern Command and nominated to role-play the Chinese army commander in Tibet.

The methodology and impact of the exercise was absorbed across the Indian Army's war colleges and can rightly be considered the wellspring of India's contemporary military strategy against the PLA in Tibet. Jimmy shares more about why he felt it was an opportune moment to brainstorm contingencies and possible scenarios along the LAC in the backdrop of a possible revival of a more robust forward policy.[32] He says that at that time the Chinese in Tibet were not prepared. They had observed that border defences were neglected, their units had many unwilling soldiers of Tibetan origin and logistical support was poor. Chinese troops were fed mostly on dry rations. 'In the Wangdung sector, the Chinese sentry was just a few metres away from our forward post,' he recalls. He adds, 'The smell of curries cooking in our camp drove them nuts. When no one was watching, the sentry accepted hot food offered by our troops. Finally, we had upstaged the Chinese in a sector from where we were driven out in 1962, and restored the confidence of our troops.'[33]

Ruminating on the possibility of limited and shallow offensive thrusts across roadless terrain in Tibet, Jimmy reckons that using helicopters for moving infantry, artillery guns and logistics supported by gunships and air power to gain air superiority, provide close air support, and interdiction of rail and road links in Tibet were essential to shape such an environment. 'The key to tackling the Chinese in Tibet is air power,' Jimmy argues.

The concept of a reorganized army mountain infantry division emerged from Operation Falcon.[34] Three decades later, such ideas still reverberate in debates on how to militarily manage the Dragon. The idea of a mountain strike corps and integrated battle groups in the mountains stems from Sundarji's idea of an offensive formation in the mountains. The success of Exercise Him Vijay in Arunachal Pradesh in October 2019, which was conducted to test the efficacy of Intergrated Battle Groups (IBGs), is testimony to that vision.

Operation Falcon was undoubtedly one of Sundarji's successes as the Indian army chief. It's clearly specified aims were to take a forward position in the Tawang Sector to prevent intrusion, strengthen India's defensive positions and assert India's claim on the McMahon Line. Fulfilling these aims risked provoking a war with China. Jimmy is certain that had it flared up into a localized conflict, the PLA would have received a bloody nose – if not across the entire LAC, certainly in the Tawang Sector. Rajiv Gandhi's visit was followed by continued negotiations on maintaining peace and tranquillity along the LAC through simple mechanisms like instituting a no-fly zone of 10 km for military aircraft and apprising each other of scheduled military exercises. It can be argued that the Indian Army's actions at Sumdorong Chu led to respect for the Indian military from its principal adversary. On the flip side, it shook the Chinese and precipitated a concerted military capacity building in Tibet that would leave the Indians far behind and constantly playing catch-up over the next three decades.

10

PEACEKEEPING IN SRI LANKA: WAS INDIA PREPARED?

'Tamils in Sri Lanka are a minority fighting a majority domination that is of relatively recent origin.'[1]

– CHANNA WICKREMESEKARA

AUTHOR'S NOTE

When India decided to militarily intervene in Sri Lanka, it perceived all the Sri Lankan Tamil secessionist groups as insurgent groups. However, from a Sri Lankan perspective, the Liberation Tigers of Tamil Eelam (LTTE) had clearly emerged as a terrorist group by the mid-1980s. India only politically proscribed the LTTE as a terrorist group in 1992, a year after its former prime minister, Rajiv Gandhi, was assassinated by an LTTE suicide bomber. The Indian Army, however, experienced the transformation of the group into a deadly terrorist outfit over three years of bitter fighting and several instances of brutal killing of its soldiers by the LTTE after being captured. It is in that context that the LTTE has been termed a terrorist organization across timelines in the chapter. The term insurgent describes the other groups which were involved in the secessionist struggle.[2]

SEEDS OF CONFLICT

Operation Pawan – the military intervention in Sri Lanka by the Indian Peacekeeping Force (IPKF) between August 1987 and March 1990 – marks an important moment in the ethnic conflict between the LTTE and the Sri Lankan government. It was one of the longest ethnic conflicts of contemporary times, and came to a bloody end in May 2009. The conflict started in the decades after Ceylon's (Sri Lanka from 1972 onwards) independence from British colonial rule in 1948. It was a result of Sinhala majoritarianism and the perceived and actual neglect of the aspirations of the Tamil minority. The liberation movement was mainly centred in northern and eastern Sri Lanka, comprising the Jaffna Peninsula, Killinochchi, Mannar, Vavuniya, Trincomalee and Batticaloa. The conflict was further exacerbated by the misplaced fear of the Sinhala majority that they would be overwhelmed by the minority Tamils with the overt and covert support of India.

The Sinhala majority of Sri Lanka claims its descent from King Vijaya, who is said to have fled the Indian province of Kalinga (the territory that coincides with the modern Indian state of Odisha) with hundreds of his followers and settled in the central part of the island.[3] The influx of Tamils into Sri Lanka began between the tenth and thirteenth centuries. It followed the arrival of the Chola and Pandyan rulers of southern India into areas around what is modern day Anuradhapura. The kingdom of Jaffna was carved out of these Tamil conquests. The Tamil rulers of Jaffna resisted Sinhala attempts to recover their lost territory in a series of battles over the centuries. Then from the seventeenth century onwards came the colonial settlers – Portuguese, Dutch and the British. This was followed by the East India Company in 1815.[4] Cinnamon, rubber, tea and coffee plantations sprang up in the northern and eastern parts with an accompanying inflow of cheap Tamil migrant labour from southern India, altering the demography of the island. Sri Lanka measures no more than 330 km from north to south and 218 km from east to west, and the entry of the Indian Tamils created an ethnic divide in the tiny island nation.[5] A collision between the cultures was thus inevitable.

Tamils constituted almost 30 per cent of the total population of Ceylon at independence. The initial secular character of the Ceylonese government ensured peace in the 1950s and 1960s, and Tamils held key positions in government, business and civil society. However, the emergence of the Janatha Vimukthi Peramuna (JVP) – a radical, leftist and militant political party with distinctly Sinhala characteristics – changed the political discourse.[6] In the 1950s and 1960s, the differences between the Tamil minority and the government triggered a slew of restrained, civilized and legitimate demands for greater autonomy for the Northern and Eastern Provinces. The Tamils, led by S.J.V. Chelvanayakan, repeatedly won elections in Jaffna and united the Sri Lankan Tamils and Tamils of Indian origin to democratically take on the Sinhala parties. His failure to convince Colombo to initiate reforms led to demonstrations and violent protests in Tamil-dominated areas across Sri Lanka.

The younger sections of the Tamil diaspora, led by Kandipan and Velupillai Prabhakaran, took to arms in the early 1970s. The assassination of the Tamil mayor of Jaffna in 1975 led to sporadic violence – it was symptomatic of more to come. In a prescient cable dated 23 November 1976, Donald Camp of the US embassy in Colombo wrote: 'Both the adamancy of the Sinhalese on the language issue and the poor economic and employment prospects will contribute to continued ill-feeling between the two communities and may lead to a gradual shifting of Tamil opinion toward the more extreme solution of separatism for their problems.'[7]

In 1977, security personnel burnt down the Jaffna Library along with its thousands of rare Tamil books and manuscripts, sparking a violent response from the Tamils and exacerbating matters.[8] The insurgency gradually expanded over the next few years as cadres from various Tamil organizations started attacking small Sri Lankan army camps in the Jaffna Peninsula. They progressively eroded the writ of the state and declared independence as their goal. Among the major insurgent groups were the LTTE led by Prabhakaran, Tamil Eelam Liberation Organization (TELO) led by Sri Sabaratnam, People's Liberation Organization of Tamil Eelam (PLOTE) led by Uma Maheswaran, Eelam Revolutionary Organization of Students (EROS) led by Velupillai Balakumar and Eelam People's Revolutionary Liberation Front (EPRLF) led by Padmanabha.[9]

LTTE Rises – India Gets Sucked In

By the mid-1980s, the LTTE had assumed leadership of the struggle for Tamil self-determination in Sri Lanka even though there were other groups also jostling for power and influence. The struggle flared up into a full-scale military conflict in July 1983, when the LTTE officially declared war against the Sri Lankan state by ambushing a Sri Lanka Army night patrol in the heart of Jaffna.[10] Thirteen Sri Lankan Army soldiers were mowed down in a vicious ambush by the waiting LTTE insurgents. This triggered the Sri Lankan security forces to unleash a disproportionate response against Tamils in Colombo. The widespread killings, arson and rape of innocent Tamils that followed led to the complete alienation of the Tamils. 'Black July', as this period was termed, could well be considered the beginning of the Eelam (homeland in Tamil) War 1. Eelam Wars 2, 3 and 4 would come in the bloody decades that followed, till the LTTE was finally defeated in 2009. India got drawn into the conflict because of the growing misunderstanding between New Delhi and Colombo over ways of resolving the crisis without further bloodshed. There were two main reasons for this. First, the proximity of northern Sri Lanka – comprising the Jaffna Peninsula and Mannar – to the southern Indian state of Tamil Nadu led to a continuous influx of refugees and insurgents into Tamil Nadu. This was after the Sri Lankan security forces initially unleashed violence against Tamils across the Sinhala-dominated areas of Colombo and the central highlands. The targeting of Tamils gradually expanded northwards in what many termed as 'ethnic cleansing'.

The Sri Lankan armed forces were poorly trained and equipped, and had no answers for the hit-and-run tactics of the terrorists and insurgents. However, the period between 1983 and 1986 saw them revive under Lalith Athulathmudali, the dynamic minister for national security. According to Shekhar Gupta, one of India's few journalists with a deep understanding of war and conflict and someone who reported from the conflict zone of Sri Lanka for several years, Athulathmudali was a 'rising star in Sri Lankan politics and one of the most brilliant and articulate politicians' he had ever met.[11] Under Athulathmudali's leadership, the Sri Lankans went scouting across the world for arms and equipment. They acquired assault rifles and rocket propelled guns (RPGs) from China, recoilless guns and mortars from Pakistan, light attack aircraft from Italy and Bell helicopters armed with MMGs. The navy too was reinforced with warships and Israeli patrol boats armed with powerful 20mm cannons.[12] India watched these developments with concern and was genuinely worried that Sri Lanka was preparing itself for a protracted and ruthless war against the Tamils. They received military and intelligence training from Israel, acquired sophisticated weaponry from all over the world and created a special task force[13] to counter the armed secessionist movement.

This escalated the conflict and created serious security problems for India as it grappled with the over 2,00,000 Tamils in refugee camps spread across the state of Tamil Nadu. The influx of about 10 million refugees from East Pakistan in 1971 was fresh in the minds of India's strategic planners, and New Delhi realized that it had to act before the situation got out of hand. A stable Sri Lanka has always been vital for India's maritime security around its oceanic southern flank. Any instability there without a suitable response from India would have invited the attention of regional and other global players – such as Pakistan, China and the US. This was something that India wanted to avoid at all costs. A friendly or even neutral Sri Lanka was what India was looking for. The mid-1980s saw an extremely aggressive LTTE take on the Sri Lankan armed forces with some success, creating extreme instability in the region. The likelihood of Sri Lanka approaching Pakistan, China or the US for help in containing the expanding armed secessionist movement caused some unease in India. This was the possible trigger for India to step in.

Tamil Nadu Happenings

After India's independence, the Dravida Munnetra Kazhagam (DMK) emerged as the main political party in Tamil Nadu. It was later challenged by the All India Anna Dravida Munnetra Kazhagam (AIADMK) – a breakaway faction led by the immensely popular cine star M.G. Ramachandran - which became more prominent in the 1970s. The two parties competed to be the symbol of Tamil identity. The Tamil refugee crisis and struggle for Eelam crystallized in 1983 after the first thousand refugees landed up on the shores of Tamil Nadu. It became a powerful catalyst for the revival of Tamil chauvinism, albeit in a neighbouring country. Tamil Nadu's involvement in the struggle for Eelam in the northern and eastern parts of Sri Lanka must be seen through this prism.

In three superb pieces written for the *Indian Express*, Shekhar Gupta provides a clear picture of what happened in the state of Tamil Nadu during the crucial years from 1984 to 1987.[14] The first piece – which incurred the wrath of the prime minister, Indira Gandhi – was particularly interesting. He wrote about the overt presence of insurgents from several Tamil groups in training camps across Tamil Nadu, and the involvement of the Indian intelligence agency, the Research and Analysis Wing (R&AW), in training them.[15] R&AW had successfully trained the Mukti Bahini during the 1971 war that led to the creation of Bangladesh, under the stewardship of the same prime minister. Indira Gandhi was convinced of the usefulness of covert operations as a powerful tool of statecraft. To further this strategy, plans were put in place to build up Tamil militant capability. The aim was to counter any Sri Lankan attempts to involve external powers in the region as a counterbalance to India's growing geopolitical clout.

As various outfits jostled for the leadership of the Tamil struggle, they scouted the refugee camps in India to recruit cadres. According to the *The Hindu* newspaper, Kolathur – located close to the Mettur dam in the district of Salem – was the largest training camp for the LTTE.[16] The same newspaper reported that there were several such training and refugee camps in the adjoining state of Karnataka, and even in the north Indian state of Uttar Pradesh. As stories of persecutions and killings filtered into these camps from

Sri Lanka, the number of volunteers rose dramatically. By 1985, the LTTE was ready to take on the increasingly belligerent Sri Lankan armed forces in what would be a fight to the finish.

The Prabhakaran-led terrorist outfit, the LTTE, was the pre-eminent group in the Jaffna area – and had already executed many spectacular strikes against government forces. However, India's intelligence agencies also trained and expanded other insurgent groups like EROS, TELO and PLOTE. Prabhakaran had left Sri Lanka in 1983 to orchestrate the insurgency from Tamil Nadu and spearhead its conversion into a full-blown terror campaign against all who opposed the secessionist struggle. His unyielding belief in the concept of Eelam was at odds with India's long-term objective of brokering a peace between the Tamils and the Sri Lankan government. The Indian intelligence agencies felt instead that TELO and PLOTE were the most malleable outfits to train and arm. Too arrogant to play second fiddle to his Indian trainers, Prabhakaran would never forget this slight.

M.R. Narayan Swamy – the biographer of Prabhakaran and one of the most perceptive Tamil journalists to write on the ethnic conflict in Sri Lanka – posits that the main reason for the sudden escalation of the ethnic conflict was India's covert involvement, which dramatically altered the dynamics of the separatist movement. From being a ragtag band of loosely trained rebels, the organization began to acquire a cutting-edge focus.[17] Indira Gandhi had used the issue of Tamil refugees to strengthen her political base in Tamil Nadu, which had been weakened after the 1975 Emergency. Thus, she had no choice but to align with one of the power centres in Tamil Nadu to ensure adequate numbers in Parliament. This was the main political reason for endorsing Tamil militancy and providing central assistance and training to the Sri Lankan Tamil insurgents.

Indira Gandhi was still highly suspicious and antagonistic towards the US – whose leadership she never forgave for its support of Pakistan. She viewed the US attempts to gain a foothold on the east coast of Sri Lanka – by building oil storage tanks at Trincomalee – as posing a threat to India's maritime interests. Australian maritime researcher David Brewster links India's intervention in Sri Lanka to this development. He writes: 'After 1947, India effectively withdrew to the Indian subcontinent and asserted what has been called "India's Monroe Doctrine" according to which India would not permit any intervention by any "external" power in India's immediate neighbours in South Asia and related islands. While India's attempts to exclude other powers from South Asia had only limited success, India's Monroe Doctrine was used to justify military interventions in Sri Lanka and Maldives in the 1980s.'[18] The assassination of

Indira Gandhi in October 1984 was a setback for India's strategic manoeuvring in Sri Lanka. Had she lived a while longer, an India–Sri Lanka accord might have managed to secure adequate autonomy for the Tamils, before Sri Lanka spiralled into chaos.

Cycle of Violence

Junius Jayewardene, the second longest serving head of state in Sri Lanka, is believed to have initiated the tough military response against the Tamil armed secessionist struggle. It was Jayewardene who had remarked to J.N. Dixit – India's high commissioner to Colombo during the fateful years of the IPKF operation – that had Indira Gandhi survived, she would have ensured the break-up of Sri Lanka. If not a break-up, she would have surely orchestrated something dramatic. It was common knowledge that Jayewardene disliked Indira Gandhi for several reasons – the main one being her closeness to his main political rival in Sri Lanka, Sirimavo Bandaranaike.

The escalation of violence in Sri Lanka can be attributed to the hardening stance of Jayewardene's United National Party (UNP) – which was driven by two ruthless politicians, Premadasa and Lalith Athulathmudali. The year 1984 saw the cold-blooded killing of forty Tamils in Mullaitivu by the security forces. This led to a brutal reprisal by the LTTE, who killed sixty-two Sinhala convict-settlers in two large communes in the same area. The LTTE also struck a police station at Chavakacheri on the Jaffna–Kandy highway and killed twenty-four policemen. The situation worsened in early 1985, when thirty-nine Sinhala and Tamil passengers on a Colombo-bound bus from Jaffna were targeted. This was followed by a deadly bombing at Anuradhapura, the spiritual seat of Sinhala Buddhism, in May.

The increasing violence and belligerence of the LTTE resulted in the declaration of a state of emergency in Sri Lanka in 1985. An abortive truce and lull for a few months allowed both sides to regroup for renewed conflict in 1986. Remotely directing his forces around Jaffna from Tamil Nadu, Prabhakaran proceeded to systematically eliminate rival groups like the TELO and PLOTE in the humid jungles of Jaffna, Trincomalee and other parts of the Eastern Province. By March 1986, many of these rival groups had fled to India, leaving just one group standing in the Jaffna peninsula – the LTTE. This could well be the turning point when the LTTE ceased to be an insurgent outfit and became a deadly terrorist group.

Escalating attacks against LTTE strongholds in February 1986, the Sri Lanka Air Force launched several aerial attacks on terrorist positions within the city of Jaffna with their newly acquired Machetti trainer aircraft and

Bell 212 armed helicopters.[19] Drums filled with explosives and incendiary chemicals were dropped from Avro medium-lift transport aircraft, causing much collateral damage to life and property. LTTE retaliation followed. An explosion at Colombo airport on 21 May 1986 killed sixteen, while a near-concurrent attack on a post office resulted in eleven fatalities. One of the tactics employed by the Jayewardene government to counter the rising Sri Lankan Tamil terrorist movement was the creation of buffer zones between the Northern and Eastern Provinces. This was combined with a Sinhala push northwards into the Eastern Province. This was done by clearing many villages of the ethnic Tamil population (both Sri Lankan and Indian Tamils) and replacing them with large communes of Sinhala convicts, who in turn cleared the jungles and created agricultural land. This was expected to pave the way for a gradual influx of Sinhalese in search of a meaningful livelihood, break the contiguity of the Northern and Eastern Provinces and prevent their likely merger.

It was estimated that by 1985, over 3,00,000 Sinhalese were resettled in an area of approximately 2,000 sq km which was earlier inhabited by Tamils. The settlements were called 'Oyas'. Four or five such large Oyas were created in the areas around Mullaitivu, Vavuniya and Trincomalee, displacing tens of thousands of Tamils – who were forced to relocate to other areas or flee to India. It was in Weli Oya that the Sri Lanka Army is alleged to have massacred innocent Tamils in 1984. In retaliation, the LTTE waylaid a convoy of buses on their way from Aluth Oya to Colombo on Good Friday in early 1987 and massacred over 120 people in broad daylight. This was followed by a Colombo bus station bombing that killed 110. It prompted a fierce reaction from the Sri Lankan security forces, who launched a multipronged offensive in the Jaffna Peninsula. It was quite clear that both sides were going hammer and tongs at each other, unmindful of the collateral damage they were causing.

Sensing that the time was ripe, Prabhakaran decided to assume direct military leadership of the struggle. Narayan Swamy describes Prabhakaran as a person who in five years had been transformed into 'one of the world's most dreaded guerrilla leaders and one who held the key to peace in Sri Lanka'.[20] By the time Prabhakaran would next return to India in late July 1987, he would have become the unchallenged leader of the armed struggle against the Sri Lankan state.

The Sri Lanka Army launched an offensive against Jaffna in May 1987 as part of Operation Liberation. Jaffna and its surrounding suburbs was besieged for almost two weeks, and while the LTTE took significant casualties, the operation also left hundreds of civilians dead.[21] The primary objective of the operation was to capture the thin strip of land called Vadamarachchi, which was the gateway to Jaffna. This strip connected the Elephant Pass to the Jaffna Peninsula. Located to the north-west of the strip were the two important towns of Point Pedro and Velvithurai, from where Prabhakaran hailed. Sri Lankan intelligence indicated that Prabhakaran was in the area, and it was assessed that capture of this strip would mean a significant 'first' victory for the Sri Lankan armed forces. Should this operation succeed, the second phase would be the capture of Jaffna. Vadamarachchi fell within a week, and it was clear that it was only a matter of time before the three brigades closed in on Jaffna. The battle lines were clearly drawn, and the citizens of Jaffna braced themselves for a torrid time. This was when a concerned India stepped in.

A Submariner's Tale

Not satisfied with the orchestration of covert operations on land, India's intelligence agencies commenced keeping a watch on Sri Lanka's coast. This was against the backdrop of the US having shown an interest in Trincomalee as a potential offshore base and oil farm sometime in 1986. August-September 1986 – Eastern Naval Fleet, Visakhapatnam: Commander Vinayak Agashe, who served in the Indian Navy for thirty-six years, was commanding INS *Vagli,* a Foxtrot-Class diesel-electric submarine. He received verbal sailing orders for an innocuous 'operational patrol' off the east coast of Sri Lanka between Mullaitivu and Batticaloa. He recalls that 'operational patrol' was a euphemism for clandestine gathering of technical intelligence of every kind. The *Vagli's* mission was to snoop around for a few days and to go as close inshore as possible. It was to remain submerged as usual, and operate with acute risk and caution.

Ordered to rendezvous with a fishing boat abeam the lighthouse at Madras (later Chennai), Agashe was surprised to see the director of naval operations come aboard and brief him for the mission. The *Vagli* was tasked with monitoring natural changes in oceanography, access into harbours, recording acoustic and magnetic signatures of ships of every kind, radio and radar intercepts, and infiltration or exfiltration of intelligence operatives. Code-named Operation Amethyst, the *Vagli* set sail from the port of Visakhapatnam and was escorted into the operational area by the frigate INS *Vindhyagiri.* Captained by then Captain Arun Prakash (Indian naval chief 2004-06), the *Vindhyagiri* with its onboard complement of the Chetak and Sea King helicopters was tasked to provide the *Vagli* with a protective surface umbrella. It was also to assist the *Vagli's* clearance divers with evacuation by helicopter should things go awry. Entering the operational area with silent speed at 100 metres depth, the *Vagli* took up a position at the boundary of the territorial waters before sunset. Thereafter, during the dark hours, the *Vagli* would rise to a depth of 50 metres for its foray along the coastline, as close as it could get. Since the continental shelf was steep, the depth of water shown on the navigation chart of the target area was 'Bottomless' or more than 1,000 metres.[22]

On board with Agashe were four Gemini inflatable boats with clearance divers. They were clandestinely launched in the dead of the night, close to preselected beachheads to reconnoitre the water depth on the shorelines, soil conditions, tides, presence of habitation, pickets or military patrols, obstacles inland and so on. They were launched and retrieved uneventfully for two nights and after completing its mission with complete stealth, the *Vagli* set sail. Once it was back in the open ocean and international waters away from shipping lanes, Agashe radioed the code word for successful completion of the assigned mission. The *Vagli* was escorted back into territorial waters by the *Vindhyagiri* where it surfaced and sailed the final stretch to its home base of Visakhapatnam, the HQ of the Indian Navy's Eastern Fleet. Arun Prakash recollects that it was during this operation that the *Vindhyagiri* masqueraded as a Royal Navy Leander Class frigate, HMS *Phoebe*, with which it shared a pennant number of F 42. He also recalls that when challenged at night on one occasion by a patrol boat of the Sri Lanka Navy, they managed to stay clear of any suspicion.[23]

What comes to light recently is that the mission almost ended in disaster after the submarine got caught in an underwater volcanic eruption followed by a mini tsunami. This resulted in rapid changes in seawater depth which varied from almost surfacing to plunging to depths. This triggered all possible alarms inside the *Vagli* as it breached the maximum diving depths and almost went down in a crushing descent. According to Agashe '(this) would have led to the crew achieving Nirvana at the bottom of the ocean'. It was thanks to good leadership, teamwork, following correct procedures, and luck that catastrophe was prevented. A subsequent enquiry into the incident revealed the existence of deep sea volcanic activity and unpredictable oceanographic characteristics in the area where the *Vagli* was operating. Many years later, in 2004, similar deep sea volcanic activity – not far away from Sri Lanka's east coast – was to trigger a catastrophic tsunami in the region.[24]

India Responds

It had been a tough few years for India's young prime minister, Rajiv Gandhi, as he attempted to fill the shoes of his illustrious mother. Troubled by terrorism in Punjab and preoccupied with Exercise Brasstacks on the Western Front, Operation Falcon on the Eastern Front, and the ongoing slugfest between India and Pakistan over the Siachen Glacier, Rajiv Gandhi did not have Sri Lanka on his radar. Matters came to a boil in March 1987, when India's intelligence agencies reported that their insurgent trainees were giving the Sri Lankan security forces a tough time. These agencies recommended that the time was ripe to push President Jayewardene towards a viable peace plan. A couple of months of procrastination by the Indian side was all it took to pass the initiative to the Sri Lankan security forces. They used this to plan and execute Operation Liberation (for Jaffna). After the fall of Vadamarachchi in June 1987, the Sri Lanka Army tightened its noose around Jaffna. A blockade was imposed around the peninsula in preparation for what would have been a final assault on the LTTE bastion. However, President Jayewardene baulked when it came to allocating a follow-on division, much to the disappointment of General Cyril Ranatunga, who was leading the Sri Lankan security forces during this operation.

Cyril Ranatunga was at the forefront of the military action to crush the JVP rebellion in the 1970s. In 1985, he had been pulled out of retirement by Jayewardene, promoted to the rank of lieutenant general and given the clear mandate of crushing the Sri Lankan Tamil armed secessionist movement. Three reasons prevented Jayewardene from going the full distance and making the final push into Jaffna. First was the increasing criticism from the West regarding collateral damage and ethnic cleansing by Sri Lankan troops in captured areas. The second reason was the fear of a coup by the JVP, should the troop concentration in Colombo thin out. Third, and most pervasive, was the constant pressure from India to halt the offensive. The pause after securing Elephant Pass and capturing the vital Vadamarachchi strip broke the momentum of General Ranatunga's offensive. He writes in his autobiography that had Jayewardene stood firm, Eelam War 1 would have been the first and the last war with the LTTE.[25] Rohan Gunaratna, a stridently anti-Indian Sri Lankan academic and counterterrorism expert, attributes India's intelligence agencies for beginning a secret war in Sri Lanka. By covertly training thousands of Tamil refugees and strengthening Sri Lankan Tamil terrorist and insurgent groups, he argues that India prevented 'the Sri Lankan security forces from achieving a military victory'.[26]

The pause in the Sri Lankan offensive shifted the spotlight to India. Rajiv Gandhi issued a veiled warning to Colombo to stop the offensive in Jaffna or face the consequences of an Indian military intervention. Not getting the desired response, India dispatched a flotilla of relief ships on an essentially humanitarian mission to relieve the siege of Jaffna. It was escorted by a lightly armed Indian Coast Guard ship, *Vikram*. The flotilla was intercepted by the Sri Lanka Navy on 4 June 1987 and forced to turn back. Why India did not adopt a more muscular approach is baffling, as it only indicated Indian tentativeness about undertaking intervention operations. In his book *Assignment Colombo*,[27] J.N. Dixit argues in favour of India's strategic dilly-dallying, stating that adhering to absolute principles of morality is the safest and most non-controversial stance in foreign relations. This policy, however, rarely serves any purpose in the inherently amoral nature of international relations. This is where a young and inexperienced Rajiv Gandhi floundered at critical moments in the initial days of the siege of Jaffna.

As a back-up, the IAF was concurrently asked to plan an aerial operation to drop supply and relief materials in Jaffna. There was palpable excitement at the air force stations in Agra and Gwalior – the parent bases of the An-32 and Mirage-2000 aircraft respectively. Bangalore was chosen as the launch base as there was enough support to load and launch the mission. Moreover, the distance of 425 km to Jaffna was well within the radius of action of the Mirage-2000.[28] The An-32, inducted into the IAF in 1984, is a twin-engine turboprop aircraft. It has medium-lift capability and carries around 5 tons of payload or a complement of forty paratroopers with their light equipment. It has a rear ramp that opens to facilitate equipment drops, and acts as a smooth exit point for two rows of paratroopers.

The Mirage-2000 was procured by the IAF from France in 1985. It is the first fourth-generation multirole combat aircraft acquired by the IAF and forms the vanguard of its fighter fleet. The aerial relief operation was called Operation Poomalai (garden of flowers in Tamil), and was orchestrated by Air Marshal Raghavendran, the vice chief of air staff, and Air Vice Marshal Denzil Keelor, the assistant chief of air staff. Both were veterans of the 1965 war with Pakistan. Raghavendran had commanded the famed 23 Squadron, which had led the Indian fightback after the initial PAF assault on Indian airfields. Keelor had won a Vir Chakra for the dogfight that pitted IAF Gnats against PAF Sabres over the Sialkot Sector (opposite the Indian Jammu Sector).[29] The broad plan was to send five An-32s escorted by four Mirage-2000s and drop supplies over Jaffna in broad daylight. No aerial opposition was expected from the Sri Lanka Air Force, and the Sri Lankans were warned against firing on the aircraft during their dropping run. The An-32 formation was led by Group Captain B.K. (Bunty) Sunder, one of the IAF's most accomplished transport pilots of the time, while the Mirage formation was led by Wing Commander Ajit Bhavnani, the commander of 7 Squadron, also called the Battle Axes.

The failure of the sea relief mission to break the siege of Jaffna jolted India's strategic establishment into action. This time around there was no hesitation in ordering the airdropping of supplies into Jaffna. On 4 June 1987, the aircraft proceeded serenely towards their drop zone over Jaffna and dropped their load of over 20 tons of supply material including food and rations. There were loud cheers in Jaffna as the parachutes floated down from the sky. The successful airdrop was appreciated by the world community as the action of a responsible power that was ready to assume leadership of the region. It, however, drew predictable criticism from Sri Lanka and Pakistan – particularly from the latter, as it was providing military assistance and training to the increasingly aggressive Sri Lankan armed forces.[30]

The Indo-Sri Lanka Peace Accord (ISLA)

The success of the airdrop and the temporary reining in of Prabhakaran emboldened India. Sri Lanka was put under pressure to declare a ceasefire and initiate talks with the various Tamil factions. An overconfident Rajiv Gandhi and his somewhat overbearing foreign secretary, Romesh Bhandari, were sure about stitching together a watertight peace accord. They did not feel the need to draw up contingency plans. It was quite clear that in early July 1987 Rajiv Gandhi was not thinking of any kind of large military intervention and believed that a little arm-twisting was all it would take to make both Prabhakaran and Jayewardene see reason.

At the end of the hectic negotiations, the Indian government had convinced all the Tamil insurgent groups – except the LTTE – to accept the blueprint for a just settlement. It was then that Rajiv Gandhi summoned the egoistic Prabhakaran from Jaffna to Delhi to cajole or coerce him into endorsing the peace accord. However, all who knew Prabhakaran sensed that he had no intention of honouring any commitment. On the Sri Lankan side, the prime minister, Premadasa, and the defence minister, Athulathmudali, were bitterly against calling a halt to Operation Liberation just when they were at the gates of Jaffna. They fell in line only because of the immense pressure exerted by India. However, they would continue to sabotage the accord in the years ahead.

Group Captain 'Harry' Ahluwalia was selected in July 1987 to command 129 Helicopter Unit, a new raising in Jodhpur. Re-equipped with Russian Mi-17 helicopters, though half the unit had already assembled in Jodhpur, the unit was relocated to Hindon, an airbase on the outskirts of Delhi.[31] On the morning of 22 July 1987, Ahluwalia was asked by Air Marshal Raghavendran, the vice chief of air staff, to take three helicopters and head for Sulur – the airbase close to Coimbatore in Tamil Nadu – for a secret mission. Since it was already 2 p.m. by the time Ahluwalia and his formation took off from Hindon in peak monsoon conditions, they headed for Nagpur (850 km away) for a night halt. With a little luck, the formation refuelled at Khajuraho even though the airfield there was closed. The Indian Oil representative rushed to the airfield thinking that a consignment of rum that he had requested a few days earlier had arrived.

The following day, Ahluwalia and his group reached Sulur only to be told to head for Thanjavur with no further information. To their surprise, they were met there by the Commander-in-Chief of the IAF's Southern Air Command, Air Marshal R.S. Naidu. He was accompanied by a wiry Tamil gentleman who kept fidgeting nervously. Naidu announced, 'Ahluwalia, you have to head to Jaffna immediately and get Prabhakaran and his family out of there. We only know the coordinates of some temple to the north of Jaffna and no other details – this guy is an LTTE chap and he will guide you to the proposed pickup zone.' As the formation entered the Jaffna area, Ahluwalia to his horror found that the LTTE escort was disoriented and talking in Tamil, which no one understood. Why no interpreter was made available to the crew was a mystery and reflects the completely ad hoc nature of the operation. Luckily the coordinates of the temple were right.

As they approached it, they saw a convoy of cars in a cloud of dust. Prabhakaran was there, in flesh and blood. Ahluwalia does recollect that Prabhakaran was short, menacing in his demeanour and seemed fidgety and insecure. His eyes constantly darted from side to side. Also on board were Prabhakaran's wife and two sons and a few aides and bodyguards. The return sortie to Trichy was uneventful. Prabhakaran headed to Delhi via Madras in a waiting An-32. He met Rajiv Gandhi after paying a courtesy call to his benefactor and covert supporter – M.G. Ramachandran, the chief minister of Tamil Nadu.

Having seemingly convinced Prabhakaran – who was being kept under soft detention at an undisclosed location in northern India – Rajiv Gandhi flew to Colombo. On 29 July, the Indo-Sri Lanka Peace Accord (ISLA) was signed by the Indian prime minister and Sri Lankan president, watched by J.N. Dixit.[32] Rajiv Gandhi, though, had a narrow escape when a Sri Lanka Navy sailor assaulted him the next day during a guard of honour at President's House, Colombo. Not having Prabhakaran as a signatory to the accord was a mistake – though it can be argued that neither was he the accepted leader of a united separatist movement, nor was he an elected representative of the Tamil people.

The agreement focused on the following aspects:

- Preventing any forces detrimental to India's strategic interests from acquiring bases and gaining a foothold in Sri Lanka.
- Neutralizing the forces that were gaining impetus in Tamil Nadu in the wake of the ethnic conflict.
- Withdrawal of the Sri Lankan armed forces and the LTTE to pre-1987 positions.
- Implementing and enforcing a ceasefire within twenty-four hours of signing the accord. This required the surrender of weapons by the LTTE within seventy-two hours.

Preserving the sovereignty and integrity of Sri Lanka was as essential as protecting Indian interests, and the recognition of Sri Lanka as a multi-ethnic and multilingual society was key to the ultimate success of the peace process. Within this overarching template came the complex process of ensuring that the aspirations of the Tamil minority were met within existing geographical realities, historical tensions and majoritarian tendencies of Sinhala society. The accord assumed the emergence of the Northern and Eastern Provinces as a contiguous province with reasonable autonomy that balanced Tamil aspirations with Sinhala insecurities and state sovereignty.

Planning for Operations

In May 1987, the Indian Army and the various intelligence agencies were yet to receive any directives on military operations against Sri Lankan Tamil terrorist and insurgent groups. It had been six months since a small military intelligence unit had been set up in Madras to establish a relationship with the LTTE and other Tamil insurgent groups based out of the city. The unit comprised Tamil-speaking operatives of various ranks – including a young Tamil army officer hereafter identified as 'X'. It established contact with high-profile Tamil separatist ideologues and military commanders such as Anton Balasingam and Lawrence Thilagar (LTTE), Uma Maheswaran (PLOTE), Varadaraja Perumal (EPRLF) and Balakumar (EROS).

Lieutenant General Depinder Singh, the Southern Army Commander, called for a briefing on all the insurgent and terrorist groups from the officer-in-charge of the unit.[33] This was the first detailed information on the Sri Lanka situation made available to the Indian Army's senior leadership. Soon after,

Depinder extended an invitation to all the separatist leaders to have tea with him at the officers' mess in Madras. This was accepted by all except the LTTE. This was also the first opportunity that the Indian Army had of assessing the dissonance within the separatist movement. As the LTTE did not attend, the army failed to assess its motives and was unable to advise the political leadership on the usefulness of any accord without first defanging the LTTE.

The experience of the Indian armed forces in irregular or sub-conventional warfare till then was limited to counterinsurgency operations in the north-east against Naga and Mizo insurgent groups, and semi-urban counterterrorism operations in conjunction with state police forces against terrorist groups in Punjab. This time around, India's armed forces came up against a well-armed, well-trained terrorist group which was tactically proficient in guerrilla warfare. There is no evidence to suggest that the Indian Army had studied the LTTE; nor had it war-gamed the prevailing situation in Sri Lanka on any operational templates. Beyond a few operational briefings at the military operations directorate at Army HQ and Southern Command HQ, there was little discussion on what was unfolding in Sri Lanka. According to several field commanders from the IPKF,[34] there were serious flaws in Sundarji's operational orientation in such scenarios. Known more for his contribution to manoeuvre warfare in conventional operations, Sundarji was not interested in low-intensity and sub-conventional conflict.

The successes of Exercise Brasstacks (Chapter 19) and Operation Falcon (Chapter 9) further convinced him that the days of the 'big battle' were not over. When queried by Rajiv Gandhi on the military capability of the LTTE to take on the IPKF, a dismissive Sundarji indicated that it would take the Indian Army no more than two weeks to neutralize the LTTE. As this vignette is taken from J.N. Dixit's book *Assignment Colombo*,[35] one is tempted to brush it off as an attempt by Dixit to deflect attention from his own mistakes. But several senior commanders – including Brigadier R.R. Palsokar, who commanded a brigade in the Vavuniya and Mullaitivu sectors – confirm Sundarji's inadequate awareness about the operational environment in Sri Lanka and the military potential of the LTTE.[36] In trying not to pin the blame entirely on Sundarji, there are many who argue that much of the Indian Army's senior leadership was unprepared for the 'vicious and dirty fighting' that was unfolding in Sri Lanka.[37]

General V.P. Malik, a future army chief, had a ringside view of the planning prior to Operation Pawan as part of the army's military operations directorate. He reveals that Sundarji had initially earmarked 54 Infantry Division for a conventional operation against the Sri Lanka Army, should it refuse to halt its advance on Jaffna. Preoccupied with Exercise Chequerboard when the ISLA was signed, Malik recollects rushing in to the operations room to alert Sundarji of ongoing developments and their impact on the tasking for 54 Infantry Division. Sundarji remained unperturbed and decided that 54 Division would merely change its tasking to that of a peacekeeping force.[38]

Within the Indian Army and the IAF there is no record of any discussion of joint operations in a counterinsurgency or counterterrorist environment.[39] Browsing through the operational record books and diaries of the battalions and helicopter units that were eventually inducted into the various theatres of operations, one finds no account of officers being sent for counterinsurgency training nor any discussions initiated at the unit level on the nature of the enemy or the terrain.[40] The IAF was ill-equipped to deal with insurgencies and terrorism, preoccupied as it was with large-scale cross-border operations involving hundreds of aircraft. Recently inducted attack and armed helicopters were yet to operate jointly with army formations, and casualty evacuation capabilities had not been tested since the India–China war of 1962.

Like the IAF, the Indian Navy too was surprised when it was asked to support the counterinsurgency/counterterrorism campaign. The insurgents and terrorists primarily depended on sustenance from the sea. However, the navy was under-equipped and under-trained to support the mission. The navy's first direct involvement was when INS *Vindhyagiri* – a Leander-class frigate with Captain Arun Prakash in command – was deployed off the coast of Colombo during the signing of the ISLA. Arun Prakash does not recollect much discussion on the role to be played by the Indian Navy in case the accord failed, or in the possible role of peacekeeping. Rear Admiral Kapil Gupta – the navigation officer on board the *Vindhyagiri* – recollects an earlier mission where they launched helicopters to provide cover to a team of surveyors who had been sent for a beach survey from the submarine *Vagli*. 'As is the norm for such missions, it was a dark night and a Sri Lanka Navy patrol boat came close to us,' Gupta says. He adds, 'We silently avoided it. I presume the beach survey was undertaken by the naval special forces and recovered by a submarine.'[41]

Prakash confirms that at no stage prior to Operation Pawan was there any kind of major joint planning.[42] Gupta further adds, 'We were deployed off Colombo and watched live on Sri Lankan TV as Rajiv Gandhi was attacked by a Sri Lankan sailor whilst reviewing a guard of honour at Colombo.' It was 30 July 1987 and Rajiv Gandhi was about to depart for New Delhi after signing the ISLA. 'We had a unit of the 1 PARA on board our ship. Their mission was to extricate President Jayewardene from his residence in case there was an attack on him,' he recollects.'[43]

It is amply evident that in the prelude to Operation Pawan, synergy was missing at all levels. At the strategic level, the political establishment did not find it necessary to keep the chiefs of the Indian armed forces in the loop while brainstorming the contours of the accord and its ramifications for national security. Of the three chiefs, it was only Sundarji who enjoyed the confidence of Rajiv Gandhi and Arun Singh, the influential minister of state for defence. The armed forces were on completely different pages when a military intervention was discussed in the run-up to the signing of the ISLA. They looked at Sri Lanka as an extension of their regional commands – and not as an integrated or expeditionary operation as it should have been.

The army operation was handed over to the army's Southern Command, where Depinder Singh took over as the overall force commander. A tactical headquarters was set up at Fort St George in Madras. Lieutenant General A.S. Kalkat was appointed as the commander of the IPKF, reporting to Depinder Singh and to New Delhi. Inexplicably, Kalkat too was stationed at Madras instead of directing operations from Sri Lanka. Air support was to be provided by the fledgling Southern Air Command in Trivandrum without any divestment of command and control. Air detachments at places like Palaly (Jaffna), Trincomalee and Batticaloa reported to Southern Air Command rather than a central force commander. The naval component was to be controlled by Southern Naval Command based at Cochin. During the early days of the IPKF operation, it was treated as a purely peacetime deployment. Leave rotation continued as before. Soldiers, sailors and airmen told their families that they were proceeding on temporary duty and would be back in a few weeks – possibly with a Panasonic TV or a Sony music system bought from the cheaper markets of Jaffna and Trincomalee.

Deployment of the IPKF

Major General Harkirat Singh was surprised when his Secunderabad-based 54 Infantry Division was chosen to spearhead the implementation of the ISLA.[44] 54 Infantry Division had performed well during the 1971 war with Pakistan under Major General W.A.G. Pinto,[45] and was part of one of India's two strike corps. At the time, the two divisions with active counterinsurgency experience were 8 Mountain Division and 57 Mountain Division – both were deployed in the north-east. Harkirat Singh thought that those divisions would be better suited than his 54 Infantry Division for the initial induction into Sri Lanka. However, geography and command-and-control convenience was prioritized over expertise. His division came under the army's Southern

Command for peacetime administrative purposes and thus was the easiest formation to deploy.

Harkirat says that his mandate was clear – implement the ISLA by separating the belligerents, ensure that the Sri Lankan armed forces withdraw to mutually agreed positions, supervise the laying down of arms by the various insurgent groups, clear the minefields and booby traps and create a favourable environment for the conduct of provincial elections. Sundarji told him that the army was going in as a peacekeeping force, and nowhere in this initial directive was there even an oblique reference to combat.[46] Such was the strategic hubris and overconfidence in Delhi that not one of the officers in Army HQ cautioned the chief about the necessity to be prepared for combat. Instead, the force was prepared for a UN-style intervention for peacekeeping operations.

The initial induction of the IPKF commenced by air and sea on the night of 29 July 1987.[47] The IAF placed thirty-six An-32, five An-12 and three Il-76 aircraft at the army's disposal at several airbases. Simultaneously, the Indian Navy readied a small fleet of amphibious landing craft and offshore patrol vehicles. Airfields at Madras and Hyderabad were the mounting bases for aerial induction and Vizag and Madras were the ports from which troops embarked for their sea journey. They would head to Kankesanturai (KKS) – a port on the northern tip of the Jaffna Peninsula – and Trincomalee on the east coast of Sri Lanka. The IAF had also positioned several standby aircraft at Bangalore, Hyderabad, Coimbatore and Thanjavur.[48] The Palaly airbase – located a few kilometres to the south-east of KKS – was the sole airfield on the Jaffna Peninsula, and it had been identified as an ideal location for the operational headquarters of 54 Infantry Division.

Strangely, the IPKF HQ remained at Madras, against all tenets of operational wisdom. It ought to have been relocated to Palaly when the going got tough a few weeks into the deployment. Either Depinder Singh had too much on his plate, or Army HQ had grossly underestimated the magnitude of the task. By 4 August, a depleted 54 Infantry Division – with three brigades and a little over 8,000 troops – had been inducted into the Jaffna Peninsula. It deployed across a vast area that stretched from the Jaffna Peninsula and lagoon areas to Vavuniya and Trincomalee. The distance from Jaffna to Vavuniya is about 140 km, and Trincomalee is a further 95 km east of Vavuniya across inhospitable terrain dotted by jungles and lagoons. There was a single arterial road-cum-rail link that ran from Jaffna to Anuradhapura, the largest city in the Central Province. Soon, the IPKF realized that the operational area needed to be extended southwards to Batticaloa, as that area too was becoming an LTTE bastion.

The induction of troops and their supporting logistics by sea from Madras proceeded smoothly through August 1987. A few shallow-draught inshore patrol vessels belonging to the Indian Coast Guard were placed under the Navy's control. They were used for inshore patrolling in the Palk Bay, which separated India from Sri Lanka. The Indian Coast Guard's F27 aircraft, operating from Madras, carried out air surveillance extending 100 miles seaward off the east coast of Sri Lanka. To ensure the smooth induction of forces, Indian Navy liaison teams were positioned at Trincomalee, Palaly, KKS and Karainagar to ensure the smooth induction of forces.[49] An ad hoc IAF base commander was appointed at Palaly with limited helicopter assets. 54 Division consolidated its presence by mid-August, with one undermanned brigade each at Jaffna (91 Infantry Brigade), Vavuniya (47 Infantry Brigade) and Trincomalee (76 Infantry Brigade). However, the area demanded a force that was three times as large.[50] Two more brigades were inducted into Sri Lanka over the next two months, along with some supporting tanks, armoured personnel carriers, artillery and engineers.

Deceptive Welcome

The IPKF landed in the Jaffna Peninsula to a mixed reception. Many of the early inductees into Jaffna remember that they were welcomed with placards and banners. The citizens of Jaffna had high expectations that their 'big brothers' from India would usher in peace in no time. Even the Sri Lankan security forces were cordial and received the first wave of the IPKF in the right spirit. However, the IPKF was banned from entering LTTE areas. Soon there were massive demonstrations and protests orchestrated by LTTE cadres demanding the release of their leader. There was a 'Line of Control' that ran from KKS (port) and Palaly (airfield) southwards to Jaffna town, east of which was designated as LTTE territory. The IPKF needed to find a way to penetrate LTTE areas and bring back intelligence.

The anonymous covert operative mentioned earlier – X – masqueraded as a journalist sympathetic to the LTTE cause and managed to legitimately slip behind 'enemy' lines. He successfully cleared an elaborate vetting process by multiple tiers of LTTE operatives that included the new Jaffna commander, Kumarappa. X was allowed an audience with Mahattaya, Prabhakaran's deputy. A probing Mahattaya took some convincing that X was indeed an LTTE sympathizer and that he was there to report the actual situation on the ground. Heckled by a large Tamil crowd during his escorted visit around the areas of Jaffna held by the LTTE, X was also manhandled by a group of Tamil women despite speaking fluent Tamil and commiserating with them.

He had to spend the night with the family of one of the LTTE cadres, who turned out to be wonderful hosts. Expecting to turn in early after an exhausting day, he recollects that six to eight girls in their late teens and early twenties barged into the house at night. 'They started arguing with me about the accord and how India had stabbed them by holding their leader under detention in Delhi,' X says. He added, 'After trying to make them understand the situation, I realized they were not like other normal people who had discussed the issue with me that day – they were totally brainwashed cadres of the LTTE. I promised that I would take their grievances to the right quarters.' X was dropped off the next day at the same spot, and from there he was picked up immediately, and later he briefed the army commander about his experiences.[51]

At the strategic level, the wily Prabhakaran outthought Rajiv Gandhi. He managed to return to lead his cadres days after the ISLA was signed, thereby seizing the initiative. It is believed that soon after he was convinced to back the accord and issue a statement of support, Prabhakaran was quarantined at an Indian intelligence base in western Uttar Pradesh. The plan was to allow him to return to Sri Lanka only after the Tamil rebel groups had laid down their arms and a modicum of peace had been restored. However, he is said to have convinced Rajiv Gandhi to allow him to return immediately after the accord was signed. Much to the annoyance of India's intelligence agencies, he managed to gradually establish a coercive presence in the Jaffna area.

There was intense competition between J.N. Dixit and Harkirat Singh to claim credit for whatever was unfolding in Jaffna, whether it was the laying down of arms by the Tamil insurgents, the return of the Sri Lanka Army to their barracks or the shaping of the environment to restore the political process. Much has also been written about the farcical and unnecessarily ceremonial twist given to the entire process of the surrender of arms by the LTTE and other Tamil insurgent groups. While Harkirat boasts about his helicopter visit to meet Prabhakaran at Jaffna University before the arms surrender ceremony, he conveniently avoids mentioning that Prabhakaran himself was absent from the ceremony – a fact highlighted by Narayan Swamy in his biography of Prabhakaran.[52] Instead, his deputy Yogi marked the occasion by dramatically surrendering his Mauser weapon. The reality was that the LTTE surrendered barely 10 to 15 per cent of their arsenal.

As early as 4 August, Prabhakaran delivered an inflammatory speech to a crowd of 40,000 Tamils in the presence of senior Indian military officers. He thundered, 'Let me make it clear to you beyond the shadow of a doubt that I will continue to fight for the objective of attaining Tamil Eelam ... the Liberation Tigers yearn for the motherland of Tamil Eelam. I do not think that this agreement will bring a permanent solution to the Tamil question. The time is not far off when the monster of Sinhala racism will devour this agreement.'[53] This was followed by another token arms surrender. The LTTE's regional organization was systematically restructured by sending strong lieutenants to the Trincomalee and Batticaloa areas. This was to marginalize rival groups like TELO, EPRLF and EROS before it moved to take on the might of the IPKF in early October 1987. It was clear from the start that Prabhakaran had no intention of accepting any political solution from a position of weakness. In fact, he was never interested in anything other than an Eelam state with complete political and military power in his hands.

The simmering rivalry between the LTTE and rival groups such as the EROS, EPRLF, ENDLF and PLOTE – and the disruptive role of R&AW in this rivalry – added to the uncertainty. By early 1987 the intelligence agency had also mistakenly assessed that it could marginalize him and the LTTE by training and arming rival groups independently – without keeping the Indian Army in the loop. Colonel Hariharan was the head of intelligence operations of the Indian Army in Sri Lanka from 1987 to 1990. He argues that, unlike Bangladesh – where the Indian Army had been at the forefront of training the Mukti Bahini and consequently built up a rapport with them – this time around R&AW took up military training of Tamil insurgents on its own and only sought limited assistance from the army.[54] This move backfired as Prabhakaran saw through the game plan.

Despite being isolated and ignored by R&AW in the run-up to the ISLA, Prabhakaran exploited the lack of synergy between R&AW and the Indian Army in the months following the signing of the accord. This allowed him to consolidate power across the Tamil-dominated belt from Batticaloa in the south-east to Trincomalee in the east.[55] The Indian Army had no clue about the LTTE's strategic and operational prowess, and it was left to the likes of Hariharan and his band of military intelligence operatives to put the pieces together once the IPKF arrived in Sri Lanka.[56] Hindering India's politico-diplomatic military strategy was Dixit's failure to spot the gradual strengthening of anti-Jayewardene forces led by Premadasa and Athulathmudali, and the rise of a strident anti-Tamil and anti-Indian discourse across the Sinhala-dominated areas of Sri Lanka. This led to a rise in the killings of Tamils in the areas around Trincomalee and Batticaloa where the IPKF presence was thin. Driving a wedge within the Tamil population by targeting the Muslim community also aided the Sri Lankan establishment in creating a divide among the Tamils in the Eastern Province.

The Situation Worsens

54 Infantry Division was meanwhile striving to restore normalcy in parts of the Jaffna Peninsula with an undermanned brigade. To expect the IPKF to check the rise of the LTTE and concurrently restore peace in Jaffna, Trincomalee, Vavuniya and Batticaloa with just three undermanned brigades demonstrated a complete lack of foresight and planning. Adding to the woes of the IPKF was the peacetime ethos that prevailed within the ranks of the senior leadership as well as the traditional 'turf battles' over the allocation of resources. In his book, Depinder Singh laments the lack of synergy between the overall force commander of the IPKF and Southern Air Command over allocation of transport and helicopter resources.[57] Similarly, the IAF repeatedly complained that they were kept out of the initial planning process and hence, would respond to requests for air support from the IPKF on a case-to-case basis. Air Marshal Bharat Kumar argues that Harkirat gave no importance to the air force commander at Palaly and wanted all the air assets 'under command'.[58] There was hardly a war-zone environment in the divisional headquarters at Palaly. Sit-down lunches were the norm and senior newcomers and high-profile visitors were entertained at the commander's high table, where there was hardly any operational discussion.[59]

Along with the scuttling of the election process in September, the LTTE embarked on a killing spree in Batticaloa and Trincomalee. Over a hundred cadres of the EPRLF and PLOTE were killed in a coordinated strike by Mahattaya right under the noses of the IPKF and the Sri Lankan Police. A young LTTE commander called Thileepan threatened to fast unto death until several Sri Lankan Tamil political prisoners were released. This condition was stated as a prerequisite for resumption of any political dialogue. Matters worsened after Thileepan died on 26 September.

Gunrunning across the Palk Strait was a common LTTE activity. On 3 October, during one of these missions seventeen of their men – including two top commanders, Pulendran and Kumarappa – were apprehended by the Sri Lanka Navy off the coast of Point Pedro. Shrewdly taking advantage of the existing amnesty, the LTTE demanded that the insurgents be released. Unwilling to cede to these demands and claiming that the amnesty did not extend to the waters around Sri Lanka, they were detained at the IPKF-controlled Palaly airbase before being flown to Colombo to stand trial. There were some who even believed that the capture was a result of a tip-off from Prabhakaran to test the resolve of the IPKF.[60] Dixit and the company commander of 10 PARA, Major Sheonan Singh – who was entrusted with the security of the detainees – advised Harkirat Singh that handing over the LTTE men to the Sri Lanka Army would be disastrous in the given situation. However, Harkirat decided to wait for instructions from Army HQ. New Delhi first instructed Harkirat to hand over the prisoners, and then when Dixit tried to intervene, rescinded the order. By then it was too late as the prisoners – after a scuffle with their Sri Lankan captors – had bitten into cyanide pills. Twelve of the seventeen including Pulendran and Kumarappa died despite desperate attempts by doctors to revive them.[61]

X was with a friend in the Nallur area of Jaffna when he saw the bodies of the LTTE men being taken for cremation. The ceremony was telecast live on the LTTE TV channel Nidharsanam. The event sparked off riots against Sinhala in Batticaloa and Trincomalee. The next morning was even worse. X witnessed several killings of Sinhala by burning tyres being placed around their necks. Realizing that things were getting bad, X somehow managed to get a cab to Palaly. Hardly thirty minutes later, the curtains were drawn on any hopes for peace.

Lieutenant General S. Pattabhiraman, an officer from the Corps of Engineers, was posted as a major in the Directorate of Military Operations during the planning and induction of the IPKF. He was privy to the operational culture prevalent at the time and faults the entire top army leadership for misreading the ground situation and the motivation of the LTTE. He says that both during the Thileepan incident and the subsequent handing over of the LTTE gunrunners to the Sri Lankans, Army HQ delayed advising Harkirat about the situation, without understanding its ramifications.[62] One possibility was that Prabhakaran was furious that his men were being handed over to the Sri Lanka Army, making Tamil emotions run high against the IPKF. However, it is also likely that Prabhakaran had realized that the IPKF commander was unsure and indecisive, and knew that it was time to strike.

On 7 October 1987, the LTTE carried out its first terrorist-style attack on the IPKF, capturing and killing five commandos of 10 PARA in Jaffna by placing burning rubber tyres around their necks. This gruesome act jolted the entire Indian establishment. There was an immediate flurry of visits to Sri Lanka from India – including one by Sundarji – to assess the operational preparedness of the IPKF and to reinforce it with additional brigades. Sundarji ordered Harkirat to launch operations to capture Jaffna, break the back of the LTTE and capture Prabhakaran. 'How many days to Jaffna?' Sundarji had asked, and Harkirat's response was that it would take no more than three or four days to get things under control. It was 10 October 1987 and the die was cast for a conflict that India least expected and was completely unprepared for.

11

INTO THE TIGER'S LAIR

'Absence or amorphousness of strategy in war on foreign soil is singularly unprofessional... in insurgency it is strategy which is so much more important than tactics.'[1]

– Lieutenant General S.C. Sardeshpande

Battle for Jaffna

Early October 1987 saw the decision to go on the offensive against the LTTE. 54 Infantry Division was hastily reinforced with two more undermanned brigades – 18 Infantry Brigade and 72 Infantry Brigade – within five days. This ensured that the beleaguered Major General Harkirat Singh had the forces to launch a three-pronged offensive on Jaffna. As the battle progressed and Army HQ became desperate for a quick victory, 41 Brigade and 115 Brigade were also flown in between 15 and 17 October. They went into battle with hardly any pre-induction training and education.

The LTTE defences all around Jaffna were a combination of reinforced military-style positions and positions embedded within the local population. These defences took the IPKF head-on and allowed the cadres to slip into civilian areas if needed. Dr Joanne Richards has tracked the evolution of the LTTE and reckons that it was 'arguably one of the most sophisticated non-state-armed groups ever assembled'.[2] Ironically, it was India that had played a significant role in the development of its fighting abilities. She states that between 1983 and 1987, R&AW reportedly trained 'an estimated 1,200 Tamils in the use of automatic and semi-automatic weapons, self-loading rifles and

84mm rocket launchers'. They were also trained in laying mines, map-reading, guerrilla warfare, mountaineering, demolitions and anti-tank warfare.[3]

Surprised with the casualties to his force, Harkirat pressed in his tanks and attack helicopters to break the resistance of the LTTE. Mi-25 attack helicopters were first used for close air support in the final days of the assault on Jaffna town. Two helicopters attacked LTTE positions with rocket and cannon fire at the Chavakacheri bus station, 32 km east of Jaffna. The most effective resistance faced by the Indian Army during the battle of Jaffna came from the LTTE snipers.[4] Maximum casualties were caused by the systematic detonation of pre-laid mines. Most of these mines had been laid by the LTTE under the very nose of the IPKF in the two months preceding the offensive. After over two weeks of bloody fighting, the LTTE finally abandoned Jaffna on 26 October – but not before making the IPKF pay a heavy price.

Official estimates provided by the Indian Army in December 1987 stated IPKF casualties in the Jaffna sector as 214 dead, over 800 injured and over forty missing. The LTTE were said to have lost over 800 fighters – though the number was impossible to ascertain as the LTTE never left their dead and wounded behind.[5] Around ninety militants were captured by the IPKF but over 1,500 experienced fighters managed to slip away into the jungles of Vanni, Trincomalee and Batticaloa. Shekhar Gupta and Dilip Bobb – journalists who covered the battle – provide the most accurate accounts.[6] Many of Gupta's observations were confirmed by numerous soldiers involved in the action, including the adverse impact of casualties on the morale of troops.[7] Writing about collateral damage caused during the battle, Bobb stated that the ferocity of the action meant that civilian deaths would have been impossible to avoid.[8]

Disastrous Heliborne Operation

On the night of 11 October 1987, a bold attempt was made to capture or eliminate the LTTE leadership. Para-commandos from 10 PARA and regular infantry from the 13th Battalion of the Sikh Light Infantry Regiment (13 SIKH LI) were flown into the University of Jaffna in Mi-8 medium-lift helicopters. However, the attempt was doomed from the start as the key tenets essential for the success of such an operation were cast aside.[9] Official details of the operation are still classified, but it is very possible that Depinder Singh and Kalkat got the idea for a heliborne operation after meeting Prabhakaran a couple of days before the operation commenced. To assume that Prabhakaran had not considered this vulnerability is preposterous, but to plan such a major operation within three days is even more so. It demonstrated a 'cowboy' approach that completely underestimated the enemy. The mission had been vetted and cleared by staff at various levels – including at HQ 50 (Independent) Parachute Brigade – indicating the hubris and overconfidence prevailing at every level of planning.

The plan envisaged heli-landing over 300 troops in multiple waves on the University of Jaffna sports ground. The landing site was chosen by Kalkat and Depinder. The first group of troops would ensure that the landing zone was adequately sanitized and insulated from enemy interference to facilitate further landings. The landing ground was very close to the presumed LTTE HQ at Kokuvil and chosen because it offered a high probability of hitting the LTTE's top leadership, including Prabhakaran. There was no information regarding the number of terrorists in the area nor about their weaponry. It was suicidal to expect 13 SIKH LI – inducted into Jaffna barely a day prior to the

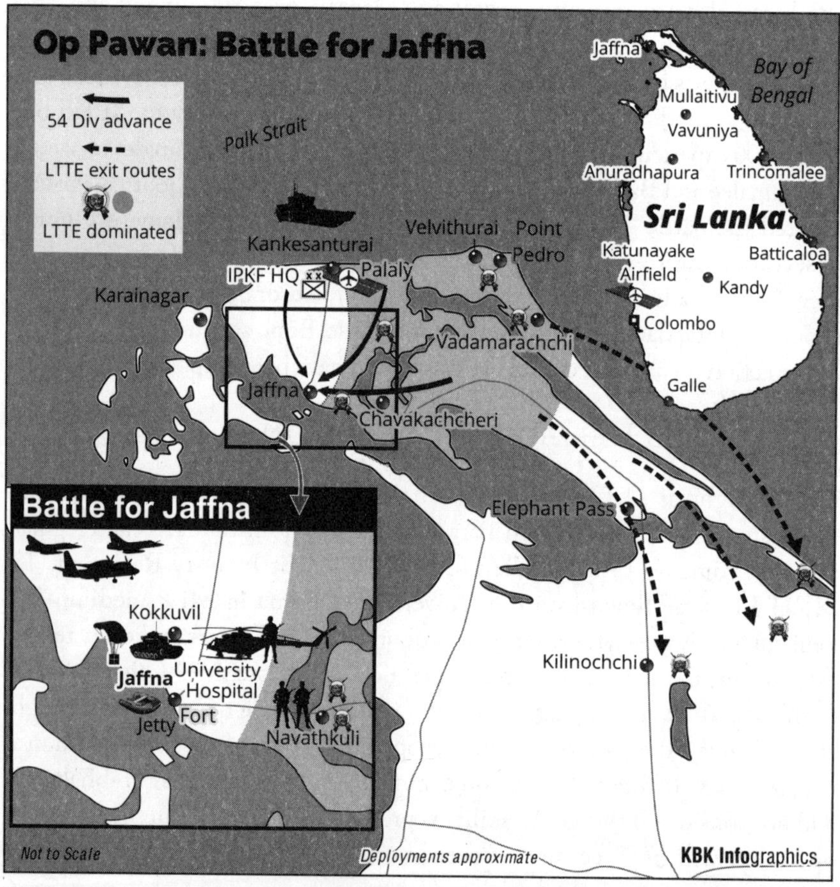

This map is for representational purposes only and does not purport to depict political boundaries

operation – to complement the paratroopers in a specialized task of hitting an urban target that they were not familiar with.

Only four IAF Mi-8s were available for the operation and there was no mock-up of the target area to brief the force upon. The experienced para-commandos were expected to get the job done while the infantry would hold off any counterattack by the LTTE. The operation was a disaster from the outset. The para-commandos found their way into the target complex under the command of Major Sheonan Singh. But instead of 200 soldiers of 13 SIKH LI, only thirty were landed. There were several reasons: the battalion arrived late at the airport; the second wave of helicopters missed the landing area; and the helicopters were severely damaged in the first two attempts. This forced the IAF to cancel further sorties.[10] At about 2 a.m. on 12 October, over a hundred para-commandos and the thirty soldiers from 13 SIKH LI were scattered around the University of Jaffna sports ground. They had lost communication with their HQ and had no means of knowing that there would be no more sorties. Come daylight, LTTE snipers picked out the infantrymen one by one. Despite a valiant fight – including close-quarter combat with bayonets – the 13 SIKH LI troops were taken down by experienced LTTE terrorists. Only one of them would survive to tell his story.

Meanwhile, Sheonan and the para-commandos had headed for the building where the LTTE leadership was holed up. Failing to identify the building, they found themselves in the streets of Kokuvil waiting for the inevitable to happen. They drew heavy fire from multiple directions and soon realized that they were hopelessly outnumbered. All they could do was fight their way into a maze of houses and streets in the hope that a large backup force would arrive. The backup force comprised two companies of the 4th Battalion of the Fifth Gorkha Rifles (4/5 GORKHA RIFLES) and tanks from 65 Armoured Regiment. Colonel Dalvir Singh, the commanding officer of 10 PARA (SF), was now the commander of the rescue force as it attempted to fight past tough LTTE defences. It was joined by soldiers of 13 SIKH LI who were not landed at the University of Jaffna the previous night. By midnight, the Gorkhas had lost three men, including their commander, in fierce fighting. When the force reached the outskirts of Kokuvil at dawn, a volley of fire at one of the tanks caused further death and injury.

By then Sheonan and his para-commandos had been fighting for over twenty-four hours and had lost six men while also causing severe attrition in the LTTE cadres. It is estimated that over fifty LTTE cadres died in the fighting. The para-commandos walked over 6 km to the Urelu temple, where they finally linked up with the rescue force. They were taken to the Palaly airfield by truck after thirty-six hours of fighting. Of almost a hundred men, they had managed to keep casualties at six killed and fourteen wounded in a professional display of courageous fighting against overwhelming odds. Though the helicopter pilots – Wing Commander Sapre, Squadron Leaders Vinay Raj and Doraiswami and Flight Lieutenant Prakash – had performed admirably in the given circumstances, an irate Harkirat accused them of landing the Sikh troops in the wrong field and exposing them to murderous fire. However, Sheonan Singh confirmed that they had done a good job and the landing was accurate. Sheonan, Dalvir, Sapre, Raj, Doraiswami and Prakash would later be awarded Vir Chakras for bravery under fire. In what was a disastrous joint operation, much was learned about the 'lungi-clad fighters' – as some Indian generals derogatorily described the LTTE terrorists. Though the LTTE had inflicted heavy losses on the IPKF, its forced withdrawal from Jaffna town into the jungles of Killinochchi, Vavuniya and Mullaitivu was a big humiliation for Prabhakaran.

Shift in the Centre of Gravity

There was much optimism in Colombo, New Delhi and the IPKF HQ after the LTTE withdrawal from Jaffna. It was widely believed that the time was ripe to push ahead with the political process. Winning the hearts and minds of the people of Jaffna was the first step towards that objective. This was partly necessitated by the highly effective LTTE propaganda regarding the excesses committed by the IPKF. It needed to be countered with an alternative narrative. Chosen to spearhead that initiative, Major General S.C. Sardeshpande replaced a fatigued Harkirat in January 1988 as the commander of 54 Infantry Division. Sardeshpande appointed Brigadier Kahlon as the town commandant of Jaffna. Roads were repaired, schools reopened and hospitals made functional. Life in the area limped back to normalcy. It is, however, rather perplexing that during this entire period (November 1987 to March 1988), everyone including Army HQ and R&AW had written off the LTTE. They had started propping up a rival militant group – the EPRLF – to align with the Tamil United Liberation Front, which was the political arm of the moderate Tamil groups.

While the Indian politico-military establishment was congratulating itself on freeing Jaffna from the clutches of the LTTE, over 5,000 LTTE cadres were busy regrouping and consolidating their position in the sparsely populated and densely forested Vanni region. Further south, it was the Indian-trained-and-supported EPRLF that dominated the Trincomalee and Batticaloa region. The IPKF commanders hoped that they would soon be able to turn the EPRLF against the LTTE and bring about a military collapse of the latter. The Indian Army recognized the need for more boots on the ground after 54 Division failed to block the escape of the LTTE cadres and leadership from the Jaffna Peninsula. It progressively inducted three additional divisions into Sri Lanka to bolster the thin deployment in Vanni, Trincomalee and Batticaloa. This allowed 54 Infantry Division to consolidate the Indian domination of the Jaffna Peninsula and create conditions that were conducive for holding elections, thereby achieving the objectives of the ISLA. However, Sardeshpande is scathing in his indictment of Delhi for inferring that conflict termination in Jaffna would automatically lead to conflict resolution across the island. He argues that there was no blended military, psychological, economic, reconstruction and rehabilitation strategy to supplement the ISLA and consolidate on the 'notional victory that New Delhi claimed in Jaffna'.[11]

By the end of February 1988, the three additional divisions were in place: 36 Infantry Division commanded by Major General Jameel Mahmood at Trincomalee; 57 Mountain Division commanded by Major General T.P. Singh at Batticaloa; and 4 Infantry Division commanded by Major General J.N. Goel in the Vanni region. Except for 57 Mountain Division – which had moved in from insurgency-ridden Nagaland – these divisions were not adequately equipped with either personnel or training to undertake classical counterinsurgency and counterterrorist operations in jungle, lagoon and semi-urban terrain. Particularly hard-pressed was 7 Infantry Brigade, a part of 4 Division that had moved piecemeal into Sri Lanka during the final stages of the battle for Jaffna in October 1987. It finally found a hostile home in the Vanni area in December 1987. Vanni turned out to be the toughest battlefield as the LTTE had consolidated its forces, logistics caches and armouries in the area. 7 Infantry Brigade would emerge as one of the longest serving and least recognized IPKF brigades, remaining in Sri Lanka until December 1989.

Overstretched Brigade

Brigadier Palsokar is probably the only IPKF brigade commander to have written a detailed account of operations against the LTTE during 1988-89 – in his book titled *Ours Not to Reason Why*.[12] There is an element of personal angst in the book, which is only to be expected from someone who commanded an underprepared brigade with little support from higher formations in conditions that were completely alien to the Indian Army of the time. However, that is

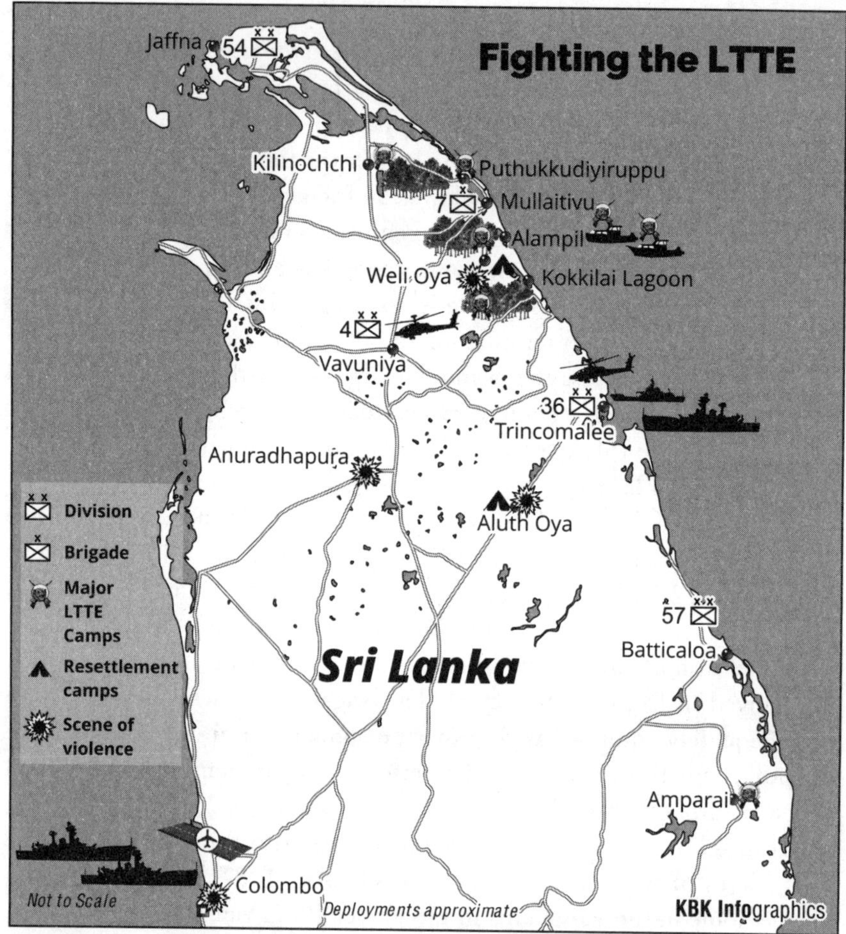

This map is for representational purposes only and does not purport to depict political boundaries

overshadowed by his meticulous retelling of events as they unfolded without covering up the failures – including his own. Palsokar is unsparing in his indictment of the senior leadership and the disconnect with operations at the divisional level and above, particularly in his sector. This objectivity makes his account a good reference when describing operations in the Vanni region.

Palsokar's brigade was totally unprepared for the missions assigned to it. Adding to the confusion was that Palsokar took over command of the brigade in Sri Lanka in December 1987 without any fresh orders or directives that spelt out the objectives for the brigade in the rapidly changing combat environment. Trained for classical infantry warfare that envisaged force-on-force defensive and offensive operations, the brigade instead had to reorient itself to combat an unseen enemy who was gradually mastering the art of guerrilla warfare. Operating in the middle of a contiguous battlespace dominated by the forests and lagoons that extended from Killinochchi in the north to Batticaloa in the east, Palsokar's brigade took time to come to grips with the fighting. Major (later Brigadier) Xerxes Adrianwalla, Palsokar's brigade major, recounted the brigade's principal tasks: 'Our major tasks were to dominate the LTTE, conduct search-and-cordon operations and man multiple Road Opening Parties (ROPs). Some of our peripheral tasks were to manage the tension between the Tamils and Sinhala settlers in areas where the two lived close to one another. Making matters worse was the continuing internecine conflict between the LTTE and rival Tamil groups and the emerging collusion between the Sri Lanka Army and the LTTE.'

After the LTTE retreated from Jaffna, it built its first bastion in the jungles immediately to the north-west of Mullaitivu. This was an area where 7 Infantry Brigade met with some early successes despite taking heavy losses during the first six months of its deployment, mainly from ambushes and improvised explosive devices (IEDs). But even so, it failed to prevent the LTTE from withdrawing southwards towards the dense forests – called Alampil and Nittikaikulam – around the Nayaru lagoon. These forests proved to be the nemesis of the IPKF and 7 Brigade for two main reasons. First, because the brigade was very thinly deployed despite reinforcements from 36 Infantry Division at Trincomalee. The second and more debilitating reason was that the wide range of competencies and specialized troops required by the brigade were hard to come by.

The exception was when the Special Forces reinforced Palsokar's brigade in several contingencies – such as extrication of a trapped company in the forests around Alampil in May 1988 and a larger operation in August and September 1988 called Checkmate IV. The former involved rescuing the 11th Battalion of the Garhwal Rifles (11 GARH RIF) as it was returning from a patrol along the coastal areas of the Nayaru lagoon and Alampil forest.[13] The latter was a concerted attempt by the IPKF to close in on Prabhakaran at a large camp in the Nittikaikulam forest. Checkmate IV commenced in Palsokar's absence. Palsokar reckons that given the casualties and the fact that a helicopter was destroyed within the forward-deployed Tactical HQ perimeter, he would have been sacked if he had been there. 'In fact, only after this operation did Kalkat realize what it meant to operate in the jungle in my sector,' he says. 'Many claims were made by IPKF HQ about the successes achieved by Checkmate IV, but these were hollow and without substance as, by then, both the army and the LTTE were opposed to the ISLA.'[14]

Though the fighting subsided in early 1989, the brigade got a respite from sustained operations only in September 1989 – when a ceasefire was formally declared and a decision was taken by New Delhi to pull out the IPKF. By December 1989, 7 Infantry Brigade had de-inducted after two tough years in the jungles of Mullaitivu. Embedded within Palsokar's narrative are vignettes of resilience, personal courage and loyalty under fire by soldiers of the Garhwal, Rajput, Sikh, Gorkha and Rajputana Rifles, and the para-commandos who operated in the brigade sector. There is also acknowledgement of the risk-taking exploits of the armed Ranjit helicopters operated by the Army Aviation Corps and the IAF Mi-17 helicopters that sustained his brigade from Vavuniya.[15]

The Alligator Strikes

If there was one weapon system that put the fear of God in the LTTE, it was the Mi-25 Akbar helicopter gunship of the IAF. Referred to as 'Mutalai' (alligator) in Tamil by the LTTE, the Mi-25 helicopter gunship had a formidable armament load of two 250-kg bombs, 256 rockets and 1,200 rounds of heavy-calibre cannons. After repeated requests from the brigades involved in the Jaffna offensive, it was finally decided to employ offensive air power against the LTTE. The 125 Helicopter Unit commanded by Wing Commander S.C. Malhan came in to Palaly with four aircraft and commenced operations on 25 October. Initial missions flown by Malhan and other senior crew members included attacks on LTTE ammunition dumps and retreating vehicles.[16]

Palaly was a busy airfield throughout Operation Pawan. Despite heavy security and constant patrolling, there was random sniper fire from the coconut groves around, particularly at dusk. This was quite frustrating and occasionally when the likely direction of fire was ascertained, an Mi-25 would be ordered to get airborne and fire at the coconut trees. This would bring down a hail of coconuts, but hardly ever a sniper. Flight Lieutenant Rajnish Malhotra was one of the several MiG-21 pilots who converted on to the Mi-25 prior to Operation Pawan. He was present at Palaly during those tumultuous times and reckons that even if a couple of snipers were brought down by the fusillade of heavy-calibre fire, there was always an LTTE party waiting to take away the bodies.

The Mi-25s were initially employed to interdict the movement of insurgents and terrorists from the Jaffna Peninsula to the neighbouring islands and mainland of Sri Lanka. This was to prevent the LTTE from bringing in reinforcements of personnel and logistics and exfiltrating its cadres from

Jaffna. In the initial weeks, several LTTE fighters were caught in the open by the Mi-25s. Additionally, Mi-25s were used in the lagoon areas to destroy LTTE boats and vehicles. On 27 October 1987, an Mi-25 piloted by Flight Lieutenant Atanu Guru of 125 Squadron fired on five LTTE heavy transports carrying massive quantities of ammunition and explosives on the old Karaitivu causeway. It resulted in the killing of over a hundred LTTE terrorists and causing explosions that could be heard 30 km away.[17]

As the conflict expanded towards Mullaitivu, Trincomalee and Batticaloa, the four Mi-25s were split into three detachments. There were two at Palaly and one each at Vavuniya (4 Infantry Division) and Trincomalee (36 Infantry Division). However, the rest of the squadron was based at Pathankot – testimony to India's preoccupation with its western front and Pakistan. Pilots recall that operations were chaotic, fluid and devoid of hard intelligence. Photo intelligence was almost non-existent till the later stages of the conflict. This was despite the IAF launching a few Jaguar missions with Infra-Red Line Scan (IRLS) pods that were designed to see through foliage and forest cover. Sometimes the air intelligence was inaccurate, such as the time when tell-tale signs of terrorist camp activity picked up by the IRLS were the dispersed remnants of cooking fires from an abandoned camp.[18]

A typical day would begin with a dawn search-and-strike mission in a large area, to see whether any LTTE cadres could be spotted as they cooked their meals. Malhotra recalled that after taking off from Vavuniya, they would land at the 7 Brigade headquarters at Mullaitivu. During his briefing to them the brigade major, Xerxes Adrianwalla, would stab his fingers on a grid on the map and say 'here' – and off they would go on another search-and-strike mission. Even the slightest movement in the area would prompt the Mi-25 gunship to pull up to about 800 metres and commence its attacks, first dropping its bombs and then firing its rockets in two passes. For those few minutes the jungles would absorb the pounding as the LTTE terrorists took cover till the 'Mutalais' left the area.

The Mi-25s were proficient at night attacks too, and several junior pilots received their training in night gunnery over the jungles of Mullaitivu. Coping with ground fire at night was a harrowing experience as tracers whizzed past. But the sheer exhilaration of spotting the location and then firing 1,200 rounds of heavy-duty ammunition was an experience the pilots would never forget. Though the Mi-25s flew tirelessly in Sri Lanka and were always in the thick of battle, their operational impact was modest. Much like 'jungle bashing' in Vietnam, firepower came off second best against a largely invisible enemy.

Baptism by Fire: Young Officers Reflect

Sri Lanka was a chastening experience for the hundreds of young officers who were baptized by fire in the semi-urban combat milieu of Jaffna, the steamy jungles of Mullaitivu or the treacherous lagoons around Trincomalee and Batticaloa. Many of them are now senior commanders who have seen action and commanded units and formations in J&K, the north-east and Siachen. They are justifiably proud of their accomplishments. But mention Sri Lanka and they can only remember how inept they were made to look by 'guerrilla fighters with unmatched motivation, sophisticated communications and a fanatic streak'.[19]

One brilliant officer from the Corps of Engineers who spent two years in Sri Lanka after the fall of Jaffna recounts his tenure with sadness, disbelief and some sardonic humour directed at the organizational apathy. His unit was rushed from a cantonment in Uttar Pradesh to Madras on 'white-hot' priority. He remembers 'eight to ten generals huddled around a tourist map and trying to make sense of what was going on in the Vavuniya, Mullaitivu, Trincomalee and Batticaloa sectors'.[20] When he joined the engineer unit attached to 7 Infantry Brigade in Vanni in the early months of 1988 there was complete chaos as the brigade was still adjusting to the move into a 'hot' operational area and was taking unduly heavy casualties. As he was proficient in Tamil, the officer was asked by the brigade commander to monitor LTTE radio chatter.

Quick to understand the LTTE's tactics, techniques and procedures, the officer observed that many units of the Indian Army would just burn any LTTE camps they came across, without bothering to collect material that could help them understand their adversary better. He also recollects that there were pamphlets on how to build a campsite and inspirational military video cassettes like *Omar Mukhtar* and *Lawrence of Arabia*. The LTTE writings found also revealed very high levels of intelligence and analysis. For example, one LTTE tactic was to hit a BMP-1 (the Indian Army's ICV) on the side – where its armour plating was the weakest. Severely injured during an operation, the young officer survived to rise to the upper echelons of the army's leadership.

Another young officer from the Garhwal Rifles on his first posting remembers disembarking at Trincomalee utterly ignorant of the location of his battalion till someone at the transit camp told him it was at Vavuniya. Once he arrived in Vavuniya, he was told that the battalion had moved to Mullaitivu. The situation was so grim that convoys were led by ICVs followed by troops on foot, with vehicles like trucks and jeeps trailing at the end. This was because of the threat of mines and the fear of crossfire. The young officer walked almost 60 km under the constant threat of an ambush. He recollects the tremendous fire discipline of the LTTE. An ambush laid by them commenced with a single shot targeting the officers, followed by a volley of fire even before the Indian troops could pinpoint where it was coming from.[21]

Para-commandos in Action

Among the few sound decisions taken by the military operations directorate in the early months of Operation Pawan was the progressive induction of three para-commando battalions into the action. 1 and 10 PARA (SF) battalions were initially deployed at Palaly. Part of the former were also positioned in Colombo and off the coast, on board the INS *Vindhyagiri* in naval uniforms and plainclothes. Their deployment on board a naval warship was undertaken at the behest of the prime minister, Rajiv Gandhi, to ensure the security of President Jayewardene and respond speedily should he be faced with a possible army coup. Jayewardene is said to have expressed these fears to Rajiv Gandhi in a private conversation.[22] Complementing 1 and 10 PARA (SF) was 9 PARA (SF) which was seconded to 4 Infantry Division and 36 Infantry Division towards the middle of 1988 as the fighting spread southwards and eastwards into the Vanni jungles and Mullaitivu.

After the fiasco at the University of Jaffna and the battle for Jaffna that followed, Colonel Rostum Nanavatty was sent to Jaffna as the commander of the para-commando task force with operational control of all three battalions initially. He is full of praise for the performance of the para-commando units in battle, terming it one of the few success stories amid the pall of gloom that permeated the IPKF. Colonel Prakash Katoch took over command of 1 PARA (SF) after his predecessor had serious differences of opinion with his divisional commander, Harkirat Singh, over operational issues. Unfortunately, the unit had also recently lost three officers in an ambush in Vavuniya. Katoch says that the dispersed deployment of his battalion was a major impediment to operations. Motivating his teams and maintaining their morale were the main challenges, and he was often faced with questions such as, 'Why are we here?'[23]

Weapons and personal equipment were a major issue for small teams and Katoch demanded AK-47 assault rifles for his unit from the IPKF leadership. In response, he was give 120 rifles out of the 1,00,000 that were imported by the Indian Army. He also requested better maps, radio sets and interpreters, and then started training extensively with IAF Mi-8 helicopters in the jungles of Vavuniya. In August 1988, the Indian Army planned a major offensive against the LTTE in the forests of Alampil and Nittikaikulam, where it had identified a large camp with multiple security rings – which suggested Prabhakaran's presence. 1 and 9 PARA (SF) both saw maximum action and took maximum casualties in the build-up to and during these operations.

The para-commandos worked together with units of 7 Infantry Brigade and 36 Infantry Division, and their presence was reassuring for the infantry battalions. The commandos would have preferred to take out the camps differently, but had no choice in the matter as Kalkat chose the conventional tasking philosophy of 'cordon, clear and move'. It took 1 PARA (SF) and a Gorkha unit three days to build a cordon. When they finally reached the camps, they found food still on the fire and Claymore mines placed on trees with tripwires laid all around. However, the large force of LTTE – including Prabhakaran – had beaten the cordon and disappeared into the jungles. The two units took eleven casualties from the overhead mines that were well camouflaged by the foliage. Seven other battalions converged on to the camps in a futile show of strength.

Katoch is still indignant when he says that it was the completely wrong way to fight the LTTE in the jungles. 'We should have inserted multiple small teams after adequate deep reconnaissance,' he laments. He adds, 'Everyone wanted to use the para-commandos, but no one wanted to listen to them.'[24] Concerned with the number of casualties, 1 PARA (SF) had to even reassess its tactics, training and procedures (TTPs) as the conflict progressed. Though Katoch was honest in his assessment of what went wrong and how he would have liked to fight, others had good things to say about the para-commando battalions. Nanavatty, who had interacted mainly with 9 and 10 PARA (SF), says that 9 PARA (SF) did brilliantly and were very well trained, fighting cleverly and stealthily. 10 PARA (SF) on the other hand was a tough unit that went forward regardless of casualties in a show of valour. In his last operation with the unit in the Vanni, Nanavatty recollects an NCO telling him, '*Sahib, goli lage to chhati mein* (If a bullet hits me, let it be in the chest).' And a little later that is exactly what happened: that about sums up the attitude of the battalion.[25] These units contributed significantly to the few operations in which the Indian Army inflicted heavy casualties on the LTTE.[26]

MARCOS in Action

Commodore Arvind Singh and Captain Prakash Chandavarkar are among the pioneers of the Indian Marine Special Force (IMSF) – later called Marine Commandos (MARCOS) – which saw action throughout the deployment of the IPKF. Arvind Singh had trained with the US Navy Seals and Chandavarkar with the Royal Marine Commando Force in the UK before they set up the naval element of India's Special Forces. The new force was then trained in India by the Special Group at Sarsawa in Uttar Pradesh. In 1986, they were moved to their base, INS *Abhimanyu*. It was not long before a handful of them were pressed into action. The Indian Navy realized that the waters around Jaffna needed protection, and it was an ideal opportunity to give the fledgling force some battle experience.

Chandavarkar remembers operating alongside 9 and 10 PARA (SF), wearing the same uniform and absorbing their fighting skills. This was a tremendous learning experience for the MARCOS. By the beginning of 1988, the MARCOS had moved to the port of Kanakesanturai, which was the hub of Indian naval activity. Supplies and personnel were offloaded here daily. Following reports that the shallow approach waters had been mined by the LTTE, the MARCOS ventured into LTTE-dominated areas. They lay in wait in their armed Gemini inflatable boats and intercepted LTTE fishing boats and trawlers that ferried cadres across the lagoons. The unit sank many such vessels in 1988. It was for several such hazardous operations that Arvind Singh and Chandavarkar were decorated with the Maha Vir Chakra and Vir Chakra respectively.[27]

Getting It Right in Batticaloa

Batticaloa town is located on a thin coastal strip in the Eastern Province, bound by the Bay of Bengal to the east and a 40-km-long lagoon to the west. The thickly forested Amparai – located about 70 km south-west of Batticaloa – was the southernmost area dominated by the LTTE during Operation Pawan. It abutted the Central Province and was primarily used as a haven to control Batticaloa and keep watch on developments in the adjoining Sinhala-dominated Central and North-Central Provinces. Part of the heterogeneous Eastern Province, it was populated by Sri Lankan Tamils and many Sinhala settlers. The hold of the LTTE in the area depended on the local cadre – as the terrorist outfit grew in strength, so did its recruitment in Batticaloa from the other insurgent groups and the local youth. As the battle in Vanni intensified, Prabhakaran moved large elements of his cadres from the south into the Vanni jungles, replacing them in Batticaloa with cadres from the north who were fatigued and needed a rest.

57 Mountain Division proved effective in its operational areas of Batticaloa and Amparai as it could function more cohesively in a smaller area. Commanded by Major General T.P. Singh, the division had gained counterinsurgency experience in the jungles of India's north-east where the

terrain was similar. It took the division two months to induct all its three brigades, and was ready for operations by the end of February 1988. The primary tasks assigned to the brigades were to seal off Batticaloa from LTTE influence, destroy the lines of communication that the LTTE had established through the jungles and lagoons and create an environment for the peaceful conduct of provincial elections in November 1988.[28] Proficient in cordon-and-search operations, it did not take the division long to sanitize Batticaloa and the villages around it.

Within months of commencing operations, the division had scored major successes in terms of capturing or eliminating LTTE cadres, or coercing them to surrender. Like other divisions, 57 Infantry Division too suffered major casualties from IED attacks and ambushes. One of the few encouraging reports from Sri Lanka came in June 1988 from Batticaloa. Anita Pratap of *India Today* wrote that the IPKF operations in and around Batticaloa had been a major success.[29] Taking over command of the division in mid-1988, Major General Ashoke Mehta continued the good work of his predecessor. He consolidated the strategy of winning hearts and minds with concurrent operations against the LTTE. Unfortunately for India and 57 Infantry Division, much of this effort went in vain. The LTTE made a startling comeback when Premadasa became president of Sri Lanka. The gradual collapse of the ISLA followed.

Stuttering Elections, Failed Mandate and Withdrawal

The IPKF consolidated its presence in the Northern and Eastern Provinces and squeezed the LTTE – but failed to deliver the final punch that would finish it off. In October 1988, the force launched Operation Mahan Kartavya to ensure a peaceful environment for holding three sets of elections. The first was the provincial elections in the Northern and Eastern Provinces in November 1988, while the second was the presidential elections in December 1988 that brought President Premadasa to power. The final set of elections was the parliamentary election in February 1989. Akin to a stability operation that relied on a show of strength accompanied by an effective communication strategy, Operation Mahan Kartavya was designed to insulate the Eastern Province from the LTTE-dominated Northern Province while trying to convince the latter to join the electoral process. Voters in Jaffna boycotted the provincial election as the LTTE refused to join the electoral fray. The elections in the Eastern Province (Amparai, Trincomalee and Batticaloa) saw the emergence of the EPRLF as the single largest insurgent group that was willing to abide by the terms of the ISLA. The India-backed EPRLF – led by Vardaraja Perumal with

K. Padmanabha as its military commander – formed the provincial government after decisively winning the November 1988 elections.

Prematurely elated that the tide might finally be turning in the direction of peace, India's intelligence agencies and strategic leadership did not pick up the ominous signs of the growing understanding between the LTTE and Premadasa. Premadasa was the leader of the nationalist United National Party. Selected as its presidential candidate – President Jayewardene had declined to contest – Premadasa scored a thumping victory over the more moderate and pro-India Sirimavo Bandaranaike in the presidential elections of December 1988. This set the stage for the gradual undermining of the ISLA. There was an emerging confidence within the United National Party that it was time to send the Indians home and sort matters domestically with the LTTE.[30] In the parliamentary elections in February 1989, the LTTE-backed EROS emerged as a clear winner in the Northern Province, revealing a completely fragmented Tamil separatist movement.

The politico-military landscape in March 1989, after all the elections, was that of an emboldened and hard-line government in Colombo led by a hawkish and anti-India Premadasa. Across the Palk Straits, the Rajiv Gandhi government faced increasing domestic flak over the Sri Lanka intervention. A fatigued IPKF had no clear direction whether to go after Prabhakaran, or let the LTTE survive. Rohan Gunaratna highlights this confusion by suggesting that Indian generals told their troops, 'This war was not to destroy your adversary but to guide him in the right direction', or suggesting: 'You must realize that your adversary is not your enemy'.[31] In such a strategic milieu, the informal ceasefire declared by the IPKF in the run-up to elections allowed the LTTE some space to initiate direct negotiations with both Indian intelligence agencies and the new Sri Lankan government.

Despite protests by IPKF field commanders that the LTTE was playing a double game, New Delhi did not want to close the door on the LTTE. It was to pay a heavy price for this as the LTTE used this ploy to build up its arsenal via the sea route from India. The new army chief, General V.N. Sharma, had many a run-in with his civilian intelligence counterparts regarding their new strategy to cultivate the LTTE.[32] He consistently argued that the LTTE was on the back foot and had suffered heavily at the hands of the IPKF through 1988 and so it was time to deliver the final blow. X agrees with General Sharma's assessment and says that sensing the weakening of the LTTE, the new government led by Premadasa made its first move in June 1989. After offering the LTTE a false hand of friendship that Prabhakaran accepted because it was better than getting destroyed by an increasingly battle-hardened Indian Army, Premadasa fired his first salvo on the eve of the SAARC (South Asia Association for Regional Cooperation) summit by telling the Indians to withdraw the IPKF. Rajiv Gandhi refused, but the die had been cast.

Soon after, in November 1989, Indian Prime Minister Rajiv Gandhi had to resign following his defeat in the general elections. The weak interim National Front government led by the new prime minister, V.P. Singh, decided to pull out the IPKF. Meanwhile, Premadasa kept hounding Dixit to advise the Indian government to hasten the IPKF's exit. Dixit went to the extent of secretly procuring forty Czech revolvers and asking General Sharma to organize some self-defence training for the high commission staff.[33] Sharma claims to have sufficiently coerced Premadasa to desist from doing anything that would jeopardize the safety of the IPKF.

Operation Jupiter

While the Indian Army readied an extra infantry division and its para brigade as part of a contingency plan to cover the withdrawal of the IPKF, the Indian Navy sailed the aircraft carrier INS *Viraat* into the waters off the Kerala coast in mid-July 1989. Code-named Operation Jupiter, the preparation and deployment was a back-up in case the Premadasa government crossed the line by undermining the ISLA completely and openly aligned itself with the LTTE to hasten the IPKF's departure. The *Viraat* was also to assist the evacuation of the staff at the Indian High Commission in Colombo should matters get rough. Commanding the *Viraat* was Captain Madhavendra Singh, a future chief of naval staff. Recalling the momentous events that commenced with a brief order on 17 July to get to operational readiness and sail south, Madhavendra had '12 hours for steam'.[34] In naval parlance that meant 12 hours to get to full operational readiness from his current position at anchorage, barely two miles off the Bombay harbour.

As they passed Goa, the Sea Harriers embarked from their base at INS *Hansa*, complementing the Sea King 42 C (commando carriers) and the Cheetah light helicopters as the aerial component of the *Viraat*. Choppy seas prevented the loading of missiles, ammunition and other aviation equipment. This meant that the *Viraat* had to stop by at Cochin to pick them up. It was only after a few days of work-up off Cochin that Madhavendra was told that he would have company on board in the form of the 7th Battalion of the Garhwal Rifles (7 GARH RIF).

Commanded by Colonel Mohan Bhandari (later lieutenant general), 7 GARH RIF was airlifted from Bareilly into Trivandrum by IL-76 aircraft of the IAF and transported by road to the Cochin airfield. In a commendable operation on 26 July 1989, approximately 400 officers and men of the battalion along with all their equipment were airlifted to the *Viraat* in five and a half hours. The *Viraat*'s Sea King and Cheetah helicopters flew 76 sorties in a stupendous display of flying in monsoon weather conditions. Originally a commando carrier with the Royal Navy in the post-WWII era, *Viraat* had adequate space to accommodate the 400 Garhwalis with spare beds for the high commission staff should an evacuation be necessary.

Madhavendra recalls that it was a good experience in planning and preparing for out-of-area-contingency operations as the *Viraat* and its Sea King and Cheetah crews spent quality training time with 7 GARH RIF over almost two weeks while they waited in Indian international waters, away from the gaze of the Sri Lanka Navy.[35] As the Garhwalis finally disembarked after the operation was called off, Madhavendra heard the troops talking among themselves in Hindi about *Viraat*, 'Arey yaar, yeh kamal ki cheez hai – mini shahar hai.' (This is a wonder, just like a mini-city).

The withdrawal of the IPKF commenced in December 1989 and was completed by March 1990. By several yardsticks, the intervention was a failure despite some commanders and foreign policy practitioners arguing that there were several positive takeaways from the two-year intervention.[36]

Lessons from Sri Lanka

The Big Picture

David Brewster, an Indian Ocean maritime security expert at the Australian National University, is among the few researchers who has tracked what he calls 'India's coercive strategies'. He has written extensively about India's strategy towards Sri Lanka and the emergence of an 'Indira Doctrine on the lines of the Monroe Doctrine'.[37] Rajiv Gandhi adopted the less risky option of attempting a 'peacekeeping intervention' rather than a muscular unilateral military intervention. He cannot be faulted for his strategic intent. Where he faltered was in his timing, and the inability to assess whether India had the operational capability to gain a favourable strategic outcome. Also, the prime minister was not cautioned by his foreign secretary, army chief or the high commissioner about the possibility of a peacekeeping operation turning into a bloody and prolonged counterinsurgency and counterterrorism campaign.

Adding to the confusion were the unprepared armed forces, and poor intelligence acquisition and dissemination by the intelligence agencies. These largely contributed to the failure of the campaign.

Intelligence

Colonel Hariharan served in military intelligence for nearly three decades and worked closely with all of India's intelligence agencies of the time. Of these, his interactions with R&AW and the Intelligence Bureau (IB) were particularly robust. One of the few officers in the Indian Army with both staff and field experience in counterinsurgency operations, he was a natural choice to head the military intelligence effort in Sri Lanka. More important, however, was his Tamil-speaking proficiency, which was imperative for operations in northern Sri Lanka. Hariharan identifies two main reasons for the lack of a comprehensive intelligence mosaic. First was the suboptimal synergy between R&AW and military intelligence; the second the shocking and complete misjudgement at every level about the capability of the LTTE. While R&AW resources were mainly focused on meeting the Indian government's aims – which were largely political – military intelligence was practically the only agency collecting daily intelligence on the LTTE for operational exploitation. Hariharan remembers that the LTTE remained neutral and aloof from the IPKF, unlike other militant groups that were quite friendly. He adds that military intelligence never considered Prabhakaran a freedom fighter, and was intensely sceptical of his vaguely worded acceptance of the ISLA – an apprehension that was not taken seriously by either Army HQ or the political establishment.[38]

At the operational and tactical levels of intelligence, X remarks that intelligence units cannot be expected to simply plug in and start giving inputs. Capability had to be slowly built up, and 'all the units did an excellent job, be it networking, operating sources or interrogation'. He also talks about the fate of LTTE detainees in IPKF detention camps in Kankesanturai, Vavuniya and Trincomalee prior to the IPKF's departure. While some of the IPKF commanders were inclined to hand over these detainees, the concern was that they would be killed by the Sri Lankan forces. X argues that since the Sri Lankan government had helped the LTTE with arms and ammunition, 'they too had to share the blame for many IPKF deaths and had no moral right to stand in judgement and decide the fate of detainees held by the IPKF'.[39] It is a pity that several undercover agents such as X have gone unrecognized over the years.

Operational Glitches

The initial euphoria with which the IPKF was received in Sri Lanka soon faded away because of the reluctance of the LTTE to lay down arms and the hesitation of the Sri Lankan forces to comply with the terms of the ISLA. The altered military objectives of the IPKF from peacekeeping to peace enforcement did not go down very well with the LTTE. Moreover, the IPKF did not have the capability to either coerce or compel its principal adversary to do its bidding. There was poor operational synergy and the successes, if any, can be attributed to individual acts of initiative and courage. General Sundarji failed to involve his fellow chiefs in any of the strategic discussions with Rajiv Gandhi, and there was no attempt to set up a joint task force. Consequently, the army units were controlled from Poona and Madras, the air force from Trivandrum and the navy from Cochin. Synergy improved when General V.N. Sharma took over as army chief, but it was too late by then. Some pin the failure of Operation Pawan on the inability to make the transition from peacekeeping to peace enforcement and counterterrorism in varied terrain. Sundarji was a brilliant mind, but he did not anticipate the vicious turn of events and the 'dirty fighting'. Harkirat was completely out of his depth and not in sync with the reality of the unfolding conflict landscape.[40] Major General Ashoke Mehta writes that while the 'LTTE varied its strategy from "confrontation" to "avoidance of contact", "hit and run" remained the mainstay of its tactics. The IPKF on the other hand could not shed its psyche of a conventional force, though it effectively engaged in small-scale counterinsurgency operations.' He adds, 'It was unable to engineer a change in mindset: fight a guerrilla like a guerrilla.'[41]

Naval and Air Aspects

The Indian Navy conducted a variety of operations during the almost three-year deployment of the IPKF, including covert operations with submarines and armed patrols by frontline warships. Over 4,00,000 troops, 8,000 vehicles and over 1,00,000 tons of equipment were ferried to and from KKS and Trincomalee. It provided naval gunfire support and carried out 152 interceptions on the high seas resulting in seventy militant boats being destroyed. Alize aircraft were based at Madurai and carried out armed reconnaissance missions to Jaffna, Trincomalee and Batticaloa in 1988, interdicting several LTTE boats. The MARCOS conducted over fifty special operations and cut its operational teeth in Sri Lanka.[42] It largely operated as a single-service entity and was constrained by the lack of political and strategic guidance on the use of maritime power in counterinsurgency and counterterrorism operations. Though using frigates to provide naval gunfire support (NGS) was tried, New Delhi had not thought through the various maritime possibilities that would have involved frequent infringement of Sri Lanka's sovereignty and territorial waters. Operation Jupiter was one such joint possibility, which ended up as a useful operational simulation.

Air operations during Operation Pawan took place under severe limitations and without adequate strategic guidance. Within the IAF itself, there was little debate and discussion during the time on the employment of air power at the lower end of the conflict spectrum. Like the Indian Navy, the IAF largely operated as a single-service entity though the synergy improved as the conflict progressed. Gradually, the Indian Army was regularly and effectively supported by transport aircraft and helicopters across the range of combat operations. The various challenges included difficult jungle terrain and urban operations with restrictive rules of engagement. The mobile and fleeting nature of the targets meant that fire was largely ineffective unless targets like enemy camps or headquarters were discovered and engaged before they were abandoned.

Navigation, reconnaissance, target identification and acquisition were complicated. Helicopters were compelled to fly low for target acquisition, thus inviting small-arms fire.[43] Several roles like Special Heliborne Operations (SHBO), interdiction of the LTTE's supply and communication lines and scout missions by the Army Aviation's Cheetah and Ranjit helicopters were tried for the first time in such an environment. Accurate intelligence has always been key for the successful execution of SHBO and real-time targeting of fleeting targets. Even though the LTTE did not have the equipment to intercept air-to-air and air-to-ground communication, they always managed to intercept the army's communications and thus were always a step ahead. This prevented many SHBO and gunship missions from achieving their aim – the University of Jaffna fiasco being a prime example.

Helicopters were inadequately equipped for night operations. There was no provision for fitting searchlights on to helicopters, which completely prevented the conduct of regular night search and patrolling. Jaguar and MiG-23 fighter aircraft flew almost 60 sorties in the reconnaissance role. Their impact in providing targeting information was minimal. While there has been widespread acknowledgement of the IAF's effectiveness from several senior army commanders, an equal number of officers who were in the field have highlighted serious deficiencies. If numbers tell stories, the IAF flew over

48,000 sorties on ten different types of aircraft during the IPKF operations. It carried 16,000 tonnes of load and 2,40,000 passengers. For the IAF, it was a significant learning experience in an out-of-area-contingency operation and the helicopter and transport fleets matured significantly after the experience.[44]

Postscript

The saga of one of the most protracted and brutal ethnic conflicts in the post-WWII period came to an end when Prabhakaran was finally cornered and killed on 18 May 2009. Sri Lankan forces stormed his hideout in the jungles of Mullaitivu, where the LTTE had given the mighty IPKF a lesson in counterinsurgency operations two decades earlier.

12

SPEEDY INTERVENTION IN THE MALDIVES

'Operation Cactus was India's first successful strategic intervention. We got it right, but only with a tremendous amount of good luck.'[1]

– Group Captain Anant Bewoor

SOS

Abdullah Luthufi and Uma Maheswaran were two desperate individuals from diverse backgrounds who found themselves co-conspirators in an audacious coup attempt in the Maldives in early November 1988. A country of several islands and atolls in the western Indian Ocean – or the Arabian Sea, as it is more commonly known in India – the Maldives was hardly on India's strategic radar when the crisis unfolded. Luthufi was an aide of Ibrahim Nasir, the Singapore-based former president of the Maldives who had extensive interests and investments in Sri Lanka. Maheswaran was the leader of the Sri Lankan Tamil rebel group PLOTE. Nasir had tried previously to unseat the Maldives President, Maumoon Abdul Gayoom, who had been elected to his post in 1978. The 1988 attempt prompted a decisive intervention by India to foil the coup. Occurring as it did during an ongoing intervention in Sri Lanka, the Maldives operation was also a demonstration of India's attempts at consolidating its position as the pre-eminent power in the region.

An early confidant and lieutenant of Prabhakaran, Maheswaran fell out with his leader in the mid-1980s and formed PLOTE. He was soon identified by India's intelligence agencies as a more approachable alternative to Prabhakaran. Prabhakaran eventually proved to be too strong for all other aspirants to the leadership of the Tamil secessionist struggle, and eliminated them systematically between 1986 and 1989. The reasons for Maheswaran to spearhead the attempted Maldives coup are a matter of much speculation – it was possibly the promise of a bounty of several million US dollars or the assurance of a haven and arms-smuggling outpost. It could have just been an escape from Prabhakaran. What is known, however, is that the plot was hatched in Sri Lanka, where Luthufi is believed to have owned a farm. It was executed with a bravado which almost paid rich dividends.

Group Captain Anant Bewoor was the commanding officer of 44 Squadron at Agra, which was equipped with the IL-76 heavy-lift transport aircraft. He would play a pivotal role in the subsequent operation and recollects that Delhi first heard of the coup from the Indian High Commission in Male early in the morning on 3 November 1988. The call was received by his brother-in-law, Kuldip Sahdev, the joint secretary in charge of the Maldives Desk in the external affairs ministry.[2] Another call followed an hour later to say that over a hundred rebels had taken over many vital installations.[3] Soon it was also confirmed that President Gayoom was in a safe house and had appealed to India and other countries like Pakistan and the US for immediate assistance.

Without any further intelligence inputs, the Prime Minister's Office in New Delhi swung into action. It instructed the Indian Army and IAF HQ to start planning for an operation in the Maldives. It also called a joint meeting at the army operations room to be attended by the prime minister. The meeting is reported to have been chaotic but with the strategic clarity that India must intervene. Brigadier V.P. Malik, who was the assistant director general of military operations, remembers being startled by Prime Minister Rajiv Gandhi's knee-jerk reaction. The prime minister had directed his newly appointed minister of state for home affairs, P. Chidambaram, to 'send the NSG there immediately'. The vice chief of air staff, Air Marshal Suri, had by then been alerted by his army counterpart, Lieutenant General Rodrigues, that there may be a need for the IAF to be ready for an operation jointly with a parachute battalion in the Maldives. Therefore, when Chidambaram asked Suri to position an IL-76 in Delhi to fly the NSG over, the latter indicated that he was already committed to a joint army-air force operation.

Soon, Rajiv Gandhi was convinced by his army chief, General V.N. Sharma, that the parachute brigade was better suited to carry out the operation. The prime minister relented on the NSG option, but not before asking Chidambaram impatiently if the NSG had flown out already.[4] Reliable sources have it that an An-12 from the Aviation Research Centre – controlled by the home ministry – was already airborne from Delhi with the NSG commandos and on course for Male, only to abort the mission when it realized that it did not have the fuel to get to Male.

By 7.30 a.m. the IAF had alerted its strategic airlift assets at Agra to be ready for departure by 1 p.m. Army HQ had also alerted its 50 (Independent) Parachute Brigade in Agra to be ready for an impending operation, but only around 10.30 a.m. However, field commanders on the ground had no idea how the operation was to be executed. By a stroke of luck, the Indian high commissioner to the Maldives, Ajay Banerjee, was in Delhi at the time. He helped in the initial stages of planning and his presence during the first briefing in Agra proved invaluable and prevented a disaster in the making. But Banerjee had not expected to be told that he would be flying with the lead intervention force to Male in the first IL-76 aircraft.

Initial Planning: Operation Cactus

Back in Delhi, the planners could not lay their hands even on an operational map of the Maldives leave alone a schematic diagram of the various airfields on the islands. They had no option but to use tourist maps to locate beachheads, dropping zones and vital installations. The first operational idea to be floated was that of a company-sized paradrop that would be followed by an air-landed operation for inducting the rest of the para brigade. A small drop zone was identified on the south-eastern edge of Male, and Brigadier Vivek Sapatnekar, a former commander of 50 (Independent) Parachute Brigade, was asked to examine its feasibility. Sapatnekar immediately ruled out the possibility on grounds that he would lose 60 per cent of his force during the drop as the prevailing winds would be detrimental for a pinpoint landing on the small drop zone.[5]

After hectic discussions involving the Directorate of Military Operations in Army HQ and the Operations Directorate at the IAF HQ, an air-landed operation at the Hulule airfield emerged as the best option in the given circumstances. It was named Operation Cactus. The scene of the action shifted to Agra, the operational hub where the Indian Army's only parachute brigade was co-located along with the IAF's strategic airlift assets. Chandigarh and Agra have always been the IAF's two largest airlift airbases. While the former is entrusted with air maintenance operations in the northern sectors of J&K, Siachen and Ladakh, the latter has emerged as the hub for strategic airlifts for overseas tasks and airborne/air-landed operations in conjunction with the parachute brigade.

Brigadier Farouk Bulsara was the commander of 50 (I) Para Brigade. He had three parachute battalions (3 PARA, 6 PARA and 7 PARA) under him along with an artillery regiment (17 PARA FIELD REGIMENT) for providing fire support when the need arose. He chose 6 PARA as his lead battalion, with 3 PARA to follow as back-up. With only two companies readily available, Bulsara placed one company of 3 PARA under Colonel Joshi's command as part of what the paratroopers term a 'spearhead battalion'. Chosen to lead the 3 PARA company was Major Navkiran Ghei.[6]

At 7.30 a.m. on 3 November 1988, Bewoor received broad directions to keep three IL-76 aircraft at operational readiness. It was Bewoor who first saw the news of a coup in the Maldives on TV. By 10 a.m., Bewoor was confident that their destination was Male, possibly via Trivandrum. He speculated whether his load would be the NSG or the parachute brigade based at Agra and still regrets that he did not pick up the phone and speak to Bulsara to ask whether something indeed was cooking. He informed his officers of an impending operation at 10 a.m., even as Bulsara ordered his units to be ready for possible overseas deployment by 11 a.m. None of the commanding officers knew where the crisis was. Bewoor too had not yet been told that he would be flying the 50 (I) Parachute Brigade out. All of them in hindsight appreciated that secrecy was important, but surely there could have been a better way to alert the forces once the decision was taken to launch the operation. Bulsara by then had a clearer picture of the situation. Somewhere between 200 and 500 mercenaries had taken control of the TV and radio stations, telephone exchange and other installations in Male. They were supposedly armed with machine guns, rocket-propelled grenades and SAMs.[7]

By 12.30 p.m. Bulsara had his entire spearhead battalion, minus the company from 3 PARA, ready for a paradrop/air-landed operation at Male. The Agra base had only seventy D5 parachutes, leaving Joshi with a smaller force than required. They were armed with Sten carbines as these were the only personal weapons that could be used with the D5 parachutes. Though two companies of 6 PARA were already at the airfield by 1.30 p.m., there was still no communication between Bewoor, Bulsara and Joshi about the operation.

Getting Their Act Together

At 3.30 p.m., the paradrop option, which was discussed again, was ruled out during the first combined briefing at Agra with the team from Delhi in attendance. Bewoor recalls that the alternative plan discussed was to drop paratroopers on a drop zone on the south-east or south-west corner of Male. If that was not suitable, the drop would be at the Hulule airfield. However, no one had assessed the capability of the drop zones to receive paratroopers.[8] Around 4 p.m. there was some clarity about the task, as it was confirmed that the Hulule airfield had not yet been taken over by the mercenaries. It was finally decided to follow the plan of air-landing 6 PARA and elements of 3 PARA at the Hulule airfield. As the Hulule plan was being discussed, Ambassador Banerjee to his horror noticed that the line diagram sent to Agra from Delhi and displayed on the briefing room whiteboard was that of Gan airfield almost 400 miles south of Hulule, on the southern tip of the Maldives archipelago. Banerjee quickly pulled out a beautiful tourist map that had a detailed photograph of the Hulule International Airport and gave it to Bewoor. This, from then on, became the main 'intelligence resource' for the task force.

By then the entire para battalion – including the company from 3 PARA – had arrived at the airfield. The three IL-76s had not yet been loaded as there was no clarity about the sequence of loading. The chaotic loading of aircraft commenced with heated arguments between the loadmasters and the parachute brigade. It was finally completed by 5.30 p.m. for a 6 p.m. take-off. Bewoor and Ghei reflect on the chaos of the moment. 'I had no opportunity to discuss the plan with Bulsara or Joshi,' Bewoor laments. They finally had their discussion somewhere between Bhopal and Hyderabad at 25,000 feet.[9] Ghei adds, 'The overemphasis on secrecy deprived the troops of preparation time. We even had to prime our grenades during the flight, contrary to all safety norms. All briefings were done during the flight on A4-sized black-and-white photocopies of the tourist map of Male provided by Banerjee.'[10]

The spearhead battalion was asked to establish a main and diversionary beachhead at Male by requisitioning local boats while the rest of the force would establish blocking and defensive positions around the airfield. The Male force would be split into two elements – one would extricate President Gayoom from his safe house, and the second would round up the mercenaries. To maintain secrecy, the flight plan of the aircraft had to indicate a destination within the Indian mainland. Instructions were hastily passed to air traffic control stations along the way not to query the two aircraft about their intended destination. However, twenty-five minutes after the two IL-76s got airborne from Agra, the BBC reported that Indian troops were on their way to Male. So much for secrecy. The rebels not reacting to this lapse by taking over the Hulule airfield says a lot about the poor situational and combat awareness of the coup plotters.

As the IL-76s cleared Indian airspace and chased the setting sun into the darkness of the Arabian Sea, Bewoor and his co-pilot readied themselves for a night landing at Hulule. They were told a password that would indicate that the airfield was safe. The second aircraft stayed close, using its navigation lights to stay in formation. The only navigation aid at Hulule was a beacon. After almost three and a half hours of flying, Bewoor spoke on his radio. 'This is Friendly One, do you have a message for me?' In relief and some panic, the air traffic controller at Hulule blurted, 'Hudia, Hudia, Hudia!' That was the password given to the airfield by the Indian high commission. They were clear to land.[11]

Hulule and Male Happenings

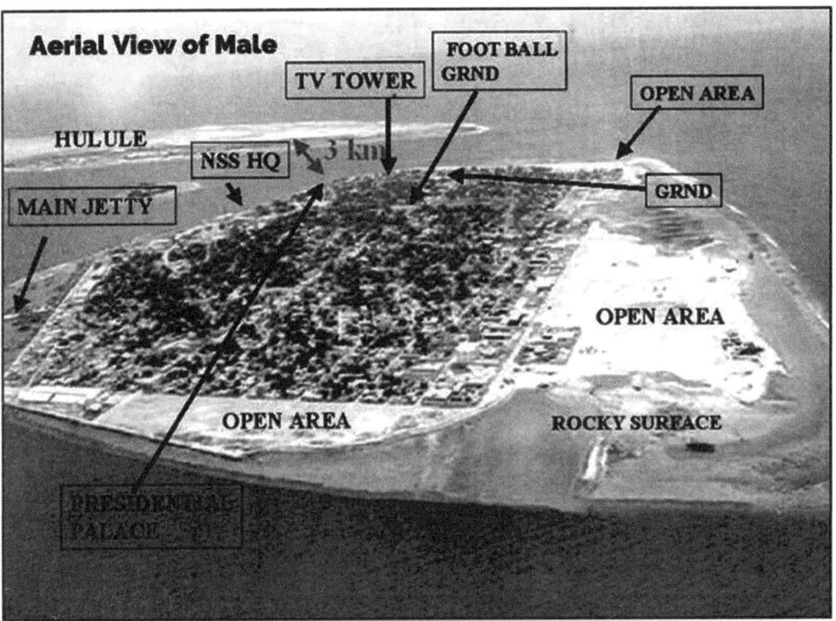

Map credit: Group Captain A.G. Bewoor

Reassured that the airfield was in friendly hands, Bewoor reduced throttle on the four giant engines and went into a gentle descent for landing. He was relieved when the runway lights came on for ten seconds on the final approach, as it allowed him to finally align himself with the centre line. When he was 100 metres from the ground, he asked the tower for the runway lights to be turned on again. It was 9.48 p.m. when the wheels touched down. The lights of Male seemed too close for comfort, and Bewoor hoped that there would be no interference while the paratroopers were exiting the aircraft and the stores were offloaded. Seeing that there was no opposition or risk, Bewoor cleared the second aircraft – which was circling over Hulule at 5,000 feet – for landing. It narrowly missed a few paratroopers crossing the runway while landing. To his dismay, Bewoor saw that all the paratroopers had exited the aircraft without offloading the cargo. It took them forty minutes to offload – hardly a template for rapid deployment.

The paratroopers secured the primary beachhead at Male by midnight, with boats requisitioned by the engineers from Kurumba Resort, the luxury resort closest to Male. A secondary beachhead was secured by a platoon from 3 PARA. Encountering no resistance, Joshi headed straight with his team to secure President Gayoom. At the same time, the other teams conducted mopping-up operations that involved cordon-and-search drills. There was some firing in which there were a few rebel casualties. President Gayoom was secured by 2.15 a.m. and spoke to Rajiv Gandhi at 4.15 a.m.

Ghei and his company from 3 PARA had by then taken up defensive and blocking positions around the western approaches to the Hulule airfield, which was separated from Male by a water channel barely a mile wide. This was also when the main leadership of the rebel force understood that they couldn't withstand the multipronged assault by crack Indian troops, and decided to flee on any anchored ship that they could seize. Observing the channel carefully, Ghei was the first to spot a ship slowly making its way out of the Male anchorage. He immediately radioed the brigade major, Major Vinod Bhatia, for further instructions. There was a brief lull as Bhatia gathered information about the ship. Then Ghei received a frantic call from him saying, 'Fire! Fire! Fire!'

Ghei recollects that all hell broke loose at that moment, as the entire lot of paratroopers around him opened fire at the silhouette with their rifles and carbines. Realizing the ineffectiveness of the fire, Ghei reacted swiftly and called upon his rocket launcher team. They fired a few 84mm explosive rounds at the ship. The team ran along the beach parallel to the ship, firing two more rockets before it glided out of range. The soldiers were certain that they had scored at least one hit.[12] The impact of this action was to emerge later during the pursuit of the hijacked ship MV *Progress Light* by the Indian Navy warships INS *Betwa* and INS *Godavari*.

By dawn the remainder of 3 PARA and 6 PARA had landed after Bewoor's squadron flew an additional three sorties during the night. 3 PARA was assigned much of the task of clearing Male as the remaining rebels surrendered by midday when they realized that they had been left high and dry by their leaders, who were by now on the high seas and sailing towards an unknown destination. Ghei recollects the mopping-up operations on 4 November and adds, 'Searching houses in a foreign land where the loyalties of the locals were unknown to us was a scary proposition. Good discipline prevailed throughout despite the stress and sleep deprivation. There were several foreign tourists in the Maldives during the operation and the entire operation unfolded in front of them. Many of them appreciated the discipline, efficiency and behaviour of the paratroopers.' 6 PARA would stay in the Maldives for an entire year at the request of President Gayoom.

What has been largely unreported was the deployment of two Mi-8 helicopters from 112 Helicopter Unit in Male. Modified for the first time with internal auxiliary fuel tanks and floats, two helicopters flew out from Trivandrum on 4 November and assisted 3 PARA in inter-island mobility for a few days till normalcy returned to the island. The helicopters returned to the mainland on 8 November.[13]

A Captain's Ordeal

Captain Jayadevan had recently joined the Maldivian state shipping company as captain of MV *Progress Light*. It was a 4,000-ton cargo carrier that mainly plied between Maldivian ports and Singapore via ports in India and Sri Lanka. The ship had arrived in Male from Singapore on 2 November 1988 with its cargo of speedboats and other items for the various island resorts. It lay anchored off the port as there were no berths for offloading available at the time. Transshipment to Male was in progress and most Maldivian crew members had gone ashore, leaving Jayadevan, his engineer and a skeleton crew on board. Jayadevan recollects hearing some gunfire that night, but it was only in the morning of 3 November that he heard continuous firing across the harbour between 7 and 10 a.m. He tried to reach his crew members on the walkie-talkie but failed to make contact. Jayadevan heard about the coup through the BBC at around 10 a.m. He braced himself for a long wait to learn of the whereabouts and fate of his crew, who were holed up in their homes.

Though the exact chronological sequence of events from over three decades ago is hazy in Jayadevan's mind, it was all action stations for him after sundown when he saw the silhouettes of aircraft landing at Hulule airport. Soon after, he heard a speedboat. There was a boat with about fourteen people on board going past MV *Progress Light*. They suddenly swerved towards his ship. The boat drew alongside and the occupants rapidly boarded his ship. They seemed to be aware that the *Progress Light* had not yet offloaded its cargo and still had enough rations and other food items on board to sustain a longish voyage. There were men armed with AK-47s among the group and accompanied by four hostages, whose identity Jayadevan could not immediately ascertain.

The armed men rushed to the bridge, where they apprehended Jayadevan, his engineer and the few crew members. They were herded into the dining room. The leader of the terrorists summoned Jayadevan to take stock of the situation. He also met the hostages, among whom were the Maldivian transport minister and his Swiss-German wife. The rebel leader made it amply clear to Jayadevan that if he tried any tricks to escape, he would be executed along with other members of the crew. Soon, a few more speedboats with escaping rebels and rations were seen approaching the ship. As soon as everyone was on board – a total of about seventy to eighty rebels – the leader of the group asked Jayadevan to start the engine and head out of port. Jayadevan objected, stating the difficulties of negotiating the channels in the dark. But his efforts in explaining to the rebels that the probability of running aground on the coral reefs was high at night were dismissed with a threat of dire consequences should he not obey their command.[14]

Jayadevan understood that he had to take his chances if he wanted to survive. As he sailed out, he heard a commotion on the airfield. Following this, the *Progress Light* came under fire. He guessed that the Indian troops had noticed a ship attempting to move out, and realized that the rebels were attempting to flee as they knew their game was up. Jayadevan recollects machine-gun fire and bullets flying around the bridge, but does not recall his ship having taken a rocket hit. He says he could be wrong, but that his ship was certainly not listing and did not slow down because of any control problems. Ghei, however, insists that the ship could finally be intercepted only because his rocket hits had forced it to slow down. Unfortunately, there is no way to corroborate this as the *Progress Light* was later sunk by the Indian Navy. Having skilfully navigated his way in pitch darkness out of Male harbour and on to the high seas, the first destination given to Jayadevan was Sumatra. Then, after some negotiations between the rebels and the Sri Lankan government, he was asked to head for the west coast of Sri Lanka. After a day's sailing, Jayadevan realized that he was being tailed by two Indian Navy ships.

Warships on the Prowl

The ships trailing the MV *Progress Light* were the INS *Betwa*, a training ship based at Cochin with Captain H.A. Gokhale in command, and the INS *Godavari*, captained by Captain S.V. Gopalchari. There is much similarity in the narratives offered by Gokhale, Gopalchari and Jayadevan about the prolonged cat-and-mouse game played on the high seas as the Indian warships attempted to force the rebels to surrender without having to resort to offensive action. Once the Indian government learned of possible negotiations between the rebels and the Sri Lankan government, it was hesitant to get involved. Then came an intelligence report that the Sri Lankans had no intentions of negotiating and were planning to sink the ship with all its occupants, as most of them were Tamil rebels from PLOTE. This forced the Indian government to contemplate action before the ship entered Sri Lankan territorial waters. Having commenced the intervention, Rajiv Gandhi had no intentions of ceding the initiative to the Sri Lankans, who were already giving him a hard time over the IPKF issue.[15]

The Indian Navy's participation in Operation Cactus commenced at 4.20 p.m. on 3 November 1988, when the *Betwa* – an air defence frigate of 1950s' vintage – sailed out of Cochin harbour. It was first asked to maintain naval presence in the waters around the Maldives following the coup.[16] By early next morning, Gokhale had been alerted that the *Progress Light* was now a fugitive ship, headed for either Sri Lanka or one of the South-east Asian countries. He was directed to intercept the rebel-laden ship, but did not have radar contact yet. Gokhale assessed that it would not be long before a US Navy ship moved into the area. He attributes the eventual visual detection of the hostage ship at around 2.45 a.m. on 5 November to the coordinates provided to him by a US Navy helicopter.

Despite repeated warnings from the shadowing *Betwa*, the *Progress Light* ploughed on towards Sri Lanka. INS *Godavari* – one of the Indian Navy's latest frigates – joined the fray later that evening. It had picked up Indian and Maldivian hostage negotiators from Colombo. As hostage negotiations failed despite concerted attempts, the drama on the high seas entered its last phase on the evening of 6 November. Jayadevan recalls with horror the execution of two hostages on the bridge right in front of him. Their bodies were thrown overboard to demonstrate coercive intent.[17]

With final Rules of Engagement (ROE) coming in from New Delhi, both ships commenced firing in the wee hours of 7 November. The firing – first with small-calibre weapons and then with medium guns – caused significant damage to the *Progress Light* and inflicted casualties among the rebels, who were foolishly refusing to surrender. Jayadevan recollects that the transport minister was hit in the leg. Small fires began breaking out on the ship. Realizing that the rebel leader was preoccupied with organizing his men,

Jayadevan ushered his engineer, crew members and the two remaining hostages (the Maldivian minister and his wife) to a dinghy. They floated towards the *Betwa*, which picked them up. The rebels eventually surrendered, and naval commandos from the *Godavari* boarded the severely damaged *Progress Light* to search for survivors on board. Jayadevan recalls identifying his crew members who had died in the firefight and were laid out with the bodies of the rebels. Then a volley of fire from the *Godavari* sank the *Progress Light*. The next day he was asked to identify and confirm that some floating debris was indeed a part of the *Progress Light*.[18] Gokhale contests this by recollecting that the *Progress Light* was scuttled by Jayadevan and the rebels. The truth may never be known in the absence of declassified action reports.

As per President Gayoom's request, all the hijackers and crew members were taken first to the Maldives. Jayadevan and his Indian crew members were separated from the Maldivian crew and taken to a guest house. The injured minister was airlifted to Pune via Trivandrum for further treatment. Jayadevan was interrogated by Indian and Maldivian interrogators who were trying to ascertain whether he was complicit in the whole operation. He was repeatedly asked why they boarded his ship when there were larger and more modern ships at anchor. Jayadevan suggested that his cargo of speedboats could have been appealing to the rebels and that perhaps they had received this information from the Maldivian crew members who were ashore. There was also a possibility that the rebels thought that the Indian crew were better at navigating the Indian Ocean than others.

After satisfying the intelligence agencies that he and his crew were merely pawns in this game, Jayadevan was permitted to return home, much to the relief of his wife and children. Once safely back in Madras, Jayadevan was surprised to receive a call from the home minister, P.V. Narasimha Rao. The minister complimented him for his conduct and poise through the ordeal, but also advised him to refrain from commenting on the incident or speaking to the press about what happened on the high seas. As a result, Jayadevan consistently refused to speak to anyone about his ordeal until finally agreeing to be interviewed for this book. He reckons that the Indian government wanted to classify details of hostage execution, the sinking of the *Progress Light* and the number of rebels who died in the shelling. Throughout the ordeal, Jayadevan kept his cool and did not do anything rash to endanger the lives of his crew members. His biggest regret was that he lost some of his crew during the gun battle. Reflecting on his experience of the Indian Navy, Jayadevan says the *Godavari*'s manoeuvring and procedures were sound, but that the *Betwa* was old and should not have been assigned for that operation. He also remembers the understandably cold treatment that he and his crew received from the crew of INS *Betwa*.[19]

Bouquets and Brickbats

From a strategic outcome perspective, the Maldives intervention was a resounding success. A floundering but legitimately elected government in India's perceived backyard was restored to power after being unable to defend itself against a ragtag bunch of mercenaries. The speed of strategic decision-making was good, even though the operational planning process was fragmented. There was good leadership and initiative at all levels.

In hindsight, it was a risky operation because there was little tactical intelligence about the mercenaries and whether they had heavy weapons such as rocket launchers that could potentially cause serious damage to the military forces. The paratroopers were organized and accomplished the mission despite the hazardous distribution of grenades and ammunition on board and the last-minute briefings over the Indian Ocean with tourist maps being used as direction finders and locators. Planning niggles and operational glitches were many and luck ultimately played a significant role in the success of the operation. The initial planning process was chaotic and operational units were not in the loop till later in the day. Compatibility of equipment and weapons was a major area of concern because the para brigade did not have personal weapons that were compatible with the D-5 parachutes.

Lack of actionable intelligence was not because of a capability gap, but because at the strategic level the Maldives was nowhere on India's intelligence horizon given the preoccupation with Sri Lanka, Pakistan and China. Operation Brasstacks, Operation Falcon and Operation Pawan had stretched the intelligence agencies completely. From a naval perspective, the absence of sophisticated navigation aids on board the *Betwa* hampered the search for the rebel ship. However, the decisiveness of Captain Gopalchari and Captain Gokhale in taking offensive action was praiseworthy. There were many things that could have gone wrong had the rebels been smarter, more zealous and organized. There is no end to such 'what-if' scenarios. The IAF's strategic airlift Concept of Operations (Conops) emerged from Operation Cactus and the IL-76 proved to be a reliable platform.

Thirty Years On

Three decades later, Bewoor reflects that the lack of bloodshed and casualties to the military forces may give the impression that the operation was nothing much to write about. But such operations are either stunning successes or dismal failures. The Entebbe rescue by Israel and the American fiasco in Iran are appropriate examples of success and failure respectively.[20]

Nearly thirty years after India intervened in the Maldives, the island nation was beset once again by internal instability that worried India. The Maldives again sought a military intervention by India in February 2018 after a widespread crackdown by the president, Abdulla Yameen, that included taking former President Gayoom into custody.[21] Further alarming the Indians was a clear strategic tilt by Yameen towards China, possibly encouraging a Chinese presence as a means of staving off any threat to his government. The Indian government speedily readied the army's Parachute Brigade as it was flown into Bengaluru along with the IAF's entire new fleet of C-130 J aircraft, and asked to await further orders. In the meantime, India's intelligence agencies and military operatives carried out a reconnaissance of Male. However, the operation was called off as Yameen understood quickly that India was not about to brook any needless overt interference in what it considers to be its own sphere of influence.[22]

13

JAMMU AND KASHMIR ERUPTS

'The terrain inside Kashmir was ideally suited for guerrilla and sabotage action. In addition, our frontier tribesmen have for centuries found India an attractive hunting ground.'[1]

– Major General Akbar Khan in 1956

Historical Perspective

Early Kashmir Rumblings

The oppressive rule of the Hindu ruler of the princely state of J&K, Maharaja Hari Singh, gave rise to two narratives in the decades that immediately preceded Partition. The first narrative emerged from the Kashmir Valley, where Sheikh Abdullah and his group of moderate Kashmiri nationalists started a movement having similar aspirations to the Indian National Congress. The difference between the two was that the Indian National Congress sought freedom from colonial rule and Sheikh Abdullah from the oppression of Maharaja Hari Singh.[2] The second narrative was the more aggressive expression of Kashmiri angst from the south of the Pir Panjal Range that separates the Valley from the plains. Here Sardar Abdul Qayyum Khan, a former soldier in the Engineer Corps of the British Indian Army, brought together disaffected Muslims from the Poonch region and attempted to overthrow Maharaja Hari Singh.

The Islamist foundation of the secessionist movement in Kashmir was laid by the Pakistan-based radical group Jamaat-e-Islami, which had strong roots in the Poonch region. (It would take India over seven decades to react to the fissiparous influence of this organization. It was finally banned in February 2019.) To further Muhammad Ali Jinnah's two-nation theory that sought division of the subcontinent based on religion, there was also the infiltration operation by the Pakistan Army in 1947-48 called Operation Gulmarg. It was poorly executed and thwarted by the spirited and professional Indian military response before it could expand into an insurrection.[3] It was a two-tier game plan. When the first tier – the planned insurrection – failed, the second tier was operationalized with the Pakistan Army joining the battle to support the armed raiders of the Jamaat-e-Islami. Though the Jamaat-e-Islami was already an influential group, it had not yet sowed the seeds of religious bigotry in the Valley. Once the raiders were beaten back and the planned insurgency fizzled out, the 1947-48 conflict panned out as a conventional military conflict.

Consequently, the argument offered by Jinnah was that Kashmir – with its predominantly Muslim population – ought to have rightfully joined Pakistan. India's prime minister, Jawaharlal Nehru, and home minister, Sardar Patel, did not agree. In an eminently readable and objective article in the *Small Wars* journal, Simon Jones articulates Nehru's reasons as to why J&K should remain with India, stating that Kashmir's diversity meant its existence was essential to the ideology of a secular state.[4] Nehru emerged rather confused about Pakistan in the aftermath of this conflict. However, he claimed to understand Pakistan's strategy on Kashmir when he said, 'The invasion of Kashmir is not an accidental affair resulting from the fanaticism or exuberance of the tribesmen, but a well-organized business with the backing of the state.' He argued that India had to deal with a nation carrying out war that, despite being informal, was a war nevertheless.[5]

And yet, despite his deep understanding of the geopolitics of the area, Nehru did little to alter the strategic landscape in the Kashmir Valley. He could have done that by ensuring good governance, strengthening political structures and bolstering them with a robust intelligence and military set-up to counter secessionist tendencies and aspirations. In the autumn of 1948, Nehru approached the United Nations for a ceasefire, trying to portray Pakistan as the aggressor. However, the US and UK supported Pakistan's assertion that Kashmir was a contested area. Nehru thus lost an opportunity to restore a semblance of status quo in the Valley. This would cost India dearly in the decades ahead.

Jamaat-e-Islami grew stronger in the region following Pakistan's continued occupation of a part of Kashmir in the aftermath of the UN-brokered ceasefire in January 1949. Sheikh Abdullah and his love-hate relationship with Nehru also dominated the political landscape, with the Sheikh's association with separatists worrying India's intelligence agencies and Patel. Patel urged Nehru to adopt a consistent but hard-line policy towards those who either propagated 'azadi' or sought Pakistan's assistance for a separatist movement. Unfortunately, Patel's death in December 1950 left India's Kashmir policy entirely in the hands of Nehru. The prime minister was rather altruistically obsessed with restoring peace in the state of his ethnic origin at any cost. This meant that he was willing to turn a blind eye to the fissures and cracks emerging within Kashmir's polity. Praveen Swami – who was the first to use the term 'informal war' – makes some very astute observations regarding the slow deterioration of the security situation in J&K in the 1950s and 1960s.[6] He writes that J&K's accession to India was challenged not only politically and diplomatically, but also militarily. J&K was thus 'a zone of continued warfare – low grade warfare, it is true, but warfare nonetheless'.[7]

Sheikh Abdullah's arrest in 1953 – for alleged secessionist and anti-national activities – followed by the installation of a pro-Congress state government in J&K ushered in a period of uncertain calm. It also paved the way for the establishment of a Pakistan-directed grid of covert actors to undermine the societal fabric of J&K. These covert cells were trained in acts of subversion and coercion. They had two objectives: first, to create fear by causing public inconvenience and disruption through bomb blasts and acts of sabotage against symbols of the state; and second, to instil fear in the minority Hindu population and polarize the communities further.

In April 1964 – still reeling from the 1962 defeat at the hands of China – Nehru decided to release Sheikh Abdullah on the advice of his cabinet. The idea was to wean him away from separatism.[8] Abdullah agreed to act as an interlocutor on Kashmir between Nehru and Pakistan's military dictator, Ayub Khan. However, a secret report of the Central Intelligence Agency (CIA) of the US shed accurate light on Abdullah's intentions, stating that his actions since his release suggested that although he knew that he had his strongest hand ever in dealing with Delhi, he was not yet ready to play it out. 'He does not believe that the Kashmir question is settled and neither does New Delhi,' said the report, 'but its public position is that the accession is final and irrevocable.'[9] Unfortunately, Nehru's death on 27 May 1964 changed things. It gave Zulfiqar Ali Bhutto, who was then the foreign minister of Pakistan, the opportunity to have an informal talk with Sheikh Abdullah while flying to Delhi to attend Nehru's funeral. The Sheikh was returning from Rawalpindi after meeting Ayub and convincing him to meet Nehru and find a lasting solution to the Kashmir problem.[10] Swami says that the plan to put in place a network of covert operators gathered steam after Nehru's death. Bhutto was emboldened to convince Ayub that he had the Sheikh's support. They decided to orchestrate a widespread people's rebellion in Kashmir, and began to plan Operation Gibraltar.[11]

The Failure of Operation Gibraltar

The Pakistan Army thought that it could force a military solution in Kashmir, especially after India's defeat at the hands of China in 1962. Operation Gibraltar was orchestrated by Pakistan's foreign office along with the ISI and the divisional commander of the Pakistan Army's 12 Division, Major General Akhtar Malik. The strategy was like the one used in 1947-48, the difference being the existence of a robust follow-on operation. This was designated Operation Grand Slam with a plan to cut off J&K from the rest of India. While the first operation was immediately thwarted by an alert Indian Army in J&K, the second almost succeeded but for a slight operational pause that allowed the Indian Army and Indian Air Force to conduct a spirited rearguard action.[12]

Brigadier Pranadhar Gaur, who served in J&K, makes an interesting observation in his doctoral thesis[13] about the absence of any radical zeal within the Pakistan Army of the 1960s, and the reluctance of Pakistan's President Ayub Khan to make Kashmir central to the India-Pakistan rivalry. One of Khan's close confidants, Major General Shaukat Riza, wrote that Ayub was 'not a wild-eyed revolutionary crazed by dreams of reshaping the world. He was a realist and in his cabinet meetings had emphasized that the security of Pakistan was not to be jeopardized for the sake of Kashmir'. Ayub knew that fighting in Kashmir would escalate to a war between India and Pakistan, and it would be a war that Pakistan could not win without foreign help.[14] Those were prophetic observations indeed.

There is a widespread belief that it was Zulfiqar Ali Bhutto who played the Kashmir card to convince a large section of Ayub's generals that the time was ripe to force a solution on Kashmir. Bhutto's opening gambit on Kashmir may have failed, but that only spurred him to find new tools that could be sharpened to drive latent Kashmiri nationalism and Islamic fervour. Despite his broadly secular leanings, Ayub did dabble in jihadi ideology. He had been influenced by Aslam Siddiqui, one of his pro-jihad aides. In his book *Pakistan Seeks Security,* Siddiqui argued that covert warriors and irregular warfare were elements of jihad that needed to be nurtured for difficult times. He also suggested that these players would be best exploited if they were nurtured outside the 'system'.[15] In her seminal work on the Pakistan Army, *Fighting to the End: The Pakistan Army's Way of War,* C. Christine Fair traces the influence of the Jamaat-e-Islami on the Pakistan Army to the late 1950s.[16]

Pakistan's Islamic Revival

The aftermath of the 1965 war with India saw Pakistan's army junta floundering. It was left to the mercurial Bhutto to drive Pakistan's political agenda. He wanted to transform Pakistan's engagement with the Islamic world and ensure that Kashmir remained central to the India-Pakistan strategic discourse. Despite an alert and resilient Indian intelligence network in J&K – led by police officer Surendra Nath – smashing the remnants of the Pakistan-sponsored covert cells, it was not enough to extinguish the embers of Kashmiri nationalism. Sheikh Abdullah's ambivalent stance in his quest to regain leadership in Kashmir also remained the same. Had Nath's early reports on J&K been heeded by Delhi – first by Lal Bahadur Shastri and then by Indira Gandhi – Pakistan's covert war strategy may well have floundered in its infancy. Unfortunately, these reports are still shrouded in secrecy.

Ayub's continuing articulation that the 'Kashmir cause' was not furthering Pakistan's national interests did not go down well with the rest of the Pakistani establishment. They forced him to agree to an elaborate plan of conducting a covert war in J&K. The strategy was to keep the pot boiling while controlling conflict escalation to levels just short of war. Such a strategy was clearly designed to exploit the established norms of 'deterrence with restraint and responsibility' that was the cornerstone of India's national security policy. Concurrently, Bhutto built close relations with other Islamic countries and created an Islamic narrative for Kashmir that would create multiple pressure points for India in the international environment. This saw Pakistan forging close ties with the United Arab Emirates, Saudi Arabia, Iran, Turkey and Indonesia.[17] Sadly, India failed to work on counter-narratives and remained cocooned in the smug discourse of constitutional sovereignty and territorial integrity.

The strategic consequences of the 1971 war with Pakistan – and their impact[18] on the trajectory of any future conflict in Kashmir – were profound. They signalled a departure from the existing discourse in the minds of the Pakistani military establishment reeling from a rather humiliating military defeat. Indira Gandhi's ill-timed magnanimity of not forcing a resolution on Kashmir in the Simla Agreement even when India held all the cards was a blunder that haunts India till today. In its moment of triumph, India neither considered the evolving situation in Kashmir, nor did it reflect on how warfare may change in the years ahead. The Indian military was sidelined in the discussions after the 1971 war and prior to the Simla Summit. This meant Indian negotiators failed to leverage the impact of holding 93,000 POWs, and let Pakistan off the hook by not insisting on a cartographic and non-interference commitment. This left a window open for the Pakistan's military, its intelligence agencies and jihadi forces to avenge the humiliation of 1971. They planned to do this by waging a constantly evolving covert war and inciting the people of Kashmir to rise against the Indian state.

Covert War Unfolds

The covert war that is currently manifesting itself in multiple forms in J&K was largely the brainchild of the late Pakistani military dictator General Zia-ul-Haq.[19] He came to power in a military coup in 1977, overthrowing the civilian government of Zulfiqar Ali Bhutto. Bhutto had elevated Zia as army chief barely a year earlier as he was perceived to be a subservient general who would be amenable to take orders from a civilian government. Little did Bhutto realize that the 'pliant' general would soon send him to the gallows. Zia also set in motion the process of the 'Islamization' of the Pakistan Army by introducing a Quranic concept of war.[20] These became the key drivers of the covert war strategy to 'bleed India by a thousand cuts', a phrase adapted from Mao's tested strategy of 'death by a thousand cuts'.[21]

The defeat of the Russians in Afghanistan in the mid-1980s made J&K a soft target for jihadis, who received active support from Zia. This is a rather simplistic summary of the origins of what has been a troublesome secessionist movement for India. The covert war since the late 1980s is but a phase in what has been a constant struggle of narratives in J&K, right from the days preceding Partition. While India chose to develop as a secular, multi-ethnic and multicultural democracy, Pakistan emerged as a theocratic Islamic state with constant jousting for political power. One of India's biggest strategic challenges has been to combat Pakistan's 'two-level strategy' of subverting India and forcing the secession of J&K. This strategy is prominently discussed in various writings about the fractured relationship between these two nations.[22]

Brigadier Gaur's Ph.D. thesis analyses the evolution of this strategy from a practitioner-scholar's perspective. Then there is Praveen Swami's book *India, Pakistan and the Secret Jihad: The Covert War in Kashmir, 1947-2004,* an academically robust and brilliant piece of investigative writing, among several others written by him in the troubled decades of 1990-2010. Other worthy references are works by US-based Professor Sumit Ganguly, one of the most prolific writers on the fractured contemporary India-Pakistan relationship.[23] Also serving as invaluable resources in the chapters on J&K are inputs from field commanders who led formations in the Kashmir Valley during this period, including Lieutenant Generals M.A. Zaki, R.K. Nanavatty, J.R. Mukherjee, K. Nagaraj, S.A. Hasnain, D.S. Hooda, Ravi Thodge and General Bipin Rawat.

The Rise of the JKLF

Swami suggests that Pakistan-trained Kashmiri jihadis became common after the establishment of the Al-Fatah master cell in the mid-1960s. It was led by Ghulam Rasool Zahgir, a clerk who recruited radicalized youth from Kashmir University in Srinagar. It executed the first recorded killings of security personnel and vandalized and desecrated places of religious worship to whip up communal passions.[24] The Al-Fatah cell expanded over the next few years, bolstering its cadres with educated youth who would focus on the twin pillars of the covert war – political activism and military action. During their numerous trips to Pakistan across the porous border, its cadres were trained in political subterfuge, military intelligence and warfighting with weapons, explosives and bombs.[25] The movement fizzled out by early 1971 just as it was ready to expand its activities. This was due to both a strange reluctance on the part of the Pakistani government to support it further and the sudden alertness of India's intelligence agencies that completely smashed the Al-Fatah.

The National Liberation Front (NLF) was set up in the mid-1960s by Maqbool Butt, a maverick student leader. The group floundered after the hijacking of an Indian plane to Lahore in 1971. Butt was arrested and given the death penalty by India. This led to the emergence of Britain-based Amanullah Khan and the reinvention of the NLF into the Kashmir-oriented Jammu and Kashmir Liberation Front (JKLF). This group offered the first real military challenge to the Indian state in the early 1980s. Initially set up in London, it operated out of Muzaffarabad, the capital of PoK.[26] The choice of location of the HQ was symbolic; the tribal lashkars had launched the first attack on Kashmir in October 1947 from Muzaffarabad.[27]

The JKLF drew blood in 1984 by kidnapping and executing an Indian diplomat in Birmingham, an act that was immediately followed by the judicial execution of Maqbool Butt by India. The expulsion of many JKLF cadres – including Amanullah Khan – by Britain to Pakistan led to its expansion in PoK. Many Kashmiri youth crossed over into PoK to be trained in the basics of infiltration and weapon-handling. The 1987 election in J&K was a watershed event in which the National Conference party and the Congress alliance came to power after a highly fractured and reportedly rigged mandate. Several JKLF leaders – such as Yasin Malik and Javed Mir, who were campaigners for the Jamaat-e-Islami and had backed the Muslim United Front – were disillusioned by the widespread rigging. They became even more committed to the secessionist agenda.[28]

Also disillusioned with his failed election foray and attempts to join the mainstream was a fiery student leader, Syed Salahuddin. He would later emerge as the leader of the Hizbul Mujahideen (HM) and head of the Kashmir-focused terrorist umbrella organization called the United Jihad Council.[29] The state descended into a spiral of violence marked by rising confrontation between separatists and the security forces. The increasingly politically aware population sat on the fence watching. A combination of poor governance and effective mobilization of cadres by the secessionists proved to be the tipping point for the escalation of an insurgency into a full-blown covert war. The JKLF was largely secular and drew inspiration from the Palestine Liberation Organization (PLO) and its cadres were committed to the idea of 'azadi'. General Zia was preoccupied at the time with the covert war in Afghanistan. But this did not prevent him from inducting the ISI in the Kashmir Valley to work alongside the JKLF. Well versed in the art of covert war and black operations, the ISI had honed its skills under the CIA in Afghanistan. It was ready to expand its operations into J&K.

Operation Topac

Personally, the defeat at the hands of India in 1971 rankled General Zia. Nationally, getting even with India remained at the heart of Pakistan's politico-military strategy. Zia represented the new face of the Pakistan Army which increasingly viewed Islam as the glue binding the army and the nation. Realizing that India was growing more powerful, Zia decided to wage a sophisticated covert war and complemented it with a strategy of internal radicalization. He already had an insight into the response mechanisms of India's security forces through his support to Bhindranwale's Sikh secessionist forces in the early 1980s.[30] However, Zia did not live to see his plans fructify. On 17 August 1988, he perished in a mysterious air crash along with many of his generals, including the ISI chief and the US ambassador to Pakistan. But Zia had done enough to give his vision a self-sustaining momentum. There are many who believe that the radicalization of the Pakistan Army rapidly followed the gradual radicalization of Pakistani society. Soon its visceral hatred for the Indian Army morphed into the desire to wage jihad against India and its mostly Hindu citizens.

In 1979, one of Zia's trusted lieutenants, Brigadier S.K. Malik, wrote a seminal treatise on the 'Quranic Concept of War'. It highlighted the relationship between Islam and jihad and recommended that Pakistan's armed forces must embrace Islamic tenets. This was a doctrinal departure from the hitherto purely Western way of warfighting. Zia endorsed Malik's philosophy and beliefs, and shared his zeal for jihad. Together, they believed that jihad was the collective responsibility of the Muslim ummah (the whole Muslim community) and not restricted only to soldiers. Zia emphasized that an Islamic military professional must have a 'godly character'. He wholeheartedly backed Malik's 'Quranic Concept of War' as the 'only pattern of war' that an Islamic state may wage.[31]

Zia's sustained alteration of Pakistan's military ethos and structure also had an impact on its civil society. There was an increase in the number of Deobandi clerics and madrassas during Zia's rule. This radicalization of Pakistan ought to have alarmed the Indian strategic establishment. Joseph C. Myers, a US Army lieutenant colonel who was senior advisor at the US Air Command and Staff College, offers insights into the reasons for the successful and rapid Islamization of the Pakistan Army through the 1980s. He argues that radical Muslims are more likely to adapt to and execute an asymmetric approach to war. He writes, 'With respect to global jihad terrorism, as the events of 9/11 so vividly demonstrated, there are those who believe in and will exercise the tenets of the "Quranic concept of war".'[32]

Operation Topac first came to public notice in 1989, in an article written by Major General Afsar Karim in the *Indian Defence Review*.[33] The article was clearly based on leaks from Indian intelligence sources in Pakistan. Written as part truth and part fiction, it was an ingenious attempt at sensitizing the Indian political establishment and military of the ominous nature of Pakistan's designs. The operation – also called 'Tupac', after a Peruvian prince – slowly took shape under the guidance of ISI chief Major General Akhtar Abdur Rehman.[34] It got an indirect boost from the Russian invasion of Afghanistan. A myopic CIA-led initiative by the US saw it give Pakistan billions of dollars in arms and military equipment, and critical intelligence in the 1980s. The US wanted to build the military capability of the Afghan mujahideen for their armed struggle against the Russians. But the aid also led to the further empowerment of Pakistan's ISI.[35]

What the Americans did not anticipate was that after the Russian defeat in Afghanistan, all this new war-waging capability would be redirected towards J&K. However, its direct impact on India in the form of a formal 'covert war' in J&K took a decade to evolve. In April 1988, Zia outlined the framework of Pakistan's strategy at a top-level meeting attended by loyal corps commanders, ISI leadership and elements of Afghan and Kashmiri mujahideen. Making a conscious attempt to steer clear of all the mistakes Pakistan had made in

1947-48 and 1965, Zia directed the first phase of the strategy at supporting widespread infiltration, subversion, shock and attacks on military strongpoints. The aim was to spur a people's revolt against the Indian government and initiate gradual disintegration of peace in J&K.

The second phase of Zia's plan would see Pakistan taking control of Kashmir and setting right the historical aberration of Partition.[36] Zia described the Kashmiri people as 'simple-minded folk' who nonetheless 'have a few qualities' that Pakistan could exploit – such as being good at 'political intrigue'. 'If we provide [a Kashmiri person] means through which he can best utilize these qualities, he will deliver the goods…'[37] Though several Western commentators believe that Operation Topac was a figment of the imagination of the Indian Army, there is much evidence to suggest that there indeed was a well-orchestrated politico-jihadi-military plan to undermine India' security with Kashmir as the prized target. Sean Winchell, a prolific writer on the ISI, believes that the ISI was perfectly positioned at the time to assume the lead role in Zia's Kashmir strategy. Writing in the *International Journal of Intelligence*, Winchell argues that 'since Partition, no political force within Pakistan has driven the nation's domestic and international political agenda as has its army' and more specifically, the ISI.[38] He corroborates the existence of such an operation, stating that in addition to supporting Afghan mujahideen fighters, 'the ISI began to assist the Kashmiri separatists in their effort to make Kashmir a part of Pakistan. In 1988, as part of that support, then-president Zia created Operation Tupac (the Indians termed it as Topac).'[39]

According to the South Asia Terrorism Portal, 1988 formally marks the beginning of the externally abetted covert war in J&K. That year saw 391 incidents and twenty-nine civilian fatalities, with one terrorist and one Indian security personnel also killed.[40] This was when India's external intelligence agencies and its army were preoccupied with the Sri Lankan quagmire. Its internal intelligence agencies were handicapped by a coalition government that paid no heed to warnings of veteran intelligence experts. On 6 September 2019, Ajit Doval – India's current NSA – confirmed in a media interaction that there indeed was a paper on 'Operation Topac that had emerged or leaked in 1988-89'.[41] Reflecting on the reasons that forced Pakistan to seriously rethink its Kashmir strategy, Simon Jones writes that 'India never once went to war specifically to retain control over the state. Its actions have always been defensive with respect to its national integrity. This indicates that while India is unwilling to lose more territory, it is content to live with the status quo. Besides this, the Indian military has proven its dominance in the field beyond a doubt and can weather almost anything that the Pakistan government throws at it, short of nuclear weapons.'[42]

Collapse of the JKLF

Following the commencement of Operation Topac, the Kashmir Valley became a fertile recruiting ground for the JKLF. It expanded in the urban areas around Srinagar, building up an 'azadi' euphoria that thrived because of the complete abdication of control on the part of the state government. Rajiv Gandhi and the coalition government of V.P. Singh were equally responsible for India's weak-kneed Kashmir policy during the late 1980s. A comprehensive analysis of the rise and fall of the JKLF[43] and the corresponding rise in the number of incidents during 1989-92[44] is highly revealing. The analysis highlights that had the J&K state government under Dr Farooq Abdullah taken serious note of the collusion between the ISI and JKLF, the insurgency could well have been crushed before it expanded into an escalated covert war.

The JKLF fragmented in 1990 after its first military commander, Ishfaq Majeed Wani, was neutralized in an encounter with security forces.[45] The JKLF therafter could not reorganize itself militarily to face the might of the Indian Army, which by 1991 had put together an effective counterinsurgency grid. Consequently, many J&K-based JKLF cadres escaped into PoK and joined the pro-Pakistan jihadi forces that were getting ready to stoke widespread rebellion in the Kashmir Valley.[46] The ISI's decision to stop funding and logistics support to the JKLF hastened its collapse as it ceased to be an effective force by the mid-1990s. Some prominent former JKLF cadres such as Yasin Malik then attempted to join the political mainstream as part of what came to be known as the All Party Hurriyat Conference. Amanullah Khan's dream of an independent Kashmir finally evaporated in 1996 when all remnants of the JKLF's militant wing were systematically eliminated by Indian security forces.

The Real Jihad

In his book *Shadow War*, Arif Jamal writes about the role played by the ISI in stoking the rebellion in Kashmir. He posits that a meeting between Zia and a prominent Jamaat-e-Islami leader in 1980 laid the foundation for the 'new covert war' in J&K and that Zia convinced the CIA that their money was being used to train jihadi fighters in Afghanistan when the real objective was to unleash the mujahideen in Kashmir.[47] Jamal portrays the Kashmir secessionist movement as being a by-product of Kashmiri angst and dissent exploited by the ISI. It was then given a jihadi focus by the Jamaat-e-Islami. Later,

Zia and the larger Pakistani security establishment adopted it as an effective and low-cost tool for containing India. However, the only groups that Jamal designates as proxies of the ISI are the JKLF and the HM. He conveniently ignores the emerging Pakistan-based groups that included foreign fighters, such as the Harkat-ul-Ansar (HuA), Harkat-ul-Mujahideen (HuM), Jaish-e-Mohammad (JeM) and the Lashkar-e-Taiba (LeT). These groups emerged as viable alternatives to the milder Kashmir-based groups, with whom the ISI was fast losing patience. However, in a later book, *Call for Transnational Jihad: Lashkar-e-Taiba (1985-2014)*, Jamal acknowledges the predominant role of the LeT in leading the ISI-sponsored jihad in J&K.[48]

Rise of Hizbul Mujahideen

Zia was sceptical of Kashmiri aspirations for independence which motivated the JKLF and its leader, Amanullah Khan. However, he played along as the JKLF sporadically attacked state police forces and government buildings from 1984 to 1988, without taking on the might of the Indian Army. But the JKLF's non-jihadist attitude and belief in Kashmiriyat did not endear it to secessionist groups like the Jamaat-e-Islami. Jamaat-e-Islami equated the fight for Kashmiri independence or secession to Pakistan with jihad. Under the fiery Syed Salahuddin, the HM became the first Kashmiri secessionist group. Salahuddin was disillusioned with mainstream politics in J&K after the rigged 1987 elections catapulted Dr Farooq Abdullah to power, and derailed his own political ambitions. He took to the gun under the umbrella of the powerful Jamaat-e-Islami. Exploiting the ISI's growing impatience with the JKLF's persistence with Kashmiriyat, he rallied thousands of disgruntled youth to follow suit. Concurrently, he bolstered the military capability of his outfit with weapons from across the border that were supplied to Pakistan by the CIA for the jihad in Afghanistan.

Through much of 1988 and 1989, the Valley witnessed numerous ISI-organized strikes and rallies. These gradually progressed into attacks on government establishments. It is said to have spent over Rs 100 crore a year to train and radicalize fighters and subvert individuals and institutions in Kashmir. Sophisticated weapons such as assault and sniper rifles, explosives and rocket launchers enabled terrorists to attack the Indian security forces.[49] As the Valley entered the turbulent 1990s, the HM became the first heavily armed ISI-sponsored jihadi group to engage the Indian Army in frontal firefights. However, the HM too soon fell out of favour with the ISI because of its largely Kashmiri flavour. Frequent fratricidal infighting made matters worse for the indigenous terrorist groups and eroded their capacity to mount a serious challenge to the Indian Army.[50] The stage was thus set for the entry into the Valley of mercenary, battle-hardened, highly radicalized and violent groups like the HuA, HuM and the LeT.[51] These groups comprised a mix of mujahideen fighters who hailed from regions as diverse as Chechnya, Sudan, Yemen and Afghanistan complemented by highly radicalized Kashmiri youth. Older and disgruntled members of various Kashmiri secessionist/terrorist groups acted as local guides for these groups. The Indian security forces soon realized that they had a serious fight on their hands.

Entry of the Lashkar-e-Taiba and Jaish-e-Mohammad

Every new proxy network that sprang up in J&K was proof of the messianic zeal of the ISI and the inability of the Indian government to convert military successes in the area into political outcomes. As the Indian security forces gained ascendancy over the HM in the mid-1990s, the ISI unleashed the HuA and HuM into the Valley. These groups came under Western censure following the kidnapping of six tourists and killing of five of them in July 1995 by the HuA.[52] Next came the LeT and JeM, with the former group working as the ISI's principal proxy. Under Hafiz Saeed, the LeT emerged as the lynchpin of the jihad in J&K for over a decade even though it was labelled as a terrorist organization by the US.[53] India began alerting the global community of the need for collective action against the two groups from the late 1990s onwards. However, the world took note of them only after the Mumbai attacks of 2008, in which 139 Indians and 26 foreigners – including several European, Israeli and American citizens – were killed.

The Markaz-ud-Dawa-wal-Irshad (MDI) was a Salafi jihadi organization that emerged in Saudi Arabia in the 1980s. It gained military momentum during the Afghanistan jihad. At the time, Hafiz Saeed was a lecturer in Islamic Studies at a university in Lahore. He was recruited into the group and honed his skills to incite terror in Kunar province of Afghanistan. Inspired by the incendiary oratorical skills of Hafiz Saeed, LeT fighters led by Zakiur Rehman Lakhvi were radicalized and trained to take on the might of the Indian Army. On 25 January 1990, the LeT claimed that it had killed four unarmed IAF pilots in Srinagar. However, the evidence gathered since points at the active involvement of the JKLF and its leader Yasin Malik in the planning and execution of the attack.[54] The attack was originally planned for the previous October, but had to be postponed for operational reasons.[55] The LeT thereafter expanded its operations by engaging in prolonged encounters with the Indian Army from 1990 to 1994. LeT fighters would keep sections and platoons of the army engaged for hours while others slipped through cordons and spread out in the Valley.

Lieutenant General Nanavatty commanded 19 Infantry Division at Baramulla as a major general during this period. He recollects that for the first time his units noticed a fanatical streak among the terrorists. They appeared to be willing to die fighting and even engaged the army in close and unarmed combat.[56] After studying the tactics of the LeT, Nanavatty informed all units engaged in counter-infiltration, counterinsurgency and counterterrorism operations about five conclusions he had reached. The first was that the LeT was the ISI's favourite proxy tool in the covert war in J&K. His second and third inferences were that it would not be too long before the LeT expanded its operation and that it had organizational, theological and financial support. The fourth conclusion was that since LeT was refraining from targeting Westerners in J&K and was not expanding its networks elsewhere, India would have to sort it out by itself. Lastly, Nanavatty concluded that the LeT was more willing to execute fidayeen attacks, which differed significantly from suicide attacks. He explained, 'Fidayeen attacks involved fighting to the death and avoiding capture by trained fighters, while suicide attacks merely involved blowing oneself up by indoctrinated but untrained fighters.'[57]

The LeT attacks progressed from encounters with security forces to directly targeting civilians from the Hindu and Sikh communities. The group was emboldened by its initial successes and its terrorist base swelled with increased funding from the ISI. It then attacked the Red Fort in December 2000 and the Indian Parliament in Delhi exactly a year later. These attacks nearly sparked off a war between India and Pakistan in 2002. The LeT continued its spree of terrorism by attacking the Akshardham temple in Gandhinagar, Gujarat, killing thirty-three people in 2002. The group is also alleged to have provided active support to the Dawood Ibrahim gang for the Mumbai serial blasts of 2003.[58] Facing heat from security forces in J&K prior to the ceasefire of 2003, the LeT diversified its repertoire. It began supporting indigenous jihadi groups and banned Islamist organizations like the Indian Mujahideen and Students Islamic Party of India. The free run of the LeT gradually slowed down after the notional censure by the US and Pakistan in the aftermath of 9/11. It morphed into the Jamaat-ud-Dawa (JuD) in 2002 and continued to wage a covert war till it was proscribed by the UN after the 2008 Mumbai attacks.

However, the one jihadi who has inflicted most damage on innocent civilians and Indian security forces in recent times in J&K is Masood Azhar, the head of the JeM. Azhar rose from being a preacher in the Deobandi-dominated madrassas of Bahawalpur and Karachi to a fully indoctrinated jihadi. Endowed with fiery and inflammatory oratory skills, Azhar was identified by the ISI as one who, along with Hafiz Saeed, could energize the floundering HM-led insurgency in Kashmir.[59] It was in this milieu that the HuA – whose core cadres comprised veterans of the Afghan Jihad and ISI-trained Punjabi jihadis – emerged as a concurrent military threat to the Indian security forces in the early 1990s. Supporting them were Kashmiri youth who were indoctrinated by Masood Azhar and his band of terrorist preachers and trained in camps that had sprung up all along the LoC in PoK.

Masood Azhar first entered Kashmir via Delhi in early 1994. He was sent by the ISI to rein in his military commander 'Afghani', who had escalated the fight with the Indian security forces to levels that made the ISI uncomfortable. Azhar's task was to recalibrate the conflict to levels that would enable the ISI to orchestrate the 'proxy war' as planned. Azhar, Afghani and other HuA terrorists were captured by the Indian Army in late 1994, interrogated and interned in different Indian jails.[60] Colonel Pavan Nair, who was a staff officer at 15 Corps HQ at that time, recalls numerous occasions when Azhar would be sitting meekly outside the office of Brigadier Arjun Ray waiting to be interviewed about the jihadi network in the Valley.[61]

An analysis of the total fatalities in J&K in the years that followed Azhar's capture indicates that the jihadi movement had acquired self-sustaining momentum.[62] This was due to the ISI's efforts and Azhar's ability to galvanize large numbers of Kashmiri youth into crossing the LoC. His three attempts to escape from Jammu's Central Jail further reinforced his aura among the jihadis. Azhar was released from jail following the hijack of Indian Airlines flight IC-814 in December 1999. Encouraged by the ISI and the Taliban – who were keen on establishing their presence in J&K – Azhar launched his own outfit, the JeM. UN reports also indicate that Azhar was supported by none other than Osama bin Laden. This allowed him to emerge at the head of the pack of jihadis in Kashmir.[63] Azhar was furious when the JeM was portrayed as having played second fiddle to the LeT during the attack on the Indian Parliament in December 2001. He soon urged the ISI to assign an exclusive JeM team to execute an attack on an Indian Army camp. The attack happened at Kaluchak near Jammu in July 2002. Thirty-one people were killed – three army personnel, eighteen family members of army personnel including several children, and ten civilians.[64]

A combination of geopolitical factors limited the JeM's activity to the Kashmir Valley. These included the 2003 ceasefire across the LoC, the ISI's preoccupation with Afghanistan, the LeT being designated as a global terrorist group after the Mumbai attacks of 2008 and the reconfiguration of

Kashmir-centric jihadi groups. However, US pressure on the LeT and Chinese intransigence towards censuring Masood Azhar has given the JeM a free run in Kashmir and a platform for expanding its network in Punjab. The massive expansion of the JeM's headquarters in Bahawalpur, Pakistan, is also testimony to the blind eye that the Pakistani government has turned to Azhar's status as the pivot of terror in J&K.

Despite the setback to the JeM after the Indian Army's surgical strikes on its camps following the 2016 Uri suicide attacks, the political vacuum in J&K gave Masood Azhar a respite from relentless operations by India's security forces. The Pulwama attack in February 2019 – which was undertaken to avenge the death of his nephew, who was neutralized by security forces in November 2017 – highlights the extent to which Masood Azhar continues to be on India's 'most wanted' list. Both these attacks and their consequences are covered in Chapter 19. For now, the narrative moves on to the late 1980s, when the Indian Army moved into the J&K hinterland in strength to tackle the ISI-led covert war that had morphed into jihadi terrorism.

14

THE INDIAN ARMY RESPONDS

'ISI is our first line of defence and stands out as the best intelligence agency in the world.'[1]

– Prime Minister of Pakistan Imran Khan in 2018

Strategizing after Punjab

Punjab was India's first brush with terrorism. Terrorism differs from insurgency in that the perpetrators coerce non-combatants instead of seeking popular support for a cause. A largely urban and semi-urban phenomenon in India, it has similarities with violent and organized crime.[2] The change in character of the terrorism in J&K and its morphing into externally abetted communal terrorism from the late 1980s, was not surprising to Indian intelligence agencies. Intelligence officers like Surendra Nath with extensive experience in J&K between the 1960s and 1980s had recommended a judicious mix of force and good governance to ensure that the indigenous terrorism led by the JKLF and HM was not hijacked by Pakistan-based jihadis led by the LeT and HuA.[3] Not helping matters was the weak and dilatory leadership in New Delhi starting with Prime Minister V.P. Singh's coalition government, which had little stomach for using force as an enabler of statecraft and allowed Kashmir to drift for much of the late 1980s and early 1990s. They let the situation fester till there was no choice but to deploy the Indian Army in strength in counter-infiltration and counterterrorism roles in the early 1990s, also called CI and CT operations in the Indian Army.

The absence of any strategic and operational analysis of secessionist terrorism in Punjab resulted in the fading away of the lessons from that period. Consequently, its impact on the contours of the terrorism and proxy war in J&K rarely figures in current discussions on the subject. A deeper examination of the Kashmir crisis by Swami and Hamish Telford – a Canadian professor of political science – reveals its linkages with the Punjab's secessionist movement in the 1980s and early 1990s. It escalated the covert war in J&K from a mere irritant for India's security forces to a siege from within.[4] Telford is a keen analyst of counterterrorism operations in Punjab and J&K and writes that India's current counterterrorism strategy in J&K is much like the one it followed in Punjab. Any further evolution has come through 'trial and error'.[5] While he may be right to some extent, the evolution of India's counterterrorism strategy has also come from a flexible process driven by experiential learning.

The lessons of the Naga insurgency and the experience of the IPKF in Sri Lanka are studied at the counterinsurgency school in Vairangte in Mizoram. This is also being undertaken at the corps battle schools that have been set up in 15 and 16 Corps; the two corps of the Indian Army that are actively involved in CI and CT operations in J&K. Army intellectuals like Chibber and Nanavatty have contributed immensely to the evolution of the CI/CT strategy as it exists today. Adding value to the discourse have been academics like Rajesh Rajagopalan who have written extensively on issues such as counterinsurgency operations.[6] Even in the early 1990s, when the Indian Army's divisional commanders like Nanavatty were commanding divisions along the LoC, there was adequate clarity on the emerging templates of terrorism and the unfolding covert war in J&K. Nanavatty has often argued against the temptation of conveniently branding all conflict in J&K as terrorism because of the terror attacks against the minority Hindu population. He says that it conformed more closely to a calibrated Pakistan-supported covert war and that Pakistan uses terrorism as an instrument of state policy to 'destabilize and diminish India'.[7] Several journalists like Shekhar Gupta and Nitin Gokhale have also indirectly enhanced our understanding of the different facets of counterterrorism over the years after their extensive sojourns in battlegrounds like J&K, the north-eastern parts of India and Sri Lanka.

India's Kashmir strategy has largely been bereft of continuity and strategic vision. It has invariably evolved from personality-centric attempts by Delhi to initiate a meaningful political process. A failure in this process has generally led the centre to blame the state government for the deteriorating law and order situation and the subversion of the political process. Following the inability of the state government to manage the security landscape, the centre has invariably attempted to bring the situation under control by deploying the military and central armed paramilitary forces with adequate constitutional provisions. Some of these that merit attention and further study are Article 356, Armed Forces Special Powers Act (1956), the National Security Act (1980), the Unlawful Activities Prevention Act (1967) and the lesser known Terrorist Affected Areas (Special Courts) Ordinance (1984) and the Armed Forces (J&K) Special Powers Act (1990).[8]

This has often been followed by the deployment of large forces in the affected areas to fight an attrition battle. The forces were expected to spread out and squeeze the infiltration/terrorism, confining it to a few areas and to prevent its contagious spread. As the force consolidated its hold, it turned its focus on the leadership of the movement. This was by way of offering a window of opportunity to both the leaders and their followers to abandon their cause. This strategic model is a coercive one which is employed by the state to psychologically exhaust the terrorist/secessionist. It seeks to highlight the physical futility of continuing with a secessionist movement. In J&K, this has been the longest and most exhausting phase for both the security forces and the terrorists/secessionists, and more so, the common people. In this battle of attrition, there are moments when both the hunter and the hunted lose focus and resort to the indiscriminate use of force. This leads to collateral damage, human rights abuses and diminishing public support for terrorists/secessionists or security forces. The entry of the media into the fray makes matters worse in this information age. Over the years, the Indian Army has complemented this strategy with embedded intelligence-driven operations by its Special Forces. These have proved particularly effective in the systematic elimination of leadership of the jihadi networks.

The last phase of the strategy is the stabilization and conflict resolution phase and the reintroduction of the political process. This is always the most difficult stage in conflicts of this nature. In Punjab, this resolution gradually took place over three elections (1985, 1992 and 1997). But in J&K, despite four elections (1996, 2002, 2008 and 2014), the covert war has continuously escalated since the late 1980s. Assessing the fault lines in India's CI and CT strategies in J&K over the years, Lieutenant General Syed Ata Hasnain, commander of the Srinagar-based 15 Corps between 2010 and 2012, laments the absence of a sustained government approach and continuity whenever there has been a 'stabilization phase' after extensive kinetic operations. Reflecting on a much-debated issue within the Indian Army of defining the centres of gravity in the conflict that has raged in J&K since 1947, Hasnain argues that these have alternated between 'the people of Kashmir' and the 'terrorist leadership'.

Important as they are, he reflects on a more important centre of gravity which gained traction as the secessionist movement gathered steam in the mid-1990s. Referring to this as the ideological idea of 'azadi' or freedom that occupied the mind space of radical elements of the secessionist movement,[9] he laments that this was not adequately addressed. This would prove costly for India as the secessionist movement has transformed since 2008 into a jihadi and Pakistani Deep State-led hybrid war. Instead, India has largely preferred the direct kinetic route to defeating terrorism in J&K. A better way may have been a more flexible 'indirect approach' that 'separates the fish from the water', as suggested by John Nagl in his seminal work, *Learning to Eat Soup with a Knife: Counterinsurgency Lessons from Malaya and Vietnam.*[10]

Boiling Over

Despite the ominous warnings spelt out during 1983-84 by Lieutenant General Chibber, the commander of the Indian Army's Northern Command, India was unable to control events in J&K in the mid- and late 1980s. This happened because India had partly deluded itself that Kashmir would sort itself out, given that Pakistan was too preoccupied with Afghanistan to stoke the secessionist movement further. Chibber insisted that it was time for the Indian Army to understand the socio-economic, religious and ethnic diversity of J&K and recognize its vulnerability to fissiparous forces from across the LoC. From this emerged the Indian Army's first strands of what would be globally known a few decades later as the counterterrorism strategy of 'Winning Hearts and Minds' or WHAM. Tasking a study group to write an easily digestible narrative that was titled *Soldiers' Role in Jammu and Kashmir,*[11] Chibber exhorted his officers to disseminate it widely, an exercise that Hasnain participated in as a company commander of his Garhwal Rifles battalion in the Poonch Sector, and in the divisional battle school at Naushera in late 1983.[12] Chibber's prescient understanding led him to believe that this was necessary if the Indian Army was not to be perceived by the people of J&K as an occupation army in the years ahead.

Jagmohan, who twice served as governor of J&K between 1984 and 1990, sensed an ominous change in the security landscape of the state. Writing to Rajiv Gandhi in early 1990, he said, 'In August 1988, after analysing the current and undercurrents, I had summed up the position thus: The drumbeaters of parochialism and fundamentalism are working overtime. Subversion is on the increase. The shadows of events from across the border are lengthening. Lethal weapons have come in. More may be on the way.' In April 1989, he desperately pleaded for immediate action: 'The situation is fast deteriorating. It has almost reached a point of no return.' Jagmohan noted that 'things have truly fallen apart'.[13] There was political instability and apathy at both the centre and state level along with mass mobilization of an educated populace and increasing penetration of Kashmiri civil society by radical elements from the Jamaat-e-Islami and the ISI.

This made it impossible for the Indian Army to stem the rot that had set in. It was clear that the Indian Army served as a border protection force along the LoC and was too thinly spread to prevent large-scale infiltration of local and foreign terrorists into the state from PoK. The time was now ripe for Zia's successors within the Pakistan Army to operationalize his Quranic Concept of War. Systematically following the first operational tenet of his strategy, they directed well-trained subversive elements to avoid confronting the Indian Army and first test their combat skills against police and paramilitary forces. An analysis of attacks during 1989-91 corroborates this accurately.[14] There was free movement on the roads of J&K and there was no way to seal the highly porous LoC and even stretches of the demarcated International Border (IB). Those were days of conventional conflict, and routine patrols were undertaken to prevent infiltration across the LoC. Artillery engagements were rare, and opposing post commanders regularly exchanged memos, pleasantries and sweets.

The Indian Army knew that youth were crossing over into PoK, but force availability and absence of an obstacle prevented the plugging of all infiltration routes. Brigadier 'R' served in 2009 as a battalion commander in a sector in North Kashmir that was known to be one of Pakistan's favourite infiltration points. Among his many tasks was to mingle with the people and establish a rapport with the elders of society. This was to convince them to counsel the youth not to take up the gun. He spoke about one such meeting with a Gujjar (hill tribesman) in his seventies. The man had set up the rendezvous at a desolate place to not be seen interacting with the officer. At the meeting, the old man spoke at length about his role in the ongoing secessionist movement and how he was among the initial set of guides recruited by the ISI to lead disgruntled Kashmiri youth into PoK in the early 1980s. He then volunteered to acquaint the battalion with numerous infiltration routes that he had traversed as a guide for the JKLF and other groups in the 1980s. He did so because of his disillusionment with the movement and the ISI's exploitation of Gujjars who had historically used grazing grounds astride the LoC.[15]

The years 1989 and 1990 were scarred by sporadic violence and a marked rise in the number of fatalities suffered by the security forces.[16] There was a complete absence of law and order under the chief ministership of Farooq Abdullah, who came to power on the back of a dubiously managed election.[17] His government failed to stop the pogrom unleashed by the Jamaat-e-Islami-led gangs that forced over 2,00,000 Hindus to flee their homes in the Valley in the winter of 1989 and seek refuge in Jammu and other cities of India. This forced Delhi to call on the army in right earnest to restore normalcy in J&K.

Lieutenant General M.A. Zaki – a distinguished infantry officer from the Maratha Regiment who had won a Vir Chakra for gallantry in the 1971 war – took over command of 15 Corps in Srinagar in October 1989. The Ministry of Defence reckoned that the appointment of a Muslim officer would send the powerful message to both the common people and the secessionists that a secular India was serious about reining in the separatists. However, Zaki could do little to stop the persecution of the Hindus and their exodus in the winter of 1989-90. Lamenting the heavily filtered flow of intelligence from Delhi, Zaki is highly critical of the then Intelligence Bureau chief, A.S. Dulat. He alleges that he was not given any detailed intelligence briefing either by the civilian or military intelligence agencies before he took over 15 Corps. There seemed to be no urgency in Delhi about the deteriorating situation in J&K, and the information he received was that 'there is no real problem in J&K'.[18] By the time Zaki assumed command in Srinagar, the JKLF had already moved to the next phase of the insurrection. The key objectives during this phase were to disrupt infrastructure and various lines of communication. Targets included the Jawahar tunnel across the Banihal Pass and key points on the Jammu-Srinagar highway.

On 9 December 1989, Rubaiyya Sayeed, the daughter of Union home minister Mufti Mohammed Sayeed, was kidnapped by a group of JKLF terrorists led by Yasin Malik. This was Zaki's first major challenge. He was only apprised of the situation by the J&K police at 8 p.m. – nearly nine hours after she was abducted. Zaki knew by then that the kidnappers would be well outside the limited security dragnet that was in place in and around Srinagar. He was told that the delay was because of backchannel negotiations between the kidnappers, Delhi and Farooq Abdullah. While Abdullah is believed to have initially taken a strong stand against negotiating with the kidnappers, his political rival Mufti Sayeed convinced New Delhi to negotiate his daughter's release. She was eventually released in exchange for jailed terrorists of the JKLF. The success of this operation gave a clear indication to secessionist forces that India was not prepared for a covert war in J&K.[19] The incident also spelt the end for Farooq Abdullah's beleaguered government. This eventually forced Delhi to declare President's rule in J&K and call on the army to

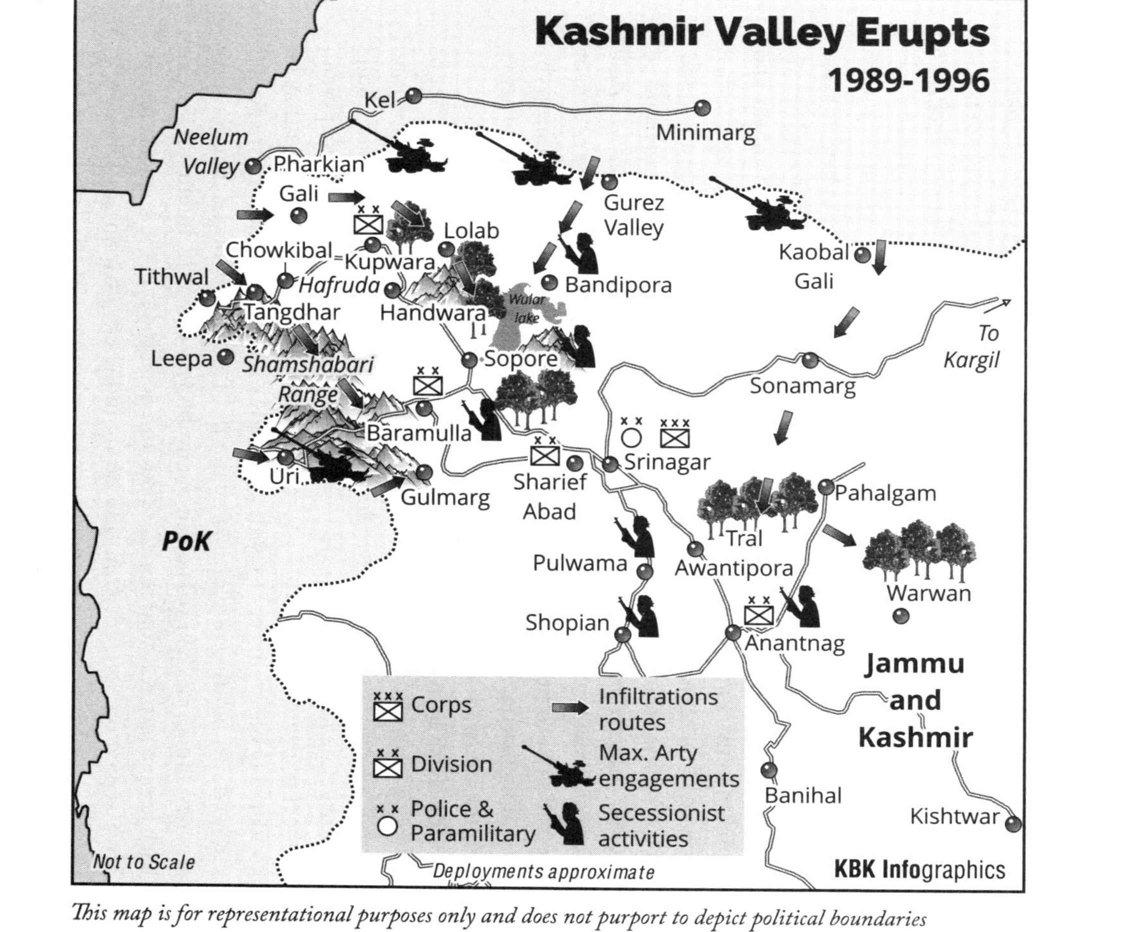

This map is for representational purposes only and does not purport to depict political boundaries

restore normalcy in J&K. General Krishna Rao resigned as governor of J&K and Prime Minister V.P. Singh's coalition government in Delhi once again appointed Jagmohan as his successor.

Coming to Grips

The Indian Army stepped in immediately, without the necessary resources. 19 Infantry Division – one of the three divisions under 15 Corps – was the only infantry division deployed in the Valley with its HQ in Baramulla. It was primarily configured for deployment along the LoC in a border protection role It had to now take on the additional counter-infiltration and counterterrorism roles. Zaki was desperately short of troops to create an effective internal security grid in northern Kashmir. Completing his force were two army battalions for counterterrorism operations in the capital city of Srinagar and a mix of central armed paramilitary and police forces. Considering the vast expanse of the area of its deployment from the Banihal Pass to Eastern Ladakh, 15 Corps was clearly undermanned and ill-equipped for counterterrorism and counter-infiltration duties. Following attacks on army camps and convoys, Zaki requisitioned additional troops and deployed his air defence regiment as convoy protection in addition to putting a counter-infiltration grid in place. Given the prevailing inertia, Zaki could well be considered the first orchestrator of active counter-infiltration and counterterrorism operations in J&K

The JKLF increased its attacks on soft targets, killing the vice chancellor of Kashmir University and his aide in March 1990. The encounters became more protracted and attacks included looting of banks and destruction of public infrastructure like bridges. The JKLF's chief military commander, Ashfaq Wani, was neutralized by the security forces on 30 March 1990. Zaki says that he accidentally blew himself up with a grenade during the engagement and did not go down fighting as glorified by the JKLF.[20] In view of the deteriorating security situation, Zaki persuaded Army HQ to move 28 Infantry Division back to northern Kashmir from Ladakh and deployed it in the Kupwara region. He assigned one brigade from the newly inducted 8 Mountain Division to bolster the counterterrorist operations in Pulwama and the Tral forest areas of southern Kashmir. This caused significant attrition on the JKLF and other terrorist groups in the Valley. But it was still not enough to plug all infiltration routes – despite the three layers of defences along major ingress routes.

By the end of 1990, there were two infantry divisions deployed along the LoC from Uri in the west to Dras in the east. Complementing them in the Budgam, Pulwama, Anantnag and Tral Sectors of southern Kashmir was the newly inducted 8 Mountain Division. In addition, there were three battalions in the city of Srinagar along with the police and CAPF. This totalled to a presence of about 80,000 to 1,00,000 personnel in the J&K at the time. The major routes of infiltration were down the Shamshabari Range through Gulmarg and Sonamarg, from the south across the Pir Panjal Range and through narrow valleys in the Gurez, Naushera, Machil, Neelum and Tangdhar Sectors. The towns of Kupwara, Sopore and Baramulla emerged as safe havens for the terrorists, who were actively supported by locals in these semi-urban areas. Srinagar continued to be the intellectual hub of secessionist activity despite heavy security presence.

Zaki recollects that the troops had no respite, with a cycle of three days in operations followed by a one-day recuperation period. Many initial army operations were unsuccessful because of the lack of an effective military-intelligence grid and a network of informers. One such operation was mounted after intelligence reports from Delhi indicated that hundreds of infiltrators had taken over the Shamshabari Range and were waiting for an opportune moment to come down into the Valley. Responding to this input, Zaki sent two battalions on a futile search operation that had to be called off a few days after not finding any infiltrators. In response to Zaki's pleas for a dedicated intelligence unit, General V.N. Sharma assigned one from Sri Lanka to 15 Corps. Despite the lack of intelligence, the number of terrorists killed rose dramatically in 1991 from the previous year. This indicated the firm resolve of the security forces.[21]

Zaki recalls meeting three young travellers from Maharashtra who were cycling in Kashmir. They told him, 'Sir, there are a lot of problems – the clocks everywhere are set to Pakistan Standard Time and we are often told that the next time we came, we would need a Pakistan visa.' Zaki confirms that thousands of misguided Kashmiri youth had crossed the LoC during 1988-89 to be trained in camps set up at Muzaffarabad, Chakoti and Kel. They subsequently infiltrated into the Valley – mainly as armed porters – with a few having received specialized training from the ISI in handling weapons and explosives among other battle skills. They would set up arms caches at various places as part of a supply chain network. The crossings were tracked with inputs from varied sources that Zaki had cultivated. One of them was an ex-army officer who had been posted with him in 19 Infantry Division, but was now setting up an ITDC hotel in the Valley. Zaki soon realized that the numbers were far higher than what was estimated in the routine intelligence briefings. He was alerted to thousands of cheap fur-lined boots and jackets being bought in the local markets in the autumn of 1989.[22]

Another operational strategy that evolved during Zaki's tenure was targeting Pakistani bunkers and positions along the Neelum-Gurez and Machil Sectors with concentrated artillery fire. This disrupted movement along the only road from the Pakistan Army's Kel Cantonment eastwards towards Minimarg, which was being developed as a brigade HQ opposite the Mushkoh Sector. Zaki recalls moving a battery of 105mm guns and mortars to 11,000 feet and mounting a fire assault in response to the infiltration in the sector. People-centric operations was another facet of Zaki's strategy. He instituted a surrender policy that assured Kashmiri terrorists of rehabilitation. Engaging with families, he gradually built up a network of informers and pro-government militants. New Delhi missed a trick by not engaging similarly with Kashmiri terrorists housed in jails across the country. Thus, when many of these terrorists were released for want of evidence they again crossed over to PoK. Pakistani flags were widely flown in the home town of Syed Salahuddin, an impoverished village called Soibug in the Budgam district of southern Kashmir.[23] Salahuddin was arrested for anti-national activities in 1990. But as the charges could not be proved, he was released later that year and crossed over into Pakistan.

Responding to a credible tip-off that a convoy of a hundred mules accompanied by armed terrorists and porters was making its way across the Shamshabari Range, Zaki ordered an infantry brigade into action. Surrounded and given opportunities to surrender, the group, however, chose to fight and were all killed – over seventy in all. Huge amounts of arms and ammunition were recovered from hidden caches in the area as such encounters and intercepts became frequent. Another major encounter followed a tip-off from a young paratrooper from 3 PARA who had spotted two large columns of men going towards Sonamarg from Kaobal Gali. Zaki surrounded the area with two battalions, tactically deploying them to cut off all routes of escape. This time around, over 200 porters and raw recruits surrendered; only one was killed as he tried to escape. Zaki was amazed by the cache of arms that included heavy weapons – including rocket launchers – and huge quantities of ammunition.

In June 1991, Zaki had completed almost two years as corps commander. He hoped to spend the twilight of his career at the Indian Military Academy, where he was sent as the commandant. But this was not to be as his services were requisitioned by the new governor of J&K, Girish 'Gary' Chandra Saxena. Saxena's predecessor, Jagmohan, had been removed from the post the previous year after taking blame for violence in the state following the assassination of a religious leader by terrorists of the HM.[24] Zaki continued in the role of advisor until 1995, when he retired following differences with then governor General K.V. Krishna Rao.

Matters came to a head when terrorists led by the notorious Mast Gul from the Khyber Pakhtunkhwa region of Pakistan slipped through the elaborate grid laid by Indian security forces and set a sacred shrine, Charar-e-Sharif, on fire in May 1995. They had literally occupied it for almost five months with the security forces in cordon. Not permitted to move in to avoid damage to the shrine, the security forces remained mute spectators for months as the terrorists consolidated their hold within.[25] This, according to Zaki, was a major reverse for the security forces and was a result of poor coordination between the army, central paramilitary forces and the local police which had allowed the terrorists to dig themselves in. Political indecisiveness in New Delhi allowed the situation to completely go out of hand. Making matters worse was the escape of the terrorists through the security dragnet after setting the shrine aflame.

Prime Minister P.V. Narasimha Rao's government lost an opportunity to seize the political initiative between 1993 and 1996, when the Indian Army was going hammer and tongs at the secessionist movement. To address the root of the problem, Zaki had suggested comprehensive de-radicalization initiatives and institutional interaction with the families of youth who had crossed the LoC. He blames the ostrich-like attitude of bureaucrats and politicians who refused to listen to the military at crucial junctures of the crisis. When Mast Gul returned to Pakistan after the desecration of the shrine, he was a hero and hailed as a freedom fighter. No one exemplifies the perception that 'one man's terrorist is another man's freedom fighter' better than Mast Gul, who was branded a 'terrorist' by the Pakistani state after masterminding the Peshawar attacks in February 2014.[26]

Securing North Kashmir

Nanavatty assumed command of 19 Infantry Division at Baramulla in June 1993, after his predecessor was wounded in a firefight, just as the HM was losing momentum in its fight against a buoyant Indian Army and the ISI had turned to the HuA, HuM and LeT to intensify their attacks in the Valley. The four brigades in his division were broadly responsible for the areas around Uri, Baramulla, Rafiabad and Naugam. 28 Infantry Division covered Kupwara, Sopore, and the Shamshabari Range, while 8 Mountain Division was responsible for the southern portions of the Kashmir Valley, which broadly comprised the Anantnag, Budgam, Bandipora, Pulwama and Tral Sectors.

Nanavatty's strategy of clearing Baramulla of all pockets of terrorists was much like the one the British had adopted in Northern Ireland. Self-contained detachments would maintain a sustained presence in the town of Baramulla – both to the south and north of the Jhelum River – by occupying abandoned and derelict buildings across town. This differed from the strategy in nearby Sopore town, where 28 Infantry Division was attempting to take control street by street and house by house.

The peculiarity of Baramulla was that Old Baramulla, to the north of the Jhelum, was a hotbed of secession and radicalism, while the area to the south of the river was controllable. However, Nanavatty recollects that within three months a battalion had restored a modicum of normalcy in Baramulla without any untoward incident. The battalion even set up a healthcare clinic that was well received by the locals. There was gradual rebuilding of trust. Nanavatty also remembers that by late 1993 the influx of foreign terrorists had reached alarming proportions. Comprising fighters of Pakistani, Chechen and Arab origin who had been trained by the Al-Qaeda and Taliban, they posed a significant military challenge to the Indian Army. The forests of Rafiabad, Hafruda and Handwara were used by large groups of these foreign terrorists to create caches and hideouts. They would emerge from these forests to engage Indian Army patrols. It was a time of experimentation for the Indian Army as well.

One of these experimental operational strategies was to try and exploit the fractured opposition by undertaking 'pseudo gang' operations.[27] This was a strategy first employed by the Rhodesian Army against anti-apartheid militant groups in South Africa. Lawrence Cline adds that:

> pseudo operations, in which government forces and guerrilla defectors portray themselves as insurgent units, have been a very successful technique used in several counterinsurgency campaigns. Pseudo teams have provided critical human intelligence and other support to these operations. These operations, although of considerable value, also have raised several concerns. Their use in offensive missions and psychological operations campaigns has, at times, been counterproductive.[28]

Volunteers from the Indian Army were tasked to create pseudo groups with the help of surrendered terrorist-turned-informers. They would then gather intelligence about other outfits, fraternize with them and even join them on operations to win their trust. Then, at an opportune moment, these pseudo groups would capture or liquidate them. The volunteers were tactically and physically proficient. They would wear local civilian attire, grow beards, speak the local dialect and perform namaz five times a day. The hardest part was establishing contact with the infiltrating foreign terrorists and gaining their confidence. The former terrorists in these pseudo gangs often exceeded their briefs and engaged in petty crime. This incurred the wrath of local villagers, who stopped providing information. There was also a competition for honours, kills and awards among pseudo gangs, which diluted their effectiveness.

A few gruesome losses led to significant downscaling of such operations by the mid-1990s. Nanavatty argues that though these operations were initially effective, the Indian Army did not approach them scientifically nor with a long-term perspective. According to him, such operations ought to have been run by the Special Forces as they had by then gathered adequate covert warfare experience in Sri Lanka. As the Indian Army tightened its grip over Baramulla, Kupwara and Sopore, Srinagar emerged as the new hotspot and intellectual hub for secessionist and terrorist operations. The army had not yet taken over operational control of this urban epicentre of secession. The inability of the army leadership to convince the chief minister or Delhi to dismantle the emerging secessionist networks in Srinagar proved consequential.

Hardening Stance and Window for Stabilization

Colonel Pavan Nair, who served in HQ 15 Corps between 1994 and 1996, recollects that by then the RR had emerged as the main counterterrorism force in J&K. He recounts, 'Those were challenging times, with three or four IED blasts every day. One such blast killed the brigade commander of the Uri-based 12 Infantry Brigade. Electronic devices recovered during raids and from IEDs revealed Pakistani ordnance factory markings. The gloves were completely off as nobody really knew how many terrorists had crossed over. Grenade attacks and firing were commonplace in Srinagar and bullets often ricocheted off roofs in the cantonment. In response, 28 Infantry Division was hitting the Pakistan Army in the Neelum-Gurez Sectors with rocket launchers, anti-aircraft guns and medium artillery.'[29]

Feeling the heat from the sustained kinetic operations in North Kashmir, separatists and jihadis searched for fresh pastures to extend the covert war. South Kashmir and areas south of the Pir Panjal Range emerged as new hotspots because of this strategy. Lieutenant General Pattabhiraman, a former vice chief of army staff, commanded 33 Infantry Brigade in the Jammu region in the early 1990s. He recounts that infiltrations had significantly increased in the Poonch and Rajouri Sectors of the Jammu region resulting in the large presence of terrorists in the areas of Doda and Kishtwar. However, the strategy adopted by the infiltrating jihadis was not the same as before. They had started targeting communities, hamlets and villages that had Hindu populations. This was the period that General Hooda, who has commanded the Indian Army's Northern Command in more recent times, refers to as the 'expansion of the arc of instability' in J&K. The tightening of the counterterrorism grid in the Kashmir Valley had resulted in the opening of an effective second front by the ISI and the jihadis. Pattabhiraman reckons that escalation in the terrorism in the areas of Rajouri, Poonch, Doda and Kishtwar in the mid-1990s proved to be an effective smokescreen for what was unfolding in Kargil.[30]

Syed Salahuddin made one last attempt to return to the Valley in 1994. He spoke to the Indian Army about alternative alignments and support. But the discussions proved fruitless and Salahuddin succumbed to the immense pressure from the ISI. He made his way back across the LoC to PoK and set up the United Jihad Council as a figurehead and puppet of the ISI. Meanwhile, the RR had amalgamated well into the counterterrorism grid and by 1996 the pipeline of foreign terrorists too had dried up. This forced the ISI to work on a fresh strategy of propelling the LeT as the vanguard of the jihad in Kashmir. Northern Command assessed that the military had done its job and it was time for the state and New Delhi to take over. Unfortunately, two years of political instability in New Delhi between 1996 and 1998 saw two ineffective prime ministers – H.D. Deve Gowda and I.K. Gujral – squander away the operational gains of the preceding five years. This allowed the ISI and the LeT to tighten their grip over the secessionist struggle in J&K.

Understandably, the newly elected Bharatiya Janata Party government in 1998 under Atal Bihari Vajpayee wanted some time to consolidate its position before initiating any comprehensive dialogue with the people of Kashmir. Making matters more difficult for Vajpayee was the controversy created over land acquisition for better facilities for Hindu pilgrims to the sacred Amarnath shrine. No more than a move to build facilities like shelters and toilets, it sparked off a politically motivated agitation that led to the collapse of the government in J&K, a coalition of the Congress and the Peoples Democratic Party. The initiation of a fresh political process distracted both the army and New Delhi[31] as the window for conflict resolution further closed when Musharraf assumed command of the Pakistan Army in 1998. He provided fresh impetus to secessionist terrorism in the Valley, particularly in South Kashmir and the Jammu region. He did this while hatching his sinister plan in Kargil to undermine the ongoing peace process initiated by Vajpayee and Pakistan's prime minister, Nawaz Sharif.

15

SURPRISE AND RIPOSTE IN KARGIL

'Come October, we shall walk in to Siachen to mop up the dead bodies of hundreds of Indians left hungry, out in the cold.'[1]

– Lieutenant General Mahmud Ahmad of the Pakistan Army

Getting Even with India

At the strategic level, the Kargil conflict of 1999 was a result of the insecurity of the Pakistani Deep State (meaning the Pakistan Army and its jihadi affiliates). Threatened by the very real prospects of the success of peace talks between Prime Ministers Vajpayee and Nawaz Sharif, the Pakistan Army sought to destabilize the subcontinent with an operation they thought was covered by a nuclear umbrella. With both countries having demonstrated nuclear weapons capability in the preceding year, the Pakistan Army leadership felt that they had the upper hand in the 'nuclear coercion' game. Consequently, they felt they could extract significant gains by surreptitiously occupying Indian territory in the Kargil Sector.

At the operational level, the Pakistan Army needed to get even with India after its stunning capitulation in 1971. The pre-emptive occupation of the Saltoro Ridge by the Indian Army in 1984, and the aggressive localized action by successive Indian commanders of the Siachen Brigade created tremendous pressure on the FCNA[2] to redeem the Pakistan Army's honour.[3] Surprisingly, the impact of the Indian occupation of the Saltoro Ridge on operational events that unfolded between 1985 and 1999 was not adequately war-gamed in

India. There was still an obsession with large-scale exercises such as Exercise Brasstacks and other massive manoeuvre exercises that were conducted in Rajasthan and Punjab. The concept of 'limited war' had not yet been thought about in detail. Brigadier Devinder Singh, who played a pivotal role during the Kargil conflict as commander of 70 Infantry Brigade, took part in a war game conducted by the Indian Army's 15 Corps in early 1999. Role-playing an enemy commander, he correctly assessed that he would easily capture several of the heights in the Mushkoh Sector. His assessment was rejected by the corps commander and the army commander.[4] They would eat humble pie months later when the same heights fell to the infiltrating Pakistani forces.

The area of Kargil has featured prominently in the history of conflict between the two nations. In late 1948, tribal Lashkars[5] supported by the Gilgit Scouts attempted a winter run into Leh via Dras and Kargil, only to be thwarted by the Indian Army's spirited pushback.[6] The initial thrust of Operation Gibraltar in 1965 to destabilize J&K was also in the Kargil sector, where the Indian Army could not prevent infiltrators from capturing Point 13620 and Black Rock overlooking Kargil town. In May 1965 – months before the main India-Pakistan conflict – the 4th Battalion of the Rajput Regiment (4 RAJPUT) of the Indian Army's 121 Infantry Brigade fought tough high-altitude battles supported by 85 Light Regiment, an artillery unit, to evict the infiltrators from these heights. Prominent among these heights was Point 13620, which was captured twice during the 1965 war. The attacking Indian forces suffered heavy casualties and felt let down when the height was returned to Pakistan after the Tashkent Agreement.[7] During the 1971 war, an ambitious Indian offensive across the Kargil heights by 121 Brigade and the Ladakh Scouts recaptured Point 13620. However, the broader offensive was thwarted by the weather and the eventual ceasefire.[8]

Pakistan's Kargil Plan is widely believed to have been mooted as early as 1987 – when Zia was the military dictator – but had been shot down as too risky and untenable by Pakistan's foreign minister, Yakub Khan.[9] It resurfaced in 1998 when General Jehangir Karamat was chief of army staff but derailed for similar reasons.[10] It is highly likely that Musharraf saw the plan as an opportunity to make history. Colonel Vivek Chadha is an Indian Army scholar who has tracked the career of Musharraf. He suggests that Musharraf's close association with the Special Service Group (SSG) was the operational catalyst for the Kargil Plan.[11] Musharraf's extensive operational experience in the area included a stint as the brigade commander of 323 Infantry Brigade in 1986-87. The desire for payback increased with each failure by his brigade to convert their assaults on Indian positions on the Saltoro Ridge into tangible operational successes.[12] An example of this was when a major attack on Bilafond La planned by him at the time was repulsed by a battalion of the Gorkha Rifles of the Indian Army (see Chapter 7). He was later responsible for the ruthless military suppression of a Shia uprising in the area which gave him the name of the 'Butcher of Baltistan'.[13] His operational experience in the area led him to believe that the chances of success were high.[14]

Some Pakistani analysts tend to downplay the importance of the Kargil conflict and argue that it was merely a tactical counter to the rising Indian Army pressure on Pakistan's 10 Corps in the Neelum, Gurez and Kel sectors.[15] Whatever the final motivation, the Kargil Plan of infiltrating and occupying dominating heights to threaten the Srinagar-Kargil-Leh highway was a bold one, which banked on speed, surprise and psychological domination. It was underpinned by the conviction that India would offer a tepid response, and the high possibility that international opinion would drive a negotiated settlement to Pakistan's advantage in a nuclear-charged environment. Musharraf had read the West well, and felt encouraged by a widespread feeling within the Clinton administration in the US that even a limited conflict in the subcontinent could lead to a nuclear face-off. This, he assessed, would force the Americans to intervene, thereby offering Pakistan significant geopolitical space to manoeuvre towards its primary objective of bringing Kashmir back into international focus.

The Battleground

Srinagar-Kargil-Leh National Highway 1A (NH-1A) winds its way up the Great Himalayan and Zanskar Ranges and enters the Mushkoh Valley Subsector at Kaobali Gali through the Zoji La Pass. This marked the western limits of the undermanned 3 Infantry Division's area of responsibility at the time. It had four brigades on paper defending an area that extended from Kaobali Gali in the west to the Daulat Beg Oldi area in the east, and all the way to Demchok in south-eastern Ladakh.

3 Infantry Division's brigade in charge of the entire Kargil Sector was 121 Infantry Brigade, with four infantry battalions and its HQ located at Kargil. It was deployed along with the Ladakh Scouts across the large area between Mushkoh and Batalik. 70 Infantry Brigade – which was assigned the Batalik Subsector – was the second. It had two battalions in the Central Sector of the Siachen Glacier under command of the Siachen Brigade on a three-month rotational basis, while the rest of its battalions were on counterterrorism duties in the Kashmir Valley. The third brigade – 114 Infantry Brigade – had

seconded one of its battalions to the Siachen Brigade to man the Northern Glacier Sector on a three-month rotational basis. The fourth brigade was 102 Infantry Brigade, with one battalion each assigned to the Northern, Central and Southern Sectors of Siachen with a fourth battalion assigned to an area called Sub-Sector West (SSW).

Except for 102 Infantry Brigade, 3 Infantry Division's other three brigades were barely sufficient to even hold ground. Colonel Kuldip Mehta was posted at the divisional HQ in February 1999 and had a ringside view of events at the tactical and operational levels. He reckons that the disposition of troops was barely sufficient to 'establish contact with the enemy, leave alone hold ground and contain further expansion'.[16] This was validated in subsequent weeks when patrols barely contacted several likely enemy positions – the red dots on Kuldip's map in the division's operations room that sprang up in the following weeks.

As NH-1A descends from Zoji La to Matayan along what can roughly be called the Mushkoh Subsector, the distance between the LoC and the highway is over 20 km. From Matayan, the road climbs to Dras. Along with Kaksar and Kargil further to the east, Dras is among the Indian Army locations closest to the LoC. About 50 km east of Dras is the critical Kaksar Subsector, which acts as a pivot for operations in the entire region. Domination of this subsector is essential for converting any success in Dras and Mushkoh into decisive operational outcomes. Batalik (121 Infantry Brigade) and Turtuk (SSW of 102 Infantry Brigade) were the easternmost subsectors. Though the distance between the LoC and NH-1A is the most in these areas, their importance lies in their proximity to the Siachen Glacier, even though the vulnerability has been overplayed at times.

The Indians had dominated operations in this area since the late 1980s. Any inroads made into this area would strengthen the communication lines between Skardu and Gultari, which served as Pakistan's main gateway to the Siachen Glacier. However, there was a small vulnerability in the Indian defences in the region between Tyakshi on the western edge of the Siachen Brigade's area of responsibility and Chorbat La on the eastern edge of the Kargil Brigade's area of responsibility. Here Indian posts were vacated during the winter. There were two main reasons for doing this. First, there was inadequate high-altitude equipment and limited logistics support for occupying these posts through the year. The second and more disturbing reason was the incorrect assessment that since Pakistan faced similar problems, it would refrain from attempting anything audacious in this area, especially given its tenuous position in Siachen. Brigadier Prakash Katoch, the brigade commander of the Siachen Brigade from 1997 to 1999, recalls cautioning 3 Infantry Division about the neglect of SSW and Batalik whenever the Siachen Brigade was asked to patrol that area.[17] Many of the posts in the sector were at heights that ranged from 13,000 to 18,000 feet and reaching them involved difficult climbs from valley floors at 7,000 to 8,000 feet.[18]

Audacious Infiltrators

Till mid-June 1999, many Western commentators misled by the effective Pakistani narrative were describing the infiltrators as 'Islamic guerrillas' and 'Taliban fighters'.[19] The truth dawned on them only after the Indian Army displayed the identity cards of several dead soldiers that clearly identified them as soldiers of the Northern Light Infantry (NLI), a paramilitary force under operational control of the Pakistan Army.[20] As casualties mounted during the conflict, the NLI was reinforced by troops from the Bajaur and Chitral Scouts from Pakistan's Frontier Corps. Most battalions of these regiments were under the FCNA and were distributed among its three brigades. Of these brigades, 323 Infantry Brigade was deployed in Dansam, 80 Infantry Brigade at Minimarg and 62 Infantry Brigade at Skardu. An additional brigade at Kel (32 Brigade) made up the eastern flank of the division-sized force along the Neelum and Gurez Subsectors.

It is widely believed that 62 Infantry Brigade was entrusted with operations in the Kaksar and Batalik Subsectors, while 80 Infantry Brigade was assigned with making inroads into the Mushkoh and Dras Subsectors. Reinforced by a couple of battalions from the other brigades, the intruding force comprised approximately seven to eight battalions[21] – which is approximately 4,500 to 5,000 frontline troops. The troops were spread over fifty posts, with the logistics hubs for each valley manned by a reserve force from defending battalions of almost twice the strength. Overall it was a force of approximately 10,000 to 15,000 personnel. Reputed Pakistani historians such as Nasim Zehra claim that about 140 posts were established, indicating the possibility of two additional battalions. These were likely to have been inducted following the success of the initial infiltration.[22]

Small cohesive groups of twenty to forty soldiers from these units sporadically patrolled snowbound areas along the LoC. They seized strategically important high points from which they later attacked the Indians with mortar fire and medium-range artillery fire. The combat zone was approximately 150 to 160 km long. It was divided into multiple subsectors by the FCNA. The subsectors allotted to the various infiltrating battalions were Tiger Hill and

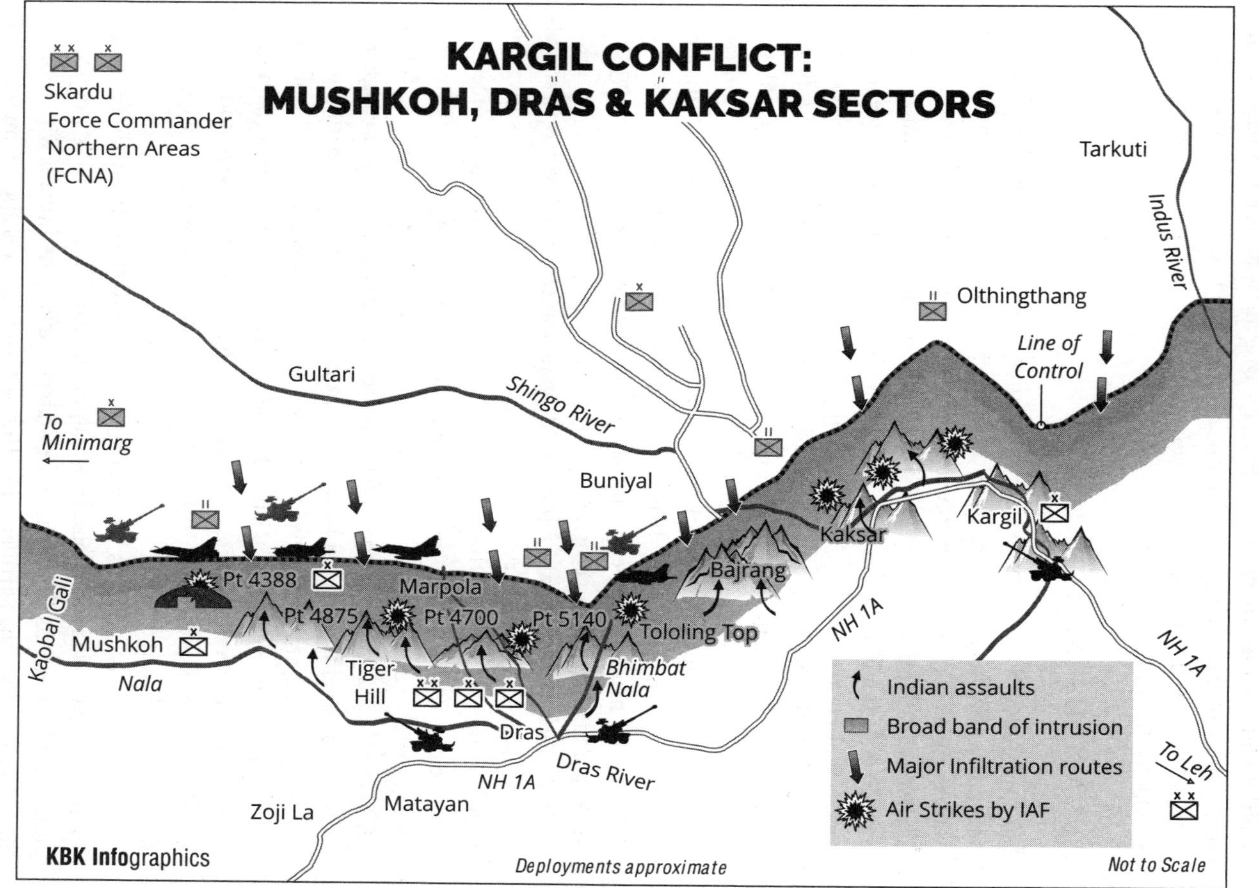

This map is for representational purposes only and does not purport to depict political boundaries

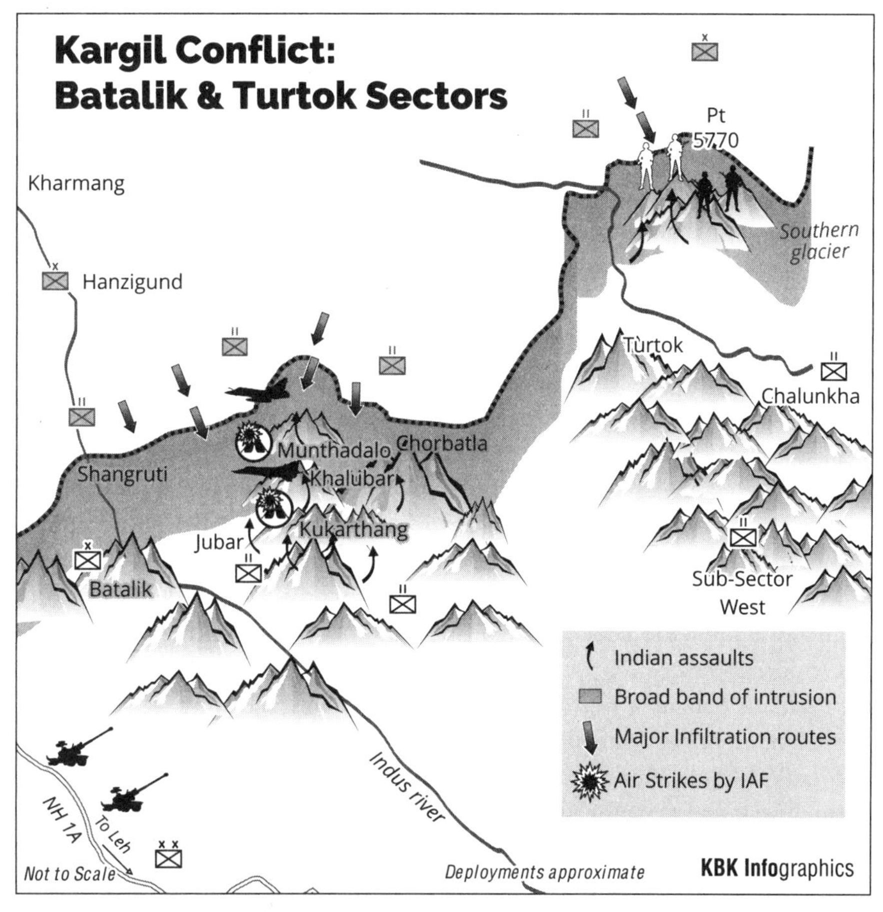

This map is for representational purposes only and does not purport to depict political boundaries

Mushkoh, Dras, Tololing, Kaksar, Batalik, Chorbat La and Turtok. Most of the officers who led the NLI battalions during the Kargil conflict were from other regiments and included Punjabis, Mohajirs and Pathans. This was done to ensure that a specific demographic group did not feel that it had been singled out to execute what was clearly a hazardous operation.

The Overconfident Generals

General Musharraf had built up an excellent operational reputation over the years. A founding member of the SSG, he had a band of loyal generals across the sectarian divide who ensured that the Kargil operation, named Operation Koh Paima by the Pakistan Army, was planned in complete secrecy. In Rawalpindi, the plan was orchestrated by Musharraf's chief of general staff, Lieutenant General Muhammad Aziz Khan, along with Lieutenant General Mahmud Ahmad. It was executed by Major General Javed Hassan, who was the FCNA. Brigadier Nusrat Sial was in tactical command of 62 Infantry Brigade.

An infantry officer, Aziz Khan's strident anti-India beliefs and Islamic leanings – along with his experience as a brigade commander in Siachen – made him perfectly suited to this role. Aziz Khan and Musharraf were no doubt the generals with the greatest knowledge of the terrain and operational requirements for mounting the operation. Mahmud Ahmad, also an artillery officer, was a regimental colleague of Musharraf and an Islamic hardliner. He was specifically brought in by Musharraf as the corps commander of 10 Corps at Rawalpindi. He later executed the coup that overthrew Nawaz Sharif in October 1999.

Ikram Sehgal, a retired officer from the Pakistan Army and a defence analyst, describes Ahmad as 'a professional soldier with a good reputation'.[23] Shaukat Qadir, another Pakistani analyst, has described him as 'sharp, intelligent and arrogant' and that he was not religious 'until he discovered the force of Islam late in his life'. Then, Qadir says, Ahmad 'became dangerous in the way that anyone can become if they believe they are incapable of doing wrong'.[24] Ahmad was without doubt the principal orchestrator of the Kargil operation.

Javed Hassan provided the last-mile connectivity for the operation as the FCNA and was the intellectual pivot of the operation. Praveen Swami has written that Hassan was of the belief that the Indian military was driven by 'the incorrigible militarism of the Hindus'. 'For those that are weak,' Hassan said, 'the Hindu is exploitative and domineering.'[25] Christine Fair offers instructive insights into Hassan's operational orientation through a dissection of his 'infamous account of India's numerous shortcomings' in his book *India: A Study in Profile*.[26] Written in 1990 when he was a faculty member at the Pakistan Army's Command and Staff College, Quetta, the book highlighted several infirmities in India's strategic psyche including its 'dismal absence of any popular resistance against foreign domination', and 'hopeless performance in protecting its own freedom and sovereignty'. The deductions from his research seemed to offer Pakistan 'two starkly different but equally dire choices as regards India: Either she acquiesces to the designs of Indian hegemony or she stands up to the challenge; which would mean as an ultimate military conflict provoked by the stronger military power.'[27] Clearly, there was adequate belief – albeit a delusionary one within the upper echelons of Pakistan's military leadership – that India would wilt in the face of this operation.

The Tentative but Resilient Defenders

At the strategic and policy level, Prime Minister Vajpayee was convinced that there was a clear opportunity for normalizing relations with Pakistan. This belief stemmed from the encouragement shown by the civilian government in Islamabad led by Prime Minister Nawaz Sharif. Vajpayee's major strategic error in the run-up to the Kargil conflict was to overlook the fact that the Pakistan Army was not on board for any peace initiative. Though a large segment of the BJP – including the home minister, Lal Krishna Advani – favoured a more hawkish Pakistan strategy, they deferred to Vajpayee. However, to infer that Vajpayee read Pakistan wrong would be to simplify a complex mindset that cut across the political spectrum, particularly for a generation of leaders who had an emotional connection with the memory of an undivided subcontinent and the lingering belief that an enduring peace was possible with Pakistan.

At the forefront of India's military response was India's Chief of Army Staff, General V.P. Malik. A highly experienced infantryman, he had completed several successful field commands and experienced a ringside view of the Sumdorong Chu, Sri Lanka and Maldives operations as part of the army's military operations directorate. He took some time to come to grips with the enormity of the intrusion as he was away on an official trip to Poland and Czechoslovakia, when the situation morphed into a crisis. There has been much criticism of his decision to go on that trip, but it is likely that given the information available, he was confident that the Northern Army Commander, Lieutenant General H.M. Khanna, would deal with the 'intrusion'. Khanna's role in the conflict finds little place in both the analytical and journalistic discourse relating to the conflict. As the chairman of the Chiefs of Staff Committee, Malik's major challenge was to concurrently direct army operations and orchestrate joint operations. While he immediately took charge of the former with ease on his return, the latter was to prove to be a challenge.

Lieutenant General Krishan Pal, the commander of 15 Corps, was preoccupied with the secessionist terrorist movement in J&K and managing an acrimonious relationship with Chief Minister Farooq Abdullah. His leadership during the conflict has been widely criticized for its lack of foresight and its stagnant counterterrorism mindset. Major General Mohinder Puri, the commander of 8 Mountain Division, speedily moved his division from Kashmir to Dras. It was under his leadership that three Indian Army brigades fought some of the most important battles of the conflict. His book *Kargil: Turning the Tide* is a detailed week-to-week account of operations conducted by 8 Mountain Division.[28]

Air Chief Marshal A.Y. Tipnis, an accomplished fighter pilot with an immaculate career profile who also happened to lead the Mirage-2000 induction project in the mid-1980s, was India's Chief of Air Staff at the time. He suggests that the IAF was not kept in the operational loop during the early weeks after the intrusions were detected.[29] Consequently, the pressure on him to deliver was immense when he had to employ offensive air power without the necessary intelligence. This led to the IAF taking too many risks during the early days of the conflict before recalibrating tactics. Marshalling the IAF in battle was the commander of the IAF's Western Air Command (WAC) and a decorated airman with extensive battle experience in the 1965 and 1971 wars against Pakistan, Air Marshal Vinod Patney.

Based on the initial intelligence, Patney was confident that his resources would suffice to fight the limited air campaign. Though the high-altitude bombing campaign took time to evolve, his aggressive tactics contributed significantly to the capitulation of the NLI.[30] The task of managing the aerial element of joint operations between the WAC and the army's Northern Command during the chaotic initial days fell on the soft-spoken and amiable Air Officer Commanding (AOC), J& K Area, Air Vice Marshal 'Nana' Menon. Nana did a tremendous job, orchestrating air efforts of all kinds and smoothing ruffled feathers as he flitted between Srinagar and Avantipur where several IAF squadrons were operating from, and Udhampur, the headquarters of Northern Army Command. He was the ideal foil to Patney in the field.

Operational Disposition

The LoC in the Kargil Sector on the Indian side was undermanned,[31] with Indian posts vacated in the winter months to strengthen the counter-infiltration and counterterrorism deployment in J&K.[32] On the Pakistani side, however, three brigades were gearing up for the intrusions. The force ratios were completely unsustainable once it was clear that India had to go on the offensive. Brigadier Surinder Singh, the brigade commander of the 121 Infantry Brigade, had to use augmented battalions that were rushed up from the Valley during the first attacks on Tiger Hill. This was in the second week of May once the intrusions were officially declared.[33]

At the commencement of conflict, the IAF fleet for the operations broadly comprised two MiG-21, two MiG-27/MiG-23 BN, two Jaguar and two Mi-17 squadrons for offensive operations. There were also two MiG-29, one MiG-21 and one MiG-23 MF squadrons for air defence missions. Both the IAF's Mirage-2000 squadrons would later be inducted for offensive operations, reconnaissance and air defence duties as the conflict progressed. With a Canberra and a MiG-25 also available for operational and strategic reconnaissance, the IAF had sufficient aerial platforms to execute an integrated offensive battle plan. However, training for high-altitude bombing of this kind had never been anticipated earlier in any air force; there was a shortage of bombs for delivery against targets at high altitude; and self-protection electronic warfare (EW) suites for attacking aircraft and armed helicopters (mainly infrared flares) were inadequate. The IAF would pay dearly for these 'grey areas' during the initial stages of the conflict.

Early Warnings

'Oh God! This has been a colossal intelligence failure,' said India's revered strategic guru K. Subrahmanyam when he visited Leh as head of the Kargil Review Committee.[34] Despite the claims of various intelligence agencies that they had warned the government about the intrusion, there was no clear integrated picture of what was happening. Senior journalists, R&AW operatives and diplomats have indicated that there had been adequate intelligence inputs about hectic military activity in Skardu and stray reports of unusual military activity in the Kargil and Batalik Sectors since the previous winter.[35] However, General Malik is emphatic that the initial 'fog of war and our inability to identify the intruders for some length of time cost us heavily'. He says this was the result of a 'major weakness in our intelligence system'.[36]

While India's civilian and military intelligence agencies have been blaming each other for the fiasco ever since, there is sufficient evidence that it was a collective failure. There was no consolidated strategic, operational and tactical intelligence that could provide a 'stereoscopic mosaic' of the situation to the political leadership. This explains the lack of initial political direction for a response to the intrusion.

At the operational level, local military commanders had been voicing their concerns regarding the thinning of troops in the area from mid-1998 onwards. But these apprehensions had been repeatedly brushed aside by both Khanna and Pal.[37] Ahluwalia was an air commodore at the time and was commanding the important high-altitude airbase of Leh. He recalls that early in May 1999, he was at the airfield to receive the defence minister, George Fernandes, who was on one of his many morale-boosting trips to the Siachen Glacier. Waiting along with him as is customary during such visits were Pal and Major General Budhwar, the commander of 3 Infantry Division. The overstretched division had recently been stripped of the critical 70 Infantry Brigade in Batalik, after a local operational assessment in 1998 suggested that 121 Infantry Brigade could take on the responsibility of patrolling that 'relatively benign part' of the LoC. Ahluwalia recollects that the two generals had discussed the multiple intrusions between themselves, but underplayed their magnitude and seriousness. What surprised him further was that his offer to help with aerial reconnaissance was not taken up.[38] At no stage during the defence minister's visit to Leh were the intrusions discussed with him, indicating that either 15 Corps was hesitant to admit that it had been caught napping, or that there were instructions from New Delhi not to raise the matter. Had the IAF and the Aviation Research Centre (ARC) assets been employed for operational and strategic reconnaissance even at this stage, the scale of the incursions would have been revealed.

Even the PAF was not officially informed about the operation till 12 May 1999. Writing in his widely read and professionally acclaimed blog *Aeronaut,* Kaiser Tufail – an accomplished PAF fighter pilot – claims that India's few covert operatives should have picked up the hectic activity in Skardu as 'troops in battle gear were to be seen all over the city'. He 'wonders how Indian intelligence agencies failed to read any such signs' many weeks before the operation unfolded.[39] The PAF got its first detailed briefing from Mahmud Ahmad. Kaiser Tufail recollects that during the briefing Ahmad broke the news that a limited operation had indeed started two days earlier. He further added that it was nothing more than a 'protective manoeuvre' to foreclose any further mischief by the local Indian formations, which had been a nuisance in the Neelum Valley. He then elaborated that a few vacant Indian posts had been occupied on peaks across the LoC overlooking the Dras–Kargil road. He added that these would serve as observation posts (OPs) for directing artillery fire with greater accuracy.

Artillery firepower, Ahmad added, would be provided by a couple of field guns that had been heli-lifted to the heights piecemeal and reassembled over the previous few winter months. He also suggested that the Indian Army had failed to detect this activity. The target was a vulnerable section of the Dras–Kargil road, the crucial lifeline of the Leh–Siachen Sector. Ahmad's hope was that this stratagem would isolate and choke the Indian Army in that vital sector for up to a month, after which the monsoons would prevent vehicular movement and airlifts due to landslides and other environmental factors.[40] Demonstrating an obsession about getting even with India, Ahmad said, 'Come October, we shall walk in to Siachen to mop up the dead bodies of hundreds of Indians left hungry, out in the cold.'[41] This gave an insight into his operational mindset and the smug conviction that his strategy of surprise and firepower would be sufficient to stun the Indians.

Complete Surprise

The creeping infiltration across the LoC in the Mushkoh, Dras, Kaksar and Batalik Subsectors commenced as early as October 1998[42] and was completed by May 1999. According to the Pakistanis, it took so long because there were a surprising number of vantage heights to take over. This resulted in a scramble for additional resources to sustain these posts. There is much evidence to suggest that the last week of April 1999 had seen some firefights in the Turtuk Sector. These went unreported by the Indian Army and were downplayed as localized intrusions. However, these were intended by the Pakistan Army to deflect attention from the major intrusions that had taken place further west.

The first sightings of intruders in non-military clothing were reported in the Batalik Sector on 3 May by a group of local shepherds. This was on the Jubar Ridge,[43] which would later see some of the fiercest fighting of the Kargil conflict. Following reports of multiple sightings, the local infantry battalion, the 3rd Battalion of the Punjab Regiment (3 PUNJAB) promptly dispatched four patrols to the area over the next four days. The first two patrols detected a few intruders on ridgelines; the next two suffered casualties when they closed in on the intruders and engaged them. This raised some alarm in 3 Infantry Division and 15 Corps HQ. Between 6 and 14 May, there was machine gun fire directed at Cheetah helicopters on surveillance operations and further reports of widespread incursions and sightings in all the sectors. However, no action was taken beyond sending two battalions from the 70 Infantry Brigade from the Kashmir Valley to the Batalik Sector. The FCNA had clearly succeeded in deceiving the Indian commanders into believing that the intruders were a 'mujahideen force' and that their area of focus was in the Batalik and Turtok sectors.

In early May 1999, Colonel Ghei received orders to head from Agra to Leh with his battalion, 7 PARA. He was immediately summoned to Kargil to join Budhwar's strategizing on the response to the early encounters. Ghei recalls troops huddled along the highway from Leh to Kargil, awaiting orders. There was complete chaos in the 121 Brigade sector with all three battalions (4 JAT, 16 GRENADIERS and 3 PUNJAB) unprepared for what was unfolding. Ghei was asked to plan an assault on an enemy-occupied post at 16,500 feet in the Batalik Sector with just one artillery fire unit for support. He said that it would be a suicidal attempt but added that his unit would attempt it if ordered into battle. Better sense prevailed and the plan was abandoned. Along with two other commanding officers from 1 and 6 PARA, Ghei was then summoned to Srinagar to plan a three-battalion assault on Gultari, a major Pakistan Army base across the LoC. However, the plan was aborted when Vajpayee banned operations across the LoC once India officially went to war on 26 May.[44]

On 10 May, Pakistani 105mm guns destroyed a large ammunition dump in Kargil, jolting the Indian Army into action.[45] This was followed by further setbacks between 14 and 17 May in the Kaksar Sector[46] as Pakistani guns continued to harass movement on NH-1A till they were silenced a few weeks later by Indian counter-bombardment. Lieutenant Saurabh Kalia of 4 JAT was leading a five-man patrol on 14 May near the Bajrang post in the Kaksar Sector. His men came under heavy fire from the winter-vacated post, which had been occupied by about thirty soldiers of the NLI. Unable to withdraw and out of ammunition, the Indians were surrounded and captured. They would be held captive for over three weeks, tortured and decapitated.[47] Led by Lieutenant Amit Bharadwaj, a rescue team of thirty attempted a frontal assault on the Bajrang post on 17 May. However, they were forced to withdraw under fire from well-fortified positions. Bharadwaj and a havildar were killed in action in this aborted attack. Repeated attempts by the unit to retrieve their bodies failed till the post was finally overrun by another unit in late June. The strength and preparedness of the intruders had been underestimated. Bharadwaj's courage under fire matched many of the exploits that would be rewarded in the weeks ahead, but his valour would sadly go unrecognized in the aftermath of the larger fiasco that was unfolding.[48]

Cranking a Response

Stung by the initial losses and clearly losing faith in Pal and Budhwar, General Malik took over operations on his return. Left with no choice but to undertake large-scale operations, Army HQ finally declared the commencement of Operation Vijay on 23 May and moved in additional formations into the area. Though Malik grasped the situation well, he chose to initiate a risky response with widespread and direct infantry assaults. He did this because 'there was immense pressure from the top' that 'something needed to be done immediately'.[49]

121 Infantry Brigade was now confined to the Mushkoh, Dras and Kaksar Subsectors and reinforced by 70 Infantry Brigade, which was responsible for the Batalik Subsector. These were followed over the next two weeks by 56 Infantry Brigade inducting and taking over Dras and 79 Infantry moving into Mushkoh.[50] The 1st Battalion of the Naga Regiment (1 NAGA) and the 8th Battalion of the Sikh Regiment (8 SIKH) were the first battalions of 56 Brigade to be moved up with little acclimatization. They were temporarily placed under the command of 121 Brigade. They were followed in quick succession by the 18th Battalion of the Grenadier Regiment (18 GRENADIERS), the 18th Battalion of the Garhwal Rifles (18 GARH RIF), the 2nd Batallion of the Rajputana Rifles (2 RAJ RIF) and the 13th Battalion of the Jammu and Kashmir Rifles (13 JAK RIF). Last to be inducted was 192 Infantry Brigade. Gradually, a new command structure emerged as HQ 8 Mountain Division was moved into the Dras and Mushkoh Sectors under Puri and took over major operations from 3 Division. Malik had commanded the same division in the early 1990s and was confident that it was best suited for the task. Three regiments from its integral artillery brigade were also moved up to provide the missing fire support that had severely hampered the initial assaults.

John Gill – a former faculty member at the National Defence University in Washington, DC, and a prolific writer on the Indian military – says that Malik outlined three key operational tasks for Operation Vijay. The first was the clearing of the Tololing and Tiger Hill complexes, as they were the closest infiltrations to NH-1A. Next was the clearance of heights around the Jubar Ridge in the Batalik Subsector, as they had the potential to threaten the logistics lines to Siachen. The third task was to isolate the Turtok and SSW areas from the Kargil battle.[51] 56 and 192 Infantry Brigades in Dras and 70 Infantry Brigade in Batalik would perform creditably in the weeks ahead.

North of the windswept Dras War Memorial – where the mercury dips to almost minus 50 degrees Celsius in winter – is an imposing ridgeline called the Tololing complex. Apart from Tololing Top, the other prominent feature on the ridge is its northern edge, known as Point 5140. Two other prominent heights – Hump and Knoll – make up the main posts. It was the closest set of heights captured by the NLI as it offered a commanding view of NH-1A on a clear day. Tiger Hill is 5,000 metres west of the Tololing complex. The ridgeline between the Tololing complex and Tiger Hill was occupied by the intruders. Point 4875 is about 2 km south-west from Tiger Hill, and along with Rocky Knob and India Gate, comprised the Tiger Hill complex. This too was occupied by the Pakistanis. The recapture of both the Tololing and Tiger Hill complexes was critical to the success of the Indian operation.

Confronted with the sudden unfolding of a threatening tactical situation, Brigadier Surinder Singh was under immense pressure. However, the divisional and corps commanders were still under the illusion that this was nothing but a set of intrusions and could be tackled immediately. Surinder Singh first ordered 1 NAGA to capture Tololing and Point 5140. Then, on 18 May, he told 8 SIKH that 'there are a few mujahideen on top, go throw them off'. (The 'top' he was referring to was Tiger Hill, which along with Tololing would remain a thorn in the Indian Army's flesh for over six weeks.[52]) 8 SIKH commenced operations that very night. It was soon joined by some troops from 1 NAGA. Both units took heavy casualties over the next few days. Their repeated attempts at frontal assaults were beaten back by enemy mortars and 105mm guns. It was then assessed that both complexes were heavily defended as the Nagas and the Sikhs had to abort their attack and dig defences on the lower slopes to recoup before their next assault. Over 140 men from these two units were lost during this initial assault. After these reverses, 56 Infantry Brigade was moved to Dras and 18 GRENADIERS[53] relocated from the Kashmir Valley and started operations without any acclimatization. 18 GARH RIF followed shortly after.

Colonel (later Major General) Samir Chakravorty, the commanding officer of 18 GARH RIF, insisted on at least a week's acclimatization before being pushed into battle, and this stood them in good stead in the weeks ahead. Surinder Singh was desperate by now and told the Grenadiers to 'just go up and bring them down by their neck'.[54] As the two initial assault units dug in around Tiger Hill and Tololing, 18 GRENADIERS and the remainder of 1 NAGA prepared for attack on the latter. The battle for Tololing commenced on 22 May and despite the initial reports that the enemy positions were well manned, the assault commenced without adequate artillery fire support. Here too the Nagas and Grenadiers became sitting ducks for the well-entrenched Pakistanis as the Indians struggled to make much progress over the next few days.

Preliminary Air Operations

Air Marshal 'Nana' Menon recollects that the first formal request from the army for armed helicopter support came on 12 May, after a Cheetah was shot at in the Dras Sector from Tololing Top.[55] The Indian Army could not provide target coordinates nor information about the kind of air defence weapons the enemy had. The IAF wanted greater clarity before committing the slow-moving armed helicopters into operations at unfamiliar altitudes.[56] By the time General Malik returned from his overseas trip, the operational picture had become quite clear: the Indian Army was faced with an infiltration by two oversized brigades in prepared defences at over a hundred locations across a front of over 100 km. Even by conservative estimates, the Indians would need a minimum of six brigades supported by heavy artillery and air power if they wanted to evict the intruders before the snow came in. However, the differences between the army and air force over committing armed helicopters persisted. This led to some animosity between Malik and Tipnis.[57] Tipnis finally relented, but only after Vajpayee approved the use of offensive air power with the stringent restriction of not crossing the LoC. During these discussions, Foreign Minister Jaswant Singh – a former army officer himself – continued to oppose the widespread use of air power, terming it as escalatory.[58]

Was the IAF caught napping about the spectrum of conflict it was dealing with? Had it adequately gamed and trained for offensive operations at high altitudes? Why were no exercises conducted with the army for such contingencies? Air Marshal Patney admits that he was taken by surprise when – at 3 p.m. on 25 May – the air chief told him that he should commence Operation Safed Sagar, the name given to offensive air operations during the Kargil conflict. Shackled by the prime minister's restriction placed on the IAF not to cross the LoC during aerial attacks, Patney's main battle plan in the sector had to be reworked. The original plan revolved around interdicting Pakistani lines of communication and supplies across the LoC. 'That would be the end of his battle plans,' he told Khanna at a briefing in Srinagar a few days before offensive air operations commenced. Patney was also constrained by the lack of actionable and accurate target intelligence which was essential for hitting targets in proximity to own troops. However, he contests the proposition that his force suffered from a lack of adequate high-altitude expertise and says that the flexibility of his force allowed it to quickly recalibrate its missions after the initial setbacks.[59]

Between 5 and 15 May, the Indian Army kept the IAF completely out of the 'investigating loop'. It merely demanded helicopter support. Therefore when the time came to develop an operational plan, it took some time for the IAF to come to grips with the reconnaissance missions required to identify targets. Between 15 and 21 May, Mi-17s attempting to carry out visual reconnaissance were shot at and damaged. Jaguars carried out long-range oblique photography that provided some target details, while MiG-21s carried out photo reconnaissance with scanty intelligence . This needed to be followed up with a Canberra mission as a Canberra bomber modified with powerful cameras was the only platform for long-range tactical recce. On 21 May an IAF Canberra was damaged by Chinese-built Anza shoulder-fired missiles. The pilot,[60] Squadron Leader Alagaraja Perumal, somehow managed to fly the damaged aircraft back to Srinagar.[61] MiG-25 strategic reconnaissance aircraft were also used extremely effectively during the later stages and were responsible for facilitating several accurate attacks by Mirage-2000s.[62]

The attack on the Tiger Hill complex began on 26 May with Mi-17 armed helicopters. These were be complemented by MiG-21s, MiG-23s and Mig-27s. Unknown to most, MiG-27s from 9 Squadron and MiG-21s from 51 Squadron were among the first over the target area in the Tiger Hill and Tololing complexes respectively. Wing Commander Sameer Joshi (then a flight lieutenant) clearly recollects the attack profiles on Tololing and that 'they scared the daylights out of them' while carrying out pull-up rocket and gun attacks against hazily reported targets that were supposed to be concealed 'Sangars', or rock-based defences. The aircraft were met with ack-ack fire and shoulder-fired missiles from the mountaintops. The IAF reacted quickly, changing plans from attack to gathering information through reconnaissance that would aid subsequent aerial attacks and infantry assaults. The main problem that the ad hoc Strike and Air Defence Planning Cell at Srinagar Airbase faced was that there was a complete mismatch in methodologies in fixing target locations between them and the army.[63]

Several air force officers highlighted the Indian Army's senior leadership's lack of understanding of air power abilities at high altitudes during the early days of the conflict. On the other hand, given that the army was suffering heavy losses, its leadership wanted offensive air power over the peaks immediately. In such a combat milieu, the IAF was unable to explain to them the importance of target information before committing fighter assets. There appeared to be a dissonance in operational synergy between the two services in May. However, Patney again does not agree, and suggests that the IAF demonstrated flexibility of the highest order in a complex battlefield milieu.[64]

MiG-21s from 17 Squadron flew photo reconnaissance missions to add to the information brought back by the Canberra. Using this intelligence, Patney decided to target locations around Tiger Hill and Tololing. After confirming the presence of snow tents and bunkers at both locations, strikes by MiG-27s and MiG-23s of 9 and 221 Squadrons and MiG-21s of 108 Squadron commenced. MiG-21s from 17 Squadron also pitched in with bomb damage assessment missions. During the initial days, the IAF used rockets, guns and iron bombs, and attacks were carried out by flying low over the crest tops and then pulling up to deliver weapons in a dive. This resulted in the attacking aircraft remaining within range of the ack-ack guns, Stingers and Anzas for the entire duration of their attack. The attacking aircraft only had an inadequate protective shower of infrared flares and the IAF was soon suffering losses.

Air attacks were halted temporarily on 28 May after the loss of two fighters and a helicopter. The first to go down was a MiG-27 piloted by Flight Lieutenant Kambampati Nachiketa Rao from 9 Squadron, which suffered engine failure after attacking the Munthadalo logistics camp in the Batalik Subsector. After having executed a successful rocket attack, Nachiketa went in for a gun pass and experienced an engine surge followed by an engine failure. Ejecting in Pakistan-held territory, he was taken prisoner and held for several days before being repatriated.

Air Chief Marshal Birender 'Tony' Singh Dhanoa was the commanding officer of 17 Squadron during the Kargil conflict. It is this tenure during a period of uncertainty, tragedy and achievement under tremendous odds that holds a special place in his heart. Getting into Srinagar on 21 May, he realized that everyone's morale there was low after Perumal's Canberra bomber-cum-reconnaissance aircraft got shot. Discussing the damage caused to the Canberra, the squadron came up with a standard procedure on how to cope with a missile hit at those altitudes. Deciding that they would stay with the aircraft and try to glide into a valley rather than eject over the jagged peaks, little did they realize that days later one of them would be confronted with exactly the same situation.[65] Highlighting the difficulties in identifying specific targets around Tiger Hill in the first week of aerial operations, Dhanoa recollects that the commanding officer of 129 HU went up for an aerial recce with the 2 I/C 8 SIKH, which had assaulted Tiger Hill a few days earlier. Unfortunately, the 2 I/C could not identify any targets for the IAF pilots despite having attempted an assault as they were well concealed and blended into the rocky terrain.

Dhanoa clearly recalls the loss of his flight commander, Squadron Leader Ajay Ahuja, on 27 May. Ahuja was waiting at the take-off point with his No. 2, Flying Officer Reddy, for a reconnaissance mission in the same area that Nachiketa's formation was returning from when he heard that Nachiketa had been shot down. The leader of the MiG-27 formation radioed the coordinates of Nachiketa's ejection area and wanted someone to ascertain whether Nachiketa had ejected safely by orbiting in the area. Ahuja and Reddy flew to the area, descending lower and lower to locate the crash site. Reddy's fuel level became too low for him to continue, so Ahuja stayed on alone. This was not wartime procedure, and Ahuja paid the price for staying over the ejection area for too long – he was consequently targeted and shot down by a Stinger-class of man portable air defence system (MANPADS). He did not eject immediately, stuck to the procedure that had been decided in the squadron, succeeded in identifying a valley and glided into it. Unfortunately, it was on the other side of the LoC. Eventually ejecting safely, he was captured. Unlike Nachiketa, however, Ahuja was brutally beaten up and killed in action. It was a rude awakening for the IAF. It understood that the intruders were no pushovers, but well-trained and ruthless troops who were prepared for aerial attacks.

The next day, 28 May, Tololing was attacked by four Mi-17s led by Wing Commander Sinha, the commanding officer of 129 HU. Sinha was familiar with the target having attacked it the previous day. Following one of the main aircraft in the formation becoming unserviceable prior to mission take-off, a standby from 152 HU slotted in at the last minute. It turned out to be the only aircraft in the formation without infrared flares. Third in the attack sequence, it was shot down after the preceding aircraft had managed to evade hits from several Stinger-class missiles that were launched by the defenders thanks to the IR flares that were dispensed.[66] Major General Alok Deb, commanding a field regiment, was positioned near Dras and witnessed the Mi-17 attack.[67] He says it was effective in its use of firepower. However, the tactical soundness underlying all the mishaps merit serious reflection. Two decades later, Patney accepts that they were costly errors of judgement. Ahuja and Sinha were the only IAF officers to be decorated with Vir Chakras during Operation Safed Sagar.

Air Chief Marshal Major – among the most experienced helicopter pilots in the IAF – was an air commodore at the time and attached to Srinagar during the conflict to assess the offensive helicopter operations. After flying a couple of sorties and observing the flight path of approaching helicopters in a benign area, he realized that the noise level of approaching helicopters in valleys and mountaintops would render them vulnerable to easy sighting. They could subsequently be taken down by SAMs and air defence guns. He had therefore recommended strikes only at dusk, dawn or night, accompanied by a heavy artillery barrage in the same area to mask the sound of the helicopters.[68]

The Pakistani intruders and their missile fire had surprised the IAF.[69] One squadron commander recollects that in the first week they literally went in 'blind' in terms of intelligence about the presence of Stingers on the hilltops and paid the penalty.[70] The IAF eventually abandoned all low-level attacks and stuck to medium-level attacks, where attacking aircraft would pull out in such a manner that they largely stayed out of the range of the Stingers. Conventional bombs of 100, 250 and 500 kg dropped by the MiG-21s, MiG-23s and MiG-27s had limited effect during the initial days. Among other reasons, some of them had delayed fuses that were bouncing off rocky hillsides and bunkers and exploding some distance away, causing shock but not enough damage. When this was changed to an instantaneous impact fuse, the effects improved significantly. When aerial operations resumed, the Mirage-2000s made a big impact with 250 kg Spanish bombs and 1,000 lb bombs,[71] the latter also being fitted with a kit that converted it into a precision bomb.

18 GRENADIERS suffered the heaviest losses, losing Major Rajesh Adhikari and five others in close combat around Tololing Top on 28 May. Caught in a vicious crossfire while attempting to recover the bodies of Adhikari and his fallen comrades on 2 June, the unit's 2 I/C, Lieutenant Colonel Visvanathan, was killed in action too. Following this, the army top brass called a halt to such suicidal and knee-jerk assaults.[72] The second wave of attacks on Tiger Hill, Tololing and the other objectives had cost the Indians dearly: the Indian Army had lost 56 men, with over 100 injured as battle casualties. The IAF had lost three aircraft and five aircrew. It was clearly time to reflect, regroup and come up with fresh operational plans and ideas.

16

A COSTLY VICTORY

'In tactics as in strategy, superiority of numbers is the most common element in victory.'[1]

– Carl von Clausewitz

Fresh Thinking

Hedging against a possible PAF intervention that never came, Air Marshal Patney added 7 Squadron (Mirage-2000s) and 5 and 14 Squadrons (Jaguars) to his initial attacking force. A detachment of 1 Squadron (Mirage-2000s) was also inducted to provide air defence cover. There was now more firepower to assault the other important heights on and around Tiger Hill and the Tololing Ridge – such as Point 5140 and Point 4700. Risky visual attacks were replaced by ones assisted by GPS and inertial navigation. Instead of rockets and guns, 250 kg, 500 kg and 1,000 lb bombs were used. Some of these were mated with Indian fuses and Israeli 'Litening' targeting pods on Jaguar and Mirage aircraft.[2]

The aerial attacks against entrenched defences on the hilltops continued with increased physical and psychological degradation due to improved weapon delivery accuracy. The IAF also identified larger targets, the destruction of which could decisively impact surface operations. To achieve this, reconnaissance platforms were tasked to locate logistics hubs.

The Mirage-2000 was the best option available to lead a high-altitude bombing campaign because of its precision capability. The challenge was how best to integrate the Litening pod with hastily modified 1,000 lb bombs with the Paveway-II guidance kits that would be strapped on to the front and rear of the bomb.[3] Air Marshal Raghunath 'Namby' Nambiar was part of the first group of flight lieutenants to be trained in India on the Mirage-2000 aircraft. A tech-savvy and passionate test pilot from those early days, he had been an integral part of any upgrades on the Mirage-2000. Associated with the Litening Project from 1996, Nambiar recalls that the Israeli Litening was chosen over the French 'Damocles' and British 'TIAD' pods because it was much cheaper at $25 million for six pods.

Patney also considered night bombing to keep psychological pressure on the enemy in the dark.[4] He was supported in this by Dhanoa, who recollects that his squadron did a trial in late June at Toshe Maidan – a high-altitude firing range – dropping four bombs with fair results. 'Attacks at night were conducted at 1 km Above Target Level (ATL) and commenced a few nights before the final assault on Tiger Hill,' recalls Dhanoa. 'It entailed flying below the crest level if need be, but since the mountains were snow-covered and it was a moon phase, everything was brilliantly lit.'[5]

Gunners Make an Impact

As the battle progressed, the 105mm guns and howitzers supporting the infiltrators caused significant attrition on the Indians. It became clear that counter-bombardment was essential if the Indians were to gain the upper hand. Silencing enemy guns and putting pressure on the infiltrators by relentless firing through the day and night became a critical operation of war. In mid-May, 121 Infantry Brigade was being supported by one artillery regiment with around sixty pieces of light mortars, 105mm guns, a few howitzers and mortars. While the mortars had a range of 4 to 6 km, the guns had a maximum range of 10 to 16 km. By mid-June, the artillery brigade of 8 Mountain Division added to the firepower with three field regiments equipped with more 105mm guns and one light regiment with 120mm mortars. A regiment of the formidable 155mm Bofors gun was also brought in from the Kashmir Valley. Pakistan had not factored this gun into its assessment of the Indian response. There were now over 150 guns with ranges varying from 10 to 35 km spread out across the three sectors. By late June, Grad B rocket launchers and the Pinaka multi-barrel rocket launcher system were inducted for field trials. By the end of June, there were approximately six regiments with over 200 guns spread across all sectors.[6] These guns in combination with sustained pressure from repeated aerial bombardment would cause tremendous attrition and psychological degradation of morale to the enemy, and contribute significantly to their eventual capitulation.

Mohinder Puri's planning of a combined ground assault was to be accompanied by relentless aerial and artillery bombardment and followed by sustained infantry assaults. 'A 100-gun fire assault' was the euphemism used by the gunners during the later stages of the conflict. Colonel (later Major General) Alok Deb, who commanded one of the artillery regiments in the conflict, orchestrated fire plans in the Dras sector, coordinating with the air force and infantry units, as troops closed in on enemy positions. The unorthodox use of the Bofors gun for direct firing was among the several bold initiatives in the employment of firepower by the gunners, turning the tide in India's favour.

Tololing Falls

As the psychological impact of air power and artillery had not yet manifested itself, the attacking Indian infantry battalions were facing stiff resistance from a determined adversary. According to John Gill, 'The NLI troops demonstrated great skill in siting their positions and great tenacity in holding out against repeated attacks, often literally to the last bullet and last man.'[7] It was time for the Indian Army to make its decisive move. The first concerted attack on Tololing had taken a heavy toll on 18 GRENADIERS and 1 NAGA, and it was time for fresh legs to consolidate the limited gains. On 1 June, 2 RAJ RIF was moved to Dras from J&K. Camping at Draupadi Kund a few kilometres short of Dras, the battalion acclimatized for a few days while receiving all the required information for executing its task. It then gradually moved up to the launch pads that had been created for them by 18 GRENADIERS. Led by Major Vivek Gupta, it managed to climb its way to within 600 metres of Tololing Top before commencing its final assault at 9 p.m. on the night of 12 June.[8] Though Gupta was killed in the assault, a young artillery officer called Captain M.K. Singh continued the attack. Tololing Top fell on the morning of 13 June after an all-night operation that left eleven dead and over fifty injured.

Years later the commanding officer of 2 RAJ RIF during the operation, Colonel Ravindranath, would recall with sadness that while the operation changed an adverse situation in India's favour, it came at an enormous cost of human life. The battalion launched another ferocious and successful attack on 29 June on another height called Three Pimples, in which nine soldiers were killed.[9] A young lieutenant wrote an account of the final battle for Tololing in a letter to his friend, saying that their 'orders were explicit – Tololing had to be taken at all cost. We took the objective but the price my company paid was a heavy one. My leading section was wiped out, everyone either dead or injured. The rest of my platoon was in tatters. Going to battle was a terrible and frightening experience.'[10]

After 17 Squadron also lost its flight commander, Dhanoa led the first mission once air operations recommenced and dropped the first bombs of the squadron since the 1971 war. The target was Point 5140, a key height in the Tololing complex. Dhanoa recollects that his formation was part of an eighteen-aircraft strike over Tololing that set the tone for subsequent medium-altitude bombing. Bomb damage assessment sorties from his squadron filmed huge black impact spots, but Dhanoa admits that there was still room for innovation and improvement in accuracy. Facing resistance from some quarters in Air HQ, Patney asked the squadrons to come up with something quickly, which they did: 221 Squadron devised an improvised bombing profile that allowed aircraft to stay outside the range of the Stingers by using GPS to calculate weapon-throw distances and improve final accuracy. This new strategy allowed them to stay at almost 30,000 feet but still bomb with reasonable accuracy.[11] Between 3 and 13 June, the IAF flew approximately 125 sorties. One of the most effective strikes was carried out on the ridge leading to Point 5140 on the morning of 13 June after the fall of Tololing Top, to ensure that the gains accrued by 2 RAJ RIF were consolidated.

Reposing continued faith in diplomacy even as the fighting intensified, India hosted Sartaj Aziz, the foreign minister of Pakistan, who arrived for talks in Delhi on 12 June. The final phase of the battle for Tololing coincided with the failed talks between Aziz, and his Indian counterpart, Jaswant Singh. As joint combat operations in Kargil entered the third week with no decisive tactical victories, both the army and IAF chiefs were seriously contemplating asking the government for permission to open another front. They calculated that it would otherwise be impossible to recover the lost heights before the fighting season ended.[12] Prepared for escalation, the IAF had issued preliminary orders to 9 and 17 Squadrons to strike Skardu and other targets in PoK on 13 June. Fully armed MiG-27s taxied out in the morning only to be recalled. The stray reports in the media regarding this escalatory move are corroborated by participants in this mission from both squadrons.[13]

It was during these seesaw battles of attrition around Tololing that 13 JAK RIF captured the imagination of the country with its courage and dogged persistence. Having arrived in the area only on 6 June, the battalion had hardly acclimatized when it was pitchforked into battle. Its mission was to relieve an exhausted 2 RAJ RIF and consolidate the capture of Tololing by taking all the other surrounding heights still in the hands of the enemy. Captain Vikram Batra led this assault as they advanced along the Tololing Ridge and captured Point 5140. The unit was then pulled back for a period of recuperation before their next assault around Tiger Hill.[14] The battles around the Tololing Ridge marked the reversal of fortunes and the gradual ascendancy of the Indian Army over the Pakistan Army.

The Story of 18 Garhwal Rifles

While the stories of 2 RAJ RIF and 13 JAK RIF have been widely narrated in the media, there were other battalions that performed equally creditably but remained away from the limelight. 18 GARH RIF was one such unit. Mohinder Puri acknowledges the contribution of the battalion after it captured Point 4700, saying that it had displayed 'exceptional valour and dogged determination' to 'overcome initial setbacks with competence and professionalism'.[15] The battalion had been operating in the Lolab Valley of northern Kashmir at a significantly lower altitude and after a week's acclimatization it was inducted into battle. It was early June and 18 GRENADIERS had dug in a few hundred metres below their objective of Tololing Top, creating a base for a final assault. 18 GARH RIF was initially given the task of securing Tololing Top, which was then reassigned to 2 RAJ RIF. The Garhwalis were instead ordered to assault the formidable Point 5140 from the east through the Bhimbat Nala (rivulet). 13 JAK RIF would simultaneously attack it from the south and 1 NAGA from the west. A multipronged attack was considered essential to keep the enemy guessing, but it was fraught with danger as the attackers were vulnerable to fire from multiple enemy locations on the ridge. Climbing slowly up a 7 km stretch, 18 GARH RIF came under constant fire from all the heights to its west. They managed to avoid too many casualties. This was the same route that had been unsuccessfully attempted by 1 NAGA two weeks earlier, leading Colonel Chakravorty, the commanding officer of 18 GARH RIF, to term his mission as a 'reinforcement of failure'. Between 12 and 15 June, the battalion was beaten back from Point 5140, but after a couple of firefights, the enemy decided to vacate the feature. By 17 June, Point 5140 was occupied by India.

18 GARH RIF returned to base and, after a few days of recuperation, was assigned another set of tricky heights north-west of Tololing including Point 4700. This was an equally tough proposition and by the time the unit captured the height, it had been fighting for over three weeks and had lost fifteen men, with another fifty-five injured. Chakravorty is among the few senior

commanders who have been consistently critical of the way the Indian Army went into battle and the attitude of its senior leadership. Recounting several verbal encounters with his brigade and divisional commanders over battle plans and tasking, he is cynical about the 'guts and glory' stories recounted later. Chakravorty reckons that it is time to confront the truth about Kargil and the several shades of war that emerged from those tough days.[16]

Despite the large number of offensive bombing sorties by the IAF between 3 and 15 June against targets in the Tololing complex, Chakravorty says that the impact on the defenders was largely psychological. As troops closed in, he reckoned that it was natural for air strikes to reduce because of the proximity of own troops. The artillery started becoming effective just before the final assault on Tololing, once all the regiments fetched up. Chakravorty, however, agrees that minimal losses to friendly fire was a result of excellent coordination of firepower – despite having six shells land perilously close to his troops' position on one occasion. Deb was coordinating the guns at that time and initially dismissed it as enemy fire, but after a quick check he ordered his guns to hold their fire immediately.[17]

Chakravorty remembered that when incoming units in Kargil came face-to-face with casualties from units they were replacing, 'there was fear and doubt that they may be next'. It was a leadership challenge, but added that 'good leadership can isolate the outside pressures, concentrate on the task at hand and fight battles as trained and rehearsed'. Contrary to the jingoistic reaffirmation of the victory at Kargil every year, he says, 'The margin between our victory in Kargil and having to accept defeat was wafer-thin.'

The IAF also had leadership dilemmas at the tactical level. Dhanoa and Nambiar both recall the gloom and despondency that had descended on Srinagar and Avantipur when the Canberra was shot at on 21 May and then again a week later when the IAF lost three aircraft in quick succession. Nana Menon found that the morale in the squadrons depended on the dynamism of the squadron commander and his willingness to go into battle and recollects some tough decisions to raise mission effectiveness. Wing Commander K.T. Sebastien, who had just finished a command of a MiG-29 squadron, had a ringside view of the action from the Strike Planning Cell at Srinagar. Calling the two MiG-21 squadrons (17 and 108 Squadrons) as the most 'dynamic and proactive of the strike squadrons', he recalls that both squadrons had an unusually large number of young and relatively inexperienced pilots who benefited immensely from their commanding officers, 'who led from the front'.[18] Leo Murray, a British military analyst and former soldier, observes in his book *The Psychology of Combat: War Games* that 'if the conditions are right then almost any man will fight, change those conditions and almost everybody will stop fighting' and 'training and experience set the psychological backdrop for a battle'.[19]

Ground Battles and Air Power in Batalik

The Batalik Subsector made up the eastern edge of the Kargil Sector and had some of the most inaccessible and logistically challenging operational areas. During the mid-1990s, 70 Brigade was deployed at Chumathang with a focus on Siachen and not on Batalik. However, as the proxy war in J&K intensified, the brigade was pulled out with two battalions deployed for counterinsurgency operations in the Kashmir Valley. Two battalions of the brigade remained in Ladakh for rotational deployment on the Siachen Glacier. In a routine move in late 1998, the brigade HQ moved back to Chumathang leaving the two battalions in the Valley. Thus, it was left to the overstretched 3 PUNJAB from 121 Brigade to patrol Batalik. This was a huge tactical mistake that was exploited fully by Brigadier Sial, the brigade commander of Pakistan's 62 Infantry Brigade. The operational significance of this sector in the run-up to operations is significant. It is highly probable that Musharraf wanted the infiltration to be first detected in this sector to draw significant Indian forces eastwards into the region. By doing so, he hoped that the more critical intrusions in the Mushkoh, Dras and Kaksar sectors could consolidate, causing significant harassment along the Srinagar–Leh highway. This would force the Indians to negotiate a ceasefire from a positional disadvantage.

Musharraf chose 5 NLI and 8 NLI for the operation and set up two large logistics hubs at Munthadalo and Kukarthang. These gradually expanded as the operation progressed. It was only after the first Canberra recce missions and subsequent tactical recce missions by MiG-21s that the extent of intrusion emerged. The NLI had occupied four ridges, of which Jubar, Khalubar and Kukarthang were the most critical. In response, 3 Infantry Division moved the HQ of 70 Infantry Brigade to Batalik and deployed the maximum number of battalions here because of the vast area that had to be covered as compared to the other sectors. With some overlap and rotation, almost ten battalions were inducted into the area, with four battalions in operations at any given time. While the 1st Battalion of the Bihar Regiment (1 BIHAR) carried out most of the operations during the early days, 1/11 GORKHA RIFLES fought the most successful battles towards the closing stages of the conflict, taking over multiple ridgelines. Lieutenant Manoj Pandey from the latter unit was the sole Param Vir Chakra winner in the sector during the battle for the Khalubar Ridge.

As the war progressed, there was a greater need for the IAF to support operations in the Batalik Sector. To do this, it committed significant reconnaissance effort to identify the major logistics hubs for sustaining Pakistani posts in the area. One such hub was the Munthadalo logistics camp, which had grown from eight to ten fabricated tents to about fifty to sixty igloo tents by mid-June. Following a dummy run in a trainer with Litening pods to exactly locate the camp the previous day, on 17 June six Mirages of 7 Squadron dropped thirty-six 250-kg bombs on this camp[20] – one of the most impactful air attacks of the campaign. The sprawling hub was razed to the ground. This effectively choked Pakistani supplies to the Batalik and Kaksar sectors, thereby sealing the fate of all their posts there.[21] This strike was followed closely by the MiG-27 strikes at Kukarthang, which turned out to be a fuel supply dump that was seen smoking for days. General Malik acknowledges the impact of air power in the Batalik sector and reckons that IAF pilots would not have been able to carry out their attacks without crossing the LoC. A senior Mirage-2000 pilot admits that it did happen several times, particularly during air defence escort missions.

Tiger Hill and Mushkoh

Following the capture of the Tololing complex, Puri shifted his focus westwards on to Point 4875 in the Mushkoh area and the formidable Tiger Hill. 13 JAK RIF captured Point 4875 on the morning of 3 July after a punishing climb and brutal close combat. Batra was killed in action by enemy artillery fire during the battle and was posthumously awarded the Param Vir Chakra.[22] Puri had sequenced his assault on Tiger Hill a day after the one on Point 4875 to confuse the enemy. The Pakistanis on the Tiger Hill complex withstood a continuous assault for over a month despite 'food and ammunition shortages and India's nerve-wracking air power', writes Nasim Zehra.[23]

From 23 June onwards, Mirages targeted key nodes and bunkers on Tiger Hill that had been clearly located. The first mission with Wing Commander Nambiar and Flight Lieutenant Monish was hampered by clouds that obscured the Litening pod's field of view and had to be aborted. However, over the next two days, they managed direct hits on bunkers and a communication node. Images of enemy soldiers running was captured by the Litening pods. An Aviation Research Centre (ARC) long-range photography (LORAP) mission followed by a MiG-25 recce located a hangar-like structure (probably Nissan

Huts) at Point 4388. Situated behind and to the west of Tiger Hill, it served as a forward logistics and heli-base. Between 5 July and 9 July, Nambiar and Flight Lieutenant Tokekar were again in the thick of action as Mirage-2000s from 7 Squadron flew two missions that destroyed the hangar and then carried out a reconnaissance mission to check the damage.

For Puri, Point 4875 was of greater priority than Tiger Hill given the former's closer proximity to NH-1A.[24] Also, the sheer physical challenges of assaulting Tiger Hill would make it the last major post to fall. Puri assigned 18 GRENADIERS with the task of delivering the final blow with 8 SIKH in support. They successfully reclaimed Tiger Hill on 4 July after several personal acts of courage in extremely bitter close combat. Among them were the exploits of Grenadier Yogendra Singh Yadav, who was part of the lead assault team and is one of the two surviving recipients of the Param Vir Chakra from the Kargil conflict along with Rifleman Sanjay Kumar from 13 JAK RIF. By 8 July, the entire Tiger Hill complex had been taken over by the Indian troops. On 9 July, Pakistan commenced negotiations for a ceasefire, farcically holding on to the lie that they had convinced the Mujahideen to withdraw.[25]

The Silent Service Pitches In

While the Indian Navy did not directly participate in the Kargil conflict – the aggressive deployment in the northern Arabian Sea of a combined task force of its Western and Eastern Fleets – reflected its coercive intent and readiness to interdict Pakistani shipping and naval assets. Vice Admiral Madhavendra Singh (later Admiral and Chief of Naval Staff) was the Commander-in-Chief of Western Naval Command and modestly recounts the likely impact of the deployment of India's vastly superior naval forces. He reckons that it was a significant threat and had the potential to effectively choke the Makaran coast, considered by many to be Pakistan's soft underbelly. In an operation code-named Talwar, Madhavendra deployed his submarines and warships as far forward as was feasible. He also assessed that the deployment would be inevitably picked up by US satellites and could result in some pressure on Pakistan at the strategic level to pull back from Kargil.[26] In the final analysis, it is possible that this created a doubt in the minds of Pakistan's security planners that India was serious about expanding the conflict, and when that would happen, the Indian Navy was in an effective position to commence a naval blockade of Karachi and choke its sea lines of communications (SLOCs).

LESSONS FROM KARGIL

Wide-angle Lens

Notwithstanding all the subsequent criticism in Pakistan and the Indian narrative that Musharraf's Kargil operation was a misadventure, the first reaction of the Indian strategic establishment was a muted acceptance of the surprise element. A body of strategic experts led by India's strategic guru K. Subrahmanyam assessed that 'strategic surprise comes from actions that are not anticipated by the adversary. Surprise was achieved by Pakistan by carrying out an operation considered unviable and irrational.'[27] Peter Lavoy offers the most objective and comprehensive Western analysis of the conflict. He writes, 'Kargil dispelled the common notion that nuclear-armed states cannot fight one another.' The only other instance was the Ussuri River clashes between China and the Soviet Union in 1969.[28] Lavoy was proven right again two decades later in 2019, when India and Pakistan engaged in a short but sharp armed face-off. There were air strikes and aerial battles, but only a muted escalation rhetoric and nuclear bluff from the Pakistani military establishment.[29]

Military historians like John Gill argue that Kargil was somewhere in the 'grey zone' of conflict between low-intensity conflict and all-out war. Pakistan nearly convinced the global media that their army was not involved in the conflict and even Indian correspondents writing for Western media began to believe that the intrusion was the handiwork of 'militants and jihadis'.[30] In line with the Indian propensity to downplay the impact of conflicts, Vajpayee chose to describe it as a 'warlike situation'.[31] However, it is best described as a limited high-intensity conflict. 'Limited' as it happened within a confined geographical space and time frame and not all tools of war-fighting were employed by either side; 'high intensity' because of the ferocity of combat and use of heavy artillery and air power. This is also a term that the Indian armed forces are comfortable with because of the increasing possibility of such contingencies unfolding along a stressed LAC with China.

Pakistan incredulously thought that by not supporting its troops with air power, logistics or casualty-evacuation operations it could convince the world that the intruders were jihadis. India wanted to seize the moral high ground in the conflict by concentrating on the violation of territorial sovereignty and resisting the temptation to expand the conflict. Despite Western concerns, Pakistan never came close to exercising the nuclear option. The operation was always considered expendable and did not violate any of Pakistan's nuclear red lines, which are primarily concerned with significant enemy gains in Punjab and Sindh.[32] Had India expanded the conflict, the situation may well have been different.

US President Bill Clinton and NSA Sandy Berger were condescending about the ability of the Indians and Pakistanis to comprehend red lines and the limits of deterrence. After extensive discussions with Prime Minister Nawaz Sharif in Washington, DC, in early July, they were convinced that the two countries were never closer to a nuclear conflict than in 1999.[33] Aggravating the Americans' concerns after the discussions was the abject ignorance of Nawaz Sharif of what his army chief was up to, both in the operational and in the nuclear domain.[34] They, however, erred in placing India in the same bracket as Pakistan and did not publicly acknowledge that Vajpayee's decision not to permit his military to cross the LoC was precisely because he understood the red lines. To be fair to Clinton, though, he did mention that Vajpayee had taken a 'risk for peace' by going to Lahore before the outbreak of the conflict.[35] Lavoy is also critical of the American media's propensity to see 'lurking around every corner of this India-Pakistan crisis a validation of their arguments about nuclear instability in South Asia and, more generally, the perils of nuclear proliferation'.[36]

Why Pakistan Stumbled

What made Pakistan take the calculated risk of occupying Indian territory in Kargil? Two decades down the road, there can be no denying that the initial plan was audacious and sought to exploit the strategic slowness of a large democracy like India. Had the infiltration succeeded and Pakistan managed to hold on to even a few heights, General Musharraf would have been a hero.[37] However, in his book *In the Line of Fire*, Musharraf has all but disowned the operation despite being its principal orchestrator. His reluctance to write about some of the major battles in the Kargil conflict and highlight conspicuous acts of individual gallantry reveals a clear unwillingness to claim ownership of the conflict as the leader who put his men in the line of fire.[38]

The flawed planning led to a string of oversights and failures by Pakistan. The wider military and diplomatic ramifications had not been accounted for. It also failed to correctly predict the response of a powerful enemy, and the absence of political guidance and objectives led field commanders to needlessly expand the scope of the operation to unmanageable levels. History shows that possession of high ground does not always translate into operational advantage in defence, especially when the attacker has a preponderance of integral firepower at its disposal. When this firepower is supplemented by air power, the advantage becomes overwhelming. This was seen in Greece in

1941 when Germany's 5 Geibrigs Division overran the seemingly impregnable Metaxis line at 6,000 to 8,000 feet with Stuka dive-bombers.[39] The final nail in the coffin for Musharraf's Kargil misadventure was when he failed to sustain communication and supply lines as the battle progressed. Had he read Clausewitz more carefully, he may not have done so. According to Clausewitz, 'The second crisis most commonly occurs at the end of a victorious campaign when lines of communications have begun to be overstretched. This is especially true when the war is conducted in a thinly populated and possibly hostile country.'[40]

If at all there was a positive from a Pakistani perspective, it was the performance of the NLI. Despite being abandoned in the closing stages of the conflict and mortified by Pakistan's refusal to accept the bodies of their fallen comrades, they fought on. Zehra wrote that 'many were confronted with tough dilemmas of whether, as lone survivors, to vacate the post or fight on'.[41] After Kargil, the NLI was upgraded from being a paramilitary force to the status of regular infantry.

Indian Reflections of a Bloody Victory

Politico-strategic Issues

Was the tremendous loss of life worth it, or was Kargil a Pyrrhic victory for India? India yet again missed an opportunity to leverage its tactical victories into long-term operational and strategic gains. Notwithstanding combat fatigue, the political push for early conflict termination and the desire to come across as a responsible and restrained power, the LoC should have been made more defensible in the Kargil Sector by consolidating the gains in Batalik and north of the Tiger Hill and Tololing complexes. Like the Henderson-Brookes report after the 1962 debacle, the Kargil Review Committee had no mandate to assess the quality of India's strategic responses. It stayed clear of assessing the effectiveness of strategic national leadership, and commented only on operational issues. Despite this, many recommendations of the committee were prescient and reformative.[42]

Preoccupied with his efforts to lead a historic peace dialogue with Sharif, Vajpayee was also handicapped by the lack of any firm threat assessment that could convince him early on about Pakistan's sinister motives. His defence minister, Fernandes, was focused more on consolidating the gains made in Siachen, managing the counterterrorism campaign in J&K and building strategic consciousness in India on the security threat posed by a resurgent China. He could have only raised an alarm about the Kargil intrusions had he received a clear and decisive threat assessment from the Indian Army and the intelligence community. He had received no such intelligence. At the strategic level, the Cabinet Committee on Security (CCS) did little to validate the reports of hectic military activity in the Skardu and Kargil Sectors – an oversight that either escaped the notice of the review committee or was deliberately ignored.

To deny that there was intelligence failure – as J.N. Dixit has sought to do in his writings – is as fallacious an argument as General Malik's assertion that India's armed forces had little or no warning of the intrusion.[43] The mudslinging and accusations that flew thick and fast in the years following the Kargil conflict only increased the lack of synergy in the upper echelons of India's national security apparatus. This takes much of the sheen away from the adaptable warfighting capabilities displayed by the Indian Army and the IAF at the unit level during the conflict. Malik takes ownership for India's military response and provides a fairly accurate operational account in his book *Kargil: From Surprise to Victory*. However, he attributes the Indian Army's initial response mainly to the suboptimal intelligence provided by the civilian intelligence agencies.[44] The IAF leadership similarly has never acknowledged that the force was not completely tuned for limited conflict, and was underprepared for 'a never attempted before high altitude offensive air campaign in the mountains'.

Indian Army Reflections

At the operational level, could the Indian Army have insisted on better intelligence rather than hoping that the sheer size of the force would be enough to evict the entrenched and acclimatized NLI troops? Manekshaw, when asked to move into Bangladesh in early 1971 by an anxious Indira Gandhi,[45] categorically told the government that he needed more time to initiate operations. Did we forget history so soon? On the one hand, time was of the essence as the Kargil-Dras-Leh highway – the lifeline to Ladakh – was under threat, and it was critical to secure it quickly. The destruction of the ammunition depot at Kargil on 10 May probably precipitated the hasty response. In hindsight, a measured induction of troops and extensive use of artillery and air power before committing ground forces may have allowed the Indian Army to reoccupy the heights just as swiftly, but with significantly lower casualties. It was a tough choice for Malik to make and he chose the former.

Artillery had a big role to play in the Kargil conflict. The progressive Indian artillery assault degraded the physical and psychological capacity of the

NLI to withstand multiple infantry assaults. Likening the impact of India's firepower to a sledgehammer, Zehra highlights the devastating effect of 100 to 120 guns being fired simultaneously. Though many Indian artillery officers will argue that the 105mm guns performed as effectively as the Bofors, Zehra conveys the awe that the Pakistanis developed for the Bofors gun, writing that 'it spread terror amongst the defenders and had a devastating effect in the destruction of enemy bunkers'. Its maximum range of 30 km – enhanced a bit by the rarefied atmosphere at high altidues – enabled deep strikes on the enemy's gun positions, administrative installations, ammunition dumps and headquarters.[46]

Air Power Outcomes

The escalatory nature of air power was at odds with India's counterterrorism strategy of restraint. There was dissonance within the CCS on the doctrinal use of air power with Foreign Minister Jaswant Singh emerging as an important voice against the use of air power. As it was initially unclear whether these incursions were anything more than jihadi infiltrations, it was inevitable that there would be hesitation to commit offensive air power resources to the fight. In retrospect, though air power contributed significantly towards conflict termination, a golden opportunity to pave the way for truly integrated operations in mountainous terrain was lost. While the IAF's effectiveness in providing close support during assaults was both appreciated and criticized by several senior army commanders, very little has been said about the sequencing of the ground operations that gave little time for the IAF to decisively exert its influence.

Like the Indian Army, the IAF took some unnecessary risks in the early days of the air war and paid a heavy price. It also took time to visualize operations in the mountains at unusually high altitudes with limited and localized objectives. It wanted instead to take the war to the enemy by hitting strategic targets in enemy territory without being fettered by the constraints of fighting in one's own territory. The Indian government's refusal to allow the IAF to cross the LoC helped India to occupy the moral high ground, but it prevented the IAF from operating to its full potential. Summarizing the broad lessons learnt by the IAF, Patney says that they had 'prepared for a different kind of war' and that 'the learning curve was steep'. He adds emphatically, 'Today, if Kargil were to be repeated, our combined strategy should be to allow the IAF to first clean out the hilltops with sighting assistance from the army.' This would reduce the army casualties.[47]

Suboptimal Jointmanship

The military objectives of the Indian Army reflected a conventional mindset – it looked to fight a high-altitude battle on its own.[48] Had the objective been simply to evict the intruders with the application of integrated combat power, air power could have been included in the strategy from the outset. The operational sequencing may have turned out quite differently and evicting the intruders could perhaps have been achieved with fewer casualties.

Artillery played a dominant role in providing fire support during Operation Vijay and vital time was lost because of the mobility constraints of artillery guns in such terrain. Air power could have helped in that situation as it is capable of both area and precision firepower.[49] With better targeting intelligence and technology at its disposal, it may have been possible for the IAF to provide battlefield air strikes with handheld laser designators, better communication sets and well-trained FACs. Much of the understanding and appreciation of the IAF's role in Kargil has been cosmetic, and there was much uninformed criticism of the IAF leadership's reluctance to commit helicopters to the fight.[50] However, Zehra highlights the impact of Indian air power, writing that it 'psychologically hit the Pakistani troops' and they felt 'unnerved and terrorized by it'.[51] Another respected PAF practitioner-analyst, Kaiser Tufail reckons that 'though the Indians had been surprised, the IAF supplemented and filled in where the artillery could not be positioned'. He argues that 'clearly the Army-Air Joint Operations had a synergistic effect in evicting the intruders'.[52] Patney also highlights an important aspect that indicated close coordination of firepower and points out that there were no fratricidal losses due to friendly fire from the air throughout the conflict.[53] Though the synergy between the Indian Army and the IAF has improved significantly since 1999, leveraging the competencies of offensive air power in high-altitude conflict continues to trouble military planners at all levels.

In Hindsight

While Malik, Puri, Tipnis and Patney had to think on their feet and retrieve a delicate situation, a historian has the luxury of reflecting with the benefit of hindsight. An integrated plan launched simultaneously as a single operation rather than separately would have highlighted the strengths of the two services and compensated for their individual deficiencies. The initial strategy should have been to apprise the government clearly of the intrusion as soon as it was detected, and ask for complete authority to employ the full range of combat power against the intruders. The IAF could then have committed its entire range of reconnaissance resources to find and fix enemy locations within the operational tramlines laid down by the government without worrying about escalation. This could have been followed by a concerted shaping of the battlefield by offensive air power and artillery even as infantry units acclimatized for assault operations. Attacks on concealed positions on the heights along with a systematic targeting of logistics hubs would have significantly depleted the intruders' fighting potential. Finally, infantry assaults would have cleaned up the heights with lower casualties as the enemy would have been demoralized by the sustained punishment meted out by artillery and air power.

The only flip side to this sequenced and calibrated plan would have been that its prolonged execution could have subjected India to immense international pressure to negotiate a ceasefire. Consequently, the possibility of having to settle for a ceasefire with the Pakistan Army still holding on to several heights was high. It would have succeeded only if the government held firm till the stated military objectives were achieved. In the given circumstances, particularly in a nuclear-charged environment – the Americans would have been breathing down Vajpayee's neck sooner than later.

Two decades after Kargil, it is important to check whether doctrinally and operationally the Indian Army and the IAF are now better prepared for another Kargil-like situation.[54] Kargil was a highly 'unconventional' conflict because the operating environment was significantly different from any other experienced worldwide during joint operations. Existing and established doctrines and tactics had to be replaced with new and untried ones.[55] In the final analysis, while the outcome was determined by the dogged infantry, which moved up the slopes and wore down the NLI in a classic attrition campaign, flexibility and ingenuity saw air power and artillery being used innovatively and decisively. Reflecting on the conflict, Patney, who may well be among the few commanders on either side to have been in the thick of action in 1965, 1971 and 1999, remarks that the 'Pakistani military leadership was brash and overconfident'. He adds, 'And they had forgotten the lessons of 1965 and 1971. On the other hand, even after being surprised, we applied common sense, were more resilient, thought instinctively, grabbed the initiative and sustained it.'[56]

17

HYBRID WAR IN JAMMU AND KASHMIR

'The Government of India has no policy about a possible solution to the Kashmir issue but hopes that as long as the issue is kept out of international attention and the insurgency and terrorism are contained through attrition, the problem will go away.'[1]

– K. Subrahmanyam in 1988

Valley Ignited

Major General Harsha Kakar, a security analyst, has attempted to simplify the nuances of the current nature of conflict in J&K. He argues that it reflects several features of hybrid war in its various hues. Offering a home-grown perspective on hybrid war, he classifies hybrid warfare as 'an all-encompassing term which goes beyond destroying an enemy's military capabilities ... It remains below the threshold of an all-out war and continues during peace and war.'[2] In that respect, the secessionist and terrorist violence in the Kashmir Valley and Jammu region while the Kargil conflict was raging can well be considered the onset of the hybrid war in J&K.

Reflecting on operations in J&K during the Kargil conflict and its aftermath, Lieutenant General J.R. Mukherjee, a highly respected counterinsurgency expert and chief of staff and commander of the Srinagar-based 15 Corps HQ between July/August 1999 and December 2001, argues that the existing narratives on the Kargil and post-Kargil operations have been incomplete. His view is that 'besides cutting off Ladakh and Siachen, Pakistan's larger game plan was also to 'set the whole of Kashmir on fire', by exploiting the large-scale side-stepping of resources from Kashmir and Jammu to Ladakh, to deal with the Pakistani intrusions'. This created gaps and voids along the LoC and the CI grid, which allowed Pakistan to infiltrate more than 3,000 terrorists into Kashmir and the 16 Corps Zone (Doda, Kishtwar, Poonch and Rajouri Sectors) during the summer of 1999.

Reflecting on the violence, he explained that though 15 Corps suffered heavy losses on the counter-infiltration and counterterrorism grids, it also killed over 2,000 terrorists, including several Pakistani regulars. Suicide attacks by highly radicalized Pakistan-trained terrorists and shallow cross-border strikes by both sides were quite normal and were managed at the operational level.[3] Mukherjee also emphasized how involved the senior Indian Army leadership was in exploring options to combat the very sophisticated covert war being waged by Pakistan. These included his own engagement in psychological operations to create doubts in the minds of local Kashmiri insurgent and terrorist groups like the Hizbul Mujahideen, about the sustainability of their operations.[4]

These efforts of 15 Corps coincided with the attempts of the Vajpayee Government in Delhi to take forward a peace initiative. The prime minister involved the Farooq Abdullah government in Srinagar and moderate elements within the HM, such as Abdul Majeed Dar. Delhi announced non-initiation of combat operations from October 2000 to March 2001. This, however, did not mean that there was an absence of violence. The initiative was a failure and was called off in June 2001. Nearly 500 civilians, 635 terrorists and 285 security personnel lost their lives between October 2000 and June 2001 in violence that spanned the full spectrum of conflict.[5]

Divisional commanders like Nanavatty had urged HQ 15 Corps to deploy the Indian Army in Srinagar as it was emerging as the intellectual hub of the secessionist movement. However, until 1999, the Indian Army avoided the presence of infantry units in Srinagar city in deference to political directions. Around the same time when Mukherjee was at the helm of operations in 15 Corps, Colonel Ranjan Kumar Singh (RK), who later retired as a brigadier, was in command of the 4th Battalion of the Kumaon Regiment (4 KUMAON), one of the Indian Army's most decorated battalions. It was located about 30 km from Srinagar and was rushed into the city's iconic Badami Bagh Cantonment in November 1999 following an LeT suicide attack that killed the army's public relations officer and several others. 4 KUMAON was soon followed into Srinagar by another infantry battalion, the 3rd Battlion of the

Garhwal Rifles (3 GARH RIF). Together they set up an elaborate urban counterterrorism grid that would over the next two years, effectively combat the LeT. Terming the time as one of great concern for commanding officers, RK does not remember anyone in his unit having slept for more than a few hours at a stretch for almost two years.

Among the several close shaves, he recollects the sheer horror of being cornered in the narrow bylanes of Srinagar with a twenty-man patrol. With kerosene oil being poured on the unsuspecting Kumaonis by an LeT team from several rooftops, RK instinctively ordered his men to remove their bulletproof vests, cover their heads and make a run for it with bullets raining down. Luckily for the Kumaonis, they timed their exit perfectly with minimal casualties or injuries. Fighting fire with fire in those days became commonplace with the Kumaonis launching an operation the very next day to eliminate the LeT group responsible for the previous night's ambush. Commenting on the reckless and fanatical zeal of the LeT in the early 1990s, RK reckons that most of the suicide bombers or fidayeen were heavy on drugs. It was during one such operation after having eliminated four of the five terrorists they were after, RK recollects being led-on to the fifth by a trail of Calmpose vials and syringes. When finally cornered, the terrorist was found shivering with a pistol in his hand but unable to squeeze the trigger.[6] Nanavatty's fears of the debilitating impact of the army being kept away from Srinagar were coming true.

A Commanding Officer's Tale

The 2nd Battalion of the Parachute (Special Forces) Regiment or 2 PARA (SF) was being blooded in combat in J&K during one of the most violent phases of the proxy war post-Kargil, having been moved into the Valley to replace 9 PARA (SF). Within months of assuming command, Colonel Gurdeep Bains, the commanding officer of 2 PARA, was surprised to hear that his battalion was being pulled out of J&K. He wrote to the army commander (Nanavatty) explaining that the unit needed more combat experience to consolidate in its new role. The army commander agreed and 2 PARA continued to operate independently in seek-and-destroy and deep-ambush missions, or as part of a larger force. The unit added significant value during the high-intensity counterterrorism operations in the Valley.[7]

However, Bains felt that the performance of the battalion had been below the high expectations reposed in it. In 2001, though the battalion had eliminated twenty-one terrorists and recovered sizeable quantities of arms, ammunition and equipment, their casualties were inordinately heavy, as they had lost four soldiers and had nine injured. 'I bear responsibility for these setbacks and have instituted remedial measures,' Bains wrote in a letter to his battalion's officers after intensifying the unit's training regimen. He concluded the letter by adding, 'I hope that the rigorous training carried out will manifest itself in good results.'[8]

2 PARA was assigned to 15 Corps and deployed with 19 Infantry Division and 28 Infantry Division. The unit spent its first year with the Kilo Force in North Kashmir before joining Victor Force in South Kashmir, where it notched up a stupendous tally of terrorist kills by December 2002. The unit was also allotted special missions with 6 Mountain Division and 1 Corps during Operation Parakram. Bains recollects that during the peak of operations in the summer and autumn of 2002, as many as six to seven teams would be participating in operations at multiple locations. This diffused and dispersed concept of operations demanded exceptional decision-making skills and a team dynamic that developed as the unit gained battle experience. Victor Force wrote that the performance of the battalion had been 'exemplary'.[9] In three years under Bains's command, 2 PARA neutralized eighty-three terrorists but lost seven comrades and had seventeen wounded.[10] He said that these casualties still haunted him and at times, he still wakes up at night wondering what he could have done to reduce them.[11]

In October 2002, soon after the local elections in J&K, there were reports of widespread disruption of peace in various areas. One such area was the Warwan Valley. Situated in the upper reaches of the Himalayas at around 7,000 feet, Warwan is bounded by the Kashmir Valley on one side and Ladakh on the other. It remains completely cut off from the rest of the world for around seven months of the year.[12] The valley was within the area of responsibility of Victor Force. The 'C' team of 2 PARA and a section of the Indian Navy's MARCOS were inducted into the Warwan Valley along with some strength of the J&K Police and other army units. A week later, the others were withdrawn to indicate to the locals and the terrorists that an assessment of the return of normalcy had been made by the district authorities.

However, 'C' team and the MARCOS moved into the adjoining hills of the Kishtwar ranges, where they established hideouts and continued to observe the developments in the Valley. Three days later, they noticed suspicious activity. In a swift operation at daybreak, three terrorists were neutralized with no loss to civilians or friendly forces.[13] The MARCOS are now considered to be an integral part of the SF deployment in the valley. Admiral Arun Prakash recalls that they had blended into the environment perfectly – unshaven, speaking

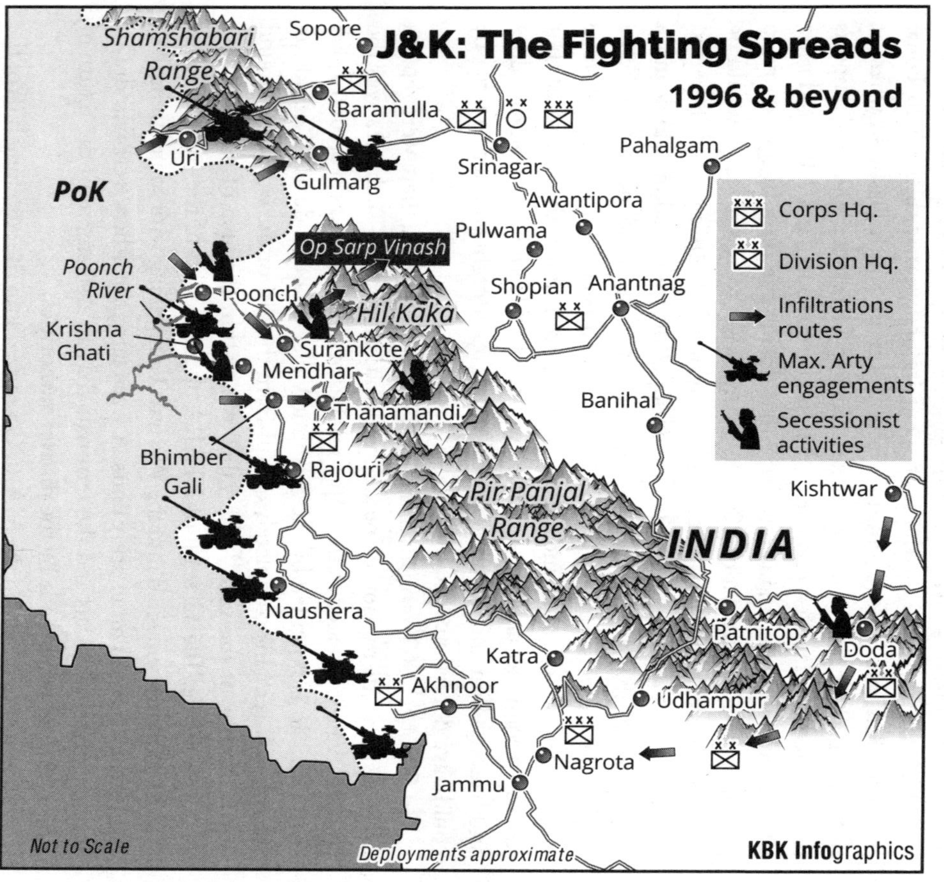

This map is for representational purposes only and does not purport to depict political boundaries

the local dialect and wearing the local robes – and that 'the army had a lot of faith in them'.[14]

In another intelligence-driven operation, a joint seek-and-destroy operation with a battalion of Rashtriya Rifles and a unit from the J&K Police's special operations group commenced at Durapur village at 10 a.m. on 30 December 2002. A team of 2 PARA joined the encounter at midday, by when several terrorists had spread out in the village. In a well-coordinated operation with minimal collateral damage and casualties, a total of eight terrorists were killed over a period of eighteen hours.[15] Bains put this success down to the ability to operate isolated in small teams and blend into a hostile environment. He recognizes the importance of leveraging the collective strengths and capabilities of the diverse security forces operating in the area.[16]

Expanding the Arc of Terror

Surankote is a small town in the Poonch Sector south-west of the Pir Panjal Range. The Poonch River flows through this town, and it is flanked by the Hil Kaka subsidiary range where the Gujjar and Bakarwal tribesmen graze their livestock in the summer. Like Sopore in the 1980s, Surankote and the adjoining hilly areas of Hil Kaka had become a haven for terrorists. From here they would fan out into the Jammu region to take the covert war deep into what the ISI termed as 'enemy territory'. Constantly searching for fresh areas to expand the covert war, Pakistan revived the traditional infiltration routes in the Poonch area to consolidate forces in the area. Led by the LeT, JeM and Al-Badr, the terrorists brazenly felt secure enough to play cricket with the locals in Surankote. For almost four years, the Surankote area remained a haven for terrorists south of the Pir Panjal Ranges till the Romeo Force of the Rashtriya Rifles was tasked to make the final push to clear Surankote-Hil Kaka.

The Romeo Force was commanded by Major General H.S. Lidder. After some discussion with the army chief, Lieutenant General Nanavatty chose 63 Infantry Brigade to undertake the operation. He was allotted teams of 1, 9 and 10 PARA for this operation.[17] Nanavatty had suggested 'Operation Rat's Nest' as the name for the operation. However, Lidder chose the more dramatic Operation Sarp Vinash ('destroy the snake'). In April and May 2003, Mi-26s and Mi-17s were employed to build helipads at key locations, lifting bulldozers and construction machinery on to hilltops. Employing over three battalions, the Romeo Force inflicted significant casualties on the terrorists, recovered large caches of arms from the many abandoned Gujjar dwellings on the hillsides and cut off most routes of escape. Though the number of kills claimed by the Indian Army were questioned and contested by a section of the media,[18] Nanavatty says that what mattered to him was that they had cleaned up Surankote and the army has not had a problem in the area since then.[19]

Lieutenant General D.S. Hooda, who commanded a brigade in the Uri Sector, 16 Corps in Nagrota, and was the Northern Army Commander from 2014 to 2016, has spent a lifetime in J&K like several officers interviewed by the author. He confirmed that there indeed had been massive infiltration into the Poonch-Rajouri Sectors as part of the ISI strategy of 'spreading the arc of terrorism' into the areas south of the Pir Panjal Range.[20] Thana Mandi, Poonch and Rajouri were the main infiltration routes for terrorists and the hills of Doda and Kishtwar emerged as safe havens. The Gujjar and Bakarwal communities have played an important role in counterterrorist operations in the Jammu region. Hooda explained that Gujjars raised cattle and had semi-permanent settlements while Bakarwals raised sheep and were largely nomads. In the winter, both communities would concentrate around Reasi, Udhampur and the lower reaches of the Pir Panjal Range. In the summer, they crossed the range into the Kashmir Valley in search of grazing grounds. The more adventurous even crossed the Zoji La Pass into the Kargil and Batalik Sectors. Along the way, they were exploited in various ways by the residents of the Valley, who extracted a heavy price from them.

Thus, there was no love lost between these communities and the Kashmiris. They were also exploited by the terrorists, who took their cattle, sheep and women, and killed those they suspected of acting as informers for the Indian Army. Hooda feels that not enough credit has been given to the two communities in the fight against terrorism in the Jammu region. He adds that some Gujjars were used as guides and porters by the Romeo Force during Operation Sarp Vinash. Hooda also recounts the setting up of village defence committees (VDCs) following the massacre of Hindus in remote villages in the Poonch and Rajouri regions. While the initial VDCs were predominantly manned by Hindus, several all-Muslim VDCs sprang up in the area, particularly in the Surankote and Hil Kaka regions. Indicating the proactive role of women in the counterterrorist campaign, an all-women VDC still exists. The concept of community-specific VDCs is now being discouraged as it is seen to polarize communities.

Heat, Ceasefire and a Fence

Quasi-official figures reveal the hit taken by the Pakistan Army and the jihadis prior to the ceasefire of 2003. From 1 January 2000 to 15 October

2002 (roughly corresponding to the period between the cessation of the Kargil conflict and the end of Operation Parakram*)*, Indian artillery and mortar firing across the LoC caused 700 fatalities to the Pakistan Army and its associated border management forces. Retaliatory fire caused about 140 fatalities on the Indian side. Approximately 2,30,000 mortar rounds and 1,02,000 artillery shells were fired by the Pakistan Army, the Indian Army responding with 2,70,000 mortars and 1,33,000 artillery shells. Small-team engagements around the LoC were widespread and caused approximately 130 fatalities among both Pakistani regulars and mujahids, while fatalities on the Indian side were much lower, at just under 50. The most telling statistic of this period was that the number of terrorists killed per encounter went up from 1.7:1 to 2.3:1.[21]

Pakistan offered a comprehensive ceasefire in November 2003 after feeling the heat from sustained Indian military action and diplomatic pressure following the attack on the Indian Parliament by ISI-trained LeT terrorists in December 2001. India accepted the offer, but it was never formalized into a binding agreement. This was because of India's insistence that it be linked to a comprehensive commitment from Pakistan to stop supporting the Kashmiri secessionist struggle and using terrorism against India. The lull in the relentless operations allowed General N.C. Vij, the army chief, to push through his ambitious project of fencing almost the entire 700 km of the LoC – which runs from what the Indian Army calls Zero Point in the Akhnoor Sector to the very edge of the Gurez Sector in the Mushkoh Valley. The anti-infiltration obstacle system (AIOS), also known as a fence, required 300 tons of steel per kilometre and was completed in early 2005 at a cost of over Rs 1,150 crore. It took 25,000 men of the Indian Army eighteen months to accomplish this. The fence made infiltration extremely difficult till the ISI discovered and designed tactics to overcome it.

Lieutenant General Hasnain was then commanding 12 Infantry Brigade in Uri and remembers General Vij insisting that the fence come up as a continuous obstacle despite the protests from local commanders who felt that it was an impossible task given the terrain. Hasnain also had to cope with the chief coming to his brigade HQ every twenty days to get a status update on the progress of the fence. Hasnain said, 'Much credit for the fence must go to General Vij. His strategic vision cannot be faulted as between 2004 and 2007 the combination of the ceasefire and the fence had impacted the mathematics of the infiltration and significantly reduced the number of ceasefire violations (CFVs).'[22]

The double-layered fence is 12 feet high and about 12 feet wide. It is made up of coils of concertina wire strung between rows of pickets and is electrified at places. Unlike the one built by the Israelis to control the infiltration of terrorists from Palestine,[23] this fence has not come under a lot of international scrutiny as it follows the alignment of the LoC and is well within Indian territory. There was also surprisingly muted opposition from the Pakistanis, as it suited Musharraf's 'dovish' strategy at the time to depict attempts to control anti-India terrorist groups. As no obstacle can prevent movement without surveillance, the Indian Army has deployed motion sensors, thermal imaging devices and night-vision equipment.[24] It has also divided the ceasefire zone into grids so that officers can be held accountable for movement in designated areas.

Amy Waldman wrote in the *New York Times* quoting Umar Farooq, a pro-'azadi' Kashmiri political leader: 'People who want to come and are determined to come, they will come. They have routes and maps, and they will use them. It's a waste of money.' Farooq thought that it was better to pursue a political settlement. Waldman quoted senior Indian military officials saying that they see 'tentativeness' among terrorists and that 'the fence has allowed the army to foil many crossing attempts'. However, terrorists in Pakistan say that the fence has made 'crossing the ceasefire line riskier' but assert that they have 'enough men and ammunition already inside Kashmir to sustain the insurgency for years'.[25] Hooda knows the fence intimately and reckons that it was easier to manage a two-layered fence in the Jammu region and instal surveillance devices. It did not collapse in the winter under the weight of snow except in some areas of the Poonch Sector. However, northwards into the Valley the fence practically disappears in the upper reaches of the Tangdhar, Neelum and Gurez Sectors and repairs must start every year in May. This is a herculean task as sand, cement and wire are needed to repair and rebuild many kilometres of damaged fence. While he was a sceptic when it was being built, Hooda acknowledges that the fence has done its job as a serious obstacle for infiltrators.[26]

Force Levels and Military Civic Action

The constant movement of security forces in and out of J&K since the early 1990s has led to intense speculation regarding their profile and strength. There was a time in the 1980s when 15 Corps in Srinagar had only one oversized division (19 Infantry Division), a couple of additional brigades and a few BSF battalions. This added up to around 35,000 troops for defending the LoC in the Kashmir region. However, in 2002 – after over a decade of violence and heightened infiltration – the deployment of counter-infiltration forces along the LoC had almost doubled to 50,000 to 60,000 troops. This was a significant rise in the numbers of security forces involved in counter-infiltration and counterterrorist operations across the Valley. South of the Pir Panjal Range in the Jammu region, the Indian Army had three infantry divisions under 16 Corps, with an extra division moving in when required. This four-division counter-infiltration and counterterrorist force had a total strength of 1,00,000 to 1,10,000 troops.

3 Corps in the north-east and 16 Corps in the Jammu region are the Indian Army's largest corps, and reflect India's security focus and concerns. Adding in the personnel of the J&K Police, there were over 4,00,000 security personnel deployed in J&K in the 2000s. Ajai Shukla has assessed that this figure may be closer to 4,70,000 in 2018. The latest figures endorsed by the Indian Army point at a lower strength.[27] However, Pakistan puts the number at one million.[28] These figures do not include the Indian Army and Indo-Tibetan Border Police (ITBP) deployments in Ladakh.

India's armed forces, particularly the Indian Army and the IAF, have been constantly engaged in civic action in the remote areas of the country since Independence. Major instances are the aftermath of Partition, the months after the cessation of 1947-48 hostilities with Pakistan, in Nagaland and Mizoram during the peak years of the insurgencies and during natural calamities across the country. The Indian Navy has effectively contributed in every humanitarian assistance and disaster relief (HADR) operation in the maritime domain since Independence.

In 1998, the Indian Army launched a military civic action programme in J&K called Operation Sadbhavna. While most commanders acknowledge the utility of military-civic programmes in remote areas, some like retired Lieutenant General Rakesh Sharma think the Indian Army committed excessive resources to Operation Sadbhavna. Hooda, however, argues that initiatives like the army goodwill schools and healthcare centres have had a great impact, particularly in the rural areas of J&K where there is a heavy army presence but hardly any civil administration or police. He recollects meeting a group of parents who had requested that the army take back a school that had been handed over to the civil administration. However, Hooda agrees that getting into infrastructure projects like constructing microhydel units was a mistake as they were not sustainable unless run by the civil administration. He recollects another high-impact initiative was the setting up of youth clubs in the hotbeds of secessionist activity – such as Anantnag and Shopian – because of their potential for deradicalization. Overall, Hooda thinks that military-civic action must be used in a measured manner without diluting the core responsibilities of the military.[29]

The Lost Years: 2003-12

The earthquake that ravaged J&K and large portions of PoK in October 2005 could have been a turning point had the Manmohan Singh government moved decisively to win over the people of Kashmir. The speed with which the Indian Army and the IAF swung into action for relief operations was in stark comparison to the lukewarm response to the natural calamity in PoK. People living in the districts of Uri and Tangdhar were the hardest hit on the Indian side. They were rehabilitated in no time. However, those in Muzaffarabad in PoK languished for months amidst the destruction. The Srinagar-Muzaffarabad bus service – started as a confidence-building measure – had allowed the locals to compare the development in J&K with that in PoK. Soon many who had crossed the border in 1989-90 as teenagers realized that it was time to go back. Now in their mid-thirties, they had married locals and been disillusioned with the jihadi movement. However, after the initial amnesty to about a hundred hardcore terrorists who came across, the initiative fizzled out in 2007 following resistance from hardliners within the Indian Army and the intelligence agencies. Hooda thinks that this was a possible lost opportunity.

General Bipin Rawat, then a brigadier, commanded an RR sector in the Sopore Sector as part of Kilo Force between 2006 and 2008. He recollects that though the ceasefire of 2003 was holding, the fence-based counter-infiltration grid had not stabilized in his sector and infiltration was continuing. This was because the thickly forested bowl-shaped Lolab Valley immediately south of the Shamshabari Range was an ideal post-infiltration staging halt for infiltrators before they climbed over the only ridge that separated Lolab from Sopore. Then they could join locals in buses and other vehicles running on the solitary road connecting Sopore with Kupwara. Among the successes that Rawat recollects are the operations conducted by his units inside and on the fringes of the Lolab and Handwara forests. They often had the help of former terrorists who penetrated the HM terror gangs and acted as double agents. They provided Rawat with critical information that led to several successful encounters. These operatives would be extricated from the jihadi groups after a few operations and not one of them was compromised during Rawat's tenure. A few of them were recruited into Territorial Army battalions of the JAKLI and are still serving.[30]

Hasnain's first attempt at seriously influencing the intellectual dimension of the covert war against the Indian state was during his divisional commander's tenure in Baramulla in 2008. Attempting to bridge the cultural, social and religious divide, symposiums for maulvis of different sects met with some success. But such ideas could not be sustained because of an inherent resistance to digress from the more visible kinetic attempts at tackling the problem. The idea, however, remained with Hasnain who went on to delve deeper into understanding Islam during his next assignment as head of the Junior Command Wing of the Army War College. Since then, Hasnain has been at the forefront of a healthy debate within the Indian Army on the importance of targeting the intellectual dimension of the 'azadi' movement in J&K.

Prime Minister Manmohan Singh was an idealist and an internationalist like his predecessor, Vajpayee. He too believed in taking the path of reconciliation in India-Pakistan relations. The five expert groups he set up in 2006 to address the varied facets of the Kashmir imbroglio made several useful recommendations that were not implemented.[31] However, it seemed that his parleys with President Musharraf for exploring out-of-the box solutions for the Kashmir conflict were headed in the right direction. Analysing the situation prior to the Mumbai attacks of November 2008, Hooda says that there was a steep decline in the number of deaths due to terrorism and insurgency – from the 2001 peak of over 4,000 to below 1,000 in 2007. This, along with the rapid progress of the Manmohan-Musharraf discussions, made the ISI derail any nascent peace initiatives.

The Indian security establishment was at the time preoccupied with the widespread protests in Kashmir over innocuous issues such as the transfer of 100 acres of land around the sacred Amarnath shrine for construction of temporary shelters for pilgrims. Initiated by environmentalists and exploited by secessionists who linked it to a dilution of their autonomy, the protests in May and June 2008 led to the resignation of the governor and the fall of the elected coalition government led by Ghulam Nabi Azad of the Congress party.[32] This led to the first manifestation of a people's movement that was called 'Chalo' or 'let's go'. 'Chalo Muzaffarabad' was the first of many such slogans that sparked a gradual spike in violence in J&K.[33] With Delhi now focused on Kashmir, the field was open for the LeT to plan attacks in India. The Mumbai terror attacks were followed by the souring of India-Pakistan relations, Western pressure on Musharraf to dismantle terror networks in Pakistan and a deterioration in the security situation in Kashmir.

While terrorist attacks and infiltrations reduced following the Mumbai attacks, civilian protests and mass mobilizations commenced in right earnest as an evolving 'strategy of the weak'. These presented the Indian Army with a new threat – stone pelting and mass mob protests designed to provoke a violent response. The year 2010 was a violent one, with 112 deaths, including both protesters and security forces. Meanwhile, Hasnain was firmly ensconced as the corps commander of the army's third strike corps, 21 Corps, till he was asked to move to Srinagar in September by the army chief, General V.K. Singh. Hasnain reflects that this was a challenge he was waiting for. He reckoned that by the end of 2010 the agitation had reached an inflection point wherein fatigue had set in amongst the populace. Education had suffered; the apple crop had wasted away; and tourism had reached an all-time low. The separatist leaders had to make a decisive move if they wanted to spark an uprising.

Syed Shah Geelani, the pro-Pakistan leader of the All Party Hurriyat Conference,[34] appealed to the people to surround military camps and raised 'Chalo UN' and 'Chalo Baramulla' calls to paralyse the civil administration. This is when Lieutenant General Marwah, Hasnain's predecessor as corps commander, put out a stern warning that if the army camps were threatened, the army would retaliate decisively. The issue was discussed at the Unified Command in Srinagar and clear instructions and guidelines were passed to the police, RR and army units to stamp out what was threatening to become a major rebellion. While the J&K Police and RR managed to control the mobs of stone pelters, soldiers from the regular army battalions often got unnerved by them. Had it not been for a steep learning curve demonstrated by young officers, there may well have been several cases of retaliatory firing by outnumbered troops.

Hasnain remembers several instances of unarmed young officers confronting mobs, dialoguing with them to return to their homes, and even daring them to target them. Like always they rose to the occasion with alacrity and fearlessness.[35] Retired Lieutenant General Ravi Thodge was commanding Kilo Force in northern Kashmir as a major general under Hasnain. He recollects that when cornered by a huge mob his troops were compelled to open fire, killing two mobsters. When he made it clear to the protesters that troops would fire in self-defence, the intensity of the agitation reduced in his area. Worried by the changing trend of violence in the Valley, Manmohan Singh sent a group of civilian interlocutors to the Valley in late 2010. It was led by senior journalist Dileep Padgaonkar and included an academic and author, Professor Radha Kumar, and an academic-turned-civil servant, M.M. Ansari.

The principal mandate for the group was to study the situation and initiate a dialogue with various stakeholders. General Thodge recollects that they were clueless about military matters, underestimated the potential of the ISI and downplayed the growing menace of the mobs. Thodge tried to explain their counterterrorism operations to the group and point out the ominous signs that the youth in Kashmir were being brainwashed to believe that 'azadi' (freedom) was around the corner. Questions such as 'Why don't you identify the terrorists before opening fire?' clearly showed that they were unaware of the restraint shown by the Indian Army during cordon-and-search operations, during which it was the army that took casualties, thus yielding the initiative to the terrorists. Thodge told the interlocutors that no heavy weapons or air power were used in such operations, and that the Indian Army was probably the most restrained counterterrorism force in the world. The Kilo Force had several successes in 2011 after the government agencies began helping with communication intelligence on the LeT and JeM. These operations were particularly effective in the Gurez sector, where Kilo Force experienced several successes during Thodge's tenure. It was clear from this experience that operations driven by intelligence and technology would be the way forward.[36]

In the mind games that followed, the separatists wilted and there appeared to be a window for Hasnain to apply a healing touch to a tired but angry and sullen local population. The years 2011 and 2012 were relatively quiet, with Hasnain building on the good work done by his predecessors like Lieutenant Generals Vinayak Patankar and Nirbhay Sharma, who had started several citizen outreach programmes. Apart from exhorting his troops to understand the cultural terrain and institute citizen-friendly initiatives such as rescheduling daily-life-disrupting military convoys through populated areas, he was clear that there would be no let-up along the LoC and in targeting terrorist leadership, particularly in North Kashmir. He regrets, however, that New Delhi and the Indian Army were impatient, and wanted the speedy conversion of the stabilization phase into a conflict resolution phase. This prevented the detection of the migration of the separatist movement from North to South Kashmir.

What slipped under Srinagar's and New Delhi's radar was the emergence of a new crop of local terrorist leadership in 2012 led by a younger generation of heavily radicalized youth like Burhan Wani who had seen nothing but violence during their impressionable years of growing up in the Valley. Exploiting a protective local population and creating a Robin Hood-like reputation with fanatic jihadi fervour, South Kashmir's locally recruited terrorists soon made it the epicentre of the separatist movement. When asked whether there was an element of overreach in his version of the 'Winning Hearts and Minds' strategy, and whether he had unrealistic expectations of any meaningful politico-strategic outcomes from his initiatives, Hasnain was candid in his reply. He was emphatic that he had correctly identified the centre of gravity within the secessionist movement. He also reckoned that there was a lack of adequate institutional continuity and an understanding that the stabilization phase in Kashmir would take a few more years before a push for conflict resolution could be made. Hasnain reckons that this resulted in the reversal of gains made between 2010 and 2012. He realized, however, that he may have built unrealistic expectations of what could or could not be achieved in a limited two-year tenure as the corps commander of 15 Corps.[37]

Escalation

Hooda was the commander of 16 Corps by 2012, a time when there was little presence of terrorists south of the Pir Panjal Range. This was because local support had dried up and some headway was being made in the political process. Total killings were at an all-time low of 107 and tourism was showing signs of revival. Senior commanders of the security forces told the Omar Abdullah government of J&K that it was the right time to improve state-driven governance, pursue deradicalization initiatives and restore law and order. However, both the state and the Centre failed to exploit the window, leaving room for the ISI to keep the Kashmir pot boiling.

Nawaz Sharif returned as prime minister of Pakistan in June 2013 and wanted to revisit the India-Pakistan peace process. That was when the General Kayani-led Pakistan Army decided to up the ante in the Jammu region by embedding their border action teams with SSG commandos. First an Indian soldier was captured during a cross-border operation by Pakistanis and beheaded. Thereafter a police station was raided and stripped of hundreds of weapons. This was followed by a hit on 16 Armoured Regiment of the Indian Army at Samba by the LeT. Outfits like the LeT and JeM were desperate for action after almost five years of forced restraint following the Mumbai attacks. As infiltrations rose, there were massive exchanges of fire across the LoC. This led to a meeting between the director general of military operations of both armies in December 2013 where de-escalation was discussed.

Taking over the Northern Command in June 2014, Hooda was immediately confronted with a massive flood-relief operation in J&K. The Indian Army and IAF carried out their roles well, but subsequent relief, rehabilitation and reconstruction initiatives were suboptimal. This caused a great deal of angst against the newly elected Mehbooba Mufti J&K government. The winter of 2015 was a restive one because, as Hooda cautioned New Delhi, there was much anger and radicalization in the Valley. He suggested a flexi response, that included the possibility of offering a ceasefire. Concurrently, in a change of strategy, the ISI scaled down the infiltration. They used the terrorists mainly to conduct strikes against military bases and as handlers for the large numbers of radicalized and disenchanted Kashmiri youth who were joining the HM in droves. Designated as a local commander, Burhan Wani soon emerged as a poster boy of the new wave. Wani was finally cornered by the security forces in Kokernag in July 2016. He was neutralized after being given several opportunities to surrender. Hooda recounts that despite the operation being an intelligence-driven one, no one had been aware that Wani was holed up in that location. A policeman was injured in the firefight and two HM terrorists were neutralized – one of whom was Wani. The turnout at Wani's funeral and the ripple effect it created across the valley surprised everyone and heralded the second wave of stone-throwing protests.

The Indian security establishment had dismissed the 2010 protests as a one-time expression of angst, but that was not the case this time. Hooda says that he was surprised at the scale of the uprising that followed in 2016. It was far more widespread than the ones in 2009-10, which were restricted to urban areas. 'As local recruitment rose, women joined the protests and helped trapped terrorists escape cordons,' he remembers. Shopian and Bandipora emerged as hotbeds of protests in southern and north-eastern Kashmir, while Kupwara in northern Kashmir saw mass protests. Mobs in Kupwara tried to set the military hospital on fire and loot armouries of police stations. 'Equally worrisome was the radicalization, which saw families divided on the mosques (Hanafi/Barelvi vs Salafist/Wahhabi Ahle-Hadith)[38] they visited to offer prayers,' Hooda says. 'Eleven-year-olds were getting radicalized in Salafist/Wahhabi mosques and joining street mobs.'[39]

Garuds in Action

The Garud Forces were formed in 2004 as the special forces unit of the IAF. To gain experience, they were initially embedded in small numbers within units of the Indian Army's special forces in Kashmir. However, this did not prove to be of any great operational value. They were not involved in any major intelligence-driven operation because of their inexperience. It took the IAF almost a decade to convince the defence ministry and Army HQ that the Garuds were capable of operations. Following this, two large teams of Garuds were sent on a six-month tour of the central Kashmiri district of Bandipora along with the RR.

Squadron Leader 'R' was assigned command of an element of Garuds in February 2017 and led his team into the Valley in July 2017. They were fully supported by the IAF with the best weapons, clothing, night vision and communication devices. The teams plunged into active operations after two weeks of rigorous training at the 15 Corps Battle School at Khrew. They were then assigned to Hajun, a densely populated town of 35,000 on the banks of the Jhelum River. Hajun had emerged as a den of secessionist activity and the Garuds soon discovered that it was easy for the town to mobilize a stone-throwing mob of up to 10,000 people. 'R' recalls that women would hide stones in their phirens (gowns) and distribute them to the young boys and men, who would throw them at the security forces. 'R' was injured by these stones and needed stitches on his left shoulder and right hand.

'R' soon developed a feel for the situation and the importance of intelligence-driven operations. North and Central Kashmir at the time were largely LeT-dominated, while the JeM controlled South Kashmir. He realized the HM was a spent force – with its local fighters more of a liability because of their poor fighting ability – and understood why they were being eliminated in large numbers by the security forces. When cornered, the HM terrorists would call up family members to rally a crowd and facilitate their escape. This was a different kind of warfare and required great restraint, skill and patience.

The first major operation that 'R' and his team were involved in took place at Rakh Hajun – a hamlet of about ten houses to the north of Hajun town. The J&K Police provided confirmed intelligence of the presence of eight to ten LeT terrorists in the hamlet. A dense cordon was laid by three SF teams from the Garuds, 9 PARA and an RR battalion. The Garuds were the blocking force to the rear, where it was anticipated that the terrorists would attempt to break through the cordon to make a run for the apple orchards. The operation commenced at around 9 p.m. on 10 October 2017. It took over twelve hours for the teams to close in on the target house. When the terrorists finally made a run for it, they ran into the Garuds. Two militants were shot down immediately and another was severely injured in a firefight that lasted no more than three or four minutes. The Garuds too lost two men during this operation – their first casualties.

Following this operation, there was talk that the Garuds may be reassigned to a quieter sector. 'R' requested his sector commander to have faith in the team and give them the opportunity to avenge the loss of their comrades. What followed was a month of painstaking intelligence collection with the active assistance of the J&K Police. This involved the continuous tracking of a terrorist's communication by intelligence agencies and the J&K Police. His

Lieutenant Prakash Chandavarkar and his team on a harbour sanitization mission

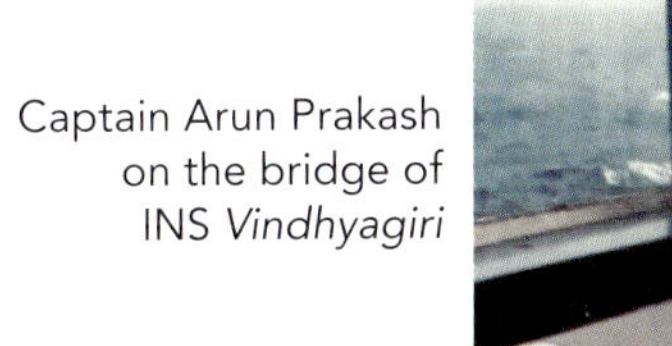

Captain Arun Prakash
on the bridge of
INS *Vindhyagiri*

Vindhyagiri trailed by the Indian Navy's new aircraft carrier *Viraat* off the Sri Lanka coast in July 1989

Mi-25 landing at the 7 Brigade HQ, Mullaitivu

Typical improvised explosive devices (IEDs) used by the LTTE

7 Brigade officers with a legend from the 1971 war, HH Maharaja Bhawani Singh (seated second from left). Brigadier R.R. Palsokar is seated on his left

Troops from 7 GARH RIF practising Helo-Assault from *Viraat*

Captain Madhavendra Singh, captain of the *Viraat*, inspecting troops of 7 GARH RIF

A Jeep of 7 GARH RIF being embarked on *Viraat* by a Sea King helicopter

An Indian Naval Sea King helicopter and its crew from INS *Godavari* with 3 PARA in Male. Major N.S. Ghei is at the extreme right

Brigadier Farouk Bulsara (left) and Group Captain Anant Bewoor (right) engaged in the final planning for Operation Cactus at Agra

IL-76 taking off from Agra for Hulule on 3 November 1988

A relieved President M.A. Gayoom accepting a memento from Colonel S.C. Joshi, commanding officer, 6 PARA

Convoys lined up on the national highway in the Dras-Kargil Sector

Typical infantry assaults with rifles, LMGs and rocket launchers

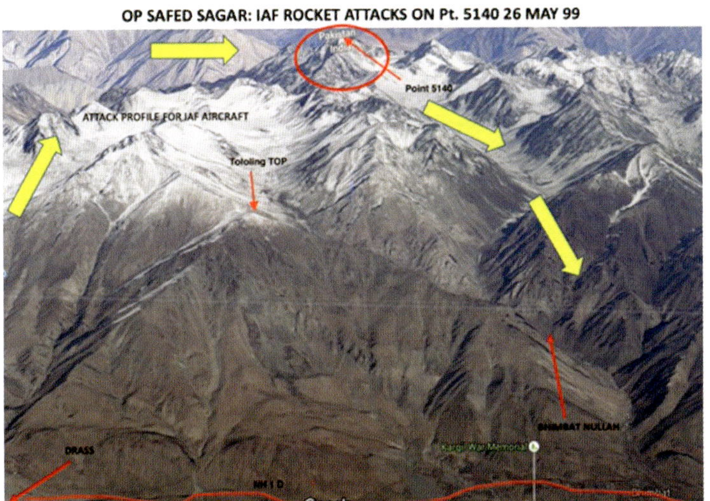

An attack profile by MiG-21s of 51 Squadron on Point 5140 during Day 1 of the air war

Flight Lieutenant Sameer Joshi with his MiG-21 Bis armed with the R-60 missile

The Bofors gun in action in Dras Sector

Colonel Sameer Chakravorty (Chaks), commanding officer, 18 Garhwal, inspecting a captured enemy air defence gun on Point 4700

CO's bunker on Point 4700 and with the men amidst the cold rocks of Kargil

Chaks with his men and with Major General Mohinder Puri, General V.P. Malik and Air Chief Marshal A.Y. Tipnis after the Garhwalis captured several key heights

Wing Commander Anil Sinha (standing, centre), commanding officer, aircrew and engineers of 129 Helicopter Unit, the Mi-17 unit, prior to a mission from Srinagar airfield during the early days of the Kargil conflict

Craters around Tiger Hill following the Mirage-2000 attacks

Air Chief Marshal Tipnis and General Malik inspecting a captured medium machine gun

Peripheral but important action – the capture of Point 5770 on the southern glacier region of Siachen by 27 RAJPUT and Ladakh Scouts

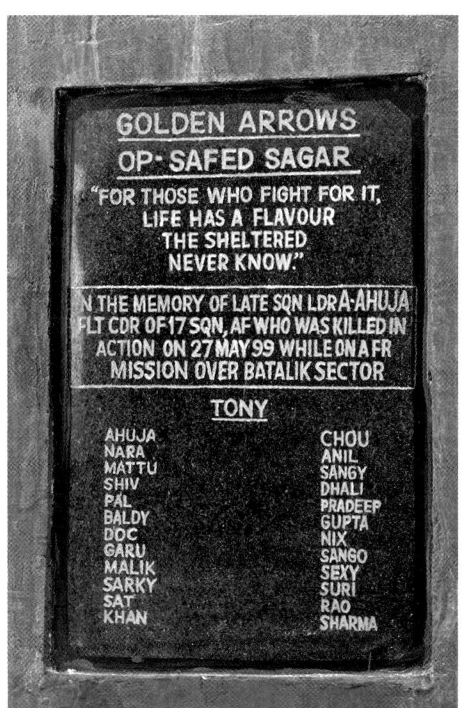

A stone plaque in memory of Squadron Leader Ajay Ahuja in 17 Squadron

A rare picture of Prime Minister A.B. Vajpayee and Defence Minister George Fernandes after the conflict. General Malik (partially hidden) showing them captured weapons from the heights

60 Para Field Ambulance embarking on their mission at Calcutta Port in November 1950

Attending to a wounded soldier from the 27th Commonwealth Brigade

Lieutenant Colonel A.G. Rangaraj receiving his Maha Vir Chakra from President Rajendra Prasad

Major Rangaraj (third from right) with an unidentified Canadian officer and fellow doctors from 60 Para Field Ambulance

IAF Canberra bombers from 5 Squadron at Kamina airfield as part of UNOC (1961-63)

Wing Commander Saroj Jena, the commanding officer of 5 Squadron (second from left), examining the aircraft logbook before a sortie

The funeral of Captain Gurbachan Singh Salaria in Congo. He remains the only Indian to be awarded the Param Vir Chakra in UN operations

Major General I.J.S. Rikhye, the Indian Army's most accomplished peacekeeper

Group Captain N.J.S. Dhillon in conversation with a UN official on the tarmac of Goma airfield, flanked by Major General Bikram Singh

A night shot of IAF Mi-17s lined up at Goma

IAF pilots Wing Commander Rajiv Puri (extreme right) and Squadron Leader Dushyant Singh (with sunglasses) with DRC troops

Securing an Mi-35 during approaching bad weather and an Mi-35 landing against the backdrop of approaching bad weather

Deinduction of IAC-1, Kigali

INS *Tabar*, the first Indian naval warship to see action in anti-piracy operations, escorting the MV *Jag Arnav*

Indian naval frigate INS *Teg* escorting a Maersk cargo freighter in the International Transit Corridor

(From top) 'The Company' Colonel Gurdeep Bains, the commanding officer of 2 PARA (SF) (front row, second from left) and his boys; IAF's Garud commandos in central Kashmir; Indian Navy's MARCOS in the Kashmir Valley

Major General Bipin Rawat with locals during his command tenure of the Baramulla-based 19 Division

A Mirage-2000 armed with a Spice-2000 PGM that was used against the Jaish-e-Mohammed training camp at Balakot on 26 February 2019

Colonel S. Dinny, commanding officer, 14 RAJPUT, with his officers and troops on a patrol on the North Bank of the Pangang Tso

A T-72 tank being transported in a C-17 to Leh

Prime Minister Narendra Modi exhorting officers and men of the army and air force to stand firm in Ladakh on 3 July 2020

location was finally identified as Chandargeer village, 7 km from Manasbal town. A dangerous physical recce of the town confirmed these findings.

On 17 November 2017, there was a tip-off that there was heightened activity in the town and announcements from the mosque that the local people must rise in response to any provocation by the Indian Army. Learning from their previous encounter, the terrorists had chosen a haven next to a mosque. They were not expecting the army to attack by day. The Garuds and RR drove into the town at around 3 p.m. and parked undetected next to a sawmill. It was the time that the terrorists would be resting, having completed their midday prayers at the mosque and eaten lunch. What 'R' did not know, however, was that the entire top LeT leadership in J&K was in the house, with several other cadres waiting at other locations in the village. It was later assessed that the group could have well been planning a major strike. The area was cordoned by the RR's modest but heavily armed blocking force. 'R' had the rear exit covered with his Garuds.

A few hours later, the trapped terrorists responded by rushing out from the rear exit firing their AK-47s. Some were shot down immediately, while the others took cover in a ditch and started lobbing grenades. 'R' had two grenades ready and responded with an accurate grenade throw. Luckily for him, one of the two grenades thrown at him hit a tree some distance away, while the other was deflected back at the terrorists. Corporal Nirala of the Garuds charged at the remaining lot but was fatally shot in the head. When the six neutralized terrorists were identified, it became clear that the Garuds had scored a major success by hitting the LeT where it hurt the most. Four of the slain terrorists were relatives or confidants of the LeT chief Hafiz Saeed and Zakiur Rehman Lakhvi, the military commander who had masterminded the Mumbai attacks. 'R' and his slain comrades were awarded gallantry medals. This operation established the Garuds as a trained force that could be called upon to deliver in multiple situations.

Fighting Fairly

If one compares the ratios of terrorists, security forces and civilians killed in encounters during counterterrorist and counter-infiltration operations in J&K over a ten-year period with several ongoing conflicts of similar nature, the Indian Army is shown to be extremely restrained and mindful of collateral damage. In the process, it has taken unusually heavy casualties. Admiral Arun Prakash calls for a better understanding of the dilemmas that face the military when it is asked to participate in internal security operations. He wrote in the

Indian Express that most insurgencies rooted in alienation and socio-economic factors are aggravated by political venality and apathy. After the serial failure of the elected government, civil administration and police, the area is declared as 'disturbed'. The AFSPA is then invoked and the military is asked to restore order. 'Even when the army restores relative peace and normalcy, the local police and administration repeatedly fail to resume their normal functioning,' Arun Prakash laments. He continues, 'The prolonged imposition of the AFSPA is therefore a fig leaf used by successive governments to hide egregious failures of governance. The governments knew that deployment of the army without the AFSPA would be illegal and that any orders issued would constitute "unlawful commands".'[40] Prakash goes on to say that 'soldiers, being human, do make mistakes and violations of human rights have occurred from time to time. But the army as a highly disciplined body is acutely conscious that violation of human rights is a crime that sullies the organization's good name.' He insists that 'strict and comprehensive codes of conduct have been laid down by the army's leadership and drastic punishments are meted out where infringements are proved'.[41]

On the Indian Army's human rights record in Kashmir, Hooda claims that 95 per cent of the allegations made by human rights activists are false. He adds the Indian Army has a record of fair investigation and punishment for those found guilty.[42] Statistics put out by the Indian Army till 2019 reveal that of the 1,053 allegations received from J&K by the human rights cell of the Indian Army, 1,030 were investigated and 999 were found to be baseless. In the cases of the thirty-one allegations that were found to be true, seventy personnel were given punishments that included dismissal from service and rigorous imprisonment. Compensation was awarded in eighteen cases. Twenty-three cases are still under investigation.[43]

The Way Ahead

Understanding Pakistan's Strategy in Kashmir

Is Pakistan's strategy in Kashmir trapped by history, driven by revenge and propelled by radicalization? Is the crisis in its present form a security dilemma for both India and Pakistan, or is it that India is preventing a revisionist and greedy Pakistan from severing Kashmir from India?[44] From an Indian perspective, there is no security dilemma. Should Pakistan stop fomenting the covert war in the state, it can successfully manage the internal dynamics at play there. What is it, then, that has forced Pakistan to embark on its futile attempt to force a secession of J&K? One reason is an unfinished agenda from

Partition, which according to Sumit Ganguly has converted Pakistan into a 'predatory and greedy state'.[45] Another is the deeply ingrained obsession of the Pakistan Army to get even with India for its humiliating defeat in 1971. The Pakistan Army realized that fomenting a fear of India among the common people of Pakistan is the only way to maintain the myth of their army being the only entity that can 'save Pakistan' from being gobbled up by a predatory India. A third reason is the radicalization of large sections of Pakistani society as well as the Pakistan Army and the ISI. This has given traction to the desire to see Kashmir as part of an 'Islamic republic'.

Aided by poor governance by successive state governments, J&K has become a testing ground for new, disruptive and low-cost jihadi strategies[46] of radical Sunni Islam from Rawalpindi and Islamabad. Driven by jihadists such as Masood Azhar and Hafiz Saeed – and supported by secessionist elements in J&K like the All Party Hurriyat Conference – these strategies seek to fuse the traditional 'covert war' methodologies with the more nebulous strategies involving proxies and hybrid tools. They seek to exploit social media and the cyber domain and foment public unrest that spirals into violence and tests the state's resilience to the limit. A senior army officer recalls that in the 1970s and 1980s, the Indian Army had a very friendly image in the Kashmir Valley. 'However, the army did not correctly read the signs of the changed profile of visits across the LoC over the years,' he says. 'Earlier, travellers from India to PoK on a fourteen-day visa would return within three days, lamenting the state of affairs across the LoC. However, in the late 1980s, the number of youth who overstayed in PoK increased. These youths would return after three or four weeks, radicalized and having received limited arms training. They had been sent back with the message "we will contact you and the weapons will reach you".'[47]

The same officer pointed out that from 2010 onwards the separatists started to attract younger worshippers to more radicalized discourses in new foreign mosques even as the elders continued to attend the prayers in traditional family mosques. Religious teachers in these 'youthful' mosques were forced under the pressure of the gun to read a page to the congregation before commencing the traditional prayer. That page began with: 'We are Muslims and the Quran says that there is no way Hindus and Muslims can live together.' However, Muslim preachers have confirmed that the Quran does not say this. The rest of the page quoted inflammatory portions of rhetorical speeches that punctured the moderate argument against 'azadi' by making false and unfounded allegations that Muslims in the eastern parts of India were deported to Bangladesh.

The preliminary sermon concluded by saying: 'If we join India, all Muslims will be pushed out.' This led to the proposition that the future line of action for the Muslim youth in Kashmir was either fighting for independence or joining Pakistan. Clearly acknowledging that India is a powerful country, the sermon would cite the example of David and Goliath and conclude that jihad was the only way forward. Indoctrination of women also commenced after 2005 and peaked around 2010. Virulent separatist leaders like Asiya Andrabi – the leader of the Dukhtaran-e-Millat (Daughters of the Nation) – would engage with women telling them that the best form of governance was a caliphate and that 'it is sacrilegious to vote'.[48]

Practitioners Reflect on Conflict Resolution in J&K

After taking over as army chief in 1997, General Malik sought to disengage from active counterterrorism operations after almost seven years of relentless operations. He suggested to Chief Minister Farooq Abdullah that it was time for the army to return to its primary task in a phased manner. This prompted a panic call from Abdullah to then Prime Minister I.K. Gujral. The prime minister tentatively asked Malik to remain engaged. His assessment was that Abdullah was not confident of overseeing the return of normalcy through governance and maintaining of law and order only with the state police and other assigned paramilitary forces.[49]

Nanavatty was relentlessly targeting the jihadi and militant leadership in the Kashmir Valley and adjoining regions of Kishtwar and Doda in the summer of 2001. However, he was also thinking about peace. He drafted a holistic and all-encompassing document entitled 'Jammu and Kashmir (J&K): Strategy for Conflict Resolution (Updated 2003)'. The clarity, constancy, boldness and contemporary relevance of his arguments seem particularly prescient fifteen years later, especially after the abrogation of Articles 370 and 35A of the Constitution by the Modi government.[50] Nanavatty and his team submitted the strategy document to Army HQ and copies were later sent to many senior government officials including Home Minister L.K. Advani, Home Secretary N.N. Vohra and Foreign Minister Jaswant Singh. Jaswant Singh discussed the strategy document with Nanavatty but the others showed little interest in it.

Recalling his interactions with Abdullah, Nanavatty says that he was nothing more than an opportunistic politician who only wore his patriotism on his sleeve without being serious about dealing with core issues. Nanavatty tried to hold discussions with Abdullah on three core issues – dealing with Pakistan, addressing the aspirations of the Kashmiri people and acknowledging the fact that J&K was being held hostage by agitating Kashmiri Muslims. Abdullah's response was to direct Nanavatty to discuss the matter with the chief secretary of the state. Nanavatty says that he was never able to hold Abdullah's attention and that he was never consistent. 'I used to urge him to initiate an intellectual discussion on Kashmir on the lines of the highly popular debates on Palestine that Tim Sebastian of the BBC would host in Doha, but he would not listen', recalls Nanavatty.[51] Nanavatty's assessment was proved correct as in the year ahead Abdullah would urge the government to engage with the pro-Pakistan Hurriyat Conference – particularly when he or his son Omar were out of power.

The opening argument of Nanavatty's document is that the internal conflict in J&K is as much a consequence of the people's alienation, poor governance and lack of development and employment as it is a by-product of Pakistan's covert war and support for terrorism. The strategy aimed at restoring normalcy in the state where democratic institutions, including those responsible for law and order, can function unimpeded. The key points of the strategy were:

1. Persuade, dissuade and if necessary, deter Pakistan from pursuing its strategy of covert war and support for terrorism in J&K.
2. Seek a peaceful resolution of the conflict within the framework of the Constitution of India.
3. Fulfil the legitimate political and economic aspirations of the state.
4. Ensure the sanctity of the LoC, the AGPL and the International Border in J&K.
5. Suppress and neutralize all terrorist groups.
6. Prevent the spread of conflict to the unaffected areas of Ladakh and Jammu.
7. Synergize the functioning of the central and state governments and the various instruments of government within the state.
8. Improve administration and governance within the state.
9. Mould public opinion in support of a peaceful resolution of conflict.

By April 2003, Vajpayee had begun talks on peace and moving forward on J&K with Pakistan and had created a special group for engaging with all stakeholders in J&K. Addressing this group, Nanavatty had said that Pakistan was waging a relentless covert war using a mix of jihadi fighters and subverted indigenous youth. He added, 'They are employing tactics of terror supported

– albeit grudgingly and wearily – by an alienated population. It is a complex situation that demands an all-encompassing strategy.' He ended his briefing by arguing, 'Unfortunately, the questions being asked and the limited interaction we have had suggests an overriding and continuing preoccupation with security-related strategy alone. We are naïve if we believe that the solution lies in mere neutralization of terrorists. Conflict resolution demands simultaneous and vigorous implementation of political, social, economic, administrative, psychological and security strategies.'[52] Voicing the frustration of every corps and army commander who had served in J&K since the early 1990s, Nanavatty urged the special group to reflect on his paper. He admitted that the army was not asked to comment on political, diplomatic, social and economic matters, but that he was 'compelled to do so with the hope of stimulating an informed debate that could lead to a blueprint for a strategy'. 'Any failure to address the issue holistically will condemn security forces to manage the conflict at great cost,' he warned.[53]

A serving lieutenant colonel noted the metamorphosis of the brutal proxy war of yesteryears into the sophisticated hybrid war of today. Reflecting on the challenges he is likely to face during counterterrorism operations in J&K, he says, 'They are blurred and span multiple domains. It is time we countered the hybrid threat with a hybrid response.' About holistic strategies, he says, 'It is time for the armed forces and the government to undertake planned campaigns to target the youth by engaging with them, educating them and empowering them with opportunities.' Comparing the threat to a hydra, he says that if not eliminated, it 'will resurface again'.[54]

18

UNDER THE UN FLAG

'India's commitment to peacekeeping is strong and will grow.'[1]

– Prime Minister Modi at the UN Peacekeeping Summit, 2015

Early Years: Impact in Korea

The UN Charter was signed in San Francisco on 26 June 1945. Two of its initial nineteen chapters – Chapters VI and VII – dealt with maintenance of peace and security.[2] All the Security Council mandates for UN Peacekeeping Operations (UNPKOs) have since largely been defined by these two chapters. The major tasks of these operations have been to stabilize conflict situations and create an environment for belligerents to negotiate lasting peace agreements. India has participated in the entire range of UNPKOs and observer missions since Independence, including operations that have long faded from public consciousness – such as the ones in Korea in the early 1950s and Congo in the 1960s.

The face-off on the Korean peninsula in the early 1950s was the first major war between communist North Korea and a South Korea that was emerging as a key ally of the US. The alliance was critical for the US in its quest to stem the surge of communism in East Asia. An offensive across the 38th Parallel by the North Koreans in June 1950 saw them overrun Seoul. A US-led UN force – backed by Security Council Resolution 83 – came to the assistance of the South Koreans in September. Under General Douglas MacArthur, the UN force first outflanked the North Koreans with an audacious amphibious landing at Incheon on 15 September 1950, and then pushed the North Koreans north of the 38th Parallel. The UN force did not stop there and continued its advance towards the Yalu River, which for the Chinese was a 'red line' that threatened Chinese sovereignty. China entered the Korean War in October 1950 as General MacArthur pressed on with his offensive. He had underestimated the Chinese resolve to follow through on their warning. Mao committed almost three million troops and the PLA pushed the UN force back across the 38th Parallel.[3] After a bitter war of attrition that lasted over two years, the UN-sponsored armistice with active Indian participation[4] was signed in July 1953. This effectively – but not officially – ended the war and created a demilitarized zone.

Not enough credit is given to India for being one of the key drivers of the Korean armistice of 1953. Jairam Ramesh – a minister in Prime Minister Manmohan Singh's cabinet between 2010 and 2014 – set the record straight in an article written in *The Hindu*. He wrote that Nehru and his ambassador in China, K.M. Panikkar, used their good offices with Mao to convince China to come to the negotiating table. This paved the way for a cessation of hostilities. Among other Indian initiatives was the formation of the Neutral Nations Repatriation Commission (NNRC) for monitoring the repatriation of about 1,50,000 PoWs – the bulk of them being Chinese and North Korean – many of whom did not want to return to their countries.[5] The commission comprised five neutral nations; Sweden, Switzerland, Poland, Czechoslovakia and India. Its primary mandate was to take custody of all prisoners and coordinate their repatriation.[6]

Lieutenant General K.S. Thimayya from India was nominated as chairman of the commission. Supporting the NNRC was a brigade-sized Indian force called the Custodian Force India, commanded by Major General S.P.P. Thorat. This was independent India's first foray into the realm of peacekeeping. Despite facing stiff opposition from the South Korean government, the Custodian Force India carried out the process of interviews and repatriation with professionalism.[7] Thimayya's deft handling of the situation was praised by everyone including US President Eisenhower, who lauded the mission as a difficult and delicate job well done. According to Ramesh, Thimayya became a hero at the end of the NNRC's tenure in February 1954. He was feted both at home and abroad for having executed a most thankless task courageously.[8]

The honour of being the first unit to be deployed overseas for UNPKOs rests with 60 Parachute Field Ambulance led by Lieutenant Colonel A.G.

Rangaraj. It was initially attached to the US 8th Army in November 1950 as it retreated from North Korea, and then transferred to the British Commonwealth Brigade as a medical evacuation unit. It comprised 346 men, including four combat surgeons, two anaesthesiologists and a dentist. When the Chinese swarmed through UN lines in November 1950, the unit had to evacuate its position. However, it had no transport and was reluctant to abandon its medical equipment. Stumbling on an ancient steam locomotive, the men filled its boilers with water, loaded the train and chugged across the last bridge south before it was blown. Rangaraj later said that they had first-class equipment and it would have been a great pity to leave it all behind. 'We would have been of little use without it, and could not afford to lose it,' he remarked.[9] The Indian medics stuck with the troops during the horrific rearguard fighting that winter, and refused to abandon the wounded.

On 23 March 1951, a dozen medics of the unit parachuted behind the lines into Munsan-ni along with 4,000 US troops. It was the second biggest airborne operation of the war – Operation Tomahawk. A US commander recalled that he was immediately struck by the efficiency of the Indians. 'That small unit, adapted for an airborne role, carried out 103 operations,' he said, and added that 'probably fifty of those operated on, owed their lives to those men'. He also wrote, 'in freezing conditions, with the wounded lying in the open, the Indian medics dug trenches to shelter them and covered them with parachute silk to keep them warm'.[10]

Their services while fighting alongside Canadian and Australian troops of the British Commonwealth Brigade in April 1951 have been acknowledged by Canadian veterans in their accounts of the Battle of Kapyong.[11] Following more fierce fighting in September 1951, the unit treated 448 casualties over the six days of fighting and a month later evacuated under fire another 150 wounded. 60 Parachute Field Ambulance not only received many decorations from its own country but also from South Korea, the UN, the US and a unit citation from MacArthur. Rangaraj was awarded the Maha Vir Chakra, India's second highest wartime gallantry award, on 10 March 1955.[12] The medics were also given several awards. India issued a postage stamp to honour their heroism. In all, the unit conducted 2,300 field medical operations and trained several Korean doctors and nurses. Without taking away anything from Nehru, Krishna Menon, Thimayya or Thorat, the real heroes of India's contribution to the Korean War belonged to the 60 Parachute Field Ambulance. Rangaraj and his band of paratrooper-medics braved over two years of fierce fighting and the icy winter in Korea to save thousands of lives.

Joint Operations in Congo

Congo gained independence from Belgian colonial rule on 30 June 1960. However, within seven months it plunged into chaos after its first president, Patrice Lumumba, was assassinated by Belgian mercenaries. The assassination had been orchestrated by the US because Congo appeared to be gravitating towards the USSR. It opened multiple fissures in the fabric of the young state.[13] The trouble leading to the assassination of Lumumba began in Katanga in the south-eastern part of Congo bordering the then British colony of Northern Rhodesia (now called Zambia), almost 2,400 km away from the capital Kinshasa. Belgian and South African mercenaries were unwilling to let go of this mineral-rich province. Supported by Northern Rhodesia and led by Michael 'Mad Mike' Hoare, the mercenaries propped up a rebel leader, Moise Tshombe. Tshombe declared himself president of the breakaway state of Katanga on 11 July 1960.[14] The secession set in motion a chain of events that led to the assassination of Lumumba and a civil war that lasted four years.

On 14 July 1960, Organization des Nations Unies au Congo (ONUC) was launched after the Security Council resolution 143 was passed. A UN Peacekeeping Force (UNPKF) under the command of a Swedish general with 4,000 troops from Tunisia and five other African states arrived in August. Despite overseeing the withdrawal of Belgian troops from most of Congo, the UN peacekeepers were shackled by a weak mandate that abjured the use of force. Even while the civil war intensified, it would take almost a year for the UN to authorize the unrestricted use of force against the Katangan rebels. At various stages during this unstable period, the crisis took on the characteristics of an anti-colonial struggle. It became a war of secession between the province of Katanga and the UN force, which eventually managed to disarm the rebels and restore some semblance of normalcy.[15]

India played a pivotal role in this transformation. The fiercest fighting during UNPKO involved an Indian contingent. It suffered heavy casualties during ONUC operations. The mandate of the ONUC was subsequently expanded to include the maintenance of the territorial integrity and political independence of Congo, preventing a civil war and ensuring the removal of all mercenaries and foreign military, paramilitary and advisory personnel not under UN command. With about 20,000 personnel, the ONUC contributed significantly to the eventual reunification of Congo. Reflecting the importance India attached to being a pivotal member of the UNPKO, Major General Rikhye was pulled out of a critical command assignment in Ladakh and posted as the military advisor to Dag Hammarskjöld, the UN

Secretary-General. He would continue in this role till the end of the ONUC operations in 1964.

Hammarskjold was killed in a mysterious air crash not long after Rikhye joined him. Investigations into the crash continue till today. A recent report in the *New York Times* suggests that the plane was possibly brought down by 'colonial-era mining interests, perhaps backed by Western intelligence agencies'[16] and executed by 'South African or Belgian mercenaries.'[17] The Katangan rebels immediately violated a two-month ceasefire and repeated attacks on UN peacekeepers followed. This prompted acting Secretary-General U Thant to direct the peacekeepers to use maximum force against the rebels. The Security Council Resolution 169 of 24 November 1961 ratified this decision. However, Tshombe ordered attacks on UN peacekeepers at the airfield to prevent them from advancing on Elizabethville (renamed Lubumbashi in 1966) – which was the largest city and capital of Katanga province.

In November 1960, the IAF had sent C-119 Packet transport aircraft from 12 Squadron in support of these UNPKOs. The aircraft were to assist with logistics operations between Leopoldville, the capital, and the ONUC HQ at Elizabethville. The Indian brigade group was under the command of Brigadier K.A.S. Raja and based in Katanga. Supporting this ground force initially were fighter, bomber and transport aircraft from the Canadian Air Force based at the Kamina airfield. In early October 1961, six IAF Canberra aircraft from 5 Squadron commanded by Wing Commander A.I.K. Suares arrived at Kamina. Fighting by then had intensified and the Katanga rebels had inflicted some casualties on UN peacekeepers.

During a hostage rescue mission in late November 1961, Major Ajit Singh of the 3rd Battalion of the First Gorkha Rifles (3/1 GORKHA RIFLES) was the first Indian officer to be killed. On 5 December 1961, the same Gorkha Rifles battalion attacked a Katangese roadblock between the rebel HQ in Elizabethville and the ONUC HQ at the Elizabethville airfield. A platoon from the same battalion attempted to reinforce the attack but ran into rebel opposition.[18] The rebel position was manned by about ninety men, whereas the Indian peacekeepers led by Captain Gurbachan Singh Salaria comprised only sixteen soldiers. Despite being outnumbered, the Gorkhas overwhelmed the enemy. They fled, leaving behind over forty casualties. Captain Salaria was shot in the neck, but continued to fight until he succumbed to his injuries. The ONUC HQ, however, was saved from encirclement.

Salaria became India's fifth awardee of the Param Vir Chakra, the highest military award for courage in war. He remains the most decorated Indian to have served in a UNPKO. Fighting was intense the next day too. Lance Naik

Ram Bahadur single-handedly charged a rebel machine-gun post, killing nine rebels before succumbing to his injuries. Ram Bahadur was posthumously awarded the Maha Vir Chakra. From July 1960 to June 1964, the Indians suffered a total of 147 casualties, including thirty-nine peacekeepers killed in action. This was the most number of casualties any Indian peacekeeping contingent has suffered in almost six decades of UNPKOs.

Authorized only to use their 20mm cannons – despite their capacity to carry over 2,000 kg of bombs – the Canberra bombers began strafing missions against rebel troop positions around the town of Kolwezi and the airbase there.[19] Sensing that Indian troops were within closing distance of capturing Elizabethville, the air effort shifted to supporting the ground battle.[20] On 9 December, Suares was briefed by Raja on the various targets in and around Elizabethville which had to be engaged from the air by Canberras of the IAF.[21] Later that day, Flight Lieutenant Dushyant Singh and Squadron Leader Charanjit Singh attacked a post office in the heart of Elizabethville that was serving as the rebel HQ. Charanjit's aircraft was hit by ground fire and he nursed the damaged bomber back to Kamina. The ground crew discovered five bullet holes – including one that had passed perilously close to the pilot and shattered the windscreen – and one on the left engine.[22] Dushyant's aircraft took four hits, including one in the nose that passed inches away from where the navigator lay. In their prone position in the nose, Canberra navigators had no ejection seat and only a narrow hatch to wriggle through in an emergency. This gave them little chance of escape if the aircraft had to be abandoned.[23]

The Canberra squadron, which played a critical role in the Indian brigade's battle for Elizabethville, continued limited offensive and recce operations for the next few months. By 18 December, the city was under UN control. In mid-1962, Raja handed over command of the Indian brigade to Brigadier Noronha and Major General Diwan Prem Chand came in from Gaza to take over command of the UNPKF in Katanga. 5 Squadron too saw a concurrent change in command and crew as it shifted base to Leopoldville. A detachment operated out of Kamina whenever an operational need for photo and visual reconnaissance came up.[24] There was some action involving the Indian brigade and Ethiopian troops in late 1962, and the last vestiges of rebel resistance crumbled by mid-1963. The ONUC finally wound up six months later in 1964. Nearly four decades later, Indian peacekeepers returned to what was then known as the Democratic Republic of the Congo (DRC) as part of the United Nations Organization Mission in the Democratic Republic of the Congo (MONUC).

After the Cold War

The UNPKOs underwent significant changes in the years after the collapse of the Soviet Union as new security challenges emerged across the world. Nationalism, anti-colonialism and ideological moorings were the principal drivers of most of the conflicts that necessitated UN intervention during the Cold War. This changed in the 1990s and beyond as conflict now was mostly ethno-religious laced with regional power struggles and stray expressions of angst against economic exploitation. The primary objectives of the UNPKOs during the Cold War era were restoration of political stability and reconciliation between the warring parties. However, the current UN mandate assumes more of a concept called Responsibility to Protect or R2P, i.e., preventing genocide and mass killings in fractured and weak countries. This shift was spurred by the Rwandan genocide and the ethno-religious strife in the Balkans in the 1990s.

The outcomes of the peacekeeping initiatives in these emerging hotspots were suboptimal, and India continued to contribute significantly to these missions. Lieutenant General Satish Nambiar was appointed as the commander of the United Nations Protection Force for Yugoslavia (UNPROFOR) in 1992 as part of the increased Indian contribution to UNPKOs. This was part of a larger strategy by India to expand its influence and achieve its medium-term objective of securing a permanent seat on an expanded Security Council. However, the mission struggled to achieve its anticipated operational outcomes of healing the deep fractures in the Balkans. Bringing the Serbs and the Croats – the two largest ethnic communities in the region – to the negotiating table proved to be a bridge too far. Among the several reasons for this, according to Nambiar, were a weak mandate, inadequate manpower and half-hearted support for the mission from the various European and Western stakeholders in the region including the US and the UK.[25]

Muscular Peacekeeping in Sierra Leone

India deployed peacekeeping forces in Sierra Leone (1999) and Somalia (2003) that included sizeable army and air force contingents. It was in Sierra Leone that the Indians engaged in serious combat with rebel forces. Prior to the large deployment in Sierra Leone, India had participated in UNPKOs in Rwanda where UN deployment had been delayed and ineffective in preventing mass killings or separating warring factions. The rising presence of warlords, mercenaries and mineral bounty hunters in African countries had changed the rules of engagement, and the UN was not prepared to take on this new dynamic. The changing character of war and conflict demanded adjustments in the existing mandates for peacekeeping and peace enforcement. Not learning quickly enough from the suboptimal experience in the Balkans, the intervention in Sierra Leone quickly exposed the irrelevance of existing peacekeeping procedures and mandates.

The United Nations Mission in Sierra Leone (UNAMSIL) was authorized in October 1999 as per Security Council Resolution 1270 with a mandate to implement the Lome Agreement. The agreement had brought the legitimately elected government of President Ahmad Tejan Kabbah and two rebel groups to the negotiating table after two years of fierce civil war. However, militia from the main rebel force, the Revolutionary United Front (RUF), made a run for Freetown, the capital. Sensing that the country was heading for a bloodbath, the UN had no other option but to intervene. Major General Vijay Jetley from India was appointed the first commander of UNAMSIL, with a Nigerian officer as his deputy. The force initially had 6,000 troops from Nigeria, India, Kenya and Ghana and was later complemented by British troops. This was woefully inadequate for undertaking any kind of robust peacekeeping. By May 2000, the rebel forces had begun testing the resolve of UNAMSIL in Makeni and Magburarka, which was rebel territory. The RUF began disrupting UN camps and escalated the confrontation by taking its peacekeepers hostage at Kailahun and Makeni. The hostages included a large complement of Indian and Zambian soldiers and UN military observers.

Bolstered by the presence of British troops in Freetown and aided by their Chinook helicopters, which complemented the Indian Mi-8s and Mi-35s, Jetley launched Operation Khukri in July to rescue the hostages. The 3,000 Indian troops in Sierra Leone were from the Gorkha Rifles, the Mechanized Infantry Regiment and the Special Forces. They had adequate logistics and engineering groups. There was also an IAF unit with eight Mi-8 and three Mi-35 helicopters. The Indian headquarters was at Daru and main deployment was at Kailahun. The IAF contingent was commanded by Group Captain B.S. Siwach and operated out of Hastings near the capital city of Freetown. The Indian battalion group was assisted by troops from Ghana and Kenya and caused much attrition to the RUF. The soldiers held hostage in Kailahun staged a fighting breakout from their besieged positions and linked up with the other forces that advanced on Kailahun from Daru. On 7 May 2000, there was a daring rescue operation by two IAF Mi-8s of Kenyan troops and UN observers from Makeni under heavy firing from RUF rebels.[26]

While Operation Khukri was successful at the tactical level, a hard look reveals that it was a reactive operation that failed to retain ground. UNAMSIL did not have enough troops nor the necessary will to seize the initiative and dominate the RUF. In May 2000, the Indian battalion group was split into two locations in eastern Sierra Leone. The Kenyan battalion in the north had been attacked and overrun by the RUF, while the Nigerian forces were not yet fully deployed. The local population had lost trust in UNAMSIL. Since the UNAMSIL contingents were not initially mandated to fight, there was very little that Jetley could do. Soon, the weaknesses of the UN military system in terms of force, training, capabilities, intelligence and surveillance mechanisms all became very apparent. The hostage crisis dealt a severe blow to the UN's reputation and confused the transition between peacekeeping and peace enforcement.

Adding to the confusion were the British troops under the command of Major General David Richards,[27] who was appalled at the brutality of the RUF and perplexed by the inaction of UNAMSIL. Richards recalls arguing with Jetley over his reluctance to respond strongly to the brutality of the RUF and his decision not to expand the mandate of the force from peacekeeping to enforcement. Richards is also quite scathing about the unwillingness of the UN force to fight despite being attacked and challenged.[28] Jetley questioned Richards's moralistic approach considering that British troops had generally not been part of UNPKOs in Africa, unlike the Indians, who better understand the concept of undertaking operations with restraint.

However, the British force did play a role in defending Freetown and Lungi airport against the RUF. They also made substantial contributions to the stabilization of Sierra Leone even after the disbanding of UNAMSIL in 2005. This was among the few successful long-term intervention stories of recent times.[29] Not enough credit has been given to Jetley for initiating the turnaround in July 2000 and freeing the hostages in eastern Sierra Leone. Instead, his differences with his Nigerian deputy and his accusing Nigeria of attempting to undermine the success of UNAMSIL have been highlighted in most Western narratives on UNAMSIL. In the *Journal of Strategic Studies*, American academic David Ucko writes that 'even the successful Operation Khukri envisaged UN forces falling back to secure positions rather than seize RUF territory around Kailahun'.[30]Among the few positives was that, for the first time in nearly four decades, the Indian Army and the IAF operated jointly under the UN flag in a sustained operation involving large forces. From May to September 2000, IAF helicopters flew about 100 sorties including offensive missions, armed reconnaissance, insertion and extrication of troops, casualty evacuation and logistics support. Troops of the Gorkha Rifles made considerable headway in limiting the recruitment of child soldiers by the RUF in the areas under their jurisdiction.

Two months after Operation Khukri, Jetley was recalled to New Delhi. It is likely that the move was initiated by New Delhi to register an Indian protest against regional bullying, and the undermining of its leadership. Matters were complicated by the fact that UN Secretary-General Kofi Annan was a West African. He tended to side with the Nigerians when Jetley accused them and proxies from neighbouring Liberia of colluding with the RUF and indulging in illegal diamond mining. Soon after, much to the surprise of the UN, India gradually pulled out its entire force from Sierra Leone.[31] India was just recovering from the Kargil conflict and the Vajpayee government was in no mood to suffer needless casualties in a foreign land. The decision was also influenced by the security crisis that followed the attack by LeT terrorists on the Indian Parliament in December 2000. The Indian experience in Sierra Leone led to a heated debate in Parliament over committing Indian troops to UNPKOs in distant lands where India had little to no strategic interest. Responding to British criticism of Jetley's leadership, Brigadier Anil Raman – who was posted with the Indian contingent in Sierra Leone as a captain and involved with planning operations during the siege of Kailahun – dismissed the British accounts of UNAMSIL as inaccurate. 'The British general was speaking rather expansively,' Raman said, 'without a realistic appreciation of the situation on ground.'[32]

Continued Presence in Congo

After the departure of UN peacekeepers in 1965, Congo endured three decades of misery under dictator Mobutu Sese Seko. Seko first changed the country's name to Zaire and then to the DRC in 1971. The second largest African nation was ruled by Seko till a coalition of neighbouring countries led by Rwanda and Uganda overthrew him in May 1997. The fragile nation continued in chaos as ethnic conflict and greedy neighbouring countries undermined the authority of President Laurent Kabila's newly formed government in Kinshasa, which had remained the capital. The epicentre of the conflict remained in eastern Congo with its several ethnic divides and huge deposits of mineral wealth. Though the intervention succeeded in ousting Seko, Kabila remained a puppet of the foreign regimes that put him in power.

To increase his own domestic support, Kabila began to turn against his foreign allies and expelled all foreign forces from the DRC on 26 July 1998. The Second Congo War[33] began almost immediately in the form of a Hutu insurgency in Rwanda's western provinces that was supported by extremist

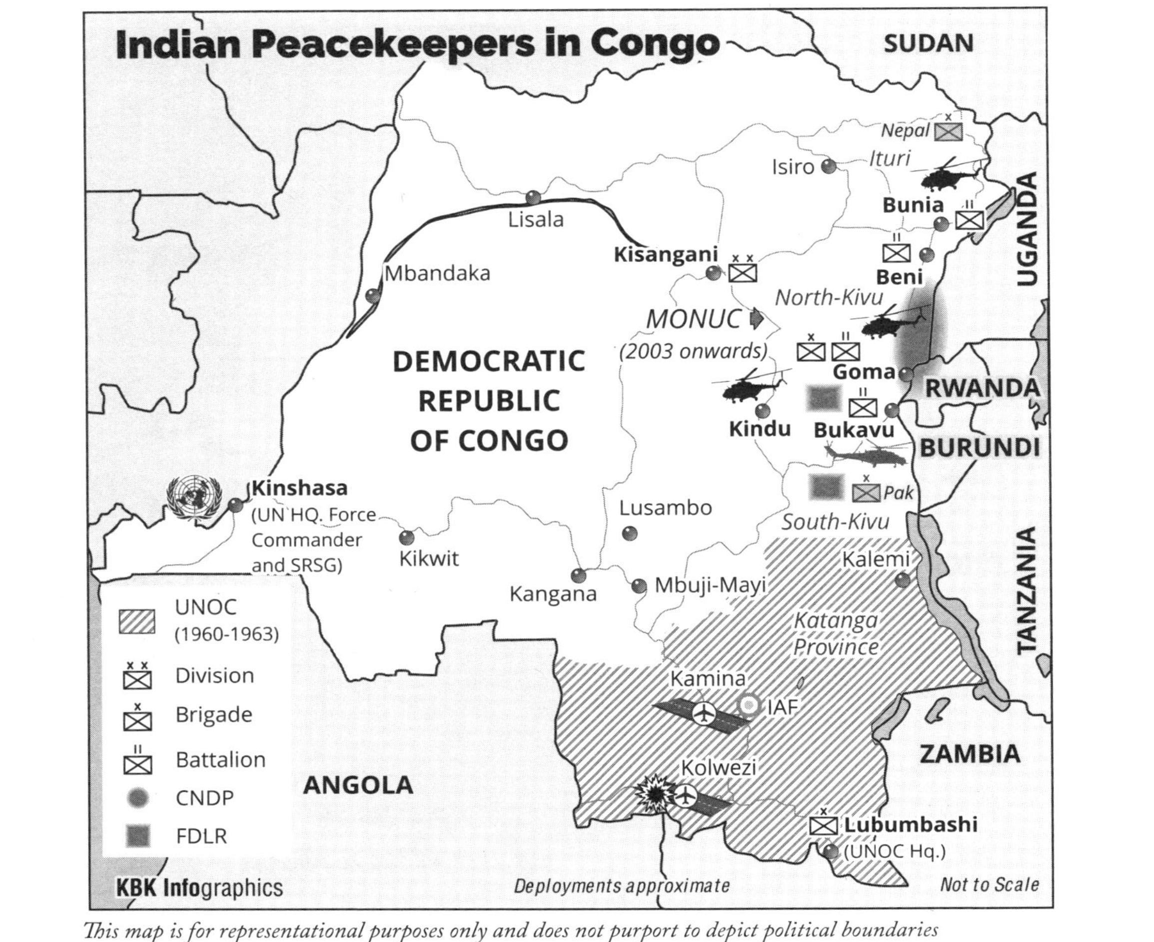

This map is for representational purposes only and does not purport to depict political boundaries

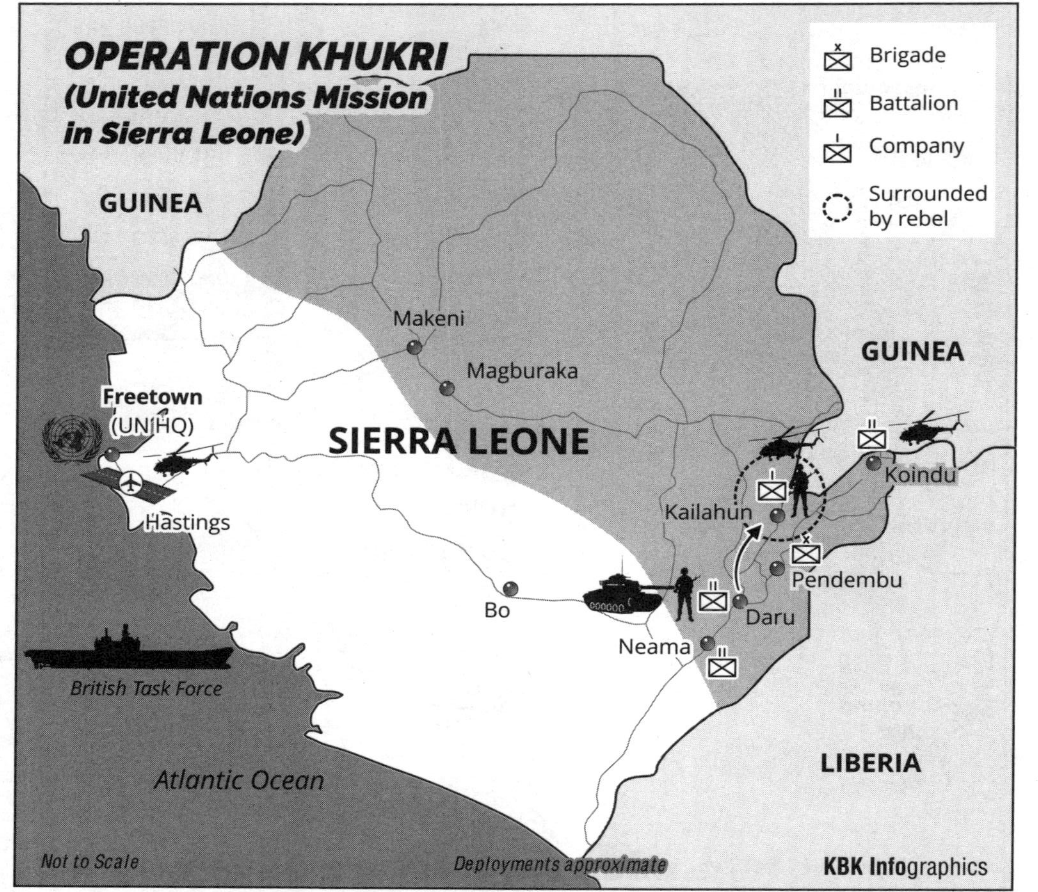

This map is for representational purposes only and does not purport to depict political boundaries

Hutu elements in eastern DRC. Unable to effectively fight the insurgents, the government sought a coalition with Uganda and Burundi to quell the rebellion. In August 1998, two brigades of the DRC army rebelled against the government and formed groups that worked closely with the neighbouring countries. The Second Congo War has since directly involved nine African countries, as well as approximately twenty separate armed groups.

The UN had a series of unsuccessful peacekeeping initiatives in the Balkans, Rwanda and Somalia in the 1990s. However, its first African Secretary-General, Kofi Annan, redefined its role as the world's conscience keeper.[34] The peacekeeping norms were amended and the concepts of protection of civilians and R2P were introduced. The UN intervened to ensure that the Second Congo War did not escalate to levels that could lead to a genocide of the kind that rocked Rwanda in 1994. Mandated by Security Council Resolution 1279, the MONUC was set up to oversee the Lusaka ceasefire of July 1999 between the DRC and five neighbouring countries – Angola, Namibia, Rwanda, Uganda and Zimbabwe. Despite these initiatives, the war and its aftermath have caused millions of deaths, principally because of disease and starvation. It has become the deadliest conflict in the post-WWII era.[35]

In 2003, after four years of negotiations, the Vajpayee government decided to send a large Indian brigade group with a strong IAF contingent to support MONUC operations. Air Vice Marshal Rajesh Isser wrote about his experiences of commanding the Mi-17 Squadron during this operation in his book *Peacekeeping and Protection of Civilians: The Indian Air Force in Congo.*[36] He recollects that IAF chief Krishnaswamy told them that the contingent would get all it needed from the IAF, but 'heads would roll' if the mission did not fare well.[37] The Indian brigade group set up its headquarters in the town of Goma. The battalions were deployed at Goma, Beni, Ituri and Bukavu. Five Mi-17 helicopters were based at Goma and four Mi-25 attack helicopters were positioned at Bunia in North Kivu, with an additional support unit at Kindu. The aviation contingent was further expanded in 2005 with the induction of upgraded Mi-17s and Mi-35 attack helicopters at Bukavu in South Kivu.[38] A divisional headquarters was set up at Kisangani to ensure close control of operational forces.

In June 2005, reports of a massacre in Ituri province, which was about 100 km north of Bunia, led to the launch of a special operation. IAF Mi-17s and Mi-35s executed a risky mission to land Pakistani troops in the area. This required a high-speed approach, a low hover, and a quick exit. The mission was successful and the MONUC sent a strong message that it would not hesitate to take military action. Isser recalled that he only later realized that the Pakistani troops belonged to none other than the NLI. They had been the enemy the Indians fought at Kargil, and were now comrades. UN peacekeeping made for strange bedfellows.[39]

Brigadier (now General) Rawat was the most senior Indian Army officer in eastern Congo between August 2008 and August 2009, and led the military action by the Indian contingent which was largely responsible for the ceasefire of March 2009.[40] He explained the complicated relationship between the peacekeepers, the Rwanda-supported and Tutsi-dominated rebel group CNDP (the National Congress for the Defence of the People), the pro-government and Hutu-dominated rebel group FDLR (the Democratic Forces for the Liberation of Rwanda), and government forces known as the FARDC (the Armed Forces of the Democratic Republic of the Congo). There were several occasions when firepower in the form of mortars, rocket launchers and attack helicopters had to be used to protect civilians from a rebel attack. Rawat argued that these were essential to coerce rival factions towards a ceasefire. In 2008, the Indian brigade group and its aviation contingent were largely deployed in the North Kivu province of the DRC along the border with Rwanda and Uganda, where most of the action was taking place. The Indian brigade group was part of a division that also comprised a Nepali brigade in Ituri, a Pakistani brigade in South Kivu and a brigade from Ghana.

Soon after Rawat took command, he sensed that a major operation was around the corner as his forward locations reported that the CNDP was massing forces barely 2 km from the border. The FARDC was flying in large stocks of ammunition into the Goma airfield, which was a few kilometres from the Indian HQ. Rawat ordered the Indian battalions to start digging trenches and preparing defences for what he envisaged were serious operations. Another issue was that while the CNDP managed to communicate with the Indian troops in English, the FARDC and FDLR spoke only French and had to rely on an interpreter at the Indian brigade HQ. There was a feeling within the FARDC and FDLR that the Indians were partial towards the CNDP and that it was time to take matters into their own hands.

As fighting intensified between the two sides, Rawat had to deploy Mi-35 attack helicopters to destroy the advancing tanks of the CNDP. It was quite clear to Rawat and the Senegalese UN force commander, Lieutenant General Babacar Gaye, that the CNDP needed to be cut down if there was to be a ceasefire. Serious differences surfaced when they sought formal clearance from the Senior Representative of the Security General (SRSG), the de facto head of the MONUC, to increase military action against the CNDP. Gaye resigned in September 2008 after the SRSG refused to authorize attacks against the CNDP. His departure meant that Rawat had to officiate as force commander, a proposition that was unacceptable to the Pakistani-led brigade in South Kivu despite the other brigade commanders from Nepal and Ghana having no problems.

Eight UN battalions created a buffer zone of 10 km between the warring forces. There were no roads to support the thin deployment and the forces had to be supported by air. Mi-17 helicopters of the IAF and Bangladesh Air Force sustained the battalions. In late October 2008, a Spanish general was appointed the force commander. He too insisted on extensive use of firepower and air power from the SRSG. By December, the Spanish general too had resigned because of differences with the SRSG. The UN found it difficult to find a replacement and asked Babacar Gaye to reassume command on 15 December. The border town of Goma became the focus of attention around Christmas because it was understood that CNDP forces would attempt to take over the town to engage in looting to pay its cadres. They planned to then retreat into Rwanda. However, this time around Gaye authorized the unrestricted use of firepower against the CNDP.

Prior to embarking on offensive operations, Rawat decided to study the situation. He sought an audience with the CNDP commander, who called himself General Bosco Ntganda. Describing the meeting as 'quite an experience,' he recollects that Ntganda was of short stature and was wearing a hat with stars and 'Bosco' embossed on it. Rawat offered Ntganda 10,000 US dollars to distribute among his men in return for calling off his Goma assault. 'As we speak, my men have gone around your area,' Rawat threatened, 'and if you advance further, we will have no option but to bring down fire on you.'[41] Ntganda did not comply. By 16 December, over 2,000 CNDP troops had lined up across Goma for an advance. Rawat ordered his battalions to fire warning and illumination rounds the moment the CNDP force started advancing. When the CNDP force came within 500 metres of the Indian line, they started to suffer casualties. Soon they broke ranks and all of them, including Ntganda, turned around and fled. This incident was followed by the arrest of CNDP commander Laurent Nkunda and the peace process gained momentum.

The IAF operating in the DRC from 2003 to 2011 became the longest-serving air contingent in any UNPKO worldwide. It has won many accolades for its ability to easily switch between peacekeeping and enforcement operations.[42] The IAF's impact inspired Isser to write that the DRC rebels were 'afraid of only two things in the world – God and the IAF attack helicopter'.[43] Group Captain Navkaranjit Singh Dhillon was the IAF contingent commander at Goma from 2007 to 2008 and worked alongside Rawat for three months. He recollects that Mi-35 helicopters destroyed CNDP tanks and several armoured vehicles during some of the critical joint operations. The Indian aviation contingent was organized quite loosely with assets being regularly swapped between the three locations at Goma, Bukavu and Bunia, to ensure that the Indian battalions had aviation support across the extended front that the Indian brigade group defended.

The UN mission name was changed from MONUC to MONUSCO in 2010 to reflect the stabilization phase, in the hope that peace would follow. In July 2010, Lieutenant General Chander Prakash was appointed force commander of the MONUSCO to take the peace process forward. A fragile peace prevailed with ex-rebels from the CNDP and FDLR continuing their activities in their areas of domination with minimal interference from either the MONUSCO or the Congolese government. With Nkunda in UN custody, the CNDP had been amalgamated into the FARDC under the ceasefire guidelines. Under threat of imminent capture in early 2012, Bosco Ntganda broke away from the CNDP with Rwandan assistance and formed the violent M23 group.

In November 2012, the M23 captured Goma with assistance from Rwandan forces. They faced only a token resistance from UN forces, who withdrew from the city after having failed to stall the advance despite the IAF Mi-35 helicopters being pressed into action. The UN forces could have stopped the raiders only before they mingled with the local population, and their failure to do so was widely criticized. Chander Prakash received most of the flak. However, the M23 withdrew eleven days later after hectic diplomatic parleys. There has been much debate on UNPKOs in the DRC since. The recent formation of an intervention brigade is believed to be the result of the 2012 experience.

Anti-piracy Operations

In 2008, the Security Council authorized the use of force against piracy off the coast of Somalia when a Saudi supertanker ship was hijacked in November. The previous month, a Hong Kong-based tanker with a large Indian crew was hijacked in the same area, creating immense pressure on the Indian government to deploy the Indian Navy on anti-piracy duties in the area. The INS *Tabar,* a Russian-built frigate, became the first Indian Navy warship to be deployed in the Gulf of Aden that month. Commanded by Captain P.K. Banerjee, the *Tabar* struck fear into the hearts of pirates with its immediate offensive action in early November. Banerjee recalls that the *Tabar* had just returned to Mumbai from the Persian Gulf on the eve of Diwali, in late October 2008. It was soon ordered to deploy in the Gulf of Aden on the morning of 29 October with only a day to prepare for the move. The operation was not under the UN umbrella and was a new experience for India's armed forces. 'We deployed independently,' Banerjee says, 'but in close cooperation with the US and other European navies in a common cause to ensure safety of seafarers transiting the piracy-infested waters.'[44]

On 11 November, there was a distress call from a merchant ship called the MV *Jag Arnav.* It was operating under an Indian flag and was manned by an all-Indian crew. The *Tabar*'s helicopter chased[45] the pirate skiffs away and escorted the *Jag Arnav* out of troubled waters. On November 18, the *Tabar* detected a suspicious vessel that matched the description of a known pirate mothership. When threatened by the pirate vessel, the *Tabar* engaged it with firepower and set it ablaze. This was a stern warning to the pirates that set the template for future operations. The *Tabar* was replaced on anti-piracy duties by INS *Mysore,* a new destroyer. The latter recovered a huge cache of arms and ammunition and took twenty-four Somali and Yemeni pirates into custody. This action had legal implications, because no government was willing to take the pirates into custody in the region. It was only after intense negotiations between the Indian and Yemeni governments that the latter accepted custody of the pirates.[46]

Reacting to the Indian initiative, the Kenyan newspaper *Daily Nation* wrote: 'This incident is one of the many decisive actions that the Indian Navy has come to be reputed for in the fight against piracy in the lawless Somalia waters. Most foreign navies patrolling that coast have been reluctant to detain suspected pirates because of uncertainties over where they would face trial, since Somalia has no effective central government or legal system. However, the Indian Navy – the fifth largest in the world – has shown that it is cut from different cloth and its entry may soon deal a permanent blow to Somali piracy in the Gulf of Aden. The navy's recent achievements attest to its transformation from a "brown-water coastal defence force to a formidable blue-water fleet",' wrote David Scott in the *Journal of Military and Strategic Studies.*'[47]

Recognizing the threat to world shipping around the Horn of Africa, several global navies – including those from the US, European Union and NATO – joined the Indian Navy's initiative in deploying task forces. An international transit corridor 500 nautical miles in length and 20 nautical miles in width was established in the Gulf of Aden. Merchant vessels were advised to transit along this corridor under escort. Secure communications protocols

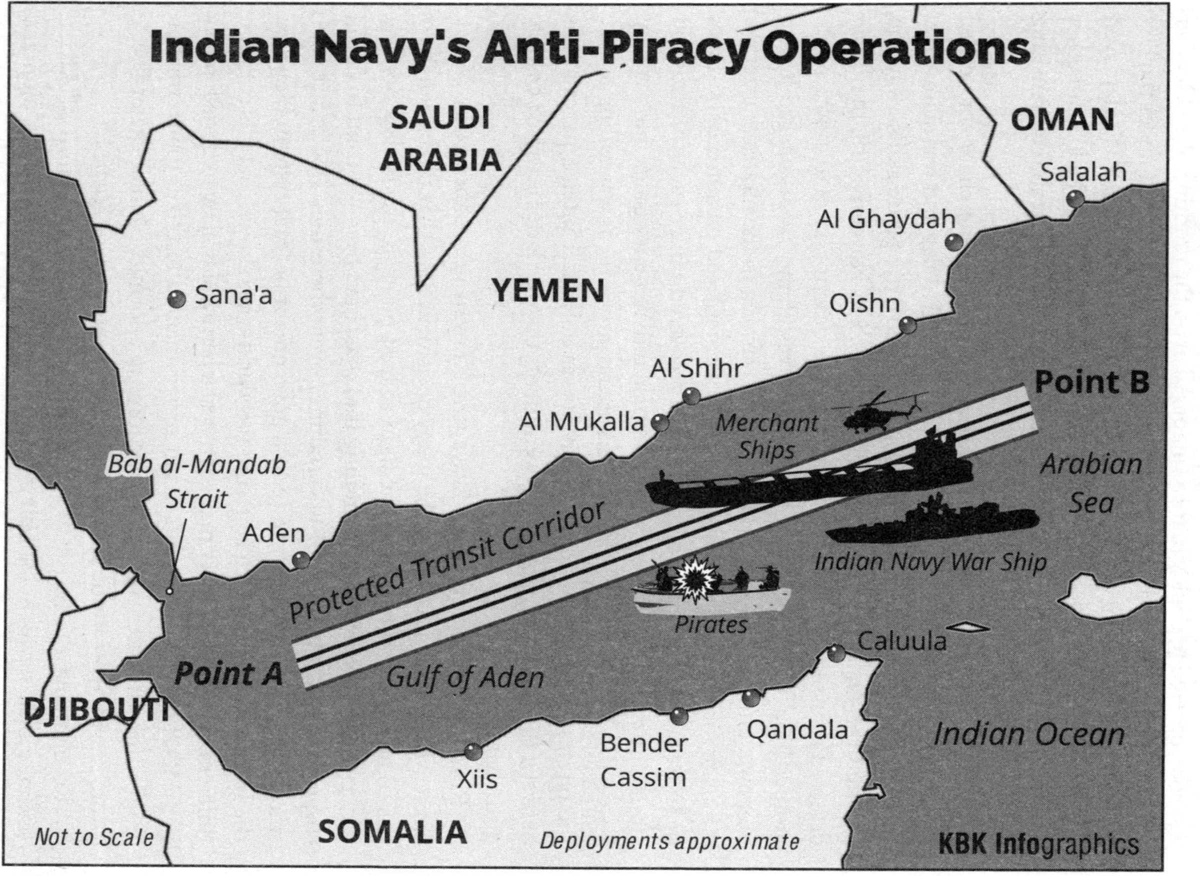

This map is for representational purposes only and does not purport to depict political boundaries

allowed patrolling navies to establish a safe way for conducting patrols. The Indian Navy established a deployment pattern after a few patrol cycles and with critical inputs from Banerjee and the other captains. After initially using the port of Djibouti, the navy then switched to Salalah in Oman. To counter intense international patrolling in the Gulf of Aden, pirate groups ventured into the high seas of the Indian Ocean with larger motherships that allowed them to extend their operational radius to shipping lanes around Seychelles, Maldives and even the Indian island chain of Lakshadweep.

Responding to these threats, the Indian Navy launched Operation Island Watch. The operation saw the sinking of a couple of Thai trawlers in the seas to the west of Lakshadweep. The navy captured several pirates and seized huge caches of arms. These trawlers had been hijacked by pirates off the Somali coast, equipped with motorized skiffs and converted to motherships. They were then used to attack unsuspecting merchant vessels in the Indian Ocean. The anti-piracy operation closest to the west coast of India was conducted about 700 km from Kochi on 11 March 2011. A pirate mothership called *Vega* was sunk by Indian naval ships and over sixty pirates were arrested and put in the custody of the Mumbai Police.[48] This resulted in an anti-piracy bill being tabled in Parliament.

As the world rallied against piracy, the number of attacks fell from 237 in 2011 to 75 in 2012.[49] It had dropped to less than ten in 2015 and the global naval presence was wound down in the wake of the diminished pirate threat. However, an uptrend has been detected since 2017.[50] In March 2017, Somali pirates hijacked a Comoros-flagged oil tanker, marking the first seizure of a large commercial vessel since 2012. They later unconditionally released the vessel when it emerged that it was a Somali charter. On 1 April 2017, the Indian dhow *Al Kausar* with eleven crew members was hijacked off the island of Socotra and taken to the port of Hobyo. An Indian naval ship on deployment in the area at the time was diverted to the east coast of Somalia to monitor the situation. Negotiations between the owner and the hijackers resulted in the dhow being released eleven days later.

Since 2017, the Indian Navy has transitioned to a new philosophy of mission-based deployments across the Indian Ocean. Drawing on the lessons learnt from anti-piracy operations, it has chosen to maintain a near-permanent presence in certain geographical areas and chokepoints. The warships deployed in these areas are fully prepared and poised to respond to all contingencies whilst being perfectly placed to monitor all other forces operating in the region. These mission-based deployments have paid rich dividends.

The Indian Navy had been operating with foreign navies for several decades before the commencement of the anti-piracy operations. However, this was the first prolonged operational exposure for Indian naval ships in a defused multilateral environment. The exposure significantly enhanced standard operating procedures in actual operational scenarios. The Indian Navy is the only one that maintains a continuous escort cycle in the international transit corridor during the monsoon season. Regular deployments in the Gulf of Aden have enhanced its situational awareness in the western Arabian Sea and allowed it to gain substantial operational information and intelligence. There is also a deeper understanding of the PLA Navy after these deployments. There is little doubt that the Indian Navy has emerged as a navy of significant capability that has made it a much-coveted maritime partner in the Indian Ocean and Indo-Pacific regions. The unbroken patrol by seventy Indian Navy ships in the Gulf of Aden over the last ten years has ensured that no merchant ship under its escort has ever been captured by pirates.

Indian Legacy

India has a legacy of being a willing participant in UNPKOs and peace enforcement operations since its inception. It has participated in forty-nine UNPKOs and has been the largest troops contributor with over 2,40,000 personnel deployed so far. There have been fifteen Indians appointed as force commander and two as military advisors.[51] India has also suffered the largest number of battle casualties till date with 168 killed in action. Its contingents have been fair, restrained and responsible while conducting operations in diverse lands and in strife-torn communities. There will be questions about whether India has been able to strategically leverage its contribution in its quest to become a permanent member of the Security Council. However, despite diverse internal and external security challenges, India is unlikely to dilute its commitment to UNPKOs.

19

OPERATIONS OTHER THAN WAR ALONG THE WESTERN FRONT

'He (Sundarji) brought a new line of thinking to the Indian military establishment with his systems-management-scenario approach...'[1]

– Chidanand Rajghatta

Doctrinal Evaluation or Muscle Flexing?

The IAF's only electronic warfare (EW) squadron in 1986 was 35 Squadron. It was equipped with the Canberra bomber-cum-recce aircraft and MiG-21 aircraft that had been innovatively modified to carry Swedish EW pods. In the winter of 1986, the entire squadron was moved to two forward airbases – Ambala in the Haryana and Punjab Sector and Nal near the town of Bikaner in Rajasthan – and spent over two months escorting Jaguars and MiG-27 aircraft on simulated strikes as part of Exercise Brasstacks. These exercises were part of an operational plan orchestrated by General Sundarji, India's army chief. On occasions, they even crossed a few kilometres over the border to check the alertness of the PAF's air defence network. The moment the radar warning receivers beeped or if a warning was received over the radio, the entire formation would turn back. The game of cat and mouse continued for two months before all forces de-inducted.

Several of those Jaguar missions were led by Flight Lieutenant Bhadauria (now Air Chief Marshal) from 14 Squadron. 'Chotu' as he is still known, was probably the youngest large-mission leader during that period and was someone to look up to. He was crisp in his briefings, cool in the air and struck targets all the time. Several new mission profiles emerged during these exercises as the IAF grappled with the danger posed by the PAF's Crotale SAM system. Among them was a Toss Bombing profile by Jaguars and MiG-23s/27s that involved a steep climb to 15,000 feet with a weapon release during the climb and a sharp break downwards to stay outside the Crotale envelope. Unable to keep up with the Jaguars and the MiG-27s because of their heavy configuration with pods, the MiG-21s from 35 Squadron would stay low and skirt the target and rendezvous with the formation at a pre-planned point, gazing skywards to pick up their buddies and head back to base. For the pilots and navigators of 35 Squadron, it was just another instance of intensive training in near-warlike conditions. The absence of any detailed briefings on what was going on gave rise to much speculation and discussion in the crew room on whether war was indeed around the corner.[2]

When Sundarji took over as army chief in 1986, he had several ideas for strengthening deterrence in the subcontinent. He was also convinced that a strong, modern and well-trained military was essential if India was to emerge as a leading power. However, barring a brief face-off in the Rann of Kutch during the prelude to the 1965 war, Sundarji did not have much combat experience. He made up for that with his varied operational assignments and powerful intellect. With his ideas about manoeuvre warfare and nuclear warfighting, Sundarji felt he was well prepared to spearhead the transition of the Indian Army into a potent fighting force. Lieutenant General Pattabhiraman served in the military operations directorate as a major during the tumultuous period when Sundarji was chief. He describes Exercise Brasstacks as an exercise with troops that was undertaken when mistrust between India and Pakistan was at its peak. Pattabhiraman says that Sundarji was close to the defence minister, Arun Singh, who was a keen student of contemporary military affairs. The two of them advised Rajiv Gandhi on all matters related to national security – the nuclear dimension, manoeuvre warfare and expanding India's influence in its strategic neighbourhood.[3]

Brasstacks, Trident and Hammerhead

Lieutenant General Shamsher (Shammi) Mehta, who headed the Western Command during the second half of Operation Parakram, was Sundarji's military advisor for much of the latter's tenure as chief. He said that Sundarji looked at developing capability with an eye on the future. 'Training this capability and exercising it was a logical progression in Sundarji's mind, and if it did send a signal to an adversary, did it not meet the demands of deterrence?' asked Mehta. He adds, 'Incorporating all three dimensions of conflict (land, air and maritime) was also merely putting doctrine into practice and taking forward what he had initiated in Exercise Digvijay when he was the Western Army Commander. Analysts and so-called experts have read too much into the whole thing. Exercise Brasstacks and Exercise Trident were not any brazen muscle-flexing or expression of intent to go to war.'[4]

An ardent proponent of manoeuvre and mechanized warfare as the sword-arm of conventional warfare in the plains, Sundarji was influenced by the US Army's FM-100-5 (Air-Land Battle concept) and the Russian operational manoeuvre groups. He created the Mechanized Infantry Regiment[5] by mechanizing some of the most accomplished battalions of acclaimed infantry regiments. Using these, he converted some standard infantry divisions into the Reorganized Army Plains Infantry Division (RAPID). When the RAPIDs were grouped with armoured divisions that were equipped with the recently inducted T-72 tank, the Indian Army had a mobile offensive element with the potential of making deep inroads into the desert-dominated terrain of Pakistan's Punjab and Sindh provinces opposite the Indian states of Rajasthan and Gujarat. Sundarji strengthened the RAPID formations further by embedding an armoured brigade, and was impatient to test out the capability of the RAPIDS despite the prevailing volatile security situation in the subcontinent. This led to Exercise Brasstacks being undertaken to translate this reorganization into actual capability.

Sundarji planned Exercise Brasstacks as a massive air-land exercise that was conducted in three phases spread over several months with a final culmination by concentrating and exercising his forces in the Rajasthan sector.[6] Sceptics, however, claim that Sundarji had little time for the air force, deeming it his manoeuvre arm in the third dimension.[7] In essence, Exercise Brasstacks involved two strike corps (1 and 2 Corps) executing a main and a subsidiary thrust with speed and surprise. It was carried out in the Rajasthan and Gujarat sectors to determine whether they could cover good distance by night against moderate opposition. This raised alarm bells in Rawalpindi and Washington, and the Pakistan Army put its own operational plans into unscheduled play by moving its offensive formations towards India's areas of vulnerabilities in Punjab and Jammu.

Lieutenant General Praveen Bakshi was then a tank squadron commander as a major in Skinner's Horse, a T-72 tank regiment. Deployed for months in the desert during both Exercise Digvijay and Exercise Brasstacks, his recollections corroborate the conservative view that Sundarji had no intention of going to war. He says that though 7 Cavalry was the first unit to convert on to the T-72 tanks, Skinner's Horse was the first to get deployed during Exercise Digvijay. 7 Cavalry joined them in Exercise Brasstacks. They easily covered 60 to 70 km in a night and Bakshi recollects having done 800 km on tracks. Despite pushing the T-72 to its limits, there were no breakdowns. As per him, the only drawback in the tank was the lack of effective night-vision devices.[8] Exercise Brasstacks, he adds, was more of the same: long manoeuvres in the open deserts, simulated isolation and capture of small townships while engaging in tank vs tank battles. Bakshi says they never loaded ammunition into the tanks, so there was little chance of going to war. 'We wouldn't have flogged the tanks so much if we had to cross the border,' he says. 'It was more of posturing and preparing ourselves for the future, as also sending a strong message across to the adversary of our overwhelming strength with modernised equipment like T-72 tanks and ICVs.'[9]

Riding on the long-standing Indian aspiration of recovering lost territories in PoK, Sundarji also had Gilgit and Skardu in his sights. Some hawkish analysts believe that Exercise Brasstacks was a smokescreen to deflect attention from Sundarji's focus on the northern areas. He was also ready to validate offensive operations in the mountains and other sectors of J&K with Exercise Trident.[10] To suggest that this was Sundarji's plan was not entirely correct, because its origins lay in the minds of the operational commanders who executed Operation Meghdoot. Brigadier V.K. Channa, who led a force that assaulted the Saltoro Ridge in April 1984, wanted to press on down the western slopes of the Saltoro Ridge. According to Channa, pushing through the Bilafond Glacier to capture Gayari, the town that was a virtual gateway to the glacier and served as a Pakistan Army battalion HQ, was essential if India wanted to recapture Skardu and restore historical boundaries. However, his plan was shot down at higher formations because of logistical overreach and fear of escalation.

Exercise Trident, while feasible, ran the risk of logistical overreach. The advance into PoK via the Burzil Pass was entrusted to 19 Infantry Division, while the main thrust from the Kargil Sector was to be executed by 28 Infantry Division and 3 Mountain Division. These divisions were already acclimatized and waiting in the Ladakh sector. 6 Mountain Division was flown in from Bareilly to replace 3 Mountain Division in the defensive role in the Ladakh Sector, with the IAF flying over seventy sorties into Leh from various bases in central India.[11] There are varying perspectives on the reasons for all these moves. Mehta says that there was no political directive to go to war. In the absence of such guidance, Sundarji was not so foolish as to take his country to war. General V.N. Sharma – who succeeded Sundarji as army chief – was the chief umpire for Exercise Brasstacks. He confirms that there was no plan to go across the border, and termed the Pakistani mobilization as a natural fallout of a volatile situation. He reckons that Sundarji and Arun Singh wanted to convince Rajiv Gandhi of the need to adopt a harder posture vis-à-vis Pakistan and China.

In the summer of 1987, Sundarji decided to militarily resolve the Siachen Glacier imbroglio once and for all. He asked the Parachute Brigade's commander, Brigadier Sapatnekar, to plan an ambitious airborne operation at Khapalu, some 60 km across the LoC.[12] Code-named Operation Hammerhead, the operation's aim was to sever the Pakistani lines of communication to the Siachen Glacier. The paratroopers were then to join up with advancing formations from Chalunkha before capturing key hubs such as Dansam and Gayari. The plan was bold but Sapatnekar's checks proved it to be rather impractical and risky. The essential unsustainability of the plan stemmed from three issues. First, the existing parachutes were not designed for high-altitude landings. This could endanger the safety of the paratroopers in the landing phase as the rates of descent would be significantly higher than what they were used to. Second, it was not possible to adhere to the time frame for linking up with an earmarked ground formation as suggested by Sundarji. This would make the paratroopers vulnerable to a concentrated enemy riposte, which could include air strikes by PAF's newly inducted F-16s. The third issue was the inability of the IAF to undertake a simultaneous two-battalion drop because most of their An-32 and Il-76 aircraft were committed to the ongoing Operation Pawan in Sri Lanka. This would mean a secondary drop without the benefit of surprise, vulnerable to interception.

The plan was dropped because of its huge accompanying risks and because Sundarji, nearing the end of his tenure as army chief, could hardly afford another setback. While Sapatnekar concurs with Sundarji's belief in the huge pay-offs of airborne and heliborne operations, he is clear that there was a wide gap between the concept and its conversion into an implementable and practical plan insofar as Hammerhead was concerned.[13]

Mehta defends Sundarji, saying that Exercise Brasstacks, Exercise Trident, Exercise Chequerboard, Operation Falcon and Operation Hammerhead were all expressions of Sundarji's desire to push the limits of deterrence and dissuasion. 'His purpose really was the achievement of strategic objectives without having to fight a war,' says Mehta. 'If you see the geographical span, it covers the entire length of contested frontiers and all the army commands. They were all moves on the same chessboard. Let's give him credit for having a perspective and communicating it to his commanders. However, a visionary does not have the wherewithal to ensure that his successors follow through.'[14] Sundarji's critics question the overall effectiveness of his attempts to change mindsets and the conduct of operational art in the Indian Army, and the impact it had on deterring India's traditional adversaries.[15] A fair analysis would be that it yielded mixed results. While it did enhance deterrence along the LAC and rattled Pakistan, it also hastened the build-up of Chinese military capability on the Tibetan Plateau and forced Pakistan to hasten its nuclear weapons programme and evolve fresh low-cost military strategies.

Alerting America

Generally dismissive of Indian strategic thinking and clouded by India's Cold War leanings towards the USSR, General Sundarji's muscular military posturing and attempts to infuse fresh thinking into the Indian Army forced the US to take note of these stirrings. Adding to this concern was the interest expressed by General Sundarji in nuclear war fighting through his writings while posted at the Army War College.[16] Concerned thus far only with India's and Pakistan's nuclear ambitions as a danger to regional stability in South Asia, a new possibility had emerged: India's rise as a regional hegemon. Interestingly, despite the geopolitical hostility, the US saw value in testing the waters in the realm of defence technological cooperation. India's Light Combat Aircraft (LCA) programme received a major fillip when the US cleared the export of the General Electric GE-404 jet engine to power it.[17]

Brasstacks was the first occasion when the US considered acting as a neutral interlocutor in an emerging India-Pakistan crisis. Among the several reasons for this change in tack was the realization that Pakistan was not as reliable an ally as it had been in the past and that it had been less than transparent about its nuclear weapons programme.[18] Chari, Cheema and Cohen argue, 'Brasstacks was a "typical" Cold War crisis for the United States. While no vital American interests were engaged, larger, global concerns were present: containment and nonproliferation.'[19] They also conclude that 'Brasstacks had no immediate impact on US-Pakistan relations because the two countries were so closely intertwined in Afghanistan'.[20] Though the exercise delayed normalization of relations between the US and India, it hastened the introduction of the concept of CBMs into the subcontinent at the behest of the US.

While the Indians were certain that the exercise was merely a validation of emerging operational thinking, the Americans looked at it as a crisis that 'had the potential to trigger a conflict as much by accident and misperception as per design'.[21] Bruce Riedel confirms the general American perception of the escalation dynamics associated with Brasstacks. He writes, 'Whatever India's motives – and they were clearly muddled – the deployment in January 1987 of two armoured divisions, one mechanized division, and six infantry divisions along the border with lots of supporting air power prompted a major Pakistani response.'[22]

Atlantique Down[23]

It was 10 August 1999, a regular day at the Air Force Station in Naliya, a marshy region in Kutch, Gujarat. 45 Squadron (Flying Daggers) had just returned from its deployment in the Kargil conflict, and the station was busy preparing for the impending visit of Air Chief Marshal A.Y. Tipnis. Flying Officer Sanjeev 'Nanu' Narayanen was asked to head to the operational readiness platform (ORP) and relieve the No. 2 pilot at around 11 a.m. Little did he realize that his life would never be the same again. Narayanen prepared his aircraft and greeted his leader, Squadron Leader 'Bandy' Bundela, who would be No. 1 on the mission. The tannoy – a secure buzzer between the platform and the controlling radar unit – startled the two when it alerted them that there was an unidentified aircraft close to the border. It was in the general hostile area and a 'scramble' was imminent.

Bundela and Narayanen readied themselves for a possible scramble. They were put on Standby 2 – a readiness state that raises the alert levels and has pilots starting up engines and waiting for take-off. When they heard the call 'scramble, scramble, scramble', it was time to taxi on to the runway and take off with maximum afterburners. Bundela took off a minute before Narayanen, but the No. 2 was the first to pick up the intruder on his Almaz radar at about 40 km – surprisingly good for the 'ancient' Russian airborne radar. Soon after, Bundela picked up the intruder visually, identifying it first as a slow-moving transport aircraft and then confirming that it was the highly capable Atlantique maritime reconnaissance aircraft of the Pakistan Navy. The IAF pilots were surprised when the Atlantique turned towards them. Bundela manoeuvred to stay on the Atlantique's port side and draw the intruder's attention through standard radio or visual procedures. Narayanen stayed high and behind his leader in visual contact, clearing Bundela's tail from possible PAF interceptors.

Not getting any response from the Atlantique, Bundela received clearance from ground control to fire his R-60 missile. The missile hit the port engine of the Atlantique and sent it down in a trail of smoke. The MiG-21 pair immediately returned to base for a debrief. It was only after landing that

Narayanen realized the enormity of what had happened. Reports came in from border patrols that an aircraft had gone down near the marshy border of Kutchh with no survivors. News reports later pegged the toll at five officers and eleven sailors. Reflecting on the events twenty years later, Narayanen writes, 'While there is no remorse on a job done in the line of duty, one can't but help call the incident an unfortunate one for the lives lost on board the Atlantique. If it indeed was a probing mission, it was a foolhardy move just a few weeks after cessation of hostilities. If the aircraft had crossed over inadvertently, then it was a costly mistake.'[24]

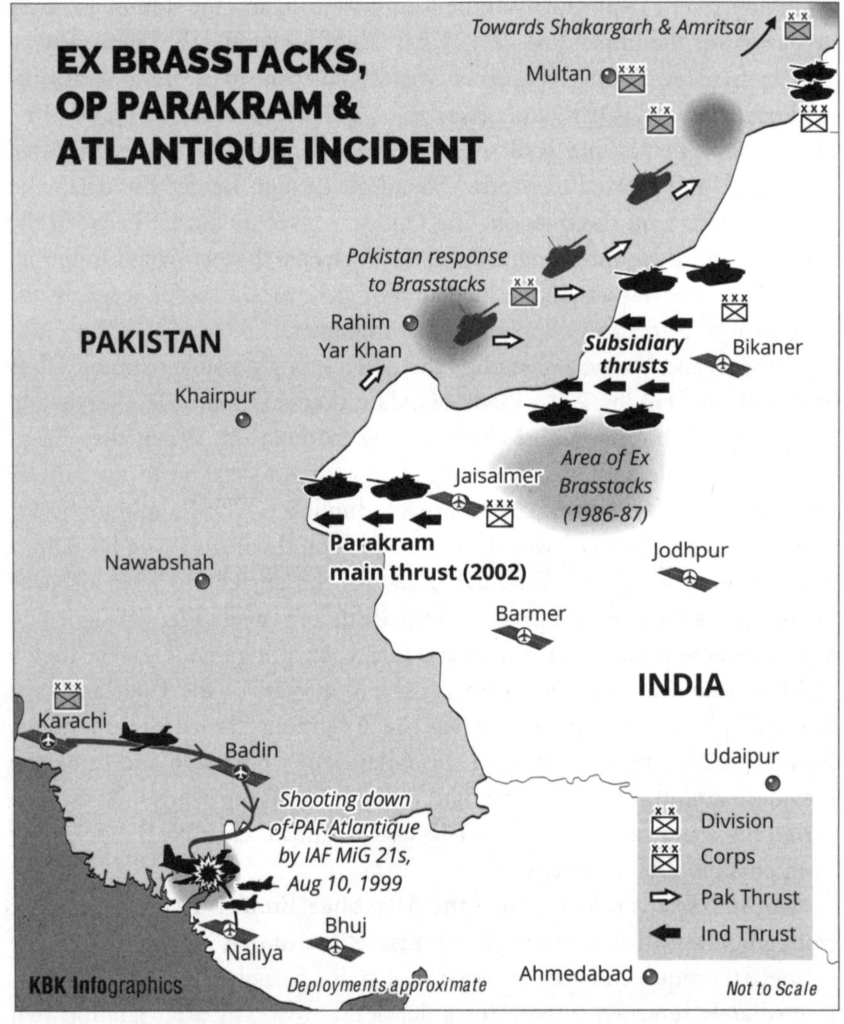

This map is for representational purposes only and does not purport to depict political boundaries

Operation Parakram and Related Operations

Operation Kabaddi

The withdrawal of the ceasefire in June 2001 allowed concerted counterterrorist operations by the Army's Northern Command. It wanted Army HQ to lift restrictions on the use of mortars and artillery for direct fire on Pakistani posts. In a briefing to the army chief, General Padmanabhan, in mid-2001, Nanavatty said that it was time to clearly articulate and adopt a punitive policy to respond to any violation of the LoC, including those by jihadis. The action would be taken by any of the three services, be proportionate and retain the element of surprise by choosing the time and place of application. Approved in principle by the army chief, but subject to final political clearance, preparations for Operation Kabaddi were initiated in autumn 2001 with the aim of redefining and redrawing the LoC as part of the Indian Army's offensive strategy in J&K. The plans included attacks to take out enemy posts and capture and hold ground for a limited duration. Forces were earmarked to be drawn from command and corps reserves without upsetting the counter-infiltration grid.[25] Operational training too commenced in pursuit of this operational objective.

Responding to collective ideas for straightening out and redefining the LoC by capturing shallow objectives, the chief agreed that it offered immense operational benefits and displayed aggression towards the adversary.[26] Lieutenant General H.S. Panag, who would later command Northern Army Command, was a brigade commander in the Batalik Sector and clearly remembers Nanavatty visiting his brigade and even identifying the posts that were to be captured by Panag's brigade in early October 2001. Nanavatty reckoned that if the action threatened northern Punjab, which is the heartland of Pakistan, and provided some northern protection for India's vulnerable Chhamb sector, it had the potential to be a major game changer.[27]

In hindsight, though the plan was bold and fitted into the template of a calibrated limited conflict in J&K, it may be argued that there was an element of overreach in Nanavatty's plans. He thought that he could change the rules of the game and introduce a new punitive paradigm in J&K. However, he may not have considered the absence of a trigger to convince the Vajpayee government to adopt an offensive posture in J&K. Then 9/11 happened and with US President George Bush declaring the global war on terror, the window for coercive action closed. With Musharraf drawn into supporting the US in Afghanistan, things got further complicated for India. Operation Kabaddi never saw the light of day, and the entire operational scenario on LoC and the western border with Pakistan had to be reassessed following the deadly suicide attack on the Indian Parliament by the LeT on 13 December 2001.

Mobilizing for Parakram

After the attack on Parliament, Vajpayee instructed the military to formulate a response and called for a meeting of the three service chiefs. Air Chief Marshal 'Kichcha' Krishnaswamy, India's air chief, was the first to respond and immediately indicated that he was ready for both a limited response against targets in PoK or a conventional response across multiple sectors in J&K, Punjab and Rajasthan.[28] While the former was eminently doable with the right intelligence, the latter assertion had an element of overreach though several IAF planners felt that the PAF was at a lower readiness state than the IAF. The naval chief, Admiral Sushil Kumar, indicated likewise. Understandably, it is believed that General Padmanabhan sought some time to formulate his response. Consulting with his army commanders, he decided that a full mobilization of the Indian Army was required to be able to respond to a strong multisectoral Pakistani reaction to possible air and naval strikes. This effectively squashed any element of surprise and closed the window for India to calibrate the escalation ladder by exploring limited options.

By the third week of December, India's armed forces had commenced mobilizing for operations across the entire International Border and LoC with Pakistan. While the offensive plans for Western and Southern Army Commands were largely the same as the ones practised during Brasstacks with minor variations, Northern Command was tasked with executing an ambitious offensive in the general area south of the Pir Panjal Range. A hastily put together offensive corps comprising two divisions from the east and an additional division from Northern Command reserves were placed under the command of Lieutenant General V.K. Jetley. Nanavatty asked for time to prepare his corps-sized offensive. Lieutenant General Nagaraj, who later commanded the Indian Army's South Western Army Command, was the major general, general staff (operations), under Nanavatty. Closely involved with Jetley during the planning, he remembers that 'there were several valid reasons why a decisive offensive was almost impossible given the lack of cohesion among the formations and inadequate medium-range artillery support'. Offering a realistic assessment, Nanavatty still maintains that it was the wrong way of going to war. He exactly knew what was in store for him as it was just over two years since he had moved his Corps HQ from the east to J&K during the Kargil conflict in anticipation of its escalation. He says, 'In Northern Command, we were conducting counterterrorism, counter-infiltration and conventional defensive operations. I was now given three ad hoc divisions which had not operated together to create a strike formation.' Nanavatty pleaded, 'I need time to ready my forces. If you want to start elsewhere, I will be ready in a couple of months.'

In the author's assessment, the Indian strategic establishment missed a trick or two by going ahead with a full mobilization of India's armed forces for Operation Parakram. It was quite clear that despite the limited success in Kargil, the concept of a limited war under the nuclear umbrella had not yet been formalized. In hindsight, since Northern Command did have limited brigade-sized offensive plans ready for multiple sectors, it is surprising that both Nanavatty and Padmanabhan did not think of selectively putting Kabaddi into play and integrate the IAF into those plans since the air chief had indicated that he was ready to hit targets in PoK with the necessary intelligence. This could have come as an immediate punitive response to the attack on Parliament without infringing on any of the red lines that could have triggered a possible Pakistani nuclear response. That would have been the India's best option for a limited response. Instead, army commanders were asked to disengage from regular operations and reshape everything. Queried by the author on this possibility two decades later, Nanavatty ponders and says, 'I had never thought about it then, but in hindsight, yes, that was a possibility.'[29]

The broad mobilization plan was sequenced to support an immediate offensive option in Northern Command in the areas south of the Pir Panjal Range. Western Command was to focus on making gains in the North Punjab Sector with the entire panoply of offensive air operations complementing it. Most of the gains were anticipated to be in the Rajasthan Sector where the IAF would support deep incursions by two of the Indian Army's strike corps. A possible outcome if war had broken out would have been an attrition-based scenario with heavy casualties on both sides. Panag, who had by then taken over 1 Armoured Division as a major general, assesses that while the going may have been tough in the northern sectors, the armoured divisions in the Rajasthan Sector would have made deep inroads towards the first obstacle, the Nara Canal.

Acknowledging very candidly that while several of his contemporaries felt that it was his reluctance to rush into battle that stalled Parakram, Nanavatty is firm in his assessment that it was 'an incorrect way of going to war and in my heart of hearts, I am glad we did not go to war'. Reflecting further, he says, 'My inputs may have been among the several issues that confronted Paddy (General Padmanabhan), but had it been the principal contributory factor, I am sure he would have told me.'[30] Nagaraj concurs entirely with his army commander on this issue, and recalls the extensive briefings in Army HQ that he and Nanavatty gave with Jetley in attendance.

On 14 May 2002, terrorists of the JeM carried out fidayeen attacks in Kaluchak near Jammu. One attack was on a bus and another on a military camp that included family members. Thirty-one were killed and forty-seven injured in the attack.[31] This was the second trigger that almost led to war between India and Pakistan, with a clamour from across the spectrum of leadership for retributive action. Hooda recollects that the Indian Army commenced the movement of 1 Corps northwards to supplement 2 Corps in the Shakargarh sector even as Padmanabhan waited for the order from the political leadership to commence hostilities. With the Pakistan Army having moved all its formations into battle positions, the Indians had no room for surprise. It is possible that when faced with the prospect of an attrition battle, Vajpayee realized the futility of going to war. It is believed that large armoured formations from 2 Corps under Lieutenant General Kapil Vij moved into dangerously provocative offensive positions in northern Rajasthan in February 2002, and were detected by US satellites. This alarmed both Washington, DC, and Islamabad. Vij surprisingly resigned and has not spoken since, even though many feel it is time for the truth to come out.

Mehta, who had taken over as the Western Army Commander towards the closing phases of Operation Parakram, says that Padmanabhan is the only one who can tell how close they were to going to war. Voicing an opinion shared by several others based on the existing readiness of Pakistan's armed forces, he says, 'As far as I am concerned, we would have sorted them out.' He adds, 'The force levels were huge and with so many complex movements at night, we will never know whether Kapil Vij suffered because he was an aggressive commander or whether he was the fall guy for a mistake made by a subordinate commander.'[32]

Jointness and Synergy

Air power has often been used in recent times for successful coercion in less-than-war situations, but it is not widely known that India also employed air power as a tool of forceful persuasion during Operation Parakram. In a written reply to a question in Parliament in November 2002 – four months after the incident in question – the defence minister, George Fernandes, categorically stated that IAF fighters had been used to evict intruders from Point 3260 (about 10,000 feet) in the Machil and Neelum-Gurez sectors in late July 2002. This sector has the Kishanganga River, the beautiful Neelum

Valley and a series of ridges that run almost parallel to the LoC. The town of Kel in PoK is a Pakistan Army cantonment from where an operation was said to have been launched by the SSG in tandem with the jihadis to occupy positions on a ridge line about 800 metres inside Indian territory. This would have allowed a continuous observation of Indian positions in an area where Pakistan has always been vulnerable. In an operation that was reminiscent of the methodology adopted by Pakistan during the Kargil conflict, vantage positions were occupied stealthily in darkness. Even temporary bunkers were built to provide shelter to troops. However, 15 Corps detected the intrusion in late July 2002 and decided that it had to be dealt with firmly.

Lieutenant General Vinayak Patankar, the commander of 15 Corps, ordered a brigade from the Kupwara-based 28 Infantry Division to evict the intruders. Not wanting to repeat the mistakes of Kargil, Northern Command convinced Delhi of the perils of acting in haste. Then an operation was planned to use air power before launching an infantry assault. Air Marshal Menon recollects getting a call from Army HQ in early July 2002 about stray intrusions in the Kel area that needed air power to be repulsed and had alerted Western Air Command about the same. Air Marshal Adi Ghandhi, the commander-in-chief of Western Air Command, received the same intelligence from Nanavatty. Realizing that Patankar was under tremendous pressure from Army HQ to evict the intruders, Nanavatty chose to bring in air power before committing to a ground assault. Getting a green signal from Air Chief Marshal Krishnaswamy, Ghandhi moved four Mirage-2000s to Adampur from Gwalior in late July. Wing Commander Rajesh Kumar, the commanding officer of 7 Squadron, was given a set of coordinates the following day for a dummy run. They conducted a simulated strike based on those coordinates and were then given the actual ones. The next day, four Mirage-2000s armed with a combination of conventional and laser-guided bombs attacked the position and destroyed the bunkers. This resulted in the immediate withdrawal of the SSG and the jihadis.[33]

Enemy communication intercepts revealed that the intruders suffered several casualties, but these figures were never released into the open domain nor corroborated by the Indian Army.[34] A mopping-up operation by the Indian Army later that evening and the next day reported that there were no intruders at the location. The other locations were also vacated in fear of further air strikes. It is important to highlight that the limited application of air power in a localized action in high-altitude terrain reinforced the utility of air power in coercion as it proved decisive, forceful, legitimate and non-escalatory.

US Perspectives and Interlocutors

Strobe Talbott, President Bill Clinton's Deputy Secretary of State and a close friend of Jaswant Singh, India's foreign minister, emerged in the post-Kargil era as a key US interlocutor in crisis situations involving India and Pakistan. Clearly acknowledging Musharraf's complicity in the continued infiltration of jihadis into India after the 9/11 attacks, he writes of US concerns following intelligence reports that India was readying its nuclear arsenal to respond to a possible first strike by Pakistan. He attaches great significance to the visit of his successor, Richard Armitage, to Islamabad to defuse the crisis following the 'nuclear alarm' as Operation Parakram was escalating towards possible war.[35]

Chari, Cheema and Cohen offer a critique of the US response after Parakram and argue that 'the United States again played an ambiguous role, being uncertain as to which side to come down on'. They also call out the unwillingness of Washington, DC, to mount a long-term strategy of regional conflict resolution. 'Washington was interested in crisis *management*, not in conflict *prevention* or *resolution*.'[36] Clearly, the crisis of 2001-02 came at a wrong time for the US to make a choice between India and Pakistan as its long-term strategic partner in South Asia. Though the preference had emerged in the aftermath of the Kargil crisis, Pakistan remained a critical ally in the ongoing war on terror in Afghanistan.

India's Proactive Doctrine

Even though the Kargil conflict ended without any talk of nuclear options, every operational or doctrinal recalibration by India's armed forces since has been viewed by Western military analysts with some alarm. They see India as wanting to upset the military balance in the subcontinent 'leading to a breakdown of deterrence which could have serious consequences, including the potential use of nuclear weapons'.[37] The 'Cold Start Doctrine' was one such tweaking of existing operational concepts.

Discussion on improving the Indian Army's mobilization schedule commenced in the military operations and operational logistics directorates in Delhi after Operation Parakram was aborted in late 2002. It gained traction during the tenure of General Nirmal Vij as India's army chief. As part of the operational logistics directorate, Hooda recollects that there was nothing overtly aggressive about the strategy. He calls it a much required logistics and mobility recalibration to cater for the emerging paradigms of limited conflict in which the more powerful of two adversaries (in this case, India) sought to claim what it considered a legitimate advantage it ought to have aspired for.

The strategy mainly involved moving offensive formations to fresh locations in the desert sector, where India sought to create any asymmetry it felt would strengthen deterrence rather than weaken it.

There was also a move to regroup armoured elements belonging to the defensive, or pivot, corps into battle groups that could launch an initial offensive. This could shape the wide desert spaces for further exploitation by India's strike corps. The cooling of tensions along the LAC in 2003 also allowed the Indian Army to create dual-tasking divisions that would rely on the growing air mobility capability of the IAF to move large units from the east to the western desert. This move was aimed at freeing up elements of the pivot corps to supplement ongoing offensive operations based on their familiarity with the terrain. Washington, DC, believed that the Indian Army's improving synergy with the IAF would allow it to make decisive thrusts in the deserts of Sindh and trigger Pakistan's nuclear red lines. With concurrent naval strategies, the proactive doctrine appeared to have all the pieces of an offensive strategy in place. Hooda though argues that despite having good synergy with the IAF in the air mobility realm, there was much that still needed to be done at the time to ensure that the IAF's offensive air capabilities blended seamlessly into this process. Despite a clear doctrinal shift in 2012, it is only in the last few years that the IAF has truly embraced parallel operations.[38] Several Western narratives on the cold start doctrine were heavily influenced by the desire to 'protect' Pakistan and ensure that it remains at the frontline of the global war on terror. It also offered an excuse for the West to remain engaged in the 'potentially catastrophic'[39] India–Pakistan rivalry despite strong assertions from India that there was no room for external players there. Not helping India's cause has been the lack of Indian narratives on the proactive doctrine in Washington, DC, and London. This is in contrast with the effective Pakistani counter-narratives by retired and serving practitioners and military scholars, who are quite prolific with their writings and presence during seminars.[40]

An Eye for an Eye across the LoC

In July 2011, the Indian Army's 28 Infantry Division suffered six battle casualties from two battalions as they changed over duties at a post on one of the ridgelines north of Kupwara. The post had been targeted differently by the Pakistanis[41] as the casualties were different to those caused by routine firing or an artillery barrage – they were brutal and premeditated. Two Indian soldiers were also decapitated. It called for an immediate retaliatory response. Resisting the urge to strike back immediately, divisional commander Major General Samir Chakravorty sought permission from the Northern Army Commander,

Lieutenant General K.T. Parnaik, to explore options for retaliatory strikes after surveillance and reconnaissance of potential targets. Seven intrusive reconnaissance missions were conducted between the towns of Kel and Neelum in PoK and a target identified about a kilometre across the LoC. Two days before Eid, Indian commandos ambushed two parties of four Pakistanis each. The Indian troops killed the enemies with IEDs, grenades and gunfire. It was a typical revenge operation.

On 18 September 2016, four terrorists from the JeM stormed a camp of 12 Brigade in Uri, killing eighteen and wounding more than twenty soldiers.[42] It put the Indian Army under tremendous pressure with commanding officers questioning the leadership on how long they were expected to sit back and do nothing. Lieutenant General Hooda, the Northern Army Commander at the time, recollects that in the autumn of 2015 Northern Command had brainstormed a few such contingencies. He had then decided that two of the SF units involved in counterterrorism operations had to be pulled out and trained for cross-border raids. He recalls, 'A fair amount of preparatory work had already been done by the time the Uri attack happened. Once the political decision was taken, it took us no more than ten days to launch five cross-border strikes across the LoC – two of them in northern Kashmir and three opposite the Poonch-Rajouri Sector.' These camps were chosen as they were within 10 km of the LoC and were established terror launch pads. The prospect of Pakistan Army posts being near these terrorist camps was not ruled out. Therefore, he adds, 'It was decided to carry out fire assaults to minimize the risks and ensure no casualties.'[43]

The strikes took place between 1 a.m. and 6 a.m. on 29 September 2016 and were monitored by Hooda via UAVs. There were a number of risks inherent in this operation. One was that over a hundred SF troops were involved, which would have alerted the enemy. This meant that the troops faced danger as they returned after having executed the attacks. Another was the lack of actionable intelligence on one of the targets. Rather than aborting the attack – which would have disappointed the troops who had trained hard for the mission – Hooda approved the plan based on the report of a surveillance team. He reckons that even one casualty would have diluted the mission's effectiveness.

Mounting a near-simultaneous fire assault, heavy casualties were inflicted on the camps with Nitin Gokhale assessing that as many as seventy to seventy-five terrorists and their handlers were neutralized during the stealthy operation. Hooda was close when he suggested that radio intercepts and an assessment by the commanders of the two units estimated the casualties at about eighty.[44] Both units had earlier operational experience in the sector and had punitive plans chalked out. Though the strikes were understandably denied by Pakistan and India did not feel the necessity to provide evidence of destruction of the camps, there was a quiet sense of confidence within the Indian Army that punitive strikes would no longer be taboo as far as standard responses to terrorist attacks were concerned. Unconfirmed reports also suggest that there were 'revenge strikes' conducted the previous night too. Soldiers from the unit that suffered losses in the Uri terrorist attack are said to have crossed over with 'pathfinder' support from the special forces and neutralized several terrorists at a launch pad.[45] Nineteen personnel from the two SF units were given gallantry awards including a Kirti Chakra (second highest gallantry award for peacetime operations) for the major who led one of the strikes.[46]

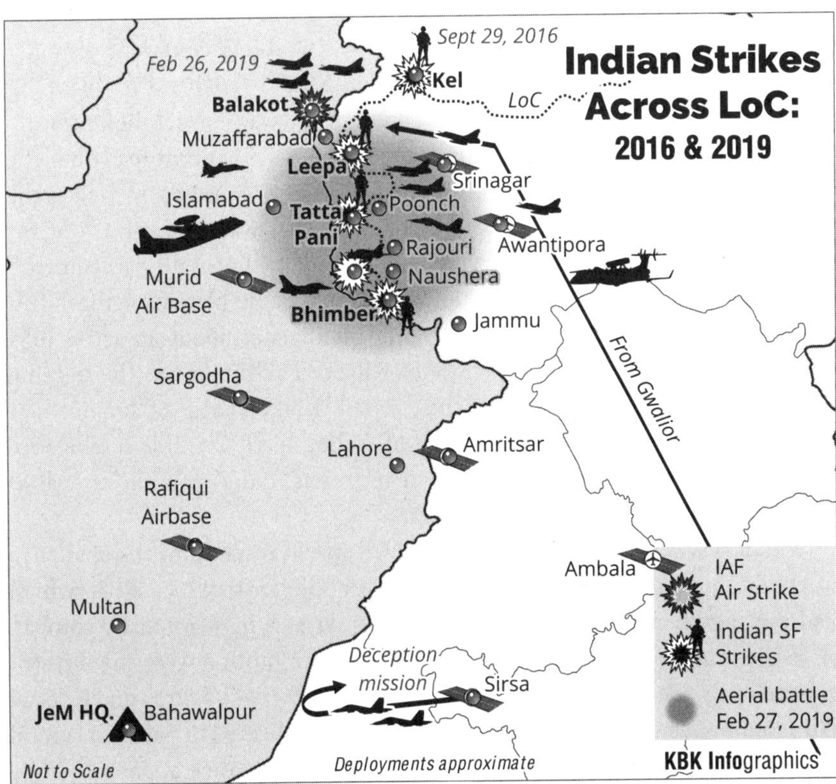

This map is for representational purposes only and does not purport to depict political boundaries

Peeling the Mask at Balakot

On 14 February 2019, a CRPF convoy was attacked along the Jammu–Srinagar highway at Pulwama by a JeM suicide bomber, killing forty-four security personnel. The event changed the trajectory of India's response mechanisms.

The Indian strategic establishment – which in 2016 had responded to the Uri terror attack with cross-border surgical strikes by SF – realized that Pakistan would be ready for any kind of surface retaliation following the Pulwama attack. This meant that air and naval strikes against non-military targets remained the only viable coercive option given that India was keen on calibrating the escalation ladder.

The three service chiefs had met a few weeks before the attack to brainstorm joint operational responses to various contingencies. Hence there was clarity when Prime Minister Modi asked them to respond with an air strike after due deliberations with the NSA and the defence minister. A senior government official – who was also present when a military response was hesitantly contemplated by the Manmohan Singh government in 2008 after the Mumbai terrorist attack – was struck by the chiefs' confident response and the alacrity with which they responded to Modi's 'free hand' for planning India's punitive response.[47] This time around, there was no such hesitation.

Rawat remarked that the Indian Army was only 75 per cent ready, but the adversary was not even at 50 per cent. The Indian Navy was not worried as the asymmetry between the Indian and Pakistani navies was enormous.[48] As for the IAF, Dhanoa was always known to possess excellent operational acumen.[49] It did not take his team long to put together a viable plan after the NSA, Ajit Doval, handed him reliable targeting intelligence about an active JeM training camp in the remote province of Khyber Pakhtunkhwa. The training camp was located at Juba Top near the town of Balakot, about 60 km north of the Pakistan Army's cantonment town of Abbottabad. Credible intelligence confirmed the presence of hundreds of terrorists under training as well as senior cadres, trainers and commanders.

Dhanoa was also confident that the IAF would respond to the challenge of escalation following the massive Exercise Gaganshakti in 2018, which had put together an operational plan for ten days of high-intensity combat. Assisting him in putting the operational plan into motion were the director general of air operations and the commanders-in-chief of Western and Central Air Commands. Dhanoa's confidence would be vindicated in part, but several shortfalls in the performance of the IAF would also become apparent.

Air Strike

On the early morning of 25 February 2019, Squadron Leader 'A' from 9 Squadron returned from a rehearsal sortie with no idea of the actual target. It was only at around 8 p.m. that he got to know that he was part of a large formation from the Mirage fleet that was striking a non-military terrorist target in Pakistan. After a comprehensive briefing at 10 p.m., it was time for a pep talk from Air Commodore 'W', an experienced Mirage pilot with combat experience in Kargil. 'This is what you have trained for and now it is time to deliver,' 'W' told them. The group split up and headed to their respective squadrons. They would now see each other only after landing at the designated recovery base after the mission.[50]

The air force station at Gwalior hummed in the wee hours of 26 February 2019. While the ground crew were busy strapping air-to-ground weapons and air-to-air missiles on the Mirage-2000s, all the commanding officers of the three Mirage squadrons in Gwalior – 1 Squadron, 7 Squadron and 9 Squadron – were going through their individual element briefings, contingency plans and escape drills. It was made clear that there was no possibility of a planned rescue in case anyone ejected in enemy territory.

The target was Juba Top and the strike force comprised twelve Mirage-2000 aircraft mostly armed with a single Spice 2000 bomb and a few with the older Crystal Maze bombs to ensure a 3X overkill factor. Escorting them were several upgraded Mirage-2000s with MICA Beyond Visual Range (BVR) missiles – the closest the IAF had to counter the potent AIM-120 Advanced Medium Range Air-to-Air missiles (AMRAAM) that were carried by PAF F-16s. 'A' recollects that the MICA BVR missiles on the tarmac were the most intimidating sight of his life. Four SU-30 MKI aircraft from 15 Squadron joined the Mirages for additional air defence protection while a diversionary package of Jaguars and SU-30s headed south towards Bahawalpur in Pakistan – the JeM HQ – to draw away PAF air defence fighters and AWACS that had been seen orbiting near the PAF airbase of Murid.

The weather over the target area had prompted a rethink and a possible delay. However, the IAF leadership took a call that was vindicated by the ability of the Spice 2000 to gather adequate target discrimination details despite the cloud cover and strike the target accurately. Demonstrating reach and precision while maintaining complete radio silence, the fuel-efficient Mirages flew over 1,300 km one way with an aerial refuelling. They used the mountains to mask their entry into PoK airspace and dropped five Spice 2000 bombs with unerring accuracy on to selected buildings that housed terrorists. Contrary to reports that the PAF had been caught napping, a post-strike IAF review claims that several pairs of PAF interceptor aircraft had been scrambled but had failed to intercept the Mirages, or were drawn away by the IAF deception aircraft seemingly headed towards Bahawalpur. The decoys turned back short of the international border, allowing a free run to the Mirage aircraft to the north.

The lack of clear evidence of the actual destruction caused by the Spice 2000 bombs does not trouble either the IAF or India's political leadership. They argue that they have enough evidence that the strike achieved its objectives. Communication intercepts between top JeM leadership about a strike on their facility as well as the reluctance of the Pakistani establishment to allow foreign journalists to access the IAF hit site even as late as April only reinforce the post-strike assessment of the Indians. Sources who wish to remain anonymous confirm that recent satellite forays over the area point at an increased sulphur content in specific areas around the Juba Top camp, indicating that large numbers of bodies hurriedly buried are decomposing.[51]

A better understanding of the Spice 2000 bomb is important for putting the pieces together. The 1,000 kg Spice 2000 glide bomb used by the IAF has an explosive charge of merely 60 to 80 kg. Planting this charge against the door of a building or strapping it around a suicide bomber would produce very different results from using it in a penetrative weapon. The explosive in the Spice 2000 bomb is enclosed within a casing weighing over 900 kg. It did not detonate instantaneously on impact with the roof as it had a time-delay fuse that allowed it to penetrate through concrete before detonating. Informed sources indicate that the time delay was just enough to cause detonation after minimal penetration to prevent an excessive upheaval effect. The primary shock wave of the explosion is first transmitted to the casing, which fragments and disperses at velocities ranging from 1.3 to 1.8 km per second (approximately 5,000 to 7,000 km per hour). In effect, the lack of destruction on surrounding structures can be attributed to the release of pressure within the large room – which would have merely blasted open the windows and doors.

Vipin Narang, an associate professor at the Massachusetts Institute of Technology, has been a vocal supporter of the larger strategic narrative that India should have exploited after the Balakot strikes, but is critical of the ensuing tactical and operational narratives. Nevertheless, he adds, 'Let analysts like me say whatever, who cares? Though I maintained from day one that the resolve to hit mainland Pakistan was the game changer. The rest is noise.'[52]

Pakistan Responds: Operation Swift Retort

Expecting an immediate riposte, the IAF's air defence radars and combat air patrols were on high alert. The PAF attempted to catch the IAF by surprise with a raid in broad daylight the following day. They had succeeded in surprising the IAF in 1965 and 1971, but this time around they failed. However, they still managed to catch the IAF out of phase during the recycling of air defence assets. India's sole AWACS is said to have been pulled further east from its normal patrolling position, which meant that the IAF's 'eye in the sky' was not available when the PAF planes approached. It was thanks to an alert fighter controller, Squadron Leader Minty Agarwal, that the two airborne pairs of Sukhoi and Mirage aircraft were vectored (directed on radar) on to the incoming PAF aircraft. Agarwal controlled multiple pairs of interceptors, including MiG-21 Bisons that were scrambled from Srinagar.[53] Simplifying one of the largest aerial battles in a less-than-war situation in recent times can only be done based on bits and pieces of selective information that have been made available by the IAF in its efforts to combat Pakistan's fake narrative.[54]

The PAF aircraft were the JF-17 and Mirage-III armed with H4 weapons.[55] Their target was the Indian Army's Naushera brigade. There were also F-16s armed with AMRAAMs and targeting pods. These were meant for keeping the IAF's Mirage-2000s and Su-30s engaged while the other aircraft delivered their weapon loads. An analysis of the rules of engagement followed during the manoeuvring reveals that both forces strictly stayed on their side of the LoC. In this cat-and-mouse aerial combat, both sides attempted to get a shot on the target from a distance while trying to not get shot themselves.

The IAF aircraft could not take shots due to the weapon range advantage enjoyed by the PAF F-16 aircraft. This meant that if the IAF fighters had to attempt a BVR launch, they had to fly into the range of the AMRAAMs. However, even though they had a weapon advantage, the PAF F-16s were surprised by the sophisticated and synergized tactics of the IAF. There is adequate evidence through monitored radio calls that four or five AMRAAMs were launched by the F-16s but missed their target either due to electronic countermeasures or a combination of timely offensive and defensive manoeuvring by the IAF aircraft. Avenger formation from the IAF's Su-30 fleet surprised the PAF with its synchronized and excellent manoeuvring, both during the offensive mission on 26 February and the air defence response the following day. The IAF chief later remarked that if he had Rafale aircraft armed with Meteor BVR missiles, the outcome of the aerial engagement would have been very different.

Meanwhile, radio transmission intercepts by the Indian Army revealed that several H4 weapons had been launched by the JF-17s and Mirage-IIIs, but had missed their targets because faulty digital elevation maps had been fed into the weapon computer. Realizing that the Sukhois and Mirages needed support, Agarwal scrambled four MiG-21 Bison aircraft from Srinagar. This is where Wing Commander Abhinandan Varthaman entered the fray. First to arrive into the area where the Sukhois were earlier battling the F-16s,

Abhinandan came into the fight from above. He locked on to an F-16 that had sneaked closer to the area where weapons were supposed to have been dropped, possibly to film the damage from just across the LoC. No aircraft had yet crossed the LoC.

Even as Abhinandan approached the LoC at top speed, Agarwal ordered him to 'go cold', which means 'turn around'. However, his aircraft was equipped with an old radio set (that should have been replaced by an indigenously manufactured software-defined radio years ago). He missed the instruction, possibly because of the PAF's communication jamming, and fired a shot at the receding F-16, taking it down. Seconds later, even as he initiated a turn to get back home, Abhinandan was probably shot down by another F-16. Ejecting a few kilometres inside enemy territory, Abhinandan attempted to escape from the pursuing locals and Pakistan Army personnel and head back to India across a rivulet. He was lucky not to have been lynched when the locals caught up with him. The Pakistan Army quickly arrived on the scene and took him into their custody. After much drama, he was repatriated to India a few days later in full media glare and after conducting himself with courage and dignity while in captivity.[56] Abhinandan soon returned to active fighter flying duties and was awarded a Vir Chakra for 'courageously engaging the enemy aircraft package with utter disregard to his personal safety', and 'displaying exceptional air combat acumen'.[57] Squadron Leader Minty Agarwal, the alert fighter controller, and five Mirage and Sukhoi-30 pilots were also recognized with awards for distinguished service during war, conflict or hostilities.

Lessons from Balakot

Notwithstanding the political rhetoric and hyperbole that followed the attacks, Pakistan got the message that India would resort not only to diplomacy to expose Pakistani machinations but also to suitable punitive action. No country – not even Pakistani ally China – criticized the Indian air strikes, which were termed as preventive strikes against non-military targets comprising an established terrorist camp.

An objective analysis of the operation and tactics reveals both positives and negatives. The preventive air strikes were planned in utmost secrecy and executed with finesse and surprise, but there were also a few hiccups that diluted the overall impact of the strikes and denied the Indians real-time information on target destruction. The synergy between the armed forces was good and the army chief understood the importance of surprise as he held back and closely monitored any surface movement of large ground formations till the attack was over. The air defence response by the IAF kept at bay a potent and numerically superior adversary, though the orchestration of air defence resources could have been better in terms of the speed of recycling airborne air defence fighters.

The downing of an IAF Mi-17 by friendly fire[58] is said to have unsettled the air defence network in J&K. The Su-30s and Mirage-2000s acquitted themselves well as they did not allow the F-16s to manoeuvre into launch ranges – despite the PAF planes having BVR missiles that outranged the Indian missiles by about 20 per cent. The MiG-21 Bisons acted as classic disrupters. The flurry of emergency acquisitions of critical weapons by the IAF in the months[59] following Balakot indicates that there will be no let-up in building capability for coercive deterrence.

Deterring a Seemingly Irrational Adversary[60]

Pakistan's irrational strategic behaviour along India's western borders – influenced in no small measure by jihadi and Salafi/Wahhabi extremism – is apparent across the political and military spectrum. Adding to the confusion are the few rational segments in Pakistan's beleaguered diplomatic corps and civil society that harbour hopes of a rapprochement with India. However, it could be that Pakistan is rational but tries to appear irrational to plant a seed of doubt in its principal adversary. Even if a ceasefire is restored along the LoC, what guarantee does India have that the Pakistan Army will honour it? Pakistan's army chief, General Qamar Javed Bajwa, has clearly indicated that he thinks it is correct to segregate the 'good terrorist from the bad one' thereby endorsing terrorism as a strategy for Pakistan.[61] Will Pakistan abandon its obsession to force the secession of Kashmir in the irrational expectation of getting even with India for 1971, Siachen and Kargil? Will India's political establishment engage with the Pakistan Army to gauge whether it is serious about restoring peace along the LoC? These are among the several questions that loom large over the India-Pakistan conundrum.

20

STRESS ALONG THE LINE OF ACTUAL CONTROL

'The overarching reality seems to be that both India and China have been subtly but profoundly influenced by the possibility that the other side might use military force.'[1]

– John Garver

Deterrence and Probing

Following the Sumdorong Chu face-off in 1986-87, there was a realization in Beijing that India would be no pushover in any form of conflict. Consequently, both sides felt the need for some form of recessed deterrence mechanism. They decided on an agreement to control escalation along the LAC in 1993. Much of the credit for this must go to then Prime Minister Narasimha Rao. He first created a political consensus in India for this agreement and then signalled to the Chinese that India was willing to negotiate the first bilateral agreement since the 1962 war.[2] The agreement, called Maintenance of Peace and Tranquillity Along the Line of Actual Control, outlined the procedures to be followed for periodic high-level military contacts and put in place several CBMs for maintaining the status quo along the LAC. Among these were prior intimation of military exercises in areas close to the LAC and establishment of a no-fly zone for fighter aircraft of 10 km within the LAC. It worked well and led to the pullback of some forces from the LAC. However, in the absence of a clearly delineated border, neither side let its guard down. This delineation of the LAC is considered by both countries as an essential first step for settling the boundary issue. Clarity on the LAC will reduce the risk of accidental conflicts by removing the reason for intruding across it. It will also set the stage for the final settlement of the boundary question. Joint working groups, interlocutors and special representatives have made slow progress. This is despite the signing of a Border Defence Cooperation Agreement (BDCA) in 2013 during Prime Minister Manmohan Singh's visit to Beijing.[3] This agreement is just a slight variation of the 1993 agreement. Its value is as a deterrent as it offers no roadmap for conflict resolution.

The power asymmetry between China and India widened rapidly in the first decade of the twenty-first century. It was only a matter of time before China – under an assertive Xi Jinping – tried to test Indian resolve in two sectors. In 2013, PLA forces first intruded into and then set up camp for a week in the Depsang plains of northern Ladakh, close to the Indian advance landing ground at Daulat Beg Oldi. A year later, even as Xi was exchanging pleasantries with the recently elected Prime Minister Narendra Modi during a state visit to India, PLA and Indian troops were engaged in pushing and shoving at Chumar in eastern Ladakh. Both Depsang and Chumar saw fierce battles in 1962, and the Chinese wanted to remind the Indians of their focus on these disputed enclaves. The PLA's attention soon shifted eastwards as it carried out probing intrusions in areas of Arunachal Pradesh. The Indian Army calls those areas Fishtail 1 and 2 because they appear like fishtails on the map. China then went for a 'big push' in Doklam that led to a two-month stand-off in 2017.

Depsang and Chumar Face-offs

Located a few kilometres south-east of the Daulat Beg Oldi airfield and the Chip Chap region, the Depsang plains are part of an area known in the Indian Army as Sub Sector North (SSN). It is flanked by the Sasoma Range to the west, the Karakoram Range to the north and the Kun Lun Range to the east. It is part of a huge area that has been defended by a single Indian infantry brigade for long. But Indian Army deployments in the area depended on the trajectory of the insurgency in J&K. It is only after the Depsang face-off that the Indian Army enhanced its troop strength in the region and seriously considered deploying tanks in the area. However, a metalled road for supporting operations remains a work in progress.

Lieutenant General Vinod Bhatia, a former director-general of military operations, explains the technicalities of maintaining a presence in one of the several disputed areas in eastern Ladakh.[4] He says the PLA routinely conducts four or five vehicular patrols in a month but their total monthly stay in the area was only fifteen to twenty hours as a return trip from their nearest camp took about four hours. India was constrained by the lack of roads into the region and instead conducted six-day foot patrols into the area twice every month. This irritated the Chinese immensely as they construed it as a prolonged presence in a disputed area. In the early morning of 15 April 2013, an officer from the Ladakh Scouts on a routine surveillance and observation helicopter sortie spotted something abnormal in the Raki Nala area on the desolate Depsang plains. This was well inside the Indian Army's limit of patrolling the LAC in eastern Ladakh. A closer look confirmed that the PLA had erected four or five tents overnight with the clear intention of staying put.

The Indian Army had only one platoon in the area at the time. Within forty-eight hours, additional troops were called in from acclimatized infantry battalions, Ladakh Scouts and the ITBP. They quickly set up camp opposite the PLA camp and troops were deployed as a physical wall to prevent any further intrusion. The overarching message from Army HQ to the officers and troops there was 'No blinking and no brinkmanship'. There was much pushing and shoving over the three-week face-off before a series of flag meetings between the two brigade commanders and higher-level diplomatic parleys defused the situation.[5] Interestingly, the intrusion took place weeks before Chinese premier Li Keqiang's visit to India.[6]

Bhatia recollects that NSA Shivshankar Menon was supportive throughout the crisis even though he had often advised against adopting a hawkish approach towards border management. Bhatia is also convinced that not having enough troops in large spaces like the Depsang plains and SSN is risky. Nanavatty offers a contrarian perspective and argues that many posts and locations in eastern Ladakh are indefensible. Describing the strategy in the early 2000s as a policing strategy and not a defensive line, he invoked Frederick the Great who said, 'You defend everywhere and you defend nowhere.' Cautioning against mirroring the Chinese in every respect, he was against the strategy of 'fingering or needling' that was being propounded by some commanders on both sides.[7]

Bhatia characterizes the PLA as a rule-based force that largely follows the templates of patrolling as laid down in various border agreements. He has studied the behaviour of PLA commanders particularly in Tibet and discounts the view held by several Indian commanders that it is the local PLA commanders who flex their muscles periodically.[8] However, he acknowledges that despite largely maintaining restraint and responsibility, patrols from both sides have often transgressed the limit of penetration. This was done to acquire an updated situational awareness of the LAC in the absence of roads and tracks, and Bhatia justifies this as being 'necessary at times'.

The Chumar incident of April and May 2014, barely a few months after the signing of the BDCA, was an exercise in coercive signalling and posturing by the Chinese. Chumar is in southern Ladakh and to the west of the prominent frontier outpost of Demchok. The disputed area to the south-west of it has a vehicular track that links it to both the Indian and Chinese sides. Chumar was constantly visited by Chinese motorized (and even horseback) patrols. Indian patrols established a post near the disputed area of the LAC on a plateau called 30R. Matters came to a head when the Chinese brought in construction vehicles with the intent of extending their track beyond 30R. This move was followed by rapid troop inductions on both sides. Human chains of several hundred infantry soldiers and personnel from the ITBP blocked a prominent river crossing and the adjoining plateau where the PLA wanted to build a road. The Chinese even landed helicopters on the plateaus for resupply. This prompted Hooda, who was the Northern Army Commander at the time, to reach out to the IAF and ask for Mi-17s to drop supplies. In a lighter vein, he recollects some drops falling on the Chinese side and the PLA troops were seen to be enjoying Indian chocolates.

A significant and unreported de-escalatory event occurred when a PLA officer who had fallen off the plateau during a patrol and been left behind by his comrades was rescued by the Indians. He was treated for his injuries and immediately sent back. This cooled the frayed local nerves and ended the sixteen-day face-off. Media reports of the PLA demolishing Indian bunkers were unsubstantiated. However, it was clear that the Chinese objective was to establish themselves on the plateau south-west of Chumar and signal that they did not agree with the contours of the LAC in the area. Having understood China's strategic behaviour, Hooda is certain that the operation would have had the blessings of its top leadership as part of periodic and continuous probing along disputed areas of the LAC. The face-off demanded extreme operational restraint from the local Indian brigade commanders who had to ensure that junior commanders refrained from taking reactive tactical decisions. Instead, Northern Command had to seek continuous updates from the field and urge caution all the time.[9] Eastern Ladakh continues to simmer as recently as May 2020, when the Pangang Tso Lake and the Galwan Valley emerged as the scenes of clashes between the PLA Border Guards and the Indian Army that involved stone throwing and resulted in injuries on both sides. As always, the incident has been downplayed by both sides following a meeting between sector commanders on both sides at the brigade level.[10]

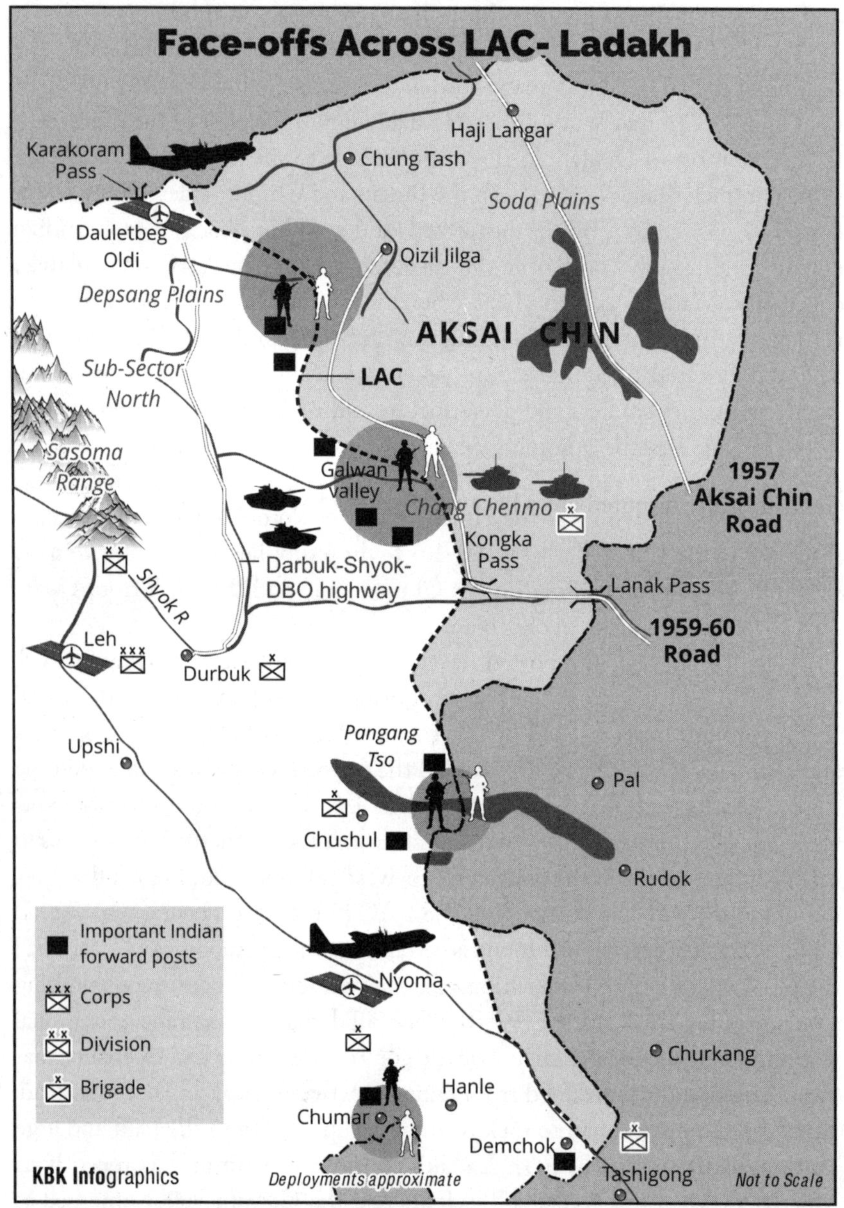

This map is for representational purposes only and does not purport to depict political boundaries

Stress in Arunachal Pradesh

The LAC in Arunachal Pradesh stretches for almost 1,000 km, which makes it impossible for the Tezpur-based 4 Corps to defend the whole region. Therefore, eastern Arunachal Pradesh has been segregated from the Tawang (Kameng) Sector. The area is now under 56 Mountain Division and 2 Mountain Division, forming part of an expanded 3 Corps zone. Along with SSN in Ladakh, eastern Arunachal Pradesh, also called Rest of Arunachal Pradesh (RALP), has the poorest infrastructure and roads. Advanced landing grounds at Mechuka, Tuting and Walong are the lifelines of the region.

Soon after the Doklam crisis, China and India accused each other of violating the LAC in the areas around Longju and the areas west of it called Asaphila, a place of religious significance for the locals near the border town of Taksing. India also charged the Chinese with unduly provocative road-building activity 1 km inside the LAC in the area close to Tuting. The Chinese in turn alleged that India had damaged the road equipment they left behind during the winter season. There is constant jousting in the areas north of the village of Chaglagam, which the Indian Army identifies as Fishtail 1 and 2. These are historically disputed areas because of cartographic errors.[11] In September 2019, a local politician alleged that the Chinese had built a bridge across a rivulet on the Indian side of the LAC in Fishtail 1.[12]

The pace of infrastructure and road development in the area has visibly accelerated over the last few years, with several roads being built by the Border Roads Organization. The construction of sixty-one strategic roads along the borders with China and Pakistan has been hastened.[13] In addition, the 9-km-long Dhola Sadiya bridge on the eastern extremities of the Brahmaputra and the 5-km-long Bogibeel bridge connecting the town of Dibrugarh with eastern Arunachal Pradesh have also been built. These are not only lifelines for the common citizen but are also critical communication nodes for the Indian Army. What remains now is to ensure last-mile connectivity by building a network of metalled roads that run up to the LAC.

An Indian commander recollects the farcical and benign – but very real – face-offs in the Fishtail region. It usually started with a group of ten or fifteen PLA border guards intruding into areas that are claimed by India. They would unfold their tripod stools and sit around the whole day before heading back to their camp for the night. The Indians would respond in a similar manner. Finally, a border patrol meeting would be called to record each other's protests. Given the significant infrastructure asymmetry in this area and the propensity of the PLA to continuously probe the Indian defensive line for weaknesses, this could be the next area of concern.[14]

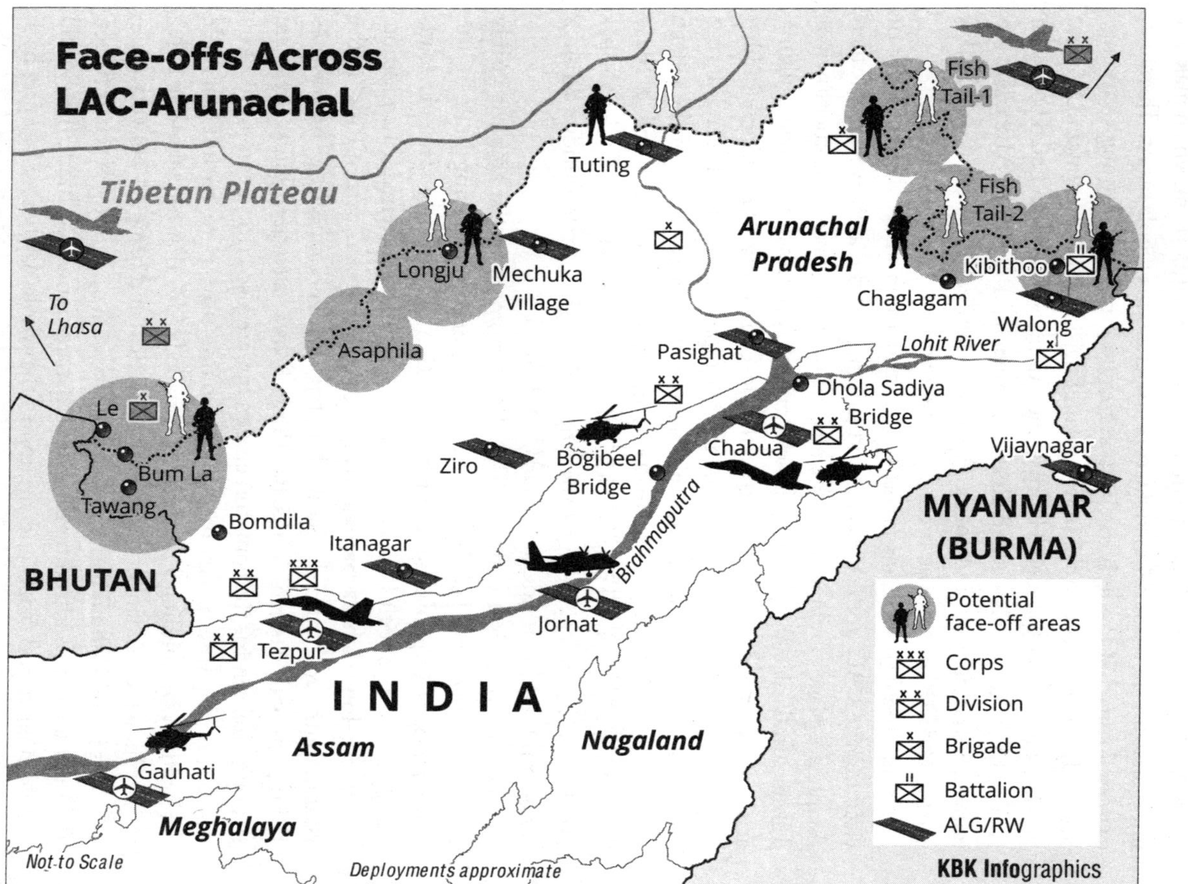

This map is for representational purposes only and does not purport to depict political boundaries

The Doklam Crisis

The Chumbi Valley is a narrow, 100-km-long dagger-shaped sliver of traversable but mountainous terrain that emerges from the Tibetan town of Yatung and connects to the trijunction of the India-China-Bhutan border and the 100-km-long Siliguri corridor that leads into Bangladesh. Any attacking force that manages to penetrate through 70 km of tough Indian terrain after coming through this valley would have a free run across the Siliguri plains.[15] The inability of the PLA to operationally dominate Indian positions on the mountain ridgelines overlooking the Chumbi Valley means that any Chinese attempt to cut off the Siliguri corridor would be a risky one. Any advance would be covered by Indian fire from tactically superior positions overlooking the valley.

Tactically, therefore, the Chumbi Valley has the potential to become a killing ground for the PLA. This has been the operational conundrum facing PLA commanders for decades, and led them to encroach on to the Dolam Plateau and attempt to dominate the Jampheri Ridge south of Batang La, a pass that marks the trijunction. The PLA's continued attempts in the region to gain tactical advantage have been foiled by the Indian Army, which along with the strong IAF deployment, is well positioned to offer adequate deterrence in the region. For ease of understanding, the crisis has been commonly called the Doklam crisis as the area around the Dolam Plateau is called Doklam by the Bhutanese and Indians, while the Chinese call it Donglang.

In the summer of 2017, India's 33 Corps and the PLA had a faceoff on the Dolam Plateau in south-western Bhutan that lasted for seventy-three days. It was a continuation of the periodic and worrisome encounters that have taken place across the LAC since India and China went to war in October 1962.[16] Much has been written about the crisis and its aftermath.[17] The Dolam Plateau lies south of the highest point on the crest line (Merung La) and the mountain pass of Batang La. China's claim over the plateau rests on an agreement signed between Britain and China in 1910 that settled the Sikkim and Tibet boundary without Bhutan as a signatory. It marked Mount Gyomochen as the point of the trijunction – however, it was later confirmed cartographically that Merung La and not Mount Gyomochen was the highest point on the watershed. Therefore, India thinks the trijunction would be at that point.[18]

Over the years, it has been acknowledged by both India and China that the Dolam Plateau was disputed territory even though maps showed it as a part of Bhutan. The Chinese had been actively eyeing the area since 2007 and had constructed a track that facilitated regular visits by PLA border patrols to the plateau. They were always met by Indian patrols, who sent them back after the usual arguments and symbolic pushing or shoving. They justified their actions with the treaty of 2012, which clearly stated that the status quo shall not be altered by any side unilaterally.

The Indian Army's Eastern Command was aware of China's desire to occupy the Jampheri Ridge and plans were in place to thwart any such misadventure. Therefore, in June 2017 when the Indian Army noticed seventeen pieces of heavy road construction equipment being moved towards the centre of the Dolam Plateau, they knew that it was not the Dolam Plateau that the PLA wanted to occupy but the Jampheri Ridge. Their assessed objective was to build a road from the Dolam Plateau to the Jampheri Ridge, thus effectively claiming it as Chinese territory. This ridge would afford the PLA good visibility over the Chumbi Valley and parts of the Siliguri corridor. Since this move was anticipated by the Indian Army, it responded quickly.

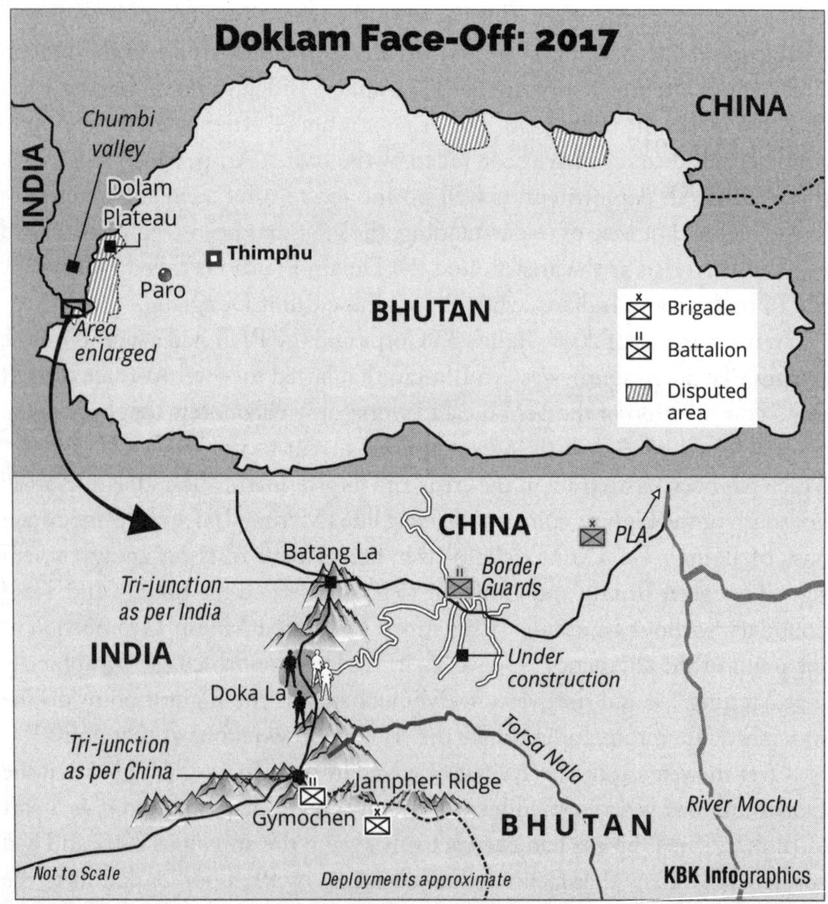

This map is for representational purposes only and does not purport to depict political boundaries

Cranking a Response

Lieutenant General Praveen Bakshi, the Eastern Army Commander at the time, understood Chinese articulation and posturing in the area. A Chinese general, Zhao Zongqui, visited Kolkata in December 2016 to meet Bakshi. There was much bonhomie, but also an element of sizing one another up. Both commanders affirmed adherence to the BDCA, but also expressed concerns regarding the other's moves in their respective areas of interest. This general's visit was followed up by a large PLA delegation visiting in February 2017.[19] However, soon after, field commanders started to report significant increase in patrolling and face-offs in Sikkim – especially in the hitherto relatively quiet northern plateau of Sikkim, eastern Arunachal Pradesh and western Kameng.

Bakshi suggests that there was an emerging mindset within the Indian strategic and intelligence community that the Daulat Beg Oldi and Depsang areas in eastern Ladakh, and Chumar were more important for the Chinese due to their proximity to the China-Pakistan economic corridor. They assumed that the Chinese now wanted to use Arunachal Pradesh only as strategic leverage. The first signs of Chinese intent emerged towards the end of May 2017, when the PLA asked the Indian Army to demolish two old unoccupied bunkers located on the Indian side of the border near the Dolam Plateau. The Indians did not comply. The PLA waited for a week and then demolished one bunker on 8 June, warning that they would destroy the second one too. On the morning of 16 June, Bakshi got a call from the commander of 33 Corps, Lieutenant General Sanjay Jha, alerting him that a PLA column was heading towards the Dolam Plateau with heavy road construction equipment. As per standard practice, the matter was reported by Bakshi to the army chief.

Bakshi initiated standard protocols to obtain permission from Army HQ to intervene and prevent the PLA from laying a road towards the Jampheri ridge, as this had adverse operational implications for India. After a call in the evening from New Delhi saying, 'You are free to take action as deemed appropriate,' Bakshi gave immediate directions to Jha to stop the PLA from building the road, even if this involved crossing the India–Bhutan border. Operational parameters were laid down whilst giving full freedom to the troops and formations in contact for executing the task at hand. Defending that stretch of the LAC was a brigade which was commanded by Brigadier Gambhir Singh. Gambhir's men crossed the border immediately and ordered the PLA troops to halt all construction activity. He set up a continuous blocking position on the plateau in front of the construction equipment, rotating his troops to ensure that they remained fresh and did not crack under any kind of pressure. Initially, Gambhir had 250 men but soon this number increased to 450. The men were replaced every two hours because of weather conditions. The Indian troops were fully acclimatized, which greatly facilitated the task. In the meantime, Bakshi ordered a media ban.

On 26 June 2017, the Chinese foreign and defence ministries issued a press release stating that India had invaded their territory. Anti-India newspaper *Global Times* from Beijing made not-so-veiled threats to India to back off from what they claimed was Chinese territory.[20] The Chinese followed this up by suspending the Mansarovar Yatra from Nathu La and moving troops closer to the Bhutan border from Yatung, which was a divisional HQ. However, they were outnumbered throughout the period of the stand-off. By early July, diplomatic efforts kicked in and a gradual downsizing of troops on the Dolam Plateau took place. China initially demanded an Indian withdrawal. India refused. Finally, after much negotiation, both sides simultaneously withdrew to previous positions.

There has been some criticism from strategic commentators – such as Lieutenant General Prakash Menon – that India has not contested the continued PLA construction of tracks leading to the Jampheri Ridge from further east. Menon argues that by staying quiet about this continued buildup, India runs the risk of a swift PLA move towards the Jampheri Ridge should the Chinese plan another incursion.[21] Bakshi responded to this apprehension by pointing out that the topography favours India as all tracks currently being built by the PLA must traverse down to the Torsa Nala or around it, and then wind up to the Jampheri Ridge. This makes it tactically unsound to assault the ridge from that direction. This is a view that many officers who have served in the area concur with. Therefore, there is little chance of the PLA occupying the Jampheri Ridge.

Bakshi feels there is too much hype around the Doklam incident as well as the forward stationing of PLA troops in certain areas along the LAC. He dismisses it as window dressing because of the tremendous tactical advantage enjoyed by the Indian troops in this area. In fact, he sees the forward deployment by the PLA as a tacit admission by the Chinese of their vulnerability in view of India's growing military capabilities in those areas. Notwithstanding this, he says it is time for India to ramp up the use of technology and limited mechanized warfare assets – such as light tanks and BMPs that can be easily deployed at high altitudes – along with UAVs, air power and strategic road building.

The démarche issued by Bhutan to China in July to restore the 'status quo' by stopping the road building immediately gave the initiative to India and allowed it to occupy the moral high ground.[22] Calling the bluff on Chinese ambiguity, Bakshi argues that it may well have been a misadventure by a local military commander who did not expect a strong military response from India. This view is contested by several military analysts as being improbable considering the vicelike grip that Xi has established over the PLA. However, the assessment after the face-off commenced was that it was toned down after seeing the Indian reaction.[23] Reconciliatory talks between Modi and Xi at Wuhan were also criticized by some as being a climbdown, as the military response was not followed by robust deterrence. However, the episode clearly reveals that neither India nor China is ready to change the nature of deterrence along the LAC. Both nations are more concerned about the possibility of peace and tranquillity being shattered inadvertently by troops in contact – something which must be avoided at all costs.[24] It is India's turn to 'bide its time', as Deng had advised China to do in the 1980s.[25]

No War, No Peace

The 'Army Tour' sees groups of fifteen course participants from the National Security Programme conducted by the National Defence College (NDC) accompanied by a faculty member visiting an operational area. These include a corps zone near the LAC, the LoC, and the border with Pakistan in the Punjab, Rajasthan and Kutch Sectors. The purpose of the trip is to give the 100 participants, including 25 from friendly foreign countries, a perspective of the continuing large-scale deployment of the Indian Army along India's stressed borders and frontier areas. The trip is also an opportunity to showcase the enabling roles of the IAF and provide an insight into why India's armed forces are always on a high state of operational readiness through the year. On such trips, it is easy to understand the prevailing situation of 'no war, no peace' that prevails in J&K and the north-eastern states of Sikkim, Arunachal Pradesh, Nagaland and Manipur.

Dimapur – a bustling and crowded frontier town at the Nagaland-Assam border – serves as the headquarters of 3 Corps, the largest corps in the Indian Army. Its area of responsibility includes much of lower Assam, some parts of northern Assam, two-thirds of the state of Arunachal Pradesh, the 'hot' states of Nagaland and Manipur and the peaceful states of Mizoram and Tripura. The corps has multiple responsibilities, the largest of which in recent years is ensuring deterrence along the LAC with China. There are also the insurgencies, which span ethnicities and tribal complexities, ranging from the still-festering Naga problem to the violent Manipuri internecine conflict and the residual embers of the Assamese dissent. Lastly, the corps must maintain vigilance along the international borders even with friendly countries such as Myanmar and Bangladesh. This is because of the challenges of illegal immigration, human trafficking, drug running and more.

Located at the north-eastern edge of the corps zone is the Lohit Valley which lies close to the trijunction between India, China and Myanmar. The Tsangpo River in southern Tibet takes a sharp turn southwards and becomes the Brahmaputra in north-east Assam at the mouth of the Lohit Valley. The Lohit River is the easternmost of the tributaries of the Brahmaputra that flows down from the watershed between India and China. It is close to Parashuram Kund, a holy spot where warrior-ascetic Parashuram is believed to have performed penance in search of military prowess. North of the Lohit Valley is the area of a brigade belonging to 2 Infantry Division. Located here are the border outposts of Walong and Kibithoo, which saw fierce fighting during the 1962 war. The Battle of Walong remains one of the few bright spots for India in the otherwise dismal story of 1962. It is the sector where the Sikh and Kumaon Regiments supported by IAF Otters and Mi-4s launched counterattacks on the advancing Chinese. After suffering heavy casualties, the Chinese radioed to their headquarters that they had entered the 'tiger's lair'.[26]

From the northern part of the valley, one can clearly see the Chinese built-up areas through a gap in the ridgeline. The battalion commander from the Sikh Light Infantry who briefed the NDC group was confident and aware of his responsibilities in the sector. He was clear that 1962 would not be repeated and that should he be forced into fighting a defensive battle, he would do so from advantageously located and well-stocked positions that had fire support. 'I know how to fight my battle, and I will not wait for directions from brigade,' he said.

Transport aircraft and helicopters are important for sustaining operations in the region, as a convoy from the closest major railhead of Tinsukia or the airport at Dibrugarh would take at least three days to reach Kibithoo in good weather; it could take a week in inclement weather. There are two IAF Mi-17 squadrons at Mohanbari to serve the Lohit Valley. For larger loads, the brand-new advance landing ground at Walong can now receive the C-17 heavy-lift aircraft. There are seven advance landing grounds (ALGs) in Arunachal Pradesh – Mechuka, Tuting and Walong constitute the forward tier, while Itanagar, Ziro, Pasighat and Vijaynagar form the rear chain of connectivity to Myanmar and the adjoining states.[27]

The 132 HU at Air Force Station Chabua is a busy unit. Whenever there is clear weather in the Lohit Valley, helicopters are packed with multiple loads – rations, barrels of K-oil, a rare bag of mail and much more. According to the unit's flight commander, the Lohit Valley is one of the broader valleys and it is a surreal experience to appreciate the pristine beauty of the pine forests and green grazing grounds overlooking the gushing torrent of the Lohit River as one flies into Kibithoo. Once the briefing was completed on a sand model by the commander at Kibithoo overlooking the LAC, a wreath was laid at the war memorial. Having grabbed a handful of shakarpara (an indigenous energy snack that Indian soldiers love), and a glass of steaming chai, it was time to heed the urgent request of the captain of the Mi-17, who was anxiously looking at the approaching dark rain clouds, that it was time to head back.

As the group trooped into the helicopter an earnest-looking young Sikh soldier got into the chopper with the group. Shyly grinning, he sprang to attention and sought permission to take a lift to get to his hometown in Punjab in time for his wedding. He would be there two days ahead of schedule, he said, and wanted to surprise his fiancée. Such are the daily tales from the east. The enduring image as the rotor blades of the Mi-17 picked up speed was this group of officers led by the commanding officer waving out as if to say – tell them about us and more importantly, tell them not to worry!

Standing Firm

Deterrence by denial accompanied by diplomacy has for long been the Indian response to China-related national security challenges. However, there have been some expressions of proactive state resolve from India, such as at Nathu La, Sumdorong Chu, Depsang and Doklam. Since 1993, deterring China has been a work in progress. However, fear is no longer the primary driver of strategy formulation. A deeper analysis of some of India's decisions vis-à-vis China reveals an apprehension of the consequences, which is exactly what China seeks.[28] It also forces India to revisit some of its strategic aspirations and alter its decision-making process rather frequently. This does not reflect India's growing power as it must realize that Doklam-style incursions are low-cost Chinese strategies to coerce adversaries by staying below the thresholds of deterrence by punishment.

Deterrence by denial must include a clear communication of India's core security concerns and that disruption of the mutually accepted 'peace and tranquillity' along the LAC will exact a mutual cost unless a comprehensive political settlement is reached. More importantly, India's neighbourhood policy is the key to limit Chinese influence in South Asia through robust economic and military engagement. Concurrently, India must continue to enhance its strategy of deterrence by deepening the security dimension of its relationship with partners such as Vietnam, Japan, America, France and Australia. The last few decades have seen some convergence between diplomacy and hard power within India's strategic establishment, and one hopes that this will continue.

Ambiguity may have been the hallmark of Chinese strategy in the Deng Xiaoping and Hu Jintao era, but contemporary Chinese strategy is not just about Sun Tzu, Wei Chi or Confucius. Xi Jinping has shown that China has learnt from Russia and the West and is ready to take on the world in an overtly aggressive manner. India needs to demonstrate a consistent and robust policy of deterrence by denial; acquire dissuasive capability of varied kinds; and practise sophisticated diplomacy in its relationship with China. Given the adversarial and competitive profile of the India-China relationship, it is remarkable that despite the huge military build-up on both sides, not a shot has been fired across the LAC since 1967.

The Indian Army has almost five divisions deployed across the LAC in the eastern sector as the superb Chinese infrastructure on the Tibetan Plateau allows the PLA to speedily reinforce deployments in case of a potential conflict. In Ladakh, however, it has only recently beefed up its deployment on the LAC to almost a complete division strength including an armoured brigade.[29] The IAF enjoys significant advantage over the PLAAF when it comes to the number of bases, quality of platforms and aerial capabilities around Tibet, but the overwhelming superiority of the PLARF has the potential to neutralize this advantage in a first strike by the PLARF against IAF bases using a variety of SSMs. This vulnerability could prove decisive during the early stages of any future limited conflict.[30] The establishment of a mountain strike corps to launch offensives into the region has been put on hold by the Modi government. It is proposed instead to form leaner integrated battle groups from internal resources.

Both sides have engaged in posturing and periodic incursions, waiting and testing the other's patience. As per the unofficial Indian figures for 2013, Chinese troops have violated the LAC on over 200 occasions, while the Chinese claim a similar number of Indian troop incursions. Most of these remained unreported. A recent report from the Observer Research Foundation mentions only thirty reported incidents of incursions and face-offs from 2003 to 2014.[31] The absence of firefights means that these incursions remain on the periphery of national consciousness in both countries. While such face-offs have led to hectic diplomatic parleys and subsequent de-escalation, a few have involved protracted physical jostling that keep local commanders on tenterhooks. Ensuring that they do not lead to a firefight requires great restraint and professionalism from both sides.

RESOLUTION?

L.M.H. Ling is a professor of international affairs at The New School in New York City and offers an interesting perspective on the mood swings that afflict the security dimension of the India-China relationship. Identifying the four cyclical phases of the relationship, she lists them as 'dangerous mood swings, stunted growth, alienation and systemic neurosis'.[32] Suggesting a line of treatment that may seem strange to the military mind, she draws on the ancient Indian and Chinese therapies of Ayurveda and Zhongyi to suggest that a systemic transformation of the relationship through balance offers immense potential for reducing the trust deficit.[33] She argues that India and China need to evaluate their respective outlooks and move away from their inflexible and egoistic positions on the border dispute.

For India, a bipartisan political consensus is needed for revisiting the parliamentary resolution on regaining all lost territories. China would need to negotiate with India based on clear cartographic templates, and revive some of the quid pro quo proposals floated by Chou En-lai and Deng Xiaoping. These proposals broadly looked at formalizing a swap deal where India recognizes Aksai Chin as an integral part of Tibet in exchange for China accepting Arunachal Pradesh as an integral part of the Indian Union. Any deal would also have to look to stabilize the China-Bhutan boundary situation so that it does not pose a security threat to India. Once this is achieved, the demarcation, delineation and ratification of all disputed enclaves in all sectors can be achieved through a mutual spirit of give and take. China last showed geopolitical sagacity in 1960, when it formally delineated its boundary with Myanmar. It needs to do the same if it is serious about demilitarizing 4,000 km of its shared boundaries with India and Bhutan.

In 2003, an unambiguously worded media release from the Ministry of External Affairs put the entire boundary question in perspective, stating that the 1962 Parliament resolution on regaining every square inch of the 'lost' territory from China was no longer relevant. The statement went on to say: 'Parliaments are sovereign bodies and reflect the political sense of the times, rather than a mere commitment to past resolutions. Any final settlement of the boundary dispute with China will have to be based on a broad agreement within the Indian political class. As negotiations move forward, the cries of "sell-out" will be heard with greater vehemence than ever before.' However, it acknowledges that 'persuading the Indian public to accept a recasting of the Indian territorial map that many generations have grown up with is not going to be easy' and warns that 'while the new Chinese leadership appears amenable to a productive political dialogue, India should be fully prepared for the unexpected'.[34] Whether a post-Covid-19 world will offer some scope for a negotiated settlement or result in opportunistic aggression by the PLA along the LAC is anybody's guess. India will have to tread cautiously.

21

THE GAP CRISIS

Face-off in Eastern Ladakh

The ongoing face-off with China in Eastern Ladakh in the areas of the Depsang Plains, Galwan Valley and along the Pangong Tso Lake (named as the GAP crisis by the author), which commenced on 5 May 2020, continues to occupy significant strategic space as both India and China attempt to negotiate a face-saving settlement to the crisis. The escalatory trajectory of the face-off that involved over 300 troops from both sides and resulted in violent clashes between Indian troops of 16 BIHAR and regular PLA troops in the Galwan Valley on the night of 15 June 2020 is cause for serious concern. These were preceded by several minor scuffles and clashes at several points along the LAC, prominent being the ones at Pangong Tso on 5-6 May and on 9 May at Naku La.

The last firefight between India and China took place in November 1975 when a patrol of the Assam Rifles was ambushed by PLA Border Guards in Tulung La in Kameng Sector of Arunachal Pradesh and four Indian troops were killed.[1] However, the two countries have never been closer to a major localized firefight after the clashes at Nathu La and Chola in 1967 than they are now, even after a partial disengagement that commenced in February 2021, almost six months after India responded to the Chinese aggression by seizing strategic heights on the northern and southern banks of the Pamgang Tso. It is therefore appropriate to ponder on the causes and consequences of the current face-off, which is more complex than any of the previous ones that have been highlighted in Chapter 20.

Preliminary analyses point at a growing Chinese irritation with India's change in status quo with respect to the configuration of the erstwhile state

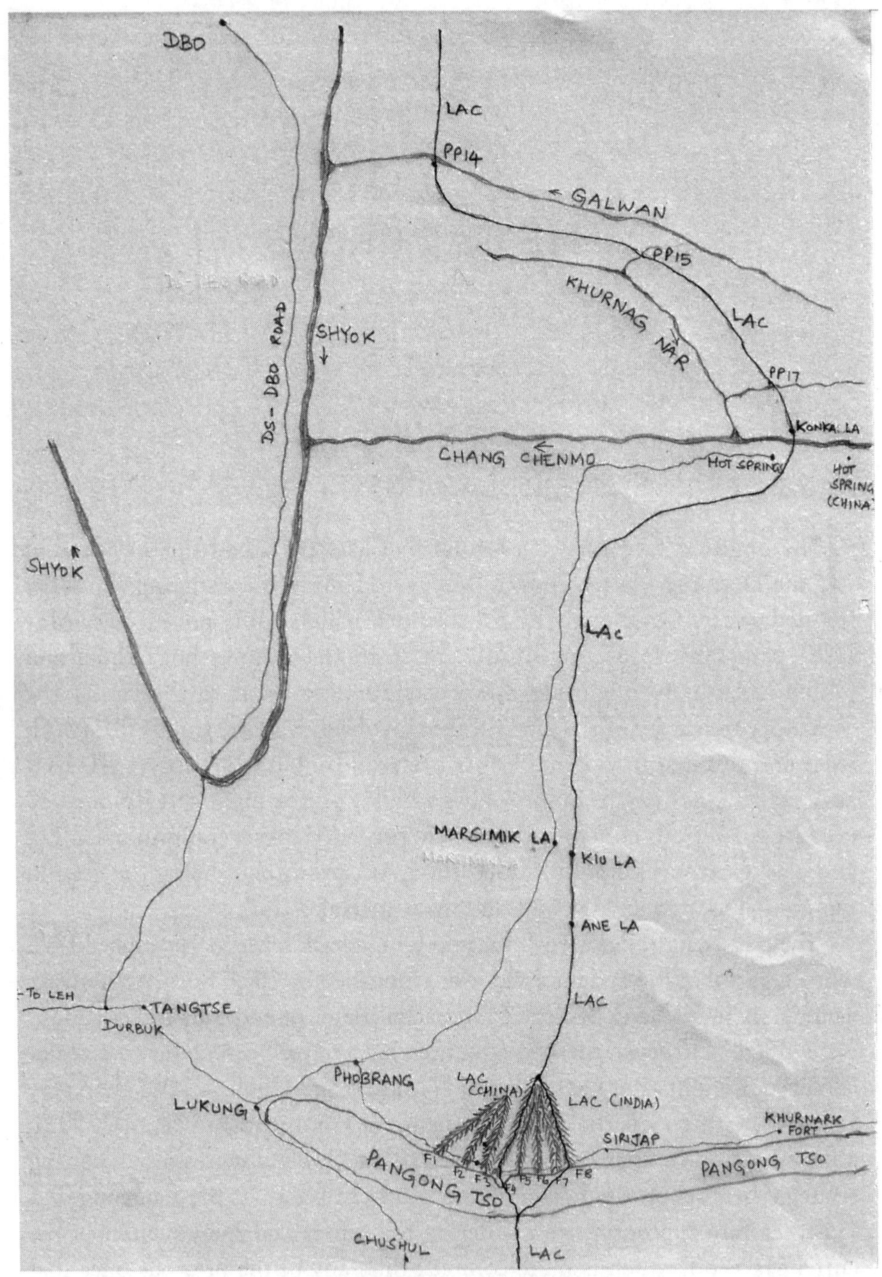

Sketch of the GAP crisis area by Colonel S. Dinny (retired), not to scale. This sketch is for representational purposes only and does not purport to depict political boundaries.

of Jammu and Kashmir – specifically, the creation of Ladakh as a separate Union Territory. The other trigger is said to be the imminent completion of the Darbuk–Shyok–Daulat Beg Oldie road fifteen years after its construction commenced. The road significantly adds on to the defensive potential of the Sub-Sector North in Eastern Ladakh, and reduces China's traditional operational advantage in that area. Consequent to these perceived threatening moves by India, China, which has historically been obsessed with stability on its periphery to the point of paranoia, is now worried about the security of the segment of its ambitious Belt Road Initiative (BRI) that runs close to the LAC. Using this as sufficient reason to change the operational narrative in areas close to the LAC where it started feeling threatened, the PLA commenced its current operation. The Galwan Valley and the Gogra Post area of the Hot Springs Sector are two such areas that were given special attention by the Chinese during the current set of face-offs. The PLA has also significantly increased its presence and fortifications in the disputed areas of the LAC where there are significant differences in the Indian and Chinese perceptions of where the LAC runs, particularly along the Pangong Tso Lake (Finger 4 to Finger 8). Speculative and uncorroborated transgression by the PLA across their own claim lines have also been reported in the strategically important Depsang Plains, close to the Indian ALG of DBO.[2]

How one views these transgressions depends on how both countries assess the physical lie of the un-demarcated LAC and the status and ownership of the disputed areas where both sides sent in patrols over the years but refrained from establishing a permanent presence. The difference between earlier and now is that by setting up camps and semi-permanent structures close to/across the Chinese claim lines, the PLA has violated established border protocols and attempted to change status quo. By doing so it has directly threatened the sanctity of the LAC and India's territorial sovereignty. In an operational strategy that has succeeded both in rattling and provoking the Indians, but not to the point of accepting the change, any outcome that results in skirmishes or a limited conflict is not favourable for Beijing as it would lead to significant casualties and a loss of face for Xi Jinping. Western assessments of the crisis have been measured but critical of China for its disproportionate response and paranoia over the recent constitutional changes involving Jammu and Kashmir. However, they have also been critical of India's response mechanisms and having to face the difficult challenge of restoring status quo in a highly asymmetric operational environment.[3]

Both Indian and Chinese forces suffered grievous casualties after the Galwan encounter that was spread across the night of 15 June 2020 and more resembled a savage medieval fight with clubs, sticks and metal rods than a twenty-first-century firefight with precision weapons. It is estimated that the total casualties on both sides (killed and injured) could be over 100, including two commanding officers, one from both sides. Colonel Santosh Babu, the Commanding Officer of 16 BIHAR, led from the front as he first attempted to convince the PLA troops to dismantle an observation post on the Indian side of the LAC. When they refused, he ordered the post to be demolished. Ambushed on the way back and killed in action, the infuriated Bihari troops, led by other officers and assisted by troops from the Punjab Regiment and an artillery regiment, mounted a spirited revenge operation for over two hours that resulted in most of the deaths. The icy Galwan River proved to be unforgiving and deadly as several Indian and Chinese soldiers tumbled off steep ledges in hand-to-hand combat into the freezing waters.[4]

Pointedly, the last time the PLA suffered large casualties was during the war against Vietnam in 1979. The Indian Army, on the other hand, has continuously suffered casualties in a variety of duels across the LoC and the Saltoro Ridge; during Operation Pawan in Sri Lanka; and during CI/CT operations in J&K and the northeast. While this is nothing to be proud of, it offers insights into the ability of both the belligerents to absorb the psychological impact of battle casualties. This is something that surely would be playing on the minds of PLA commanders as they evaluate various options. While military commanders search for ways to initiate a disengagement and de-escalation, the international community will hope for a political settlement led by none other than Prime Minister Modi and President Xi Jinping. At worst, India and China may well be heading for a limited conflict wherein the exchange ratios in every domain could puncture the carefully manicured Chinese narrative of military modernization. For the Indians, it could derail the fragile economy and slow down the charge to leading power status. Assessing the impact of the clashes, Brahma Chellaney, a professed China hawk and among the few who has been a consistent critic of India's China policy irrespective of the government in power, argues on his Twitter handle that while the clashes at Pangong Tso and Nakula were a 'draw', the outcome of the Galwan clash was a 'humiliation for China'.[5]

Despite marathon meetings between senior military commanders on both sides through the summer and announcements of a disengagement, the PLA continued to build up its forces all the way up to the northern extent of the LAC that is marked by the Depsang Plains in the area around Daulat Beg Oldie. While significant withdrawals from several locations were announced by the Chinese foreign ministry spokesperson Wang Wenbin,[6] tens of thousands of troops with artillery and tanks were amassed by the PLA, seemingly for a major operation before the winter set in. The Indian Army and the Indian Air Force responded in strength, beefing up offensive capability, including the induction of heavy armour at multiple locations.

By early June 2020, flying activity by both the IAF and the PLAAF had increased exponentially and reports indicated that the airfield of Hotan in Southern Xinjiang saw the deployment of large numbers of J-7, J-11 fighter aircraft along with other supporting platforms.[7] Similarly, flying operations in Ladakh by the IAF saw an exponential increase, with both fighters (newly inducted Rafales, Mirage-2000s, Su-30 MKIs, MiG-29s) and helicopters (Apaches and Chinooks) going through complicated operational drills and acclimatization. Though several strategic commentators have pointed out gaps in intelligence gathering and assessments prior to the crisis,[8] it is too early to evaluate this based on speculative assessments. Tara Kartha, a former Director in the National Security Council Secretariat, mounted a spirited defence of the intelligence process with respect to the strategic and operational intelligence gathering prior to the crisis.[9] Whatever be the facts, these face-offs must be followed by serious introspection and bolstering the combined intelligence gathering process along the LAC if the ghosts of 1962 and Kargil are not to appear again.

As the winter season of 2020 approached, India's strategic establishment brainstormed on possible response strategies even as the Indian military continued to demonstrate its capability to reassure its citizens that it was ready to meet any contingency posed by the Chinese. There was, however, a realization that the situation was not likely to result in a return to the pre-May 2020 status quo until this capability was exercised in a show of coercive intent. What this meant in real terms was quite simply that a smaller and weaker India would have to consider harder options, including a threat of the use of force, for the Chinese to return to the pre-May disposition. Options to launch combined assaults on selected positions that seriously threaten Indian sovereignty to cause attrition with surprise and firepower were considered even though such actions ran the risk of escalation. Other options included a more calibrated and nuanced application of combat power, with Special Forces seizing high ground that could be used to negotiate with the Chinese after a display of intent, initiative and coercion. There was much speculation and debate on whether India had finally reconciled to the reality that the language of power and coercive posturing was the only strategic language that the current Chinese dispensation would take seriously.[10] If that was so, did it have the stomach for escalation?

For those in India who advocated a tough response, it meant reversing a DNA of diffidence and reactiveness that India has been comfortable with for decades except on three occasions: the Nathu La skirmish, the occupation of the Saltoro Ridge and the envelopment of the PLA positions in the Sumdorong Chu Valley. Notwithstanding all talks of economic posturing, there is a widespread acceptance that India may not have the economic muscle or diplomatic heft to reverse the negative fall-out of the GAP crisis. As the face-off approached September 2020, the two sides realized that a series of localized skirmishes along the LAC could be costly for both nations and that a limited conflict would always be the last option.

Two concurrent intellectual articulations in the media necessitated some deep introspection within India's strategic community, particularly the politico-diplomatic-military-intelligence structures. The first was a piece by Chris Buckley in the *New York Times* titled 'Clean Up This Mess: The Chinese Thinkers Behind Xi's Hard Line'. Quoting a frontline Chinese scholar, Tian Feilong, who primarily addressed Western liberal constituencies, the article quoted him as arguing: 'Back when I was weak, I had to totally play by your rules. Now I am strong and I have the confidence, so why can't I lay down my own rules and values and ideas?' Several such views have emerged over the last few years from a group of uncompromisingly anti-liberal and pro-authoritarian Chinese intellectuals who have been termed as 'statists'. Essentially, Tiang is only invoking an old Thucydidian principle called the Melian Dialogue, which emerged during the Peloponnesian War prior to the siege of the island of Melios by Athens, that says: 'The strong will do what they can and the weak suffer what they must.'

The second articulation was by none other than India's foreign minister, Dr S. Jaishankar. In a statement made during an interview with the *Times of India*, he argued, 'Reaching an equilibrium with China is not going to be easy. We will be tested and we must stand our ground.'[11] He also asserted that the state of the border and the future of bilateral ties cannot be separated. India at last may slowly be realizing at its own elephantine pace the sub-optimal outcomes accrued so far from its existing China policy. Coming as it did when the current crisis in Ladakh entered its fourth month, it offered some pointers that India may finally be coming to grips with a possible fait accompli and a new status quo that the Chinese are likely to offer it. Will it be a case of the Melian Dialogue playing all over again, or is it time for India to emerge out of the cocoon of a post-independence strategic culture and DNA?

India's Strong Response

Resisting strident calls from diverse domestic constituencies to respond immediately to PLA provocations, the Indian Army, supported by the Indian

Air Force, steadily built up its forces in Eastern Ladakh during July and August to over two divisions. Sensing the futility of talks from a disadvantageous strategic position, the Indian government nevertheless continued to engage the Chinese in regular corps commander-level talks, with five rounds being held between mid-June and mid-August 2020. Concurrently weighing several coercive options within a carefully calibrated escalatory framework, the Indian Army, ably supported by the Indian Air Force, gradually created an operational mosaic in Eastern Ladakh that would cover the entire spectrum of retaliatory responses that the PLA could offer in case India decided to launch a retaliatory operation.[12]

As mentioned earlier, flying activity by both the IAF and the PLAAF increased through August, and reports indicated that the Hotan airfield had seen the deployment of large numbers of J-7 and J-11 fighter aircraft, along with other supporting platforms. Similarly, IAF operations in Ladakh increased exponentially in an area that had been a no-go for several decades, owing to the ongoing confidence-building measures that restricted air activity on both sides. Fighters and helicopters underwent complicated operational and acclimatization drills, with senior IAF commanders relishing the opportunity to train maximum crews in multiple roles in terrain that was largely unfamiliar.[13]

In a deliberate, stealthy and well-planned operation, the Indian Army moved to occupy several tactical heights on the northern and southern banks of Pangong Tso on the night of 29-30 August. Of strategic importance were the heights on the Kailash Range on the South Bank that overlooked the Moldo Garrison of the PLA and included Rezang La and Requin La, which had seen much action in the 1962 conflict. Executed by a mix of specialized units made up of Special Forces from the elite Establishment 22 and well-acclimatized regular troops from several battalions, the operation, code-named Snow Leopard, rattled the PLA and offered the Indians adequate manoeuvre space to negotiate disengagement and de-escalation. Apart from surprising the PLA, the action demonstrated that India was prepared to respond to Chinese aggression at a time and place of its own choosing.

India's Chief of Defence Staff, General Bipin Rawat, attributed the success of Operation Snow Leopard to the deliberate planning and systematic build-up of the Indian Army and the IAF. Commending the calm and resolute approach of the army chief, General M.M. Naravane, who firmly resisted any call for an immediate riposte without having the wherewithal to cope with an escalation, he was surprisingly candid in a conversation with the author when he confessed that he was among those who had pushed for an early action.[14] When asked to comment on the impact of Operation Snow Leopard in mid-

September, General Naravane was measured and circumspect when he offered that it was too early to assess the impact, and rightly so.[15] It would take another five months through a tough winter and four more rounds of talks for the PLA to realize that the Indian Army would continue to hold fast on the strategic heights. Consequently, the first signs of a thaw emerged after the ninth round of talks, where it was agreed that Phase-1 of the disengagement would involve a pull-back from both sides along the Pangong Tso, with China withdrawing to the east of Finger 8 and India pulling back to Finger 3.[16]

It is still too early to assess the long-term impact of this exercise. Getting the Chinese to withdraw from the other areas they have transgressed into is going to be even more difficult as Gogra, Hot Springs and the Depsang Plains offer greater visibility and proximity to the Darbuk–Shyok–DBO highway, the construction of which seems to irk the Chinese. As the summer of 2021 approached, there still existed several 'hot spots'. While India must build on the intent it had displayed, it must be prepared for further PLA aggression in sectors where it enjoys tactical advantages, particularly in Eastern Arunachal Pradesh. Commenting on events post the partial disengagement, Ashley Tellis called the 'Indian handling of China and its determined resistance and refusal to capitulate a lesson to the world'. But he also cautioned that this showed the 'Chinese ability to move back and forth and risk the use of force'.[17]

Diffident or Restrained

India's preference over the years for reactive and overly restrained response strategies against belligerent adversaries can be perplexing to some. When Generals Sundarji, Narahari and J.M. Singh suggested in 1987 that a limited offensive by a well-prepared Indian Army supported by the IAF could result in limited gains across the LAC in the Tawang Sector, New Delhi would have none of it. It is easy to understand why India has been circumspect and wary of China given the growing power differential, particularly on the Tibetan plateau and in the maritime domain. Its unwillingness to follow through with sustained punitive action in response to Pakistan's repeated provocations on multiple sub-conventional fronts has also been frustrating. Several times over the troubled 1980s and 1990s and during the first decade of this century, India's political establishment has contemplated embarking on what Jonathan Renshon terms a 'preventive war' against Pakistan. It is believed to have considered pre-emptive aerial strikes against Pakistan's nuclear facilities in the early 1980s. Largescale attacks in multiple sectors to counter Pakistan's support for the proxy war in J&K in the late 1980s and early 1990s were also considered, as were aerial strikes on Pakistani targets across the LoC during the

Kargil conflict. Offensives in J&K and massive armoured attacks in the Desert Sector accompanied by airstrikes were debated during Operation Parakram in the aftermath of the 2001 Parliament attack.

In his book *Why Leaders Choose War*, Renshon, an American political scientist, suggests that among Britain, France, the US, Israel and India, it is only India that does not subscribe to the idea of preventive war as a solution to actual or perceived security threats.[18] His views draw attention to the larger question of whether India has been diffident or wise when it comes to 'waging war' in modern times. His list of preventive war factors[19] broadly looks at a declining power differential, sustained hostility and rigidity of thought that lead to conflict and the windows of opportunity to engage in preventive military action. He has mainly used the India–Pakistan template to prove his hypothesis and identified India as a country that has not resorted to preventive military action despite all supporting factors.

However, between 1982 and 2002, India did in fact undertake two significant military actions that could be characterized as preventive limited military action. The first was the swift occupation of the Saltoro Ridge in April 1984 – this action was both preventive and pre-emptive as the Pakistanis were a few days away from doing so themselves. The second was the IPKF intervention in Sri Lanka in 1987. While the primary aim in the latter was to broker peace between the LTTE and the Sri Lankan government, Rajiv Gandhi and his strategic advisory team also perceived this as an opportunity to cement India's strategic position along its southern flank and prevent the entry of external players. Though Operation Pawan was an operational failure, it did send a message to the rest of the world that India would not hesitate to engage in limited preventive military action to further its national interests. Operation Pawan infused an element of circumspection within India's strategic establishment about the effectiveness of pre-emptive and preventive military action in a nuclear neighbourhood –particularly against Pakistan, which was inclined to indulge in brinkmanship after the heady success of the ISI in Afghanistan.

Like several liberal democracies, India has struggled to cope with the changing character of war in the twenty-first century. It slowly understood the complexities of hybrid warfare and its effectiveness when the situation in J&K remained volatile despite the overwhelming presence of the Indian Army. India has been more successful than many Western countries in combating radical and extremist Islam but has failed to capitalize on this success because of poor governance in border states such as J&K.

Do the punitive Indian strikes of 2016 and 2019 following the Uri and Pulwama attacks by the JeM indicate a shift in deterrence and security strategies? Have the fierce clashes at the Galwan Valley and the subsequent action by the Indian Army with strong IAF presence in Eastern Ladakh demonstrated that there will be a new normal along the hitherto stressed but relatively peaceful LAC? Have these occurrences lowered India's threshold for considering punitive action as a regular response to security provocations, not only against Pakistan, but against an increasingly aggressive China? No immediate answers are available as India searches for an equilibrium in its rise as a power of consequence. As much as its economic and demographic potential have contributed to this rise, its resolute, responsible and restrained use of force as an instrument of statecraft has also played an equally important role. Political probabilities and aims have generally determined military outcomes – such as the timing of the cessation of the Kargil conflict, or the withdrawal of the IPKF from Sri Lanka. These decisions may not have always gone down well with the military leadership, but have generally been consistent with the rather sceptical attitude of India's postcolonial political establishment towards the use of force.

Fractured civil–military relations and the lack of political interest in military strategy have resulted in a lack of congruence between policy, strategy and doctrine in the areas of national security and the study of war and conflict. The need for wide-ranging reform and remedial measures within the Indian military has often been articulated in recent times by Prime Minister Modi, but there has been lack of political continuity in the MoD to ensure a top-down approach to military reform. The appointment of a Chief of Defence Staff by the government and the impending restructuring of the military can only be steps in the right direction. The 'whole of government approach' in tackling the crisis in Eastern Ladakh offers hope for the future, should the government be firm in its assessment that national security and development in a fractured world are like conjoined twins.

Recalibrating its relationships with its adversaries can help India define the extent to which it is willing to be pushed by them. There is a growing willingness by India to move from reactive to proactive deterrence, but it is too early to assess whether it will be possible for India to walk the talk given the capability deficit that exists across the national security architecture. 'Willing and capable' is a phrase that is commonly used in contemporary strategic debates. 'Willing' implies intent, resolve and a risk-taking propensity, while 'capable' signifies the state's capacity to employ all elements of statecraft from a focused national security perspective to deter an irrational adversary. Is India emerging as a 'willing and capable' state with respect to security challenges?

Reflecting on the OODA Loop

Among the most important elements of warfighting in the contemporary world of unstructured warfare is the Observe, Orient, Decide and Act (OODA) Loop.[20] So pervasive has its impact been that it is now discussed not only in war studies courses and military operational rooms across the world, but also in corporate boardrooms as part of business strategy. The OODA Loop emerged as a key operational concept in modern warfare in the early 1980s, thanks to a maverick United States Air Force fighter pilot, Colonel John Boyd. Boyd argued that split-second decision-making during air combat was dependent on four main sensory actions that he attractively packaged as the OODA Loop.

Thus, a pilot who managed to observe the enemy first and analyse the combat environment in all its complexity – either with the help of a radar or with his eyes and orientated himself in time and space quicker than an adversary – gained a few seconds over the enemy to decide how to act. This lead of a few seconds invariably resulted in an action that marked the difference between victory and defeat, or even life and death. Boyd argued that the OODA Loop could be made shorter by complementing human ingenuity and reflexes with training and rapid advances in technology. He also suggested that organizational lethargy and lack of imagination could slow down the loop and allow nimble adversaries to seize the advantage. The OODA Loop has turned modern warfare on its head and offered a level playing field to decision makers across the spectrum of conflict to operate inside each other's loops and gain disproportionate advantages. A point to ponder over is whether over the past few decades both China's and Pakistan's Deep State, India's principal military adversaries, have managed to operate within the OODA cycle of the Indian strategic establishment.

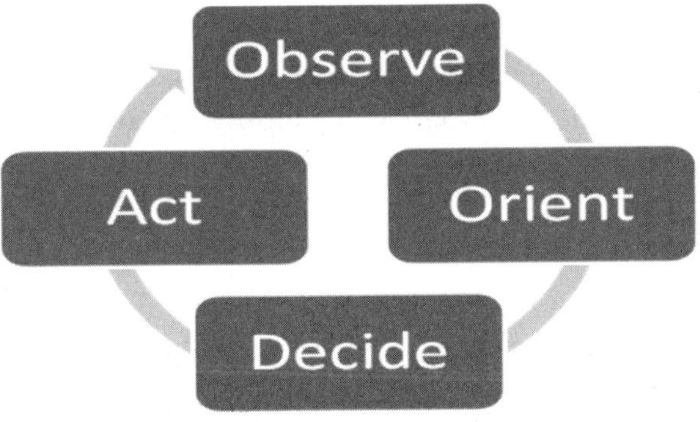

OODA LOOP OF MILITARY DECISION MAKING[21]

FINAL THOUGHTS

The disruptive impact of the Covid-19 pandemic is likely to seriously impede capability building in the Indian military over the next five years, and the maxim of 'do more with less' and 'manage all the emergent crises' may well be the clarion call from the political establishment. This may also force India to adopt a cautious 'wait and watch strategy' against belligerent adversaries, rather than make the transition to more proactive and preventive strategies that seemed to be emerging after the cross-border strikes of 2016 and the Balakot strike of 2019. The speed of change in the regional security environment has forced India's security establishment to change its orientation from one that anticipated fewer instances of traditional conflict across the spectrum in the next few years to a sudden possibility of full spectrum conflict across multiple fronts. The Indian military will have to find the ways and means of keeping the traditional sharp end of the sword ready to be wielded whenever called upon to do so in less-than-war, limited conflict and full spectrum contingencies in all three domains. Least expected, however, is the reality that this capability could be called into action sooner than later in the wake of the ongoing border crisis with China. Concurrently, it will need to build intellectual capital, evolve strategies and train to cope with the new ways of war. Domains as dispersed as space, cyber, social media, internal security and military diplomacy will no longer be considered peripheral as India's military must remain a critical instrument of statecraft as it continues its march towards becoming a leading power.

Postscript: It was difficult to strike a balance between seeking the truth and telling a credible story within the parameters of the Official Secrets Act. Some will argue that there is far too much advocacy in the book. However, the advocacy has been accompanied by the right amount of introspection, respect, transparency and criticism, which hopefully makes for a balanced piece of work. If you have reached this far, thank you for reading and understanding India's armed forces. *India's Wars II* has been written as a book for a wide readership. If it achieves that aim, I will consider it a mission accomplished.

22

ESSENTIAL READING

'That men do not learn very much from the lessons of history is the most important of all the lessons that history has to teach.'

– Aldous Huxley

While this volume completes a detailed examination of contemporary Indian military history, it merely scratches the surface of what has been a fascinating period of modern Indian history. The post-1972 period has also seen an increased involvement of India's strategic community with the world at large. Consequently, there has been much good writing by western scholars on various facets of the Indian armed forces, its adversaries, and the complex security environment in South Asia. It is only right therefore to complement this book with several others to arrive at a holistic assessment of war and conflict in independent India and its impact on the growth of the Indian state, the development and sustenance of its democracy, and the armed forces' role in India's emergence as a leading power.

Backgrounders

Srinath Raghavan's *1971: A Global History of the Creation of Bangladesh* and the author's first book, *India's Wars I: A Military History, 1947-1971*, offer a multi-disciplinary introduction to politics, diplomacy, war and conflict in independent India. Of all the books by western authors on capability development in the Indian military in recent decades, none is better than the slim volume by Stephen Cohen and Sunil Dasgupta, *Arming without Aiming: India's Military Modernization.* K. Subrahmanyam is the doyen of contemporary Indian strategic thinking and *Shedding Shibboleths: India's Evolving Strategic Outlook* is a collection of essays on national security that offer a strategic framework to track the trajectory of the growth of Indian hard power.

The existing literature on the changing character of war is vast and suggesting a few books to understand the complexities of contemporary warfare was a daunting task. David Kilcullen's *Accidental Guerrilla*, John Nagl's *Learning to Eat Soup with a Knife: Counterinsurgency Lessons from Malaya and Vietnam*, Colonel Thomas X. Hammes's *The Sling and the Stone: On War in the 21st Century* and Hew Strachan's *Direction of War: Contemporary Strategy in Historical Perspective* offer good Western perspectives. Rajesh Rajagopalan's *Fighting Like a Guerrilla: The Indian Army and Counterinsurgency* and Lieutenant General Nanavatty's *Internal Armed Conflict in India* are among the few Indian offerings to address the conceptual and theoretical aspects of the complexities of modern conflict from an Indian perspective.

Naga and Mizo Insurgencies

Among the early books written in India on the Naga insurgency, four merit a revisit. Y.S. Gundevia's *War and Peace in Nagaland* offers an excellent overview of the origin of the Naga people, their tribal diversity and distribution and the reasons for their alienation from the fledgling Indian state soon after independence. D.R. Mankekar's *On the Slippery Slope in Nagaland* is a mainstream Indian journalist's outsider view of the secessionist flavour of the Naga revolt. Colonel R.D. Palsokar's *Forever in Operations* is a detailed operational account of 8 Mountain Division which saw extensive operations in Nagaland from the early 1960s to the late 1980s. Along with Major General Palit's *The Sentinels of the North-East,* they remain the best offerings on the early years of counterinsurgency operations in Nagaland.

Nirmal Nibedon's *Night of the Guerrillas* and Sanjoy Hazarika's *Strangers in the Mist: Tales of War and Peace from India's Northeast* offer local perspectives of the Naga and Mizo rebellions that are distinctly anti-New Delhi, sympathetic to the insurgents' cause, but highly relevant to understanding ground realities. Hazarika's *Strangers No More,* published nearly two decades after his first book is a scathing indictment of New Delhi's approach to conflict resolution in Nagaland and is critical of the security forces. The solitary civilian scholarly perspective on the Mizo insurgency comes from the Mizo scholar-turned-politician Dr R.V. Hluna and his daughter, Rini Tochwang. It is titled *The Mizo Uprising: Assam Assembly Debates on the Mizo Movement, 1966-1971.* Colonel Vivek Chadha, an Indian Army scholar, offers a nuanced assessment of the army's successful counterinsurgency campaign in Chapter Two of an edited volume by Sumit Ganguly and David P. Fidler, *India and Counterinsurgency: Lessons Learned.*

Operation Blue Star and the Insurgency in Punjab

The military dimension of the operation to storm the Golden Temple in Amritsar has been succinctly described by Lieutenant General Brar, the commander of the division that was tasked to storm the temple. *Operation Blue Star: A True Story* is a searing account from a Sikh general who did his duty in what was a thankless military mission arising from a wrong politico-military decision. Mark Tully and Satish Jacob have written an almost immediate account of the operation from their recollections of on-the-ground reporting. *Amritsar: Mrs Gandhi's Last Stand* is a balanced narrative that offers deep glimpses into the murky politics of the time and the circumstances that led to a wrong strategic decision by Prime Minister Indira Gandhi. A deeply hurt Sikh perspective of the entire operation comes from Harminder Kaur in her book *Blue Star over Amritsar.* Operation Blue Star exacerbated Sikh angst and the insurgency in Punjab escalated to dangerous proportions before it was defeated in the early 1990s. Ved Marwah's *Uncivil Wars: Pathology of Terrorism in India* and a volume edited by K.P.S. Gill, *Terror Containment: Perspectives on Internal Security,* are offerings from accomplished police officers who played an important role in stamping out terrorism in Punjab.

Siachen Operations

With no periodic declassification of operational details from either India or Pakistan, there is little academic writing on the nearly four decades of operations on the glacier. However, the closest is a book by a former divisional commander of the area, Lieutenant General V.R. Raghavan. His book, *Siachen: Conflict Without End,* offers an excellent Indian perspective on the geostrategic dimension of the conflict. There is no matching analysis from Pakistan though General Pervez Musharraf offers glimpses into his personal experiences on the glacier in his autobiography, *In the Line of Fire.* Nitin Gokhale's racy account of how the Indian Army first occupied the Saltoro Ridge, *Beyond NJ 9842: The Siachen Saga,* is an accurate journalistic and easy-to-read narrative that is based on several visits to the glacier and interviews with officers who have extensive operational experience on the glacier. Despite all the early setbacks and the inability to displace the Indians from the vantage heights, the Pakistan Army was the first to support the writing of a book on the Siachen operations. Lieutenant Colonel Syed Ashfaq Ali's *Fangs of Ice* is a jingoistic account of the Pakistan Army's exploits on the glacier during the peak years of fighting (1984-91).

IPKF in Sri Lanka and Operation Cactus

Two academically robust books that have several chapters on the IPKF operations in Sri Lanka are Channa Wickremesekara's *The Tamil Separatist War in Sri Lanka* and Rajesh Rajagopalan's *Fighting Like a Guerrilla: The Indian Army and Counterinsurgency*. Of all the accounts of Operation Pawan by generals from the Indian Army, only *Assignment Jaffna* by Lieutenant General S.C. Sardeshpande meets the criterion of an honestly objective account of the operation. *Assignment Colombo* by J.N. Dixit, the Indian high commissioner in Colombo during the crisis, is an erudite exposition of the diplomatic and geostrategic happenings during the run-up and postscript to Operation Pawan. Though the narrative is highly personalized and self-adulatory, it offers the best 'big picture' of the time. Rohan Gunaratna's brilliantly researched but biased account of the role of India's intelligence agencies in the ethnic conflict in Sri Lanka, *Indian Intervention in Sri Lanka: The Role of India's Intelligence Agencies*, is a Sri Lankan perspective that must be read. Finally, General V.P. Malik offers a crisp analysis of both Operation Pawan and Operation Cactus from a vantage position of being involved with the planning of both operations in his book *India's Military Conflicts and Diplomacy*.

Terrorism and the Covert War in J&K

Much essential reading on the India-Pakistan conflicts of 1947, 1965 and 1971 is available in *India's Wars I: A Military History, 1947-1971*. It is considered that the book offers a good take-off point to navigate the complex covert, proxy and hybrid war that has emerged in J&K since. Two books from that list merit attention. The first is Major General Akbar Khan's *Raiders in Kashmir* and the second is Sumit Ganguly's *Origins of War in South Asia: Indo-Pak Wars since 1947*. They offer a Pakistani and an Indian perspective of the early years of the covert war. A more recent book by Sumit Ganguly, *Deadly Impasse: Indo-Pakistan Relations at the Dawn of a New Century* is an excellent follow-on reading of the ongoing proxy and hybrid war in J&K. By far the most rigorous academic examination of the growth of the Kashmir insurgency, its morphing into a covert war aided and abetted by the Pakistan Deep State as an asymmetric counter to India's growing military superiority, is Praveen Swami's *India-Pakistan and the Secret Jihad*. Selected chapters from Christine Fair's in-depth and commendably researched books, *Fighting to the End: The Pakistan Army's Way of War* and *In their Own Words: Understanding Lashkar-*

e-Tayyaba, offer deep insights into the obsession of the Pakistan Army with Kashmir as the prize to get even with India over several military defeats, and an understanding of India's principal Jihadi adversary, the LeT. At a peripheral level, Hussain Haqqani's book, *Between Mosque and Military*, offers a pragmatic Pakistani perspective on the use of terrorism and jihad as an instrument of the Pakistani Deep State to weaken India.

Kargil

General V.P. Malik's *Kargil: From Surprise to Victory* is a comprehensive personal account through the lens of India's army chief during the conflict. Detailed and reflective, it is more a 'setting the record straight' kind of a narrative. It is, nevertheless, an essential read. Nasim Zehra's *From Kargil to the Coup* – a very recent account of the conflict from a Pakistani perspective – is a rather balanced narrative of the conflict, the military coup that unseated Prime Minister Nawaz Sharif from power, and the ensuing political turbulence in Pakistan during Musharraf's tenure as President of Pakistan. By far the best edited volume on Kargil that offers a wide-angle Western perspective on the Kargil conflict is an edited volume by Peter Lavoy, *Asymmetric Warfare in South Asia.* It has contributions from a wide range of experts and academics from the US, India and Pakistan and is the most academically robust offering on Kargil. The last book is the declassified version of the official Indian strategic and operational critique of the Kargil conflict. Put together by a committee of experts headed by the doyen of Indian strategic discourse K. Subrahmanyam and titled *Kargil Review Committee Report,* it is a repository of accurate information that is essential for any focussed study of the conflict.

Operations Other than War

Although the skirmishes, face-offs, encounters and less-than-war situations that have occurred on the LoC and LAC with Pakistan and China have been reported on extensively in the Indian and Western media, there is little declassification of such operations other than media briefings. Consequently, much of the writing is interpretive and speculative. Ravi Rikhye's *The War that Never Was* is the only Indian book that offers a reasonable analysis of Exercise Brasstacks, while Lieutenant General V.K. Sood and Pravin Sawhney's *Operation Parakram: The War Unfinished* is a well-written account of the causes and consequences of India's massive military mobilization that fell well short of the impact it was expected to have on Pakistan.

Four Crises and a Peace Process, written collaboratively by P.R. Chari, Pervaiz Iqbal Cheema and Stephen Cohen, is an attempt to balance US, Indian and

Pakistani perspectives on the several crises that have erupted involving India and Pakistan under the overhang of a charged nuclear environment. When complemented with Strobe Talbott's eminently readable *Engaging India: Diplomacy, Democracy and the Bomb* and Bruce Riedel's *Avoiding Armageddon: America, India and Pakistan to the Brink and Back*, readers will get a holistic overview of how the West views the continuing military tension between India and Pakistan. Completing the list is a recent book by Happymon Jacob, *Line on Fire: Ceasefire Violations and India-Pakistan Escalation Dynamics*, which offers an academically rigorous quantitative look at the continuing ceasefire violations by both countries along the volatile LoC.

The continued stress along the LAC with China since the 1962 war is very opaque and undocumented given the remote and inaccessible terrain on both sides, and the lack of any official narratives other than news reports. John Garver's *Protracted Contest* and Bertil Lindtner's *Great Game East: India, China and the Struggle for Asia's Most Volatile Frontier* offer informed and well-researched narratives on the jostling for strategic space along the LAC and along India's volatile north-eastern frontiers. The only other operational account of the skirmishes and face-offs that have occurred along the LAC at Nathu La, Cho La, Sumdorong Chu and Doklam comes from Probal Dasgupta whose *Watershed 1967: India's Forgotten Victory Over China* is a racy and interesting account with extracts from war diaries and detailed interviews.

UN Operations

Despite its enduring contribution to UN Peacekeeping Operations since the inception of the world body, there is no consolidated account of the Indian military's participation in these widely dispersed operations. While several practitioners have written personalized accounts of their tenures on several missions, much of the information is only available through journal articles, newsmagazines and newspaper papers. Lieutenant General Satish Nambiar's *For the Honour of India: A History of Indian Peacekeeping* is the only Indian book that merits inclusion in a reading list. *The Oxford Handbook of United Nations Peacekeeping Operations* remains the main repository of information on these operations even though it is mainly a European perspective.

Finally, the Indian website www.bharat-rakshak.com has an excellent repository of material of all kinds on India's wars after Independence and about the Indian armed forces. It is a must visit. By no means is the suggested reading list all-encompassing. Any omissions are unintentional and solely reflect the limitations of the author. Happy reading!

ACKNOWLEDGEMENTS

This was a tough one to write – more so because it was a sequel to a book that had no expectations. It was written under pressure and dislocation following a premature retirement from the IAF to pursue teaching and writing after failing to garner any institutional financial support to avail of two prestigious fellowships at Harvard and Oxford. The no-strings-attached financial support from the Tata Education Trust and the British Ministry of Defence enabled me to pursue my dreams. I owe gratitude to several unnamed well-wishers who helped me obtain the Tata support, while Brigadier Mark Goldsack, defence attaché at the British high commission, who had been a student of mine, ensured that I got to Oxford.

Professor Sugata Bose recommended me for the fellowship at the Harvard Asia Center, and was also a mentor during my stay there. I am also deeply indebted to the Changing Character of War programme at Oxford University and its director, Professor Rob Johnson, for giving me the space to write and receive feedback from the diverse participants of the programme.

Teaching a course on War and Conflict in Contemporary South Asia at the Fletcher School of International Law and Diplomacy in the fall of 2018 allowed me to share ideas with the faculty, students and the US military fellows. I am grateful to Admiral Stavridis and Professor Richard Shultz for welcoming me into the International Security Studies Programme and to Professor Ian Johnstone for his continued support. Professor Raj Echambadi from Northeastern University supported my writing in Boston by offering me a concurrent fellowship at the D'Amore McKim School of Business. Shekhar Gupta may not have realized but publishing a weekly column in The Print for over six months helped me make ends meet in exorbitant Boston and Oxford.

I am grateful to Ashoka University and the Jindal School of International Affairs for offering me teaching assignments in 2019. I could finish my manuscript in peace because of that cover. General Rawat and Air Chief Marshal Dhanoa were particularly supportive of my endeavour during the last lap of research and writing. They spent quality hours with me recounting their operational experiences and offering critical senior leadership perspectives.

I laboured on with valuable assistance from battle-hardened military veterans such as Lieutenant Generals Zaki, Nanavatty, Shammi Mehta, J.M. Singh, Ghei, Katoch, Hooda and Bakshi; Major Generals Chakravarty and Deb; Brigadiers Palsokar and Adrianwala; Colonel Gurdeep Bains; Admiral Arun Prakash, Air Marshals Patney, Menon, 'Harry' Ahluwalia, Nambiar and several others, who infused credibility and context into my narrative. Air Chief Marshals Tipnis, Krishnaswamy and Fali Major, General Malik and Admiral Madhavendra Singh have been frank in their recollections of their operational careers. I am lucky to have spoken with them. Several colleagues, course mates, students from the war colleges I have taught in, friends and military history enthusiasts who believed in my mission offered assistance whenever I asked. I cannot name all of them here, but I am grateful to them all. The National Defence College in New Delhi remains close to the heart of this endeavour too: *India's Wars I* was published during the last lap of my service career as a faculty member there and *India's Wars II* sees me back at the institution as a mentor and academic advisor.

Kiran Sahni was incisive and responsive with her initial editing. I would have struggled without her interventions. Lieutenant Colonel Akshat Upadhyay, a serving military scholar, was brilliant in his microscopic examination of my manuscript and caught several inconsistencies and factual errors. I am grateful also to an anonymous reviewer who helped me refine my narrative and caution me wherever he felt that I had engaged in overreach. Krishan Chopra, Siddhesh Inamdar, Saurav Das and the team at HarperCollins were good to work with as they deftly managed the last-mile navigation. Ramneek Singh has been great with the maps as always. Thank you, folks!

My wife, Mowthika, has sacrificed much for me to write these books and acted as a sounding board for my ideas as they emerged. Shruti and Meghna, our two daughters, have been tolerant of my eccentric behaviour and erratic parenting over the years. My parents will always be an inspiration in any intellectual endeavour – particularly my father, a brilliant academic who did not get an opportunity to read any of my writing. This book is for all of them.

LIST OF INTERVIEWEES

This is a list of serving and retired officers formally interviewed, informally spoken to, or corresponded with during the research for this book.

General Bipin Rawat
General V.N. Sharma
General V.P. Malik
Admiral Madhavendra Singh
Admiral Arun Prakash
Air Chief Marshal A.Y. Tipnis
Air Chief Marshal S. Krishnaswamy
Air Chief Marshal F.H. Major
Air Chief Marshal B.S. Dhanoa
Lieutenant General M.H. Zaki
Lieutenant General R.K. Nanavatty
Lieutenant General Shamsher Mehta
Lieutenant General J.M. Singh
Lieutenant General J.R. Mukherjee
Lieutenant General S. Pattabhiraman
Lieutenant General P.C. Katoch
Lieutenant General S.L. Narasimhan
Lieutenant General N.S. Ghei
Lieutenant General S.A. Hasnain
Major General Alok Deb
Major General Samir Chakravarty
Major General Gajendra Joshi
Major General H. Dharmarajan
Major General Devinder Kumar
Major General Gurbirpal Singh
Major General A.K. Ramesh
Air Vice Marshal H.S. Ahluwalia
Air Vice Marshal Rajesh Isser
Brigadier Vivek Sapatnekar
Brigadier Ravi Palsokar
Brigadier Xerxes Adrianwalla
Brigadier V.M.B. Krishnan
Commodore P.K. Banerjee
Commodore Srikant Kesnur
Air Commodore Shashank Mishra
Air Commodore Tejinder Singh
Air Vice Marshal M. Fernandez
Colonel Gurdeep Bains

Lieutenant General D.S. Hooda
Lieutenant General Praveen Bakshi
Lieutenant General K.H. Singh
Air Marshal Vinod Patney
Air Marshal Teshter Master
Air Marshal N. Menon
Air Marshal C. Hari Kumar
Air Marshal R. Nambiar
Air Marshal N.J.S. Dhillon
Air Marshal R.D. Mathur
Air Marshal V.R. Chaudhuri
Group Captain K.P.S. Lamba
Lieutenant Colonel T.P. Rajkumar
Wing Commander Rajiv Chauhan
Wing Commander K.T. Sebastian
Commodore Arjun Nair
Colonel R. Hariharan
Colonel A. Jairam
Colonel Navdeep Cheema
Colonel Vijayant Singh
Group Captain Anant Bewoor
Group Captain Unni Kartha
Group Captain Raju Srinivasan
Group Captain Sanjeev Narayenan
Group Captain S. Tokekar
Wing Commander R. Malhotra
Wing Commander Dushyant Singh
Captain Jayadevan
Lieutenant General K. Nagaraj

The author is also deeply grateful to Mr Sanjay Mitra, a former defence secretary, for his candid views on several issues of vital importance. Over fifty officers and men of various ranks and ages shared their perspectives on the operations they participated in, but requested anonymity. These include several officers from the Indian Army's Special Forces, MARCOS of the Indian Navy and pilots from the squadrons that participated in the Kargil conflict and the Balakot strikes. My deepest gratitude goes out to them.

PHOTO CREDITS

Indian Ministry of Defence, Photo Division
Air HQ
Artillery School, Deolali
218 Medium Regiment
17 RAJPUT
7 Squadron
48 Squadron
IAF Garud Flight
Lieutenant General J.M. Singh
Lieutenant General Rostum Nanavatty
Major General Devender
Brigadier Adrianwalla
Colonel S. Dinny
Admiral Arun Prakash
Commander Vinayak Agashe
Air Marshal R. Nambiar
Air Vice Marshal Vikram Singh
Wing Commander Rohit Rai
Wing Commander K. Ramji
Wing Commander Sameer Joshi

Army HQ (ADGPI)
IAF PRO
60 PARA FD
Angad Singh
Pushpindar Singh
60 PARA FD
17 Squadron
114 Helicopter Unit
General Bipin Rawat
Lieutenant General M.A. Zaki
Major General Samir Chakravorty
Major General Ramesh
Colonel G.S. Bains
Admiral Madhavendra Singh
Captain Chandavarkar
Air Marshal Teshter Master
Air Marshal N.J.S. Dhillon
Group Captain A.G. Bewoor
Wing Commander A. Samtani
Wing Commander Dushyant Singh
Probal Dasgupta

PHOTO CREDITS

NOTES

Chapter 1: Introduction

1. Bernard Brodie in Carl von Clausewitz, *On War*, eds. Michael Howard and Peter Paret (New Jersey: Princeton University Press, 1976), pp. 53-54.
2. Arjun Subramaniam, *India's Wars I: A Military History, 1947-1971* (New Delhi: HarperCollins India, 2016, and Annapolis: US Naval Institute Press, 2017).
3. Ibid, pp. 369-70.
4. Lawrence Freedman, ed., *War* (Oxford: Oxford University Press, 1994), p. 8.

Chapter 2: Chameleon Wars

1. K. Subrahmanyam, *Security in a Changing World* (New Delhi: D.K. Publishers, 1990), p. 219. The book is a collection of essays on national security and analyses the strategic framework that directed military capability developments through much of the 1980s.
2. My comfort with the term 'Limited War' was prompted by a thought-provoking talk by Professor Dan Stoker, US Naval Post-Graduate School, during the 'Changing Character of War' programme at Oxford on 23 January 2018. The talk was very provocatively titled 'How to think about Limited War (without limiting your thinking)'.
3. A detailed practitioner's perspective on the contours of twenty-first-century warfare is available in the early chapters ('Introduction and Chapter 1') of Colonel Thomas X. Hammes, *The Sling and the Stone: On War in the 21st Century* (St Paul: Zenith Press, 2006).
4. This is a personal geo-military perspective that the author has arrived at after extensive discussions over years with both Indian and Western military leaders and security experts who have been involved in internal armed conflict across the globe.

5. Hew Strachan, *The Direction of War: Contemporary Strategy in Historical Perspective* (Cambridge: Cambridge University Press, 2013), pp. 82-83.
6. Ibid.
7. See Chapter 9 for a detailed examination of the Nathu La crisis and firefight.
8. For a detailed examination of this conflict see Chapters 8-12 in Arjun Subramaniam, *India's Wars I: A Military History, 1947-1971* (New Delhi: HarperCollins, 2016).
9. Ibid, p. 251.
10. Ibid, p. 326.
11. Ibid, p. 427.
12. This is the broad methodology followed by India's armed forces in operational formations and war colleges.
13. An excellent analysis of the Air-Land Battle Doctrine is Douglas W. Skinner, *Air- Land Battle Doctrine* (Center for Naval Analyses, September 1988). Accessed online at http://www.dtic.mil/dtic/tr/fulltext/u2/a202888.pdf.
14. An equally good monograph on sequential military operations is Major Richard Dixon, *Operational Sequencing: The Tension between Simultaneous and Sequential Operations* (Kansas: School of Advanced Military Studies United States Army Command and Staff College Fort Leavenworth, September 1994). Accessed online at http://www.dtic.mil/dtic/tr/fulltext/u2/a284087.pdf.
15. Parallel operations have emerged as a dominant concept of conventional warfighting in recent years due to the increasing ability of air power to influence joint operations – See Proposition 6 in Colonel Phillip S. Meillinger, *Ten Propositions Regarding Air Power.* Accessed online at https://www.airuniversity.af.edu/Portals/10/ASPJ/journals/Chronicles/meil.pdf.
16. Impressions based on Sundarji's writings, study group sessions with him during the 49th Staff Course at Wellington and exhaustive interviews with Lieutenant General Shamsher Mehta, who was on Sundarji's staff when he was chief.
17. Jasjit Singh, *Air Power in Joint Operations* (New Delhi: Knowledge World, 2003).
18. For clarity on EBO, see Meilinger, *Ten Propositions Regarding Air Power.*
19. See Benjamin Lambeth, 'American and NATO Airpower Applied: From Deny Flight to Inherent Resolve', in *Airpower Applied: US, NATO and Israeli Combat Experience,* ed. John Andreas Olsen (Annapolis, Maryland: Naval Institute Press, 2017), pp. 124-216.

20. Lieutenant General Prakash Menon, *The Strategy Trap: India and Pakistan Under the Nuclear Shadow* (New Delhi: Wisdom Tree, 2018), pp. 176-77.
21. Hammes, *The Sling and the Stone,* pp. 5-29.
22. Integrated HQ of Ministry of Defence (Army), *Doctrine for Sub-Conventional Operations* (December 2006), p. 65.
23. Ibid.
24. Ibid.
25. Indian MoD, *Joint Services Glossary of Military Terms* (Delhi: 2003), p. 119.
26. From the Indian Army's Doctrine for Sub-Conventional Operations, 2006, p. 66. Also see Russel D. Howard and Reid L. Sawyer, *Terrorism and Counterterrorism: Understanding the New Security Environment, Readings and Interpretations* (New York: McGraw Hill, 2009), p. 26. Bruce Hoffman offers different definitions and perspectives of terrorism from contemporary times in Chapter 1.
27. Praveen Swami, 'Failed Threats and Flawed Fences: India's Military Responses to Pakistan's Proxy War', *India Review,* Vol. 3, No. 2 (April 2004), p. 147.
28. Parvez Hoodbhoy, 'Views from Pakistan: Bleed India with a Thousand Cuts Policy in a Shambles'. Accessed online at http://www.openthemagazine.com/article/views-from-pakistan/bleed-india-with-a-thousand-cuts-policy-is-in-a-shambles.
29. H.P.S. Sidhu, 'Understanding Hybrid Warfare and Developing a Response', from a paper presented at the National Defence College on 5 May 2016 and published in *Understanding Strategy,* a collection of seminar papers with limited distribution.
30. F. Hoffman, 'Conflict in the 21st Century: The Rise of Hybrid Wars', Potomac Institute for Policy Studies, December 2007.
31. David Kilcullen, *Accidental Guerrilla* (London: Hurst, 2009), p. 25.
32. Qiao Liang and Wang Xiangsui, *Unrestricted Warfare* (Beijing: PLA Literature and Arts Publishing House, February 1999).
33. Kilcullen, *Accidental Guerrilla*, p. 3.
34. H.R. McMaster, former National Security Advisor in the Trump Administration, in Patrick Radden Keefe, 'McMaster and Commander', *New Yorker,* 30 April 2018, pp. 36-49.
35. John Boyd, 'Patterns of Conflict', from a series of presentations made by Boyd at various war colleges in the US. Despite not having written a book, Boyd's impact on contemporary warfighting has been phenomenal. See http://www.projectwhitehorse.com/pdfs/boyd/patterns%20of%20conflict.pdf.
36. Ibid.

37. This was before Nagaland was granted statehood.
38. Rostum K. Nanavatty, *Internal Armed Conflict in India* (New Delhi: Pentagon Press, 2013), pp. 65-69. Also see 'The Armed Forces (Jammu and Kashmir) Special Powers Act (1990). MHA website accessed online at https://www.mha.gov.in/sites/default/files/The%20Armed%20Forces%20%28Jammu%20and%20Kashmir%29%20Special%20Powers%20Act%2C%201990_0.pdf.
39. Vivek Chadha, ed., *Armed Forces Special Powers Act: The Debate* (New Delhi: Lancer, 2013), pp. 10-21.
40. Sanjoy Hazarika, *Strangers No More* (New Delhi: Aleph, 2018), pp. x-xi.
41. Nikhil Raymond Puri, 'Assessing Disturbance in Jammu and Kashmir's Disturbed Areas', ORF Issue Brief # 104, September 2015. Accessed online at https://www.orfonline.org/wp-content/uploads/2015/12/ORFIssueBrief104.pdf.
42. Nanavatty, *Internal Armed Conflict*, p. xvii.
43. Carl von Clausewitz, *On War*, eds. Michel Howard and Peter Paret (New Jersey: Princeton University Press, 1976), p. 594. See Book Eight of the section on 'Scale of the Military Objective and of the Effort to be Made'.

Chapter 3: India's Military Renaissance

1. John F. Burns, 'India's New Defense Chief Sees Chinese Military Threat', *New York Times*, 5 May 1998. Accessed at https://www.nytimes.com/1998/05/05/world/india-s-new-defense-chief-sees-chinese-military-threat.html.
2. Subramaniam, *India's Wars I*, pp. 401-06.
3. Several interviews and conversations with Lieutenant General Shamsher (Shammi) Mehta between 2013 and 2019.
4. International Institute of Strategic Studies (IISS), *Military Balance*, Vol. 73, Issue 1, 1973. Online version (1973) Asia and Australasia, 73:1, 45-58, DOI: 10.1080/04597227308459833, accessed on 29 March 2018, https://doi.org/10.1080/04597227308459833. All comparisons with the situation at the end of the 1970s have been made by referring to Vol. 79 of the same series at https://doi.org/10.1080/04597227908459894.
5. Interview with Shammi Mehta.
6. *Military Balance*, Vol. 73, see note 4. The annual Military Balance series of consolidated reports and analyses from the IISS, London, analyses military capability from a global perspective. Indian and Chinese GDP and defence spending figures may vary.
7. Ibid.
8. Ibid.

9. Vice Admiral G.M. Hiranandani, *Transition to Eminence: The Indian Navy, 1976-1990* (New Delhi: Lancer Publishers, 2004), p. 27 (tabular compilation of various warships).
10. Subramaniam, *India's Wars I*, pp. 415-17.
11. The story of the HF-24 is well narrated by Sushant Singh in 'In Fact: Before the LCA, India had its own fighter – Marut', *Indian Express,* 8 July 2016. Accessed online at https://indianexpress.com/article/explained/tejas-hf-24-marut-tejas-combat-aircraft-indian-air-force-2894021/.
12. *Military Balance,* Vols. 73 and 79.
13. Interview, Air Marshal Patney, 6 August 2018.
14. *Military Balance*, Vols. 81 and 90.
15. Ibid, Vol. 90.
16. Amit Gupta, 'Determining India's Force Structure and Military Doctrine: I Want my MiG', *Asian Survey,* Vol. 35, No. 5 (May 1995), pp. 441-58. Accessed online at https://www.jstor.org/stable/2645747?seq=1.
17. Ibid.
18. Interview with Lieutenant General Pattabhiraman (retd), former Vice Chief of the Indian Army, at Wellington, 15 March 2017.
19. Selig Harrison and K. Subrahmanyam, eds., *Superpower Rivalry in the Indian Ocean: Indian and American Views* (New York: Oxford University Press, 1989) and Rear Admiral Raja Menon (retd), *Maritime Strategy and Continental Wars* (London: Frank Cass, 1998).
20. *Military Balance,* Vols. 80, 81 and 90. Also see Gupta, 'Determining India's Force Structure'.
21. For a perceptive piece on the legacy of K. Subrahmanyam and his contribution to contemporary Indian strategic thought, see Anit Mukherjee, 'K. Subrahmanyam and Indian Strategic Thought', *Strategic Analysis,* Vol. 35, No. 4 (July 2011), pp. 710-13.
22. Interview with Air Marshal Patney, 6 August 2018.
23. *Military Balance,* Vols. 91, 98 and 100.
24. Personal recollection of the author of getting Romanian engines in the 1990s for MiG-21s in his squadron.
25. 'Army's elite counterinsurgency unit Rashtriya Rifles celebrates 25 years', accessed on 15 February 2017, https://economictimes.indiatimes.com/news/defence/armys-elite-counter-insurgency-unit-rashtriya-rifles-turns-25-tomorrow/articleshow/49171891.cms?from=mdr.
26. 'New Army Chief for Debate on Security', *Hindustan Times,* 1 July 1993.
27. 'New Army Chief Suggests Restructuring to Fight Militancy', *Financial Express,* 1 July 1993.

28. George Fernandes, 'Examining the Concept of National Security', in *General B. C. Joshi Memorial Lectures on National Security,* ed. Prof. Gautam Sen (Pune: University of Pune Press, 2006), pp. 54-55.
29. Interview with Air Marshal Patney, 6 August 2018.
30. John F. Burns, 'India's New Defense Chief sees Chinese Military Threat', *New York Times,* 5 May 1998, accessed on 18 November 2017, https://www.nytimes.com/1998/05/05/world/india-s-new-defense-chief-sees-chinese-military-threat.html.
31. Ibid.
32. *Military Balance* comparison.
33. 'Army inducts three artillery guns including US' M777 howitzers,' 9 November 2018, https://timesofindia.indiatimes.com/india/k9-vajra-m777-howitzers-to-be-inducted-today-sitharaman-to-attend-event/articleshow/66552262.cms.
34. For a succinct evaluation of the PLA Navy see Christopher Yung, 'China's Evolving Naval Force Structure: Beyond Sino-US Rivalry', *China Brief,* Vol.18, Issue 9, Jamestown Foundation. Accessed on 12 November 2017. https://jamestown.org/program/chinas-evolving-naval-force-structure-beyond-sino-us-rivalry/.
35. Arjun Subramaniam, 'Closing the Gap: A Doctrinal and Capability Appraisal of the IAF and PLAAF' in *Defence Primer: An Indian Military in Transformation,* eds. Pushan Das and Harsh V. Pant (New Delhi: ORF, 2018).
36. Lt Cdr Kalesh Mohanan, 'Indigenous Warship Building', *Indian Defence Review,* Vol. 27, No. 2 (April-June 2012). Accessed on 12 January 2017. http://www.indiandefencereview.com/spotlights/indigenous-warship-building/.
37. Interview with Admiral Arun Prakash at the Naval War College, Goa, on 30 October 2016 with inputs from Captain Srikant Kesnur, who commanded the same ship (F-42).
38. For an excellent chronological evolution of the Nilgiri class of warships and the transformation of Indian naval design, see Vice Admiral Hiranandani, *Transition to Eminence: The Indian Navy, 1976-1990* (New Delhi: HarperCollins, 2004).
39. Phillip Rajkumar and Pushpindar Singh, *First to the Last: 50 Years of MiG-21 with the IAF* (New Delhi: Society for Aerospace Studies, 2013), p. 11.
40. Interviews with Air Marshal Patney.
41. A presentation by USAF Colonel Terrence Forn during Exercise Red Flag (2008). Accessed on 13 January 2018. http://www.f-16.net/forum/viewtopic.php?t=21258.

42. 'Bofors: Getting Away', *India Today,* 15 September 1989, pp. 25-30. Accessed online at http://media1.intoday.in/indiatoday/bofors/pdf/bofors_low.pdf.
43. Ibid.
44. Army Guide, accessed online at http://www.army-guide.com/eng/product4673.html.
45. Prabhash K. Dutta, 'Kargil: How Bofors guns made Pakistan eat humble pie', *India Today,* 26 July 2019. Accessed at https://www.indiatoday.in/news-analysis/story/bofors-the-controversial-gun-that-won-kargil-war-for-india-1573814-2019-07-26.
46. Mandip Singh, 'Lessons from Somdurong Chu Incident'. Accessed online at https://idsa.in/idsacomments/CurrentChineseincursionLessonsfromSomdurongChuIncident_msingh_260413.
47. Email correspondence and conversation with Lieutenant General Ahuja, 10 October 2019.

Chapter 4: The Naga Rebellion

1. D.R. Mankekar, *On the Slippery Slope in Nagaland* (Bombay: Manaktalas, 1967), p. 11.
2. For a detailed profile of Bob Khathing see H. Bhuban Singh, *Major Bob Khathing: The Profile of a Nationalist Manipuri Naga* (P. Haoban Publishers, 1992). The book is out of print but is available with the library in the Assam Rifles Regimental Centre.
3. Ibid.
4. Vikram Singh, *Spitfire in the Sun* (New Delhi: Ambi Knowledge Resources, 2017), pp. 75-76.
5. Archives of the Assam Rifles Regimental Centre.
6. Singh, *Spitfire,* pp. 75-76.
7. Ibid.
8. Colonel R.D. Palsokar, MC, *Forever in Operations, A Success Story: A Historical Record of the 8th Mountain Division in Counterinsurgency in Nagaland and Manipur, and in the 1971 Indo-Pak Conflict* (Pune: HQ 8 Mtn Div, 1991), p. 26.
9. Lieutenant General J.R. Mukherjee, *An Insider's Experience of Insurgency in India's North-East* (London: Anthem Press, 2005), p. 27.
10. Associated Press, 'Angami Phizo, 83, fought for Secession in North Indian state', *New York Times,* 4 May 1990. Accessed 17 September 2017 at https://www.nytimes.com/1990/05/04/obituaries/angami-phizo-83-fought-for-secession-in-north-india-state.html.
11. 'Revolt in the Hills', *Time,* Vol. 67, Issue 16, 16 April 1956, p. 33.

12. For a succinct review of the origin of the Naga people and their migration into the hilly tracts of northeast India see Y.D. Gundevia, *War and Peace in Nagaland* (Dehradun and New Delhi: Palit & Palit, 1975), pp. 1-6.
13. Ibid, pp. 29-51.
14. Ibid, p. 42.
15. Ibid.
16. Nirmal Nibedon, *Nagaland: The Night of the Guerrillas* (New Delhi: Lancer, 1978), pp. 20-25.
17. Bhuban Singh, *Major Bob Khathing*.
18. Nibedon, *Nagaland*, p. 29.
19. Ibid, pp. 32-35. This section also includes the gist of the dialogue between the NNC and Mahatma Gandhi.
20. Phizo was first arrested by the Indian government in 1949 for delivering inflammatory speeches against India.
21. Sanjoy Hazarika, *Strangers No More* (New Delhi: Aleph, 2018), p. 54.
22. Nibedon, *Nagaland*, p. 63.
23. Palsokar, *Always in Operations*, p. 26.
24. Nibedon, *Nagaland*, p. 63.
25. Palsokar, *Forever in Operations*, p. 30.
26. Ibid, p. 31.
27. For a detailed profile of Lieutenant Colonel Chitnis, see https://www.honourpoint.in/profile/lieutenant-colonel-jagannath-raoji-chitnis-ac/.
28. Harish Chandola, *The Naga Story: First Armed Struggle in India* (New Delhi: Chicken Neck, 2012), pp. 57-62.
29. Palsokar, *Forever in Operations*, p. 35.
30. Ibid, pp. 35-36. Also see Nibedon, *Nagaland*, pp. 90-91.
31. Email correspondence with Wing Commander Chandrashekhar Misra. Also see http://www.bharat-rakshak.com/IAF/Database/Aircraft/HJ-233.
32. From the squadron diaries of 43 Squadron.
33. Email correspondence with IAF veterans and air power historians.
34. Email correspondence with Air Marshal Bharat Kumar, the IAF's foremost historian, on 6 September. Samir Chopra, an air power historian, co-author of *Eagles over Bangladesh* and professor at NYU, recollects having seen entries in his father's logbook of live strafing missions in the early 1960s from Tezpur: email correspondence in late August 2018.
35. Major General D.K. Palit, *The Sentinels of the North-East* (New Delhi: Palit & Palit, 1984), p. 224.

36. Extracts from operational record book of 29 Squadron for the period October-December 1961, compiled by Flying Officer V.S. Bhavnani and sent to the author by Polly Singh.
37. This was possible due to the efforts by Group Captain Sartaj Singh from the Historical Cell at College of Air Warfare and Group Captain Unni Kartha, who served for many years in the region.
38. Bashas are portable dwelling units made of bamboo and reed and found in all parts of northeast India.
39. Operational record book of 29 Squadron for the quarter ending 31 December 1961, pp. 1-3. Compiled by Flying Officer V.S. Bhavnani.
40. Ibid.
41. For a brief mention of air operations against Naga insurgents in the early 1960s also see Brigadier S.P. Sinha, 'CI Operations in the Northeast', *Indian Defence Review,* Vol 21, No. 2, Apr-Jun 2006. Accessed online at http://www.indiandefencereview.com/spotlights/c-i-operations-in-the-northeast/0/ Also see http://vayu-sena.tripod.com/other-coin-offensive-fighter-ops-ne.html.
42. Subir Bhaumick, *Troubled Periphery: India's Troubled North-East* (New Delhi: Sage, 2009), pp. 44-47.
43. The Battle of Walong was one of the few sectoral battles in NEFA in which the Indian Army gave the PLA a bloody nose in the 1962 war, before being overwhelmed by sheer numerical superiority. For a detailed overview of the battle see Subramaniam, *India's Wars I*, pp. 245-46.
44. Nanavatty diaries and interviews, 18 February 2017, 13 March 2017 and 18 August 2018.
45. For a detailed narrative on the Goa operations, see Subramaniam, *India's Wars I*, pp. 180-94.
46. Palsokar, *Forever in Operations.*
47. For a detailed analysis of the threat posed by external actors to stability in the north-eastern part of India since the early years of the Naga insurgency, see Brig. (Dr) S.P. Sinha, 'Northeast: The Threat Posed by External Actors', *Indian Defence Review,* 14 February 2016. Accessed online at http://www.indiandefencereview.com/spotlights/northeast-the-external-dimension/.

Chapter 5: Mizo Angst, Nagaland Festers

1. Brigadier Sushil Kumar Sharma, 'Lessons from Mizoram Insurgency and Peace Accord 1986', Vivekananda International Foundation, June 2016. Accessed at https://www.vifindia.org/sites/default/files/lessons-from-mizoram-insurgency-and-peace-accord-1986.pdf.
2. Mukherjee, *An Insider's Experience,* p. 49.

3. Ali Ahmed, 'Mizo Hills: Revisiting the Early Phase'. Accessed online at http://www.claws.in/images/journals_doc/1607757556_AliAhmed.pdf. This journal piece is by far the best all-encompassing analysis of the Mizo insurgency from a politico-military perspective.
4. Sharma, 'Lessons from the Mizo Insurgency'.
5. Interview with Lieutenant General Thomas Mathew, 12 November 2014.
6. Email exchanges on the IAF History Yahoo group, following the author's request for personal accounts of IAF veterans who had participated in extensive aerial operations in the northeast through the 1960s.
7. Email from the late Air Marshal Teshter Master on the IAF Yahoo group.
8. Anand Ranganathan, 'A Brief History of Mizoram: From the Aizawl Bombing to the Mizo Accord'. Accessed at https://www.newslaundry.com/2015/08/06/a-brief-history-of-mizoram-from-the-aizawl-bombing-to-the-mizo-accord.
9. Email from Air Marshal Bharat Kumar on the IAF Yahoo groups.
10. Times News Network, 'Silent Rally Echoes Mizo Pain of'66 IAF Attacks, 5 March 2011. Accessed online at https://timesofindia.indiatimes.com/city/guwahati/Silent-rally-echoes-Mizo-pain-of-66-IAF-attacks/articleshow/7636603.cms?referral=PM.
11. Conversation with Colonel Vivek Chadha, 11 April 2020.
12. Dr J.V. Hluna and Rini Tochwang, *The Mizo Uprising: Assam Assembly Debates on the Mizo Movement, 1966-1971* (Newcastle: Cambridge Scholars Publishing, 2012), p. xix.
13. Rinchen Norbu Wangchuk, 'Mizo Peace Accord: The Intriguing Story behind India's Most Enduring Peace Initiative', 2 July 2018. Accessed online at https://www.thebetterindia.com/148387/mizo-peace-accord-laldenga-rajiv-gandhi/.
14. Mukherjee, *An Insider's Experience*, p. 52.
15. 'An Incident in Nagaland', a personal account by Group Captain Anil Bendre of an incident in Nagaland on 20 May 1974 in an email through Air Vice Marshal Ahluwalia to the author, 29 September 2018.
16. *Citizen's Voice*, 18 December 1969, p. 1. Accessed at the Kohima public library.
17. Nishit Dholabhai, '70-plus and still going strong in BSF', *Telegraph*, 9 May 2004. Accessed online at https://www.telegraphindia.com/states/north-east/70-plus-and-still-going-strong-in-bsf-septuagenarian-naga-sentinels-continue-in-service-thanks-to-fudged-age/cid/1557309.
18. Interview with General Narasimhan at Coimbatore, 15 February 2017.
19. Ibid.
20. Interview with Lieutenant General Prakash Katoch, 13 May 2019.

21. Brigadier Sushil Sharma, *The Complexity Called Manipur: Perceptions and Reality* (New Delhi: Viva Books, 2019).
22. Interview with Nanavatty, Dehradun, August 2018.
23. Ibid.
24. Ibid.
25. Patricia Mukhim, 'A Deal at Last', *Hindu,* 28 March 2019. Accessed online at https://www.thehindu.com/opinion/op-ed/a-deal-at-last/article26656012.ece.
26. Interview with General Bipin Rawat, Chief of Army Staff, 21 April 2019 and 7 July 2019.
27. Interview with General Rawat, 21 April 2019 and 7 July 2019.
28. For a gripping people-centric narrative of this operation see Shiv Aroor and Rahul Singh, *India's Most Fearless: True Stories of Modern Military Heroes* (New Delhi: Penguin Random House, 2017), pp. 37-64.
29. Times News Network, 15 August 2015. Accessed online at https://timesofindia.indiatimes.com/india/7-medals-for-Special-Forces-team-that-hit-Myanmar-camps/articleshow/48490051.cms.
30. 'Terror Camps on India-Myanmar border destroyed', *Economic Times,* 15 March 2019. Accessed online at https://economictimes.indiatimes.com/news/defence/terror-camps-on-india-myanmar-border-destroyed/articleshow/68432469.cms.
31. Ibid.
32. General Rawat interviews.
33. For a poignant description of the arrival of Phizo's body at the Dimapur airfield on 11 May 1990 see Pieter Steyn, *Zapuphizo: Voice of the Nagas* (London: Kegan Paul Limited, 2002), pp. 159-63.
34. Samudra Gupta Kashyap and Praveen Swami, 'Explained: Everything you wanted to know about the Naga insurgency', *Indian Express,* 4 August 2015. Accessed online at https://indianexpress.com/article/india/india-others/everything-you-need-to-know-about-nagaland-insurgency-and-the-efforts-to-solve/.
35. Ibid.
36. Interview with Lieutenant General Hooda at Panchkula, Chandigarh, 20 July 2019.
37. Kashyap and Swami, 'Explained'.
38. Palit, *Sentinels.*
39. Shekhar Gupta in a YouTube video that is part of a series called 'Cut the Clutter' for The Print. Accessed at https://www.youtube.com/watch?v=CcI4NOsmw4I.

40. Namrata Goswami, 'India's Counterinsurgency Experience: the "Trust and Nurture" Strategy', *Small Wars and Insurgencies,* Vol. 20, Issue 1, 2009. Accessed online at https://doi.org/10.1080/09592310802573475.
41. Colonel Sanjeev Hazarika, 'Genesis of Naga Imbroglio, Status of Underground Groups, Prevailing Situation, Prognosis and Army Activities', *Infantry Journal,* pp. 31-34.

Chapter 6: Operation Blue Star: Ours Is Not to Question Why

1. Lieutenant General K.S. Brar, *Operation Blue Star: The True Story* (New Delhi: UBS Publishers, 1993), p. 10.
2. Lieutenant General S.K. Sinha, *A Soldier Recalls* (New Delhi: Lancer Publishers, 1992), pp. 278-80.
3. The Damdami Taksal in the late 1970s and 1980s was the fountainhead of Sikh fundamentalism and the nerve centre of anti-government extremism. It has over the years, particularly in recent times, reinvented itself as a moderate centre of Sikh religious teaching.
4. Sinha, *A Soldier Recalls,* pp. 289-91.
5. The Nirankaris are a secular, spiritual sect, unaffiliated with any religion, and deny that Sikhs have any authority over them. See 'Who are the Nirankaris,' *Indian Express,* 18 November 2018. Accessed online at https://indianexpress.com/article/who-is/who-are-nirankaris/.
6. Sinha, *A Soldier Recalls,* p. 290.
7. Harminder Kaur, *Blue Star over Amritsar* (New Delhi: Ajanta Publications, 1990), pp. 117-18.
8. Mark Tully and Satish Jacob, *Amritsar: Mrs Gandhi's Last Battle* (New Delhi: Rupa, 1985), pp. 10-14.
9. Brigadier R.K. Chopra, Internal Security Environment in India, 28th NDC course thesis, 1988. Accessed 26 March 2019, NDC library.
10. 'Suspected Sikh Extremists Slay Editor'. Accessed online at https://www.upi.com/Archives/1984/05/12/Suspected-Sikh-extremists-slay-editor/3839453182400/.
11. Michael Kaufman, 'Sikh separatists hijack Indian jetliner to Pakistan', *New York Times,* 30 September 1981. Accessed online at https://www.nytimes.com/1981/09/30/world/sikh-separatists-hijack-indian-jetliner-to-pakistan.html.
12. Rajshri Jetly provides an excellent overview of the Khalistan movement in, 'The Khalistan Movement in India: The Interplay of Politics and State Power', *International Review of Modern Sociology,* Vol. 34, No. 1 (Spring 2008), pp. 61-75. Accessed online at https://www.jstor.org/stable/41421658?seq=1.

13. Praveen Swami, *India, Pakistan and the Secret Jihad* (New Delhi: Routledge, 2007), p. 147.
14. Data sheets of annual fatalities in terrorist-related violence, 1981–2019, accessed online at https://satp.org/satporgtp/countries/india/states/Punjab/data_sheets/annual_casualties.htm
15. Brar, *Operation Blue Star*, pp. 33-39.
16. Mark Tully, 'Operation Blue Star: How an Indian Army Raid on the Golden Temple ended in Disaster', *Telegraph,* 6 June 2014. Accessed online at https://www.telegraph.co.uk/news/worldnews/asia/india/10881115/Operation-Blue-Star-How-an-Indian-army-raid-on-the-Golden-Temple-ended-in-disaster.html.
17. For a detailed description of SFF involvement in Operation Blue Star, see Claude Arpi, 'Special Frontier Force and Operation Blue Star'. Accessed online at http://claudearpi.blogspot.com/2014/01/special-frontiers-forces-and-operation.html.
18. Brar, *Operation Blue Star*, p. 88, and extrapolated from attached map on the same page.
19. Interview with Lieutenant General Prakash Katoch, 13 May 2019.
20. Arjun Subramaniam, *India's Wars I,* pp. 355-57.
21. Tully and Jacob, *Amritsar*, pp. 88-89.
22. Ibid.
23. Brar, *Operation Blue Star*, pp. 100-15, and battle narrative by Katoch.
24. Ibid, Brar, *Operation Blue Star.*
25. Katoch interview.
26. Based on personal conversations over the years.
27. Brar, *Operation Blue Star*, p. 124. Also see Kaur, *Blue Star*, pp. 46-48.
28. Interview with Chief of Army Staff General Bipin Rawat, 21 April 2019.
29. Email correspondence with General Ghei.
30. Rashi Lal, 'When LU became Ground Zero for PAC Revolt', *Times of India*, Lucknow edition, 1 June 2018. Accessed online at https://timesofindia.indiatimes.com/city/lucknow/when-lu-became-ground-zero-for-pac-revolt/articleshow/64417667.cms.
31. 'The secret behind Operation Blue Star: Britain's dilemma explained', ET Online, 13 June 2018. Accessed online at https://economictimes.indiatimes.com/news/et-explains/the-secret-behind-operation-blue-star-britains-dilemma-explained/articleshow/64569757.cms?from=mdr.
32. Katoch interview.
33. 'Golden Temple attack: UK advised India but impact limited', 7 June 1984. Accessed online at https://www.bbc.com/news/uk-26027631.
34. Tully and Jacob, *Amritsar*, p. 194. Also see Kaur, *Blue Star*, p. 49.

35. Apurba Kundu, 'The Indian Armed Forces' Sikh and Non-Sikh Officers Opinions of Operation Blue Star', *Pacific Affairs* (Spring 1994), Vol. 67, No. 1, pp. 46-69. Accessed online at https://www.jstor.org/stable/2760119?seq=1.
36. Ibid.
37. Colonel Gurnam Singh, 'Secularism in the Indian Army'. Accessed online at https://www.speakingtree.in/blog/secularism-in-the-indian-army.
38. Sumit Mitra, 'Rajiv–Longowal Accord: Mathew Commission delivers an unexpected anti-climax', *India Today,* 15 February 1986. Accessed online at https://www.indiatoday.in/magazine/cover-story/story/19860215-rajiv-longowal-accord-mathew-commission-delivers-an-unexpected-anti-climax-800593-1986-02-15.
39. Suman Dubey, 'Shiv Sena militarily gears itself to protect Hinduism and Hindu interests in Punjab', *India Today,* 15 April 1986. Accessed online at https://www.indiatoday.in/magazine/cover-story/story/19860415-shiv-sena-militantly-gears-itself-to-protect-hinduism-and-hindu-interests-in-punjab-800756-1986-04-15#ssologin=1#source=magazine.
40. Swami, *India, Pakistan*, p. 47.
41. Chopra, *Internal Security Environment.*
42. For a detailed narrative of Gill's tenure as DGP in Punjab and his efforts to stamp out terrorism in the state, see K.P.S. Gill, ed., *Terror Containment: Perspectives on India's Internal Security* (New Delhi: Gyan Publishing House, 2001), pp. 23-83.
43. Gobind Thukral, 'Extremists, AISSF leaders once again use Golden Temple as an occasional hideout', *India Today,* 15 May 1986. Accessed online at https://www.indiatoday.in/magazine/indiascope/story/19860515-extremists-aissf-leaders-once-again-use-golden-temple-as-an-occasional-hideout-800876-1986-05-15.
44. For a detailed narration of Operation Black Thunder, see Ved Marwah, *Uncivil Wars: Pathology of Terrorism in India* (New Delhi: Indus, a reprint of HarperCollins, 1995), pp. 188-200.
45. Ibid.
46. Dr A. Suryaprakash, 'The President corrects some historical facts, gives Narasimha Rao his due'. Accessed on 4 April 2019 at https://www.vifindia.org/article/2016/may/04/the-president-corrects-some-historical-facts-gives-narasimha-rao-his-due.

Chapter 7: Siachen: An Icy Battleground

1. Edward W. Desmond, 'War on High Ground', *Time*, No. 29, 17 July 1989, pp. 6-13.

2. Harish Kapadia, *The Siachen Glacier: A Historical Review* (102 Infantry Brigade: Partaker, 2011), p.1. The booklet was specially written by Harish Kapadia for officers and men who serve on the glacier.
3. Professor Giotto Dainelli, 'My Expedition in the Eastern Karakoram:1930', *Royal Geographical Journal,* pp. 46-55. (The article was attached to a letter written by Harish Kapadia to Nanavatty when he was Northern Army Commander, following the discovery of an old stone from Prof. Dainelli's expedition by Captain Nitin Shreshtha, an officer from 7/11 Gorkha Rifles. Also see *The Himalayan Journal,* Vol. 4, 1932. Available at https://www.himalayanclub.org/hj/04/4/my-expedition-in-the-eastern-karakoram/.
4. The Grid Square 9842 represents an area on the map and not a point.
5. Interview with Nanavatty, 13 March 2017.
6. Kapadia, *The Siachen Glacier*, pp. 5-6.
7. Omer Farook Zain, 'Siachen Conflict: Discordant in Pakistan-India Reconciliation', *Pakistan Horizon,* Vol. 59, No. 2, April 2006, pp. 73-82. Accessed online at https://www.jstor.org/stable/41394127?seq=1.
8. Ibid, p. 74.
9. Literally translated from Sanskrit, Meghdoot is the messenger of the clouds.
10. Lieutenant General M.L. Chibber, 'Siachen – The Untold Story', *Indian Defence Review,* January 1990, pp. 146-52.
11. The Cheetal is a re-engineered version of the Cheetah optimized by Hindustan Aeronautics Limited (HAL) in 2002 for better high-altitude performance. All the three variants are offshoots of the French Alloutte light helicopter.
12. M.M. Bahadur, 'The Buildup to Operation Meghdoot', 10 December 2017. Accessed online at http://www.bharat-rakshak.com/IAF/history/siachen/1046-meghdoot.html.
13. Kevin Fedarko, 'The Coldest War,' updated 22 April 2012, https://www.wesjones.com/coldest.htm. Also see https://hassaanrabbani.wordpress.com/2011/09/10/experiencing-siachen-war-part-5-by-kevin-fedarko/.
14. Chibber, 'Siachen', p. 149. Also see Farook Zain, 'Siachen Conflict', p. 79.
15. Based on multiple conversations with Indian and Pakistani veterans who have served on the glacier.
16. The best operational account of the initial assault is by Nitin Gokhale in his book *Beyond NJ 9842: The Siachen Saga* (New Delhi: Bloomsbury, 2014). Also see a review of the book in *Strategic Analysis*, Vol. 39, No.1 (IDSA, 2015), pp. 97-99.
17. Telephonic interview and email correspondence with Group Captain Rohit Rai, 10-17 June 2020.

18. Nitin Gokhale interviews Sanjay Kulkarni. Accessed online at http://www.abplive.in/blog/meet-the-man-who-planted-the-first-indian-flag-on-siachen.
19. Rohit Rai interview.
20. Ibid.
21. Lieutenant Colonel Syed Ishfaq Ali, *Fangs of Ice* (Rawalpindi: Pan America Commercial, 1991), p. 24.
22. Ibid, pp. 29-30.
23. Martin A. Shurgarman, *War Above the Clouds* (California: Shurgarman Productions, 1996), p. 9. From Farook Zain, 'Siachen Conflict', p. 79.
24. Interview with Lieutenant General Ghei at NDC, New Delhi, 12 October 2016.
25. Kumar FLB was moved east of the Siachen Glacier in 2001-02 – on to terra firma instead of glacial ice – and was converted into an advanced base camp for mountaineering expeditions. It has the potential to be converted into a scientific research station in the future.
26. Major General Raj Mehta, 'Bravery Beyond Comparison: Hony Captain Bana Singh, PVC', *Scholar Warrior* (New Delhi: Autumn 2013), pp. 132-36.
27. Onkar Singh, 'True Valour', *Illustrated Weekly of India,* 28 March 1988, pp. 38-39. From the personal documents of Nanavatty.
28. Ishfaq Ali, *Fangs,* pp. 56-68.
29. Mehta, 'Bravery Beyond Comparison', p. 135.
30. Ishfaq Ali, *Fangs*, pp. 56-68.
31. Ibid, p. 67.
32. Singh, 'True Valour', p. 38.
33. Nanavatty interviews, 2017-18.
34. Nanavatty interviews and email correspondence of 18 November 2019.
35. Nanavatty interviews.
36. Interview with Brigadier Devender Kumar, NDC, New Delhi, 13 May 2017.
37. All these posts are named by the Indian Army and as they are still manned, their names are represented by letters.
38. Nanavatty interviews.
39. In army parlance, Point 6400 refers to an unnamed height that measures 6,400 metres. It is called 'Point six-four-zero-zero'.
40. Ishfaq Ali, *Fangs*, pp. 87-117.
41. Ibid. Force Command Northern Areas or FCNA is a division-sized force deployed in Pakistan's Northern Areas comprising Gilgit and Baltistan and includes the Siachen Glacier.

42. Nanavatty interview and compilation of operational reports from varied sources.
43. Nanavatty interviews.
44. Nanavatty diaries.
45. Telephonic interview with Captain Vijayant in August 2019.
46. For a second Pakistani perspective on the Battle of Chumik, see Lieutenant Colonel S.M.H.Y. Naqvi, 'The Battle of Chumik', *Pakistan Army Journal,* Vol. XXX. No. 4, December 1989.
47. Email exchange between the author and Nanavatty, 18 November 2019.
48. Write-up on Bofors sent to author on email by Lieutenant General Ahuja on 10 October 2019. See Chapter 3 for further details.
49. Interview with Brigadier V.K. Sharma, NDC, New Delhi, May 2017.
50. Edward W. Desmond, 'War on High Ground', *Time,* 17 July 1989, p. 8.
51. The figures are mainly representative and may not be accurate. From the discussion on modalities of arty engagements on the glacier – Nanavatty interview.
52. Interview with Brigadier Ramesh, NDC, New Delhi, May 2017.
53. Nanavatty interviews.

Chapter 8: Flyboys over the Glacier

1. W.P.S. Sidhu, 'Tenuous Lifeline', *India Today,* 31 May 1992, p. 99.
2. Interviews and email correspondence with Air Commodore Shashank Mishra, October 2016 to March 2017.
3. Ibid.
4. From the squadron diary of 114 Helicopter Unit.
5. Email correspondence with Mishra.
6. A.V.M. Manmohan Bahadur, 'In 1990, there was another daring rescue of an IAF helicopter from Siachen glacier', The Print, 28 December 2018. Accessed online at https://theprint.in/opinion/in-1990-there-was-another-daring-rescue-of-an-iaf-helicopter-from-siachen-glacier/170068/.
7. 'Siachen Glacier: Roll of Honour'. Accessed online at http://www.bharat-rakshak.com/IAF/Personnel/Martyrs/198-4-99-Siachen.html.
8. Ibid.
9. Interview with Air Vice Marshal 'Harry' Ahluwalia, 16 December 2016.
10. Ibid.
11. Email correspondence with Group Captain Lamba.
12. Conversation with squadron pilots of 48 Squadron at Chandigarh.
13. Arjun Subramaniam, *India's Wars I,* p. 8.

14. From multiple conversations with pilots from the MiG-23 MF squadrons. Correlated with logbook entries.
15. Interview with Air Commodore Tejinder 'Tango' Singh, NDC, New Delhi, April-May 2017. Tango had meticulously maintained a diary and recorded his impressions of life on the Siachen glacier.
16. Lieutenant General Prakash Katoch, 'Tryst with Deceit', *Outlook*, 23 April 2012. Accessed online at https://www.outlookindia.com/website/story/tryst-with-deceit/280653.
17. Email correspondence and telephonic conversation with Air Chief Marshal Major.
18. Telephonic conversation with Colonel Jayaram on 15 July 2019.
19. These comprised Grenadiers, Gorkhas, Rajputs, Jats, Dogras, Mahars, Marathas, Jammu and Kashmir Rifles and more. From email correspondence with Mishra.
20. Nanavatty interviews.
21. Interview with Subedar Major Satheesan at the Madras Regimental Centre, Wellington, 21 April 2016.
22. Presentation by Nanavatty made to cadets of the Rashtriya Indian Military College, Dehradun, 16 October 1992. From the Nanavatty diaries.
23. Ibid.
24. '869 soldiers have died in Siachen since 1984' , 13 July 2018. Accessed online at https://economictimes.indiatimes.com/news/defence/869-indian-soldiers-have-died-in-siachen-since-1984/articleshow/50138852.cms?from=mdr.
25. 'Siachen: 879 deaths and still counting', *Indian Express*, 11 February 2016. Accessed online at http://indianexpress.com/article/india/india-news-india/siachen-avalanche-hanumanthappa/.
26. 'Avalanche traps 135 people near Siachen', 7 April 2012. Accessed online at https://tribune.com.pk/story/361097/avalanche-traps-over-100-pakistani-soldiers-report/.
27. Anna Orton, *India's Borderland Dispute: China, Pakistan, Bangladesh, Nepal* (New Delhi: Epitome Books, 2010), pp. 96-98.
28. Katoch interview.
29. 29. Shyam Saran, *How India Sees The World* (New Delhi: Juggernaut, 2017), pp. 90-92.
30. 'When M.K. Narayanan stalled the Siachen deal', 7 September 2017. Accessed online at http://www.dnaindia.com/india/report-when-mk-narayanan-stalled-siachen-deal-2543556.
31. A. Linsbauer, H. Frey, W. Haeberli, H. Machguth, M. Azam and S. Allen, 'Modelling glacier-bed overdeepenings and possible future lakes for the glaciers in the Himalaya Karakoram region', *Annals*

of Glaciology, Vol. 57, No. 71 (2016), pp. 119-30. Accessed online at https://www.cambridge.org/core/journals/annals-of-glaciology/article/modelling-glacierbed-overdeepenings-and-possible-future-lakes-for-the-glaciers-in-the-himalayakarakoram-region/C18FD61BBB68E27ECCF5657074A8246A.

32. Karan Kharb, 'Why China and Pakistan want demilitarization of Siachen', 19 May 2014. Accessed online at http://www.indiandefencereview.com/news/why-china-and-pakistan-want-demilitarization-of-siachen/.
33. Hooda interview.
34. Javed Hassan, 'The Fight for Siachen', *Express Tribune*, 22 April 2012. Accessed online at https://tribune.com.pk/story/368394/the-fight-for-siachen/.
35. Colonel Vinayak Bhat, 'Fresh Provocation: China building a 36 km-long road in strategic J&K valley near Siachen', The Print, 15 January 2018. Accessed online at https://theprint.in/security/china-building-a-36-km-long-road-valley-siachen/28812/.
36. Nanavatty diaries and interview.
37. Farook Zain, 'Siachen Conflict', p. 82.

Chapter 9: Standing Up to the Dragon

1. J.M. Singh was the divisional commander of 5th Mountain Division during Operation Falcon and at the forefront of all defensive and offensive plans for countering the PLA incursion into the Sumdorong Chu Valley.
2. Anit Mukherjee, *The Absent Dialogue: Politicians, Bureaucrats and the Military in India* (New Delhi: Oxford University Press, 2019), pp. 66-67.
3. For a brilliant account of the build-up to the battles at Nathu La and Cho La, also see Probal Dasgupta, *Watershed 1967: India's Forgotten Victory over China* (New Delhi: Juggernaut, 2019), pp. 51-81.
4. See Inder Malhotra, 'Indian Tonic at Nathu La', *Guardian*, 18 September 1967, p. 8. At Pro Quest Historical Newspapers.
5. Ibid.
6. Dasgupta, *Watershed 1967*, p.100.
7. Major General Sheru Thapliyal, 'Nathu La and Cho La Clashes of 1967: How the Indian Army Dealt with Chinese Trouble', *Indian Defence Review*, 22 September 2014. Accessed online at http://www.indiandefencereview.com/when-chinese-were-given-a-bloody-nose/.
8. Ibid.
9. P.K. Roy, 'The Scene of the Incident', *The Baltimore Sun*, 17 September 1967, p. 12. At Pro Quest Historical Newspapers.
10. Interview with Sapatnekar, December 2012. Also see Dasgupta, *Watershed 1967*, pp. 138-39.

11. Joseph Lelyveld, 'India: New Troubles', *New York Times,* 17 September 1967.
12. 'PM hopes firing is local affair', *Times of India,* 2 October 1967.
13. Tanvi Madan, ' How the US viewed the 1967 Sikkim skirmishes between India and China'. Accessed online at https://theprint.in/2017/09/13/how-the-us-viewed-the-1967-sikkim-skirmishes-between-india-and-china/.
14. Arunachal Pradesh was declared the twenty-fourth state of India in February 1987.
15. For a detailed account of the Battle of Namka Chu in October 1962, see Arjun Subramaniam, *India's Wars I,* pp. 232-34.
16. For a short journalistic overview of the crisis, see Claude Arpi, 'The Sumdorong Chu Incident: A Strong Indian Stance', *Indian Defence Review,* 4 May 2013. Accessed online at www.indiandefencereview.com/the-sumdorong-chu-incident-a-strong-indian-stand/.
17. Email correspondence with J.M. Singh, 15 June 2019.
18. Ibid.
19. Class 9 indicates that the track can support a 9-ton vehicle.
20. Ibid.
21. FACs are normally young air force officers who are deployed with forward army formations to control and direct fighters and helicopters during offensive missions over the TBA.
22. Interview with General V.N. Sharma, 21 August 2019.
23. Emails and telephonic conversation with J.M. Singh between July and December 2019.
24. Email correspondence with Wing Commander Raju Srinivasan, 15 June 2019.
25. Email correspondence with Air Chief Marshal Fali Major, June 2019.
26. Email correspondence with J.M. Singh.
27. Ibid.
28. Email correspondence with Lieutenant General Ahuja, 10 October 2019. Also, conversations with Lieutenant General V.K. Ahluwalia, 14 October 2019.
29. Email correspondence with Lieutenant General J.M. Singh.
30. Ibid.
31. 'Rajiv Gandhi's 1988 visit broke ice between India and China: Chinese diplomat', *Hindustan Times,* 13 October 2017. Accessed online at https://www.hindustantimes.com/india-news/rajiv-gandhi-s-1988-visit-broke-ice-between-india-and-china-chinese-diplomat/story-JiQdkXFbI5jcNsE7c6pG0J.html.

32. Subramaniam, *India's Wars I*, pp. 220-24.
33. Email correspondence with J.M. Singh.
34. Amit Gupta, 'Determining India's Force Structure and Military Doctrine: I want my MiG', *Asian Survey*, Vol. 35, No. 5 (May 1995), pp. 441-58. Accessed on 14 August 2018 at http://jstor.org/stable/2645747.

Chapter 10: Peacekeeping in Sri Lanka: Was India Prepared?

1. Channa Wickremesekara, *The Tamil Separatist War in Sri Lanka* (Oxford: Routledge, 2016), p. 6.
2. Sunil Dasgupta, 'Why Terrorism Fails While Insurgencies Can Sometimes Succeed', Brookings Op Ed, 4 January 2002. Accessed online at https://www.brookings.edu/opinions/why-terrorism-fails-while-insurgencies-can-sometimes-succeed/. Refer Chapter 2 for understanding the difference between an insurgent and a terrorist.
3. John M. Senaveratna, *The Story of the Sinhalese from the Most Ancient Times up to the End of the Mahavansa or Great Dynasty* (New Delhi: Asian Educational Services, 1997), pp. 7-20.
4. Wickremesekara, *Tamil Separatist War*, pp. 6-9.
5. V.S. Sambandan, 'A Promise of Identity', *Frontline*, Vol. 20, Issue 5, 1 March 2014. Accessed online at http://www.frontline.in/static/html/fl2005/stories/20030314000805700.htm.
6. Shankar Bhaduri and Afsar Karim, *The Sri Lankan Crisis* (New Delhi: Lancer, 1990), pp. 7-15. Also see Wickremesekara, *Tamil Separatist War*, pp. 31-34.
7. Recently declassified 'Airgram A-97 from the Embassy in Sri Lanka to the Department of State', 23 November 1976. Accessed online at https://history.state.gov/historicaldocuments/frus1969-76ve08/d102.
8. J.N. Dixit, *Assignment Colombo* (New Delhi: Konark Publishers, 1998), p. 12.
9. Rohan Gunaratna, *Indian Intervention in Sri Lanka* (Colombo: Gunaratne Offset, 1993), pp. 135-36. Also see, Wickremesekara, *Tamil Separatist War*, pp. 11-13.
10. M.R. Narayan Swamy, *Inside an Elusive Mind: Prabhakaran* (New Delhi: Konark Publishers, 2003), pp. 3-9.
11. Shekhar Gupta, 'Such a Long Lankan Journey', *Indian Express*, 11 September 2013. Accessed online at http://indianexpress.com/article/opinion/columns/such-a-long-lankan-journey/.
12. Wickremesekara, *Tamil Separatist War*, pp. 36-37.

13. Ibid, pp. 39-42.
14. Gupta, 'Long Lankan Journey'.
15. Ibid.
16. 'The largest LTTE training camp was located at Kolathur', the *Hindu,* 28 August 2014. Accessed online at https://www.thehindu.com/news/national/tamil-nadu/the-largest-ltte-training-camp-was-located-at-kolathur/article6357629.ece.
17. Narayan Swamy, *Elusive Mind*, p. 94.
18. David Brewster, 'An Indian Sphere of Influence in the Indian Ocean?' *Security Challenges*, Vol. 6, No. 3 (Spring 2010), p. 15. Accessed online at https://www.jstor.org/stable/26459796?seq=1#metadata_info_tab_contents. Also see James R. Holmes and Toshi Yoshihara, 'India's "Monroe Doctrine" and Asia's Maritime Future', *Strategic Analysis*, Vol. 32, No. 6 (November 2008), pp. 997-1011. Accessed online at https://www.tandfonline.com/doi/abs/10.1080/09700160802404539.
19. Barbara Crossette, 'Sri Lanka Air Force Raids Tamil Guerrilla Bases', *New York Times,* 23 April 1987. Accessed online at https://www.nytimes.com/1987/04/23/world/sri-lanka-air-force-raids-tamil-guerrilla-bases.html.
20. Narayan Swamy, *Elusive Mind*, p. 149.
21. Crossette, 'Sri Lanka Air Force'.
22. Email exchange and telephone conversation on 6 April 2020 with Commander Vinayak Agashe (retd), who now lives in Nagpur.
23. Arun Prakash interview and conversation on 6 April 2020.
24. Agashe conversation.
25. For a detailed Sri Lankan perspective of Operation Liberation see Cyril Ranatunga, *Adventurous Journey: From Peace to War, Insurgency to Terrorism* (Colombo: Vijitha Yapa Publications, 2009).
26. Rohan Gunaratna, *Indian Intervention*, p. iii.
27. Dixit, *Assignment Colombo*, pp. 326-50.
28. For a detailed account of Operation Poomalai see Bharat Kumar, *Operation Pawan: Role of Airpower with IPKF* (New Delhi: Manohar, 2015), pp. 54-66.
29. For a detailed overview of their exploits see Arjun Subramaniam, *India's Wars I,* pp. 297-319.
30. Dilip Bobb, 'Sri Lanka: Tackling the Tigers', *India Today,* 30 June 1987. Accessed online http://indiatoday.intoday.in/story/indias-decision-to-airdrop-supplies-over-jaffna-opens-up-a-diplomatic-pandora-box/1/337218.html. Also see Dixit, *Assignment Colombo*, pp. 100-109.

31. Interview with Air Vice Marshal H.S. Ahluwalia, 7 September 2016.
32. Accessed online at https://peacemaker.un.org/sites/peacemaker.un.org/files/IN%20LK_870729_Indo-Lanka%20Accord.pdf.
33. A reliable anonymous source.
34. Interviews with Brigadier R.R. Palsokar and Brigadier Sapatnekar at Pune, January 2013.
35. Dixit, *Assignment Colombo*, p. 156.
36. Palsokar interview.
37. Interview with Nanavatty, 14 February 2017.
38. Interview with General V.P. Malik, 31 January 2020.
39. There was no mention of any impending operations in the operational record book of 7 Squadron.
40. Interview with Major General Bhaduria. Bhaduria's unit was among the early units that were inducted into Jaffna.
41. Email correspondence between Admiral Arun Prakash and Rear Admiral Kapil Gupta, 17 October 2019.
42. Interview with Arun Prakash, Naval War College, 30 October 2016.
43. Email correspondence, Prakash and Gupta.
44. Major General Harkirat Singh, *Intervention in Sri Lanka: The IPKF Experience Retold* (New Delhi: Manohar, 2007), pp. 30-34.
45. Subramaniam, *India's Wars I*, pp. 411-12.
46. Singh, *Intervention in Sri Lanka*, p. 33.
47. Ibid, pp. 28-33.
48. Kumar, *Operation Pawan*, p. 79.
49. Vice Admiral G.M. Hiranandani, *Transition to Triumph: The Indian Navy 1976-1990* (New Delhi: Lancer Publishers, 2004), pp. 192-94.
50. Lieutenant General Depinder Singh, *The IPKF in Sri Lanka* (New Delhi: Trishul Publications, 1992), p. 43.
51. Interview with 'X', the anonymous covert operative.
52. Singh, *Intervention in Sri Lanka*, p. 47. Also see M.R. Narayan Swamy, *Tigers of Lanka: From Boys to Guerrillas* (Colombo: Vijitha Yapa Publications, 1994), pp. 252-54.
53. Vellupilla Pirabakaran, 'On the Indo–Sri Lanka Accord', Tamilnation.org, 4 August 1987. Accessed online at http://tamilnation.co/ltte/vp/87suthumalai.htm.
54. Interview with Colonel R. Hariharan. Accessed online at http://www.internationallawjournaloflondon.com/interview-with-indian-peacekeeping-forces-intelligence-corps-chief-col.-hariharan.html.

55. Gupta, 'Long Lankan Journey'. For an equally insightful peek into the activities of R&AW, see Shekhar Gupta, 'The Espionage Game', *India Today,* 31 December 1993. Accessed online at http://indiatoday.intoday.in/story/the-espionage-game/1/303572.html.
56. Hariharan interview.
57. Singh, *IPKF in Sri Lanka*, p. 59.
58. Kumar, *Operation Pawan*, p. 88.
59. Interview with Nanavatty. He was privy to these conversations during his short stint with the IPKF.
60. S. Murari, *The Prabhakaran Saga: The Rise and Fall of an Eelam Warrior* (New Delhi: Sage, 2012), pp. 39-41.
61. Rohan Gunaratna, *Indian Intervention,* pp. 235-36.
62. Interview with Lieutenant General Pattabhiraman, 13 December 2016.

Chapter 11: Into the Tiger's Lair

1. Lieutenant General S.C. Sardeshpande, *Assignment Jaffna* (New Delhi: Lancer, 1992), p. 158.
2. Dr Joanne Richards, 'An Institutional History of the Liberation Tigers Tamil of Eelam', CCDP Working Paper No. 10, November 2014. Accessed online at http://repository.graduateinstitute.ch/record/292651/files/CCDP-Working-Paper-10-LTTE-1.pdf.
3. Ibid.
4. Shekhar Gupta, 'India's Blackhawk Down: Incompetence and Heroism in a Commando Raid', 14 October 2018. Accessed online at https://theprint.in/opinion/indias-blackhawk-down-incompetence-heroism-in-a-commando-raid-gone-wrong-at-jaffna-univ/134316/.
5. Singh, *Intervention in Sri Lanka*, pp. 174-76.
6. For a detailed account of myriad facets of the Jaffna battle, see Shekhar Gupta, 'In Rush to Vanquish', *India Today,* 13 January 1988, and 'Uncovering the War', 13 September 2013. Accessed online at http:/indianexpress.com/article/news-archive/print/uncovering-the-war/. Also see Dilip Bobb, 'A Bloodied Accord', *India Today,* 15 November 1987. Accessed online at intoday.in/story/after-16-days=of-bloody-fighting-ipkf-finally-captures-ltte-stronghold-jaffna/1/337703.
7. Ibid.
8. Ibid.
9. Jagan Pillarisetti, 'Descent into Danger', 7 March 2015. Accessed online at https://swarajyamag.com/politics/descent-into-danger-the-jaffna-university-helidrop.

10. Ibid.
11. Sardeshpande, *Assignment Jaffna*, pp. 46-47.
12. Brigadier R.R. Palsokar (retd), *Ours Not To Reason Why* (Pune: Sunidhi Publishers, 2017). My narration of the trials and tribulations of 7 Brigade are a fusion of my understanding of Palsokar's narrative, several email exchanges and conversations with him, and conversations with many who served in the brigade or supported it.
13. Palsokar, *Ours Not to Reason Why*, pp. 106-107.
14. Email correspondence with Palsokar.
15. Emails and interviews with Palsokar and others.
16. Kumar, *Operation Pawan*, pp. 148-59.
17. Unni Kartha, 'Stroll through the killing fields of Sri Lanka', 31 October 2018. Accessed online at http://cyclicstories.blogspot.com/2018/.
18. Several conversations with Group Captain Rajnish Malhotra (retd).
19. Interview with Nanavatty, 14 February 2017.
20. Off-the-record conversations with currently serving officers in the Indian Army who wish to remain anonymous.
21. Ibid.
22. Interview with Colonel Hariharan.
23. Katoch interview.
24. Ibid.
25. Nanavatty interview.
26. Ibid.
27. Email correspondence with Captain Chandavarkar, 16 July 2019. Also see Hiranandani, *Transition to Triumph*, pp. 241-42.
28. From the 57 Division operational diaries. Also see Rohan Gunaratna, *Indian Intervention*, p. 258.
29. Anita Pratap, 'Sri Lanka: IPKF gains public acceptance in Batticaloa', *India Today*, 15 June 1988. Accessed online at https://www.indiatoday.in/magazine/neighbours/story/19880615-sri-lanka-ipkf-gains-public-acceptance-in-batticaloa-797341-1988-06-15.
30. Shyam Tekwani, 'Sri Lanka voters back United National Party but peace remains elusive'. Accessed online at https://www.indiatoday.in/magazine/neighbours/story/19890315-sri-lanka-voters-back-united-national-party-but-peace-remains-elusive-815847-1989-03-15.
31. Rohan Gunaratna, *Indian Intervention*, p. 259.
32. Interview with General V.N. Sharma, 21 August 2019.
33. Ibid.

34. Telephonic conversation with Admiral Madhavendra Singh, 2 May 2020.
35. Hiranandani, *Transition to Triumph*, p. 195. Also, interview with General V.N.Sharma.
36. Ashoke Mehta, 'Tackling the Tigers'. Accessed online at http://www.india-seminar.com/1999/479/479%20mehta.htm. Also see, 'Revisiting interventionism:India's peacekeeping force in Sri Lanka', Discussion held at Brookings India on 5 May 2019. Accessed online at https://www.brookings.edu/events/revisiting-interventionism-indias-peacekeeping-force-in-sri-lanka/.
37. Brewster, 'An Indian Sphere of Influence'.
38. Email correspondence with Hariharan, 19 September 2019.
39. Interview with X.
40. Nanavatty interviews.
41. Mehta, 'Tackling the Tigers'.
42. Hiranandani, *Transition to Triumph*, p. 196.
43. Ibid.
44. Arjun Subramaniam, 'The Use of Air Power in Sri Lanka: Operation Pawan and Beyond', *Air Power Journal*, Vol. 3, No. 3 (Monsoon 2008), pp. 15-35.

Chapter 12: Speedy Intervention in the Maldives

1. From a presentation on Operation Cactus at the Defence Services Staff College in 1990 by Group Captain Anant Bewoor and Brigadier S.C. Joshi. The presentation has been refined over the years and widely presented across India at war colleges and universities. The presentation was shared with the author by Bewoor.
2. Conversation with Group Captain Bewoor, March 2020.
3. Sushant Singh, *Mission Overseas: Daring Operations by the Indian Military*, (New Delhi: Juggernaut, 2017), pp. 18-20.
4. Interview with General Malik, 31 January 2020.
5. Presentation by Bewoor and Joshi and several conversations with Bewoor.
6. Email correspondence with Lieutenant General Navkiran Singh Ghei, 9 June 2019.
7. Telephone conversation with Bewoor.
8. Presentation by Bewoor and Joshi.
9. Ibid.
10. Email correspondence with Ghei, 9 June 2019.

11. Presentation by Bewoor and Joshi.
12. Email correspondence with Ghei, 9 June 2019.
13. Email correspondence with Wing Commander Raju Srinivasan, 15 March 2021.
14. Interview with Captain Jayadevan on 2 and 4 June 2019.
15. Anonymous sources.
16. Commodore H.A. Gokhale, 'Operation Cactus: A Naval Perspective', from the presentation by Group Captain Bewoor and Brigadier Joshi, Defence Services Staff College, 1990.
17. Jayadevan interview.
18. Ibid.
19. Ibid.
20. From the Bewoor papers and briefings.
21. Nayanima Basu and Amiti Sen, 'India mulls intervention as Maldives crisis deepens', *Hindu Business Line,* 6 February 2018. Accessed online at https://www.thehindubusinessline.com/news/world/india-mulls-intervention-as-maldives-crisis-deepens/article22670700.ece
22. Inputs from a now-retired senior IAF officer who was involved in the operation and has requested anonymity.

Chapter 13: Jammu and Kashmir Erupts

1. Major General Akbar Khan, *Raiders in Kashmir* (Delhi: Army Publishers, 1999), pp. 11-32.
2. Sheikh Abdullah, *Flames of Chinar* (translated by Khushwant Singh).
3. Arjun Subramaniam, *India's Wars I*, pp. 121-31.
4. Simon Jones, 'India, Pakistan and counterinsurgency operations in Jammu and Kashmir', *Small Wars and Insurgencies,* Vol. 19, No. 1 (March 2008), p. 4. Accessed online at https://www.tandfonline.com/doi/abs/10.1080/09592310801905736.
5. C. Dasgupta, *War and Diplomacy in Kashmir: 1947-1948* (New Delhi: Sage Publications, 2002), p. 102.
6. Swami, *India, Pakistan*, p. 46.
7. Ibid.
8. 'Sheikh Abdullah and the Kashmir Issue', a declassified CIA report, 18 April 1964. Accessed online at https://www.cia.gov/library/readingroom/docs/DOC_0000283431.pdf.
9. Ibid.
10. Swami, *India, Pakistan*, pp. 53-55.

11. Subramaniam, *India's Wars I,* pp. 275-282.
12. Ibid, pp. 261-335.
13. Brigadier Pranadhar Gaur, 'Use of Force in Regional Conflicts: A Study of Pakistan's Two-Level Strategy in Kashmir since 1987', Jawaharlal Nehru University, July 2000. Accessed online at http://shodhganga.inflibnet.ac.in/handle/10603/15150?mode=full.
14. Ibid, p. 78 and Major General Shaukat Riza, *The Pakistan Army War 1965* (Lahore: Wajid Ali's Ltd, 1984), p. 20.
15. Hussain Haqqani, *India vs Pakistan: Why Can't We Just Be Friends* (New Delhi: Juggernaut, 2016), pp. 115-16. Also see Aslam Siddiqui, *Pakistan Seeks Security* (Lahore: Longman Green, 1960), p. 67.
16. C. Christine Fair, *Fighting to the End: The Pakistan Army's Way of War* (New Delhi: Oxford University Press, 2014), p. 101.
17. Gaur, 'Use of Force', pp. 105-07.
18. Subramaniam, *India's Wars I,* pp. 423-38.
19. Fair, *Fighting to the End,* pp. 81-82. Zia's theological implant into the Pakistan Army is well brought out in chapter 4, 'The Army's Defense of Pakistan's Ideological Frontiers.'
20. S.K. Malik, *The Quranic Concept of War* (New Delhi: Himalayan Books, 1986). For an excellent review of the book see, Gurmeet Kanwal, 'Misinterpreting the Quran to Justify Jihad, CLAWS Issue Brief, No. 13, 2009. Accessed online at https://www.claws.in/static/IB13_Misinterpreting-the-Quran-to-Justify-Jihad.pdf.
21. Zia's derivative sub-conventional strategy against India bore a striking similarity to Mao's guerrilla warfighting strategy.
22. Fair, *Fighting to the End,* pp. 40-65. Chapter 3, 'Born an Insecure State', offers insights into the origins of Pakistan's deep sense of insecurity vis-à-vis India.
23. Of the numerous books written by Sumit Ganguly, I found *Conflict Unending: India-Pakistan Tensions since 1947* (Columbia University Press, 2002) and *Deadly Impasse* (Cambridge University Press, 2016) to be the most instructive.
24. Swami, *India, Pakistan*, pp. 78-85.
25. Ibid.
26. Ibid, pp. 125-30.
27. Subramaniam, *India's Wars I,* p. 119.
28. Swami, *India, Pakistan*, pp. 158-60.
29. 'Who is Syed Salahuddin, and why is he designated as a "global terrorist"?', *Hindu,* 27 June 2017. Accessed online at https://www.thehindu.com/

news/national/who-is-syed-salahuddin-and-what-is-a-global-terrorist/article19154173.ece.

30. Ved Marwah, *Uncivil Wars: Pathology of Terrorism in India* (New Delhi: Indus, 1995), pp. 166-75.
31. Ibid.
32. Joseph C. Myers, 'The Quranic Concept of War', *Parameters* (Winter 2006-07). Accessed online at http://insct.syr.edu/wp-content/uploads/2013/03/MyersJoseph.Quranic-Concept-of-War.pdf.
33. Major General Afsar Karim, 'Operation Topac', *Indian Defence Review,* July 1989.
34. Ibid, pp. 35-48.
35. Sean P. Winchell, 'Pakistan's ISI: The Invisible Government' *International Journal of Intelligence and Counter Intelligence,* Vol. 16, No. 3 (Fall 2003), p. 374. Accessed at https://www.tandfonline.com/doi/abs/10.1080/713830449.
36. Gaur, 'Use of Force', Chapter V.
37. Ibid.
38. Winchell, 'Pakistan's ISI', p. 374.
39. Ibid, p. 379.
40. Fatalities in terrorist violence 1988-2017, South Asia Terrorism Portal. Accessed online at http://www.satp.org/satporgtp/countries/india/states/jandk/data_sheets/annual_casualties.htm.
41. 'Ajit Doval says not one bullet fired in Kashmir in the past month, a record since 1988'. Accessed online at https://theprint.in/india/ajit-doval-says-not-one-bullet-fired-in-kashmir-in-the-past-month-a-record-since-1988/288279/.
42. Jones, 'India, Pakistan', p. 7.
43. Paul Staniland, 'Organizing Insurgency: Networks, Resources and Rebellion in South Asia', *International Security,* Vol. 37, No. 1 (Summer 2012), pp. 142-77. Accessed online at https://www.jstor.org/stable/23280407?seq=1. This piece offers an excellent overview of all the major terrorist networks and groups in J&K.
44. South Asia Terrorism Portal.
45. Siddhartha Gigoo, 'In Search of Stories Lost'. Accessed online at https://www.livemint.com/Leisure/AIQpbcotgcNTeiGf7lzF0I/In-search-of-stories-lost.html. Gigoo wrote this story twenty-six years after he was forced to leave his home as part of the widespread pogrom unleashed on Kashmiri Hindus by radical Kashmiri separatists led by the Jamaat-e-Islami.

46. For a detailed account of this period see Manoj Joshi, *The Lost Rebellion: Kashmir in the Nineties* (New Delhi: Penguin, 1999). Also see Praveen Swami, 'Terrorism in Jammu and Kashmir in Theory and Practice', *India Review,* Vol. 2, No. 3, 2003, pp. 55-58.
47. Arif Jamal, *Shadow War* (New York: Melville Publishing, 2009), p. 109.
48. Arif Jamal, *Call for Transnational Jihad: Lashkar-e-Tayyaba (1985-2014)* (New Delhi: Kautilya Books, 2015), pp. 92-119.
49. Winchell, 'Pakistan's ISI', p. 380.
50. Staniland, 'Organizing Insurgency', p. 167. Also see Swami, 'Terrorism in Jammu and Kashmir', pp. 58-59.
51. Jones, 'India, Pakistan', pp. 9-10.
52. Praveen Swami, 'Remains of Another Day', *Frontline,* Vol. 17, Issue 2, 22 January 2000. Accessed online at https://frontline.thehindu.com/static/html/fl1702/17020100.htm.
53. For a list of terrorist organizations as declared by the US, see https://www.state.gov/j/ct/rls/other/des/123085.htm.
54. Pandita, 'Beyond Balakot', *Open,* 28 February 2019. Accessed online at https://openthemagazine.com/cover-stories/beyond-balakot/.
55. C. Christine Fair, *In Their Words: Understanding Lashkar-e-Tayyaba* (New Delhi: Oxford University Press, 2019), p. 77. Also, IAF archives and operational diary at the air force station in Srinagar.
56. Nanavatty interviews.
57. Ibid.
58. A detailed overview of major terrorist attacks in India prior to the 2008 attacks is available in Gurmeet Kanwal and N. Manoharan, eds., *India's War on Terror* (New Delhi: KW Publishers, 2010), pp. 283-96.
59. Adrian Levy and Cathy-Scott Clark, *The Meadow: Kashmir, Where the Terror Began* (New Delhi: HarperCollins, 2012) pp. 31-57. The best profile of Masood Azhar can be found in the chapter 'A Father's Woes'.
60. Shujaat Bukhari, 'From a calm moulvi to a dreaded militant', *Hindu,* 17 October 2001. Accessed online at https://www.thehindu.com/thehindu/2001/10/17/stories/02170003.htm.
61. Interview with Colonel Pavan Nair, Pune, 30 March 2019.
62. South Asia Terrorism Portal.
63. United Nations Security Council, 'Jaish-i-Mohammed', https://www.un.org/securitycouncil/sanctions/1267/aq_sanctions_list/summaries/entity/jaish-i-mohammed.
64. 'Kaluchak Massacre, 14 May 2002', Ministry of External Affairs press release. Accessed online at https://mea.gov.in/in-focus-article.htm?18990/Kaluchak+Massacre+14+May+2002.

Chapter 14: The Indian Army Responds

1. Imran Khan speaking during a visit to the ISI HQ in September 2018. Accessed online at https://economictimes.indiatimes.com/news/defence/isi-is-pakistans-first-line-of-defence-says-pakistani-pm/articleshow/65796885.cms.
2. Nanavatty interviews. Many of Nanavatty's briefings and letters to his commanders reflected a continuous attempt to differentiate between insurgency and terrorism.
3. Interview with Lieutenant General M.A. Zaki, Hyderabad, 1 July 2019.
4. Swami, *India, Pakistan*, pp. 145-49.
5. Hamish Telford, 'Counterinsurgency in India: Observations from Punjab and Kashmir', *Journal Of Conflict Studies*, Vol. 21, No. 1 (Spring 2001). Accessed online at https://journals.lib.unb.ca/index.php/JCS/article/view/4293.
6. Rajesh Rajagopalan, *Fighting Like a Guerrilla* (New Delhi: Routledge, 2008), and Rostum Nanavatty, *Internal Armed Conflict in India* (New Delhi: Pentagon Press, 2013).
7. Nanavatty interviews.
8. Kaushik Adhikary, 'Combating terrorism in 21st century: The legal and institutional responses with special reference to Indian security laws', thesis, University of Calcutta, 2017. Accessed online https://shodhganga.inflibnet.ac.in/handle/10603/172205. See Chapter V.
9. Skype interview with Lieutenant General Syed Ata Hasnain, 6 April 2020.
10. John A. Nagl, *Learning to Eat Soup with a Knife: Counterinsurgency Lessons from Malaya and Vietnam* (Chicago: University of Chicago Press, 2005), p. 28.
11. HQ Northern Command Study Group, *Soldiers Role in Jammu and Kashmir* (New Delhi: HQ Northern Command, 1984).
12. Hasnain interview.
13. Letter written by Jagmohan to Rajiv Gandhi in April 1990. Accessed online at http://www.newindianexpress.com/nation/2019/aug/17/potatoes-one-day-the-pope-the-next-2020117.html.
14. Gaur, 'Use of Force', p. 287.
15. Interview with Brigadier 'R'.
16. Swami, *India, Pakistan*, p. 175.
17. Jagmohan, *My Frozen Turbulence in Kashmir* (Bombay: Allied Publishers, 1991), pp. 162-65. Also see Inderjit Badhwar, https://www.indiatoday.in/magazine/special-report/story/19870915-rising-unpopularity-threatens-kashmir-accord-799268-1987-09-15.
18. Zaki interview.

19. Pradeep Thakur, *Militant Monologues* (Parity Paperbacks, 2003). Also see Barbara Crossette, 'Abducted Woman Freed in Kashmir', *New York Times,* 14 December 1989. Accessed online at https://www.nytimes.com/1989/12/14/world/abducted-woman-freed-in-kashmir.html.
20. 'Ashfaq Majeed Wani remembered', *Greater Kashmir,* 5 July 2019. Accessed online at https://www.greaterkashmir.com/news/kashmir/ashfaq-majeed-wani-remembered/.
21. Swami, *India, Pakistan*, p. 175.
22. Zaki interview.
23. A detailed profile of Syed Salahuddin. Accessed online at *Economic Times*, 14 July 2018, https://economictimes.indiatimes.com/news/defence/syed-salahuddin-tale-of-a-preacher-turned-terror-chief/articleshow/59343807.cms?from=mdr.
24. Pankaj Pachauri, 'Mirwaiz fiasco sparks off a change in guard in Kashmir', *India Today,* 15 June 1990. Accessed online at https://www.indiatoday.in/magazine/indiascope/story/19900615-mirwaiz-fiasco-sparks-off-a-change-of-guard-in-kashmir-812692-1990-06.
25. Bilal Handoo, 'Charar after Mast Gul', *Kashmir Life,* 17 May 2016. Accessed online at https://kashmirlife.net/charar-after-mast-gul-issue-09-vol-08-105467/.
26. 'Mast Gul, a freedom fighter turned terrorist attacks Peshawar', *News*, 7 February 2014. Accessed online at https://www.thenews.com.pk/archive/print/636032-mast-gul,-a-freedom-fighter-turned-terrorist-attacks-peshawar.
27. Lawrence E. Cline, 'Pseudo Operations in Counterinsurgency: Lessons from other countries', SSI Monograph, US Army War College. Accessed online at https://www.globalsecurity.org/military/library/report/2005/ssi_cline.pdf. The paper does not cover operations conducted by the Indian Army as these were never openly publicized. Also see Staniland, 'Organizing Insurgency'.
28. Ibid.
29. Interview with Colonel Pavan Nair, 30 March 2019.
30. Interview with Lieutenant General Pattabhiraman.
31. Hasnain interview.

Chapter 15: Surprise and Riposte in Kargil

1. Briefing to senior PAF officers, 12 May 1999, Rawalpindi.
2. The FCNA leads a division-sized formation under Pakistan's 10 Corps with four brigades, including the brigade fighting in Siachen.
3. Interviews with Nanavatty and Katoch.

4. Telephonic conversation with Major General Alok Deb, 22 November 2019.
5. Lashkars are tribal militias from Pakistan's north-western frontier provinces who have been used as proxies by the Pakistan Army since 1947.
6. Subramaniam, *India's Wars I*, p. 142.
7. Ibid, pp. 275-78.
8. For a detailed overview of the battles to capture Point 13620, see http://www.scoopnews.in/det.aspx?q=49500.
9. Vivek Chadha, *Low Intensity Conflicts in South Asia: An Analysis* (New Delhi: Sage Publications, 2005), p. 141. Also see Shaukat Qadir, 'An Analysis of the Kargil Conflict 1999', the *RUSI Journal,* 2002, pp. 24-30. Accessed online at https://doi.org/10.1080/03071840208446752.
10. Owen Bennet Jones, *Pakistan: Eye of the Storm* (New Haven: Yale University Press, 2002), pp. 94-96.
11. Chadha, *Low Intensity Conflicts*, p. 141.
12. Many Indian officers interviewed have acknowledged the professional capabilities and raw courage of the SSG.
13. Ajai Sahni, 'Area of Darkness', *Outlook,* 18 September 2009, accessed online at https://www.outlookindia.com/website/story/an-area-of-darkness/261931.
14. Chadha, *Low Intensity Conflicts*, p. 141. Also see Alok Bansal, 'Gilgit-Baltistan: The Roots of Political Alienation', *Strategic Analysis*, Vol. 32, No. 1 (January 2008), p. 84.
15. Zafar Iqbal Cheema, 'The Strategic Concept of the Kargil Conflict', in *Asymmetric Warfare in South Asia*, ed. Peter Lavoy (New York: Cambridge University Press, 2009).
16. Telephonic conversation with Colonel Kuldip Mehta, 15 August 2019.
17. Katoch interview.
18. This overview of the area of operation on the Indian side was put together by a combination of personal visits to the region and discussions with several Indian Army officers who served in the region.
19. Rahul Bedi, 'Intel Failures made Indian attacks in Kashmir inevitable', *Jane's Intelligence Review,* Vol. 11, Issue 6 (1 June 1999).
20. Rohit Saran, Harinder Baweja and Raj Chengappa, 'Kargil conflict shows signs of intensifying as India gains, Pakistan remains resilient', *India Today,* 5 July 1999. Accessed online at https://www.indiatoday.in/magazine/cover-story/story/19990705-kargil-conflict-shows-signs-of-intensifying-as-india-gains-pakistan-remains-resilient-824618-1999-07-05.
21. Nasim Zehra, *From Kargil to the Coup* (Lahore: Sang-e-Meel Publications, 2018), pp. 96-97.
22. Ibid, p. 100.

23. Ikram Sehgal, 'Choosing Merit over Friendship', Media Monitors Network, 9 October 2001. Accessed online at https://www.mediamonitors.net/perspectives/choosing-merit-over-friendship/.
24. Qadir, 'Analysis of Kargil Conflict'.
25. Praveen Swami, 'General Kayani's Quiet Coup', the *Hindu,* 3 August 2010. Accessed online at http://www.thehindu.com/todays-paper/tp-opinion/General-Kayanis-quiet-coup/article16117389.ece.
26. C. Christine Fair, *Fighting to the End,* pp. 163-64.
27. Ibid. Fair devotes an entire chapter to how the Pakistan Army perceives India through multiple lenses.
28. Lieutenant General Mohinder Puri, *Kargil: Turning the Tide* (New Delhi: Lancer, 2016).
29. Conversation with the former air chief on the sidelines at Western Air Command, Subroto Park, New Delhi, after an air power seminar to commemorate 20 years of the Kargil conflict, 16 July 2019.
30. Patney interviews.
31. *From Surprise to Reckoning* (New Delhi: Sage Publications, 1999), pp. 85-86. Also see John Gill, 'Military Operations in the Kargil Conflict', in *Asymmetric Warfare in South Asia*, ed. Peter Lavoy (New York: Cambridge University Press, 2009), p. 101.
32. Ibid.
33. General V.P. Malik, 'The Capture of Tiger Hill: A First-hand Account', Indian Ministry of Defence Media Centre, 26 July 2002. Accessed online at http://mea.gov.in/articles-in-indian-media.htm?dtl/14805/The+capture+of+Tiger+Hill+a+firsthand+account.
34. Telephonic conversation with Mehta.
35. See J.N. Dixit, *India-Pakistan: In War and Peace* (London: Routledge, 2002) and Praveen Swami, 'Skeletons in the Generals' Cupboards', *Hindu,* 10 August 2009. Accessed online at http://www.thehindu.com/todays-paper/tp-opinion/Skeletons-in-the-Generalsrsquo-cupboards/article16530736.ece. Also see B. Raman, 'Should We Believe Gen Malik', 5 May 2006. Accessed online at http://m.rediff.com/news/1999/jul/16akd.htm.
36. General V.P. Malik, *India's Military Conflicts,* p. 120.
37. Swami, 'Skeletons'.
38. Interview with Ahluwalia, 21 February 2019.
39. Kaiser Tufail, 'Kargil Conflict and the Pakistan Air Force', *Aeronaut,* 28 January 2009. Accessed online at http://kaiser-aeronaut.blogspot.co.uk/2009/01/.
40. Ibid.
41. Ibid.
42. Zehra, *From Kargil,* p. 101.

43. Praveen Swami, 'The Kargil War: Preliminary Explorations'. Accessed online at http://www.satp.org/satporgtp/publication/faultlines/volume2/Fault2-SwamiF.htm. unfolded/articleshow/59754091.cms.
44. Interview with Lieutenant General Ghei, Chandigarh, 19 July 2019.
45. Gill, 'Military Operations'.
46. Rahul Bedi, 'Paying to Keep the High Ground,' *Jane's Intelligence Review*, Vol. 11, Issue 10 (1 October 1999).
47. General V.P. Malik, *From Surprise to Victory* (New Delhi: HarperCollins, 2006), p. 209.
48. Josy Joseph, 'Three battalions ignored as the nation honours martyrs of Kargil'. Accessed online at https://www.rediff.com/news/2000/jul/25kargil.htm.
49. Malik interview.
50. See Gill, 'Military Operations'; Malik, *Kargil;* and Zehra, *From Kargil.*
51. Gill, 'Military Operations'.
52. Ibid.
53. Sumit Walia, 'Head Hunters in Kargil-Naga Regiment, *Indian Defence Review*, 28 July 2017. Accessed online at http://www.indiandefencereview.com/spotlights/head-hunters-in-kargil-naga-regiment/.
54. 'Tololing Peak: The Battle that Probably Changed the Course of the Kargil War', *India Today*, 5 July 1999. Accessed online at https://www.indiatoday.in/magazine/cover-story/story/19990705-tololing-peak-the-battle-that-probably-changed-the-course-of-kargil-war-824608-1999-07-05.
55. Interview with Air Marshal 'Nana' Menon, Bengaluru, 21 January 2019. Also see Benjamin Lambeth, 'Air Power at 18,000: The Indian Air Force in the Kargil War', Carnegie Endowment for International Peace, 20 September 2012. Lambeth's monograph is a most authoritative and well-researched document that was written after extensive research conducted by the author in India over two visits.
56. Interview with Air Marshal Patney.
57. Conversation with Air Chief Marshal Tipnis.
58. Interview with General Malik, 31 January 2020.
59. Patney interviews.
60. Lambeth, 'Air Power'.
61. Official records and Kargil diaries, IAF History Cell, Air HQ, New Delhi. Also see Squadron Leader Alagaraj Perumal, 'Missile Strike', Lambeth, *Air Power*, 12 June 2017. Accessed online at http://www.bharat-rakshak.com/IAF/history/kargil/1060-perumal.html.
62. Conversation with Group Captain Tokekar, an active participant in the conflict as part of 7 Squadron.
63. Ibid.

64. Telephonic conversation with Patney, 25 November 2019.
65. Interview with Air Chief Marshal Dhanoa, 27 June 2019.
66. Air Commodore Sinha's narration in the squadron diary of 129 HU.
67. Vivek Chadha, 'Artillery in Op Vijay: Perspective of a Commanding Officer', 28 June 2019. Accessed online at https://www.youtube.com/watch?v=6V_XiMHyP08. Also see Major General Alok Deb, 'Artillery in Operation Vijay: Perspective of a Commanding Officer', in *Surprise, Strategy and Vijay – 20 Years of Kargil and Beyond,* ed. V.K. Ahluwalia and Narjit Singh (New Delhi: Pentagon Press, 2019), pp. 77-85.
68. Email correspondence with Air Chief Marshal Major.
69. Marcus P. Acosta, 'The Kargil Conflict: Waging War in the Himalayas', *Small Wars & Insurgencies* (2007), pp. 397-415. Accessed at https://doi.org/10.1080/09592310701674325.
70. An IAF squadron commander who requested anonymity.
71. Conversations with Bhanoji Rao, a weapons expert, and Mirage pilots who dropped the Spanish bombs, 12 October 2019.
72. L.N. Subramanian, 'A Ridge Too Far: Battle for Tololing', 12 October 2009. Accessed at http://www.bharat-rakshak.com/ARMY/history/kargil/307-battle-for-tololing.html?tmpl=component&print=1&layout=default&page=.

Chapter 16: A Costly Victory

1. Carl von Clausewitz in *On War,* eds. Michael Howard and Peter Paret (New Jersey: Princeton University Press, 1976), p. 194.
2. Lambeth, 'Air Power'.
3. 'Secret Revealed of Kargil War: Indian Air Force Used a Juggad', at https://defenceupdate.in/secret-revealed-of-kargil-war-indian-air-force-used-a-jugaad/. Also see Lambeth, 'Air Power'.
4. Patney interview.
5. Dhanoa interview.
6. Gill, 'Military Operations', p. 113. Also refer interviews with Alok Deb, 15 September 2019.
7. Gill, 'Military Operations', p. 120.
8. A dramatic description of the assault by Havildar Digendra Singh is available on YouTube. Accessed at https://www.youtube.com/watch?v=qzkm-yWXmdc. Also see account by Colonel Ravindranath, 26 July 2015. Accessed online at https://www.thequint.com/news/india/victory-in-kargil-war-lessons-learnt-at-great-human-cost.
9. Ibid.
10. Diksha Dwivedi, *Letters from Kargil* (New Delhi: Juggernaut, 2017).

11. Dhanoa interview.
12. Interview with Malik, 31 January 2020.
13. Vishnu Som, 'In Kargil War, India was minutes away from bombing Pak bases'. Accessed online at https://www.ndtv.com/india-news/exclusive-in-kargil-war-india-was-minutes-away-from-bombing-pak-bases-1433345.
14. Puri, *Kargil*, p. 78.
15. Ibid, p. 87.
16. Several personal interviews and conversations between July 2019 and March 2020.
17. Email correspondence with Deb, 19 February 2019.
18. Conversation with Wing Commander K.T. Sebastian (retd), 4 May 2020.
19. Leo Murray, *War Games: The Psychology of Combat,* (New Delhi: Jaico Publishing, 2019).
20. Conversations and formal interview with Air Marshal Nambiar and conversations with Wing Commander Anupam Banerjee.
21. Ibid. Also refer telephonic conversations with Group Captain Tokekar, who participated in both missions as a flight lieutenant.
22. Nishtha Gupta, '10 heroes India will always be proud of', *India Today,* 26 July 2019. Accessed online at https://www.indiatoday.in/india/story/10-kargil-heroes-india-will-always-be-proud-of-1574014-2019-07-26.
23. Zehra, *From Kargil*, p. 230.
24. Puri, *Kargil*, pp. 90-95. Also see Malik, *Surprise to Victory*, pp. 169-175 and Harinder Baweja, 'Kargil war: Army took over a month planning to recapture Tiger Hill in Dras Sector', *India Today,* 19 July 1999. Accessed online at https://www.indiatoday.in/magazine/cover-story/story/19990719-kargil-war-army-took-over-a-months-planning-to-recapture-tiger-hill-in-drass-sector-824832-1999-07-19.
25. Malik, *Surprise to Victory*, p. 263.
26. Interview with Admiral Madhavendra Singh.
27. Kargil review committee report, p. 160.
28. 'Introduction' in *Asymmetric Warfare in South Asia,* ed. Peter Lavoy (New York: Cambridge University Press, 2009).
29. Sushant Sareen, 'Balakot air strikes: the end of the madman theory', *ORF Commentary,* 5 March 2019. Accessed online at https://www.orfonline.org/research/balakot-air-strikes-the-end-of-the-madman-theory-48730/.
30. Bedi, 'Paying to Keep'.
31. Gill, 'Military Operations'.
32. Peter Lavoy, 'A Conversation with Gen Khalid Kidwai', Carnegie International Nuclear Policy Conference, 23 March 2015. Accessed online at https://carnegieendowment.org/files/03-230315carnegieKIDWAI.pdf.

33. Strobe Talbott, 'The day a nuclear conflict was averted', *Yale Global Online*, 13 September 2004. Accessed online at https://yaleglobal.yale.edu/content/day-nuclear-conflict-was-averted.
34. Strobe Talbott, *Engaging India: Diplomacy, Democracy and the Bomb* (Washington, DC: Brookings Institution Press), pp. 154-69.
35. Ibid.
36. Lavoy, *Asymmetric Warfare*, p. 4.
37. Ibid.
38. Pervez Musharraf, *In the Line of Fire* (New York: Free Press, 2006).
39. Arjun Subramaniam, 'Kargil Revisited: Air Operations in a High-Altitude Conflict', *Claws Journal* (Summer 2008), pp. 183-95.
40. Clausewitz, *On War*, p. 340.
41. Zehra, *From Kargil*, pp. 219-20.
42. Kargil review committee report, pp. 252-64.
43. Dixit, *India-Pakistan*. Swami largely goes along with Dixit's hypothesis in his writings, blaming the Indian Army for gross dereliction of duty.
44. Malik, *Surprise to Victory*, pp. 85-112.
45. Subramaniam, 'Kargil Revisited', p. 191.
46. Ibid, p. 215.
47. Patney interview.
48. Vinod Anand, 'India's Military Response to the Kargil Aggression', *Strategic Analysis*, Vol. 23 (October 1999), p. 56.
49. Marcus Acosta, *High Altitude Warfare: The Kargil Conflict and the Future*, Naval Postgraduate School, Monterey, California, June 2003, pp. 18-45.
50. Lieutenant General Mohan Bhandari, 'Kargil Controversy: Army Trashed IAF Perspective', *Indian Defence Review*, Vol. 25 (April-June 2010). Accessed online at http://www.indiandefencereview.com/spotlights/kargil-controversy-army-trashes-iaf-perspective/.
51. Zehra, *From Kargil*, p. 232.
52. Kaiser Tufail, 'Kargil Conflict and Pakistan Air Force', 28 January 2009, accessed online at http://kaiser-aeronaut.blogspot.com/2009/01/kargil-conflict-and-pakistan-air-force.html.
53. Telephonic conversation with Patney, 25 November 2019.
54. Subramaniam, 'Kargil Revisited', p. 194.
55. Ved Shenag, 'The IAF in the Kargil Operations 1999'. Accessed online at http://bharat-rakshak.com/IAF/History/Kargil/1055-VedShenag.html.
56. Patney interviews.

Chapter 17: Hybrid War in J&K

1. K. Subrahmanyam, 'A proactive Kashmir policy', *Economic Times*, 7 September 1988.
2. Harsha Kakar, 'Has Pakistan started losing the hybrid war in Kashmir', Raisina Debates, 2018, ORF Online. Accessed online at https://www.orfonline.org/expert-speak/has-pakistan-started-losing-hybrid-war-kashmir-46027/.
3. Extensive email correspondence in August 2019 between the author and Lieutenant General John Ranjan Mukherjee (retd).
4. Ibid.
5. Rajesh Ahuja, 'Looking back, the ceasefire in Kashmir in 2000 saw more violence but lasted longer', *Hindustan Times*, 17 June 2018. Accessed online at https://www.hindustantimes.com/india-news/looking-back-the-ceasefire-in-2000-saw-more-violence-but-was-longer/story-eD1BIfi109TFgopG.
6. Extensive conversation with Brigadier R.K. Singh (retd) in Dehradun on 11 and 12 March 2019.
7. Email correspondence with Colonel Gurdeep Bains, October 2018.
8. Letter written by Bains to his battalion on 11 December 2001.
9. Letter from Victor Force to Army HQ on 28 May 2002.
10. From a letter written by Bains to his battalion on 23 April 2003.
11. Email correspondence with Bains.
12. Firdaus Tak, 'Warwan Valley: A Hidden Beauty', Greater Kashmir, 24 July 2012. Accessed online at https://www.greaterkashmir.com/news/news/warwan-valley-a-hidden-beauty/125718.html.
13. Personal papers of Bains.
14. Interview with Arun Prakash, 30 October 2016.
15. Personal papers of Bains.
16. Interview with Bains, Bengaluru, 10 February 2019.
17. Nanavatty interviews.
18. Praveen Swami, 'Hype and the folly', *Frontline*, Vol. 20, Issue 13, 20 June 2013. Accessed online at https://frontline.thehindu.com/static/html/fl2013/stories/20030704007300400.htm.
19. Nanavatty interviews.
20. Hooda interview.
21. Nanavatty interviews and diaries.
22. Hasnain interview, 6 April 2020. Also see Happymon Jacob, *Line on Fire: Ceasefire Violations and India-Pakistan Escalation Dynamics*, Table 4.1 in

chapter 'Lull Before the Storm' (Oxford Scholarship Online: May 2019). Accessed online at DOI: 10.1093/oso/9780199489893.001.0001.

23. Amy Waldman, 'India and Pakistan: Good fences make good neighbours', *New York Times*, 4 July 2004. Accessed online at 'https://www.nytimes.com/2004/07/04/world/india-and-pakistan-good-fences-make-good-neighbors.html.
24. Ibid.
25. Waldman, 'India and Pakistan'.
26. Hooda interview.
27. Snehesh Alex Phillip, 'What Imran Khan says is 9 lakh soldiers in Kashmir is actually 3.43 lakh only', The Print, 12 November 2019. Accessed online at https://theprint.in/defence/what-imran-khan-says-is-9-lakh-soldiers-in-kashmir-is-actually-3-43-lakh-only/319442/. For an earlier report, see Ajai Shukla, 'India has 700,000 troops in Kashmir? False !!!', Rediff.com, 17 July 2018. Accessed online at https://www.rediff.com/news/column/india-has-700000-troops-in-kashmir-false/20180717.htm.
28. 'India has deployed more than 1 million troops in held Kashmir: Foreign Office', *Dawn*, 30 November 2016. Accessed online at https://www.dawn.com/news/1299621/india-has-deployed-more-than-1-million-troops-in-held-kashmir-foreign-office.
29. Based on discussions with Nanavatty, Hooda and Rakesh Sharma.
30. Rawat interviews.
31. Harsha Kakar, 'Pace the key for interlocutor success', ORF Online, 20 October 2017. Accessed online at https://www.orfonline.org/expert-speak/pace-key-interlocutors-success-kashmir/. Also see, G. Parthasarathy and Radha Kumar, *Frameworks for a Kashmir Settlement,* (New Delhi: Delhi Policy Group, 2006).
32. 'Chronology of Amarnath land row', *Times of India*, 6 August 2008. Accessed online at https://timesofindia.indiatimes.com/india/Chronology-of-Amarnath-land-row/articleshow/3331566.cms.
33. Hasnain interview.
34. The Hurriyat, as it is known, is a twenty-six-party alliance of separatist parties that was formed in 1993 with enduring support from the Pakistani Deep State.
35. Hasnain interview.
36. Discussion with Lieutenant General Thodge during one of the Rawat interviews.
37. Hasnain interview.
38. Aarti Tikoo Singh, 'Here's how schools of faith, mobiles are radicalising Kashmi', *Times of India*, 9 July 2017. Available at https://timesofindia.

indiatimes.com/india/how-mosques-and-mobiles-are-radicalising-kashmir/articleshow/59507200.cms.

39. Hooda interview.
40. Arun Prakash, 'Who Defends the Defenders', *Indian Express*, 22 August 2018. Accessed online at https://indianexpress.com/article/opinion/columns/independence-day-afspa-indian-soldiers-miliatry-army-act-ministry-of-defence-5318222/.
41. Ibid.
42. Q&A during a talk by Hooda at Ashoka University on 18 September 2019.
43. Annexure 1 of the human rights cell and handling of human rights violation cases in the army. Accessed online at https://indianarmy.nic.in/Site/FormTemplete/frmTempSimple.aspx?MnId=xc6s3otnoaeLSkagPIPQRg==&ParentID=HyPoMmCZnm SA9FT9WPkFlw==.
44. Sumit Ganguly, *Deadly Impasse: Indo-Pakistan Relations at the Dawn of a New Century* (Cambridge: Cambridge University Press, 2016), pp. 1-2.
45. Ibid, p. 19.
46. Ibid.
47. Interview with a very senior officer in the Indian Army who requested anonymity.
48. Ibid. Also see Ananya Bharadwaj, 'Asiya Andrabi: Kashmir's first separatist who also dreamt of marrying a mujahid', The Print, 10 December 2018. Accessed online at https://theprint.in/india/governance/asiya-andrabi-kashmirs-first-woman-separatist-who-also-dreamt-of-marrying-a-mujahid/160138/.
49. Malik interview.
50. Sushant Sareen, 'Pakistan punched by Article 370 move', ORF Online, 9 August 2019. Accessed online at https://www.orfonline.org/research/pakistan-punched-by-indias-article-370-move-54261/.
51. Nanavatty papers.
52. Ibid.
53. Ibid.
54. Conversation and email correspondence with a serving officer from the infantry currently posted in J&K who has requested anonymity.

Chapter 18: Under the UN Flag

1. 'Full text of statement by PM Modi at UN peacekeeping summit'. Accessed online at https://timesofindia.indiatimes.com/india/Full-

text-of-statement-by-PM-Modi-at-UN-Peacekeeping-Summit/articleshow/49145092.cms.

2. 'UN documents: Gathering a body of global documents'. Accessed online at http://www.un-documents.net/charter.htm.
3. Odd Arne Westad, *The Cold War: A World History* (Penguin Random House, 2017), pp. 159-82.
4. Robert Barnes, 'Between the Blocs: India, the United Nations and Ending the Korean War', *Journal of Korean Studies,* Vol. 18, No. 2 (Fall 2013), pp. 263-86. Accessed online at https://doi.org/10.1353/jks.2013.0022.
5. 'Agreement on Prisoners of War (Official UN Documents)', *American Journal of International Law,* Vol. 47, No. 4, October 1953. Accessed online at https://www.jstor.org/stable/2213914.
6. Jairam Ramesh, 'India's Role in Ending the Korean War', *Hindu,* 3 May 2018. Accessed online at www.thehindu.com/opinion/op-ed/india's-role-in-ending-the-korean-war/article23750989.ece.
7. Kim Chan Wahn, 'The Role of India in the Korean War', *International Area Review,* Vol. 13, No. 2 (Summer 2010), pp. 22-24.
8. Ramesh, 'India's Role'.
9. War Diary of 60th Para Field Ambulance.
10. Battle accounts from the US Army recovered from the war diary of 60th Para Field Ambulance.
11. From a detailed account of Canadian experiences in the Korean War. Accessed online at https://www.veterans.gc.ca/eng/remembrance/history/korean-war/valour-remembered.
12. From the archives of the Indian Army's parachute regimental training centre, Bengaluru.
13. Georges Nzongola-Ntalja, 'Patrice Lumumba: The most important assassination of the 20th century', *Guardian,* 17 January 2011. Accessed online at https://www.theguardian.com/global-development/poverty-matters/2011/jan/17/patrice-lumumba-50th-anniversary-assassination.
14. A. Walter Dorn and David J.H. Bell, 'Intelligence and Peacekeeping: The UN Operation in the Congo, 1960-64', *International Peacekeeping,* Vol. 2. No. 1 (Spring 1995), pp. 11-33. Also see Robert D. McFadden, 'Mad Mike Hoare, Irish mercenary leader in Africa, dies at 100'. Accessed online at https://www.nytimes.com/2020/02/03/obituaries/mike-hoare-dies.html.
15. Ibid.
16. Rick Gladstone and Mike Ives, 'UN report bolsters theory that Hammarskjold plane was downed', *New York Times,* 8 October 2019. Accessed at https://www.nytimes.com/2019/10/08/world/africa/dag-hammarskjold.html.

17. Ibid.
18. 'Elizabethville fighting rages as plan found', *Desert Sun*, 5 December 1961. Accessed online at https://cdnc.ucr.edu/cgi-bin/cdnc?a=d&d=DS19611205.2.10&e=-------en--20--1--txt-txIN--------1.
19. Dr K.K. Sharma, 'Congo: First African War and Indian Soldiers (1960-64)'. Accessed online at https://www.academia.edu/32888328/CONGO_FIRST_AFRICAN_WAR_AND_INDIAN_SOLDIERS_1960-64_.doc.
20. K.S. Nair, *Ganesha's Flyboys: The IAF in Congo* (Hyderabad: Anveshan Enterprises, 2012).
21. Ibid.
22. Ibid.
23. Ibid.
24. Group Captain A.S. Ahluwalia, *Airborne to Chairborne: Memoirs of a War Veteran Aviator-Lawyer of the Indian Air Force* (Bloomington: Xlibris, 2012), p. 189.
25. Satish Nambiar, 'An Indian General Recalls how the world failed Srebnica Years Ago'. Accessed online at https://thewire.in/external-affairs/an-indian-general-recalls-how-the-world-failed-srebrenica-20-years-ago.
26. 'IAF Contingent 2000 to UNAMSIL'. Accessed online at http://indianairforce.nic.in/content/sierra-leone.
27. Chris McGreal, 'What's the point of peacekeepers when they do not keep the peace?' *Guardian,* 17 September 2015. Accessed online at https://www.theguardian.com/world/2015/sep/17/un-united-nations-peacekeepers-rwanda-bosnia.
28. Ibid.
29. David H. Ucko, 'Can Limited Intervention Work: Lessons from Britain's Success Story in Sierra Leone', *Journal of Strategic Studies*, pp. 847-77.
30. Ibid.
31. Colum Lynch, 'India to withdraw large UN force from Sierra Leone', *Washington Post*, 21 September 2000. Accessed online at https://www.washingtonpost.com/archive/politics/2000/09/21/india-to-withdraw-large-un-force-from-sierra-leone/33c46528-678d-4014-b8b2-8aa299a3658b/?utm_term=.e2dfe7d4c37f.
32. Email correspondence with Brigadier Anil Raman.
33. Timothy Longman, 'The Complex Reasons for Rwanda's Engagement in Congo' in *The African Stakes of the Congo War,* ed. John F. Clark (New York: Palgrave Macmillan, 2002), pp. 131-32.
34. Christopher Bangert, 'Kofi Annan, who redefined the UN, dies at 80', *New York Times,* 18 August 2018. Accessed at https://www.nytimes.com/2018/08/18/obituaries/kofi-annan-dead.html.

58. Manjeet Singh Negi, 'Indian Air Force probe finds friendly fire caused February 27 Budgam chopper crash, 5 officers in dock', *India Today,* 23 August 2019. Accessed online at https://www.indiatoday.in/india/story/indian-air-force-budgam-chopper-crash-friendly-fire-officers-guilty-1590764-2019-08-23.
59. Manjeet Singh Negi, 'Indian Air Force signs Rs 1500 crore deal with Russia for R-27 air-to-air missile', *India Today,* 29 July 2019. Accessed online at https://www.indiatoday.in/india/story/indian-air-force-r-27-air-to-air-missiles-russia-defence-deal-1574898-2019-07-29.
60. Arjun Subramaniam, 'Raising costs for infiltration without abandoning India's core principles of restraint', The Print, 16 March 2018. Accessed online at https://theprint.in/opinion/raising-costs-infiltration-without-abandoning-indias-core-principles-restraint/41752/.
61. Harsha Kakar, 'Pakistan's "good" and "bad" terrorists', ORF Raisina Debates, 8 March 2018. Accessed online at https://www.orfonline.org/expert-speak/pakistan-good-bad-terrorists/.

Chapter 20: Stress Along the Line of Actual Control

1. John Garver, *Protracted Contest: Sino-Indian Rivalry in the Twentieth Century* (Seattle: University of Washington Press, 2002), p. 4.
2. Shivshankar Menon, *Choices: Inside the Making of India's Foreign Policy* (New Delhi: Penguin Random House, 2016), pp. 26-29.
3. 'Border Defence Cooperation Agreement between India and China', Press Information Bureau, Government of India, Prime Minister's Office, 23 October 2013. Accessed online at https://pib.gov.in/newsite/PrintRelease.aspx?relid=100178.
4. Interview with Lieutenant General Vinod Bhatia, 2 August 2019.
5. For a detailed academic paper that assesses the strategic dimension of the Depsang crisis, see Manoj Joshi, 'Depsang incursion: Decoding Chinese signal'. Accessed online at https://www.orfonline.org/research/depsang-incursion-decoding-the-chinese-signal/.
6. 'Chinese incursion of April 2013 in Depsang, Ladakh', *Takshashila Issue Brief,* May 2013. Accessed online at http://takshashila.org.in/wp-content/uploads/2013/05/TIB-ChineseIncursions2013-May2013.pdf.
7. Nanavatty interviews.
8. Bhatia interview.
9. Interview and several telephonic conversations with Hooda.
10. Rajat Pandit, 'Several soldiers injured in clashes in Ladakh and Sikkim as border tensions flare up between India and China', *Times of India,* 11

May 2020. Accessed online at https://timesofindia.indiatimes.com/india/several-soldiers-injured-in-two-clashes-between-indian-chinese-troops-along-the-border/articleshow/75660665.cms.

11. 'China objects to India's transgression in Arunachal Pradesh, India says it's our land', 8 April 2018. Accessed online at https://www.outlookindia.com/website/story/china-objects-to-indias-transgression-in-arunachal-pradesh-india-says-its-our-la/310746.
12. Pawan Bali, 'BJP MP alleges Chinese Intrusion in AP's 'Fishtail', *Asian Age*, 5 September 2019. Accessed online at https://www.asianage.com/india/all-india/050919/bjp-mp-alleges-china-intrusion-in-aps-fish-tail.html.
13. Manjeet Singh Negi, 'India Building 61 Strategic Roads along Pakistan, China Border'. Accessed online at https://www.indiatoday.in/india/story/india-building-61-strategic-roads-along-pakistan-china-borders-1569516-2019-07-15.
14. Rawat interviews.
15. Lieutenant General H.S. Panag, 'India-China Standoff: What is happening in the Chumbi valley?' Accessed online at https://www.newslaundry.com/2017/07/08/panag-india-china-sikkim-bhutan.
16. Interview with Lieutenant General Praveen Bakshi, Chandigarh, 20 July 2019.
17. The most detailed Indian analysis of the Doklam crisis is a discussion document from the Takshashila Institution, a multidisciplinary and bipartisan Indian think tank based in Bengaluru. See Anirudh Kanisetti and Prakash Menon, 'Doklam Imbroglio', September 2018. Accessed online at https://takshashila.org.in/takshashila-discussion-document-the-doklam-imbroglio/. For a Chinese perspective on Doklam see Liu Lin, 'India-China Doklam Standoff: A Chinese Perspective', 27 July 2017. Accessed online at https://thediplomat.com/2017/07/india-china-doklam-standoff-a-chinese-perspective/.
18. Ibid.
19. 'To boost ties, Chinese army delegation visits Indian Army's Eastern Command in Kolkata', *Hindustan Times*, 24 February 2017. Accessed online at https://www.hindustantimes.com/india-news/to-boost-ties-chinese-army-delegation-visits-indian-army-s-eastern-command-in-kolkata/story-Oa1RqC1Iu3LazyPNhA5rFL.html.
20. Shen Yi, 'China prevails in Doklam standoff but India attempts to distort public opinion', *Global Times*, 3 September 2017. Accessed online at http://www.globaltimes.cn/content/1064491.shtml.

24. Ibid.
25. Ibid. Also see Happymon Jacob, *Line on Fire,* pp. 1-6.
26. Nanavatty interviews.
27. Ibid.
28. Conversation with Air Chief Marshal Krishnaswamy at a reception at Air House, New Delhi, October 2019.
29. Conversation with Nanavatty, 25 April 2020.
30. Ibid.
31. Press release from Ministry of External Affairs, 14 May 2002. Accessed online at https://mea.gov.in/in-focus-article.htm?18990/Kaluchak+Massacre+14+May+2002.
32. Mehta interview.
33. The entire operation has been reconstructed based on conversations with Lieutenant General Nanavatty, Air Marshal Menon and Air Marshal Rajesh Kumar. Also see Arjun Subramaniam, 'From Kargil to Parakram: A Lesson in Forceful Persuasion', *Hindu,* 27 July 2012. Accessed online at https://www.thehindu.com/opinion/op-ed/from-kargil-to-parakram-a-lesson-in-forceful-persuasion/article3687855.ece.
34. Input from one of the key planners of the operation who was then posted in Western Air Command.
35. Strobe Talbott, *Engaging India: Diplomacy, Democracy and the Bomb,* (Washington, DC: Brookings Institution Press, 2006), pp. 214-15.
36. Chari, *Four Crises,* p. 183.
37. Walter C. Ladwig III, 'A Cold Start for Hot Wars', *International Security,* Vol. 32, No. 3 (Winter 2007), pp. 158-90. Accessed online at https://www.belfercenter.org/sites/default/files/files/publication/IS3203_pp158-190.pdf.
38. For a clear understanding of parallel operations, see *Basic Doctrine of the Indian Air Force* (New Delhi: Air HQ, 2012), p.11. The document is the first unclassified and publicly distributed doctrine document of the IAF.
39. Ladwig, 'A Cold Start'.
40. This is the impression the author got during his various interactions at think tanks in Washington, DC, and London during his sabbatical in 2017 and 2018 where he noticed the significant participation of serving and retired Pakistan military officers in seminars and discussions.
41. Interview with Major General S.K. Chakravarty, 20 September 2019.
42. Manjeet Singh Negi, 'Uri attack: An inside account of how it happened'. Accessed at https://www.indiatoday.in/india/story/uri-attack-inside-story-pashtun-map-pakistani-ammunition-jash-e-mohammed-341761-2016-09-18.

43. Hooda and Chakravarty interviews.
44. Nitin Gokhale, 'The Inside Story of India's 2016 Surgical Strikes', *Diplomat,* 23 September 2017. Accessed online at https://thediplomat.com/2017/09/the-inside-story-of-indias-2016-surgical-strikes/. Also, Hooda interview.
45. Conversation with a serving officer who wishes to remain anonymous.
46. PTI report, 11 July 2018. Accessed online at https://economictimes.indiatimes.com/news/defence/heroes-of-surgical-strike-honoured-with-gallantry-medals/articleshow/56782741.cms?from=mdr.
47. Conversation with a senior government official who wishes to remain anonymous, 7 August 2019.
48. Rawat interview. Chapter Six: Asia, 'IISS Military Balance Report 2019', https://doi.org/10.1080/04597222.2018.1561032. The report highlights the stark asymmetry between the Indian Navy and the Pakistan Navy.
49. A personal assessment shared by many in the IAF.
50. Anonymous sources.
51. Specialist sources who wish to remain anonymous.
52. Twitter exchange with Professor Vipin Narang.
53. 'I witnessed Wing Commander Abhinandan shooting down Pak's F-16 aircraft: Squadron Leader Minty Agarwal'. Accessed online at https://www.indiatoday.in/india/story/i-witnessed-wing-commander-abhinandan-varthaman-shooting-down-pakistan-f-16-aircraft-squadron-leader-minty-agarwal-1581180-2019-08-15.
54. Short info briefings by IAF press relations office.
55. 'Why is Pakistan being secretive about JF-17's recent "Smart Weapon" Test', 14 March 2019, https://www.theweek.in/news/world/2019/03/14/pakistan-secretive-smart-weapon.html.
56. The narrative of the Balakot strike and the aerial engagement the next day have been deconstructed based on a combination of unclassified information provided to the author by the IAF PRO during the crisis, several articles by experts in the open media, Open Source Intelligence (OSINT), stray conversations with IAF leadership and participants in the mission, and the author's consolidated analysis that is reflected in two analytical pieces. See https://www.firstpost.com/world/balakot-and-after-iaf-demonstrates-full-spectrum-capability-6236391.html and https://www.orfonline.org/research/the-indian-air-force-sub-conventional-operations-and-balakot-a-practitioners-perspective-50761/.
57. Shiv Aroor, 'Revealed: Wing Commander Abhinandan's Elusive Vir Chakra Citation', 29 January 2020. Accessed online at https://www.livefistdefence.com/2020/01/revealed-wing-commander-abhinandans-elusive-vir-chakra-citation.html.

35. The Upsala conflict data programme. Accessed at http://ucdp.uu.se/#/exploratory.
36. Ibid.
37. Email correspondence with Air Vice Marshal Rajesh Isser.
38. Air Commodore Rajesh Isser, *Peacekeeping and Protection of Civilians: The Indian Air Force in Congo* (New Delhi: KW Publishers, 2012), pp. 73-84.
39. Ibid.
40. Rawat interviews.
41. Ibid.
42. Isser, *Peacekeeping*, p. 78.
43. Ibid, p. 90.
44. Interview with Commodore P.K. Banerjee.
45. 'Navy saves vessel in pirate channel', *Telegraph,* 11 November 2008. Accessed online at https://www.telegraphindia.com/india/navy-saves-vessel-in-pirate-channel/cid/524854.
46. Patrick Mutahi, 'India plays globo cop of Somali coast as Western navies play safe', *Daily Nation,* 18 December 2008. Accessed online at https://www.nation.co.ke/news/africa/1066-504022-7e1nn7z/index.html.
47. Ibid.
48. Press Information Bureau, 'Indian Navy nabs 61 pirates and rescues 13 crew, neutralizes pirate mother vessel Vega 5', Government of India, Ministry of Defence, 14 March 2011. Accessed at http://pib.nic.in/newsite/PrintRelease.aspx?relid=70909.
49. '2012 Annual IMB Piracy Report'. Accessed online at https://www.scribd.com/document/305029896/2012-Annual-Imb-Piracy-Report.
50. 'ICC IMB Piracy and Armed Robbery against Ships: 2017 Annual Report'. Accessed online at https://www.icc-ccs.org/reports/2017-Annual-IMB-Piracy-Report.pdf.
51. 'India and United Nations: Peacekeeping and Peace Building'. Accessed at https://www.pminewyork.gov.in/pdf/menu/submenu__455847884.pdf.

Chapter 19: Operations Other Than War Along the Western Front

1. Chidanand Rajghatta, 'The country's foreign and military policies need to be disciplined', *Times of India,* 1 January 1991. From ProQuest Historical Newspapers.
2. The author was part of the deployment and operations with 35 Squadron during Exercise Brasstacks.
3. Interview with Lieutenant General Pattabhiraman in Wellington.

4. Interview with Lieutenant General Shamsher Mehta in Pune.
5. For a brief history and organization of the Mechanized Infantry Regiment of the Indian Army, see https://indianarmy.nic.in/Site/FormTemplete/frmTempSimple.aspx?MnId=yZlkklVdHhGdbY1CE+KXUw==&ParentID=+ngVrzsh95uOjf39RLAeIg==.
6. Mehta interview.
7. Ravi Rikhye, *The War That Never Was: The Story of India's Strategic Failures* (New Delhi: Prism Paperbacks, 1988), pp. 34-40.
8. Email correspondence with Lieutenant General Praveen Bakshi.
9. Ibid.
10. Rikhye, *The War*, pp. 209-11.
11. Ibid, pp. 192-204. The author too recollects hectic activity at the Bareilly airfield during the period.
12. Conversations with Brigadier Sapatnekar and Brigadier Palsokar, December 2012.
13. Sapatnekar interview.
14. Mehta interview.
15. Sharma interview.
16. Publishing the proceedings of a seminar on nuclear issues when he was commandant of the Army War College catapulted Sundarji to the forefront of the Indian military's attempt to become a major stakeholder in the emerging domain of nuclear strategy within India's strategic establishment. See Ali Ahmed, 'In tribute: Recalling the Sundarji Doctrine', *USI Journal of India* (January-March 2008). Accessed online at https://usiofindia.org/publication/usi-journal/in-tribute-recalling-thesundarji-doctrine-2/.
17. Srinath Raghavan, *Fierce Enigmas: A History of the United States in South Asia* (New York: Basic Books, 2018), p. 341.
18. P.R. Chari, Pervaiz Iqbal Cheema and Stephen P. Cohen, *Four Crises and a Peace Process: American Engagement in South Asia* (Washington, DC: Brookings Institution Press, 2007), pp. 73-79. A detailed overview of the American perspectives on Ex Brasstacks is available in the chapter titled 'The Brasstacks Crisis of 1986-87'.
19. Ibid.
20. Ibid.
21. Ibid.
22. Bruce Riedel, *Avoiding Armageddon: America, India and Pakistan to the Brink and Back.*
23. From a detailed account by Group Captain Sanjeev Narayanen by email on 6 September 2019.

21. Prakash Menon, 'Stand Up Against China', *Pragati,* 20 April 2018. Accessed online at https://www.thinkpragati.com/opinion/4291/stand-up-against-china/.
22. 'Construction of roads by China a violation of pacts: Bhutan', *Times of India,* 13 July 2018. Accessed online at https://economictimes.indiatimes.com/news/defence/construction-of-road-by-china-direct-violation-bhutan/articleshow/59376510.cms?from=mdr.
23. Bakshi interview.
24. Arjun Subramaniam, 'For Modi and Xi, not achieving much at Wuhan may be the best thing', The Print, 5 May 2018. Accessed online at https://theprint.in/opinion/for-modi-and-xi-not-achieving-much-in-wuhan-may-be-the-best-outcome/55393/.
25. Interview with former Australian prime minister Kevin Rudd: 'Emperor Xi's China is Done Biding its Time', 3 March 2018. Accessed online at https://www.belfercenter.org/publication/emperor-xis-china-done-biding-its-time.
26. Extract from transcripts at the Walong war memorial.
27. Deepshika Hooda, 'IAF to have seven operational advanced landing grounds in Arunachal Pradesh in a month', *Economic Times,* 13 July 2018. Accessed online at https://economictimes.indiatimes.com/news/defence/iaf-to-have-7-operational-advanced-landing-grounds-in-arunachal-pradesh-in-a-month/articleshow/49809013.cms?from=mdr.
28. The Wuhan meeting between Modi and Xi following the Doklam incident is one such instance.
29. Dinakar Peri, 'Third regiment of T-72 tanks to be moved to Ladakh soon', *Hindu,* 19 July 2016. Accessed online at https://www.thehindu.com/news/national/Third-regiment-of-T-72-tanks-to-be-moved-to-Ladakh-soon/article14497629.ece. A recent assessment of force levels by the Belfer Center at the Harvard Kennedy School of Government is instructive. See, Frank O'Donnell and Alex Bollfrass, 'The Strategic Postures of China and India: A Visual Guide', Project on Managing the Atom, Belfer Center for Science and International Affairs, Harvard Kennedy School. Accessed online at https://www.belfercenter.org/publication/strategic-postures-china-and-india-visual-guide.
30. Iskander Rehman, 'Hard men in a hard environment: Indian special operators along the border with China'. Accessed online at https://warontherocks.com/2017/01/hard-men-in-a-hard-environment-indian-special-operators-along-the-border-with-china/. Also see Arjun Subramaniam, 'Closing the Gap: A Doctrinal and Capability Appraisal of the IAF and PLAAF', in *Defence Primer: An Indian Military in Transformation,* eds. Pushan Das and Harsh Pant (New Delhi: ORF, 2018), pp. 35-43.

31. Mihir Bhonsale, 'Understanding Sino-Indian border issues: An analysis of incidents reported in the Indian media', ORF Occasional Paper, 12 February 2018. Accessed online at https://www.orfonline.org/research/understanding-sino-indian-border-issues-an-analysis-of-incidents-reported-in-the-indian-media/.
32. L.M.H. Ling, 'Border Pathology' in L.M.H. Ling, Adriana Erthal Abdenur, Payal Banerjee, Nimmi Kurian, Mahendra P. Lama and Li Bo, *India China: Rethinking Borders and Security* (Ann Arbor: University of Michigan Press, 2018), p. 123.
33. Ibid, p. 122.
34. Media Center, Ministry of External Affairs, 'Settling the border question', 3 July 2003. Accessed online at https://www.mea.gov.in/articles-in-indian-media.htm?dtl/13537/Settling+the+China+border.

Chapter 21: The GAP Crisis

1. Ananth Krishnan, 'Forgotten in fog of war, the last firing on the India-China border,' *The Hindu,* 14 June 2020. Accessed online at https://www.thehindu.com/news/national/forgotten-in-fog-of-war-the-last-firing-on-the-india-china-border/article31827344.ece
2. Rahul Shrivastava, 'How much of Indian land is occupied by China? As Centre, Congress trade barbs, the truth lies in Parliament records,' *India Today,* 23 June 2020. Accessed online at https://www.indiatoday.in/india/story/how-much-of-indian-land-in-ladakh-is-occupied-by-china-1691859-2020-06-23.
3. Vipin Narang and Christopher Clary, 'India's Pangong Pickle: New Delhi's options after its clash with China,' *War on the Rocks,* 2 July 2020. Accessed online at https://warontherocks.com/2020/07/indias-pangong-pickle-new-delhis-options-after-its-clash-with-china/.
4. Shiv Aroor, '3 Separate brawls, outsider Chinese troops & more: Most detailed account of the brutal Galwan battle,' *India Today,* online report, 21 June 2020. Accessed online at https://www.indiatoday.in/india/story/3-separate-brawls-outsider-chinese-troops-more-most-detailed-account-of-the-brutal-june-15-galwan-battle-1691185-2020-06-21
5. Brahma Chellaney on Twitter @Chellany, 7.42 p.m., 25 June 2020. Accessed online at https://twitter.com/Chellaney/status/1276156416269713418
6. Shubhajit Roy, 'Ahead of Military Talks, China claims troops have disengaged at most sites,' *Indian Express,* 29 July 2020, pp. 1-2.
7. Vinayak Bhat, 'A peek at China's aerial preparedness along the Ladakh borders,' *India Today,* 20 July 2020. Accessed online at https://www.indiatoday.in/india/story/a-peek-at-china-s-aerial-preparedness-along-the-ladakh-borders-1702508-2020-07-20

8. AVM Manmohan Bahadur (Retired), 'Indian Intelligence failure again? Heroism at Galwan must lead to reforms,' *The Print,* 23 June 2020. Accessed online at https://theprint.in/opinion/indian-intelligence-failure-again-heroism-at-galwan-must-lead-to-reforms/446865/
9. Tara Kartha, 'Calling LAC Conflict "intelligence failure" is lazy. It ignores India's real problem,' *The Print,* 26 June 2020. Accessed online at https://theprint.in/author/tara-kartha/
10. Arjun Subramaniam, 'Can Counter-Coercion work against a belligerent China?', Expert Speak at ORF Online, accessed online at https://www.orfonline.org/expert-speak/can-counter-coercion-work-belligerent-china/.
11. Indrani Bagchi, 'China shouldn't view us through US lens. That would be a great disservice, says S Jaishankar,' *The Times of India,* 2 August 2020. Accessed online at https://timesofindia.indiatimes.com/india/china-shouldnt-view-us-through-us-lens-that-would-be-a-great-disservice-says-s-jaishankar/articleshow/77307398.cms
12. Arjun Subramaniam, 'To the brink and back in Ladakh,' *The Hindu,* 17 September 2020. Accessed online at https://www.thehindu.com/opinion/op-ed/to-the-brink-and-back-in-ladakh/article32624934.ece
13. Arjun Subramaniam, 'IAF has enhanced India's deterrent and coercive posture in Ladakh,' *The Indian Express,* 23 November 2020. Accessed online at https://indianexpress.com/article/opinion/columns/power-in-the-air-7061634/
14. Conversation with General Rawat, 28 September 2020, when the author went to present him with a copy of this book.
15. Conversation with the army chief, when the author went to present him with a copy of this book in early October 2020.
16. 'Pangong Lake: India and China complete pull-back of forces', *BBC News,* 21 February 2021. Accessed online at https://www.bbc.com/news/world-asia-56147309
17. Jyoti Malhotra interviews Ashley Tellis for *The Print,* 4 March 2021. Accessed online at https://www.youtube.com/watch?v=0zCmmhr2JHo
18. Jonathan Renshon, *Why Leaders Choose War* (New York: Praegar Security International, 2006).
19. Ibid, p. 149.
20. John Boyd, *Patterns of Conflict,* from a series of presentations made by Boyd at various war colleges in the US. Despite not having written a book, Boyd's impact on contemporary warfighting has been phenomenal. See, http://www.projectwhitehorse.com/pdfs/boyd/patterns%20of%20conflict.pdf.
21. Ibid.

INDEX

ABOUT THE AUTHOR

Air Vice Marshal **Arjun Subramaniam** is an accomplished military historian and the author of *Shooting Straight: A Military Biography of Lt Gen. Rostum K. Nanavatty* and the two-volume *India's Wars: A Military History*. Subramaniam was the President's Chair of Excellence in National Security Affairs at the National Defence College, New Delhi, from February 2021 to March 2023; a Visiting Fellow at the Harvard University Asia Center and the Changing Character of War Programme, Oxford University; and Visiting Professor, Fletcher School of Law and Diplomacy. He is currently a Visiting Faculty at Kautilya School of Public Policy, Hyderabad, and several war colleges across the three services.

ALSO BY THE AUTHOR

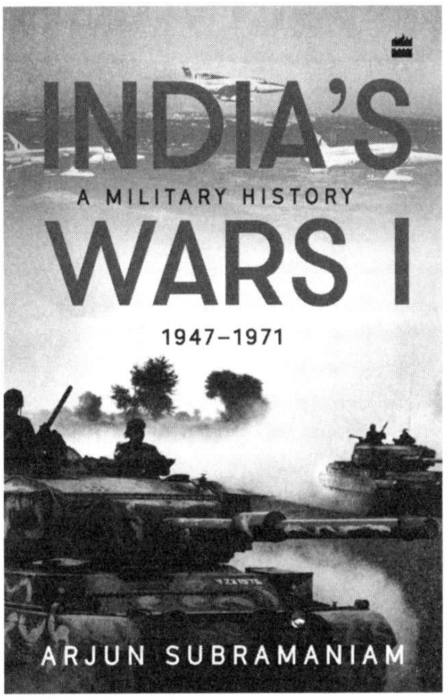

The armed forces play a key role in protecting India and occupy a special place in people's hearts. Yet, standard accounts of contemporary Indian history rarely have a military dimension.

In *India's Wars I*, Arjun Subramaniam seeks to give India's military exploits their rightful place in history. Beginning with a snapshot of the growth of the armed forces, he provides detailed accounts of the conflicts from Independence to 1971: the first India-Pakistan war of 1947-48, the liberation of Hyderabad and Junagadh, the campaign to evict the Portuguese from Goa in 1961, and the full-blown wars against China and Pakistan.

At the same time, *India's Wars I* is much more than a record of events. It is a tribute to the valour of the men and women in olive green, white and blue in the hope that it reaches out to a large audience, specially the youth. It highlights ways to improve the synergy between the three services, and emphasizes the need for wider discussions on matters related to national security.

Laced with veterans' exhilarating experiences in combat operations, *India's Wars I* fuses the strategic, operational, tactical and human dimensions of war with great finesse. Deeply researched and passionately written, it unfolds with ease and offers a fresh perspective on independent India's history.

HarperCollins *Publishers* India

At HarperCollins India, we believe in telling the best stories and finding the widest readership for our books in every format possible. We started publishing in 1992; a great deal has changed since then, but what has remained constant is the passion with which our authors write their books, the love with which readers receive them, and the sheer joy and excitement that we as publishers feel in being a part of the publishing process.

Over the years, we've had the pleasure of publishing some of the finest writing from the subcontinent and around the world, including several award-winning titles and some of the biggest bestsellers in India's publishing history. But nothing has meant more to us than the fact that millions of people have read the books we published, and that somewhere, a book of ours might have made a difference.

As we look to the future, we go back to that one word—a word which has been a driving force for us all these years.

Read.